# REDEMPTION OF A HARDROCK MINER

## ADVENTURES IN DIVINE PROVIDENCE IN THE LAST DAYS

By JOHN H GERGEN

9/1/2017

Severely Edited By Lori A. Gergen

JOHN GERGEN

Copyright © 2018 by John H Gergen
All rights reserved

Unless otherwise noted all Scripture quotations are from the New King James Version (NKJV)
of the Bible Copyright © 1979, 1980, and 1982 Thomas Nelson, Inc.

Cover photograph by John H Gergen

ISBN Number 978-0-692-08908-8

Library of Congress Control Number 6354299101

www.facebook.com/RedemptionofaHardrockMiner

## Dedications

I would like to dedicate my life story to the expansion of the Kingdom of God and to my Awesome Heavenly Father, His Holy Spirit, and to my Lord, Savior, and my loving Master Jesus Christ, who orchestrated and directed this entire "ordeal".
I love you guys, and I can't wait to get back home for some real "face time"!

– And –

I dedicate this book to my beloved soulmate, best friend, partner, and beautiful wife, Lori, who never gave up praying for me and has always stood strong by my side – literally, for better or for worse.
Sorry I drug you through so many years of doing things "my way"… You deserve so much better.
Sooo… I'm gonna let you pick out our new house in Heaven!
I love you, always and forever.


*And*

To ALL Prodigals, Everywhere.
Be a seeker.
Seek and you will find.
It's the Ultimate Treasure Hunt.

## Acknowledgments

To my mentors, those who are so dear to me who shared with me their faith, and in so doing, built up and encouraged mine, to do what the Lord called me to do.

Joe Solomon

Phil "The Unk" Davis

My father and best friend,
William "Bill" Gergen

And particularly to my dearest friend and mentor, and my beloved Brother in Christ,
Armando V. Munoz

"By the grace of God I am what I am, and His grace toward me was not in vain,"
1 Corinthians 15:10

And neither was yours.
I will always honor you in my prayers.
Thank you.

# Table of Contents

**INTRODUCTION** ..................................................................................vii

A Flaw in My Plan .................................................................................1

My God of the Mountains .....................................................................7

Not the Good Ol' Days ........................................................................12

When the Metal Hits the Bone ...........................................................21

The Boys From The Brush .................................................................25

God Sends Love, And Love Changes Things. ...................................32

Surrealistic Pillow, Staking, And a Small Mine Story ........................37

The Search for Dark Treasure ............................................................49

When Things Get Crazy...er ...............................................................64

TOMMYKNOCKERS ...........................................................................72

Tales of Gooseberry ...........................................................................82

The Tallahassee Cache ......................................................................90

Tramming and Nine Bells ...................................................................98

Cinderella Shanty Town ....................................................................106

Gypo Raise Mining ............................................................................113

Remnants of Death ...........................................................................118

Our Ticket Home ...............................................................................129

False Accusations, Grace, and the Iron Mast Mine .........................134

You Reap What You Sow-For Good or Evil .....................................145

Sorcery, Drugs, and Some Help Navigating the Road through These End Times .................................................................................................154

| | |
|---|---|
| The Lure of Mohave Gold | 163 |
| The High Cost of Gold Fever | 169 |
| It's in the Blood | 180 |
| When the Hunter Becomes the Prey | 191 |
| A Voice in the Cold | 199 |
| Let's Make a Deal | 207 |
| Deals & Covenants, Rainbows & Circumcision | 220 |
| Good Ol' Ely | 226 |
| A Clean Start | 232 |
| ...What Is Truth...? | 240 |
| Back to the Mohave | 246 |
| Animals, Unicorns and Dragons | 250 |
| Calador and the Wildcat | 256 |
| Summer of Freedom and Hippies-1972 | 261 |
| Here We Go | 265 |
| The "Criminal" Justice System | 270 |
| Back to My God of the Mountains | 277 |
| Running the Backroads | 285 |
| Lerdo | 296 |
| The Deal that Saved My Soul | 303 |
| Oh, Hell No! | 314 |

| | |
|---|---|
| The Miraculous Begins | 325 |
| Going Out Shackled | 332 |
| Catching the Chain | 339 |
| Free Indeed | 350 |
| No Greater Feeling | 357 |
| Guns for a Sword | 364 |
| Stumbling into My Calling | 373 |
| Angels, Demons, and Jailhouse Religion | 379 |
| Integrity | 389 |
| Mayhem to Miracles, and a Peek at Heaven | 394 |
| Dances, Road Trips and Doing Business for the Lord | 400 |
| The Open Door | 407 |
| Breakfast With An Angel | 417 |
| Healing on the Mountain | 429 |
| EPILOGUE...EULOGY...WHATEVER | 434 |
| APPENDIXES | 445 |
| ABOUT THE AUTHOR | **488** |

# INTRODUCTION

I have lived many days of love, of light and of laughter. I have also lived through many days of profuse darkness. I always felt, for the most part, that I was in control, but that's not the case. Most of the time, the truth be known, something was controlling me or I had no control at all over certain events that unfolded in my life. Some good and some...not so good. Even though God, in His mercy and grace, has granted me forgiveness, regret remains my constant companion, even to this day. I am truly remorseful for the things I did, and eternally thankful for the things my Heavenly Father did not allow me to do. And, of course, I learned a few things along the way; some very important things that sometimes came at a very high price.

Because I still live at the time of this writing, and wish to continue to do so, much has been, buffered, edited, left out, white washed, sugar coated and omitted. Forgive this please. I dearly love my daughter, Brandy, who is and has always been my counselor, mentor and my confidant, who I never wish to embarrass (too badly) or bring shame upon, however, it is my hope to leave a legacy of God's continual work and His Divine Providence in my life to my grandchildren and others. Furthermore it is never my intent to glorify my enemy or his work in my life. It is my deepest desire that this testimony give hope and instruction to my son, Bill, by presenting him with a road map as to how to get out of the darkness and into the light of our Lord and Savior Jesus Christ and the victorious life God has for him. I believe in you. It can be done. You're not alone. It ain't an easy road and time is very short, but "There's still time to change the road you're on" (Led Zeppelin, Stairway to Heaven, 1971). Please hurry up, son; we have a lot of catching up to do!

And my deepest prayer for this writing is that it compels YOU to seek out the truths, for yourself, which are embedded within these pages. Although it is my story, there has to be more to my life than simply telling of how Divine Providence unfolded in my life, so the actual intent that I have written in the following pages is specifically designed to help you with your story.

So here it is……..a tale that may or may not have happened. Any similarities between fictional characters in this book and real people, names or places are pretty much coincidental…sort of.

Too bad, so sad. That's just the way it is.

Because my memory is fading, I have also had to fill in a lot of "blank spots" as best I could; but its fiction so what does it matter, rieeeght? That's the importance of writing a fictional work…it maintains an incredibly high level of deniability. We'll just say it's a fiction based on my true life experiences, and for the safety of others, I have become very reticent as I write it. Sooo… in any event, it's my story and I can tell it any ol' way I want, and please know that, in so doing, it is my full intent to bless you, the reader. It is my fondest goal that you will clearly now see what it has taken me over twenty years to recognize – God's Divine Providence in orchestrating the events in the life of one so seemingly unworthy and hell bent on self-destruction. To gain full knowledge and understanding of this story, you will benefit greatly by having access to a Holy Bible in order to see various scriptures as they pertain to the story and are referenced.

Finally…may the blessings and protection of our Lord be upon you as you embark on your next adventures, and I pray that my story will set you on to the road that will begin the greatest adventure of your life!

Now, come and see what the Lord has done!

# CHAPTER 1

## A Flaw in My Plan

Spring 1990. The old mine was ungodly dark. You could put your hand in front of your face until it touched your nose and still not see it. You could feel the density of the darkness pressing in around you. It felt thick. There is no darkness like underground darkness. Crazy as it sounds, it always seemed peaceful to me.

I always loved being underground and felt kinda at home here, totally free from all the drama going on above, on the surface. Escapism, I guess. All the years I worked underground it was just you and the rock, and nothing else really mattered; not the bills, not the argument with my wife, not anything…you put on your earmuffs, open the water valve to your drilling machine, then kicked on the air, and all hell broke loose for the next six or so hours, as you drilled out your "round". Then you loaded the holes with dynamite and BOOM! You shot your round as you came off shift and you barred down and mucked it out at the beginning of shift the next day. Did it every day, "round in, round out." Just you and the rock. The smell of rock drill oil and powder, the deafening scream of a Gardner-Denver "83 Drill, and always the rock. A split second warning is all you get, and you better not miss it, so you're always watching every crack in the rock for movement, feeling for down pressure on the steel, and always keeping your partner in the corner of your eye. His life is in your hands and yours in his. No mistakes. Hardrock mining is a very unforgiving business and you don't survive many mistakes. You don't daydream; you don't lose your focus. Also unique to the underground mining profession is the universal understanding that everything that goes wrong is either the fault of "Tommyknockers", small mischievous elf like creatures that live in the cracks and holes in the rocks, or, more likely, the fault of the "dumbasses" on the other shift.

Even though I and my brother Bill as well, survived several cave-ins and near death experiences, we never considered quitting. Adrenaline addiction maybe…anyway, when it's in your blood, it's what you do, as our family has always done for hundreds of years…you would think that someone would have paid attention in school, somewhere down the line in my family tree. When I was growing up and attending school in a mining town, if you didn't pay attention, they would pat you on the back and say "Don't worry about it, just get your butt on up to the mine, we got a job for you," and that's how your career in the Hardrock mining business usually began.  (In actuality, Mackey School of Mines has bestowed several hard earned engineering degrees, etc. on my brother and cousins Mickey and Sam "Smed" that have secured their rightful positions in the family Miners Hall of Fame, and my awesome daughter recently graduated at the very top of her class from Boise State with her Bachelor of Health Science in Respiratory Therapy! Whoot! Whoot! How, if at all, any of this inadvertently contributes to my retirement portfolio, only time will tell.)

But this was different.  My partner John (we called each other "Jones") and I were standing silent in a pitch black abandoned mine.  I had turned the light off to listen into the darkness and search for any other trace of light that might reveal the hidden presence of someone else.  Nothing.  Just blackness.  Turning our lights back on, we moved slowly and quietly down the tunnel and around a couple more turns.  Jones was keeping behind me about five feet and watching our backs.  Around another turn and we came to an old ore chute that led up into one of the old open stopes above.  It was empty, the ore being pulled out by the "old timers" probably over a hundred years ago.  There was a much newer rope hanging in the old chute that disappeared up into the darkness of the open cavern above.  Very unsettling.  I struck a match and the flame flickered and leaned toward the open stope.  Air was moving up there which meant another possible opening to the surface above us.  That could be bad.

Jones and I had watched each other's backs a dozen times before, mostly treasure hunting and chasing Spanish silver and gold in central Nevada.  We stuck together and proceeded down the tunnel.  Soon the dim light of the entrance could be seen as a small dot in the distant darkness.  It must be getting late in the day outside.  Most of the old underground workings we had covered in the last five hours were only about six feet high, and I am 6'1" tall.  My back was getting pretty sore from being crouched over for so long, but now was not the time to get in a hurry.  As we got closer to the portal we slowed even more to allow our eyes to adjust to the days fading light outside, otherwise we would be blinded when we stepped out into the light.

About ten feet from the entrance we could look out and see the brush and trees on the facing hillside, as the mine portal came out in a ravine.  For a long time we sat in the darkness of the tunnel and scanned the hillside in front of us. For some reason, I had a bad feeling about this but couldn't see anything to cause the warning bell that was going off in my head. I whispered to Jones "I'm hungry" he grinned that grin of his and nodded. "Let's go" I said, and stood up. WHAM! Something hit me hard in my chest, slamming me backwards into a mine timber on the hanging wall. The timber kept me from being slammed to the ground. I was gasping for air in short breaths. I don't remember hearing the shot, I just remember the impact…and how incredibly clear my mind became over the next few minutes. Seemingly apparent is the possibility that there may be a flaw in my plan. Jones, hunkered down behind a timber on the other side of the tunnel, said "what the hell was that?" as he looked from the pistol in my hand to the growing red stain on my t-shirt. "I'm hit," I said matter of factly, and fired into the visible hillside across the gully, until my first magazine was gone. I ejected it and slammed a second fifteen round magazine in place, and emptied it until I had covered the entire hillside that was visible from inside the tunnel entrance.

The roar of the Beretta 92FS inside the small mine entrance was deafening. Somehow I knew I only had a few more moments before the shock wore off my body and I would be down, "We gotta go, Jones," I said, as the dust on the opposite hillside began to drift away, and we leaped through the entry way and into the light. I dove to the left behind a boulder and Jones went to the right, behind an old steam compressor. Nothing. Silence. The only sound was my panting for air and the hideous sucking noise my chest and back were making. My right lung had collapsed, and I was getting "tunnel vision" at a very fast rate. Then Jones was by my side and helping me up. With my arm around his shoulders, we followed the mine rail around the face of the mountain to the main mine workings, where our truck was parked by an old miners shack.

At the truck we ripped off pieces of material from the bottom of my tee shirt. I could plug the hole in the right side of my chest but I had to have Jones plug the exit wound in my back in order to get it to stop sucking air. He wasn't real happy with the idea, but he didn't hesitate, either. That's what friends do. I made him shove a piece of twisted t-shirt into the hole with his finger, then we wrapped the rest of the t-shirt, now in long strips, around my chest, and then he tied it tight. The shock was wearing off and the pain was blinding, causing white flashes in front of my eyes, as we headed down the long, bumpy mountain trail and into Railroad Valley.

"What the hell just happened?" Jones asked. "I don't know" I told him, "but you gotta stay calm and take it easy till we get to the County road." Every little bump and bounce was excruciating now. It's not like in the movies where it hurts so bad that they "pass out." I wished to God that I could have passed out, but with that extremely intense pain, believe me there is no chance of eluding consciousness. After a few miles on the County dirt road that clung along the foothills of the mountain range, Jones said "I know the people at this ranch up ahead and his wife is a paramedic. They're good people. They will know what to do." For the first time ever I realized that my partner was scared and I was in serious trouble. I told him to just keep going to Ely, but he wasn't having any of it. Can't exactly blame him… I wouldn't want to explain me dying in his truck either. We still had about 30 miles of dirt road then another 65 miles of highway to the nearest hospital, in Ely. I don't think Jones thought I would make it. All I knew was that, somehow, I had to stay calm and control my breathing and slow my heartbeat, or I wouldn't last till Ely. That seemed crystal clear to me "somehow." Somehow, I "knew it" on the inside of me. Jones opened his door and hit the ground running for the ranch house, almost before the truck came to a stop. Seconds after he entered the house, I could see people jumping up and moving through the front window of the house. A woman picked up a phone and Jones and another man came running out of the house towards me. "We're gonna put you in my wife's truck and get you to town. The ambulance is on the way to meet us," the man said. I tried to object but they were lifting me out of Jones' truck already. I would have preferred to stay with Jones. At least if I died I would be with my friend and not strangers, but I think Jones was scared. He was doing what he thought was best for me, and you can't ask for more than that.

And there was no "we" and "us." The woman jumped in, dumped the clutch, spun gravel for about 100 yards, and off we went. The truck started "fishtailing," swinging from ditch to ditch across the road as we quickly picked up speed. I looked up to see a cattle guard approaching and tried to tell her to slow down, but as I tried to speak, she went off yelling "don't you leave me, damn you, don't you die on me," over and over! We hit the cattle guard so hard that the back of my head hit the roof of the pickup! "Hang in there buddy, don't die on me," she yelled. Finally, I managed to reach across the seat with my left hand and get a hold of her by the face. My thumb went into the side of her mouth and my fingers dug into her flesh behind her neck and I squeezed with everything I had left, and pulled her face toward me. She hit the brakes, and the truck slid sideways to a stop in the middle of the road. I looked into her terrified eyes as she tried to pull my thumb out of her mouth and said as clearly as I could "you gotta calm down or you're gonna kill me – DO YOU UNDERSTAND?" She stopped struggling and nodded as tears started running down her face. I removed my hand. She stared at me for a moment, and through her tears said "I'm sorry, I'm ok." Better. "And stop telling me not to die, ok?" "Ok, sorry," she said, taking a deep breath. Then, I don't "know" why but I said "relax I'm gonna be ok." Where that came from I have no clue, but I believed it when I said it, even though I didn't "know" if I would live through the night. Anyway, it seemed to calm both of us down quite a bit.

As we rolled on through the night we finally came to highway 6, and the much welcomed, and smoother, pavement. We hung a right and headed towards Current Creek and Ely. God I was beat. As we drove I laid back and looked up into the beautiful Nevada night sky. Nothing like it. The stars and half-moon glistened brightly as my mind drifted back to other days and star filled nights when I was a boy at Keystone Mine in Hot Creek Valley.

## CHAPTER 2

## My God of the Mountains

*I will lift up my eyes to the hills –*

*From whence comes my help?*

*My help comes from the Lord*

*Who made Heaven and earth. Psalms 121: 1-2*

Most of my boyhood summers back in the 60's, were spent in the mountains and high deserts of Northern and Central Nevada. Star Peak, Black Point, Unionville, Luning, Morey, Reveille, Troy Canyon, Tybo, Hot Creek, and I especially remember Keystone Mine in Nye County, Nevada. We slept under the stars on the ground unless it rained or snowed, then we would move into one of the old rock cabins of the Keystone ghost town down by the spring, or into the closest old mine drift or tunnel. Staring into the stars every night like that, you cannot help but be drawn to the reality of God.

My folks were awesome in this regard. My Dad was a professional prospector and hard rock miner who never left his family behind if he didn't have to! Dad handled the mining and exploration projects for famed Howard Hughes, Jack F. Grimm and Bunker Hunt, just to name a few, as my father's reputation always preceded him as an honest and trusted man. I remember as a young boy taking our Silver Tipped German Shepherd, Dan, through the casino and into the elevator of the Desert Inn Hotel and Casino in Las Vegas every month, while my Dad did his monthly report directly to Howard Hughes himself. Amazingly, people would always ask, "Is that Rin Tin Tin?" To which my brother and I always replied "Why, yes it is!"

While living at Keystone and other mining camps, we only went back to town during the summer for supplies and in the fall and winter for school. I disliked towns... still do I guess. Way too much drama. I never seemed to "fit in" anywhere. Anyway, Mom and Dad honored the Lord, and as much depended on them, taught me and my brother, likewise. I knew the Lord's Prayer way before I started kindergarten and walking and talking to God every day in the mountains came natural. Truth is, if you ever stood on a mountain side in Nevada, and listened to the wind move in the pine trees, then you have stood in my church.

Helping to raise us was my father's dear friends Johnny and Bessie Pinola, of the Shoshone Tribe. They taught us tradition and respect. When we hunted we got one bullet and if you didn't have it when you got home at night, you had better have some fresh meat. And let me tell you, when people watch a twelve or thirteen year old kid beat a deer to death with a rock because you slightly misplaced your one and only shot, they really get freaked out! And, thanks to the Pinola's teachings, if it moved across the surface of the earth, they taught us how to track it.

Looking back in retrospect, it amazes me how the prophets, and "mighty men of valor," throughout the Bible not only came down from the mountains, but also received God's leading, guidance and direction in and on the mountains. Where did Jesus go after a hard day of ministering to God's people, or before facing the cross? That's where we gather our strength, is in spending time alone with Him, in solitude.

*Who treads the high places of the earth – The Lord God is his name. Amos 4:14*

*Now it shall come to pass in the Latter Days that the mountain of the Lord's house*
*Shall be established on top of the mountains,* (please note mountains is plural!)
*And so shall be exalted above the hills; And people shall flow to it.*

Micah 4:1

And my favorite of many;
*Hear now what the Lord says;*
*Arise, plead your case before the mountains,*
*And let the hills hear your voice. Micah 6:1*

These are only a few of the hundreds of examples the Bible gives us about where to go to escape the distractions of the world and to be alone with God. Even if you can't make it to the mountains, it's vital that you find a quiet place to be alone with our Creator, especially in times of need!

John Muir was a Scottish-American naturalist, who among other things, is accredited with the foundation of Yosemite National Park in the early 1900's. His thoughts about God and the spiritual aspects of nature are well worthy of researching, as they truly are awe inspiring in the glorification of our Creator. It was John Muir who stated that:

"The clearest way into the universe is through a forest wilderness. Keep close to nature's heart… and break clear away once in a while, and climb a mountain or spend a week in the woods. Wash your spirit clean."

And,

"…full of God's thoughts, a place of peace and safety amid the most exalted grandeur and enthusiastic action, a new song, a place of beginnings abounding in the first lessons of life, mountain building, eternal, invincible, unbreakable order; with sermons in stone, storms, trees, flowers, and animals brimful with humanity." And, "everybody needs beauty as well as bread, places to play in and pray in, where nature may heal and give strength to body and soul alike."

As well as…

"Oh, these vast, calm, measureless mountain days, inciting at once to work and rest! Days, in whose light everything seems equally Devine, opening a thousand windows to show us God. Nevermore, however weary, should one faint by the way who gains the blessings of one mountain day; whatever his fate, long life, short life, stormy or calm, he is rich forever."

And finally;

"The mountains are fountains of men as well as rivers, of glaciers, of fertile soil. The great poets, philosophers, prophets, able men whose thoughts and deeds have moved the world, have come down from the mountains – mountain dwellers who have grown strong there with the forest trees in nature's workshops."

Anyway, I'm sure you get my point. God clearly appointed us to fellowship with one another in a corporate setting in order to encourage and edify each other in the faith. But what I learned (and forgot), while spending one on one time with the Lord when I was growing up in the mountains, is that when you got trouble, you better run to Him and find a quiet, secluded place to be alone with your Heavenly Father, and tell Him everything! I remember at Blackpoint Mine, 11 miles north of Eureka, Nevada, we spent a lot of summers working my grandfather's old silver mine. One chilly fall evening my brother and I, along with my cousins Bill and Mickey, had moved into the old tunnel for the night, as the skies promised rain before sunrise. We awoke the next morning to a fresh snow slide that had sealed the portal of the tunnel, and us inside. Daylight never felt so good as when we finally dug our way out that morning! That would not be the last time my brother and I would be trapped underground together.

***

My Dad gave my brother and I BB guns at an extremely young age. They resembled Winchester 30-30 carbines, which he actually gave each of us when we turned twelve years old and were legal to hunt deer in Nevada. Although I suffered (got my ass whooped!) through multiple "epic fails" (windows, birds, cats, my brother, etc.,) with the BB gun, when my Grandma Gergen died, my Aunt Neva gave us a Remington .22 caliber single shot rifle, and amazingly, my Dad let us have it! Probably because we adored our Grandmother, and our hearts were broken at her passing. For me she was the most influential person in my life, up to that time. She taught us what is was to be loved unconditionally, the Ten Commandments, how to pray and sing to the Lord, and was a living example of what a true Christian looked like. I still clearly remember gospel lessons she taught me, before I was old enough for school. When she went home to Heaven, we were all crushed.

So we got to keep the .22 rifle! When summer came, Dad put it in the back window gun rack, right along with our BB guns. Over the summer he diligently drilled into us how to safely use it. By the end of June we were out of bullets, so every time someone pulled into camp to visit with my Dad and Mom, chances are, while they were visiting, I and my brother Billy Bob would be rifling through their vehicle for .22 shells (God forgive us). I spent hours and hours every day walking the hills and mountains of Hot Creek Valley with that single shot and communing with God. I got real good at both. Mom apparently knew this as well, because when I would get "antsy" or "rambunctious" in my teen years (I had ADD before there was a name for it), she would have my older cousins, Mickey and/or Bill, take me out to Hercules Gap (all sagebrush back then – no houses) and drop me off and make me walk back to town (it took about four hours). Bill and Mickey always did what Mom instructed, but they were (usually, unless I ran my mouth) merciful in sneaking my rifle and a box of shells out of the house for me, God bless them.

## CHAPTER 3

## Not the Good Ol' Days

As we pulled over in the middle of the flat, in Railroad Valley, to meet the ambulance, I wondered how I had drifted so far from God to end up like this. Pain blasted through my body and into my head as they transferred me to a gurney and into the ambulance. The EMT's were good and recognized that I had to be elevated as my one good lung was apparently slowly filling up with blood. Time was against me. If I couldn't control my breathing (I was taking short panting breaths) and slow my heart beat down, I was gonna drown in my own blood before we made it to the hospital. We still had about 55-60 miles to go. I closed my eyes and focused on my breathing. Eventually, the EMT from Duckwater, thinking I had fallen asleep, began talking about how she and her husband were celebrating their wedding anniversary when she got the emergency call. When I could no longer "play dead", I smiled, and that ended the conversation with an embarrassing gasp on her part. Funny how you remember stuff when you're in life threatening situations (sorry, Barbara. Thank you for helping save my life that night. My bad). Going over Current and Ward summits were agonizing roller coaster rides. I tried to tell the EMT's what to say to my wife, Lori, as I felt my strength fading, but they were so adamant about saving my life, that they wouldn't hear of it. (God bless them). Finally one gal held up a defibrillator and said, "Don't worry – we're not gonna let you die"! When I tried to laugh, my pain soared to new levels and the white spots in front of my eyes literally blinded me until I refocused on my breathing. Note to self; when you're in the ambulance and the EMT's tell you to do something (i.e. calm down), DO IT.

  Meanwhile, Jones had called my wife in Ely and told her I was on the way into the hospital. She knew I would never allow my son and daughter to see me like this. After all, this wasn't the first time I came dragging myself home, all tore up. During my ride to town, Lori went through her entire Rolodex of friends and family trying to find anyone who would help watch our two young kids, so she could be at the hospital when I got there. Sad to say, that turned out to be a real eye-opener into who you could count on in an emergency, among those who claim to always be there for you. It's really amazing to me who couldn't help her with the kids, but could show up at the hospital to watch and see if I lived or died, or to try and console my lovely wife.

I thank God to this day for the people that, though not in our closest circles, stepped up to help her. Thank you, especially to those who looked after my children that night. I will never forget you helping us through this, even though I wasn't the easiest person to be friends with at that time.

Lori was trying to be strong when I saw her, but I must have looked pretty bad, because as soon as they wheeled me into the light of the ER she started crying…then praying. Now I was scared. They had to sit me up in a chair now because my lungs were so full of blood, if I laid back, I would drown. The night shift doctor came in, and when he leaned down to listen to my heart and lungs with his stethoscope I could smell alcohol, and his face was very red. Great. Only in Ely. There seemed to be no doubt in my mind that God was punishing me for all the times I had stuck my high and mighty nose in the air, and looked down and treated drunks with contempt. Of course, we won't mention my "recreational" cocaine use here, or the fact that when my parents took over the Warm Springs Bar and Café in Hot Creek Valley, in the early 70's, I could drink wholesale all throughout my teen years.

***

Although I thought I could drink with the big boys, the truth is, I really sucked at it. My system had about zero tolerance for alcohol. My metabolism refused to cooperate and I refused to believe it. So I kept drinking, puking, fighting, and as always, passing out by the time most normal people were going on their third or fourth drink. Same with marijuana. My friends and I would smoke a joint and they would go out cruising, partying, or working on their cars. I would curl up in a corner somewhere and pass out for about ten hours…right after I ate everything available in the house, including, but not limited to, cans of stewed tomatoes, cans of Rosarita refried beans, raw macaroni with catsup, etc. Forget driving, walking, and regrettably sometimes going to the toilet in a timely manner. And regardless of contrary belief, NO! These were not the "good ol' days". These were my "stuck on stupid" days. And only having the ability to see everything from my self-centered perspective, all drunks were just like me. Now you can get an understanding of my aggressive distain for this whiskey breathed doctor who is now in charge of whether or not I live or die.

Adding to the tension was the fact that by the time I was fifteen or sixteen years old, full grown drunks at my Dad's bar had wiped the floor with my inebriated backside about a dozen times, mostly because when I drink I never learned to shut my mouth. I loved to run my mouth, and as my friend A.V. Munoz put it, "I was an invincible genius". My mouth wrote multiple checks that my rear end had insufficient funds to cash. Needless to say they bounced, and so did I.

It was fifty miles to the nearest town from Warm Springs, and that was a small busted mining town called Tonopah. The mines in the area of Warm Springs (Gila, Reveille, Golden Arrow, Silver Bow, Keystone and Tybo) were booming and Warm Springs Bar and Café wasn't just the best place in town, it WAS the town. It was company owned and operated, by and for the mining companies and they "looked out for their own"…meaning the closest law of any type, other than an occasional daytime drive-by, or a Nevada highway patrol responding to an accident, was fifty miles away. So was the nearest "cathouse" and grocery store, so in the next few years, after I turned sixteen and could drive (term used loosely), I totaled out thirteen cars (not all of them mine) on that fifty mile stretch of road. Almost all of them were over 100mph and most of them rollovers or, my personal favorite, end-over-ends and usually had a cow or horse involved. One was even an end over end, six times, backwards, in a Mazda pick-up as, while dodging a cow, we went into a spin and leaving the road backwards, we hit our rear bumper on a concrete culvert, and across the desert we danced! The miracle that I even survived one of those insane, hi-speed wrecks, let alone thirteen of them must have had Gods Holy Angels pushed to the limit trying to look out for my dumb ass, but of course, by then, I was blaming God for wrecking me! Yup. He was saving me over and over and I was breaking His heart. I know I am now washed in the Blood and I am forgiven, but the regret that haunts me I will carry until I finally go Home with Him.

Warm Springs actually has an awesome mineral hot springs swimming pool where I learned to swim (and sober up as the need arose). All these years growing up in the Hot Creek Valley, I kept practicing almost every day with my guns, and I got really good. Better than most, as I won a lot of "turkey shoots" against men many times my age, and I was fast. I never practiced when I was drinking (or hung over) so eventually I began to spend more time with my guns and less time in the bar.

Definitely worth mentioning here is the reason why my children and grandchildren exist today as a direct result of Divine Providence. At one of many fast draw competitions that I competed in, I had just completed my lightning fast draw placing five out of six shots into a paper plate at 25 feet. I had stepped back to allow the next contestant into the "shooters box". As I stood there behind him reloading my six shooter, my competitor made his draw, but as his iron cleared leather, his front sight hung up on the hammer thong of his holster and he inadvertently fired his round, and the bullet drilled right through my holster! Me being left-handed, had that bullet strayed a few inches to my right... Well, you see my point. But give credit where credit is due – Hallelujah!

One Sunday morning I got up at 4:30 a.m. to leave and go back to school in Red Bluff, 475 miles away. As I came out of the back room of the bar where I slept, the smell was so overpowering that I started to gag as I made my way to the coffee pot. The night before, a barroom brawl had broken out and it was the first time ever that I remembered still being on my feet and conscious when it was over (verses being beat to hell and often knocked out). A huge personal victory for me, I can't begin to tell you how extremely proud I felt. I had been limiting myself to just one or two beers lately, and when the fight erupted, not only did I not start it, but I wasn't drunk either. Sure, I was pretty badly beat up, but I was still on my feet! I was seventeen years old.

As I poured my pounded self a cup of coffee that morning, I looked down the long bar at the men (still drunk, of course, some still nursing wounds, some passed out, and by the odor, at least one had messed his pants...typical Sunday morning in a roadhouse), and as I just kinda hovered over that first cup, I realized two things;

One, they were, as every morning, having the same macho bullcrap conversation that they were having when I went to bed five hours ago, and most importantly, the second thing was that I swore to myself that never again would I allow anyone to look at me, again, the way I was looking at them at this moment. No one respects a drunk...the truth is, not even another drunk. And you can't live with a drunk (let alone raise a family) unless you are a drunk with them. Alcoholism NEVER ends well, if left untreated. Ask anyone who has been raised in a home with an alcoholic parent, and in my experience, without exception, it always ends tragically with long term emotional and psychological damage to children and non-alcoholic spouses. Saying "I love you" over and over does nothing to heal the hurt, yet they never seem to be able to see their "disease" as a problem, let alone seek help. It's been like this for thousands of years, as maybe Satan's most efficient tool for ripping families apart. My beloved mother lived with three of us in this scenario for many years, God bless her. My misguided philosophy was ingrained into me by Johnny Hernandez, my dear friend, hero, blade operator, bartender and bouncer extraordinaire (no one on earth loved to fight more than John ), who taught it to me this way; "It don't matter how old, how drunk or how small they are, they all know what they're askin' for". That morning, also for the first time, nobody at the bar had any jokes or smartass comments for me as they usually did. Some looked at me, and then just looked away, while others wouldn't look at me at all. Except Johnny Hernandez, whose menacing facial expression and stone cold glare couldn't hide the glimmer in his eyes or the slightest hint of a smile, as he looked me up and down, and locked eyes with me for a second before going back to tending bar. That pre-dawn morning, standing in the aftermath of that ugly brawl, Satan input a "hook" of pride in me that would take over twenty years and a lot of anguish, to tear out.

Even so, realizing that I was usually picked on in the bar because I was young, tall and skinny, I began building on a reputation so that nobody was in a hurry to start something with someone who was crazy enough to always pursue extreme vengeance on anyone who hurt them, even to the point of establishing the distinction of being crazy enough to come back and maybe kill them if they hurt me bad enough. Between my red hot temper and my constant practicing with my guns out behind the bar, and a few examples of my versions of revenge, it wasn't very difficult. Hurt me, hurt you. Soon enough, people started letting me be, and I started keeping more to myself as not to instigate things by running my mouth.

On a more positive note, my brother Bill and I would sometimes enlist semi intoxicated men from the bar to accompany us on our rabbit hunts at Keystone Canyon. While my brother Bill and I walked the sides of the canyon walls, we would have our new hunting companions walk through the high brush of the canyon floor below us to flush out rabbits that only my brother and I could see from above. It worked pretty well, for the most part. On one particular warm summer evening, we were hunting with a young kid named George, who was more than content simply staggering up the canyon floor through the high sagebrush with a bottle of beer in each hand. He didn't even have a gun, much to our delight, as giving a loaded gun to an intoxicated stranger never seemed like that good of an idea to us, anyway. As George talked, sang songs and laughed his way up the canyon he flushed a lot of rabbits for us. Then, as Bill and I opened up on a rabbit that took off directly in front of George, it suddenly reversed direction and headed straight towards our young hunting companion. As we continued to lay down a barrage of gunfire from Bill's rifle and my pistols, the rabbit eventually tumbled to a stop in a crumpled, bullet ridden heap at George's feet. Except, George was no longer on his feet. He had assumed a fetal position on the ground covering his head with his arms. After he blabbed to everybody at the bar about what had transpired on his hunting expedition, it was hard to talk anyone else into going with us. It also turned out to be a very sobering ordeal for George, even though Bill and I failed to see what the big deal was and held a much more humorous perspective of the whole thing. A few weeks later, my insanity was solidly established when I shot the feces out from under a squatting man from 40 yards away (I used a rifle). Counseling and sedation were highly recommended to my parents but never attained, and nothing much ever became of it.

Before I turned 20 years old I went to jail over a dozen times, mostly in Tonopah. The last four or five times it was just because the local law saw me on the streets after they told my father to keep me out of town. At 17 years old, this complicated things because I had been kicked out of school in Ely the previous year and was now going to school, first in Reno, then in Red Bluff California. I had to drive through Tonopah on my way to and from school, on the weekends and such, to get home to Warm Springs. My best friend, Steve, and I picked up a couple of local girls one night and took them "swimming" out at Warm Springs. When we took them home, about 3 o'clock in the morning, the law was waiting for us. It seems one of the girls was supposedly the wannabe (on his part) girlfriend of a local bigmouth ("the girl of his dreams" he stated), whose father happened to be with the Sheriff's office of Nye County. They took us to jail and roughed us up pretty good, after they found a condom in my wallet and I said "I probably should have used that". Me and Steve started howling with laughter at the deputies red faced kid, and then I ( or Steve...can't rightly remember) fell over backward in my chair, laughing hysterically. By the time they threw us in our cell my ribs hurt more from laughing than anything else. That pretty much started the whole Tonopah thing. I really don't have a legitimate excuse for all the other towns I got locked up in, and (confession time) I actually knew who the girl's love-struck boyfriend was before I picked her up that night in Tonopah... No innocent coincidence there. I knew what I was asking for and did it anyway. The Sheriff's kid thought he was a tough guy and I guess I just got tired of his mouth. But of course, somehow, I managed to twist things and find a way to blame God for this, as well, obviously His punishment because I sinned (after all, it couldn't possibly have been my fault, like, direct consequences of the choices I made... No way! Of course not!). I remember hearing laughter in my head, when I used to get drunk and think it was God laughing at me. Years later I realized who it really was.

Another time, we were running from some more Tonopah trouble (no comment) in my 71 Nova. We were a few miles out of town going by the Round Mountain Junction, and the speedometer was pegged at 120 mph. I went down the oncoming lane on the left side of the traffic island to pass a car, and hit some spilled gravel, probably from an overloaded truck making the left hand turn onto Highway 376, turning north from Highway 6. We left the road, hit a drain ditch, and did a real-life "Dukes of Hazard" jump about 60 feet in the air. Unlike Dukes of Hazard, when the nose of that Nova hit the ground, my face hit the steering wheel so hard that it bent it to the dashboard (I know, I know. No seatbelt). My back was hurt so bad that Steve had to pull me out of the wreck and lay me on the side of the highway. The police finally got there, loaded us up, and even though my face and back, and Steve, were all busted up, they threw us in jail about 11:30 PM. I had a lot of blood running down the back of my throat from my busted up face, as my nose and cheeks were badly broken. About 3 AM, I guess they thought I was gonna die, so amazingly, they loaded us up in a cop car and threw us out on the sidewalk, downtown, in front of the Mizpah Hotel! They reasoned that they couldn't have me die in the jail, and to avoid answering for not taking me to the hospital, they figured that they would drop us off downtown and swear that I wasn't in that bad of shape when they did. The main street was pretty much deserted so my friend loaded me up on his back and carried me all the way back up the hill (about a mile), past the jail, to the hospital. He saved my life.

My Mom came into town the next day to see me, stuck her head in my room, looked right at me, and said "Sorry, I'm looking for my son". Your face is a mess when your own mother doesn't recognize you. Of all the regret I have in my life, hurting my dear mother like this is my greatest. She was the sweetest, loving person on the planet and she never, ever gave up on me. Lord, please give my Mom a huge hug for me, and tell her I'm sorry. I thank God for allowing my Mom and Dad to live long enough to see me get right with the Lord. Thank you, Jesus.

## CHAPTER 4

## When the Metal Hits the Bone

So here I was, back in E.R., this time in Ely. At that time, I firmly believed (wrongly) that all doctors in Ely were there because they had been malpracticed out of everywhere else. Thank God for Dr. Chris! The doctor attempting to treat me on this night, however, obviously had a "snoot full", and wasn't doing such a fine job. He would walk back and forth not knowing what exactly he was looking for, then would leave the emergency room for a few minutes, then come back, and do it over again. He finally started setting up an I.V. unit full of God - knows - what, and mumbled something about how it was going to "buy me time". But, as he tried to stick the needle in my arms (Yep! Both arms!) he would miss my veins. Then, instead of taking it out, he would turn it while it was in me, and try to hit my vein(s), which, for the most part, were collapsed anyway. Of course, me being me, I tried to yell at him, and he snapped. He stood up, looked at my wife, and said, "I can't be responsible for this", and he walked out. As in GONE!

We all knew I was gonna die, now. The Staff were trying to get ahold of the head surgeon, Dr. Chris, but couldn't reach him by phone. The police were notified and were searching for him as well. As best I could, I was trying to use my last moments with my wife to get my affairs in order and convince her that she and the kids would be all right (like, that's gonna happen). I loved her so much... That reality dominated my thinking as the tunnel vision grew much more intense and I was beginning to fade in and out of darkness. I still remember how incredibly clear my mind was. Then a "candy - striper" walked by in front of me. I don't know the technical name for this position that these young people have these days (sorry Brandy, my beautiful daughter, and respiratory therapist that I am very proud of). Anyway, she was close enough for me to grab and I got her by her arm and pulled her down to me. I looked into her terrified eyes and told her "Honey, I know it ain't your job, but you gotta stick that I.V. needle in my arm or I am gonna die". I still don't know if she was real or an angel, but, with tears running down her face, she stuck that thing in me and nailed that vein the very first time! Miracle! With the I. V. going, the tunnel vision seemed to relax a little and my vision stopped fading in and out of the blackness.

Jones was there now and we took time to collaborate our B.S. story. Why tell the truth when a lie would be better. If somehow I lived, I didn't want anybody or anything messing up the tracks around that old mine until I personally got a chance to investigate myself, or in case we had anything to "clean up". I wasn't sure what happened exactly, but when I find out there's gonna be hell to pay. Revenge is an art form to me that I have perfected and mastered. Somebodies gonna pay for this with their life, if they haven't already, and nobody is gonna save them from me. A bullet makes a distinctive sound when it hits meat and bone, but the roar of my pistol in that mine tunnel had eliminated any chance of hearing/knowing if I hit anything. Yeah, I know. I am minutes away from death, drowning in my own blood, in an emergency room, and I'm planning my revenge. How messed up is that?

In the meantime, a guy named Pope had just got home from the high school football game early, and as he walked into his house, he heard the cops looking for Dr. Chris on his scanner. He jumped back in his pickup and raced all the way back to the football field, where he had just seen Dr. Chris watching the game. Miracle, again! Perfect display of divine providence in action!

It's my understanding that Dr. Chris was a surgeon in the Korean War and apparently was the only doctor in the area with expertise in gunshot wounds. That's what I was told, in any event. However, Doc and I weren't particularly best friends, as he had not only patched me up before on multiple occasions, for various injuries, but I had also contributed to his on-the-job experience with injuries he had patched up on other people, that I may, or may not, have had something to do with. And again, running my mouth didn't help our relationship at all. That must have been a lot of it because I recollect my pal Ronnie smashing a guy's head into a slot machine after he got beer mugged by the guy, and Doc Chris got along with him okay. Hmmmm... Of course, Ronnie always had a much more charismatic character than I did.

Soon, the swinging doors of the ER room burst open and Doc Chris covered the distance across the floor to my chair in about three long strides, followed by a couple of the biggest male interns I have ever seen (apparently my mouth had preceded me). Man, he was all business, too. He looked down at me (is that disdain I see in your eyes?), and took the wrapping off of my wounds. Without a word he took one quick look at the holes, and stuck the gauze bandages back over them. He walked over to the counter and started gathering stuff out of the drawers and cabinets. By the look on Lori's and Jones's face, it wasn't a tea set he was assembling. He told Jones and my cousin Mickey that they had to wait out in the hall. He told my wife she could stay, but said it would be best if she left to. Lori stayed.

"Hold him", Doc said, as he turned around with a long bladed scalpel in one hand and a clear plastic tube, a little bigger than a thick McDonald's straw, in the other. With my arms pinned to the armrests of the chair, I was slightly leaned back and held there by another hand on my forehead. This time there was gentleness and compassion (pity?) in Doc's eyes when he said, "In a few seconds you're going to want to cough, and it's going to be very painful. Hopefully you will only need to cough once, and then it will be over". Then, assuming someone had already given me some type of painkiller in all the time I was in the ER, he shoved the blade of that scalpel into the top of the right side of my chest, about 4 inches above the bullet hole. The surgical steel glanced off of my rib bone as it bore all the way into my lung. The look on Doc's face, as he carved out the hole needed to insert the straw, told me that he clearly was surprised that I hadn't received any morphine or painkiller. No words can describe the pain I suffered over the next 15 seconds or so. It was a lifetime to me. Yup. It's true what the song says about "when the metal (bullet) hits the bone" (by Golden Earring, I think). It shot through my entire body, my entire being, and into my very soul. Instead of opening my mouth and yelling, for some reason I screamed through such tightly clenched teeth that my wife, and even Jones and Mickey out in the hall, could clearly hear distinctive "pops" as my teeth broke. As much as that hurt, it didn't compare to the cough that followed when Doc inserted that tube into the incision he had made, and down into the bottom of my lung. That cough will always be the most painful experience of my life, or in the universe, as far as I'm concerned. Then... I coughed again! I couldn't hold it back. I tried as best as I could. It was such pain that I was totally blinded in a brilliant white light that encompassed my total vision.

Amazingly, as the light began to subside, so did the pain, a little, and most importantly, I could breathe better. I felt needles going into both of my arms. Ah, morphine. As my vision came back to me I looked down to see the tube, now hooked into another tube and into a bag, pumping nasty looking blood and "stuff" out of my lung. I could hear my Lori trying to talk to me but I couldn't make out the words. Everybody sounded like they were mumbling. Eventually, I could make out Doc telling Lori that he had plugged the holes in me and re-inflated my right lung. I remember thinking, man, that sucked. As my morphine saturated mind drifted smoothly and calmly into La La Land, I remember admitting to myself that Doc was a man of integrity and had always been good to me, even when I was a total jackass, and lastly, I remember thinking what a good woman and friend my wife Lori was. She was always there for me.

# CHAPTER 5

## The Boys From The Brush

*"There is a friend who sticks closer than a brother"* Proverbs 18:24

After high school, I went to work full time for Nevada Mine Service. It was my Dad's company and we contracted to other companies, putting mines into production, mostly. I worked with the greatest bunch of hooligan tramp miners that ever terrorized the mining camps of Nevada. We were called "The Boys From The Brush". Despised by local law enforcement, feared by fathers of pretty (or not so pretty) young daughters, and loved by every cathouse madam for 300 miles (I have since then repented a 1000 times). When we came to town, it was party time! (That song from Thin Lizzy should start playing about right here...The boys are back in toooown!)

Get rowdy and tear stuff up? Yup! Get everybody pissed off? Yup! Get everybody smashed? Oh yeah! Go to jail, do not pass go, do not collect $200? Like clockwork. Get bailed out?

Sometimes, and only because the company couldn't find our replacements on the Sunday night before shift began on the following Monday morning. I can't even recall all the exploration and mining jobs, the multitude of staking contracts, or all the mines we tramped together... Reveille, Gila, New Reveille, Keystone, Rossi, Freiburg, Taylor, Cherry Creek, Cornucopia, Hamilton, Atlanta, Star peak, etc., etc., etc.

We worked hard and watched each other's backs. We lived in mining camps, ate together, partied and drank together, fought together, worked together, hunted together, and we looked out for our own. About twice a month we got to go to town, so we always were making up for lost time, it seemed, so "going to extremes" was a huge understatement in describing our days off. There was me, Stevie, my brother Billy Bob, Ronnie, and "Festus". Ronnie's younger brother Ricky drifted in and out of this conglomeration of backwoods talent, but for the most part, he had enough sense to go to Salt Lake City and get a steady job mining for Kennecott. They were, and still are to this day, my dearest brothers, even though we have gone separate paths and don't get to enjoy each other's company as much as we wish. When we do see or talk to each other we always retell the tales. Amazing that any of us lived this long. Especially when you consider that, in those days, most places served cold beer in a cold beer mug. Beer mugs were always lethal. My friend Ronnie was a champion survivor of being beer mugged. Like I said earlier, no one loved fighting more than John Hernandez, but Ronnie came really close.

One time we were all staking over 1000 mining claims for Phil (The Unk) Davis up by Soldier Creek in northern Elko County. A bad blizzard just "appeared", as is common in the Nevada Mountains, and we got separated in the storm. Billy Bob and Festus were in an M 29C track mounted "Weasel", and Ronnie and I were on foot, although Ronnie and I managed to find each other in the white out. Every now and then, Ronnie and I could hear the sound of the Weasel engine carried on the wind but couldn't tell what direction or how far away it was. We figured Bill and Festus would be okay in the Weasel as long as it was running, so as darkness set in, we started trekking cross country toward where we had left the trucks, about 4 miles away. When the sun went down the wind slowed and the snow started piling up in a hurry. There was no sound at all except our feet and legs trudging through fresh snow, and after a mile or so the snow was just below our knees. By midnight we were following Soldier Creek about a half mile from the trucks and every step was a deep ache in our legs and back. Our snow boots felt like cinderblocks, but we had to press on, knowing that if the storm broke and the sky cleared, the temperatures would plummet way below zero. Our elevation was over 6000 feet.

Ronnie was about 30 yards ahead of me breaking trail through the snow, as we took turns walking and each other's footprints to conserve energy. Though we were well dressed in winter gear, we were soaking wet with sweat. To stop would be to freeze. I knew that... Yet when we were within about 200 yards of the trucks I remember feeling quite euphoric. It seemed as if everything was just going to be fine and I wasn't cold anymore, and I thought, "The trucks are just up the hill a little ways, so I think I'll just lay down and take a short break". The wind faded from my ears and I felt warm and cozy lying in that soft, fluffy, fresh snow and my mind drifted to a sunny day in my backyard with my beautiful wife and two young children. We were barbecuing T-bone steaks. "Get your ass up, Johnny", he yelled in my face as he grabbed me by the front of my coat and literally jerked me up out of the snow and stood me on my feet. He stared straight into the eyeholes of my sub-zero facemask and said

"What the hell are you doing? I almost didn't find you! The wind covered our tracks". No doubt he was mad as hell, as well as relieved. He came back for me, and he saved my life.

By morning the storm had broken and by 10 A.M. Bill and Festus pulled up in the Weasel. When it got so bad that they had lost visibility, they had stopped and rode out the storm.

Two days later, in Battle Mountain, we had just finished breakfast at the Happy Ox. Me, Ronnie, Stevie, Festus and Billy Bob loaded up to leave in my Mom's green International Travel All, but it wouldn't start. We were parked right in front of the restaurants front windows. Ronnie and I got out, and raised the hood. I pulled out my Shrade single blade knife and proceeded to thump on the battery terminals... BOOM!

I was leaning directly over the battery when it blew up. My entire face, including both of my eyes, were drenched with plastic and battery acid. I was blind. Ronnie immediately grabbed me by the arm and swung me around towards the front door of the Happy Ox in order to get me to the bathroom and wash my eyes out. Quick thinking... A little too quick, maybe. At the double swinging entrance doors he yanked one side open and as we flew through the opening, he accidentally slammed me face first into the second unopened door! WHAM! Lights went off in my head, as I was holding my hands over my face with my head tilted slightly forward upon impact. My forehead felt like it had been smacked with a hammer. Oops! He pulled me on into the restaurant, wrapped his huge arm around my shoulders to steady me, and made a hard, fast turn to the left, and SPLAT! This time my face was in an upright, unprotected position as it met with the corner slot machine closest to the front door! I 'ma goin' down...nose smashed, blood spurting, knees buckling, lights dimming... Ronnie mutters "sorry", grabs me around my waist, and ushers me through the bathroom door that either Billy or Festus (God bless you!) are holding open. Although I probably could have splashed the ice cold water on my own face, I wasn't allowed that option. And it must have been fun because I'm relatively sure that all four of them were doing it. I tried to take a breath and sucked blood, acid and water down into my lungs and filled my sinuses. I am now drowning, trying fervently to push them away as they hold my eyes open and slam handfuls of water into them and I gasp desperately for air. Then, I achieve blurriness! I can begin to make out fuzzy shapes, and cough up the battery acid, blood, and water cocktail they so lovingly shoved into my lungs. As my vision begins to clear I can see the true concern for me etched on their faces, and although I would never say it out loud (great big tough guy me) it melts my heart. I love these guys and they love me. We are brothers all... The Boys from the Brush!

There are some people in this life that (God forgive me) you are just meant to get in trouble with. The old-timers would say "ride the river with", and I wouldn't trade my time and adventures with these boys for anything (including the ones I can't write about). They are the best of the best, and God loves them.

As I looked from face to face, they were all yelling and asking me if I could see, except Festus. As I turned and looked at him he was grinning from ear to ear and said "You're a blankety-blank mess... And your nose is broke – Baahahaha"! Then he busted up laughing! I was thinking, "What an ass", but by the time I looked in the mirror, we were all in hysterics! We laughed until our ribs hurt... And until we stepped out of the bathroom. The manager had called the cops. I cannot overstate the seriousness of dealing with "small town" law in Nevada, so I choked back the impulse to jokingly scream "Somebody, please help me", as jail time in Battle Mountain would surely suck. It might've been funny for a second, but we all would have gone to jail and I had a $200,000 staking contract to complete for The Unk.

To help matters along, a few nights later, Billy, Ronnie and Festus were drinking in a local Hispanic bar in Winnemucca, and they were the only white guys in the place. No big deal, until Ronnie gets his fill and decides it's time to head back to the motel. But, before he leaves, he plugs a dollar in the jukebox, and plays the same song over and over and over, and with his famous "up to something" devious smile, he walks out the door. Yep. Bruce Springsteen's "Born in the USA". If you run across my brother Billy Bob or Festus you'll have to ask them about it. It's their story, so they can tell it any old way they want. To say the least, bar fights were incredibly common (often including, but not limited to, pool cues, knives, beer mugs, and busted bottles) for all of us, as we were all instigators... You reap what you sow.

Needless to say, I couldn't wait for summer so we could turn these jobs into camp jobs, and get us back out into the hills, where we belonged. No jail, no bail, and a lot less drama. Out there we would pull the lead bullets out of .22 shells and replace them with soap (from a soft bar of soap) because it was more fun to shoot the flies (and each other) than smack them with a flyswatter, and it left no holes in the camp trailers. And man, could these guys shoot! Rifles, shotguns and pistols...

To go through 500 rounds a day was common, as we had no TV, telephones, or other means of entertainment to pass the time, so we hunted. The main theology that we believed at the time was that God made jackrabbits for target practice. If they could see it, they could hit it. We love the mountains of Nevada. It's what we know. It's where we were at home. It still is for me. I think, for me at least, the saddest day was when we eventually had to move to town and become "civilized" (To this day I barely know what that means).

God knows how I miss the sound of the wind blowing through the pines and the smell of sagebrush after a summer rain, and staring into the face of the starry sky as I drift off to sleep..., a cool summer breeze on my face on a sunny Nevada day in the high desert and the first rays of dawn breaking on our snow-covered mountain peaks.., And, God forgive me, the smell of gunpowder and the recoil of my pistols. Eventually, my guns would become my strength, and in them I would put my trust. My ability with them would lead me far from God, so I understand now why my Loving Father had to separate me from them in order for me to truly seek his face and rightfully put my trust in Him and Him alone. There was no other way.

And don't even get me started on our days at Warm Springs, as that would be a book in itself that should never be put into print. However, one rumor worth mentioning; me and Steve, may or may not have boosted our music collections beyond belief when we found out about Columbia house's offer of buy one album and get 11 for free, offer. Warm Springs mail came to a "general delivery" mail shelf in the corner of the bar, so when we were having a few beers every night after work, we would sift through all the magazines for the Columbia house free introductory offer cards, fill several out every night in names like Susie Peamoore, FiFi Laflamme, Ralph Schwartz and Darrell Domass.

Every week when the mail came in we packed out boxes of eight tracks, albums, and the newfangled cassette tapes. Or so the "alleged" story goes (so sorry, Lord, please forgive us if it actually did happen). And making deer antler pot pipes in the back room of the old Tybo saloon with my cousin was a definite boost to our finances, as twice a month we took them to Reno and sold them to Import Trading Post.

Things kinda came crashing down one day when Beverly Harrell, the madam from the Cottontail Ranch, came into Warm Springs with several of the girls. She was on tour trying to stir up votes as she was running for some (Congress? Assemblywoman?) political elected position. All the Boys from the Brush were sitting at the bar nursing our hangovers when Beverly and the girls came in and proceeded to call us by name and came running over to hug us... right in front of my mother. First thing, knowing that Mom would expect him to participate, Dad grinned and ducked out back through the kitchen, full well knowing that we were about to have our asses handed to us, and rightfully so. Words can't describe the shame (of getting caught) or the white-hot scolding we got. Mom's chin would quiver and her sweet cheeks would run rampant with the watershed from her blue eyes. Even without words, we were slashed to the bone and rightfully condemned to hell for our heinous crimes that caused even a single tear to fall from her loving, and always compassionate eyes. Overwhelming, unacceptable guilt! And you think your past won't come back to haunt you. You think what you do in secret won't come to light? You're losing an internal battle of wits with an unarmed person-yourself.

## CHAPTER 6

## God Sends Love, And Love Changes Things.

Even though Mom was the most forgiving person on the planet, I believe my pardon and restoration from this incident finally began when, on a hot summer night, cruising Virginia Street in Reno, I met the ultimate girl of my dreams. Stevie and I were on our way back from Eureka California on "business". We hit Reno about 9 PM and decided to "drag main" in hopes of seeing friends. We did. Our good friend Roger was cruising as well, so we pulled into the Mayfair parking lot to meet up. While we were talking, these two really hot chicks pulled up in a Chevelle to talk to my friend Roger. Cha Ching! Bata Bing! While Renée, the passenger, talked to Roger they introduced us and I immediately started impressing the super-hot driver babe, Lori, with my coolness, style, and Sauvé. Stevie hooked up with Renée and soon we were cruising in my even more impressive "75", LS6, 454 C.I.D. custom painted Chevy truck with twin stacks. It was a real nice tight fit on that bench seat, and man, this girl was not only foxy, but she had class! That was kind of a rare combination in my social circles (not that class was rare in most chicks Stevie and I picked up... I mean... umm... Never mind). And she was no easy mark. This one would take some work on my part. Then, while cruising, there was this little old man and a big old woman... Lori, I don't know how to describe the big old woman lugging five suitcases, and the little old man towing one small suitcase on a rope behind him, and nobody else would get it anyway (one of those "you kinda had to be there", things), but it's enough to say, we spent the night laughing our heads off and loving each other's company. I enjoyed just being with her and soon felt comfortable enough to let down my façade and be open about the real me. That was truly a first. Revealing this part of me, the real me, no other woman had ever been allowed to see.

    Thereafter, seeing her and talking to her was all I thought about. What the heck was wrong with me? Almost 400 miles away from her, I spent my days at the Reveille Mine, in Nye County, counting the days until I could go to Reno on my few days off to see her. Twice a month wasn't enough, so several times I would leave the mine after work and tach that LS6 454 engine to the max to get to her house in Washoe Valley, just about 9 PM. I would be allowed to "court" her by sitting beside her on her mother's couch, under the ever watchful eyes of her parents (who, by the way, were very slow to warm up to my charm and magnetic personality... Especially her Dad!).

But love was in the air. After about 30 minutes or so I/we (sometimes Stevie went with me) would have to leave and we would head into Carson City to "coffee up". Then, for the next three or four hours we would dodge cows, deer, coyotes, (never dodged a single rabbit at all) and various other critters of the night, at over 135 mph to make it back to work on time. Very long nights. Steve woke me up more times than I can count as I drifted into the other lane. Rumble strips are one of the greatest inventions of my time, and it's too bad we didn't have them back then. Lord God, please bless the holy angels that you gave charge over us all those dark nights on the Nevada desert highways!

Calls were made by riding 50 miles or so south of our mine to Union Carbide's Tempiute mine (the town is now called Rachel). They had a relay payphone that worked up on top the mountain above the mine. Oh yeah, forgot to mention, I had previously gotten not only myself, but my Dad's entire mine crew kicked out, or more precisely, 86'd, from Warm Springs by the new proprietor, who, I was confident, was a man of extremely low IQ. Something to do with shooting out some of his Christmas lights while displaying extreme belligerence (him or me, being belligerent, I wonder?)... my bad, I'm sure...even paid for the damage and he still threw us out- go figure. Probably smarter than I thought.

Then, a few days later, as Steve and I pulled in and tried to get gas and use the only public phone for 50 miles, the new proprietor came running out the front door with a pistol. I was exceedingly pleased. He was way too slow. At the gas pumps, I drew, cocked and aimed before he could bring his gun down to bare. His face went white as he realized he was about to die. I hated him and had no remorse, whatsoever, and this was a perfect opportunity. Only Steve's soft-spoken words to me saved his life that day. As the proprietor, a total ass in every sense of the word, stood before me mortified, Steve simply said, "Don't Johnny, were on probation, man". It was enough to save the above mentioned ass's life. Realizing, as I look back to that day, how eager I was to take his life, shamefully makes me shudder. How far into darkness I had gone, and how it had engulfed me. The adrenaline rush from that split-second, life or death episode became my addiction, I had to have it. I had to have a lot more.

The man dropped his gun and whispered "please". "Step away from it", I said. "Call the cops and I'll be back for you". He nodded once. We drove away.

\*\*\*

1977 – one day I was blading the road from Reveille Mine to the highway. Steve had gone back to the mine to get fuel for the grader I was operating, and I was parked at the highway waiting for him to return. Lying on top of the rear tires with my butt in the space between them, I was completely covered in "bug dust" that the open cab grader had kicked up while working my way down the hill. Lying back with my eyes closed, I heard a car slowing down as it approached the turnoff to the mine. To my delight, Lori's Chevelle pulled next to me on the dirt road! The passenger window rolled down and Renée looked at me and asked, "Is this the road to Reveille Mine?". I must've looked like the Pillsbury Dough Boy all covered in that bug dust, and with my hair in a ponytail, they didn't even recognize me! I laughed and said, "Yup! It is". Lori leaned over by Renée and they both just stared at me with squinted eyes in total disbelief. For a moment I thought they might turn around and leave. After all, what did they think I did for a living... sell Avon? They gathered their wits about them and slowly got out of the car. They said they had asked for directions at Warm Springs, and that the proprietor, who was very polite and kindly, told them how to get here (good choice by the proprietor). Steve soon arrived and we made our way back up into the canyon to camp.

The next morning Einar (the company owner) arrived. When he found out the girls had spent the night he told my Dad that we had to find a different campsite because we were living in sin. Looking back, you have got to admire a man who doesn't compromise his faith (Counsel of Twelve, Mormon Church). He was actually right and we were wrong, but there is no way I could even begin to see that, at that time. All I could see was this beautiful girl and think, "Oooh-la-la!". So we loaded up our trailers, my old three legged pet coyote, "Yotey", got ourselves a generator and moved our camp into Hyde Springs, in a side canyon, down the road a piece. It was soon dubbed "sinners camp", and not surprisingly, several of the other miners moved there with us. It was at sinner's camp that I asked Lori to marry me, and she said yes! I told my folks and all my friends, but the general consensus was, "Yeah, right. You? Married? Snicker, snicker. That'll be the day!" they chided.

That was 40 years ago at the time of this writing-snicker, snicker! Who's laughing now? And we were married in the Mormon church in Carson City to boot! Double snicker, snicker! Ha! Ha! Ha! Poor girl had no clue. Born and raised in Santa Monica, California, she thought Washoe Valley was out in the "sticks". I showed her what "sticks" were all about! It was 75 miles to the nearest town and it was Tonopah, a dust blown little busted mining town that I had already been kicked out of! At that time, I was convinced of the fact (maybe wrongly), that if God were to ever give the world an enema, I knew, for sure where the nozzle would go. And being 86'ed from Warm Springs, the closest place to take a bath was about 70 miles south of the mine at a swimming hole called Ash Springs. Otherwise, there was always the horse trough at Sinners' Camp.

In any event, the girl had moxie. We were married on January 28, 1978, one week after I turned 21, because I wanted to know what it was like to be "free, white, and 21", before I got hitched. Without doubt, it was nothing compared to being married to the hottest girl on the planet, who was quickly becoming my best friend. In late fall we moved camp around the west side of the mountain to New Reveille Mine and geared up to ride out the rest of winter. I had over 80 coyote and bobcat traps (No.3 & 4 Victors) set throughout the surrounding mountains, and ran my trap line after work, sometimes until after midnight. One bitter cold night a deep freeze came and Lori and I were running the trap line, pulling up traps so they wouldn't freeze into the ground. We didn't really expect to catch much as the weather was so cold. Near the end of the line, I left Lori in the truck to stay warm and dropped into a steep ravine, then under a cedar tree to recover two sets of my No. 4 Victors. As I got close I heard the low snarl of a cat, just before my flashlight lit up the bright reflection of its eyes. The first round in in the chamber of my pistol is a .22 short that I used to "empty" my traps, as not to make an unsightly exit wound in the hide that would later have to be sewn up, after skinning. As I took the safety off, a second growl sounded in the tree above the trapped cat and I suddenly threw my back against the bank of the ravine, behind me. As I hit the ground I fired and managed to turn my head sideways to avoid the second cat from landing directly in my face, as it lunged out of the tree at me. The shot went wild but was just enough to make the bobcat miss me. It landed right beside my head and vaulted off into the darkness, thank God, as the .22 short lacked the power needed to completely cycle another round, and the Colt Challenger pistol jammed.

My hands were shaking wildly as I dug another .22 short out of my pocket and dropped it in the snow. I managed to get the next one in the chamber and shot the bobcat that still remained in my trap, between the eyes. In the stillness that followed, I laid there in the snow with my heart pounding into my throat, as huge snowflakes began falling all around me. I pulled my traps, gathered up my cat, and as I got closer to the truck, I could hear Lori singing to the radio, totally oblivious to my peril. I was still shaking a little as I threw the cat and my two traps in the back of the truck, and just stood there for a moment and enjoyed the adrenaline that was still coursing through my veins (I know, right? No addiction there). I opened the driver's door and Lori looked at me with a big smile and kept on singing. At that moment, I knew more than ever, that I was truly in love with my perfect soulmate. However, I'm not so sure she was totally sold on the idea, especially when I dropped the oven door in our little 21 foot trailer and used it for a skinning table (I got pictures!), as it was almost 20° below zero by the time we got back to camp. She apparently had really serious problems watching me skin them, and the smell made her "launch". That, and our dog, Bear, hiding a pile of rabbit guts under her pillow didn't help much either. I suppose having a rattlesnake in a fish aquarium for a piggy bank, and a fairly mean (major understatement) three legged old coyote for a pet may have added to her discomfort. But, like I said; she had moxie. So, to make her feel better, I got her a kangaroo rat of her very own, as a pet... But, unbeknownst to me, it was pregnant and directly after giving birth to several baby rats, the new mother turned around, and right in front of my horrified wife, ate all of her young (who knew?). Run back home to mama? You would think so, but no! That's moxie.

With all the traps pulled in, Steve and I went to "calling" coyotes and cats at night. The call sounds like a wounded rabbit, when done properly, and I got pretty good at it.

This one particular night we were in the Hot Creek Valley, about 7 miles east of camp, below New Reveille Mine. Although the night started out fairly clear, it had clouded up in a hurry. We saw a lot of movement heading farther east towards the mountains when we kicked on our spotlights, and decided to head in that direction. As we reached the foothills and caught a small herd of deer in our lights, sleet began to fall.

wasn't enough, so several times I would leave the mine after work and tach that LS6 454 engine to the max to get to her house in Washoe Valley, just about 9 PM. I would be allowed to "court" her by sitting beside her on her mother's couch, under the ever watchful eyes of her parents (who, by the way, were very slow to warm up to my charm and magnetic personality... Especially her Dad!).

But love was in the air. After about 30 minutes or so I/we (sometimes Stevie went with me) would have to leave and we would head into Carson City to "coffee up". Then, for the next three or four hours we would dodge cows, deer, coyotes, (never dodged a single rabbit at all) and various other critters of the night, at over 135 mph to make it back to work on time. Very long nights. Steve woke me up more times than I can count as I drifted into the other lane. Rumble strips are one of the greatest inventions of my time, and it's too bad we didn't have them back then. Lord God, please bless the holy angels that you gave charge over us all those dark nights on the Nevada desert highways!

Calls were made by riding 50 miles or so south of our mine to Union Carbide's Tempiute mine (the town is now called Rachel). They had a relay payphone that worked up on top the mountain above the mine. Oh yeah, forgot to mention, I had previously gotten not only myself, but my Dad's entire mine crew kicked out, or more precisely, 86'd, from Warm Springs by the new proprietor, who, I was confident, was a man of extremely low IQ. Something to do with shooting out some of his Christmas lights while displaying extreme belligerence (him or me, being belligerent, I wonder?)... my bad, I'm sure...even paid for the damage and he still threw us out- go figure. Probably smarter than I thought.

Then, a few days later, as Steve and I pulled in and tried to get gas and use the only public phone for 50 miles, the new proprietor came running out the front door with a pistol. I was exceedingly pleased. He was way too slow. At the gas pumps, I drew, cocked and aimed before he could bring his gun down to bare. His face went white as he realized he was about to die. I hated him and had no remorse, whatsoever, and this was a perfect opportunity. Only Steve's soft-spoken words to me saved his life that day. As the proprietor, a total ass in every sense of the word, stood before me mortified, Steve simply said, "Don't Johnny, were on probation, man". It was enough to save the above mentioned ass's life. Realizing, as I look back to that day, how eager I was to take his life, shamefully makes me shudder. How far into darkness I had gone, and how it had engulfed me. The adrenaline rush from that split-second, life or death episode became my addiction, I had to have it. I had to have a lot more.

The man dropped his gun and whispered "please". "Step away from it", I said. "Call the cops and I'll be back for you". He nodded once. We drove away.

***

1977 – one day I was blading the road from Reveille Mine to the highway. Steve had gone back to the mine to get fuel for the grader I was operating, and I was parked at the highway waiting for him to return. Lying on top of the rear tires with my butt in the space between them, I was completely covered in "bug dust" that the open cab grader had kicked up while working my way down the hill. Lying back with my eyes closed, I heard a car slowing down as it approached the turnoff to the mine. To my delight, Lori's Chevelle pulled next to me on the dirt road! The passenger window rolled down and Renée looked at me and asked, "Is this the road to Reveille Mine?". I must've looked like the Pillsbury Dough Boy all covered in that bug dust, and with my hair in a ponytail, they didn't even recognize me! I laughed and said, "Yup! It is". Lori leaned over by Renée and they both just stared at me with squinted eyes in total disbelief. For a moment I thought they might turn around and leave. After all, what did they think I did for a living... sell Avon? They gathered their wits about them and slowly got out of the car. They said they had asked for directions at Warm Springs, and that the proprietor, who was very polite and kindly, told them how to get here (good choice by the proprietor). Steve soon arrived and we made our way back up into the canyon to camp.

The next morning Einar (the company owner) arrived. When he found out the girls had spent the night he told my Dad that we had to find a different campsite because we were living in sin. Looking back, you have got to admire a man who doesn't compromise his faith (Counsel of Twelve, Mormon Church). He was actually right and we were wrong, but there is no way I could even begin to see that, at that time. All I could see was this beautiful girl and think, "Oooh-la-la!". So we loaded up our trailers, my old three legged pet coyote, "Yotey", got ourselves a generator and moved our camp into Hyde Springs, in a side canyon, down the road a piece. It was soon dubbed "sinners camp", and not surprisingly, several of the other miners moved there with us. It was at sinner's camp

A different color of eyes lit up behind the deer herd, but they were just out of range for night shooting, so we followed them into a small canyon in hopes of catching a better shot. The sleet was really gaining momentum now and the sky was completely blotted out by the black clouds. The temperature was dropping, as we decided to call it a night. As we were turning around we snapped a U joint in the center driveline of the company Dodge (yeah, I know… Using a company truck for hunting) we were in. In this particular model, there is a short driveline between the transmission and the transfer case, where we lost the U joint, so we had no power to the front or rear wheels.

With no spare U joint, we climbed under the truck to remove a U joint from the front axle driveline and use it to replace the broken U joint in the main driveline, thus, giving us rear wheel drive to go home on. Even though it was just sitting there idling, the engine started overheating (typical 70s series dodges) so we had to shut it off.

It only took about 20 minutes to install the U joint but when we got back into the cab, the battery wouldn't turn the engine over. We were stranded about nine or ten miles from camp at about 11 PM and the sleet had now turned to huge wet flakes of snow. I suggested burning the truck down to stay warm, as the piece of junk was always breaking down on me… more times than I can remember, and we were both soaking wet to the bone. But Steve, who always seems to have more sense and patience than me, came up with plan B – build a shelter and a fire. In a ravine by the pickup we built a 6 x 4 lean-to against a huge rock. There was plenty of old trees and wood, but most of it was wet. Digging under the larger pine trees got us some much-needed dry wood and kindling, and we soon had a fire. Within an hour there was about 3 inches of snow and it wasn't slowing down. As we huddled around our small fire in the cramped space of our shelter, we realized that our wood wouldn't last much longer and surely not until morning, when we had hoped that someone would see our smoke.

Soon the snow just stopped and the silence was overwhelming. No wind, no sound at all, except our dying fire. We had to move. There was an old ghost town and mill site down in the middle of the valley, about halfway between us and camp. If we could make it there we could find dry wood and get in out of the weather, inside the old mill building.

It was pitch black. The new snow gave us just enough dim illumination to tell where the old road was (two lane cow trail is more like it), so we could find (stumble) are way off the foothills to the valley below, which I think was about 4 miles or so. As we moved as briskly as we dared in the dark, the clouds broke up and the sky began to clear. There was no moon but the stars lit things up really nice. With the cloud cover gone, the cold air descended on us like a blanket of ice, freezing our wet clothes and even our hair that stuck out from under our beanies. With about a mile to go, my wet close started to freeze to my back, shoulders and ankles. We were in real trouble. The temperature continued to drop and the wet fluffy snow was now crunchy under our boots. It had to be getting close to 0°. That's, pretty much, the Nevada high desert for you. Our elevation was just less than 6080 feet. The trees thinned out and soon large shadows loomed ahead of us, indicating we were getting close to the ghost town and the old mill building, and the air that was going into our lungs was so bitter cold that it hurt. Neither of us had feeling in our feet anymore, just numbness.

Meanwhile, back at camp, Lori was going from trailer to trailer waking people up trying to get help. She knew something was wrong and we must be in trouble.

As soon as we got into the old mill building we started gathering wood, and found an old metal box to build a fire in. We burned everything we could find; old chairs, tables, shelves, and eventually we even started pulling boards off the walls and floor, until everything we could burn had been put in the fire. The sky was entering its predawn light as I thought how stressed-out Lori must be right now. It made me wish that I hadn't told her all those bull crap stories about Bigfoot, mountain lions and bears (I know, I know... Bigfoot maybe, but bears were pushing it).

Only half-jokingly I said, "God if you're real, we could use a little help right now or we're not going to make it till dawn". The cold was crippling. All we could do now was shiver and watch the last of our wood burn down. Did I or Steve consciously push the metal box of fire up against the wooden wall of the mill building? I don't know... Maybe. I don't remember. I began to drift off, but irregardless, it probably saved our lives. Smoke was rolling out of the building and the sky was getting light and the next thing I remember was hearing the faint sound of a vehicle approaching. It kept getting louder and closer, but I couldn't bring myself to open my eyes or even try to get up. We were both lying on the floor as I heard Ray Horn's booming voice as he yelled, "Here they are! I found them". I heard him but I didn't give a damn. I just wanted to drift off into the quiet darkness of my mind.

Ray was a giant of a man. As he jerked me up off the floor and packed me outside I remember opening my eyes and seeing others throwing snow on the smoldering wall of the building. I smiled inside a little as I realized the irony of a man freezing to death while orchestrating his own cremation, as his final act. Amazingly, I would never even consider therapy as an option back then… Or ever, for that matter! Wow.

As we were getting out of the trucks, back at camp, we looked back into the valley floor to see a dark billowing cloud of smoke rising several hundred feet into the air, where the ghost town was. Apparently, they had missed an ember or two. Dad said I would have to go over to Twin Springs Ranch and tell Joe Fallini that I burnt his mill building down. Near death experiences always go better with a big pile of humiliation on top. For this reason, I told Lori that I had to go alone, regardless of her objections. The fewer the witnesses, the better, especially her.

"How about we just wait and see if he notices it's gone", I suggested. "Get cleaned up and get some coffee in you. No use putting it off", says Dad. I could think of sixty-seven reasons to put it off. First and foremost in my fuzzy, half froze brain, was sleep. Sleep would be good. But my Dad was a man of integrity and conviction, and I knew it was the right thing to do. What's more, Steve and Ray had gone to fetch that Antichrist of a Dodge truck that Satan had obviously sent to torment me till Jesus comes, so now I'm gonna have to face Big Joe all by my little lonesome.

Big Joe and Helen Fallini were the true salt of the earth and I always held them in the highest regard, and I would die before doing anything to disrespect them. I was feeling like a real piece of work as I stepped up to the ranch house door and knocked. Bobby Mike (the oldest Indian cowboy on the planet) was smoking a roll-your-own and coiling his raita as he watched me knock on the door then step back to wait. There was laughter in his old eyes… Could he somehow know?

Helen answered the door with a genuine smile and said, "Hi Johnny, come on in and have some coffee". I felt so bad that I just looked at the floor and said, "Helen, I best see Big Joe. I gotta tell him something I did last night". She looked at me kinda puzzled and said, "Go on in the back. He's in their shaving".

"What the hell are yuh up to, Johnny?", Joe says, as I walked up behind him and he looked at me in the bathroom mirror, without even missing a beat with his straight razor.

"Joe, last night, or more like early this morning, I burnt down your mill building at the old Reveille mill site. I burn it to the ground." I confessed.

He just kept on shaving.

Then, a slow, deep, chuckle… "Heh, heh, heh… The hell you did!" he says!

"Well", says Big Joe, "you look like hell. You better get in the kitchen and have some coffee".

"I'm sorry, Joe", I said, and went to the kitchen where Helen was already waiting with a cup of piping hot fresh coffee. I could hear Joe's slow, low, laughter as I left the back room.

And that was it.

In all my days I will never forget the mercy, grace, and forgiveness Joe and Helen bestowed on me that day, and I will honor them to the Lord, as it truly had an effect on me and made me a better man by the example they showed me. God bless them for allowing me to retain my dignity and some sense of honor, which I most assuredly did not deserve.

## CHAPTER 7

## Surrealistic Pillow, Staking, And a Small Mine Story

When I woke up in the hospital room, I looked over at the nurse and said, "This place stinks like dead people". My mother's visit lasted about a minute and a half until she walked out to the nurse's station and told the person on duty, "I don't know what you're giving my son but you better get him off it!" Pure hate and rage spewed out of my mouth. I don't remember it, but that's when we found out that I am allergic to Demerol. I apparently told Doc I didn't have any money, and even if I did, I wasn't gonna pay him for patching me up again, so he might as well release me from the ICU (because of my pride, I would eventually mortgage my house to pay these bills, rather than declare medical bankruptcy). A few days later he did just that. It took about 3 ½ hours for the morphine to wear off, and after four hours I was completely humbled. I blamed God, over and over, because (as my L. D. S. Bishop had taught me in counseling when I was a boy) God could never be pleased with me because of my actions/sins etc., so who else could be pre-orchestrating the horrible events in my life? (I know, right? They certainly could have nothing to do with any of MY choices.) When my aunt Neva came to visit me in the hospital, I told her about why God hated me, according to what my LDS counselor had told me. The next day she brought me an incredibly enlightening book called "The God Makers" and told me to keep it hidden or the nurses would take it, and later, while I was sleeping, they did! The book seemed to make perfect sense, but now added frustration to my confusion about God, so as what seemed my only recourse, I told God to leave me alone. I told my wife that God simply created us for his entertainment, and this is what happens when he is bored with us. Blessed Father, with all my heart I regret the ugly things I said all those times, and thank You dearly for never leaving me or forsaking me, especially in my darkest years. Thank You for Your sweet forgiveness, Your grace, and Your mercy.

The tube in my chest came out as easily as it went in (sarcasm… Ha ha!), But Doc, being a man of mercy as well as integrity, (and faith, I later found out! Divine providence, again!) sent me on a Surrealistic voyage to the Land of La La, again, via the starship/Airplane Morphine.

All I remember, as my head hit the Pillow, was an episode of the Jeffersons playing on the TV! (I did it! I used all four words, Jefferson, Airplane, Surrealistic Pillow, to describe a morphine trip! Only the wise who survived the 60s and 70s will get it. 1967 RCA Records.... Try YouTube) Uummmm... Sorry. My bad, again

Once I got home to my rock house on Campton Street, all I could do was "not move" as I healed. Every breath hurt but I got stronger day by day. I slept sitting up in a chair, and woke up every morning at 8 AM to the sound of my neighbors chainsaws.

***

Somehow, knowing who was using them, made the sound of those chainsaws comforting to me. Louie was not only my neighbor, but he is my dear friend and Boy Scout master. Anyone who knows him knows what a true man of God looks like. I, and my brother, cousins, and many close friends are responsible for many of his gray hairs, though distinguished looking as they may be. He showed us how to "walk the walk" and always lead by example. He loved us and we loved him, and we are all sorry (in our own ways) about the whole dynamite on the scout camping/fishing trips, Louie, even though I believe we can all humbly agree that nothing catches more fish than DuPont Spinners! God bless you for always sticking up for us and never calling the cops. Having Louie as a close neighbor has always been a blessing, especially since I knew he would be praying for me. Thank you.

Jamboree was the great yearly gathering of Boy Scout troops in the West, to Success Summit Campgrounds in White Pine County. A "rendezvous", if you will, of hundreds and hundreds of Boy Scouts. Politically correct? Bah ha ha ha! If little things like words offended you back then, you were a "whussy" and would probably, at some point, windup trapped in the bottom of an outhouse or tied naked to a tree and left alone in the forest for a night. I believe Louis had to set more than one whussy free every year at Jamboree. Back then, Scouting was for honing our survival and life skills, and for boys becoming men, not something weird. More realistic to me now than it was then, was our oath – "On my honor, I will do my best, to do my duty, to God and my country, and to obey the Scout Law; to help other people at all times; to keep myself physically strong, mentally awake and morally straight". In today's society, openly repeating this "politically incorrect" oath would offend so many people on so many levels, that many would have to seek medical attention and psychotherapy after choking on the words "God", "country", and the most offensive of all, "morally straight". Ironically, it looks like the "whussies" run things now. Sad. One time at Jamboree, my brother Bill was "tapped out" for the privilege of being tested in regard to see if he had what it takes to become a member of the elite group known as "Order of the Arrow". The three days of testing were painfully grueling, to say the least, requiring exceptional mental and physical abilities and extreme self-control. Very few made it through the full three day ordeal to earn their place of acceptance in the Order of the Arrow, and I am very proud to say, my brother was one of those very few who did. I will forever hold him in the highest esteem for this amazing accomplishment.

We seemed to always set up our camp right next to the Owyhee Indian Scout Troop from Northern Nevada. They were a really rough lot and other scout troops avoided them. We always seem to get along pretty good with them, outside of a couple of fights and a tomahawk whizzing past my cousin Bill's head one night (putting cellophane under their toilet seat at night got alot of fairly innocent people hurt one year!).

They had a favorite campfire game we came to love and (sort of) master, called "Pig" (meaning unknown). Played most always at night, everyone stood evenly spaced apart, in a large circle around a campfire. Everyone in the circle had a long, thick pine tree or juniper tree limb about 4 or 5 feet long. Limbs cut from pine trees, sticky with pitch, were preferred so that they would catch fire from time to time during a "round" and terrify (not to mention, burn!) your opponents. Everyone also dug about a 6 inch hole in the dirt right in front of where you stood. As long as your "stick" was in the hole, it was your "house". If you took your stick out of the hole and allowed someone else to put their stick in your "house", you were "it" (basically, homeless), and now in search of a house. To get another hole or "house" you would have to take it from somebody else, and there were two ways to accomplish this; 1) by forcing your opponent to remove his stick in an attempt to defend his house, for just a split second, from his hole/house so you could shove yours into it, or, 2) by knocking a white hot tin can (not aluminum) into his hole while his stick was still in it. By doing so, your opponent would have to relinquish possession of his "house" to you and reheat that can in the campfire until it was again white-hot, for the next round. Sticks are not allowed to be raised higher than your waist while swinging it (supposedly, only at the hot can or your opponents stick… think, shins, to be more accurate), when defending off the attacker with the can, as he approaches. Regardless, you must hit the can away from your "house" in order to defend it and keep it. As you try to hit the can away, he tries to take your house by shoving his stick or the can in your hole. As stated before, the can is heated to white-hot, and if it hits you in the legs or body, you can catch fire (blue jeans and down filled jackets, especially) or be severely burned instantly, so your hole/house isn't the only target the one who is "it" is covertly aiming at! All of us have scars on our shins to this day, mostly from clubbing each other with tree branches. This was often the result, when your closest neighbor was being assaulted by the guy with the cherry red tin can, and you leaned over and stuck your stick in his "house" while he was distracted by fighting for his life. They would then beat each other's legs while racing to your old abandoned hole/house in their attempt to take possession of it. It was considered treachery on your part, but still produced interesting and entertaining results.

Hanging out with the Owyhee's also definitely honed your skills throwing knives, tomahawks and axes. Oddly, they weren't that great at archery, probably because they all packed guns like us.

***

The nice part about owning my own corporation is that the mining and exploration work I was involved in, kept me out in the mountains most of the time. I had pretty much "opted out" of the whole 9 to 5 thing going on in town, and had enhanced my chances of feeding my adrenaline addiction through various "adventures" that always seemed to present themselves. Desert Enterprises Inc. was a full-service mining company. We did a lot of underground timbering, rehab and salvage, as well as a mass amount of claims staking.

Silver? Copper? Zinc? At the time of this writing, all hold claim to be this year's top performers. We, my brother and I, have all of them in one mine. In fact, we have 20,000+ tons of ore stockpiled in Central Nevada. We also have lead, which is typical of Nevada ore bodies, and even a little gold. It's a good mine. But unfortunately, it only has the capacity to make millions... not billions and billions, or trillions and trillions, so it's just not "Big enough." At least not for the big boys such as Barrick, Kinross or Newmont, even though they have staked well over 500 claims that totally surround us.

You would think that would be a good thing, right? No, not really. In fact, negotiations got so ridiculous that we haven't been back to the "table" in years... just can't take the B.S. anymore. Sometimes it just seems like, if you're from a small town in Nevada, you're automatically categorized as an uneducated hick. My brother has spent many decades as the senior mine planner for many large companies such as Echo Bay, Barrick, etc., and has also witnessed a decline in professionalism over recent years toward the "little guy." Whereas, in the past, they were responsible for the discovery of the majority of producing mines in Nevada, and considered a valuable asset. Now the small miner or prospector is not only near extinction, but the few I know of that still hold their properties, are commonly disrespected and preyed upon by larger companies.

Big companies know that they have no place to go with their ore, even if they could wade through the miles of bureaucracy to actually mine it. All the "custom mills" that received ore from the small mining outfits have all been dismantled, destroyed, or sit dormant in promotional stock companies that don't have the funds to put them back into operation, and probably wouldn't if they did. Remember back in the 70's and early 80's when you couldn't pick up a mining magazine or most Nevada newspapers without seeing dozens of ads by big companies soliciting small miners to "submit your mining properties to us?" My old friend Jack Grimm told me it was because "their geologists couldn't hit an ore body with their hat, even if they were standing on it", and there may be a thread of truth in there somewhere. I don't know for sure. Why don't you see those types of ads anymore? Well, because by the late 80's we had all submitted our data to these big companies, so they knew what all the small mining outfits were holding. Then, came the "Armageddon" of the small mining companies.

You see, most of us little outfits made our living doing other people's assessment work. Remember that? Remember doing actual yearly work that was the equivalent of $100 per claim, per year, on the property itself? My Dad, my brother, and I, as well as thousands of others, all had our own companies that hired about 6-10 employees and we made enough money from our clients, doing their required assessment work on their properties, to pay for the advancement of our own mining endeavors. It not only supplied a living for us and our employees, but it also allowed us "little guys" to successfully compete in the same open marketplace as major multi-billion dollar mining corporations. But, of course, we couldn't have that now, could we? Then, promoted by the big companies, I believe, the Bureau of Land Management passed the law that said we no longer would spend the $100 per claim, per year for assessment work on the properties themselves, but instead, we will all just give the money to the BLM.

With no more revenue coming into our companies through yearly assessment work, we no longer could afford to hold more than 10 claims (small miner exemption) and I was told that tens of thousands of small mining companies, including ours, were forced out of business within the first few years after the law was passed. The money the big companies saved by not having to deal with the small mine owners was more than enough to compensate for the added expense, and they simply had collected all of our data (which never seemed to be "big enough" or fit their "criteria") and they didn't need us anymore. They knew we didn't have the money coming in any longer to keep and maintain our claims, so they just waited and took them for nothing, when we couldn't hang on anymore. Basically, we couldn't afford to pay our working capital to the government and still afford to work our claims as well. Greed, by any other name is still greed.

Then, amazingly, all the custom mills that would take smaller quantities of ore from different small mines around Nevada, vanished. Interesting "coincidence" don't you think? You could dig it out, but you had nowhere to go with it. Now, the big companies are like when Pike are introduced to a fresh water lake. They eat every other fish, and then they eat each other. I'm not saying big companies are all like this. Sometimes I even hear rumors of some mystical "junior" companies and "mid-range" outfits that adhere to an old fashioned "code of ethics" or "honor system", but I have no idea where to look anymore. I'm not in the promoting business; I'm in the mining business. Times have changed and such old "ideals" are not seemingly held in very high regard these days.

There are still a few of us "old timers" who still hold on to our small mines in hopes of a custom mill magically appearing within shipping distance, or someone who is looking for a small (millions) mining project, who will be willing to build an onsite recovery system. Soon, the last of us will all be gone, and our properties consumed by the big dogs, who will publicly proclaim that "they" have made a "new" discovery, and will use our dreams to promote investors out of billions for exploration costs, I am sure, probably without any intention of productivity. Why? Because paperwork sells stock, and nothing produces paperwork like exploration projects on ore bearing ground with a production history. Hence the term "paper miners."

So be it, but know this... what killed off all the true prospectors and small miners? We were miners, not promoters. We liked it small and simple. We didn't want to grow big, we just wanted to mine... and that was our undoing. And like my Dad told me one time, when we saw a TV commercial with a Hearst pulling a U-Haul trailer; he said "No, you can't take it with you son, except just one thing, and you better pray to God that it's intact when you stand before your Maker on judgement day, and that's your honor. Integrity is everything son, and on it you will be judged." I'm good with that.

All industries evolve. I suppose like all other industries, it was inevitable, that the mining industry has evolved into what it is today. I guess I'm just missing an era of days gone by. Mega mines now employ hundreds of thousands of people and everybody that walks through the front gate of today's mine sites gets to be called a "miner", regardless of their assignment (i.e. janitor, forklift operator, etc.,) Whoot! Whoot! Yet my prayers still lift up those actual hard rock miners that descend into the darkest, deepest realms of underground mining, every day... round in, round out... God Bless and protect them! In any event, please forgive the ramblings of an old hard rock miner...

Staking mining claims, to me, was the "cream of the crop" as far as work goes. You were always deep in the Nevada Mountains, and your clients paid you an asinine amount of money while you looked for treasure, arrowheads, and old bottles, and I usually gave a substantial discount if it was close to a decent fishing hole. Lori, on the other hand, when she wasn't helping me out on the job, was up to her ears in my paperwork; maps, certificates of location, BLM filings, etc. etc. I remember rolling into town late at night between contracts, to drop off my old paperwork, pick up the new location notices and maps, then rolling out at dawn for the next job. Lori always kept things going. In winter we would swap out or rebuild the big block Chevy engines in our five trucks, repaint stuff, and service the Weasel and the four wheelers. The staking business was extremely hard on equipment and crews, to say the least. If you weren't in pretty good physical shape when you hired on, you would be in a few weeks, if you didn't quit.

Sometimes you would spend the entire day scratching and clawing your way up some unnamed mountain, in the middle of nowhere, with a stack of claim posts and gear strapped to your back. Finally, when every breath is a painful gasp and every muscle in your legs and back are spasming, you top out on a mountain where you know darn well that no other man has ever been on. No one else will ever know what you did or how you feel as you look in every direction for a hundred miles, holler at the top of your lungs, and beat yourself on the chest because it feels so good to have made it to the top of that mountain! It's between you and God. It's a personal victory that only He shares. He saw, and He knows how you feel. However, extended celebrating can be costly, as getting down off that mountain before dark usually poses its own unique challenges, as well. Up or down, you gotta keep moving.

A typical lode mining claim is 1500 feet long and 600 feet wide, and in a "claim block" (large group of claims attached to each other) the boundary markers (posts) have got to be laid out accurately in a straight line, sometimes for miles. You usually don't get the luxury of going around obstacles; you must go over or through them to maintain distance and elevation accuracy. You gotta stay in a straight line. It is not a mere stroll through the countryside, by any means. Rocks, trees, cactus, sagebrush, greasewood, cliffs, rivers, creeks, and all other natural landscaping set the tempo of the day. I sometimes had up to a 13 man crew, and then, just as often I was totally alone or just me and Lori and/or Dad. My Dad was my best pal, and he taught me the trade.

My crew, on the other hand, was usually my primary source of concern. I tried to keep them out in the hills on camp jobs as much as possible, and feed them lots of red meat and protein. Month after month, these boys taxed their bodies and spirit to the limit and were in extremely good shape after just a few staking contracts... and maybe a little wild. My brother Billy Bob, for instance, took to running up on gut-shot jackrabbits, hurtling his body into the air at full speed, and coming down full force on his back with a genuine WWF elbow slam on the screaming rabbits! Sometimes he would hit the ground so hard that he would knock the wind out of himself! Thought he was having a seizer or something. Throwing dead, shot up rabbits at each other was another kind of sick source of entertainment, and windshields were a favorite target. Often, the stench of so many dead rabbits, in certain areas, made it hard to breathe while working in them.

The mid-80s was known in the mining industry as "claim wars", as gold and silver prices were up and every company, from large multi-million-dollar corporations to small Mom-and-pop outfits alike, were out staking every available piece of ground, particularly on the "Carlin Trend", in northern Nevada. In no time at all they found themselves competing at the same time with several other companies, for the same chunk of real estate. Most companies back then were willing to invest a multi-million-dollar exploration program into their claim groups in hopes of getting in on the "Carlin Trend Gold Rush" (started by John Livermore's discovery of microscopic gold and the ability to process it with cyanide, in the 1960s) and hitting it big. For them to accept any excuse as to why you didn't (or weren't able to) stake all the ground they had contracted you for, was unheard of. Not fulfilling your contract could cost you hundreds of thousands of dollars, and sometimes there were other staking outfits with similar contracts (similar threats hanging over their heads), trying to take the same piece of ground that you were... Hence, "claim wars". Roads were blocked to deny access, fences and gates were locked shut, and "nail traps" were set out (boards or tarpaper filled with nails and buried in Creek bottoms, road crossings, under bug dust, around corners, etc. etc.), all on public lands. One major gold company in Battle Mountain had mechanics and service station personnel hired to steal claim maps, at $100 per map, out of the vehicles they serviced and worked on! "Mysterious" fights broke out, for seemingly no reason at all, in restaurants and bars to keep you in town and out of the way. It was open industrial espionage, at its lowest. All in all, it was a very exhilarating time to be in the staking business! Lots of constant cloak and dagger stuff! Multimillion dollar investment programs rested on your ability to take the ground, and little Mom-and-pop outfits could compete on the same playing field as multibillion-dollar corporations, and I know with all my heart, that my crew was the best of the best! Why? Because we NEVER lost ground, but we took ground and legally (mostly) beat out everybody we competed against, including the big dogs – Newmont, Barrick, Echo Bay, Cordex, etc., not to mention God knows how many junior Canadian stock companies. Yep, and they hated us (bonus!), and we took a lot of pride in that (God forgive us).

  That, in itself, is why I always tried to keep them out on camp jobs. They were in top shape, and after spending weeks at a time in the mountains, taking them into town and just cutting them loose had devastating results. If bail was set too high I could be out of business, as anyone worth a darn at staking, pretty much, already had a job and replacing my crew was not an option anyway, because they were my closest friends. It was a very stressful balancing act, to be sure. When we hit town we just wanted to run amuck, and raise us a little hell.

  We got into it with another staking crew at the Cattlemen's Restaurant, in Winnemucca, one night, and me, my brother and Richie Rich laid waste to the whole other crew, as well as the restaurant itself. It simply started when one of them walked over, reached across the table, and hit me on the jaw-Boom! When it was all over, we walked out... and they didn't, and let me tell you, there was a mess of them. An honest waitress, God bless her, came forward and testified that the other guy just walked over and hit me to start the fight, so we skated on $15,400 worth of damages that they were claiming (again, God bless that waitress).

I don't think we ever felt more alive than we did in those days, however, I always had to stay away from home as long as I had to, until I healed up, so my kids would never see me tore up. By the time I did get home it was all just a vicious rumor, anyways. Except to Lori. Lori knew... Lori always knew, and was a master at squeezing confessions out of me.

Out in the mountains, you had to be a lot more cautious where there is no law and often no witnesses. Nail trapping someone usually meant that they walked to town unless they had four spare tires (each of my trucks had two or three), and if you weren't very, very careful, things could go to "gun mode" really fast. One time I fired an antitank practice grenade into the door of the drill rig that was blocking the road above Rossi mine, that meant to deny us access to the area we were staking. The next practice (dummy) grenade I slid onto the barrel of my CAR 15 was painted bright red and it fooled them into thinking it was a live round, so they moved out of my way. For me, I had a $175,000 contract at stake...all they had to lose, at worst, was a paycheck.

When things got really crazy was when two outfits, with high dollar contracts, were both after the same ground. And unless somebody got seriously hurt or killed, what happened in the mountains, stayed in the mountains, because we all had to sign a one million dollar "confidentiality clause" that guaranteed that nobody is gonna talk about where they are, who they work for, for what they are doing... so, no whining to the local sheriff's department. And, as a matter of honor in keeping my word, there are probably 100 stories, though worthy, I cannot tell and will carry to my grave with me, however, reminiscing with the ones who were involved will always be an adventure shared between friends, until we go home to be with the Lord. And the Almighty already knows every one of them, good and bad, and He knows our hearts are mindful of how He and He alone, saved us through all of them. I pray that none of us will ever forget what You did for us, Lord.

It was on such a staking adventure, also in the Grant Range of Nevada, near where I got shot, that I met Norman and his brother Andy. It was through them that I was led to embark on the most bizarre and dangerous treasure hunting adventure of my life.

***

As Mark Twain so aptly put it, "There comes a time in every rightly constructed child's life when they have a raging desire to go somewhere and dig for hidden treasure".

True that.

The fact is that this "raging desire" burns in me now, as intensely as it has all my life. The mining/prospecting business is literally nothing more than a multibillion-dollar industry based on "treasure hunting" for gold, silver, or whatever precious metal or gems your heart desires. If you're in the mining biz, then treasure hunting is in your blood, as it has been in miners of the past, for thousands of years. I like to think of it as a traditional addiction, handed down from generation to generation in my family as far back as I can trace my family tree, even to Germany, Ireland, Wales and Scotland, hundreds of years ago.

When I was young, all you had to do to get into the mining business was, don't pay attention in school. Pat you on the back they would, and tell you, "Don't worry about it kid, just get on up to the mine. We got a job for ya". On the other hand, my brother Bill broke the mold, so to speak. Where did he go to college at? I'm glad you asked! Why, University of Nevada Reno, Mackay School of Mines, of course! He is highly esteemed in the mining industry with expertise in mine planning; both underground and open pit, Vulcan, mine management and engineering, and has spent the majority of his career in the upper echelon of the largest gold producing companies of the world.

As for me, I always knew what I wanted to be; an underwater archaeologist, i.e. treasure hunter who hunts sunken Spanish treasure ships and pirate booty! Dad and Mom even sent me on a bus ride to La Jolla, California when I was 14, so I could go to Scripps Institution of Oceanography to meet with them and figure out what study courses I needed to take to qualify for their world renowned school (founded and operated by Jacques Cousteau). Unfortunately, try as I might, for several years, I could never understand the mathematics required, and by my junior year of high school I knew I wouldn't make it. Dag nab it!

That, by no means, stopped me from hunting Spanish treasure on land in the southern and western United States. We have researched and hunted Conquistador and Jesuit treasures and mines, not to mention countless stagecoach, lost mine, bank robbery and immigrant trail caches, for over a half of a century. My son Billy and I have uncovered Spanish mines that were hidden for hundreds of years, by the local Indian tribes that rebelled twice against their slavery at the hands of their Spanish captors, and drove them back to the sea. Lori and I have searched out ancient Spanish arastras and silver mines in Nevada and throughout the West. We have even found Knights Templar (1178 to 1307) ornamental silver pieces hidden in central Nevada! On the coil of my metal detector is the Scripture from Isaiah 45 verse 3 because I believe it when the Lord said "I will give you the treasures of darkness, and hidden riches of the secret places". AMEN! You must also be mindful that the Lord also said, "The silver is Mine, and the gold is Mine, says the Lord of Hosts", in Haggai 2:8, so it is always a good idea to discuss with Him what it is, exactly, that you intend on doing with what actually belongs to Him, anyway... Or not, and if not, let me know how that works out for you.

Many times we have found where the treasure "was", such as the famed Ellison Creek Cache in White Pine County, and several empty strong boxes we have unearthed on the immigrant trail where the cache has either been reclaimed by the original people who put it there and came back for it later, or, as often is the case, found by previous treasure hunters. Let me tell you, digging up and opening a strong box, only to find it empty with the bottom rotted out (the reason the box was left) is the ultimate "thrill of victory and the agony of defeat" scenario, rolled into one. The adrenaline rush peaks just before you open the box, with your heart pounding in your throat to the point where you can't breathe, and a second later you're on the verge of a heart attack from the supreme disappointment of the empty strong box. The same with uncovering empty, rotten saddlebags, and I wouldn't trade the experiences for the world... Except maybe a full strong box, or an old Spanish mine with the valuable contents still inside. Yeah, that would be nice. And truthfully, the times I actually found what I was looking for, and my wife/partner wasn't with me, those were the hollowest of victories, as she was not there to share them with me.

In any event, Lori always said I was a packrat because I could never go out into the desert or mountains without bringing home something rusty (my yard in Ely looks so cool!). The point being; treasure is treasure! No matter what it's made of!

# CHAPTER 8

## The Search for Dark Treasure

*"I will give you the treasures of darkness and hidden riches of secret places"* Isaiah 45;3
*"For what will it profit a man if he gains the whole world, and loses his soul?"* Mark 8:36

I had a staking contract with Norman, that's how we met, and I took a liking to him right from the start. He was probably in his late 60s or early 70s, he was "old school", and he had a tale to tell.

It went something like this;

In the mid-1980s farmers all across the nation were losing their farms to foreclosure. This was brought about mostly by natural disasters such as drought, tornadoes, etc., that cost farmers the ability to produce a cash crop for several years in a row, thus leaving them unable to pay their mortgages. The media attention given to this predicament brought out the good in a lot of people, as well as the evil in others. On September 22, 1985 a benefit concert was held, the first of its kind since Live Aid earlier that year, to specifically help farmers. It was held in Champaign Illinois and was organized by the famous music legends, Willie Nelson, John Mellencamp and Neil Young, and was performed before 80,000 people, raising over $9 million for America's family farmers. Thus, Farm Aid was born and exists to this day, for the same purpose (see, farm aid.org).

Unfortunately, also during this time of hardship on America's family farmers, evil also arose to the occasion, through many con and scam artists, with none more so than a man from Mobile Alabama, that we will fictitiously refer to as "Jackman".

It started out in Kalispell Montana, and spread throughout the Northwest. Jackman and his cohorts would befriend farm owners that were in jeopardy of losing their farms, with the lure of salvation and redemption from foreclosure proceedings with the promise that, if the farm owners would sign over the deeds to their farms to him, he would, in turn, sign over to them (after the sale of their farm), a much more desirable income property equal to, if not worth more, than the worth of their farm. Usually, motels and small businesses were hinted at or eluded to, depending on the personal preferences of the victims.

One of the few such promotional income properties that actually existed, I visited in Winter Haven, Florida. The Hotel Orleans was purchased as one of the "income properties", and as such, was presented to the farmers in its entire splendor. Deviously kept hidden was the fact that the new freeway had bypassed Winter Haven completely, leaving the Orleans high and dry in a small town, too far off the beaten track to attract enough business to survive.

The Hotel Orleans was the primary bait that was used to get God knows how many honest farmers to sign over their farm deeds, which he sold for pennies on the dollar and left hundreds of his victims penniless and homeless (is that not diabolical?). And, amazingly, none of it could be traced back to Jackman, as multiple "dummy" corporations and offshore brokers were used to filter all of the transactions and convert them to cash. Very tricky. With nothing left, these people couldn't even afford legal counsel, let alone to start over, as most were in their later years which disqualified them from gaining financial assistance from any of the banking institutions. Eventually many of them massed together, and formed a coalition, of sorts. I don't know for sure who came up with the idea, but money was raised through relatives and such, to finance a plan to recuperate their money back from Jackman, by any means possible. Spearheading this endeavor was my friend Norman.

So it came to pass, that they hired a couple of Georgia boys to kidnap Jackman... And they did. And eventually, I am told, that they beat (more like, tortured) Jackman into arranging for a semi-truck to be loaded with (get this!) 21 million in cash and gold, with most of the gold being in Canadian gold leaf rounds, and some bars of various sizes. It is my understanding that Jackman was one of the most ruthless and cruel men who operated in the country's underworld of crime syndication, but even if he wasn't before he was kidnapped, beaten almost to the brink of death, and then robbed, I'm quite compelled to think he definitely was, afterward.

And, yup! Contrary to the plan given them, for whatever reason, after the delivery of the above mentioned truckload of treasure, they foolishly let him go, and the chase was on!

Gets better. Meanwhile, my friend Norman is hospitalized with severe cancer in his face and intestines, and not expected to make it. To protect the coalition of angry farmers, it was agreed upon by all parties involved that Norman would be the only connection our Good Old Boys from Georgia would have. So when these enterprising young men found out that Norman was as good as dead, they started looking at their truckload of "dreams come true" as free money that they had worked for and earned. That is, if they can figure out how to stay alive, as they soon became aware that Jackman and his crew of about 40 thugs were searching everywhere for that truck. And Good Old Boys that they were, they had lots of good ol' boy friends, it turns out. Starting in southern Georgia they took off due south, burying money and gold in 13 different stashes, all the way down through Florida, and finally ending, to the best of my knowledge, in Plant city. Then the Georgia boys go into hiding.

Please bear with me a little more... Ready? Here we go...

About that time, back in Montana, Norman's brother Andy returns from old Mexico with this "miracle cure" for cancer, simply referred to as "Mud" or "Black Mud". Mostly zinc, I venture to guess. Anyway, Andy isn't allowed to minister the "miracle cure" to Norman while his brother is under hospital care, so he checks Norman out of the hospital, but not before convincing a doctor there to give Norman a mass amount of prescription morphine. So at home, they take this black gooey "Mud" and stick it directly on the open legions the cancer has caused on Norman's body. There were two on his side and one on his face, right below Norman's left eye, as the cancer had spread through Norman's face like "cords" going up the bridge of his nose, above his eyes and on down and around his left ear and jaw bone. Within a couple of hours, the application of this black gooey substance begins to harden and grow into what Norman calls "cookies". As it begins to slowly draw the cancer out into the "cookie" over the next few weeks, the cookies grow larger and they continue to add more "Mud" daily. Norman described the pain to me as "piano wire under your facial skin, and wound throughout his intestines and stomach, being ever so slowly pulled toward the "cookies". Soon, more pain meds are needed, and the doctor agrees to monitor Norman until almost 3 weeks later, when the "cookie" on Norman's face simply falls off! Until that time you couldn't touch it, let alone, pull it off, without excruciating pain. Eight days after that, both "cookies" on Norman's side fell off as well. Although he has lost well over 100 pounds and now only weighs about 130 pounds (Norman was a big man to begin with), the doctor's test results confirm that Norman's face is 100% cancer free and only a slight trace is left in his intestines!

Sounds crazy, huh. That's what I thought until, in 1993, I saw it work for myself in my Cousin Mickey's friend. She had survived several bouts with chemotherapy, lost all of her hair, and finally, was sent home to die. Mickey told Norman, and a week later, Norman showed up with the "Mud". A doctor in Ely monitored her but I can't remember who it was, but like Norman, in 3 ½ weeks she was cancer free! As unbelievable as all this seems, it's God's truth that I'm telling you. I do not know where Norman and Andy got the "Mud, but when my Mom, Lori's Mom and my Dad got cancer, I wished to God that I did.

Well, as Norman is not dead, he manages somehow to get back in contact with our Good Ol' Boys from Georgia, who aren't doing so good. Somehow, Jackman has been able to seek them out a couple of times and they have barely escaped with their lives. As no one knew where they were hiding, it is believed that Jackman is using "psychics" to track them (yes. I rolled my eyes the first, second, and 37th time I heard the whole "psychic thing" too. Way too much BS for me, or so I thought). The Good Ol' Boys were running scared and wanted Norman to somehow provide protection, so they were more than willing to tell him all that they had done with the money, including brief descriptions of several of the caches. In particular, they told Norman that the largest cache, in Plant city, was in a storage unit. The crates or boxes that held the gold were falling apart due to the extensive truck ride, so they shoved a huge steel box into a large storage unit and dumped the contents of the broken crates and boxes into it. This is said to have represented the largest cache, at around 13 million in gold, at 1989 gold prices.

Norman left for Florida immediately to meet up with our Georgia Geniuses so they could show him exactly where they had hidden the money. Upon arriving at the address he had been given, Norman found the place busted up, and bloodstains everywhere, and no sign of his co-conspirators. Apparently, Jackman's people had caught up to them. Out behind the house, about 50 yards, was an old dilapidated barn, surrounded by trees and overgrowth. An old Case backhoe sat next to the wide-open main doors. Inside, Norman found a long trench, about 25 feet long, that had been cut down the center of the dirt floor, obviously by the backhoe. Upon closer investigation there were several holes, about 2' x 3' x 3' deep, dug into both walls of the trench, and a few tore up, black garbage bags were scattered about the place. The Georgia boys had told Norman that most of the caches were buried in similar fashion; a long trench was dug out, then side holes were excavated into the walls of the ditch to hide cash money in black trash bags. The reasoning was that the trench could be re-excavated without tearing up the garbage bags of cash upon recovery. Makes sense, I guess.

And, hang on, because we've barely begun to go down the "beyond bizarre" road with this story.

Soooo... The crew that caught up with our not so Good Ol' Boys from Georgia were supposedly directed to their location by a couple of female psychics out of New York City that Jackman had retained for this exact purpose. However... The four or five thugs that actually did the deed, in reality, answered directly to the two psychics, and not Jackman, personally (double agent thugs?). I suppose I must mention, that Norman says this information was obtained, later on, when some of his boys "interrogated" one of the psychic's hired thugs that was personally involved in the Good Ol' Boys from Georgia's "interrogation". So, as told to Norman by the New York City thug, the New York thugs worked over the Good Ol' Boys until they gave them several locations of the treasure caches. And in order to prove they told the truth, and stop the beatings, the Georgia boys gave up the 1+ million dollar stash in the old barn, behind the house in which they were hiding. The New York thug boys, understandably, I suppose, got pretty excited upon digging up all that cash money in the garbage bags, and when they called the two New York psychic ladies up and told them, they got real excited too! The good news for the Good Ol' Boys from Georgia is, the beatings stopped immediately. The bad news for the Good Ol' Boys from Georgia is, they immediately went for a surprise one way boat ride, each tied to a pile of cinderblocks, into the Gulf of Mexico, about 30 miles south of Tampa, near where they were holed up.

Last laugh? (Not funny). Ironically, the New York thugs and two middle-aged psychics didn't find out till it was too late that the Not – so – Good Ol' Boys from Georgia LIED TO THEM, probably full well knowing that they were gonna die anyway. Makes one wonder if it takes some kind of deep learning process to achieve such extremely high levels of stupidity. Hmmmmm... You would think so, but no.

In any event, Jackman is betrayed and double-crossed and an entirely new group of well-financed (remember the 1+ million dollar stash in the barn?), ruthless, evil cutthroats have entered into the competition to find the treasure(s). A third hunting party enters the game. They hired trigger men right off the streets of New York to search for the treasure, as well as protect them from Jackman and his crew... And they needed protection because when Norman found out about how things went down for his Georgia boys (God rest their souls), he knew he was way out manned and outgunned. But Norman, that wily old fox, made sure, somehow, that Jackman found out exactly what transpired 30 miles south of Tampa and made it perfectly clear where the fault lies in nobody knowing where the rest of the caches were buried, so now, the war was on! Jackman was overcome with rage, and for some time, he focused that rage on getting even with those two psychics from New York City. Even though Jackman was not successful in his endeavors to pay back the betrayal, it did buy Norman a much needed reprieve to reorganize his efforts, while Jackman and the New York crews were hunting and trying to kill each other.

Norman was considering getting out of the whole thing and had verbalized his decision to the Farmers Coalition. It was short-lived, however. Jackman soon realized that Norman was probably the only possible person left who might have an idea where the money was, so he kidnapped a 13-year-old female and a 16-year-old male from two coalition members' families. It was only after I was already in this thing way too deep that Norman yielded this information to me, when I reached the point that I had to demand that he render "everything" to me, as our lives spiraled into grave danger. Even so, he would not divulge certain detailed information to me, regardless of the risk of jeopardizing and possibly terminating our relationship. He did tell me that he and a few boys from Montana got the hostages back by force, somewhere in upstate Alabama, where they were being held captive... And lives were lost. That's what he told me, and that's all I know about it.

All Norman had was vague descriptions of a few of the caches. Not enough to pinpoint even one, except the plant city gold cache. So he did the only insanely logical thing he could think of – fight fire with fire. 1) he hired an 18-year-old male psychic (of course!), and 2) he hired me to put together a crew to go to Florida and retrieve the treasure(s). Of course, he didn't mention any of this psychic BS to me until I and my crew were in Florida, and it had become a real problem. What a nice surprise that was! Anyway, he probably (and rightly so) figured that I wouldn't go on this twisted treasure hunt (oh, hell no.) if he did. The truth be known, I had a super bad experience, with a Ouija board, my senior year of high school. I didn't know a lot back then, but I knew what evil was, and even before I knew much about Jesus, or his holy Angels, I damned well knew what a demon was (sarcastic pun intended). So that's why I don't mess with any of this psychic crap since then... Until now... Again. "This can't be good", I remember saying to myself. And I do distinctly remember "The Unk", Phil Davis, calling me before I left for Florida, and telling me something was terribly wrong with all of this and that he, through prayer to the One True God, believed that there was great evil involved and he felt compelled to warn me. Phil was a very devout man of God, who, to my shame, I ignored on a regular basis by this point in my life. Yet, he never gave up on me and constantly was sending me "religious" material, books and videos that mostly went unopened. Please forgive me, Unk. Thank you, dear friend, for hanging in there with me and eventually becoming one of my greatest spiritual mentors. And, thank You, Jesus, for sending such a great man of faith into my life, as You foretold in the Gospels of Luke 10:2, and Matthew 9:38.

\*\*\*

So, just a couple of weeks after surviving a gunshot wound to the chest and being released from the hospital, I find myself on an airplane to Tampa, Florida to meet up with Norman and Andy. I'm still having problems with the bullets exit wound in my back not wanting to close, and it continues to "seep" a little blood, etc. The rib it drilled through is a constant deep pain with every breath I take, but is made tolerable by pain pills, and mostly, by the lure of treasure.

Jones is waiting back in Ely to hear from me, so he and 11 other of my closest mercenary friends can begin moving our crew and our "tools of the trade" from Nevada to Florida. For some odd reason, Norman has insisted that he, Andy, and I travel separately to Florida, and he especially insists that they do not travel with my crew, or even stay in the same hotel with them when they arrive. A little strange, I'm thinking, but, whatever. It's his circus and he's paying for it so, to some degree, he can call it anyway he wants, as long as it doesn't interfere with my ability to get the deed done. On that end, I alone call the shots, and Norman knows this. It's what he hired me for. Of course, the gunshot to the chest might have made most normal folks question my decision-making ability under certain circumstances, but apparently that never occurred to Norman. Norman knew he could trust me, and with millions in cash and gold at stake, that's all he needed to know.

His trust was rightly placed in me, I might add. There was a line of integrity instilled in me by my father that I did not ever cross. I would protect Norman's trust and interests with my life, as a matter of honor (the one thing even treasure could never buy), even if it meant crossing it up with certain members of my own crew.

Like growing up with the Boys from the Brush, I learned firsthand that in these types of situations, your survival usually depended on who was watching your back. I watched Norman's back, and Jones was watching mine. Easy money, right?

Norman was waiting to meet me at the Tampa airport when I got off the plane. He had arrived a day earlier, and in that time, had managed to get himself all stressed out. He was super jittery, talking low and looking all around, at everybody and everything. "We gotta get our hands on some guns, fast, John", he told me, and he looked right in my eyes when he said it. He was dead serious, and for the first time, I saw fear in him. "Okay, okay, Norman", I said, "I'll handle it... Just take it easy". He was in no way gonna wait till Jones and the boys got here with our gear. I grabbed a local Tampa newspaper and we walked into a fairly quiet airport bar, as it was only about 9:30 AM there. I put down a couple shots of Christian Brothers Brandy to help the pain pills work on the agitated wound in my back, which had been amplified by the long plane ride. In fact, just about everything agitated it. Regardless, I dug out the "classified" section and gave the rest of the newspaper to Norman in hopes of keeping him occupied while I found what I was looking for. "You got a car, Norman?" I asked. "Yeah, outside. I rented one while I was waiting for your plane to get in", he responded.

No GPS back then so we got a city roadmap. I made a couple of calls, and we were off and running. Within an hour or so of arriving in Tampa, we had a Ruger 9 mm and a Smith & Wesson Bull Pup 9 mm semi-automatic pistols with ammo and extra clips, and nobody we got them from even asked our names, which helped to calm Norman down a little.

As Norman was acting a little weird and his eyes kind of clouded over when we talked about the gold, I thought it best if I did the driving. As we left the Tampa area, he seemed to like sitting in the passenger seat and playing with his new gun, anyway. After a couple of hours, eventually, Norman's strange behavior and his obsession with his new pistol started making me nervous, so I quietly jacked a round in the chamber of my newly acquired Smith & Wesson, the first chance I got when he couldn't see. "I like you, Norman, so please don't weird out on me" I remember thinking.

We left Tampa and drove over to Winter Haven, where Norman took me on a tour of the Orleans Hotel, as mentioned earlier, in order to add legitimacy to his crazy story, I assume. The place was really nice, but had no customers that I could see. "We gotta get out of here", he finally said, as he constantly looked around and always back over his shoulder. Truth is, I was glad to be going. This place seemed a little more than creepy for some reason, and by the time we left the hairs on the back of my neck were standing up.

As we moved down the road to Plant City, Norman divulges the "update" and "new" information he has recently acquired, as to keep me up-to-date. "New information" probably should have been a red flag, or at least I should've asked as to the source of this new info, but my adrenaline was pumping and was probably clouding my thinking process, as we got closer and closer to Plant City and that cache of gold.

Something, possibly common sense, overshadowed my giddiness to see the gold, and against Norman's ranting objections, I decided to do a couple of "drive-byes" rather than just pull into the storage unit facility like we owned the joint. Turns out, we couldn't have anyway. The sign on the closed and locked gate said, "Closed – no units available – entry by appointment only", but there was no phone number to call. Even stranger, as we drove around it a couple of times we saw several men moving about inside the fenced facility. They didn't seem to be doing anything in particular, just kind of wandering around. As not to be obvious, we pulled away from the storage facility and got a room on the second floor of the motel where we could see about one quarter of the place from two blocks away. Norman had to meet Andy, who was flying into Tallahassee (why Tallahassee?) the following day, so he got me my own rental car and bought me a pair of binoculars and left the next morning. God knows I needed a couple of days rest. The trip and stress caused by the new, unforeseen circumstances in Plant City had left me weakened. I needed to heal up a little more. Norman always seemed sure of himself and always in control, so to see him in this schizoid state of mind had put me on edge, as well.

Norman called me the next evening from the hotel room he and Andy had taken in Tallahassee. He said he had thought about it on his drive up to Tallahassee, and had devised a plan. It was basically, quite simple; call the boys down from Nevada, cut through the chain-link at both ends of the facility and rush them from both sides---in other words, go in guns blazing. Wow.

Thank God Andy was there with Norman now, and as of yet, hadn't taken leave of his senses, as well. When I talked to Andy he said he would calm Norman down by the time my crew drove to Florida from Nevada, and it would give me a few more days to "scope out" the Plant City situation. Over the next couple of days I kept the storage facility under surveillance from every possible angle and viewpoint I could find and throughout the night as well. People were in their 24/7, and often only seen in the shadows when they lit a cigarette. Sometimes as many as 11 or 12 at a time, with others coming to relieve them about every six hours. A large part of at least one row of storage units had been converted to possible barracks or living quarters, at any rate, and I could only guess at how many men were inside of them. I found several of the garage doors on the unused units slightly open and even noticed that most of the closed units didn't have padlocks on them. This whole thing was a façade.

Multiple security cameras were placed throughout the property, and were obviously active because I saw them move on many occasions, by what I assume would be remote control. And, how many storage facilities are encased in razor wire? Not barbed wire, razor wire. Or, maybe Norman's paranoia is spreading like a flu virus. If I was going to put my possessions in a storage facility, you can bet I would insist on a storage unit with high security, and razor wire, by what I've seen of Florida so far, may just possibly be how they roll down here.

I was watching the last of the sunset from out of my hotel room window, and thinking about dinner, when a quick flash of light caught my eye. It came from a dark window in the top level of a three-story office building behind the storage unit facility. Even though there was a small parking lot between the building and the storage unit's chain-link fence, the darkened third story window had a bird's eye view right down onto the units. Hmmm... Paranoia?

I went to Shoney's restaurant and had dinner, including grits (grits suck, but they give em to ya anyway). Then I found a Walmart and bought a 90 power, kind of cheesy, spotting scope. It was fully dark when I got back to my room, and I entered without turning on any room lights. Before I left, I took the precaution of closing the curtains to be sure no extra light from the motel sign, outside my room, would reveal my presence in the otherwise dark room.

I set up a small table with the spotting scope on it, in front of the window, then slowly cracked the curtain opened just enough to allow a clear field of vision through the scope. Because I had a corner room, my door was not visible from the direction of the storage unit facility. After staring into the dark windows for about 45 minutes and trying to go to the bathroom without turning any lights on, I had had about all I could handle. Finally, I spilled the last of my coffee on my bed (I'm pretty sure of what the maid is gonna think). As I reached across the spotting scope trying to find the light switch on the table lamp, I saw it; dull light in the dark third story window. I went to the scope just in time to see light from a door in the office room disappear, as the door closed. I kept watching, and a few minutes later, the door opened and briefly allowed the bathroom light to illuminate the room before it was shut off. Definitely not paranoia. Some sneaky assed "peeping Tom" wannabe was lurking around in that dark room! Ouch! That is nothing like or remotely even similar to the sneaky assed "peeping Tom" lurking around in my room. This is different.

In any event, my adrenaline was pumping, and it felt good. I slipped out for a stroll about 1:30 AM. I reasoned that whoever it was in the room obviously wasn't in cahoots with the guys in the storage facility, or they wouldn't be covertly watching the same place from a darkened room overlooking the facility... like me.

My first guess would be some branch of government law enforcement, IRS, FBI, Justice Department or possibly even the US marshals, but before I "bug out", I had to know for sure because Jones and the boys were already in route from Nevada. No cell phones back then, so we kept contact through my awesomely hot accomplice (and wife), Lori, back in Ely. We all checked in every day with her.

It amazed me how many other people are out moving around in the dark, in the few hours just before dawn. I had to move very slowly, as I was unfamiliar with this area. There were, of course, a few drunks here and there that were relatively easy to avoid, but there were also people moving about and keeping in the shadows, who definitely weren't drunks. By the time I finally worked my way all the way around the other side of the office building, it was 3:30 AM. My vantage point covered the back entrance and parking area. I was hunkered down in a 2 foot wide area between an incredibly stinky (fish, maybe?) dumpster and a corner wall of a brick building, across the back parking lot from the office building. Several older vehicles were scattered about the parking lot, but one in particular early 80s Chevy delivery type van at the back door had my focus. After just sitting, listening and watching for about 30 minutes, I crept over to the van and popped the wing window open with my pocket knife. Careful not to bump or jiggle the vehicle enough to set off a possible car alarm, I slipped my arm in the window and gently unlocked the door.

The inside light came on for a second as I quickly opened the door and slipped inside. That was extremely risky, but a chance I had to take. I sat in silence for a few minutes to see if I had drawn any attention... all good. With my tiny little Maglite that I got by sending in 300 "Camel Bucks" coupons (I know most of you know what I'm talking about), I quickly and systematically pillaged and plundered the vans interior. This is definitely not a cop van. It's a pigsty. Trash and partially eaten sandwiches, Mickey D's bags everywhere, and, ahhh...what's this? A cheesy spotting scope empty box! The registration showed the van was leased by a "research" company in New York City. Maybe I got the wrong vehicle, then again, maybe not. Under the back seat I found three handguns and one sawed-off single barrel 16gauge shotgun in a tennis bag. The pistols were "Saturday night specials", and very cheap ones at that. Two revolvers and some foreign made .380 automatic, and none of them have serial numbers. These were throwaways (please, don't ask how I would know that). I closed the wing window and hit the lock button as I gently closed the door and exited the vehicle.

Who the hell are these guys?

Predawn was approaching as I started working my way back to my room. I had no more than gotten across the parking lot to the dumpster when an old minivan pulled in next to the Chevy van; two guys get out, unlocked the back door of the office building, and disappear inside. Minutes later, two other guys came out, locked the back door, get into the Chevy van and leave.

I couldn't make out much detail in the predawn light, but I noticed all four of them wore what looked like ill-fitting suits or sports jackets fresh off the rack at a Salvation Army thrift store. Seemed kind of out of place in the middle of Florida, but would probably fit right in if they were on the streets of New York. Street thugs, maybe? Nothing is making sense here. Back at my room I slept for a few hours, then called Lori and told her about the night's events and what I had found. We both came away from it all with very unsettling feelings about these new developments, and I had warning buzzers going off in my mind. I paid a high price the last time I ignored what my senses (?) were trying to tell me.

After another day and night of surveillance, I knew that I was just seeing the tip of the proverbial iceberg. I focused on details of the people, both inside and outside of the perimeter of the chain-link fence, and soon realized they were rarely the same men in a 48 hour period. I then realized that these were two separate "crews" working on the outside, as well as the inside of the storage unit facility, separated only by the chain-link fence. They were adversaries and I became aware that they knew that each other existed by the way the crewmembers entered and exited the storage facility; always making it obvious that they entered and exited the place empty-handed – with no gold, and never in numbers more than two at a time, as not to cause conflict. So, it seems, everyone knows the gold is here, and both crews make sure that the other one doesn't try to move it.

Blatantly obvious was the fact that we were massively outgunned at least three or four to our one. Even though silencers would be a great advantage, the few we had wouldn't be enough.

One thing for certain, whoever tries to load up that huge pile of gold and makes it mobile won't survive long enough to make it off of the peninsula; and that's if you could get through all of the security and get it on a truck, somehow. It's a fool's errand that would cost many their lives. Everybody on both sides of the fence surely knows that if it goes to "gun mode" the local law will get involved in a matter of minutes and more than likely end up with all the gold. Still, something told me that they would rather kill each other and lose the gold than allow the other crew to have it, and I'm willing to bet that they have all been promised a big piece of the Golden Pie that they are guarding. This has to be the ultimate "powder keg" scenario, and I mused over the temptation of firing off a few shots, in the wee hours of the morning, that would definitely get the party started. I mean, what the heck. If we can't have it... The entertainment value this idea presented was a temptation that I barely resisted, and the regret of not doing it still bothers me from time to time, Lord, forgive me... Would a, should a, could a.

A trip to the recorder's office revealed that the storage facility had been purchased by a "mailbox" Corporation in Mobile, Alabama; eight months ago (Gee... Wonder who that could be?).

I left for Tallahassee the next day, as it was high time to find out what Norman's not telling me. I got to Tallahassee a couple of hours before Jones and my crew arrived from Nevada. It would be good to see them.

I intentionally had not told Norman of all that I had discovered until I was face to face with him. When I did, his countenance hit the floor, and when I told him about the van being leased by an outfit in New York City, he went pale as a ghost.

Omitting all the psychic junk, Norman told me he had reason to suspect another group of undesirable and un-ethnical individuals from the New York area might be involved, God bless him. I realize now that we were probably his last hope and he was just desperate, and that was why he withheld such vital information. He also told me he had booked several rooms in a motel on the other side of Tallahassee for me and my crew. That's really kind of odd, but I didn't ask why because I figured that I had interrogated him enough for one day. So when the phone rings, Andy answers it, looks at Norman and says, "It's him". Norman snaps out of his bewilderment, jumps up, and ushers me out the door jabbering about how "things are under control" and he has to take this call, and literally slams the door in my face! Man, things are gettin' weird.

It's gonna be so good to see my friends and have a somewhat sane conversation, at least from my perspective, but probably not from theirs, I suspect. And besides... my Colts were in the gear they had hidden in the secret compartments in our vehicles. That alone would be an immensely great comfort to me. When I told them what had transpired over the past week, I'm sure they had thought that I had lost my mind and wondered what I had gotten them into. The way they looked at me while I updated them was probably the same way I had looked at Norman, a couple of hours before. You know, that, "you gotta be... Kidding... me" look of disbelief combined with the eyes rolling up, and the "oh my God, I can't believe this is happening", look.

I know the feeling, boys. I need a drink.

They were dog tired from the road trip across the lower United States, so after getting them all fed I took them to a bar called "Bullwinkle's", down by the University. "Go Seminoles" didn't begin to help us fit in. It was literally 13 road warriors walking into a college bar. What's more astounding is that they kinda took to us, and without divulging our purpose, we had a pretty good time shooting pool, playing darts, and making a few friends. If nothing else, my crew knew how to maintain a high level of confidentiality concerning our business. It simply was a matter of professionalism on our part.

As I stepped outside on the front sidewalk to have a smoke, an elderly man came up the sidewalk and walked right up in front of me, and stopped. He had shoulder length long gray hair and a short well-kept gray matching beard. His dark brown eyes were so intense that it seemed, as he looked into my eyes, that he was penetrating my soul. He put his hand on my shoulder (very creepy!) and simply said, "You must think clearly – your enemy now knows you're here" (insanely crazy, creepy!). Then he turned and walked off down the sidewalk into the night.

Instantly sober, I just stood there stupefied and finished my smoke. "Oh, that's nice", I said to myself. I really hate all this macabre bull crap that I can't begin to understand. What next? Voodoo lunatics waving dead cats over my head as I sleep? Where's the safe zone? Do I even have a safe zone in my life? For a split second, my mind flashed back to when I was a boy walking in the warm, bright noonday sun along the mountain trails of Keystone Nevada, with my single shot .22 rifle. Then Jones came out the front door of the bar, and standing next to me lit up a smoke, and said, "Better head these guys for the motel and put them to bed. Their startin' to get a little rambunctious". Good advice, I thought.

## CHAPTER 9

## When Things Get Crazy...er

Room and board for my crew didn't come cheap and we were just sitting, without a target. So much for the hit and run operation we were geared up for. Norman was still struggling with the fact that we weren't going to hit on the multimillion dollars' worth of gold being held in the storage unit facility in Plant City. I didn't bring my friends down here to commit suicide. They always trusted me not to get them into anything we couldn't handle, and that trust meant more to me than my life or all the gold in the world. Norman often described the other crews from New York and Mobile with colorful names like, "mindless trigger men", and," Street urchins/punks with guns", but in so doing made his point that they had nothing to lose and that they were also incredibly obedient to their employers. They had been promised large percentages of the cash and gold they recovered (wow that sounds familiar) and were willing to die for the "once-in-a-lifetime opportunity" (not familiar at all).

Norman was more than discouraged that I and my crew were not as willing to just go in, guns blazing, and starting a war we probably wouldn't come out of. Welcome to reality, my old friend. I guess it must have sucked to realize that his crew had guns AND brains. In any event Jones and I reasoned with him that while everybody else was focused on the largest cache of gold in Plant city, it opened a perfect opportunity to go after the smallest cash stashes (I almost said cash caches) of approximately 1.1 to 2.2 million, and gain some badly needed operating capital. As far as I was concerned, we needed a target, and those other crews could kill each other for all I cared.

Norman told us that the Good Ol' Boys from Georgia hid the money on property owned by "friends they could trust", and not just random hiding places. He had researched some of the Georgia boy's relatives in Florida and that gave us a few starting points to check out. One such cache was 1.4 million hidden about 15 miles outside of Winter Haven. There were possibly two more, a 1.1 million and a 1.2 million, cash money stashes close to Tallahassee, but that would "take more time to get better information". When he told us that, Jones and I looked at each other and I could tell he and I were sharing the same questions. Where was he getting this "better information" from, considering the only two guys that knew the exact location where the money is actually buried, are fish poop by now?

A chill ran up my spine as I flashed back to the Ouija board and séance episode from my senior year in high school. Norman said he would make a call to his "source" so we stepped outside the door of his room. Jones grabbed me by the arm and led me down the sidewalk out of hearing range of anybody that might be listening. In a low tone he began, "I gotta tell you somethin' Jones", he said to me (as I stated, we always called each other Jones) "this is gonna sound weird, but hear me out. My Mom was a psychic and the way she explained it all to me is every word that everybody speaks or thinks about is floating around out there –".

"Out where?" I asked.

"Out there, I don't know, in the atmosphere I guess", he said, irritated that I had interrupted him. "Listen Jones, this is serious. She said psychics could pick through all these words looking for certain conversations and words and stuff. She said mostly, it's like looking for a needle in a haystack, unless you have a lot of people talking about the same thing at the same time. That made an easier or larger target to find".

"Awe, crap Jones, come on", I snorted, "you gotta be kidding me". But I could see in his eyes he was dead serious. And anybody else but Jones and I would have gone off in their face. But Jones I trusted and I could tell Jones was anguishing over even having to talk to me about it. He told me of how, even as a boy, he could sense evil presence in and around his Mom's house when she would "channel", go into a "trance", read Tarot cards, or do séances. He said he loved his Mom but finally had to get away from it all, so he eventually left home when he was still very young. He finally ended his story by saying, "If that's what's happening here, pard, we need to get the hell out of here".

I was thinking, yeah, right. Too much information. I think I need to go to "timeout"…for about 12 years.

We got a chance here to make a lot of money, and everybody is losing their minds. Jones, on the other hand, I trust, but I can't begin to process what the hell ever he's talking about, but out of respect, I will keep it in mind. I really wanted a couple shots of brandy but what that old man out in front of Bullwinkle's said to me came to mind, and killed the desire. Probably for the best, I guess. Things are getting complicated and I need to keep a clear head.

\*\*\*

The next morning we loaded up and headed south on the old back roads, to a roadside run down motel a few miles north of Winter Haven. What seemed to be our best and easiest shot at a quick hit on the money, was based on Norman's new intel he had received from whoever he was getting the calls from, back in Montana. The money was buried in a well house, in the middle of an orchard, on a farm owned by a cousin of one of the Dead Ol' Boys from Georgia.

Norman said we needed to all travel separately, about an hour apart. Counting our two rental cars we had six vehicles, two of which belonged to me, including a custom Chevy van with hidden gun compartments in the walls and ceiling. So you can imagine how stupid Norman's plan to space out each vehicle an hour apart must have sounded to me. I got a better idea. Will let Norman go first, then in an hour, me and the boys will come behind him, altogether, and look out for each other as we have always done. You know… Safety in numbers, etc., etc.

We rolled into the Cockroach Motel about 3:30 in the afternoon, unloaded our stuff, and Norman led me Jones and one other of the guys to the Orchard. Norman then left the three of us to do recon and headed back to the motel.

Before leaving the motel, however, Norman seemed as giddy as a schoolboy with his first kiss. He said to "come right back as soon as we get the money and he was gonna take us shopping in a Sportsman's Warehouse that was close by". Jones and I just stood there with our mouths hanging open. "What did you say?" I asked, hoping I didn't hear what I heard.

"Shopping", Norman says, "And there's an auto mall over by the freeway. I want to go look at those new Ford trucks, too".

"I'm just gonna check it out tonight, Norman. And when we do get the money, you better be packed up, cuz were gonna run like hell back to the mainland. When we take it, Norman, they're going to try and take it back. You better be ready to move, Norman, no BS… Understand?" I spoke back to him as slowly and clearly as I could manage, considering how bad I wanted to grab him by the shoulders, shake him till his teeth rattled, and scream it in his face.

Shopping… He wants to go shopping. We're probably gonna be running for our lives, from what I've seen so far. As in, Take the Money and Run (Steve Miller band), and there are only so many roads that go north out of Florida. Thinking about it, I found the whole idea very exhilarating... Good plan, I like it. Definitely my cup of tea. Let's do this deed.

We had a much harder time than you would think finding a place in the Orchard to hide my Chevy Luv pickup, as the trees are well pruned offering very little cover at eye level, beneath the branches. The road we had come in on had been built up and was slightly higher than the ground level of the Orchard, so we left the truck quite a ways from the road, inside the orchard itself.

We fanned out and slowly made our way through the vast sea of trees. The rolling topography led us to the edge of the trees, and looking downward into a clearing with two new looking metal buildings/barns, several pieces of farming equipment including a new tractor, and two old tractors, and (Yee Haw! Whoot! Whoot!) a well pump house right where it was supposed to be.

Finally, a break! And the pump house was the closest thing to us, and set quite a ways apart from the nearest building. Together, we worked our way to the edge of the tree line, and lying on our bellies, pushed up the sandy dirt in front of us. Soon we had made an indentation into the ground with a gentle hump of dirt in front of it that was just barely enough to conceal our position. There were about 35 yards of open ground between us and the pump house. Another new tractor with spraying apparatus showed up just as the sun was setting and two field workers parked it and went into the nearest metal building. A moment later they emerged on a four wheeler and drove off into the trees using a dirt access road at the far end of the clearing.

I had to see into that pump house, so when everything went quiet again I sprinted across the open ground to the shed. It wasn't even locked! I opened the door and stepped inside, on to a fresh, new concrete floor! I looked around for a second then ran back up the slope. As the sun disappeared and we lay there whispering, we heard distinct movement in the orchard behind us, directly between us and the truck to the north. We took off low and quiet in the soft dirt, skirting the tree line, and headed east. After about 100 yards or so, we started back north, avoiding the urge to move faster and create noise. The light was fading and silence was our only advantage.

We heard movement a head, so close that all we could do was hit the ground on our bellies. I was a little ahead of the other two, and as I hit the ground I glanced back and saw Jones trying to look small with his pistol out in front of him. A split second later, we froze in motion as we heard them coming. They were only three and four rows of trees away from us, moving quickly toward the clearing. Quick enough for us to hear them. At that moment, in the dim evening light I could clearly see the first two men closest to us, and at that same exact moment I realized both of my hands were in a nest of fire ants; and I dare not move. "Dear God, please don't let them see us", I remember thinking as they quickly came closer, in crouched positions. They had shotguns. In what seemed an eternity, they trotted right past us, so close that we could hear every breath they took. I wanted to scream for the agony of the ant bites I was taking but we stayed motionless, after they had passed, to make sure that we didn't stand up and run right into any more of them. Shotguns would be nasty business at this close range with hardly any cover at all.

As we zeroed in on the truck, the thought occurred to us that they may well have left a couple of their boys behind to make sure we didn't get away. The truck had a set of Florida license plates on it that we had "commandeered" the night before we left Tallahassee (Lord forgive us) and I thought about the option of leaving it to avoid a possible trap, but discarded the idea, as, being on foot in unfamiliar territory would surely not work out so good, not to mention the loss of the "gear" that was hidden in it. Jones, my other friend, and I spread out to cover the little Chevy truck as we approached it. My hands were swelling badly and gripping my pistols was terribly awkward, so we covered Jones while he ran the last few yards to the truck. He hit the ground beside the driver's door, within our line of sight, so we could cover him. Nothing. They must not have had the extra men to leave behind (safety in numbers, etc., etc.).

Jones reached up and opened the door. The inside light had been disconnected earlier, but in the dim light he could see the glovebox had been rummaged through, obviously looking for the registration that we removed earlier and was safe and sound in Jones's wallet (that Jones was a thinker!).

In only a moment we heard the engine start and we ran and bailed into the vehicle as it was already moving toward the road. My friend jumped up front with Jones and I bailed in the back. I heard a distant shot behind us, and off to the right. Then another and I saw the muzzle flash from the shotgun, well over 50 yards away.

We hit the two lane asphalt road in haul-ass mode. Another truck came out of the orchard and onto the road about a half mile behind us, and it was gaining. Jones was rapping out that Chevy Luv's little four-cylinder engine until the rods started rattling. They opened the sliding back window as we started approaching the stop sign that marked the main highway, as I dug like a madman into the bottom of the bed wide custom toolbox, and yelled, "Come to a complete stop at the stop sign".

"What?" They both screamed simultaneously in horror, as if I had lost my mind.

I had dumped all the tools and jacks out of the toolbox, and emptied it to get to the hidden compartment in the bottom. I popped the hidden latch, opened the compartment, and pulled my Ruger Mini 14 with a nine power scope, up and out of the toolbox.

"I said, I need a complete stop", I yelled at them through the open window.

The truck behind us was getting close, but with my burning swollen hands, I had to have a steady shot. Another moment and Jones yelled "hang on, Jones!" and hit the brakes causing the little Chevy pickup to go skidding for about 25 feet. We came to a complete stop for about a heartbeat, and with the Mini 14 rested soundly and my back firmly against the toolbox, I fired, and then we were smoking our tires around the corner and slamming gears down the highway. In the fraction of a second before I fired, I could see the faces of the men in the truck. They were close enough that I knew exactly where my round was going. Hot steam exploded from the radiator as the .223 armor piercing round center punched the radiator, and found its way through the water pump and into the engine block. I could actually hear the engine blow up over our screaming tires! And as we headed up the road, I could hear the rod and main bearings chattering in the Chevy Luv's little motor. As we pulled through Winter Haven we stopped at a convenience store that surprisingly had some Lucas Engine Honey on the shelf (that had to be a miracle), and it seemed to help the little engine as long as we kept the RPMs as low as possible.

I was dog tired, pissed, and my hands hurt like hell fire. The clerk at the convenience store told me what to buy to ease the pain and swelling in my hands, as well as how to care for them when I got "home".

But instead of "rest for the weary" (not to mention "the happy to be alive"), we pulled into a circus at the motel. Norman had everybody in a panic and packing up to bug out.

"They are coming! They're coming for us!" Norman said in a panicked voice, with Andy right beside him, nodding his head up and down like Mr. Bobble Head, in agreement. My crew was pretty much loaded up… and very frustrated. It was starting to rain.

"What the hell are you talking about? Who's coming? How do you know they're coming?" I yelled. I was losing it and I was right in Norman's face.

"You're gonna tell me everything! We're not going anywhere!" I said as I looked at my guys and told them, "gear up and spread out; cover both directions on the road".

Norman went wide-eyed in terror and screamed "NO! They will kill me… All of us. We gotta run!"

"I'm done running for one day." I said, "This has gone far enough."

I'm thinking, Norman's lost his mind, probably. Someone's coming after me and my boys? Let them come, if they even exist at all. We'll settle this.

The guys were pulling serious iron (high-powered weapons of mass firepower) out of the van when Andy walked up to me with tears in his eyes and quietly said, "Please John. Do like Norman says, and then we will tell you everything… I promise". The look on his face was so sincere that it sort of shocked me a little bit, and I kinda figured Andy still had his wits about him. Jones was beside me, looking back and forth between Andy and me. With his cigarette hanging out the side of his mouth, he jacked a round into the chamber of his Smith & Wesson (that I gave him, by the way!), and calmly said, "Awe, bull____, John. Let's do this". I knew he was serious about not running, because he rarely ever called me by my name unless it was his bottom line. I try never to cross that line, out of the respect and trust he has rightfully earned from me.

Everybody was looking at me now. I looked from Andy to Norman, who was standing a few feet away. Norman's mouth moved, but even though no noise came out, I could clearly hear the word "please".

"Load up", I said. "Head back to Tallahassee".

Jones added, "And split up".

I shot him a look and he said to me, We got to, Jones". In another minute we were mobile.

Jones and I headed west then north in the rental car. It gave us time to talk. "Jones", he said, "I think this is all the psychic bull____ and that's how they know how to track us".

"Well, maybe, maybe not", I responded, "But I left Ricky and Miles in the woods back there to watch and see if anybody actually shows up. Either way, Jones, I'm tired of being played".

***

Proverbs are little "Truth Bombs", if you will. There are 31 chapters of them in the Bible, one for every day of the month. You and I really need to read one per day, every day. It will literally bless you. Proverbs 1 verse 7 says, *"The fear of The Lord is the beginning of knowledge, but fools despise wisdom and instruction"*.

So the Bible literally calls the person who rejects the knowledge of God and refuses to be guided through God's wisdom, a fool.

Are you seeking His wisdom through the knowledge of the One who created you, by reading, studying and applying His Word?

Not me... At that time of my life, I was a fool, as the Bible declared me to be. That's why I was defenseless against what was happening to me and my boys, in Florida. In regard to this point in my life, I was an "unlearned" fool, as I had not the knowledge of His instructions, or His guidance.

Sooo... I will try my best to spare you the consequences of my ignorance and bring you up to par, so to speak. What you do with it, is on you.

## CHAPTER 10

## TOMMYKNOCKERS

> *"... A certain slave girl possessed with a spirit of divination met us, who brought her masters much profit by fortune-telling... But Paul, greatly annoyed, turned and said to the spirit,' I command you in the name of Jesus Christ to come out of her'. And he came out that very hour".* Acts 16: 16, 18

We've reached a place in this story where I think it's important to deal with this whole psychic thing, and now is as good a time as any. Might as well do the whole "shebang" while we're at it, so here goes...

Well, let's see... If I got this right, it usually starts with Santa Claus, the Easter Bunny, and the Tooth Fairy. It gains a little momentum at the boogie man, unicorns, monsters, dragons, gnomes, gremlins, imps, fairies, trolls, elves, and various other enchanted beings. At Halloween, the devil throws things into high gear with witches, ghosts, spooks, werewolves, the undead (recently added), zombies, and serial killers, i.e. Freddy Krueger, chainsaw killers with hockey masks, and of course, demons and devils. And sometimes, deep down inside, you get the insight that your boss is possessed (just kidding... Of course!).

So then, as adults, with common sense screaming to the contrary in our brains, not to mention contrary to what the Bible clearly defines as forbidden, we embrace every other nonsense or evil snare that the enemy of our souls lays in our path, such as Voodoo, Wicken, fortunetellers, mediums, horoscopes, witchcraft, astrology, magic charms, sorcery, New Age religion, evolution, the worship of the moon and stars, worship of mother Earth, magic, and cults (see Scripture references in Appendix A, "Cults") of all kinds, and even the darkest evil of the occult (see Appendix B, "Occult") itself, satanic worship and rituals, soothsayers, fortune tellers and psychics included.

And let me tell you a truth; when you open the door to the evil one and his minions, he's coming in. Prisons are full of people just like you and me who did just that, and it generally started with something seemingly innocent, like a Ouija board, horoscope or séance. And that "King of all Lies", the devil, will not leave when you ask – he has to be thrown out! It's best not to let him in, in the first place… Trust me in this.

Where does it all end? Often in tragedy, always in deception and separation from the One Who Is True and Holy. That's what it's all designed by your enemy to do, and, as always, its working good for him. Only the Truth of the Word of God, the Bible, can define what is and isn't from God. There is no other source for you to reference besides the Bible. Everything else is a deception. Again, please take time to review the scriptural references found in the Appendix, in the back of this book. It could literally save your life one day.

The Apostle Peter warned us; *"but there were also false prophets among the people, even as there will be false teachers among you, who will secretly bring in destructive heresies, even denying the Lord who bought them, and bring on themselves swift destruction. And many will follow their destructive ways, because of whom the way of truth will be blasphemed. By covetousness they will exploit you with deceptive words; for a long time their judgment has been idle, and their destruction does not slumber".* 1 Peter 2:1-3.

And as proclaimed by the apostle John; *"For many deceivers have gone out into the world who do not confess Jesus Christ as coming in the flesh. This is a deceiver and an antichrist. Whoever transgresses and does not abide in the doctrine of Christ does not have God. He who abides in the doctrine of Christ has both the Father and the Son. If anyone comes to you and does not bring this doctrine, do not receive him into your house nor greet him; for he who greets him shares in his evil deeds".* 2 John1:7, 9-10.

These verses seem like major understatements to me. Please also see "The Gospel" Appendix E.

We are to "test all things" (1 Thessalonians 5:21) against the Word of God, to determine their origin, whether good or evil (see Appendix C, "test all things" for Scripture references). And, yes I know… We hate homework. Sorry, but you need this. Here it is in a nutshell;

*"If someone claims to be a profit and does not acknowledge the truth about Jesus, that person is not from God. Such a person has the spirit of the Antichrist, which you heard is coming into the world and indeed is already here"* 1 John 4:3. So when you cook down all religions and their belief systems to their irreducible bottom line, there are only two results: they are either founded on and exalting Jesus of the Bible, His

work, and His deity or they are denying it. It's either Christ or the Antichrist. That's why it's vital that you get into the Gospels, Matthew, Mark, Luke and John, and get to personally know the real Jesus. Don't be fooled by a lie. For example, Jesus is not the half-brother of Satan, nor is He the Arch-Angel Michael. If you did your own Bible study instead of listening to what someone else told you, you would know this.

If you're not in The Word, then I believe you are just a slow moving target for the evil one. He will always attack you when and where you are the weakest and never where you are the strongest, so to be *"Strong in the Lord and the power of his might"* (Ephesians 6:10-12) cannot be overstated. Because *the world is under the sway of the evil one* (1 John 5:19) they have succumbed to his lie that "ignorance is bliss", when in truth, ignorance of the True Word of God is spiritual suicide. Keeping you from reading the Bible is his number one priority; how's his plan working so far with you? He loves to make sure that we are to "busy" and knows that time is on his side; all he has to do is make sure that you run out of it. If you make time daily to spend in the Word you will eventually rise to a place where *the evil one cannot touch you* (1 John 5:18) because once the Truth is in you, his lies become ineffective and he has no more power over you...or not...it's your choice. What is good and what is evil? Its source will determine that. Where did it come from? Only knowing the Word of God, the Holy Bible and no other, gives you the ability to *"discern between good and evil"* as Hebrews 5:14 explains.

Of course, at the time I was in Florida, I knew none of this and tested nothing.

Unicorns, for example, are mentioned several times in the original King James version of the Bible, but were apparently "edited out" in newer versions, as not to embarrass anybody. Check it out and see for yourself! What does the original King James say about dragons and sea monsters (Leviathan) or dinosaurs (Behemoth)?

No, Tinkerbell, leprechauns, and Tommyknockers are not in there... But I wonder if maybe Tommyknockers should be. Maybe, right there in Job 28, somewhere between verses 1 and 11 would be perfect... Like, at the end of verse 8 it could say"," only Tommyknockers". It would be kinda like this;

*"Surely there is a mine for silver, and a place where gold is refined.*

*Iron is taken from the earth, and copper is smelted from ore.*

*Man puts an end to darkness, and searches every recess for ore in the darkness and the shadow of death.*

*He breaks open a shaft away from people; in places forgotten by feet. They hang far away from men; they swing to and fro.*

*As for the earth, from it comes bread, but underneath it is turned up as by fire;*

*Its stones are the source of sapphires, and it contains gold dust.*

*That path no bird knows, nor has the falcon's eye seen it.*

*The proud Lions have not trodden it, nor has the fierce lion passed over it, ONLY TOMMYKNOCKERS!* (**My suggested input**).

*He who puts his hand on the flint; he overturns the mountains at the roots.*

*He cuts out channels in the rocks, and his eyes see every precious thing.*

*He dams up the streams from trickling; what is hidden he brings forth to light." Job 28:1 – 11.*

I love it that the Bible talks about mining and NOT that I'm telling God what to do or say in His own book… And I'm not saying that Tommyknockers are real… It's just that…

\*\*\*

I really can't recall all the underground mines that I worked in, reopened, rehabbed, salvaged or just plain plundered. My brother and I, along with our cousins, were digging tunnels all over the neighborhood before I was in kindergarten. We even made the newspaper a time or two and had a bit of trouble over undermining our neighbor's garage and "sinking" her Oldsmobile (poor quality of timber, NOT poor quality of timbering, mind you).

By the early to mid-70s, Steve and I were making pretty fair change by "high grading" a turquoise deposit in an old Spanish mine tunnel. We were working by day at the Reveille Mine in Nye County, and working the turquoise after work, at night (I got some cool pictures, too!). This was just before I met the girl of my dreams.

The vein was high up in the "hanging wall" and it was pretty rotten (unstable) ground. The old-timers who dug this mine used local pine and cedar for support timbers and they were in the latter stages of deterioration.

One night, as we were heading back about 200 feet underground to the vein, a rock bounced hard off of my hard hat. I turned on Steve as the only possible culprit, seeing how he was behind me and we are the only two in the mine.

"What was that for?" I asked.

"I didn't do it", says he.

About a dozen more steps and "doink!" A rock bounces off my hard hat and hits me on the shoulder. Before I could say anything, Steve, wide-eyed, says "I didn't do it! I saw it hit you, but I didn't do it! And it didn't come from above us!"

"We've been in and out of this old mine dozens of times and it never happened before... Fine", I said, trying to think of what I must've done to piss him off. "You go first, then".

We were almost to the area we were working when the third rock hit me in the back! It didn't hit my hard hat or my shoulders, as a falling rock would; it hit me in the back as only a horizontal moving object could! It freaked me out and I told Stevie, "deep enough!" (That means 'I quit' in miner language).

"Let's just let it go for tonight. I just got hit in the back with a rock, pard".

Steve said, "Fine by me", in an irritated tone.

We were almost to the portal when the tunnel caved in about 75 feet behind us. For probably over 200 years the ground had held... Until now.

Tommyknockers.

Sprite, imp, elfin, or leprechaun type mythical creature that lives in mining folklore as far back as the second oldest profession can be traced throughout history. Sometimes blessing with guidance to rich ore or warnings in time of danger (such as cave-ins!), to mischievous, obnoxious, and sometimes, just plain out mean doers of dastardly deeds, carried out in the darkest of dark places of the earth, hundreds of feet underground. That's probably why I like them. I even tried feeding them once... Left food laying around for them. The other miners said the mine rats ate it, but I don't think so.

Seen one ever? No... Maybe... Out of the corner of my eye, once... There was something...

Nevertheless... They take stuff and hide it; they mess with your machine, shut off your drill water, and dump out your rock drill oil so you have to go all the way out to the station to refill your jug, cuz you can't drill without it.

And you better for sure guard your lunch!

Also known as "Knockers" in Welsh, Cornish, and Devon folklore, Wikipedia describes them as about 2 feet tall and grizzled, but not misshapen, they live beneath the ground. Here they wear tiny versions of standard mining garb and commit random mischief such as stealing miner's unattended tools and food. At one mine I worked at, they got blamed for nailing lunchboxes to the benches in the "doghouse" with .60 penny nails! (Ha ha ha! J. Dugger, you know the truth!). The portable toilet was too heavy for them, so they didn't get blamed for that when it got thrown down the main shaft from the 800 level.

Their name comes from the knocking on the mine walls (ribs) that happens just before cave-ins, as well as the creaking of rock and mine timbers before they give way under the extreme pressure. That's why only Douglas fir is allowed for timbering underground – no other wood will give you a warning in the form of creaks, moans, and, sounds that are often times described as "a woman softly wailing". Miners would often tell each other "You can sure hear Mona today", or, "Mona is really talking today", as a warning that the ground is taking a lot of pressure and might possibly be dangerous.

To some miners, the Tommyknockers were malevolent spirits and the knocking was the sound of them hammering at walls and supports to cause a cave-in. To others, who saw them as essentially well-meaning practical jokers, the knocking was their way of warning the miners that a life-threatening collapse was imminent. And yep! They throw rocks at you, too!

By personal experience I obviously tend to agree with the latter. After all, why would they destroy their own habitat?

According to some Cornish folklore, the Knockers were the helpful spirits of people (contrary to the Bible) who had died in previous mine accidents in the many tin mines in the country, warning the miners of impending danger. To give thanks for the warnings, and to avoid future peril, the miners cast the last bite of their tasty pastries into the mines for the Knockers (I bet the mine rats loved that).

In the 1820s, immigrant Welsh miners brought tales of the Tommyknockers and their theft of unwatched items and warning knocks to Western Pennsylvania when they gravitated there to work the mines. Cornish miners, much sought after in the years following the gold and silver rushes, brought them to California and Nevada. When asked if they had relatives who would come to work the mines, the Cornish miners always said something along the lines of "Well, me Cousin Jack over in Cornwall wouldst come, could ye pay 'is boat ride?", and so they came to be called "Cousin Jacks".

The Cousin Jacks, as notorious for losing tools as they were for diving out of shafts and tunnels just before they collapsed, attributed this to their diminutive friends and refused to enter new mines until assured by the management that the Knockers were already on duty. Even non-Cornish miners, who worked deep in the earth where the noisy support timbers creaked and groaned, came to believe in the Tommyknockers.

And by the way, about all those hands working all those open pit mines? They are actually construction workers digging a big hole... not Hardrock Miners. We live in an era where every man or woman that steps on a mine site is called a miner... I am one of them also, but I am an "equipment operator" or "Cat Skinner", etc. when working the surface mines. That's not even close to what a miner is. And, God forgive me, I gotta say, most of those surface people who call themselves miners these days, wouldn't make a pimple on a Hardrock Miners butt (Sorry... Had to say it... My bad).

Belief in Tommyknockers in America remained well into the 20th century. When one large mine shut down in 1956, and the owners sealed the entrance (portal), fourth, fifth, and sixth generation Cousin Jacks circulated a petition calling on the mine owners to set the Knockers free so they could move on to other mines. The owners complied. Belief in Nevada still persists amongst its true Hardrock Miners to this day, however, as I stated before, more recently much of the blame for all the problems and types of misfortune incurred is squarely placed on the shoulders of the "dumb ass on the other shift"

I, too, became very comfortable with this dispersion of fault blaming, until, on my way to the 800 level shaft station at Gooseberry mine, at the end of my shift, after wrecking a seven car ore train 20 minutes before shift change, and leaving them twisted up into the timbers of the main haulage way, the reality hit me between the eyes that, I AM the ass on the other shift (as so perfectly explained by Stephen M. Voynick in his book, the Making of a Hardrock Miner).

Since then, I'm sticking with the whole Tommyknocker thing. And if you're interested, another good read, although out-of-print is a book called Mining Lore, by Wolfgang Paul. Incredibly interesting to me was the stories and illustrations of some of the most beautiful churches, chapels and hand carved cathedrals, hundreds of feet underground, hand hewn out of solid rock, salt, etc.

You see, all through history up until the 1950s, tradition mandated that the shift of the miners coming out from underground would meet with the shift about to go into the mine, and pray for them and sing hymns. God has always been ever present in the lives of miners, and I will always speak with godly pride of my family's heritage. Above all else, we are miners.

***

Moving from Santa Monica, California to Washoe Valley, Nevada, and eventually, the mining camps of Nye County, Central Nevada in the middle of nowhere, took its toll on my city girl. Looking back, it must have been excruciating for her. This was my world, and the self-centered king of selfishness that I was, this is how it's going to be. Her Mom must have been missing her because every time she would read about or see something on TV concerning some new sickness or disease, she would say she was showing the symptoms, and make a doctor's appointment not only for herself, but for Lori as well! In Reno! About 400 miles away! Not only did it eat up my days off and blow holes in my paycheck, but Lori was constantly on the road back and forth between the mine and her Mom's house. It took almost a year, but Lori finally moved back in with her Mom in Washoe Valley. She enrolled in college and eventually got accredited as a legal secretary (which paid off for me as the years rolled by, believe me).

Fine by me, I tried to convince myself. She and her Mom were driving me nuts... And she can't even cook oatmeal... Finally some peace and quiet. I made it a couple of months. I quit my gravy job with my Dad's company, hauled ass for Washoe Valley, and moved in with "Mom", too. It didn't take long before I rubbed Lori's Mom and Dad the wrong way, no matter how hard I tried not to. They obviously just didn't like me, or I think miners in general.

I worked the Savage and New Yorker underground mines up the hill in Virginia City for a while before my cousin Mickey got me hired on at the Gooseberry mine outside of Reno. Underground mining was my new addiction and escape from the reality of having to live in the city. I became a citified "hermit" or "recluse", and Lori became a fashion model for Eve Lynn Productions, as well as the lead singer in a bluegrass band. Yeah, you should've seen me try to fit in at the high society social events and cocktail parties... I always seemed to get along good with the bartenders, though. We bought an older Victorian-style house in Sun Valley, a little north of Reno, and moved out of Mom's house in 1980.

About two months later Lori's Dad, Bob, was trying to clear some land he had purchased down on Widican Road in Reno, to build an apartment complex. About 100 years earlier, the old-timers had built a huge wooden water flume system for irrigation, across the property. Now, all that was left of it was these giant 15' x 20' concrete pillars that used to support the massive flumes that channeled water from the Truckee River to the farm fields.

He had hired a dozer and couldn't budge it, and had rented a compressor and chipping hammer that they used to peck away at it for several days, with no results. It must have killed him to call me, but I went down to get a look at it, before going to work on graveyard shift at the Gooseberry mine. I told him to trade the chipping hammer for a Gardner Denver sinking (Jack) Hammer that actually drills holes. I also told him to drill six-foot deep holes about 8 inches apart, all around the base of the square concrete pillar, at 45° angles. Then I said I would be back in the morning when I got off work. I was so looking forward to making Lori's father have to rely on me and trust me, that it wasn't funny.

The next morning I got to his job site and could clearly see he was nervous. He really got fidgety when I popped open my lunchbox and pulled out a dozen sticks of "Hercules's Finest", 40% dynamite, along with electric blasting caps and a half role of blasting wire. I quickly selected and loaded the five holes I needed. The rest of the holes were to give the force of the dynamite the correct direction to break to. There was a propane tank and a plate glass window on the occupied house about 45 feet away from the concrete pillar, and the more that Bob stared at them, the whiter his face turned, as I did the final wiring and strung the role of wire over to his pickup.

As I opened the hood of his pickup to gain access to the battery, Bob went into "back out" mode. He was stammering and making partial sentences about "wait a minute" and "try something else". I can understand his fear, as he didn't really know me at all, let alone how incredibly good I really was with dynamite. I had intended to maximize his anxiety by just handing him the wire leads and saying, "there you go", then walking off to make him set off the charges himself... But it was obvious that he had talked himself into a frenzy and wanted out of the whole thing.

As he looked at me and said the words "we gotta find another way", I reached over and touched the two blast wires to the positive and negative posts on his battery. The look on his face was priceless... True "shock and awe", as the ground under our feet shook slightly, with a barely audible, deep, "WHUMP, WHUMP" sound, and that concrete pillar just kind of lifted up a couple of inches, shook a couple of times, then settled back down. There was barely any dust at all. The guy on the dozer was grinning as he hit the starter switch on his machine, and I looked at my father-in-law and said "You best windup that shot cord before somebody sees it", then, "See ya later, Bob", and then I walked off. Lori was smiling, and by the way she held her head up high when she said goodbye to her Dad, made me add a little more "strut" to my already cocky "John Wayne"(my best imitation, anyway) stride.

Me and Bob got along really good after that day, God bless him.

## CHAPTER 11

## Tales of Gooseberry

Back at the Gooseberry mine, me and the Tommyknockers were getting along just fine. I advanced quickly and was making some pretty big money. They started me out "caging" (operating the man cages and ore skips in the main shaft) and "tramming" (running the ore trains on the 800 foot level and throughout the mine), but in no time I was "driving drift" with my new pard, JD, and life is good. Round in and round out, every day. That means when we got to work, the blast smoke had hopefully just cleared from the other shift blasting their round as they came off of their shift. So you would first "bar down" any loose rock with steel tipped fiberglass poles so it didn't fall on you while you worked under the newly blasted rock. Then you would "muck out" the round (freshly blasted rock) with a Gardner Denver 22B mucking machine that literally threw the rock over the top of itself and into the ore car behind you, where you stood on the side of the thing running it, and tried not to get hit or smashed between the mucker and the rib (wall). After you cleaned up the blasted rock, you stood your timber. In this case, 12" x 12" Douglas fir posts, 9 foot tall, with a matching "cap" or beam across the top of the posts, all wedged tight against the surrounding rock to hold the fresh hole you just shot out, from collapsing in on you. Once the ground is secure, you hang your "services", water and air pipes made of Victaulic steel, hook up the lines to your Gardner Denver 83 rock drill with its three-phase air extendable leg, and drill out your next round. After completion of the drilling pattern, in this case, 66 holes, you remove your drilling equipment and load the holes with dynamite and electric, 1 to 45 second delay blasting caps.

When it's your turn at quitting time, you hunkered down behind a timber, a "safe distance" down the drift, yell "fire in the hole!", and touch off your round, counting each shot to make sure you don't have any "misfires", that can cause someone to accidentally walk or drill into a "live round". Then you go home and do the same thing the next day, and the next, and the next. "Round in, round out". And just about everything you handle on a daily basis weighs over 100 pounds; timber, machines, bags of powder, etc. When you wear out your body, you are "stoped out" meaning you don't have enough left in you to make "Gypo", or in other words, get your round in, round out, every day. It's called "deep enough" when you gotta quit and go look for work on the surface, and nobody has a clue about what you have been through, let alone what you have survived, on a daily basis.

Hmmmm.. Sometimes I wonder if maybe Tommyknockers might not more likely be, in reality, God's Guardian Angels for underground miners??? Sounds crazy? It wouldn't if you ever spent any time working underground. It always amazed me how many of my big tough friends, on the surface, found out they were claustrophobic and terrified of the dark when they went a few hundred feet underground; especially when you reach over with your "rap wrench" and bust their light out and leave them in the dark for a few hours, listening to the timbers moan and creak. If they came back the next day, which is rare, they will usually make a pretty good hand. I know it sounds mean but JD and I had to spend a lot of time breaking in new miner trainees, called "nippers", and just keeping them alive long enough to teach them what to look out for and to do and not do, until they could survive on their own, was a very frustrating and time-consuming investment of time. This was very tedious; to say the least, just to have them decide after a couple of paychecks that the money wasn't worth the risk. Better to "weed them out" as soon as possible so you weren't wasting a lot of time trying to teach someone who was going to quit anyway.

One time we had this "nipper" that was always on us about letting him drill. The sooner you can drill and be promoted to "miner" status, the sooner you make "Gypo" or contract money, which is so much extra per foot of advance, so much per set of timber you stand, so much for every "pony set" of timber, etc., that is paid over and above your days' pay. It's where the big money is.

The trick to drilling was finding the perfect balance between the drilling and hammering of the drill steel going into the rock, and the amount of pressure being applied by the three-phase telescopic "Jack leg" that was (hopefully) steadily pushing on the drill, therefore pushing the drill steel into the rock with the proper amount of pressure, without "sticking the steel" in the hole. High-pressure air and water blew through the drill steel, into the hole, and ran/sprayed back out between the steel and the rock, and usually into your face. The noise, in such an extremely confined space, is virtually deafening. You can yell and scream at the top of your lungs and not be heard.

So, much to my disapproval, JD decides to give him a shot at it, mostly I'm sure, just to get him to shut up. JD was drilling one of the top "reliever" holes right above the "burn" (center) hole that was about 7 feet up the "face". The kid, who I would love to name, but can't, was still running his mouth about how he "had this", when he kicked on the air to the drill and was drowned out by the roar of the hammer. JD had mercifully started the 6 foot steel about 8 inches into the rock so it wouldn't slip on the guy. Unfortunately, that left over 5 foot of the bendable drill steel between the face and the drill.

When our nipper turned the grenade looking air control for the leg, it seemed like nothing happened, so he gave it a hard crank. Those controls are very touchy. With way too much air hitting that telescopic leg, it shot the hammer straight up to the "back" (ceiling), bending that drill steel as it went. The nipper had both hands wrapped tightly around the control handles on the back of the Gardner Denver 83, and tried to hang on. The leg pressure shot him and the drill right on up until it stopped, slamming into the "cap" or top beam of timber above his head, pinning him by his fingers on both hands between the drill and the mine timber! His feet were about eight or ten inches off of the ground and he was kicking and clamoring trying to get his feet onto the slippery, oily Jack leg. JD and I were trying to yell over the machine and tell him to push the emergency air release button under his thumb. We held up our clenched fists and wiggled our thumbs as if pushing the button, while he kicked and flailed wildly. He was screaming and his eyes were bugging out, then a look of comprehension came on his face and he pressed the button and held it in. The leg began to retract and slowly lower him down to the ground. As his feet touched the rock beneath, for whatever reason, he let off the button and again shot right back up to the same position, pinned against the timber!

God forgive us, there was no helping him now. JD and I were on the ground, laughing hysterically while he wildly kicked and twisted through the air, again, trying to wrap his legs around the Jack leg and relieve his now broken hands and fingers. Lying right beside me was the main airline, but because I was laughing so hard, I had a hard time kinking it. Finally, with all my strength, I bent it together enough to cut off the entire air supply, and down he came, again. JD quickly shut the controls down when they came within reach. I know.... Not funny.. I guess you had to be there.

***

Gooseberry was using a "sand fill" stope mining system. We blasted and hauled out the ore and filled the open cavern we had created with wet sand that we pumped in from the surface. As the sand settled and filled the stopes to a workable level, the water separated and was pumped back to the surface. This created a mass amount of weight and exceptional ground pressure in the workings and haulage ways below the stopes.

In the 809 Haulage Way below the stopes, 12" x 12" posts and caps (timbers) were installed 6 feet apart. Within a month, "reliever sets" of 12" x 12" timbers were installed to help take the pressure off of the original set of timbers. Within two months 10" x 10" steel "I" beam supports were installed to help stop the wooden timbers from breaking. I have photographs of the steel "I" beams twisting like licorice sticks under the ground pressure, just before they had to abandon that part of the mine.

Stopes and raises were a place to make big money fast on Gypo, and I spent a lot of my career there, digging up towards the surface, rather than down sinking shaft or horizontally driving drift. For one, the ore pretty much moved itself once you shot it out. Tommyknockers were working overtime, I believe, as cave-ins were common in this type of wet, soggy environment, referred to commonly as "bad ground". Even good hard solid ground could quickly become "bad ground" when it fell on you and killed you. At least, in the stopes, you are above the sand and water.

After sand fill, it was like walking onto a beach to go to work, only hundreds of feet underground and in the dark.

Over some controversy about some "alleged" missing burritos taken off of the wall board heaters in the 800 level doghouse, I was "promoted" into the 801 – 802 sand fill stope, regardless of the fact that a remedy had already been invoked upon the alleged burrito perpetrator, and cured the alleged problem. The Mexican miners loaded up a burrito with peppers and homemade (nuclear!) hot sauce and left it for the alleged burrito snatcher. The alleged burrito snatcher supposedly took the nuclear burrito up into his raise where he might possibly have taken several bites before realizing his ill-gotten booty was incinerating him from the inside out! It burned so hot that white flashes allegedly appeared in his vision, semi-blinding him! With absolutely nothing else in the raise to combat the horrifying consequences of his alleged misdeeds, he may or may not have been forced to remove the drill water hose from his "buzzy" or "stoper" (one piece drill mounted on a solid telescopic leg, used primarily for drilling straight up, over one's head), and drinking the recycled, oily, filthy drill water that was pumped out of the sand fill sumps and "piss ditches" then recycled back to the drills. That would, in fact, be the ultimate cure for allegedly snatching burritos out of the "doghouse", (underground lunchroom usually with at least one light bulb in it) had any of this actually occurred. Enough said.

The 801 – 802 stopes, at that time, were so dangerous that mine inspectors took your word for how safe the work area was, because they wouldn't go into it to see for themselves. And it was bad. It didn't start out that way. As we mined from the 800 foot level up to about the 600 foot level we could hold our ground fairly well until we mucked out and sand filled. But about the 600 foot level we hit a huge clay "slip". It absorbed water from the sand fill and became insanely unstable. We tried going around it, through it, and we even tried leaving gigantic pillars of high-grade ore between us and the clay, but it just kept caving off around us. And of course, the ore got richer and richer around the clay slip, so the company wouldn't even consider abandoning the stope.

By that time it had grown to about 120 yards long and 20 to 60 feet wide at different places. About three weeks after hitting the clay we had lost so much ground that it was only about 50 yards long. Me and my partner, Neil, would set up and drill for a couple of days, but the back would cave in before we had a chance to load and shoot it. Man, it was scary going into that hole every day, but it seemed that every time we would try to quit, they would offer us more money, to the point where Neil and I became the highest-paid miners in the country! As it was typical in these situations, as the ore grade and extreme pay rate went higher and higher, are common sense went lower and lower. Everyone else (with any brains) had quit the stope and Neil and I had the whole mine to ourselves on graveyard to stop other work areas from causing any undue vibrations in the ground (i.e. drilling and blasting) while we were working in the stope.

If a black cat crossed my path on the way to work, I would turn around and go back home for the night. Couldn't sleep, either.

Neil and I decided to work farther apart so we could still watch out for each other, but at least, if it caved while we were drilling, one of us might still make it out or be able to help the other one.

At shift change, hardly anyone would even talk to us, and that was okay because truthfully, when we came out of the hole in the morning, our nerves were pretty well frayed anyway. I guess that makes it kinda tough to make small talk.

One night Neil had gone up to the 500 foot level, to the powder magazine, to get our blasting agents. As I walked over toward the 911 rubber tired mucker, a dreadful moan echoed up the steel lined ore chute I was walking by, and it made the hair on my neck stand up. Again it sounded as I pulled the dipstick on the mucker to check the oil, and it sounded like someone moaning the word "go" or maybe "no". I knew it was a "timber moan" echoing up the steel ore chute from below, but man, it really made my skin crawl. To shut it up I fired up the diesel engine on the 911 mucker to drown out the noise. God, I wish I hadn't of ignored that inner voice... Or those wailing Tommyknockers, maybe.

I was just going to move the mucker to the manway access raise to get it out of the way before we started loading holes. A fist-sized rock landed on the ROPS protective cage and roll bar over my head.

That's all I remember... Then darkness.

I'm not sure when I became conscious of the fact that I was conscious. Was I alive or dead? Silent, blackness. Then, I slowly became aware of the pain; some in my neck, but mostly in my right hand. I was alive. I could taste blood in my mouth as I "came to". How long had I been out? What happened? What about my light?

It was then, as I attempted to reach up and turn my light on, that I came to the cold, bone chilling realization that I had been buried...alive.

When I tried to raise my left hand off of my lap, it was stuck. My right hand was smashed down in between the two loader bucket control sticks, and was broken. Both were being held down by dirt and rock. My head and face were pressed down onto the steering wheel, but I could still lift my head up a few inches, yet I couldn't raise it all the way up to a sitting position or hold it up, so I would have to set my face back down on the steering wheel. I wiggled around and eventually worked my left hand free enough to reach up through the steering wheel and feel for my light, but it was broken out. I also realized my front upper teeth were loose and one was broken, as well.

I tried to yell but it ended up more of a groan. My right hand hurt like hell, but for the life of me, I couldn't get it unstuck and unburied. The safety roll cage had obviously been smashed down, and except for the small confined space around my head and chest, I was completely buried.

I thought of Lori and my Mom and Dad, trying to remember the last things I had said to them. Mom had sent me a birthday card the other day, with something about "she keeps me in her prayers" written in it.

How's that working for you now, Mom? It's gonna take a long time for me to die like this... "If You hear me God, please kill me quick, if that's what You're gonna do. I know I don't have the right to ask You anything after all I've done, but if You're going to do it, get on with it... Please. And I'm sorry for the things I done", I softly whispered.

A low bump. A couple of muffled thumps! I think I heard... No, I definitely heard something! I tried again to yell but with my head forced so far down, I couldn't get much out. I kept working my left arm until finally and painfully, I got it worked into the open space by my head. The thumps and bumps became steadier. With only being able to move my forearm and hand a few inches, I got a rock and hit it on the steel tubing of the steering column a few times. The thumps and bumps immediately stopped.

Then I heard it! Three louder thumps!

The proper response is to pound 10 times, but I could only make six or seven before I was gasping for breath and had to quit. I was running out of air!

It didn't matter; a few moments later I heard the five pounding knocks that meant they had located me and help is on the way! Soon the digging sounds got louder and louder as they were in a frenzy to get to me before I died, God bless them. I started drifting in and out of consciousness, again, and the last thing I remember hearing was the raspy voice of my pard, Neil, yelling and hollering orders to the other miners to "put their backs into it".

The truth is Neil and I didn't get along hardly at all on the surface... From different sides of the tracks, you could say. As a matter of fact, we were total opposites. But down here, he was my "pard" and we looked out for each other every single day. Our lives were always in each other's hands, and I knew he wouldn't let them quit till they got me out – alive or dead. I knew the gates of hell wouldn't stop Neil from digging me out, and vice versa. Thank you, Neil, and God bless you where ever you are.

And to my friends and partners over the years, that never saw it coming, rest in peace, my dear brothers, and I will see you on the other side...just not this time. Why not? Devine Providence. If those wailing Tommyknockers/moaning timbers hadn't have creeped me out so badly when they did, I probably would not have fired up that mucking machine and climbed into it, and underneath its protective roll cage, which was the only possible place that I could have survived being "slabbed" (caved in on) by such an enormous amount of rock. If I had been just a few seconds later getting into that machine, I would have been nothing more than a wet spot underneath all that rubble. Luck? No such thing. That's Devine Providence.

They never reopened that stope after that, partly due to the fact that they couldn't find anybody dumb enough to go back down into her, and that you can't reopened a work area after an accident until it has been inspected and cleared by MSHA (Mine Safety and Health Administration), and there wasn't an inspector in the country that would go down into that hellhole. I'm betting that Tommyknockers even called that one "Deep Enough", too.

■■■■■■■■■■■■■■■■■■■■■■■■■■■■■■■■■■■■■■■■■■■■■■■■■■■■■■■■■

## CHAPTER 12

## The Tallahassee Cache

> *"Now he who received seed among the thorns is he who hears the word, and the cares of this world and the deceitfulness of riches choke the word, and he becomes unfruitful"*
> *Matthew 13:22*

Back in Tallahassee, I purposely made a point to avoid Norman and Andy until Ricky and Miles caught back up with us. And when they did, they had a story to tell. Two hours after we pulled out, two vans and a dark blue sedan pulled up into the motel parking lot, got our room numbers from the office, and kicked in the doors! And, they didn't look at all like street thugs. They were organized and much more professional. They checked our rooms and were gone in the time it took the motel management to call the police. A rental sticker was visible on one of the vans; they were casually dressed in nice clothes and jackets, and from what my guys saw of their few flashes of hardware, they were packing good quality and at least one piece of high-end "equipment" (Uzi 9 mm). This could only be Jackman's crew. And somebody had to have told them how to find us... A traitor is what I'm thinking, and it ain't one of my guys, for sure. Time for Norman and Andy to come clean before somebody gets killed.

Understandably, Norman wasn't feeling very well, and Andy had regained his calm composure. I knew in my heart they were both good men; they were just obviously way in over their heads on this deal, and it was taking its toll on them, and us as well. I was more than frazzled at having another crew hunting us. I was here to do the hunting, remember? After about an hour of listening to Norman and Andy "explain things", I was way over the edge and ready to call it quits.

Jones, on the other hand, sat there riveted on Norman's every word, as cool as a cucumber and never said a thing.

Some guy named Joey hooked Norman up with a psychic named Lisa who was going to lead Norman and Andy to the stashed money and gold. Joey, a friend or relative of the deceased Georgia boys, lured Norman to Plant City and ripped him off for some undisclosed, but obviously asinine, amount of money that Norman didn't want me to know, as he was extremely embarrassed. It must have been pretty big money though, because it didn't bother him too much to tell me about the $20,000 cash that his new psychic partner, Lisa, in October 1990, had ripped him off for a few months later, in Tampa. That helped explain a lot about Norman's weird behavior. As he was accountable to the Farmers Coalition, I can relate to his frustration and desperate measures he is willing to go to. We found it very disturbing and somewhat alarming when Norman and Andy detailed how Lisa had proven her ability to not only track the money and the other "crews" in the area, but also revealed her ability to supply up to a 100 man crew of "trigger men", which I had personally witnessed part of, surrounding the Plant City storage unit facility.

Thus, it was now clear that Jackman's men were on the inside of the facility, and it was a stalemate for now.

Sonja is the psychic who betrayed Jackman, if I got this right, and now is working with Lisa and her New York crew, independently of their former employers, namely Norman and Jackman whom they both betrayed. Sonja supposedly used to live on the property of one of the Tallahassee caches.

The guy Norman keeps talking to and getting his information "updates" from, on the phone all the time, is "Robbie". Robbie is Norman's 18-year-old psychic in Montana, who is apparently more interested in his teenage screaming male hormones than treasure, and as such, is very often impossible to reach when Norman tries to call him. Yep. Robbie has our lives in his hands and is out chasing girls. And to verify what Jones told me, Robbie told Norman that they can track us easiest when we are all together and moving, and talking about the money. He says it's harder, if not almost impossible, to track us unless we are moving in a large group.

Furthermore, Robbie calls Norman and "embeds pictures or visions" into Norman's mind, over the phone, of the landscape and visual references closely related to the hiding places of the money. Robbie says he can actually see the money and gold!

The latest call Robbie made to Norman revealed that the actual Ford truck and trailer used in the transport of the treasure, was on the move just north of Tallahassee, and had several wooden crates of gold and 11 garbage bags of money in the trailer, and a guy named Eddie was following the truck. Robbie told Norman that he would keep him posted; that was several hours ago.

\*\*\*

"I need a drink…you comin'?" I said to Jones, and we left Norman and Andy in their room and went downstairs to the hotel bar. To make matters worse, I had reopened the bullet hole in my back and it was oozing pus and blood. When I had Jones look at it in the bathroom, he looked concerned and said "you probably ought to see a doctor, Jones. It's startin' to look kinda nasty".

Right… No amount of BS is gonna explain a bullet hole in your back to a doctor, without him getting the law involved. Besides, the hole in my back was the least of my concerns at the moment. If even a fraction of this ongoing episode of "Twilight Zone" that we were involved in was true, I had to get my team out of here and back home as safely, and as soon as possible. They are my first priority, and way too much of this lunacy was totally out of our control, and our rule has always been, we only play in games we control, and we control the game or we get out of it.

The treasure was big enough to fight for, even go to gun mode over for that matter and we have no qualms about that, but we are definitely not calling the shots here. Lunatics and psychics are.

As the bartender poured us another drink, we regrettably agreed to tell everything to our crew. That's gonna be tough… They're gonna wonder what the heck I got us into, and I didn't want to lose their trust in me, but they had the right to know the situation.

It was getting late and Jones and I were Marks, the bartenders, last customers, so he ambled over to shoot the breeze. Jones gives him a line about how we are in the "property recovery" business. Mark goes on to tell us how he is in his final year of college and will soon have his Master's Degree in medicine. Then he will be returning to his hometown to a career as an emergency room physician.

I said, "Yeah? And how are you with gunshot wounds?"

Top of his class, says he.

"Ever seen one? I mean a real one?" I asked.

The atmosphere of the conversation had changed, becoming a little more serious than Mark felt comfortable with, as he responds, "Sure, I mean yeah, on a cadaver (dead body). Lots of times", he said nervously, looking back and forth between me and Jones. "How come you guys call each other Jones, anyway? Its kinda weird isn't it?" Me and Jones looked at each other for a second, then relaxed our glares and smiled at him.

As I took out a $100 bill and slowly slid it toward the bartender, I said, "Well Mark, it's not really weird at all. See, my partner here's name is Jones and by coincidence, my name is Jones also". He looked at the Franklin now in front of him and back at me with deep suspicion.

"I'd like you to look at something and just tell me what you think, okay Mark"?

He faked a weak smile and said "Sure, I guess".

We went into the bathroom and he was getting really scared, until I pulled up my shirt. As soon as he saw the wound his countenance totally changed and he was all business.

I was showing signs of infection and if I didn't arrest the infection quickly, it would soon spread into the marrow of the punctured rib. It wasn't going to heal without being cleaned and the festering had to be treated. He told us what to buy and what to do, closed the bar, and laid me on the pool table, and then he cleaned it (hurt like hell!) with Everclear (almost pure Alcohol) and re-bandaged it out of a first aid kit he kept in his car. He was a Godsend to me (literally, I'm willing to wager). Looking back on that night, I say "Thank You, Father, for sending your servant to patch me up, again. Amen".

Jones and I came to the realization that if we sent everyone home at the same time, if all this psychic BS is true, then they would be able to not only know where we live, but also follow us in an attempt to extract information, as was their general mode of operation. We had to be careful. No way was I gonna allow any of this shit-storm (sorry…my bad, again) to find its way back to our families.

So Jones, who rarely does anything that surprises me anymore, makes a few phone calls to whoever, and comes up with our very own psychic! Randy is more of a "witcher" or "diviner" than a "vision seeing" psychic (God have mercy). Just when you think it can't get any better (I'm thinking, shoot myself)!

"But he's the best I can come up with on such short notice", Jones defensively exclaims. I'm so glad Jones is on my side.

Eyeballs rolled around and a few tempers flared when I downloaded all the information on my crew, and I held nothing back. We discussed our options over the next few days, until Randy confirmed the plan to send the crew home in small groups of two or three, taking different routes on different days, and laying over in Arizona and Utah a few days to see if they were tailed, before making the final leg of the journey into Nevada. They were all grilled on the seriousness of the situation and instructed on controlling what they thought and talked about as well.

Plan B (my other plan) was rejected by the majority (not all), to all travel together, lead them into the high desert Nevada Mountains of our own turf, and ambushed them (would have worked). This way we wouldn't have to worry about them ever getting close to our families... Finish it once and for all, was my way of thinking (sad to admit). Yeah, if you haven't figured it out by now, I'm really sick of all this eeby-jeeby, voodoo psychic stuff, and just want to get it done with. I don't understand it and I don't want to. I'm way out of my league of expertise and that's very uncomfortable for me, not to mention dangerous. You can't shoot what you can't see.

But, majority rules.

\*\*\*

"Is it moving? Is it moving, Robbie?" Norman is loudly and repeatedly asking into his room phone as Jones and I walk in. "Can you hear me? What? What did you say?"

Norman looks up at me, and then says "Hold on a minute", into the receiver. "I can't hear him, John, and neither can Andy with his hearing aid... Here; you talk to him", and he shoved the phone into my hand and stood up to give me his chair at the small desk.

Get real, I thought as I put the phone to my ear and said, "This is John". I almost added, "Now let's see if you can BS me, kid", but I didn't. The young kid's voice on the other end of the phone line simply said, "The truck is stopped. Are you sitting down?"

"Yeah, I'm sitting, go on... Where is it?" I said.

"This will be easier for you if you can relax a little and just close your eyes and focus on my words. I can sense your animosity toward me, and I understand this is a lot for you".

"A lot for me". So he thinks I'm an idiot. He must not be too good of a psychic or he would know how much I wish I could climb through this phone and kick his ass.

Robbie then says, "Okay, listen closely. The truck is about 16 miles past I-10. There is a dirt road with an "S" turn and it". As he spoke, vivid pictures erupted in my mind as, somehow, he transposed the pictures in his head into my mind. "And about 300 yards down the old road past an old tarpaper house, the semi and trailer are locked inside a steel building".

For a brief second, I could see it in the building as if I were there looking at it! When I finally hung up the phone, my head was exploding into extreme migraine pain. Unbearable pain. And the pain was accompanied by what I can only describe as a deep sense of dark despair, as if I had committed an evil act against my soul. Andy was right there when I put the phone down, ready with water and aspirin… Lots of aspirin.

"So this is how it is every time you guys talk to him?" I asked.

"Yeah", Andy said and nodded. "It takes an hour or so for the pain to go away. Wet washcloths help too, so it's best to just lie down until it passes".

No kidding, I thought. I'm not sure I can walk and I can barely see. After a while Jones helped me back to our room, and when I could, I wrote down what he "showed" me.

Over the past few days most of the boys had moved out in small groups and just me, Jones, and four others of our team remained, even though they understood the risk. We had spaced ourselves out in different motels across town, and it seems, as long as we aren't moving together, we were not being tracked. Randy, Jones, Norman and Robbie are trying to give me a crash course in "psychic survival 101". One good thing became absolute; none of these "spooks" could apparently tell the future.

There's a lot of thick forest growth north of Tallahassee and after a few days of searching, we finally go to the courthouse and get aerial maps and topography maps of the area, to help us narrow down the search. Finally, we closed the search area and confirmed the target area using government aerial photographs from the Department of lands.

We had to maneuver around the old house Robbie told me about, as it was occupied. It looked exactly how I saw it in my mind when he "showed" it to me… Very freaky. The old trail or road past the house down to the barn and metal building was very overgrown, but the recent passing of the truck could still be detected in the smashed down weeds and foliage. We went by some old silos, staying about 15 or 20 feet into the woods, paralleling the old road. We left two of our team at the top of the road to cover the house and our primary escape route. Two more had been dropped off to the northwest in the forest to cover our alternative escape route to the road in that direction, if the need should arise.

When we've reached the edge of the forest by the steel building, we sat down, watched and listened for a while until we were satisfied that we were alone. Jones covered me as I stood up and walked over to the side door and cut the lock off with a pair of bolt cutters. Had I walked around to the big bay doors I would've found that the padlock on it had already been cut.

Inside the building was the truck and trailer, just like Robbie had said. An empty broken wood crate was on the ground beside the rear of the trailer, and another empty crate was inside, and that was it. Otherwise it was empty. We started looking around for any signs of burial or fresh turned dirt, but found nothing. There was some fairly fresh blood on the ground in front of the Ford truck and some more by the bay doors. There were a lot of tracks in and outside of the building. At the sound of an approaching vehicle we ducked out the back bay doors and into the forest.

We moved low and quiet heading north towards a small lake, and then as we started to change our course to the west and our secondary escape route, we spotted two men coming towards us with hunting rifles. Jones was about 40 feet behind me to my left. They hadn't seen us yet and I hit the ground in the middle of a small clearing as I didn't have time to make it to cover. I burrowed, as best I could, into the forest floor of dead leaves, branches and foliage. It wasn't much cover. The two men had stopped about 50 or 60 feet from me and were looking around with binoculars, mostly towards the small lake. As they panned in my direction with their binoculars I looked back over my left shoulder at Jones. He was just sitting there on his ass, on an old fallen tree, grinning at me. I realized that he was around behind some fallen deadwood and far enough back to be out of the field of site of the hunters, if that's what they were. He seemed to be enjoying my predicament, and confirmed that this whole thing was to his liking as he smiled and waved at me! What an ass.

The guys with the rifles slowly started moving to the south east in the general direction that we had just come from. As they passed within 30 feet of me, Jones had to duck down behind the fallen tree he was sitting on... Somehow that gave me a little satisfaction, at least.

We rendezvoused with our guys and went back that evening to put a watch on the small house. After dark we planned on going in and finding out who took the money, and where it went, if possible. Nobody went down the road to that steel building and loaded out that cash and gold without whoever is in that house knowing about it. Full dark set in and no lights came on. By 10:30 PM we had waited long enough. Four of us encircled the house and two kept watch. The doors weren't locked and

I went in the front door, closed it behind me and crouched down inside the door to let my eyes adjust to the dark. As they did, I started making out vague shapes of broken furniture and as I began to move I felt broken glass under my feet. I heard my partner in the back room whisper, "Jones". I stood up and turned on my dimly lit, duct taped flashlight. A quick check of the rooms and we were clear. I increased the light by removing some more of the tape from the lens. Busted furniture, in the kitchen especially, and a lot of blood, all over the walls and the floor, the kitchen sink, and all over the floor of the small living room. We had our gloves on, for the most part, but wiped down anything we may have touched anyway. Jackman would be my guess, tying up loose ends. Great.

At least we had found hard enough evidence to prove that at least it wasn't all fantasy in an old man's mind. We were just sick and tired of coming up short. By the freshness of the blood in and around the truck and trailer, and here, we couldn't have missed it by more than a day or so… Very disheartening… so close.

## CHAPTER 13

## Tramming and Nine Bells

*"He breaks open a shaft away from people; in places forgotten by feet they hang far away from men; they swing to and fro.*
*As for the earth, from it comes bread, but underneath it is turned up as by fire; its stones are the source of sapphires, and it contains gold dust.*
*That path no bird knows, nor has the falcon's eye seen it.*
*The proud lions have not trodden it, nor has the fierce lion passed over it.*
*He puts his hand on the flint; he overturns the mountains at the roots.*
*He cuts out channels in the rocks, and his eye sees every precious thing.*
*He dams up the streams from trickling; what is hidden he brings forth to light.*
*Job 28:4-11*

My pard, JD and I were back to tramming which is operating the two underground electric trains that ran throughout the 800 level, pulling ore from the chutes beneath various stopes and raises that were being worked. It's what we did while we waited for our stope to be sand filled. The stope and raise miners would leave notes on their ore chutes as to how many carloads we were to pull out of each one. The chutes, with their steel or wooden gates, were spaced about 6 feet apart. Except for all the steel lined sand fill chutes, with their air doors, all the ore chutes in "chute row" had a piece of pipe or a hole in them that you stood on the upper edge of the 2 ½ ton ore car, stuck the handle of your "rap wrench" (similar to a pipe wrench only with a hammering surface built on it) into the hole and lifted up the chute gate. This allowed the blast rock to pour out, into the ore car, while hopefully, you got the heck out of the way as not to be buried in the ore car. When the car was full, the trick was to shove the gate back down and shut off the flow of rock before it overflowed the car and flooded the haulage way.

It seemed the asses on the other shift weren't very good at pulling chutes, so JD and I spent a lot of time, at the beginning of our shift, just digging the cars out. Nobody liked cleaning out the cars, either, so we did a lot of that as well. Drill oil and drill water would saturate the dirt and rock that we pulled out of the ore chutes, and cause it to stick and build up in the ore cars. The solution to this was a 4 foot long, 1 ½ inch in diameter blowpipe, hooked up to 325 pounds of air pressure, with a ball valve to shut it off and on with. You had to wear face shields and a rubber rain suit and gloves to survive the back spray of flying rock and dirt that it produced when blowing out the cars.

When the ore trains approached the grizzlies, or "load out" ore chutes where you dumped out the ore into bins to be loaded out on shaft "skips" (buckets) and hauled to the surface, the locomotives always entered the area first, with the cars in tow. You sat sideways on the end of the locomotive, behind the protective ½ inch thick steel plate that you peered over the top of, as you operated the train down the dark tunnels to the 800 level station and the grizzlies.

Mine mice are very easy to catch because they are usually blind from being born in the darkness. They fit nice and snug in the "barrel" of the blowpipe I previously described that is used for cleaning out compacted dirt and rock from within the ore cars. Do you remember the 325 pounds of compressed air and the ball valve? As I came around the final corner and into the lighted grizzly station, I saw JD standing with his legs straddling the track, bracing himself, a huge grin on his face and the blowpipe held firmly at hip level (kinda like the Rifleman!) and pointed right at me! I barely had time to duck behind the half inch steel safety plate before he fired. If he had hit me, that mouse would have gone right through my head! As it were, the mouse hit the steel plate just inches below the top, with a resounding bang that sounded like a hammer and made that steel ring! The mouse literally disintegrated, leaving only a bloody wet spot with a little guts and hair stuck on the safety plate. I looked up to see JDs light bouncing down the drift into the darkness as his hysterical laughter faded away and he ran to his locomotive and disappeared around the corner. It was such an awe-inspiring trick that all I could do was admire his ingenuity and laugh along with him!

Making parachutes out of sample bags and dropping the mice down the main shaft when men were working below us on the lower levels became a favorite pastime. Something about hearing your name echo up that massive two compartment shaft as men screamed it in rage was very self-satisfying. They always seemed to know who did it, but could never prove it. This way of doing things became my forte, especially in dispensing revenge, in later years, Lord, please forgive me.

As I mentioned earlier, the other type of ore chutes we had to pull from were steel lined chutes coming down from the sand fill stopes, and they had steel sliding doors with huge air rams to force them to open and close. So that the blast rock coming down the chute did not directly hit the chute doors and rip them out, at the bottom of the long straight down drop it would hit a steel plate angled at about 45° to deflect the force of the free falling rock. This plate, in turn, was about 4 feet long and dumped the falling blast rock on to another similar plate facing the opposite direction at about 45° also. On the end of this plate was the air door, controlled by the air rams, and the whole system was encased in timber and steel to eliminate any spillage.

The hand operated valve to open and close the door was on the opposite side of the tunnel from the ore chute itself. Thus, the operator could stand safely behind the ore car that was being filled when he opened and closed the air door allowing the ore from the stope up above to be emptied into the ore cars. We always tried to leave a ton or so of material in the chute to act as a buffer in protecting the doors.

Often times, when pulling the ore out of the chute, the chute would "plug". Somewhere between 20 and 200 feet up that steel lined, 5 foot in diameter vertical tube of steel, the rock would compress itself to the walls of the liner and stick leaving multiple tons of blast rock just hanging up there ready to fall. Unknown to us, we would pull out all of the rock beneath the plug, leaving an enormous open void between the chute gate and the plug. This was very dangerous and created a deadly situation to be dealt with, as we had to unplug the plugged chute. This was almost always left to "swing shift" so the administrative staff and personnel on day shift could plead ignorance of the whole affair, should things go bad.

Also, there are never mine inspectors on night shift. The easiest I ever saw a chute get unplugged was when a "shifter" (ramrod/mine supervisor/walking boss/foreman) brought an M1 carbine rifle down the hole, shoved the rifle pointing straight up into the open chute as far as his arm could reach around the "Z" pattern of the two, 45° angle plates. He fired off three rounds in rapid succession, jerked the gun out, and dove out of the way before the hundreds of tons of rock came crashing down. His partner closed the air door as soon as he was out of the way, only allowing about a ton and a half to come by the door before it closed, and into the ore car. Pretty trick, I thought, until they fired him for bringing a firearm into a mine, which is a federal offense. Too bad, it worked well, considering the alternative method.

Here's how JD and I did it…for 100 bucks a pop.

, Regardless of how high up the plug was, we would first try tying or taping a stick of dynamite on to a 10 foot flexible bamboo pole and gently shoving it up inside the chute, resting the bottom of the bamboo pole on the top angled steel plate. We would close the door and set off the charge. Sometimes the blast force would break the plug free, and sometimes it just compacted it more tightly. To do all of this, mind you, you had to literally climb through the open chute door, over the two 45° angled steel plates, and up into the open air chute below hundreds of tons of blast rock hanging right over your head, that could cut loose at any time. If it trapped you in the chute it would crush you to wet powder instantly. That's the worst case scenario. The best case scenario is, if it cuts loose while you're up in the chute, you kick your feet out from under you, allowing your body to freefall, slamming yourself through both the opposite slots of the 45° angled steel plates, and out past the air door and into the 2 ½ ton ore car. You are also praying that your pard, who is waiting with his hand on the open/close air valve on the other side of the drift, is able to throw the valve and close the door behind you before you are buried and crushed in the bottom of the ore car by the tons of rock following a split second behind you. The delay on the air door itself takes about 1 ½ seconds to fully close the door, which in a freefall, is a lifetime…your lifetime. It's best to come out of the chute on your backside so when your feet hit the floor of the ore car, you might have time to lurch forward to the far side of the car and try to get your head and chest above the wall of the car, so it is clear of the following "muck" as possible.

If your partner was a little too fast, he would cut you in two with the air door as it closed, but it would only bother you for a fraction of a second, until the rock caught up to you, anyhow. I have been buried just above my waist, when I landed in the ore car, a couple of times, and thank God and JD that my pard was ready and damn quick on that air door control valve. I returned the favor, in spades, on multiple occasions.

So that's how me and JD did business. We have both had our legs and buttocks pounded black and blue from the rocks pounding against us in that car.

The second option was much more complicated. If the first blast didn't bring the plug down, we still tied the stick of dynamite on to the bamboo pole as before, but now, we tied additional 10 foot links of bamboo pole onto the first one, with blasting wire, as we raised the dynamite higher and higher up the chute. The objective, of course, was to get the stick of powder right up against the plug of rock, before setting it off. If a Tommyknocker dropped a rock on you, you instantly "kicked out", and down the chute you went. It was apparently very entertaining to the Tommyknockers as it happened way more times than it should have, and usually several times before we got the powder close enough to blast the rock free. And yeah, those little rocks bouncing off of our hardhats and shoulders saved our lives on a lot of occasions, as we would only get the dynamite part of the way up to the plug about 50% of the time before it cut lose all by itself. You like getting high on adrenaline? Try that.

I know what you're thinking… "What a couple of numbskulls". Maybe. But back then, 100 bucks actually bought something for your family, and the adrenaline high was a bonus. If you got killed underground in those days, the company would actually take good care of your family. Today, not so much.

\*\*\*

I was at the 800 level main shaft station unloading my timber for the 854 raise, when "nine bells" rang on the stations shaft signal buzzer. Me and everybody else who ever worked underground always dreaded the sound of nine bells. It's a very sobering affair, as your stomach goes kind of sick, the hair goes up on your neck and your skin begins to crawl. A miner or group of miners are in serious trouble; usually the dead or dying kind of trouble.

I had the "man cage" tied up at the 800 station with my timber. As I frantically threw the last piece of 8 x 8 Douglas fir out of the cage, my "straw boss" (shifter/shift boss) Larry Cates, came running around the doghouse and we jumped in the man cage together. We rang for the 1000 foot level and were there and less than two minutes. As we opened the cage door and stepped out onto the 1000 foot level station, a panicked miner was yelling and hollering, "You gotta help him, it's really bad, really bad!"

"Where?" Asked Larry.

"Down the new haulage way", the miner yelled. "It's bad! For God sake you gotta help him! It's really bad!"

It must be, I thought because this guys in shock. We ran headlong down the drift. Soon we were past the steel service pipes, past the end of the vent bag, and then we were about 30 feet past the last set of timber when we found him.

He was pinned against the rib (wall) of the drift by an overturned Eimco 22B mucking machine. I think he must have hooked a solid rock with the corner of the bucket, and when it didn't give, the extreme airpower of the machine enabled it to pull itself over sideways, and came to rest with its top steel rail and controls pinning the miner to the wall, just at the bottom of his rib cage. There was a "V" groove cut into the rock that his spine had happened to go into, probably saving him from being instantly cut in half. As the top rail of the machine came down on him it had broken several sets of his ribs before coming to rest against his backbone, just above his abdomen. It was ungodly gruesome. A lot of his internal parts were visible as well as his intestines, which had been smashed out his sides. And worst of all, he was conscious and screaming.

With all of our might, we could not budge that machine. He had been in the "mucking out" phase of his shift and there was nothing in the blast face that he was working except him and the mucker... No timber, no rock bolts, no drill or drill steel. He was at least 30 feet ahead of his timber in a "bald-faced" drift. His eyes were glazed over and every time he looked down at himself he would scream again. How he was even alive I could not comprehend. We took off running back down the drift for drill steels, to use them to pry with. As I grabbed a couple of six-foot Swede steels, Cates grabbed the Gardner Denver 83 drill and Jack leg. We tried to pry the mucker up with the steels but it was just too heavy and too far over for us to move.

"Were gonna get you outta here", I told him, then Larry and I ran back down the tunnel to get the airline, rock bolts and plates, driver steel, and a come-along that we had seen at the station. As I ran back with the come-along, I stopped at the air manifold just long enough for Larry to yell, "Give me air!" I turned the ball valve on and immediately heard the "83" kick on at full bore.

The hammer was deafening and we almost immediately lost most of our visibility in a cloud of rock smoke, because we were drilling her dry, as it would take longer to hook up the drill water and time was running out. I could yet still hear the man's screams, even over the drill.

Larry bottomed out the drill steel in the hole, pulled it out and kicked it loose from the machine. I shoved a "driver steel" into the chuck (hole at the end of the machine where the steel goes), and slammed the arm down to hold it in place. I grabbed a rock bolt (split bolt---long tube of steel with the slit down the side) and slid a 6 in. steel plate down the shaft of it, and rammed it into the fresh drill hole, on the opposite side of the tunnel from the man underneath the mucker. Larry quickly jabbed that driver steel into the open end of that rock bolt, kicked on the jackhammer, and slammed that bolt all the way home into the rock. It was taking forever, it seemed.

Larry leaned the drill against the rib and left the blow-by air valve open on it to help clear the dust filled air we were now choking on. The come-along was quickly hooked behind the steel plate and the rock bolt and the other end to the mucker. Just before I started jacking the mucker off of that poor man, Larry leaned over into his face and grabbed him behind the neck to look into his wide-open eyes; "Listen", Larry said to him, loudly. The man looked back into Larry's face and stopped screaming. I couldn't hear what Larry softly said to him, but his eyes relaxed and he nodded his head up and down. I was now working that come-along for all it was worth.

A half-dozen lights were bobbing down the dust filled drift, as men were running towards us. As the huge mucker began to rise back up and off the miner, relieving the terrible pressure that was upon him, he looked right at me for a moment, and then slowly closed his eyes.

A dozen hands were grabbing him now, and pushing the mucker back to its upright position. The smell of the man's exposed internal parts flooded my nostrils as I turned toward the shaft station and half staggered up the drift. All I could see was his face as he stared at me, then closed his eyes. Even now, I need the Lord to help me with this after all these years, as I still see his face and hear his anguished cries in my dreams. I found a short side drift they used for storing their powder, and I ducked inside, and went all the way to the back. I sat down and turned off my light, and cried. I don't know for how long. Until I was empty, I suppose.

After a time, I got up, and started heading out of the side drift and back toward the main haulage way that led to the shaft station. Everyone else was gone... Except Larry. As I turned on my light, I found him sitting at the entrance to the side drift I was in, like a guard dog, waiting for me in the dark. He stood up and turned his light on, more likely as a matter of dignity so we couldn't see each other's faces behind our lights. Then, he just put his hand on my shoulder, squeezed it and simply said, "You done real good back there, Johnny. I'm proud of ya". We didn't say anything after that as we got on the man cage. I got off at the 800 level and started gathering up my timber... I had timber to stand and a round to put in and my partner was waiting on me. Round in, round out. Larry went on to the surface.

    We never talked about it after that day. After all, what is there to say?

## CHAPTER 14

## Cinderella Shanty Town

*"... The wealth of the wicked is stored up for the righteous."*
Proverbs 13:22

"Get in here quick! You gotta see this!" Andy hollered at me and Jones. We were out front having a smoke. We flipped our cigarette butts over the balcony handrail and headed into their hotel room. Norman had his chair about 5 feet in front of the TV and was leaning forward as not to miss a single word. It was a local news station broadcasting a piece on the "Cinderella Shanty Town".

Norman sat there, wide-eyed in total disbelief, saying, "That's my money. That's our money". It was all I could do not to bust out laughing (I got a slightly twisted sense of humor). The irony of the situation was inescapable. We are daily risking our very lives hunting for this money, and a bunch of poor old black people, living in squalor, simply find it! Ha ha ha! Too much!

Andy starts to climb up on his soapbox and rattle off something about God this, and God that, and I cut him off with "Don't even go there, Andy; I don't want to hear it". I already felt like I was losing round number 3847 with God as it is, and was convinced that God enjoyed screwing up my life for the sole benefit of His entertainment. I knew He didn't like me, and I was never going to be one of His "cherished chosen ones" who receives His nod of approval.

The part of the newscast that I caught talked about how a "shantytown" of about 11 shacks, with no electricity or water, on the Florida – Georgia border, seemingly overnight went from dirt floor shacks and a community outhouse that was set up over a small creek, to 9 brand-new or near new single wide and one double wide mobile homes, including electric power, septic systems, and running water. All of which was paid for in cash money, over a four month period. This drew the attention of everybody in the area, including law enforcement and eventually the state tax commission, but no one was talking. It spoke of how the local law enforcement had run countless serial numbers taken off of the money and it was "clean" (I thought that was good to know), and towards the end of the program, they had a cameraman recording as a state tax official pounded on the door of the double wide trailer which wasn't even set down on the ground yet. As we all stared in wonder at the television set, a very very old black man opened the door with a distinctive drunken suspicion.

"Are you Mr. So-And-So?" The pompous taxman asked in an overbearing voice.

"Ya, wha chew wa?" Was the proprietor's response while teetering a little, and hanging on to the doorjamb for obvious support.

"On such and such a day you purchased a double wide such and such model, serial number whatever, etc., mobile home from whoever, and took delivery on such and such a date, is that correct, sir?" The taxman asked (my paraphrase added).

The proprietor started a smile that turned into a smirk, leaned over in the face of the taxman, and said, "Yuh blind? Wha da hell is dis Ima standin' in?" Taxman goes white faced, pumps out his chest and declares, "According to the state tax statute blah, blah, blah, section blah, and as a representative of the state of Blah, (to protect that old guy, cuz I like him) I am hereby authorized to immediately impound this property and everything on it in lieu of the $9330 in state taxes you owe on the purchase of said property – unless you choose to willfully cooperate and disclose the source of capital gain you and your neighbors used to make these purchases".

The old man wasn't smiling anymore; he was just kinda hovering in the doorway, staring at the taxman, trying to mentally process all of this. He was definitely (excuse the terminology, please) shit-faced. A very long, silent pause, then it seemed as if a light bulb went off in the old guy's cloudy brain. He wrinkled his old gray eyebrows and looked the taxman in the face when he asked, "How much?"

"9,330 dollars" snapped the irritated taxman.

"Jussa min", says the old gentleman, as he steps back and closes the door.

In what seemed a long couple of minutes, he reopened the door and grabbed the taxman's hand before he knew what was happening. He slapped a stack of what appeared to be mostly $100 bills into the taxman's hand and said with a grin that was missing most of his teeth, "Keepa da change, sonny bo". As he went back inside of the doorway of his new double wide trailer, he half turned and, looking over his left shoulder at the people outside his door, asked, "We dun heah?"

Before he got an answer he simply said, "Den go!", and slammed the door shut!

The camera went to the shock and disbelief on the taxman's face, and that's where we all lost it. Even Norman was laughing despite the fact that it was his money that they were all spending!

When Norman regained his composure he called for me to get what was left of my crew together and head on up to "Shantytown" and see if there was anything left to recover. With all the publicity, I doubted if anyone from Jackman's outfit, or the New York crew would dare climb out of the darkness and show themselves in Shantytown; much too risky to possibly expose the rest of the treasure story to the public, if one of their crewmembers were caught and questioned. The place would be under government surveillance probably, for a long time to come. In light of this, I told my boys to take the day off, just as long as they stay away from Norman and Andy's part of town. They headed for Bullwinkle's.

Jones and I swapped out our rental car (something we did every few days), put on a fictitious license plate, and headed up north just to go and see. God knows those old people deserved that money a lot more than we did.

Upon approaching the area, the first thing you notice is a lot of cars parked here and there that don't belong in these backwoods. All good, we figured, because with so much public attention, nobody is gonna do anything stupid. It was kinda like being on neutral ground.

We pulled right on up and parked by the creek, away from any particular structures, either new trailers or the remaining old shacks. There was a backhoe across the way putting in a septic tank, and some guys were anchoring tie-downs on a single wide. An elderly black lady was putting up a "no trespassing" sign by her trailer and looked over at us as we just strolled along the small Creek, taking it all in. We came up to the outhouse that was built straddling the little creek, which was their original version of "running water". I wished I had a camera as I wondered who lived downstream from the outhouse.

A heavyset black woman came up to us and said, with a raised eyebrow, "We gonna have trouble from y'all?" as she looked us up and down.

"No ma'am, not from us", I said. She nodded a couple of times and turned and ambled away. That was the only contact we had with the locals. We had no intention of asking them anything... What they had was theirs.

Somehow, someway, being here and taking all of this in managed to comfort me. It was pretty country too, so Jones and I just spent the rest of the day driving around and sightseeing, and of course, making sure we weren't being tailed. We tried to imagine what it would be like to live in this lovely place, and to not have to carry a gun everywhere you went.

***

"Nothin' left", I told Norman, when we got back. He was already focused on the next cache that Robbie has recently given him information on. We geared up the next morning, in the rain, and hit the I-10 Freeway heading east. By the time we hit the 75 freeway going south, it was really pouring down. A couple of times we had to slow down to 10 mph. I never saw a rain like this before. We finally pulled over and I got behind the wheel of Norman's rental car, as we had turned mine back in before we left Tallahassee.

Our new search area was not much more than a few very vague landmarks in the Ocala area, as the proverbial "haystack" was getting huge, and the "needle" was getting smaller.

A few miles before Gainesville we were doing about 35 mph in the downpour when the back side window behind my head exploded, followed by two loud metallic thumps behind the back door of the sedan. "Plan B" engaged automatically. I have sometimes heard it said that the minute you formulate a "Plan B" or backup plan, you have admitted that you're not going to succeed. My plan B has always been to shoot my way out of whatever leaves me no other option. And it always amazed me how fast things escalated into gun or knife mode in my life, yet how few people actually had the stomach for it, once it did. It goes to prove that you better be real careful what you ask for, with some people. As I am still on this side of the grass, I believe we can agree that my Plan B has apparently been somewhat successful, up to this point.

I swerved to the right and headed off of the shoulder of the road, for the safety of the bar pit. Looking in my rearview mirror, I could tell my wife's van was taking hits also. The freeway was built up several feet above the original ground level in this area, and offered immediate cover from the fire we were taking from the northbound side of the freeway. One of the two vans that had fired upon us was attempting to turn around and come after us, when it was struck in the rear quarter panel by another vehicle that spun it around, and it slid off the road into the center median.

I had jumped out into the rain and ran back to my wife's van, which had pulled in right behind us to shield Norman's rental car, but the side door was already wide open and the van was empty. I remember hearing the eerie "smacking" sound of bullets hitting the wet trees behind us. At that same moment a barrage of semi-automatic gunfire erupted from behind the van where Jones and the boys were kneeling, just before the top of the roadway, and returning a firestorm into the van that was between the two lanes of freeway. I fired about a half of a magazine at the remaining van still sitting back up the road along the side of the northbound lane. It was extremely hard to see with all of the rain, but I made out several men jumping back into the van I was firing at as it began to speed away. A moment later, a dark blue sedan came flying up out of the bar pit on the other side of the freeway, and took off after the second van. There was no movement around or return fire from the first van, and I yelled, "Let's go", and then turned around to see my old friend Norman standing there, soaked to the bone, with his pistol in his hand, God bless him. That old man had grit.

As everyone bailed into my wife's custom Chevy van (I'm in so much trouble), I kept asking "is anyone hit?" Everyone shook their head no and Jones said, "We're good, let's get out of here". The whole thing was over in a matter of minutes.

I checked Norman and Andy when I got back to the rental car, and except for a few minor glass cuts on Andy's left face and neck, we were good to go. And go we did. Jumping off the freeway at the next exit we wound through a maze of back roads and two lane highways until we reached Trenton. There we wiped the rental car down and left it in a grocery store parking lot. My wife's beautiful blue custom van we could patch up, but no way could we fix the holes in that rental and get away with it. At a Good Guy's Auto Parts store we picked up Bondo, primer, sandpaper, etc., and then got off of the main highway on a side road, a little north of Cross City, on Highway 98.

It was about 1:30 AM when we finally came dragging back into Tallahassee. Getting the old rental car license plate number off of Norman's previous room receipt, I registered him and the rental car, into his room. Norman wasn't looking so good and Andy and I were worried about the toll all this was taking on him. We were all still soaking wet because nothing ever seems to dry out, once it gets wet, in Florida.

At 6:30 AM Norman called the car rental agency at the airport to "See if they had picked up his car for some reason". They said "no" naturally, and suggested he call the Tallahassee police, which he did. By 8 AM the police left with their missing vehicle report and the rental car agency had delivered a replacement. That extra insurance they try to sell you every time you rent a car? Buy it.

My wife's beautiful blue custom van was a different story. There were three large tinted windows down the driver's side of the van and amazingly (a little belated, but, thank You, Lord!), not one of them took a hit! Jones and I had steel plated the inside drivers compartment door and front corner around the battery box with ¼ inch steel plate, as well as the full panel behind the driver's door, all the way to the first big window. This allowed the driver to lean back behind the door window and be protected. We also armor plated both backdoors and the 16 inch metal spaces, floor to ceiling, between the windows where the hidden gun compartments were located.

The driver's door took two rounds, close together, about dead center, damaging the window roller mechanism but otherwise, was stopped from penetrating the driver's compartment by the steel plating in the door. And also, there was a bullet hole between each of the large windows on the driver's side! One of which, somehow managed to bounce around after hitting the edge of steel plating and splintered the forward piece of wooden gun stock on a AK-47 that was stored within.

The guys took the van somewhere away from the motel to work on it, and when they brought it back that evening, it didn't look too bad. The two shades of blue spray paint didn't match the original paint that well, and you could see where the edge of the tape had been, where the new paint ended and the old paint began. But all in all, it was a dog gone good job, and from a short distance away you really wouldn't notice. We had been "lucky" (blessed and protected by Almighty God, would be more like it). No one was hurt and we were still mobile. I sent the last of my friends back to Nevada in the same fashion we had sent the others, except for Jones. To be safe, we put the van in an enclosed storage unit, in case a description had been issued.

Robbie and Randy both said the only way they probably knew it was us on the freeway was "by chance" that they were passing in close proximity of us, and happened to have their psychic traveling with them; probably in the dark blue sedan. Jones pointed out that both vans had CB radio antennas on them, so I suppose it made sense. The reality was, my "give a damn" must have taken a hit on the Gainesville freeway because it wasn't working anymore. I was sick of all this. It's miraculous that none of us had been hurt or killed in all of this, and I didn't like watching Norman's health suffer due to the extreme stress he was attempting to endure. On the plus side, Robbie assured us that as we were down to just Jones and I in the field now, we would be pretty much "invisible" to the psychics, and fairly free to move about without detection. How nice. Move about, where?

Jones and I lurked around in the Florida landscape for a few more weeks chasing down every lead they gave us. Twice more we found where the money "was". Andy had taken Norman back to Montana and it was finally time to call it "deep enough". It felt so good to be back in the van and headed for Nevada. We traveled mostly at night until we got past New Orleans, then put our Nevada license plates back on and went home.

\*\*\*

A week or so after we were back, Randy "witches" a couple of our maps and claims to have found the location of a much older (Civil War, possibly) cache of silver and gold in one of the areas we had hunted in. Hmmmmmmm…

## CHAPTER 15

## Gypo Raise Mining

The 854 raise was the farthest raise on the 800 level, at the very end of the main haulage way, and was designed to follow a vein of high grade ore from the 800 foot level to the 500 foot level. A raise is a square two or three compartment hole you drive (dig) straight up. One compartment is your "manway" that has half of it used for your offset ladders and "landings" (3" x 12" lagging placed across the manway every couple of sets or levels, for you to land on if you fall), that you use to climb up into your work area. The other half of the compartment is an open hole with wooden "slides" made of 3 x 12's also that your "skip" or timber sled rides up and down on, via a hoist cable, to raise dynamite, timber, materials, tools, drills, and equipment up into your work area. The whole compartment combined is about 6 feet wide, in this case. The other compartment is simply a straight down open hole or ore chute, lined with 8 x 8 blocks that run from the top of the raise all the way down to its chute gate in the main haulage way below. In this case we had run the raise about 190 feet up, so far. It is completely lined with 8 x 8 "square sets" of timber all the way up, timbering as you go.

    Coming on shift you climb up to the top of the raise and try to peek around the temporary 45° angle or so "bulkhead" of 3 x 12 "lagging" (planks) that are installed over the manway half of the raise, just before you blast. The idea is to force the blast rock down the 3 x 12 bulkhead and into the open chute half of the raise, without any (or as little as possible) blast rock going down the manway side of the raise, and you try to peek around the bulkhead without getting a loose rock in your face… That's the trick. You remove one of the 3 x 12's to get in to the freshly blasted area and "bar down" any loose rock still hanging on the "back" (over your head, ceiling) with your fiberglass "bar". You muck all of the remaining rock down the chute, take down the 3 x 12 bulkhead/blast slide, and use the lagging to cover over the open chute so you can stand, work, and drill above it. Then you hoist up your timber and stand your "sets", including lining the chute with 8 x 8 blocks. You bring up your drill from the compartment below, set up, hook up and drill your round out straight over your head, with drill water and rock chips showering you and falling in your face as your "buzzy" (drill) bangs and grinds every blast hole 6 foot up into the rock. When you are "drilled out" you lower your equipment to the compartment below you, and bring up your powder and caps (but never together... Or so I'm told) and load your holes. You set up the 45° angled blast bulkhead again, tie in the shot wires and climb down out of the raise. You hook up your lead wires to the blast box, hit the "fire" button, count the rounds as they go off, and go home, handing the blast box to the next miners in line to shoot their round on your way out. Round in, round out. Follow the vein.

Every Friday one of the engineers, usually a college kid from Mackey School of Mines, climbed all the way up our raise and measured from the previous spray paint mark he had left on the center 8 x 8 timber, the previous Friday, to the top of our most recently installed set of timber or "cribbing "depending on the type of raise you are running. That determined how much "gypo" contract money we had made during the week. Like I said, above and beyond our hourly pay, we received extra money for every foot of advancement that we made, a hundred something dollars for every set of timber we put in daily, and so much extra for the "services" (air, and water Victaulic pipe, and vent bag) we installed as the raise went up. Our hourly pay is subtracted from the gypo total amount and we get the remaining balance in addition to our hourly wage for the week.

It usually comes out to a lot of money, so the company is always trying to "gyp" you, and that's why I personally think they call it "gypo" mining.

Yeah, so, me and JD are making pretty big money and I'm getting some serious bills paid off, including the fully muraled with pirate ships, custom van Lori and I just bought six months earlier. JD is a new Dad with a new bouncing boy named Chris (hi Chris!) and you know the old adage of "baby needs shoes!", so we're pretty much spending it about a week before our checks clear the bank. The problem is, the vein we have been chasing is getting sporadic. It "pinched out" (disappeared) on Tuesday, so we put in two more rounds and got it back. Otherwise, if we lose the vein we will be back tramming until another work area opens up, which means no more big money on gypo for a while. Can't have that, now can we?

One day as we are sitting in the 800 level doghouse eating lunch and waiting for our timber to come down, our happy-go-lucky Mackey

School of Mines pre-grad engineering student pushes his way through us and all the other men trying to eat their lunch in the small, confined doghouse with a bench down each wall. As you sat and ate your lunch your knees bumped the knees of the guy across from you. Rather than walk around the doghouse to get to the main haulage way, which would take about 30 seconds longer, most engineers and geologists would shove their way through the doghouse at lunch time (nin-come-poops) knocking your lunch around and spilling your coffee. Some kind of tradition, maybe, that I wasn't aware of. They always came at lunchtime on Friday... I know, I just need to let it go.

So this day, as our bright and bubbly engineer shoved past us, I reached up as he went by and snatched a can of paint out of the back of his engineers vest. As our raise was deepest back in the mine, he started there first and worked his way through the other stopes and raises, back to the shaft station.

Sooo... When we got back to our work area he was just coming out of our raise, as usual. When we got up to the top, there was the engineers paint mark on the center 8 x 8 post, in the center of the last set of timber we had stood this week, again, as usual. As there wasn't hardly any weight on the top horizontal timber of the new set, it was fairly easy to raise up enough to take the weight off of the painted center post that we had not nailed down yet. With the weight taken off of it, we turned the post until the paint mark disappeared around the backside of the 8 x 8, lowered the "cap" back down on it, and drove home the 60 penny spikes with our mine axes, nailing it permanently into place. We moved down to the next set of timbers below us and put a new paint mark on the 8 x 8 post next to the ladder. We got an extra 120 bucks each on our next paycheck.

The next week, we dropped down two sets and marked the timber and got 240 extra bucks apiece! I only had two van payments left when the vein "pinched off" again. Fortunately, or not, the ground we were drilling had gotten pretty "ratty" (prone to cave-ins, dangerous, crumbly) in the last few weeks and the geologists and engineers avoided coming all the way up to our "heading" (work area/face), at all costs. So basically, the only ones that actually laid eyes on our alleged vein, was JD and I.

When Lori and I lived out at Keystone Mine in central Nevada, we would load up a truck load of Keystone ore and take it to Virginia City, Nevada, and sell it to the local rock shops on our days off, as Virginia City was close to her Mom's house in Washoe Valley. Keystone ore is very beautiful rock, and very distinctive. We would get a dollar a pound, and a football sized rock weighed about 25 pounds. They would bust it up and sell it to the tourists for "Comstock ore", because Comstock ore was actually murky gray and ugly. We made hundreds of dollars every time we took a load of Keystone rock to them, as it had a lot of shiny galena, silver, lead, zinc, copper, pyrite, and especially, peacock copper in it. And as I stated, it was very distinctive. Once you saw it, you would recognize it anywhere if you saw it again.

It was also very different from the ore at Gooseberry Mine, as well. That's why I had to hide the pieces of it that I put in the bottom of the sample trays for the 854 raise that we worked in. The sample trays for all of the work areas on the 800 level were on a shelf by the grizzlies, where the ore cars were dumped. Before dumping the ore cars contents down the load-out chute to be hoisted to the surface and milled, the Trammer would take a big handful of dirt out of each car and throw it into the appropriate sample tray that coincided with the work area that particular load of ore had been pulled from. I would bury a piece of Keystone ore at the bottom of the sample tray for my work area, and we just kept on mining for weeks after the vein ran out. I know, that's pretty bad, but it paid off my wife's van.

About that time the engineers were really starting to struggle with the fact that, according to their own weekly measurements, the 854 raise not only should have broken through to the 500 foot level of the mine by now, but according to their calculations, had probably passed by or missed the 500 foot level and gone beyond it by quite a bit. In actuality, we were still about 40 feet below the 500 foot level. To complicate matters, the company had just hired a geological engineer named Tom Cannon, whose previous employer was Gold Creek Corporation, the same employer I had when I worked at the Keystone Mine... And he knew Keystone ore when he saw it.

It all came crashing down one fine day, when I laddered out of the raise to go get our blasting agents and load our round. Tom had been waiting for me to come down out of my raise, at the bottom of the manway. I turned around to have his big sausage looking finger stuck in my face, as he melodramatically and loudly proclaims, "I know it was you, and I know what you did! IT ENDS NOOOW!" as he holds out one of my Keystone Mine rocks in his other hand, accusingly at me.

"Hi Tom! When did you start working here?" Was my "caught totally red-handed" reply. But he just turns and walks off down the drift towards the shaft station without even the courtesy of a friendly reply... How rude. I sweated bullets for a week or so, but God bless Tom, he never turned me in. Probably, I believe, out of respect and friendship for my father, who was highly respected for his honesty and integrity. I, on the other hand, had to make people wonder if maybe I hadn't been adopted, as I didn't appear to be the proverbial "chip off the old block". Not being turned in made me feel worse than if I had been fired for what I did. I was ashamed, and repented (sort of, in my own way), and feared for the longest time that my father would hear of what I did. Thank you, Tom, for sparing me that, even though I had it coming. Thinking back on this incident, many years later, helped me to understand what "Grace" was all about.

When I "fessed up" to Lori what I had done, she was clearly disappointed. That hurt me bad, as it was her that I was constantly trying to impress.

## CHAPTER 16

## Remnants of Death

*"Come now, you who say, "Today or tomorrow we will go to such and such a city, spend a year there, buy and sell, and make profit"; whereas you do not know what will happen tomorrow.*
*For what is your life? It is even a vapor that appears for a little time and then vanishes away."*
James 4:13-14

Dad called us in the spring of 1981, with a 400 claim staking contract for Jack "Cadillac" Grimm of Grimm Oil Company, and another 100 claim contract for Bunker Hunt of the Hunt brothers, all out of Texas, but the actual contracts were all in eastern Nevada, north of Ely. At $100 per claim, it was an excellent opportunity to make some big money without spending my entire summer underground. There were times at Gooseberry Mine, in winter, that I would go "down the hole" to work just before the sun came up, and would come out of the mine about 30 minutes after the sun had set. I jumped at the chance to get back out into the Nevada Mountains. I quit my job at the mine, loaded up my wife, my dog, and my gear, and off to Ely we went.

My brother Bill took 200 claims on the south end of the Delcer Buttes, and Lori and I took 200 claims on the north end. As there seemed to be no hurry on Jack Grimm's part, and no competition in the area, we didn't hire any extra help. Instead we moved out onto the property and set up camp sites as the job progressed, only going to town for occasional supplies, food, and lots of ammo, as the rabbit hunting was of legendary proportion. We spent the best part of the summer there, just east of the spectacular Ruby Mountains, sleeping under the stars or in the van when rain came. However, something about the Delcer Butte Mountains attracted lightning like no other place we had ever seen. Thunder and lightning storms would roll across the desert and we would be forced to abandon camp and flee across the valley until it passed. We would sit on the other side of the desert flat to the east of the buttes and watch the most amazing and indescribable lightning shows imaginable. Bolts of fire would head straight down from the Heavens towards the valley floor, but before they struck the ground, they would do a 90° turn about 100 feet above the desert floor, and the lightning bolts would go horizontal just above the ground until they crashed into the side of the mountain! Rocks and trees would explode and tree fires would flare-up on several strikes per hour! Just plain crazy lightning, I'm telling you! When they passed in an hour or so, we would go back to camp or go over the mountains to Currie Store for a burger and soda.

At one point, about one quarter of a mile west of the Delcer Buttes, I was running a side-center line through part of the brush covered valley floor, when I came across some old scattered bones, a curled up pair of boots, some rotted denim and several rusty peach cans. Because we were working under a signed "confidentiality agreement" as mentioned before, we couldn't report it until after the claim staking contract was finished and legally filed with the court house and BLM (Bureau of Land Management), but I intended to do so as soon as possible, thereafter. I marked the spot exactly on my 7.5 scale topography work map and went on with the project. By the completion of the project, the map had been lost and we tried several times to relocate the site, but we could not, I am sad to say. I did not disturb the site any more than I had to, but now I regret that I at least should have gathered and buried the bones; maybe said some words over them or something. It had to be a hard way to die, regardless of the circumstance, be it winter or summer in the high desert mountains of Nevada. Please convey my apology to whoever he was, Lord... As You know, it still bothers me to this day.

Similarly, later that fall I was high up in the Egan Mountains when, in a sharp ravine, I came across an old stone, single room, miner's cabin. All of the "goods", such as cans of food, oil lamps, a can of carbide, pots and pans, rotted books, etc. were still in place on the shelves, bed, and a rickety old table. Part of the canvas roof was long gone exposing everything inside to the elements over the years. But in the back of the cabin the last half of the roof was made of timbers and sod, and was for the most part, still intact. Hidden up on top of the farthest back rafter I found a Winchester 30-30 Saddle Ring carbine rifle with a badly weathered front and rear stock. In the butt stock was nicely carved the word, "Nevada", and an empty hole the size of a silver dollar (quite common in those times) was on the other side. It seemed as if the proprietor of the cabin had simply gone to work or somewhere, and never came back.

I left everything intact as I found it, with the exception of the rifle, which I took with me. And nope! Even though it was my intent to do so, I never made it back to that cabin... You would think so, but no. Life happens and you get sidetracked, I suppose.

Also on top of the Egan Mountains, near Water Canyon, an old dilapidated rock cabin we found was built up against a huge rock above an old gold mine. While using our metal detectors, Lori and I found exactly 20 spent rifle cartridges, all in the same 2 foot in diameter area, just inside the door way, up against the wall. Between the slabs of rock that had been placed for flooring in the entry way, we found almost all of the pieces to an intentionally smashed and broken brass "breach" or "action" to a Henry rifle.

Upon closer investigation we found several broken pieces of at least four arrowheads in the cracks between the rock flooring and three pieces of broken arrowheads in the rock of what was left of the back wall, directly in line with the doorway. No one could possibly know with certainty what exactly happened, but the story I picture in my mind is the possibility that, when the miner, who was under siege by Indians, ran out of bullets he probably knew the end was imminent. Thinking of others like him, miners, ranchers, settlers and the like, his final act was to protect them from his own Henry rifle that would be turned against them, in the hands of his triumphant enemies. So, I believe, he smashed it apart on the rock floor as not to let it fall into the hands of the Indians, who were about to kill him. That's my best guess, anyway. I'll ask around when I get to Heaven, if I am permitted, to find out what really transpired.

I also suppose that in all three instances, none of the men in these situations woke up that morning with dying on their minds, except maybe the bones we found out in the desert. In any case, that day turned out to be the day that they met their Maker. I pray to God that they were prepared, and I pray right now that you are also. This could be your day... You never know. Are you ready? Have you settled things with the One to whom you are accountable? Life is but a "vapor" (James 4:14, and Psalms 90).

And yes, you and I are accountable... for everything. If there was any other way I would have found it, trust me. I diligently searched for years for a way not to be held responsible for my way of life and the things I did. No way could I ever survive standing in the Glory of a Holy God, or so I thought. Amazingly, the world, and all its religions, new age religions included, and even spinoffs of Christianity (Cults) such as Celestine Prophecy, Scientology, Jehovah witness, Mormonism, Islam, etc., etc., etc., all offer various versions on how to avoid hell, but none of them "hold water", or for me, could prove what they claimed and they were all based on my "works", "deeds" or my ability to be "good enough", which in fact, are the basis that each of them uses to condemn me to hell, in the first place. Dark and twisted oxymorons, if you will.

These are the very same religious folks that upset Jesus the most. In all four Gospels I found that not once did the Lord have issues with sinners, but with sin. Nor did He ever contend or battle with the sinners who He came to save. (1 Timothy 1:15-16, Luke 5:32, etc.) Jesus's battle was not against sinners, it was clearly against religious bigots and hypocrites.

What I came away with, at the end of about a six year search, was that so-called "facts" are subject to change and often do but the "Truth" never changes. Therefore, knowing the Bible is our only defense against deception, (Ephesians 6; 10-18, Proverbs 4:20-27, etc.) and a "casual Christian" is completely ignorant of spiritual warfare.

I am who I am and the only one who can change that is God, I can't. I am a sinner separated from God by my sin (Isaiah 59:2) and I can't stop falling short of the mark (Romans 3:23). There is nothing I can do in my own power, and positively nothing that any religion can do, to get me off of the imminent fast track to judgment and eternal hell.

BUT, God so loved the world (you and me) that he sent His only begotten Son, that whoever believes in Him should not perish but have everlasting life (John 3:16). And check this out; I love this part; "for God did not send His Son into the world to condemn the world, but that the world through Him might be saved. He who believes in Him is not condemned;…"!!!! (Verses 17 and 18)

"Well, what makes you think the Bible is any different than any other religion?", you might ask. Good question. First of all, if you align yourself with any other mainstream religion, such as Buddhism, Hindu, Islam, etc., you eventually find yourself following, worshiping, and likely praying to a dead guy(s). Whereas, Jesus Christ is alive, and can actually hear your prayers and help you! The truth that God (Yahweh) raised His only Son (Jesus, Yeshua) from the dead after being crucified and buried for three days is an actual historic truth!

Nonetheless, we are never to pray to or for dead people. We are to "give nothing for the dead", God warned us in Deuteronomy 26:14, and it provokes God to anger (Psalm 106:28), and please also see biblical references in Appendix D in the back of this book, as to why we cannot and should not be "baptized for the dead". In short, to pray for or to be baptized for a dead person is a slap in the face to God in regard to his judgment. You are, in essence, saying that God was wrong in his judgment of a person, and you are going to fix it.

As to God raising Jesus from the dead; the world, atheists, and all other religions have adamantly tried, and still try, to discredit the "facts" of this actual event, yet the truth of its reality stubbornly still exists today. You and I acknowledge the life, death and resurrection of Jesus Christ every time we write or see today's date! When we write, for instance, January 22, 2019, that 2019 is the representative of 2019 "A.D.", or in its full meaning, 2019 years since the birth of Christ. This has to be very frustrating to atheists! That is a very hard "fact" to change…hahaha!

When the timetable or years that are being referenced or studied were before Jesus's birth, it is referred to as "B.C.", representing the term, "Before Christ".

A.D. represents the term "Anno Domini", a Medieval Latin term which means "in the year of the Lord", or more often and rightly translated "in the year of <u>our</u> Lord". In its proper entirety it is occasionally set out more fully as "Anno Domini Nostri Lesu (or Jesu) Christi" which is, "in the year of our Lord Jesus Christ". (Wikipedia encyclopedia)

So you see, every time anyone on the planet writes or speaks a date or year, regardless of what they choose to believe, they acknowledge the existence of Jesus Christ! Gotta love it! The Lord, I'm sure, has an occasional giggle over that one, especially in light of Philippians 2:9-11, which says, "Therefore God has highly exalted Him and given Him <u>the Name</u> which is above every name, that at the Name of Jesus every knee should bow, of those in Heaven, and those of earth, and of those under the earth, and that every tongue should confess that Jesus Christ is Lord, to the glory of God the Father". Have you ever been asked what today's date is? Did you say it out loud? Did the person you know, who doesn't believe in Jesus, ever say the date out loud? Think about it! Hahahaha! Funny, don't you think?

The Smithsonian Institute recently issued a statement professing that the Bible is one of the very most archaeologically proven historical books in its possession. In contrast, the Smithsonian Institute released a document stating that the book of Mormon has no significant historical value and no evidence whatsoever to any of its historical claims; no archaeology, no coins, etc.

Please know that my purpose is not to rant on Mormonism, my goal is to share the Truth in love, as in my own experience, when the foundational doctrine of my faith was blown out from under me by a "Truth Encounter" with the Bible. Sometimes the truth hurts. Many of the people that I dearly love are truthfully seeking to follow God but have fallen prey to false doctrine; because they believed what someone told them is truth instead of seeking it out for themselves. In this regard I ask that you would take time to read the two verses in 2 Timothy 4:3-4. Please don't put all your trust in what someone else tells you; put your trust in God's only Word! And don't take my word for it, either. For God's sake, do your own homework, and read the Holy Bible yourself!

What archaeology has done to confirm and prove the Bible, is unquestionably astounding. What archaeology has done to disprove and discredit many other cults (spinoff religions of Christianity) is devastating.

"Sola Scriptura" means, "by Scripture alone – the Bible and the Bible only" as Martin Luther (1483 – 1546 A.D. German theologian and the initiator of the Protestant reformation, defender of truth and religious freedoms) proclaimed, is the only true text that has withstood the tests of time, archaeology, history, confirming historical literature, and the fulfillment of prophecy with a 100% accuracy rate!

The evidence proving the Bible as the true and accurate word of God is beyond overwhelming. Only if you close your eyes to the truth and refuse to search for it yourself, will you be able to not see it. Don't take someone else's word for it, search it out yourself. It's the most important "treasure hunt" you will ever do, I promise. I'll even give you a few interesting starting points. If I am wrong, you lose nothing. If I am right and the Bible is the true word of God, and you reject it, regardless of your lack of knowledge and regardless of who told you what, you lose your soul to hell, and miss out on the wonderful eternal life in Heaven that God intended for you, in the first place. The choice is always ours. As my friend A.V. Munoz rightly observed, "What have you got to lose that you won't lose anyway?"

*"For what profit is it to a man if he gains the whole world, and loses his own soul? Or what will a man give in exchange for his soul?"* Jesus asked in Matthew 16:26.

Biblical archaeology is an awesome place to start your search, and is probably my favorite, as I love treasure hunting. Just Google it! It's mind-boggling how much has been discovered in the last two centuries that prove the divine accuracy of the Bible! Golgotha, graves of the apostles, several chariot wheels with four spokes (significant to the time of Moses) found at the bottom of the Red Sea, and the empty tomb, for starters! No other cult, culture or religion can claim this.

Bible Archaeology – Wikipedia is fantastic and lists hundreds of recent discoveries, as well as finds over the last centuries, under the "List of Artifacts in Biblical Archaeology" section. These include everything from Egyptian hieroglyphics, Assyrian, Moabite, Aramaic, Akkadian, Phoenician, Greek, Latin, and Hebrew texts and writings on stone tablets (Cune Forms) and cylinders that give verifying accounts of the historical events and people that actually happened in the Bible, from other cultures and secular perspectives.

For instance, history records that Nero condemned the Apostle Paul to death by decapitation somewhere between 64 and 68 A.D., in Rome. It is believed that Paul's body was buried outside the walls of Rome, at the 2nd mile on the Via Ostiensis, on the estate owned by a Christian woman named Lucina.

It is here, in the fourth century, that Emperor Constantine is believed to have built the first church. The next proceeding four emperors considerably enlarged it between the fourth and fifth centuries and the present day Basilica of St. Paul Outside the Walls was built there in 1800.

In 2002 an 8 foot long marble sarcophagus, inscribed with the words, "Paulo Apostolo Mart" (Paul Apostle Martyr) was discovered during excavations around the Basilica of St. Paul Outside the Walls on the Via Ostiensis. Vatican archaeologists declared this to be the tomb of Paul the

Apostle in 2005. In June 2009, Pope Benedict XVI announced the excavation results concerning the tomb. The sarcophagus was not opened but was examined by means of a probe, which revealed pieces of incense, purple and blue linen, and small bone fragments. The bone was radiocarbon dated to the first or second century. According to the Vatican, these findings support the final conclusion that the tomb is Paul's (Wikipedia.org/Paul the Apostle/Remains).

Probably the most stunning of these discoveries of the past 100 years has been the "Dead Sea Scrolls", comprised of 981 different texts discovered between 1946 and 1956 in 11 caves in the immediate vicinity of the ancient settlement at Khirbet Qumran in the West Bank, about 1.2 miles from the Dead Sea. Scientists believe they have proven that these scrolls date from the last three centuries Before Christ (B.C.) and the first century after (A.D.). Bronze coins found at these archaeological sites support and confirm the radiocarbon and Paleozoic graphic dating of the scrolls.

"Wiki" goes on to explain the great historical, religious, and linguistic significance of these texts, because they include the third oldest known surviving manuscripts of works included in the Hebrew Bible "Canon"! So get this... In comparing these 2000 year old Bible texts to the current Bible (King James Version and the New King James Version) that we now have, especially the comparison of the Book of Isaiah (my personal favorite Prophet) we find that the Bible is not only God's Word to us throughout the centuries, but wonderfully astounding is the discovery that God has divinely preserved and protected the accuracy of His Holy Word down through all of the ages, as well! Just like 1 Peter 1:22-25 declares! Word for word! So these "supposed" churches and religions that say, "The Bible has been changed, misinterpreted, written by man," or especially "doesn't say what you think it says", don't know what they are talking about or are just plain lying to push their own agenda. And never fall for that line, "God has revealed something new to me".

Remember always, *"For such are false apostles, deceitful workers, transforming themselves into apostles of Christ. And no wonder! For Satan himself transforms himself into an angel of light. Therefore it is no great thing if his ministers also transformed themselves into ministers of righteousness, whose end will be according to their works"*. 2 Corinthians 11:13-15.

THE BIBLE IS WHAT IT CLAIMS TO BE, AND IT SAYS WHAT IT SAYS! That's a proven truth! No other religion, cult, or "other testimony" can claim this, let alone prove it!

Only the Bible is the proven Word of God. Period.

Think not? All roads lead to Heaven? What about this religion or that belief? Prove it to me. Show me the evidence.

Ancient writings and literature on and around the first century A.D., written by historical authors such as Josephus, Origin, Eusebius, and the Diary of Egeria (or, Aetheria) prove the detailed events that are depicted in the Gospels and the Book of Acts, and that they unfolded just as the Bible says.

BiblicalArchaeologySociety.org is another excellent resource, especially concerning updates on current "digs", as is Archaeology and the Bible, at ChristianAnswers.net.

The unearthing and discovery of ancient biblical cities, some lost for thousands of years, such as Jericho, Haran, Hazor, Dan, Megiddo, Shechem, Samaria, Shiloh, Gezer, Gibeah, Beth Shean, Beersheba, Lachish, and many other urban sites, notwithstanding larger existing and obvious locations such as Jerusalem, Nazareth, Bethlehem, or Babylon have to impose a blatant and unarguable slap in the face to Bible critics of all forms, to which the evidence can only be ignored by the "foolish" (really need to read the Book of Proverbs).

The Apostle Paul spoke this profound truth to the Corinthians in chapter 1 verses 18 through 25 of his first Epistle, when by the power of the Holy Spirit he stated, *"For the message of the cross is foolishness to those who are perishing, but to us who are being saved it is the power of God. For it is written; 'I will destroy the wisdom of the wise, and bring to nothing the understanding of the prudent'.*

*Where is the wise? Where is the scribe? Where is the disputer of this age? Has not God made foolish the wisdom of this world? For since, in the wisdom of God, the world through wisdom did not know God, it pleased God through the foolishness of the message preached to save those who believe. For Jews request a sign, and Greeks seek after wisdom; but we preach Christ crucified, to the Jews a stumbling block and to the Greeks foolishness, but to those who are called, both Jews and Greeks, Christ the power of God and the wisdom of God. Because the foolishness of God is wiser than men, and the weakness of God is stronger than men.*

I guess the question is, where do you stand? There is a vast eternal difference between "those" and "us" in the verses above. If you look at the evidence and sincerely do your homework, it is truly harder to not believe the Bible than it is to believe that it is the true and proven Word of God. If you want a little more information on who the Bible defines as a fool, then check out the Book of Proverbs, and as I mentioned earlier, there are 31 chapters, that's one for every day of the month, and reading one of them a day will bless you, I promise.

Listen, God did not give us a bunch of "rules" because he doesn't want you to have any fun or enjoy life. He gave us specific "do's and don'ts" because they have consequences and because we have a relentless enemy that hates our very souls, and our Heavenly Father gave us a "roadmap", if you will, to keep us from the wrecks the enemy has laid for us.

Jesus said, *"The thief does not come except to steal, and to kill, and to destroy. I have come that they may have life, and that they may have it more abundantly"*. John 10: 10.

It's Jesus who wants you to have a more abundant life! Don't ever forget that. That's the truth, regardless of what you have been told, taught, or think. It was usually our choices, for good or bad that got us where we are now. That's why it's very important to take ownership of your sins and the mistakes you have made, repent, and move on... And make better decisions.

\*\*\*

Fulfillment of prophecy

Allow me to give you the short, really short course on prophecy; here it is;

*"The Lord of hosts has sworn, saying, 'Surely, as I have thought, so it shall come to pass, and as I have purposed, so it shall stand:'"* Isaiah 14:24. If God said it, then it's gonna happen.

*"Knowing this first, that no prophecy of Scripture is of any private interpretation (origin), for prophecy never came by the will of man, but holy men of God spoke as they were moved by the Holy Spirit."1* Peter 1:20-21. Bible prophecy came from God, not man.

*"Blessed is he who reads and those who hear the words of this prophecy, and keep those things which are written in it; for the time is near."* Revelation 1:3. These End Time Prophecies are a blessing to us and not a curse; the Lord is coming! *"Behold, He is coming with the clouds, and every eye will see Him, even they who pierced Him. And all the tribes of the earth will mourn because of Him. Even so, Amen."* Apparently, not so much of a blessing to those who reject him. *"I am the Alpha and the Omega, the Beginning and the End, says the Lord, who is and who was and who is to come, the Almighty."* Revelation *1:7-8*

*"For the testimony of Jesus is the spirit of prophecy."* Revelation 19:10. Exactly as it was prophesied the first time He came, so He will come the second time, exactly as it is prophesied...so tell others!

The fulfillment of prophecy is the final and ultimate "clincher" that the Bible is the only true divinely inspired Word of God. As FaithFacts.org states so perfectly on its webpage, "No other religion has specific, repeated, and unfailing fulfillment of predictions many years in advance of contingent events over which the predictor had no control". There are no prophetic failures in the Bible! Unlike Nostradamus or Jean Dixon, whose wrong predictions are countless. Exhaustive studies of professed psychics reveal that only around 8% of their predictions come true and virtually all of these can be attributed to chance, vagueness, and a general knowledge of the circumstances.

Not so with the Bible. Biblical prophecies are very clear and extremely detailed in most cases. There are over 2000 prophecies in the Bible and over 300 of them are fulfilled messianic prophecies about the Messiahs first coming as detailed in the Gospels of Matthew, Mark, Luke and John, and are completely corroborated and verified through history, literature, archaeology, and fulfilled prophecy. How can anyone ignore that? After all my years of searching I have come to the conclusion that the Bible can be trusted, and it is the only thing that can be. It's actually harder to dismiss the truth of the Bible than it is to accept it, if it is the truth you are seeking, but whatever... We all have that choice to make, and God will honor that choice.

Chuck Missler (Chuck Missler on Bible prophecy/YouTube) breaks down the extremely conservative formula used to present the odds of one person on planet Earth actually fulfilling only eight of these 300+ detailed prophecies of Jesus' first coming over 2000 years ago. That's eight random detailed prophecies out of 300, as given in the following examples;

| Prophecy | Prophesied in; | Fulfilled in: |
|---|---|---|
| 1. Messiah born in Bethlehem | Micah 5:2 | Matthew 2:1-6, Luke 2:4-6 |
| 2. Messiah born of a virgin | Isaiah 7:14 | Matthew 1:18-25, Luke 1:26-38 |
| 3. Messiah Betrayed for 30 pieces of silver | Zechariah 11:12 | Matthew 26:14-15 |
| 4. Messiah presenting himself to Jerusalem As a king riding on a donkey | Zechariah 9:9 | Luke 19:28-40, John 12:12-16, Matthew 21:1-11, Mark 11:1-11 |
| 5. Messiahs detailed crucifixion (over 700 years before the invention of crucifixion!) | Psalm 22:15-17 | Mark 15:21-40, Luke 23:26-49 Matthew 27:34-50, John 19:28-30 |
| 6. Messiah will be pierced | Zechariah 12:10 | John 19:34-37 |
| 7. Messiahs details of suffering and death and resulting salvation | Psalm 69:21 Isaiah 53:2-12 | Matthew 26 – 27, Mark 15 – 16 Luke 22 – 23, John 18 – 19 |
| 8. Messiahs resurrection | Job 19:25 Psalm 16:10 | Acts 2:30-31, 13:32-35, 17:2-3 1 Corinthians 15:20-22, John 20 – 21 Luke 24, Matthew 28, Mark 16 |

All of the prophecies concerning Jesus the Messiah were made hundreds, and some, thousands of years before the birth of Christ! The chances of just these eight prophecies being fulfilled to the utmost detail is calculated conservatively at one chance in 10 to the 17$^{th}$ power ($10^{17}$ that's a 1 followed by 17 zeros) or, 1 in 100,000,000,000,000,000. I may have sucked at math, but I got this! And that's just eight of over 300 prophecies fulfilled! It's a tough number to wrap your head around, huh?

Honestly, I can't even begin to grasp the odds and numbers of all 300+ (333, I believe) similar detailed prophecies that have truly been fulfilled in

Jesus's life. Not one prophecy has failed- not one! The fulfillment of just the above-mentioned eight prophecies is illustrated to the equivalent of covering the entire state of Texas with silver dollars, 2 feet deep, marking one of them with a scratch, then mixing them all up and having a blindfolded person walk across the state of Texas in 2 feet of silver dollars and reach down in them and select the marked silver dollar at random, the first time.

Here is the real clincher... The majority of the remaining 1700 or so prophecies in the Bible are mostly about the "Second Coming" of Christ and the time you and I are living in right at this moment, and they are being fulfilled all around us, to the exact detail, every day! He is coming. You will see it.

So... As the amazing fulfillment of the 300+ prophecies about Jesus's first coming, to the utmost detail, is now a factual truth etched in history, how can anyone seriously think for a single moment that God will not fulfill the remaining prophecies of His Second Coming in the exact same way? You need to look into this because He truly is coming. Are you ready?

## CHAPTER 17

## Our Ticket Home

I know, I'm getting all preachy, so I'll finish this up, as short and sweet as possible, then tell you how I took a knife to a gunfight.

The Bible is obviously the undeniable Word of God. So what does it say?

There are tons of commentaries written on "the last days" to verify the days we are living in. Just remember, that they are commentaries by men, and are subject to imperfection, and you MUST always pray over them before you read them, and ask the Holy Spirit to retain what is truthfully of God and to reject from your mind and memory the things that are not in line with God's Word. This practice of prayer should always be implemented over anything you read, watch or listen to outside of the Bible itself, including this book. As my brother in Christ, Armando Munoz taught me, "Take the meat and leave the bones".

Anyway, such renowned authors as Chuck Missler, Grant Jeffrey, Jack Van Impe, Hal Lindsey, John Haggie, and David Jeremiah, just to name a few all offer their similar views on the currently unfolding prophetical events going on around us. However, God's Holy Word is the true and accurate foundation that we must all cling to. In any event, based on the fulfillment of biblical prophecies, I believe these authors as well as any Bible college 101 graduate will tell you, we are living in the final days before our Lord returns. It could literally happen at any moment. Therein lies the source of my urgency in writing this book and repeatedly harping on you about all this. Time is short. The Bible says that when He comes in all His Glory that, "every eye will see Him" (see Revelation 1:7 and Revelation 19:11-16). Here's the problem; the Bible also says we must accept Him by faith (Ephesians 2:4-9). So please... If you don't get anything else out of this book, please get this. If you wait till you see Him it will be too late, because He will no longer be your Savior, He will be your Judge. That's why I feel so compelled to keep asking at the risk of annoying you, if He came in the next few minutes, would you be ready? It's a free gift from God. Even though our sins separate us from God, *"If we confess our sins, He is faithful and just to forgive us our sins, and to cleanse us from all unrighteousness"* (1 John 1:19).

Because, *"God so loved the world that He gave His only begotten Son, that <u>whoever</u> believes in Him should not perish but have everlasting life. For God did not send His Son into the world to condemn the world, but that the* *world through Him might be saved. He who believes in Him is not condemned; but he who does not believe is condemned already, because he has not believed in the name of the only begotten Son of God" (John 3:16-18).*

The Apostles made clear that *(Acts 2:21) "and it shall come to pass that* <u>*whoever*</u> **(*that's you and me*)** *calls on the name of the Lord shall be saved"* and, *(Acts 2:38-39) "then Peter said to them,' Repent and let every one of you be baptized in the name of Jesus Christ for the remission of sins; and you shall receive the gift of the Holy Spirit. For the promise is to you and your children, and to all who are afar off, as many as the Lord our God will call".*

Peter goes on to say, *"Nor is there salvation in any other, for there is no other name under Heaven given among men by which we must be saved"* (Acts 4:12). He knew this because, as a disciple of Jesus, he was present when Jesus clearly stated, *"I and the way, the truth, and the life; no one comes to the Father except through Me" (John 14:6).* And, I might add, when you know the Truth, then you know what and who isn't.

The Bible is truthfully the greatest story ever told and should be told, as such, at every opportunity. I think we do it a great injustice when we try to narrow it down to a "salvation formula", but with this generation's attention span lasting about a minute and a half, sometimes the short course is all you get an opportunity to present. When such short opportunities do present themselves, it is vitally important to let the Holy Spirit lead us.

That said, four passages in the book of Romans, what is commonly called "Romans Road to Salvation" is often used to lay out the path of our salvation quite nicely, like this;

Romans 3:23, *"For all have sinned and fall short of the glory of God,"* We were all born under the condemnation of sin, so it's not like something we had to work at or set out to purposely do; sin comes naturally to us. No sin can stand in the presence of a Holy God, so our sins created a huge void or "chasm" between us and our Father.

Romans 5:8-9, *"But God demonstrates his own love towards us, in that while we were still sinners, Christ died for us. Much more then, having now been justified by His blood, we shall be saved from wrath through Him."*

Awesome news! That means you don't have to "get your stuff together" first! It's a "come as you are" party! Right now, the way you are! Hallelujah! It's because Jesus, the Son of God, was born into this world just like we were, lived a sinless life, and yet took all of our sins, along with their penalties, that were separating us from God, upon Himself and paid the full price (that we could not pay) for them with His own Blood on the cross. Jesus alone did this and no other, creating a "bridge" for us across that "chasm" or huge void that separated us from God. He made a way back home to our Heavenly Father for all who choose it. That's the Gospel of Jesus Christ! That's what He did for you. Gospel means "good news" and I have to say, news doesn't get any better than this!

Romans 6:23 goes on to testify, *"For the wages of sin is death, but the gift of God is eternal life in Christ Jesus our Lord."* Whoot! Whoot! And it's a free gift to us from God; we don't have to "earn" it. Not only did we not earn it, but we surely did not deserve it; we are able to receive this incredible gift from God that He has offered to us by His Grace, and Grace alone. This world, as we know it, is dying and we don't have to be a part of its death! This world is not all there is to life! Thank God.

Still with me so far? Good.

What must I do to be saved, you ask (hopefully)?

Romans 10:9-11 & 13 explain how incredibly simple it really is; *"The word is near you, in your mouth and in your heart (that is the word of faith which we preach); that if you confess with your mouth the Lord Jesus and believe in your heart that God has raised Him from the dead, you will be saved. For with the heart one believes unto righteousness, and with the mouth confession is made unto salvation. For the Scripture says, whoever believes on Him will not be put to shame. For whoever calls on the name of the Lord shall be saved."* And yup! The literal theological meaning and interpretation of the word "whoever" used in these passages actually means "WHOEVER"... You and I... Us! Hear me when I tell you this; you have not done anything that God can't forgive, when you are truly remorseful and repent in your heart, turn away (stop repeating) from your sins and change the way you think and start thinking the way the Lord thinks about sin.. That's repentance. The key to changing the way you think is found in Proverbs 4:20-27, and 2 Corinthians 10:3-5; Get into the Word and stay on it. After all, you're already thinking about something day and night already, so just replace the junk in your head. But what happens if I sin after that? Then welcome to Christianity (check out Romans 7:15 through Romans 8:17). When you sin again, you repent again and receive your forgiveness again and move on, just like the rest of us, praying and asking God to help us do a little better tomorrow than we did today. Please be aware, though, that Job 5, Proverbs 3, and Hebrews 12 all make clear that who God loves, He "corrects", so by no means are we to misconstrue this process of forgiveness as a license to sin ( Romans 6), as God will intervene if we consistently retain habitual sins. Our sins need to be dealt with. Rarely is God's intervention and correction comfortable or pleasant, but it is always done in His great love for us, as a loving Father corrects his children. During periods of correction (God's "woodshed" or "timeout") your Heavenly Father will be there to comfort you (2 Corinthians 1:3-4) and He will strengthen you and help you (Psalm 37:39-40, Isaiah 41:10). If you feel that His correction is what you are going through, I encourage you to study the "Correction" section in Appendix F in the back of this book.

Do your homework in the Bible and ask God to reveal Himself to you, especially in the Gospels. Get to know Him. The importance of reiterating this cannot be overstated because the peace He will give you is indescribable. After all these years, (and a substantial amount of correction) to finally know what it is to have peace with God, has got to be the greatest thing the Lord has ever done for me, second only to what He did to save my soul. If, like me, peace is what you are seeking then please allow me to point you in the right direction, as Appendix G, "Keys to Peace" will greatly bless you. Here's a hint; Ephesians 2:14 (in fact please read both chapters of Ephesians 1&2) reveals that Jesus is our peace, because He is the Prince of Peace (Isaiah 9:6). And the first and most important thing that you need to know as you begin your search for peace is that God is not mad at you (Isaiah 54:9)!!! I understand that I will never truly know peace as long as I am on this planet, but having peace with my Lord is what enables me to handle my time here, and keep my past, present and future in their proper perspectives, until I get home to Heaven. There will be no regret in Heaven, and I long for His return. On that day, we will completely understand and know what true peace and freedom are all about.

Then, as the above Scripture tells us, when you believe in your heart, and, confess with your mouth the Lord Jesus Christ, this is what is commonly referred to as a Prayer of Salvation or Sinners Prayer. Only God knows your heart and what's in your mind, yet angels and demons and all that is in the spiritual realm can hear your voice. So basically, this prayer is a verbal (out loud) proclamation of Jesus Christ as your Lord and Savior that forever will define the course of your soul back to God and His Heavenly Kingdom, and often goes something like this;

**Dear Lord Jesus, I call upon You to be my Lord and Savior. I know that I am a sinner and I need You to forgive me of my sins and fill me with Your Holy Spirit, and help me become the person of God You created me to be. I believe that You died on the cross for me to pay the full price for my sins and that You rose from the grave to give me life. Show me how to know You and live a life that honors You. In Jesus's Name, Amen.**

As long as this is what is truly in your heart, then there is no wrong way to say a prayer of salvation. At the time you receive Christ as your Lord and Savior ("conversion"), as my pastor correctly says, along with the Holy Spirit, you also receive the full armor of God (Ephesians 6:10-18, Romans 13:11-14), the character of the Beatitudes (Matthew 5:1-12), the fruit of the Spirit (Galatians 5:22-23), and every spiritual blessing (Ephesians 1:3-7) not to mention his grace, mercy and the forgiveness of our sins! And as you pray and prayerfully study God's Word daily, you will progressively learn to walk in them.

*"You must grow in the grace and knowledge of our Lord and Savior Jesus Christ. All glory to Him both now and forever! Amen"* 2 Peter 3:18 (NLT). And I know that sometimes it can be very difficult, but it's important that we do our best to extend grace to others, though often seemingly undeserving, as God has shown his grace upon us when we didn't deserve it either. The Lord explains

how vital this is in Matthew 6:14, Matthew 18:21-35 and Matthew 25:31-46 and we need to know this, because its how it works.

If you said this prayer with all of your heart, then welcome to God's family! God really does love you! He knows everything you have ever done and still loves you! Get into a BIBLE teaching church and Bible study group where you can learn and "grow strong in the Lord and the power of His might! (Ephesians 6:10).

And as the Lord instructed us (Matthew 28:19, Mark 16:16), be baptized in the name of the Father, Son and Holy Spirit as your public and spiritual commitment to take your place in the Body of Christ (1 Corinthians 12:12-14, Galatians 3:26-29). What is this whole baptism thing? Why be baptized? To Scripturally answer these and other questions you may have, please see the Bible references I have listed under "Baptism" in Appendix I.

***

In closing this chapter I would like to share a little something that Paul Harvey recited many years ago, on the radio;

"One raw winter night the man heard an irregular thumping sound against the kitchen storm door. He went to a window and watched as tiny, shivering sparrows, attracted to the evident warmth inside, beat in vain against the glass.

Touched, the farmer bundled up and trudged through the fresh snow to open the barn door for the struggling birds. He turned on the lights and tossed some hay in the corner. But the sparrows, which had scattered in all directions when he emerged from the house, hid in the darkness, afraid. The man tried various tactics to get them into the barn. He laid down a trail of saltine cracker crumbs to direct them. He tried circling behind the birds to drive them to the barn. Nothing worked. He, a huge, alien creature, had terrified them; the birds couldn't comprehend that he actually desired to help. The farmer withdrew to his house and watched the doomed sparrows through a window. As he stared, a thought hit him like a lightning bolt from a clear blue sky: if only I could become a bird – one of them – just for a moment. Then I wouldn't frighten them so. I could show them the way to warmth and safety.

At the same moment, another thought dawned on him. He grasped the reason Jesus was born."

To expand your understanding of this please study "The Gospels" section, Appendix E, in the back of this book.

## CHAPTER 18

## False Accusations, Grace, and the Iron Mast Mine

*"But these, like natural brute beasts made to be caught and destroyed, speak evil of the things they do not understand, and will utterly perish in their own corruption,"* 2 Peter 2:12

After Lori and I finished up our staking contract with Jack Grimm at Delcer Buttes, we went back to our home in Reno, as fall set in. We were pretty well caught up on all of our bills so we bought 2 new Honda dirt bikes and took them for their one and only ride in the hills behind our house in North Reno. They were our presents to each other after a lot of very hard work and a prosperous summer staking claims together, so the next morning, when Lori somehow woke up pregnant, I just never felt like riding without her. Eventually we sold the bikes; in brand new condition (one had 12 miles on it and the other only 16… Sad face…).

I took a job "driving drift", from the surface in, at the new Iron Mast Mine by Imlay, Nevada. It was like "old home week" as everybody who worked there was a friend or relative of mine, including my brother Bill, two of my cousins, Mickey and Bill, two of the Pierce brothers from my old neighborhood in Ely, John (the boss) and his little brother Dick (my nipper) who I grew up with, Mike H. (Mongo), Joel, Ron E., along with Mel Fox and Ray Horn from my Reveille Mine and Warm Springs days.

Lori and I first moved into a single wide trailer in Mill city, behind the Mill City Bar, with my brother and Ron. It was small to begin with, before Bill parked his 64 Harley hard tailed chopper in the living room, but it was doable… until he started it up every morning in the house. And yep, it had straight pipes. We kinda liked it as an alarm clock but the exhaust fumes sent Lori running for the toilet (morning sickness times 50) every single day, so on our days off we went home to Reno and grabbed our 35 foot camp trailer that we bought when we worked at Keystone Mine (our first new house together!). It was nice having our own place again, as we (mostly Lori) had both quit drinking (Lori never did drink much, so…) after we found out Lori flunked the "rabbit test". The curtains and couch were a little torn up from Lobo and Bear, our purebred Grey Timberwolf and our female German Shepherds "growing up" years. Other than that it was well-built and insulated, making it a warm and cozy place to spend the fall and winter.

Most mornings were cold, and as we crossed over the bridge at the Humboldt River every day on our way to work, the river showed early signs of trying to ice over. I don't remember whose idea got it started, but on the way home from the mine we would throw out all of the dead rabbits we had shot, at the base of a huge tree on the south end of the bridge. Then some of the guys started nailing them to the tree with .60 penny mine nails.

One day, coming home from work, the tree by the bridge was ribboned off with police tape and cops were everywhere, photographing everything. We smiled and waved as we drove by. When we got home to the Mill City Bar the place was abuzz with talk about how a murderous cult of evil people had moved into the area and was making ritual sacrifices of rabbits at the Jungo Bridge! Wow. We were thinking dimwits and numbskulls are obviously running this circus. Coincidentally (right?) the same thing happened at Wilson Reservoir up in Elko County, a few years earlier, when we were staking claims at Cornucopia…Hmmmm. It seems people like to always imagine the worst of the situation, don't you think? Nonetheless, I suppose we should be ever mindful that somebody is always watching so we should be careful of the impression we leave, and where we lead. After all, it was the Lord who said, "You will know them by their fruits" (Matthew 7:20) meaning people know us by what we produce in our lives and not by what we say we produce. Are we our brother's keeper? Yes. It's on us, and we are responsible and accountable where we lead other people (see Ezekiel 3:20-21, Romans 14:12-13 and 1 Corinthians 8:9). Twisted as it may seem, I think those rabbits may have sacrificed themselves, when, day after day, they ran out in front of moving vehicles, going down a secluded dirt road, that were crammed packed full of redneck miners with guns. What other outcome could there be? They expected… What? Really, poor ol' redneck miners were just trying to get home after a hard day's work (like I said… Twisted).

In any event, because most, if not all of those rabbits had huge worms eating away under their skin, which had to be miserable, probably 95% of them usually died off anyway when the temperature dropped well below freezing, and ended the rabbit hunting for this season. Even more amazing was the folks at the Mill City Bar giving credit to the FBI for stopping the "ritual killings" right after the cold winter temperatures set in for the season! Honestly, you can't make this stuff up!

***

*"You shall not bear false witness against your neighbor."* Exodus 20:16, Deuteronomy 5:20

Let me give you another example. Years earlier at 19 years of age, before I met Lori, Steve and I were working at the Eldorado Mine, about 16 or so miles east of Eureka in Nevada. At the junction of Highway 50 and Strawberry Rd., Highway 892 there was this roadhouse called the Eldorado Bar and Café. It was run by a good ol' boy and ex-miner named Bob, who previously had worked for my father for a while as well as Gold Creek Corporation when I was there.

As roadhouses go, this one was "managed" by a big, huge, self-centered, jackass of a man who called himself "Big Daddy". I'm not making this up! For some reason, Big Daddy and I never really "bonded". It seemed that his mouth and mine were always in conflict, and I believe we both enjoyed antagonizing each other.

Steve and I were living in my brother's camp trailer out behind the bar, in a rented trailer space, which made things even more complex in our relationship with Big Daddy. Out of respect for Bob, we tried to maintain a certain "line", if you will, that we really tried not to cross, such as fighting and tearing up the bar, running off customers, etc..

BUT… One night Big Daddy pushed too far, and I wasn't backing up. That night another one of my Dad's crew members was also in the bar. His name was Cobra (legally! I know… I know...) and he was a triple black belt, 6'6" tall, from Guam, and proclaiming himself to be a Samoan. I was usually pretty careful around Cobra as, even though we drank and worked together, we didn't necessarily get along very well. I always made it a point of keeping Cobra in the corner of my eye when he was present, never knowing when or where he would go off. He was truly what is referred to as a "loose cannon". You just never knew.

Anyway, this night Big Daddy was provoking me, and I was provoking him right back. The only thing holding us back was the creepy way that Cobra kept laughing at us. Big Daddy was no fool when it came to realizing there was someone in the bar that is potentially much more dangerous than the two of us, so he was edgy as well. There was no telling where Cobra would stand if things went off, and that was very unsettling. I had a 10 inch long knife holstered in my left boot, but had left my Colt 9 mm in the trailer for the evening's festivities, a choice that nearly cost me my life.

It was obvious that we were both waiting for Cobra to leave, so when he got up and headed for the bathroom, Steve moved off closer to the door and away from me to give me space. As Cobra opened the bathroom door and stepped inside, Big Daddy hissed at me, "Tonight I'm gonna kill you". As I stood by a table in the middle of the room, I brought my left foot up onto a chair in front of me. Big Daddy was moving toward the end of the bar, about 15 feet away from me, and presented himself at the perfect distance as the target for my blade. I couldn't miss. Then Big Daddy's hands dropped out of sight behind the bar as my hand curled around the bone handle of my boot knife. It was a sawed-off double barrel 10gauge shotgun that came up from behind the bar, and to me, it looked like a cannon.

As I have stated before, it always amazed me how fast things went in to "gun mode", and how equally fast your mind becomes crystal clear, especially in gun mode, particularly when I don't have one. I was 20 feet from the door and I knew I wasn't going to make it...the song "Give Me 3 Steps (towards the door) by Lynyrd Skynyrd comes to mind, huh? As I pulled my knife clear of my boot I realized I was going to die in the next split second as Big Daddy brought that shotgun to bear on my chest. I clearly heard the twin hammers click back into place at full cock, as I brought my arm back into a throwing movement that I would never complete.

As my total focus was on the triumphant look on my adversary's face and the deadly shotgun, I anticipated the imminent bright muzzle flash that would end my life. What I didn't see was Cobra moving like a shadow from the bathroom to the end of the bar where Big Daddy was leveling the shotgun on me. Cobra stepped right in front of that cocked shotgun, leaned over the top of it with his face about 12 inches in front of Big Daddy's, and said, "Can you see me over that shotgun, Big Daddy? Cuz you better pull the trigger!"

The words had no sooner come out of Cobra's mouth when the back room door to Bob's bedroom burst open and Bob came charging to the bar in his underwear. "That's enough!" he yelled as he grabbed the shotgun and yanked it free from Big Daddy's hands. "Get out!" he said to me. Steve and I were out the door so fast that Bob had no need to repeat himself. We grabbed our gear out of Billy Bob's trailer and headed for Eureka.

I now know God made him do it, but I never knew then why Cobra stepped between me and that shotgun. Divine Providence. I never got the chance to ask Cobra either, as I never saw him again after that night... He just disappeared, with not even a forwarding address for his paycheck. Was he an angel? I don't think so because no one could be around him for very long without sensing how dangerous he was, and he was a hard drinker that loved to fight. It's apparent that Big Daddy and I were simply just mere entertainment for him.

I am ashamed of the evil that was in my heart that night, as it would settle for nothing less than bloodshed and death, and yet God loved me still, and orchestrated the events of this night to spare my life. I know the blatant truth that Romans 5:8 clearly states, *"But God demonstrates his own love towards us, that while we were still sinners, Christ died for us"*. And verse 10 goes on to break it down saying, *"for if when we were enemies we were reconciled to God through the death of His Son, much more, having been reconciled, we shall be saved by his life"*. Romans 5:8 is truly a reality to me and I pray it is to you, as well. How awesome is the One who created the universe, and yet still loves YOU with such individual intensity!

A couple of days later, Steve and I were riding with Johnny Pinola from Eureka to work at Eldorado Mine. A thick layer of smoke filled the valley as we descended Pinto Summit and approached the Strawberry Road and Highway 50 junction. The source of the smoke became obvious as we slowed to make the turn onto Strawberry Road. The Eldorado Bar and Café had burnt to the ground.

As to the example I wanted to give you at the beginning of this story, for many years following this incident, many, if not most people in the area believed that I burned Eldorado to the ground in retaliation. I did not. Even almost 20 years afterwards a couple of my friends would ask me, in confidentiality, "Tell me the truth, did you really burn Eldorado down?" It kinda still hurts when it comes from a friend. No, I didn't burn Eldorado down, but you all can think whatever you want. I don't care anymore. And I'm pretty sure I know who did though, but even if I had proof I wouldn't say. Nope. It wasn't Cobra, either.

Even though I didn't do it, rumors dogged me for many years, sometimes costing me friends and many relationships in the area over the years. The only peace I have been given over all of this is when, over 10 years later, I ran into Bob and he put his arm around my shoulder and told me that he believed me when I told him I didn't do it.

Here's the point of all this drama I'm laying on you; the truth that awakens one person will often harden another. A warm sunny day in Nevada can melt ice, but it can also harden clay. As with the teachings of Jesus and His use of parables, whether someone understood the parable or not depended solely on the condition of his or hers heart. Also applicable to us, based on this heart condition, is the way we judge others in situations that we know little or nothing about. Whether we choose to only see the truth about someone or something, or prefer to think the worst of them will depend on how we have allowed our hearts to be conditioned by our own experiences.

We can assume the worst of people and jump to faulty conclusions, or we can lighten up a little and actually give people the benefit of the doubt. Maybe even show a little of the grace and mercy to them that our Heavenly Father has so lavishly poured out on us. Full well knowing the evil (as well as the good) that was in my heart, God still showed compassion and mercy on me... Me! How can I not show the same mercy and compassion on others like me who Christ died for, just as he died for me?

The world has wrongly taught us to assume the worst, but we can actively recondition our hearts to try and see the best of people and situations, regardless of how allusive they may often seem. This is what I'm trying to get across, and probably not doing very well at it.

No one is exempt from the pain of being falsely accused. Just ask Jesus. He was accepted or rejected, then as well as now, as a result of the condition of the human heart. That's probably why God does His best and most complete work through brokenness (Psalms 51:17). It doesn't have to be this way but sadly, for most people like me, it's the only way we will learn. *"What do you want? Shall I come to you with a rod, or in love and a spirit of gentleness?"* (1 Corinthians 4:21). What the Holy Spirit is trying to say, I believe, in this Scripture is, "I love you too much to let you go without a fight; how do you want to do it – the easy way or the hard way?" Guys like me, by our own choices,

have to have it the hard way. We have to be broken to our pride and self-will. Even though we chose poorly, God still did not allow us to perish without giving us every possible opportunity to turn to Him. It didn't have to be this way. We made our choices; we endured the results.

What about you? Easy way or the hard way? Don't worry, if this current affliction you find yourself in isn't enough to make you humble yourself before God and seek His intervention, then I'm sure the next one probably will be... or the next, or maybe the one after that. It's our choice. He's never gonna stop loving you so He will never stop pursuing you. Talk to Him about it, won't you?

The current condition of our heart is what is now controlling our ability to seek and accept the Truth, or reject it in favor of preconceived worst case scenarios projected by the world around us. We preferred these negative worldly views because of our worldly nature. The really good news is, we can retrain our hearts to "love our neighbor" (Mark 12:33) and see people and things much more clearly from the Lord's perspective. How do we know His perspective? You've got to read his Holy Word, the Bible, and you will get to know Him and how He looks at things. Pray and ask Him to reveal Himself to you every time you read the Bible and you will see what I mean, I guarantee.

Much prayer= much power.

No prayer= no power.

Talk to him about everything. Its okay, He already knows, and he loves you still! (See Romans 8:35-39). It just takes practice and a little help from the Lord. As it worked wonderfully for me, may I suggest that you try this prayer of David, as recorded in Psalms 51?

*"Create in me a clean heart, O God, and renew a steadfast spirit within me.*

*Do not cast me away from Your presence, and do not take Your Holy Spirit from me.*

*Restore to me the joy of Your salvation, and uphold me by Your generous Spirit.*

*Then I will teach transgressors Your ways, and sinners shall be converted to You."* (Versus 10-13)

It's the deal (covenant) that David made with God after committing, and repenting of, an outright sin. God apparently agreed and held up his end and David went on to hold up on his part too (2 Samuel 11 – 12). It worked for David and it worked for me.

Did you notice the words, create, renew, restore, and uphold in the above prayer? That's where your blessing is! Psalms 51 should rightfully be read and prayed in all of its entirety to understand the full impact of what this chapter is all about, and to experience God's profound impact on your heart as detailed in these Scriptures. It will most assuredly bless you.

\*\*\*

Back at the Iron Mast Mine winter was setting in. At the bottom of the hill, near where we stockpiled our ore, was this huge, heavy 1940-ish G.I. truck cab. One morning at our safety meeting, John announced that everyone would be required to meet at the bottom of the hill, after work, to help load this monstrosity of a truck cab on to a flatbed trailer that John was going to town to rent. Why? So John could take it to his ranch house and make a chicken coop out of it. Of course! What else could it have been? In our own private meeting, excluding John, we drew straws, and I lost.

Although no proof was ever rendered, I took the blame for this as well...but this time, rightfully so, although it was technically the "luck of the draw" and I feel that I did not act alone.

After we had all gone to work underground, I snuck back out of the new drift I was portaling off, crept through the trees around the side of the hill, past the mechanics shop, and eventually ended up, unseen, at the powder magazine. I crimped a blasting cap on the end of 28 foot of fuse, embedded it securely into a stick of "Hercules's Finest" (stick of 40% dynamite), and shoved that through a small hole I made in a full 80 pound bag of Prell (ammonium nitrate mixed with diesel, for that hard to find, disintegrating, "big bang" so commonly sought after, yet rarely achieved). Balancing my deadly payload on my shoulder, I lurked back down through the pines and mahogany trees until I connected with the main ore haulage road that ran from the mine to the stockpile, at its steepest place, just below and around a corner and out of sight from the shop. By the time I smoked a cigarette I could hear the old ore truck creeping down the steep grade above me in its lowest gear, which would be about 1 mile per hour. As it came even with the tree that I was hiding behind, I leapt up on the passenger running board, and much to the surprise of my wide-eyed friend Dick, threw the 80 pound bag of explosives through the window and onto the passenger seat. Dick was always game for stuff like this and produced a huge grin of understanding as he looked back and forth between me and the powder. We never even spoke as I climbed in the cab and rode to the bottom of the hill. He knew. There wasn't anything else to say. As we approached the old truck cab Dick, with a chuckle, slowed a little as I stepped off the running board with my bag. I used a tree branch and a rock to tilt the cab up enough to get the bag of Prell centered under it, and then I let it down, lit a smoke and waited for the ore truck to head back up the hill. After looking down the road for a few miles and making sure no one else was headed our way, I lit the fuse and jumped back in the truck as it was going by. I was back in my work area by the time Dick got his next load.

KABOOOM!!!

The ground shook and a nicely formed mushroom cloud arose from the bottom of the hill, below the mine. "What the hell was that?" I yelled as I ran towards Ray Horn and the other guys coming out of the shop building. They looked back at me in total bewilderment.

The biggest piece we could find was about 12 inches wide, and we only found four or five pieces at that. It cleared an area of about 18 feet in every direction that looked like it had been swept with a broom.

***

Soon the temperatures dropped well below freezing but I still had not driven the new tunnel far enough into the mountainside to evade the cold. Once far enough underground, the temperature of the mine does not change. I have worked in 91° day in and day out, and 61° every day also, and most temperatures in between, depending on what mine you're in.

Just to the west of the portal was a limestone rock ledge about 8 foot high and 30 feet wide. I drilled a couple of rounds into it and blew out a nice square hole between two big trees. Over the next few days I pillaged enough wood, timber, and tin, and even a window and nice old door to seal it up and form a cozy, small cabin built into the rock. I used an old 30 gallon carbide barrel for a stove, and hung it sideways from the ceiling timbers with some old chain. I could at least come out of the drift, build a fire and get warm when it got so cold I couldn't take it anymore.

One afternoon, as I was walking out of the portal and into the sunlight, I heard a loud WHOOOM sound and saw about 10 feet of flame blow out the door of my cabin, then disappear. A second later, Ron came running out the door, hung a left turn and disappeared up the mountainside into the trees, apparently heading for the main mine tunnel above us. I only saw him for a couple of seconds, but it was long enough to see he was smoking! And not smoking as in cigarettes or something like that, I mean smoking as "on fire" smoking. His cloths, his hair, and I remember distinctly, his eyebrows! I took off after him as fast as I could, to try and help him. Up the hill I scrambled, clawing and pulling myself up the steep mountain side until I finally made it over the top of the main dump and on to the level ground, about 50 yards from the main mine tunnel entrance. As I did I saw Ron running across the open area towards the Chevy Blazer parked in front of the mine, so I took off running after him. As I ran across the open area of the dump, Mel Fox, who was cutting mine timber over to my left, yelled, "What the hell did you do to Ron?"

Why would he think I did anything to Ron? Bonehead.

Ron had jumped in the front seat of the blazer on the passenger side, still smoking, and simply looked over at my brother who was sitting in the driver seat getting warm, and said, "BOOM"! My brother's classic response was, "God, you stink!" About then is when I caught up. As I recall, Ron had some nasty burns on his face and one hand. Most of his facial hair was burned off and what remained still had wisps of smoke lingering and it. Bill grabbed the first aid kit out from under the seat and went to trying to patch Ron up with burn ointment and Band-Aids.

From what we gathered, Ron, in an attempt to get warm had come down to my cabin to build a fire. He stuffed the barrel stove full of wood but couldn't get it going. He found a can of starting fluid and proceeded to spray down the wood. At this point it's a little vague, but he either tried to throw a match in, or more likely, the smoldering embers left over from the morning fire ignited the ether all at once while he was bent over with his face directly in front of the open stove.

Later that week the ore vein they had been following in the main tunnel, and the one I was supposed to drive our new haulage tunnel underneath, pinched out. It simply disappeared. Liking our paychecks, and considering the fact that eating is a hard habit to break, my brother and Ron put in three more rounds and picked up the vein again. It was much smaller and getting weaker with each round, and we never knew if the next round would be our last. That Friday I was down at the mechanics shop, having Ray Horn braze a nice new set of brass handles on my throwing knife. Ray was pretty handy at that sort of thing and we were kind of killing time as our paychecks were late…again. Last week we didn't get them in time to take them to Winnemucca before the banks closed, so we had to cash them at the Winners Inn Casino, for a fee.

That day, as Ray worked on my knife, I watched the excess brass fall and splatter on the ground. I slid a bucket of water under the vise that held our project, and let the hot liquid brass fall into the water and make really cool brass splatters. Sooo…after we finished my knife I gathered up a handful of the brass pieces and headed up to the main drift where my brother and Ron were working.

They had just shot their round and were waiting for the smoke and dust to clear so they could go in and see if the vein was still there. It was…barely. I showed them the brass I had in my pocket and they both just started laughing. We pried cracks in the vein with our knives and a screwdriver then filled the cracks we had made with brass. Finally, at about 6 PM, they showed up with our paychecks and off to town we went.

As, once again, we were too late to make it to the bank, we pulled into the Winners Inn. As we approached the cashier's cage to cash our checks, "what should appear before our wondering eyes, but" all of our paychecks from the last week, nailed to the cashiers wall! They had all bounced. We immediately headed to the bar to make a plan.

Saturday morning we loaded up everything, equipment wise, at the mine that was paid for and wasn't nailed down, took it all to my house in Reno and called the district attorney's office in Lovelock (Pershing County). On Monday the DA gave the mining company 24 hours to pay us in cash or they would forfeit all of their equipment, totaling about $60,000 worth. They flew into Reno and paid us by 4:30 PM that evening, and we even charged them for taking their stuff back on Tuesday.

Tuesday afternoon we unloaded everything and when we went into the mine to check things out, we found that the "salted" vein had been hand dug back about 5 inches and the floor of the drift below the face had been swept clean! Realizing that the brass we pounded into the vein was probably the only reason we got paid (they thought the vein was full of gold and needed us back to mine it), we unanimously decided to call it "deep enough". We were ready to move on anyway, as my boyhood friend, Dick, had died in a rollover on the way home from work a few weeks earlier.

Lori and I opted to spend the winter in our house in Reno and stay until the baby was born in June. I, along with everyone else, was offered another job in Austin Nevada at the Slaughterhouse Mine, but as much as I wanted to go, I just had a bad, unsettling feeling about it and decided to pass on the offer. My friend Festus, of "The Boys from the Brush" fame, took my place. A few months later he watched in horror as our old friend John, Dick's older brother, was "slabbed" (killed) in a cave in.

Was that Providence? Providence is the way God arranges the circumstances of our lives to accomplish His purposes. The word Providence comes from the Latin word that means "to see beforehand". I don't even begin to pretend that I understand any of this, but God, being omniscient, or all-knowing, apparently sees the events and situations of our lives in advance, based on the choices we make, before they actually take place.

I wanted to go to Austin, but I didn't because I felt weird about it. Nothing I could put my finger on exactly, just that, something wasn't right. Kind of like the "feeling" (I now believe it was the Holy Spirit) I had at Gooseberry Mine before I got buried alive. Festus went instead and it led him to end his underground career, possibly saving him from God knows what that awaited him in his future. And what about my friends John and his little brother Dick? I have no answers, but over the years I have settled into accepting the facts that I don't, and won't ever know everything as long as I am here on earth, however, it comforts me to realize that the important thing is to just know and trust the One who does know all things. I do know that John and Dick both knew the Lord as their Savior, and when I get to where they are now, I will have all of my answers, just as they do.

My wife worked at Hospice in Ely for over 16 years. It is a gift of compassion and strength that she possesses, and I do not, meaning that my heart breaks and I "lose it" when ministering to people in the last moments of their lives. Nonetheless, I have seen many people come to terms with their last days here on the planet, in many different ways. They face death differently and die differently, because they have lived their lives differently. Many I know have faced death with hope and often even a sense of anticipation.

Lori and I were with my father in his last days and moments before going home to Heaven, and the immense homecoming party that awaited him. When the doctor came into his room at St. Mary's Hospital in Reno, he told Dad that he must start chemo treatments and blood transfusions immediately. My Dad laughed! Then he said, "Listen Doc, in a few days it's gonna be my 50$^{th}$ wedding anniversary, and I am intending to dance with my wife in Heaven!" Seeing the calm resolve in my father's countenance, and his peaceful demeanor, the doctor simply asked, "What can I do for you, Bill?" Dad answered, "I just want to die with a little dignity. I would appreciate anything you could do to make me comfortable".

Others only know hopelessness and despair as death approaches their final moments. The most difficult funeral I ever presided over was a non-Christian funeral, and it is the one and only one I will ever do. The realization is just too heartbreaking for me. What can you say? "They were a good person and they had a good life, and we loved them and will miss them" only stretches so far.

I'm ready to go. As my dear friend Armando said it, "I have had enough". (By the way, I highly recommend his book, 'Radical Faith, Transforming the World, One Person at a Time, by A.V. Munoz). Come, Lord Jesus! Lori and I long to rise and meet the Lord in the air (1 Thessalonians 4:17). If not, and the Lord takes me another way, I pray its quick, like my old friends, John and Dick, where you don't even have time to think about it. In a moment, in the twinkling of an eye (1 Corinthians 15:52), you're there in Heaven (1 Thessalonians 4:13-18). Until then, I'm just trying my best to grow old, gracefully.

For further study of Scripture references on this, see; "Rapture" in Appendix J.

## CHAPTER 19

## You Reap What You Sow-For Good or Evil

*"Do not be deceived, God is not mocked; for whatever a man sows, that he will also reap. For he who sows to his flesh will of the flesh reap corruption, but he who sows to the Spirit will of the Spirit reap everlasting life."* Galatians 6:7-8. That's a major spiritual law that cannot be broken.

My son, William Robert, was born on June 3, 1981. Lori had a tough time through hours of contractions, and finally the delivery of my son. I was present the entire time and it really changed my perspective concerning my priorities. I felt so helpless to help the one I loved the most in her most painful hours before Billy's birth, yet somehow, she always maintained her dignity and integrity throughout her suffering. I will never forget that and will always regard her with the utmost respect for doing so under such travail. She never even yelled at me or cussed me, even though I may or may not have panicked, and possibly, freaked out a couple of times... allegedly freaked out... or not.

Lori's Mom, on the other hand...standing half bent over at the foot of the hospital bed, both hands white knuckled and clinching the stainless steel foot rail in a death grip, veins popping out on her neck and forehead as she leaned over the bed with her wide eyes seemingly popping out of their sockets, staring into the face of her youngest daughter, and in a deep, guttural, hissing voice that was definitely not her own, she loudly repeated over and over, the single word; "BRREEEAATHH"!

Very, very spooky. Finally, I believe for my sanity, Lori finally stared back into her face, between contractions, and with equal intensity, my loving wife slowly and clearly told her to, "Knock it off, Mom". And thank God, she did! I was about to totally lose my mind at that point. The look on Lori's face calmed me right down as well, sort of a byproduct of dealing with her Mom. More like the old adage "two birds with one stone", if the truth be told. I had seen that look before. I knew better. I took a deep breath or two and refocused, and thankfully so did Noreen.

I swore at that moment that I would do my very best not to do anything that she or my son would ever be ashamed of. Although I failed miserably to keep this vow in the years following, it definitely kept me from participating in a lot of activities, which presented themselves over many years, that had the potential to make our lives much worse. I dropped a lot of bad habits, relationships, and "Associates" in an attempt to uphold my promise, yet I was destined to fail. God had to have all of me, not just a piece of me, and my personal accountability for my actions and my pride was not something I would even vaguely consider.

Fortunately, no one is beyond the reach of God, although some of us will require more love, and long-suffering than others. It depends on the condition of one's heart, and mine was very hardened. Eventually, the hardening of my heart, over many years, would require the need for me to be broken, to be saved. God didn't do this to me, or you. It is the result (fruit) of our rejection and disobedience of Him – the results of our choices. Even with all the mistakes and sins we commit, He is quick to forgive us and help us, if we repent. If we do not, the Lord simply allows the consequences of our deeds to manifest in our lives. Blaming God for these consequences, as I did for many years, is obviously very foolish and wrongfully inappropriate.

So, amazingly, even though my heart was extremely calloused and getting harder and harder as the years of my life unfolded, my Heavenly Father had already foreseen my need and supplied the remedy over 2000 years ago! Jesus died on the cross to pay my sin debt, and yours, because our Father loved us too much to let us parish. And what father does not "correct" his child, out of love, to keep them from evil?

*"My son, do not despise the chastening of the Lord, nor detest his correction;*

*For whom the Lord loves He corrects, just as a father the son in whom he delights".* Proverbs 3:11-12

In my youth, my Mom once asked me why I always had to take the hard road, to which I answered, "Mom, what makes you think that I see two roads?" To benefit and be saved by Jesus's work on the cross, I had correction coming. It's the way it had to be for me. The end result it is designed to accomplish for God's purpose is to enable me to receive His prophesied promise made to us hard cases through His prophet, Ezekiel;

*"I will give you a new heart and put a new spirit within you; I will take the heart of stone out of your flesh. I will put My Spirit within you and cause you to walk in my statutes, and you will keep my judgments and do them... I will deliver you from all your uncleanliness"* Ezekiel 36:26, 27, 29.

It's a restoration process. Yes, we are born in sin, but we were not created in sin. Most Christians I have heard tell the of redemption story of Jesus almost always start in Genesis 3 with the sin debt, but if we correctly begin in Genesis 1 we see that we were originally created in a total realm of peace and communion with our Creator. "In the beginning" is where we should start, and not in the "this is where you messed up" part. It's about getting us back where we belong and where we came from, and not about taking us to a new place.

In Genesis, God never calls us a bunch of busted, disgusted, sinners so I don't believe we should base our Gospel message on that foundation. We are separated from God by a result of our actions, but that, by no means, is who we are, or where we are from. God hates our sins because they separate us from Him, and we should hate them to, but it's important to keep in mind that God is not in love with a future version of you, He is in love with you right now as you are. We are God's creation and His greatest love, and God has divinely provided a way, through Jesus Christ, to restore the peace and fellowship we are created to share with Him! Now that's good news, don't you think? That's where the story starts! Truly, I don't recall anyone I have met, that believed there was a God, who wasn't fully aware that they were separated from God by their sin, and knew that they weren't "good enough". What I find most commonly, is the terrible emptiness in their souls in not knowing that God loves them anyway! Just like "in the beginning", God loves them still! Try telling that to the lost! Let me know how that works for ya. It is the truth, so we should tell the truth.

When I was young, being told by the head of my "Ward" that I was never gonna be "good enough" caused me to eventually give up trying, and eventually led me to turn on God like a mad dog. Soon I could tear any church or Christian apart by simply quoting Scripture. And He loved me still. God forgave me. Then I learned that my inherent worth and value, as well as yours, is based on Who made me, and not on what I, or you, do or think. The world and the devil want to strip us of our true identity and our dignity by telling us we are not worthy. That's a lie. Don't you ever believe it. You are who God, your Creator, says you are, not who anybody else says you are; and God says you are worth dying for! Ask Jesus!

*"So God created man in His own image"*, Genesis 1:27. I hope you will please take time to look at who the God of the Bible says you really are, in the "I am's" section found in Appendix K in the back of this book. This truth you need desperately to know. The Creator of the universe loves you right now, right here where you are! He is not mad at you, either (Isaiah 54:9). He knows the choices you have made and He is here to help you, not punish you. Get alone with Him somewhere in a quiet place, pray, and ask Him about what I'm telling you. Ask Him what to do next. Then listen…open a Bible, read, and listen some more. Soon you will begin to recognize His voice in your heart. It's the real deal. Honest.

Please take time to look over "The Voice" in Appendix M.

\*\*\*

Winter came and took a long time leaving. I was choking on cabin fever and jumped at the first job opportunity that presented the possibility of getting out into the hills. I staked a couple of hundred claims for Phil Davis in northern Elko County by fall, and then I loaded up Lori, dropped my son off at Lori's mother's house and headed for the Bahamas, to do a little diving, etc., etc., etc., and treasure hunting. When we got back I got hooked up with an old miner named Jesse Wilson, who was looking to sink some exploration shafts down to bedrock, in Goler Canyon near Randsburg California. Mongo, my brother Bill and I took a camp trailer and Dad's International compressor truck, which was fitted with double drum hoists and a portable head frame, and we went to sinking shaft with a borrowed "clamshell".

Then the rains came. Goler Canyon was very narrow with at least 1000 foot cliffs on both sides in several places, and is known for its monstrous flash floods of biblical proportions. Known to everybody but us, that is. One evening after work, it started to sprinkle. Rain in the Mohave Desert is a wondrous thing. Flowers and plants that have lain dormant for sometimes many years bloom and blossom turning the dry and barren desert into a garden of immense beauty. Rain also drops the temperatures from way over 100°, down to a doable 80 or 90 degrees, at least until the summer storm passes by. Then it's right back up to "fry your brains out" temperatures as usual.

Our camp was set up about a mile or so below the mouth of the canyon, out in the valley by the highway, at the wellhead that supplied water for our operations. We had enough experience from living in the high deserts of Nevada to put our camp on high ground, and there was a berm of dirt and rock built around the wellhead to protect the area in case of such an event as this. The area that was cleared and protected inside the perimeter of the safety berm was about 75 yards square and we shared this area with a fellow named Banjo. Banjo lived with his lovely wife and two children on the far side of the cleared area, in a single wide trailer. As Banjo's wife had a gentle demeanor, I tended to feel that she was very mismatched with her loudmouth, drunken husband, who often left her and the kids alone out here in this godforsaken desert, while he went drinking in Ridgecrest.

A few days before the rains came, we were working in the canyon as usual. And as was his custom, Banjo would come charging up the canyon in his old truck to threaten, rant and rave at the people we were working for. Banjo had leased his mining claims to an investment group, who in turn hired Jesse and his boys to build a 100 ton per hour placer gold plant, who in turn, hired me, my brother, and Mike (Mongo) to sink shaft to bedrock and find the gold. Even though the "company" paid Banjo a very generous monthly fee, Banjo consistently showed up on the property, almost always inebriated and spewed threats, rants and cursing's at Jesse and his crew. He often pulled out and waved around an old Colt .45 Peacemaker that he bragged was given to him by his Dad to protect the claims with. Why Jesse and Jesse Junior tolerated this outlandish behavior, over and over, I will never know, but seeing how it had nothing to do with us, we stayed out of it.

Near the end of a scorching 120° day we had just shut down the compressor and were gathering up our tools, when Banjo came bouncing up the canyon road towards us. Jesse and his boys had taken a few days off to go home to see family back in Nevada, and we were the only ones working in the canyon. When it was apparent that he was heading our way I reached in the truck for my own Colt .45 six-gun and strapped it on my left hip. I left the door to the truck open and stood behind it as Banjo came to a stop just 30 feet in front of me. He was yelling something about how we couldn't work on his claim unless Jesse was here, before he even got out of his truck. As he got out and slammed the door he continued with his babble saying that we couldn't be trusted with the gold, if we found it, and to stop us from stealing it, we had to leave now. Then he dropped his right hand to the butt of his Colt. I slammed the door on my truck, took three long steps towards him so he could clearly hear me, and said "Don't do it, Banjo. If you pull that pistol, I'm gonna kill you". He stopped in mid-stagger, although he didn't seem quite as drunk as he usually was. The air got silent and super thick for a few seconds as Banjo looked from my face to my holstered Colt, then back to my face again. If he didn't comprehend anything else in that moment, he knew that time for talking was over.

"You can turn around and leave us be, Banjo, or you can pull that pistol". Silence again, as he tried to process what was happening. Then I heard Mongo's soft chuckle somewhere behind me...and so did Banjo. His eyes opened wide as he went for his pistol. I really never thought he would do it. I drew and cocked my .45 Long Colt, and leveled it at his face before he had a chance to bring up his gun. Wisely, he froze, wide-eyed and staring down the barrel of my pistol.

"Drop it", I calmly ordered. He just stood there.

BOOM! The shot from Mongo's 30-06 into the air was amplified 100 times as it bounced off of the canyon walls, deafening all of us. Banjo jumped about 2 feet straight up and dropped his gun into the dirt in the process. He was very sober now. He turned without a word, walked back to his truck and left.

I finally turned around to see Mongo leaning against the front fender of the pickup holding his 30-06 rifle upright with the butt stock on his right hip while he took another bite of a peach that was in his left hand.

"If you're done now, can we go eat?" He says, blank faced and matter of factly.

"What the hell was that?" I retorted. "You almost made me shoot that fool!" I started to shake a little, but did good to hide it. Mongo smiled and simply said "I'm hungry – let's go". I looked over at Bill on the other side of the truck and he just looked angry, shook his head, and got in the truck. I picked up Banjos Colt and got in. That's when I noticed my Colt CAR 15 rifle next to my brother on the seat. Big brothers got my back! The thought made me feel warm and fuzzy inside.

Banjo didn't show up back at camp for several days until the night the rains came. In the early hours of the morning we awoke to the sound of a lot of rushing water. The sky was just barely beginning to turn light as we dressed and went outside to look around. Water was moving fast and pouring around both sides of the campsite, held at bay and splitting around us by the dirt and rock berms that surrounded us. It flooded across the two lane roadway on both sides of our camp area. As the morning sky brightened we could begin to fathom the incredible amount of water that must be pouring out of the canyon. We drove north to higher ground then rode up the ridge line to a point to where we could see the wall to wall river of water coming out of Goler Canyon, however, we could not see up the canyon and around the bend to tell how our equipment was faring. Our hearts sank as we silently realized the chances of our truck and other equipment surviving this catastrophic flash flood was slim to none.

That evening we listen to the rain decrease to a steady drizzle as it fell on the roof of the camp trailer. After dinner I emptied Banjo's six shooter, stuck it behind my belt and trudged through the rain over to their single wide trailer. I knocked and his wife answered the door. I asked permission to come in and followed her through the living room to the small kitchen where Banjo sat at the table. He seemed to be sober and stared up at me with distaste and humiliation in his eyes. Whether or not he had told his wife what had transpired I do not know, but in a soft voice she asked if I would like a cup of coffee. It smelled great on a damp and gloomy night such as this, but "No thank you, ma'am" is what I replied, as not to add further awkwardness to my presence in Banjo's house. He uncomfortably leaned forward in his chair to speak, but before he could, I said, "We're not your enemy, Banjo", and I placed his Dad's Colt on the table. "We are just here to do a job and put food on the table for our families, like you".

I looked over at his two little girls coloring in the living room and finished with, "I think that's the important thing to remember and it's what we should all be mindful of and tending to, don't you agree?" I turned my gaze back to him and he nodded and said, "Yeah, it is". I nodded once to him and turned for the door. "Good night", I said to his wife as I stepped past her and crossed the living room. The girls warmly smiled up at me as I stepped past them, and I gave them a smile in return. As I reached the front door, there on a bookshelf was a hot steaming cup of black coffee. I turned and looked back across the room at Banjo's wife. With just a hint of a smile and a kind nod, she turned and went back into the kitchen. The cup warmed my hands as I stepped back out into the rain, and a deep ache hit my heart as I realized how badly I missed my wife and son. At least my heart wasn't totally calloused over and hardened solid back then, thank God. And, the truth be told, I liked the way it felt to show mercy.

Pastor Joseph said that some people are just sent into our lives as "grace growers". They are the people who irritate us crazy, yet come with the reminder to us to show the same grace and mercy to them that God has extended to us… annoying as they may seem. I believe the downside is that we learn and make habits through repetition, and that's why these types of people are always with us and in our lives.

***

When I was a young "pupil" going to Ely grade school we had to walk about 2 ½ blocks down the hill to the lunchroom in the high school cafeteria, every day at noon. Being tormented and provoked by several of his classmates, there was this kid, somewhat smaller than me that was daily trying to pick a fight with me, on the way to lunch. One day he jumped out in front of me, blocking my path, and with his fists up in his "put up your dukes" position, managed to finally press the right button. While he was still spewing insults at me I slapped him hard with an open hand, right on his right ear, then stepped back as the ringing effect sent in. I knew just exactly how intense it was because I learned about it on the playground, the year before; in the same manner he was learning it now. He still stood there with his fists up and his eyes wide. A circle of other kids hoping to see a fight had surrounded us and the loud taunts were flying. I looked over my raised fists into his eyes and said, "You don't have to do this". His eyes softened and he slowly lowered his fists. I looked over at his buddy who was the biggest mouthpiece responsible for pushing this kid into a fight he couldn't win, and said, "How about you?" He just walked off.

Later on that very afternoon, I was caught by my teacher, relentlessly teasing a girl that I had a crush on. But rather than making me bend over and grab the edge of the desk to receive my usual forthcoming "swat" with the paddle, she told me to stay after school to receive the consequences of my actions. It turned out to be a vital lesson on reaping and sowing that I never forgot. After everyone was gone I was told to come up to her desk and "assume the position", which I did. I was prepared. Never had I ever let a teacher see me cry when I took my ass-whoopin', and this time would be no different. I was A.D.D. before they ever had a name for it, and this, over many years, is what taught me self-discipline. It worked well and was very effective. My teacher picked up her wooden paddle (which, by the way, had my name with many stars beside it, along with several others written on it, including my brother's) and came around her desk. But instead of whacking my behind, she sat down on top of her desk right beside me, leaned over and said, "I saw you today, on the way to lunch. You let that other kid off the hook and you didn't have to. He asked for it. So you know what I'm gonna do? I'm gonna let you off the hook, even though you and I both know you earned your swat. I won't be so nice next time, now get outta here and go home".

I never forgot. The times I have been shown mercy, in my younger days, are extremely rare. Thank you, Mrs. Dalby. God bless you, I never forgot.

***

Sometime in the night the rain stopped. As the day dawned we could see the havoc the flash flood had had on the surrounding area, and it was devastating. "The hundred year flood", people told us. Nothing about the landscape looked the same and washed up turtles (tortoises) were everywhere. Most were dead or injured and many were in need of assistance, being upside down or wedged between rocks and stuck in the debris. We even went to town and bought a tire repair kit in an attempt to patch up a hole in the shell of a very large tortoise, but he died anyway. When Banjo saw the dead tortoise lying outside beside our trailer he asked Bill, "What are you doing with that?" To which my brother somberly answered, "We're making soup", and yeah, Banjo freaked out.

BOOM! Mongo shot a running coyote with a small tortoise in its mouth, with that 30-06 of his. Then he and Bill went to shooting crows out of the air with their rifles, causing Banjo to haul-ass back inside his trailer and locking the door behind him. Then we loaded up, locked in the hubs, and headed up the canyon.

Looking at the rock walls of the canyon we realized that a full 5 to 6 feet of earth had washed out of the entire floor of the canyon and into the alluvial in the valley below. Every bush, shrub, old cabin, and Russian olive tree was gone. The canyon floor looked to have been swept clean and leveled by the torrid floodwaters. All that remained was rock and gravel. As we rounded the bend in the canyon, we prepared to see the worst. But no amount of preparation could ready us for what we saw.

A narrow 20 foot wide, 50 foot long, 5 foot tall "island" appeared before our bewildered eyes as we came around the bend in the canyon! Just to the left of the center of what was left of the canyon floor, was this little spit of land that the raging floodwaters had separated and gone around! And the most awesome part is, on top of this little and only patch of untouched ground sat all of our equipment! The International compressor truck, the bobcat, the head frame, the clamshell…everything! We all agreed that we were staring at a miracle. Almost completely beyond belief! There was no extra room to spare either. Our stuff was all there was room for on that little island of dirt. The edges of the island's embankment looked as if they had been cut with a knife; just 5 foot high shear walls, straight up and down, and the tires of the truck were less than 18 inches from the edge!

God had blatantly showed us, (and everybody else who came up Goler Canyon over the next couple of days) His amazing mercy and deliverance! I can almost grasp the intensity of how much Moses's mind must have been blown when the Lord parted the Red Sea in front of him. At the upstream end of the island it simply came to a point of gravel where the waters had parted. There was no rock or boulder or anything there that would even suggest a reason for the water to part and go around our equipment. It was, beyond doubt, all God!

Sometimes, thinking back in retrospect (20-20 hindsight), I have considered the similarities between my fifth grade teacher, Mrs. Dalby, showing me mercy that day because I showed mercy to that other boy on the way to the cafeteria, and how God obviously and miraculously showed me mercy in Goler Canyon when the flood came because, I believe, I showed Banjo mercy, as the Lord explained in Matthew 5:7. (See also the Bible study, "Our Words" in Appendix H) I believe in an all knowing, all-powerful, and ever present God. If that is true then I have no room in my heart for "coincidence". We reap what we sow. What we put out there in thoughts, words, and deeds, is what we get back, multiplied (2 Corinthians 9:6-8). For good or for evil (Luke 6:45). It was God's first law (Genesis 1:11) that pretty much all of the other spiritual laws are hinged on. It will always remain as a covenant with Creation itself (Genesis 8:22). So if your heart, words and actions are good and bless others, this is some of the best news you're ever gonna hear! You know what type of future is in store for you, based on your obedience and faith in God's covenant with us! If negativity, cursing, and living your life according to the world and the pursuit of self-gratification, and just plain doing what you know to be wrong, is your forte…well…it sucks to be you (Proverbs 15:10).

At least be big enough to take ownership of what you have brought into your life by your own thoughts, words, deeds and your general character. Don't blame it on others, and don't expect mercy if you have shown none to others (Luke 6:37-38). Jesus said it himself; *"Blessed are the merciful, for they shall obtain mercy"* (Matthew 5:7). But, thank God, Jesus is with us to help us orchestrate any and all needed changes we have to make in our lives and characters, accordingly, to remove the darkness we have brought into our own lives and bring us back up on to the path of life and light we were designed for. We don't have to stay in the pit!

Thank You, Lord! Hallelujah!

## CHAPTER 20

## Sorcery, Drugs, and Some Help Navigating the Road through These End Times

> *"Enter by the narrow gate; for wide is the gate and broad is the way that leads to destruction, and there are many who go in by it. Because narrow is the gate and difficult is the way which leads to life, and there are few who find it."* Matthew 7:13-14.

The group of investors financing the Goler Canyon Placer Mine were a conglomerate of doctors primarily out of Riverside, California. They had just paid us for sinking almost 35 feet of shaft through the sand and gravel floor of the canyon in an attempt to reach and sample the bedrock. We had fought for every inch of shaft we had sank and fought harder to keep it, and now it was gone. The water had caused the sides of the shaft to totally collapse and the remains of the hole itself was now filled with water. They wisely decided not to pay twice for the same shaft that they had already paid for once, and lost. That would have been very inefficient and foolish, so we understood completely when they decided it was "deep enough", and being men of integrity, they paid us off in full.

We borrowed the good doctor's Terex bulldozer from the mill site and cut ourselves a rough road down the canyon to get our equipment out, and we were looking forward to going back to Nevada. Besides, since the flood we had killed over a dozen Mohave Green Rattlesnakes in less than two days, apparently washed out and displaced from their dens and holes. It was kind of creepy going outside to pee at night and hearing them "buzz" around you in the darkness, and yeah, Green rattlesnakes are incredibly deadly. They can kill you and the anti-venom, in those days, could only be found in Riverside or Ridgecrest and both were too far from our location to be of any use, so if you get struck, you're probably gonna die. They do make beautiful hat bands though and I still have one on an old brown cowboy hat hanging in my basement.

Wait! I think I'm having an epiphany here! Snakes. In the Garden of Eden. Just go with me on this for a second. In Genesis chapter 1, in the beginning, we find God creating all things that exist in our world. Then on the sixth day God created man in His own image and gave him DOMINION over the fish of the sea, over the birds of the air, and over cattle (Adam – the first cowboy?), over all the earth and over every CREEPING THING THAT

CREEPS ON THE EARTH (verse 26). Then, in verse 28, God blessed them, and God said to them, *"Be fruitful and multiply; fill the earth and SUBDUE IT ;"* ( emphasis mine). Now this is just me, but I think what God was alluding to here, and trying to warn and instruct Adam about was this; SNAKE COMING! SUBDUE IT! Hmmmm... Maybe, or maybe not, but anyway... I think Jesse Duplantis preached on this one time...

We know more than had the road to the bottom of the canyon roughed in when the first vehicle to come bouncing up the trail to our washed out job site was this redheaded Irishman in a big ol' Cadillac. Wow... That's different...

Cornelius O' Flannery, O'Fleary, O'Something or Another, from County Cork, Ireland, was his name, and he seemed bigger than life (full of piss & vinegar) and almost always had laughter in his eyes. One of those people who, even if you disagreed with them on some things, you couldn't help yourself from liking them; and his laugh was contagious.

He was putting together this deal and that deal, and wanted to buy us a drink in town before we left for Nevada, to talk some "business". He was living in the "Whatever" Motel (because I can't remember the name of the place anymore) on Ridgecrest Boulevard, mostly because it came with a small restaurant/coffee shop, and most importantly, a bar. The air conditioner worked good in the bar and that's all we cared about, until a little while later, after a few drinks, and we stepped back outside into 121 degrees of shimmering heat. It almost dropped me! They all drank Irish whiskey, of course, but I had a couple of shots of Christian Brothers Brandy instead (no, I'm not trying to justify anything here). Cornelius or "Con" as he so aptly like to be called, "felt hurt" that I wouldn't join him for a whiskey, but whiskey and me have never been very compatible. In any event, getting back home to Nevada was a long ride in that International 1600 compressor truck, so we said our goodbyes, exchanged phone numbers and addresses, and home we went.

\*\*\*

And boy howdy, was it great to be back home with my wife and son. It was not so great being unemployed. Lori was modeling for Eve Lynn Productions in Reno as well as playing guitar and singing in a very popular bluegrass band. We hung out at a place called The Depression Delicatessen on fourth Street, with my cousins, and Aunt Ramona and my awesome uncle Jim Wright, who got us involved in black powder shoots and "rendezvous", which are Mountain Man clubs gathering for shooting and knife and tomahawk throwing competitions, the sharing of "Apple Pie" which is a homemade beverage made with Everclear (instant ticket to La La land), and days of fun filled camping and general comraderies.

Money was tight and jobs were scarce that year, and I was considering taking my camp trailer to eastern Nevada to look for work in one of the many gold mines starting up in Elko County.

It was fall of "82" when Phil Davis (The Unk) called me to stake 200 load mining claims in northern Elko County, at $100 per claim, and he paid in cash. Hot Diggity dog! And I didn't even care that the jobs for Unk always came with a bunch of preaching about "how much I needed Jesus". Little did I know at these times in my life, God was using uncle Phil to plant "seeds" (the Word of God – see Matthew 13:1-8, and 18-23) in my heart, because the Lord knew I would need them to survive later on in my life when I really messed everything up bad. And God "guarantees" His seeds to work! You need to know that. He promised it through His profit in Isaiah 55:10-11;

*"For as the rain comes down, and the snow from Heaven, and do not return there, but water the earth, and* make *it bring forth and bud, that it may give seed to the sower and bread to the eater,*

*So shall My word be that goes forth from My mouth; it shall not return to Me void, but it shall accomplish what I please, and it shall prosper in the thing for which I sent it".*

I honestly knew nothing about the Lord's "spiritual laws" back then, but Phil did. And he also knew that spiritual laws of Yahweh (God) cannot be broken... and that sadly, in many cases, they will break you, and that's where God begins His finest work – in a broken heart. It's "the deal" if you will, as Psalm 51 explains it, that put it all in perspective for me in later years when my time to be broken came about. King David wrote the prayer in Psalm 51 when he was broken, and I figured if it worked for him it would work for me, so I prayed it back to God, Who is no respecter of persons (Romans 2:11, acts 10:34), and it worked! It will work for anyone. Phil knew all of this, so regardless of how many times I played it off as "religious rhetoric, no big deal", the Unk just kept planting seeds in me, praying, and then just sitting back over the years and waiting to see the results that he knew would come, eventually.

Combined with the prayers of my parents, my wife, and later, my daughter, my salvation was inevitable. They never gave up on me and neither did God (Luke 18:1-7).

I know I'm sidetracked again from the story at hand, but if you have a child or someone close to you that is walking in darkness, DON'T EVER GIVE UP! There are specific scriptures you need to know and pray about, and pray on their behalf, some of which are listed under Appendix L, Prayers for My Kids. And you need to keep placing their names before God in your prayers, no matter how weary it becomes or what the circumstances look like; and know this, that it will always seem to get worse when you start praying for them. This is called "spiritual warfare" but God, with all his resources will fight for you and your loved ones just like he did for me, and a couple of million others that I know of!

"Well John, they didn't have to deal with drugs like heroin and meth way back when the Bible was written", you might be thinking, right? "You would think so, but no!" as Pee-Wee Herman says it.

In the Old Testament the Hebrew word "kesheph" is the word commonly translated into the English words "sorcery" and sometimes "witchcraft". In the New Testament the Greek word we see that translated into the words "sorcery" and "witchcraft", most commonly used figuratively and literally is the word "pharmakeia". Yes, that sounds familiar, doesn't it? It's where we get the word "medicine", or literally "pharmacy".

The most predominant and common definition in the Bible for sorcery (sorceries, sorceress, etc.), according to Strong's Concordance, which I highly recommend, is; 1) the use or the administering of drugs! Strong's also points out its connection in, 2) poisoning, and 3) tells us that the term sorcery (drugs) is often found in the biblical connection with idolatry and is also often fostered by it...wow! Furthermore, further usage of sorcery/witchcraft (i.e. drugs) is implemented in the deceptions and seductions of idolatry. Well, yeah... I can see that.

Idolatry defined is the worship of false gods. This includes the worship of mammon (money), sins and vices springing from idolatry, and basically, anything that we deem more important than God. What is more important to you than God right now? Hmmm.

How many people can you think of, right off the top of your head that have placed self-gratification before God? They just made themselves their own god (idol). How many do you know have placed money in a more important position than their Heavenly Father? Money has become their idol or false god. Okay, try this one; how many people have placed drugs and/or alcohol before their job, family, kids, and their self-respect, and literally lost everything let alone placed their addictions before God? Yes, we can clearly see the correlation between drugs and idolatry blatantly played out in the lives all around us, and tragically, often in our own lives as well.

Isaiah 47:9-15 and Isaiah 57:1-13 are descriptive examples of the ramifications of drugs (sorcery) in Scripture. Continuing on in Isaiah 57:14-20 God shares His provision and promise for the backslider, as does Job 22:21-30. I pray these scriptures back to God on behalf of the people that I love, including my son, who are in a rerun cycle of addiction and deliverance. God clearly did not deliver you and lift you up out of the "pit" just so you could return to what put you there in the first place. That's backsliding. So, just how many times do you think the Lord should deliver us from something, over and over and over?

Painfully explained by the Apostle Paul in 1 Corinthians 10:19-22, the Bible says, *"What am I saying then? That an idol is anything, or what is offered to idols is anything? Rather, that the things that the Gentiles (us) sacrifice they sacrifice to demons and not to God, and I do not want you to have fellowship with demons. You cannot drink the cup of the Lord and the cup of demons; you cannot partake of the Lord's Table and of the table of demons. Or do we provoke the Lord to jealousy? Are we stronger than He?"*

It grieves my heart to say this, but so many of us have sacrificed everything for nothing, as this verse says. What we have sacrificed, friends, job, careers, family...our children...to our idols of self, drugs, alcohol, whatever...has been for nothing. And what's even worse is that we have opened doors into our lives to allow (yes, allow!) demonic activity. Think not? Just turn on the news, or if you are reading this while incarcerated all you have to do is look around the room to be a first-hand eyewitness. So many have done this in this last generation that men of God like Neil T Anderson have devoted their lives to the deliverance and salvation of a world of people who have gone down this road, opened the doors to their lives to allow darkness and demonic activity in, and now, cannot throw them out or reclose the doors again. Anderson's books, Victory over the Darkness, and the Bondage Breaker have helped tens of thousands regain their freedom in Christ.

So in an attempt to satisfy the desires of our "flesh" we are willing to sacrifice everything and everyone, because, well, we want what we want. We are that selfish. We become our own god and stop at nothing to appease our desires. Isn't that the truth? Nothing matters more than what we want. And I can't even begin to touch on the pain and anguish we have caused the ones we love the most, because my heart can no longer bear it.

That's why we must change direction. It's never too late. Get some help. Cry out to God and tell Him that you can't do it alone, and He will send his laborers as promised (Matthew 9:38). The battle is for your mind, but I believe our flesh determines the time, place and conditions of the battles. Many have proven that we can win these battles but we must bring our flesh into submission and under control instead of letting our flesh call the shots and ruin our lives. Repentance means "change your way of thinking" about sinful habits and "turn away from" them.

You need to know up front that the hardest battles you're ever going to face in your life are not going to be with other people, enemies, or even the devil. The hardest victories to obtain will be in your daily battle with your old nature…your flesh. Every victory is a result of the time you privately spend with God. Jesus told us that, "Apart from Me you can do nothing" (John 15:5) and our many defeats are the result of our forgetting this. Never fight alone. Spend time in prayer and worship before the battle and you will be good to go.

Galatians 5:19-21 proclaims the sobering truth; *"Now the works of the flesh are evident, which are; adultery, fornication, uncleanliness, lewdness, idolatry, sorcery, hatred, contentions, jealousies, outbursts of wrath, selfish ambitions, dissensions, heresies, envy, murders, drunkenness, rivalries, and the like; of which I tell you beforehand, just as I also told you in time past, that those who practice such things will not inherit the kingdom of God".*

Revelation 9:21 confirms this in the details of the great tribulation, whereas, *"And they did not repent of their murders or their sorceries or their sexual immorality or their thefts".*

Thankfully, the Bible also provides our cure as stated in Galatians 5:16 *"I say then; walk in the Spirit, and you shall not fulfill the lust of the flesh".*

And I love Isaiah 55:6-7; *"seek the Lord while He may be found, call upon Him while He is near. Let the wicked forsake his way, and the unrighteous man his thoughts; let him return to the Lord, and He will have mercy on him, and to our God, for He will abundantly pardon".*

Back in the last century, many Bible scholars would read end time prophecies in bewilderment, wondering how this or that prophecy could possibly ever come to pass. We read prophecies how children would turn on their parents and vice versa, and think "a good ass whoopin' would cure that". Then came meth. And in epidemic proportions it has swept the nation. This is just me talking, but, oh my God, the uncontrolled hate and rage coming out of the mouths of our kids and adults alike is bone chilling.

From all I have seen, experienced, and prayerfully studied in the Holy Bible I am convinced that the conscience is a vital tool that the Holy Spirit uses to communicate to every person. When we disobey the warnings God has given us in His Word and we use the things of this world, such as drugs, alcohol, etc. to alter our minds from the God created state that He made us in, I am convinced that we cut off all communication with God. He can no longer lead us, guide us or warn us. We are, in this drug or alcohol induced state of mind, at the sole mercy of the Prince of Darkness who temporarily (see "lake of fire burning with brimstone" in Revelation 19:19-20! Baahahaha!) now rules this world, and let me tell you my friend, there is no mercy in him. He comes only to kill, steal and destroy (John 10:10). And yeah, marijuana and peyote are weeds, not herbs. They are of the world and a direct result of the curse on the land (see Genesis 3).

And without being in the Word we have no spiritual defense, armor, or most importantly no weapon or sword, as outlined in Ephesians 6:10-18. As the Word is God's primary way of talking to us, we are surely cut off from Him without it, and are now easy prey for the devil.

So, *"Be sober, be vigilant; because your adversary the devil walks about like a roaring lion, seeking whom he may devour. Resist him steadfast in the faith..."* 1 Peter 5:8-9. No Word – no faith – no resistance. *"Faith comes by hearing, and hearing by the Word of God".* Romans *10:17.* Get in the Word!

The incredibly fantastic news is this; *"We know that whoever is born of God does not sin; but he who has been born of God keeps himself, and the evil one cannot touch him"* 1 John 5:18. We need to stop worshiping our own flesh and discipline it. It's no easy thing but it's the only way to close the doors that are allowing self-destruction and tragedy to continually reoccur in our lives. It's time to get rid of the trash and replace it with the good things of God that He intended for us. When we are no longer a slave to our flesh and we are in submission to God through faith in His Son and obedience to His Word, I promise you, we will then know what true freedom really is.

What's more, as this change occurs we will begin to produce specific characteristics that will soon become obvious to others around us, giving hope to many like us and cause them to want what we have! Seriously. And we can tell them where and from Whom we got it.

Peace is very contagious and that's just one of the characteristics we will produce in our lives when we follow the "owner's manual to our souls", the Bible's instructions. Remember that Scripture from Galatians 5? Well that's not all it says; Galatians 5:22-25 goes on to teach us, *"but the fruit of the Spirit is love, joy, peace, long-suffering, kindness, goodness, faithfulness, gentleness, and self-control. Against such there is no law. And those who are Christ's have crucified the flesh with its passions and desires. If we live by the Spirit, let us also walk in the Spirit."*

When we make our flesh "shut up" then, once again, the voice of the Holy Spirit becomes discernable above the noise of the world around us, and as our conscience becomes more and more susceptible to God's leading through the Holy Spirit, an amazing thing happens. The world's opinion on what's right and wrong becomes exposed to the Truth and begins to crumble along with our worldly way of thinking. What's right and wrong becomes much more clearly defined and that so-called "gray line" or questionable area in between them becomes very small. As we begin to see things clearly in the light of what is truly good and evil, we immediately find ourselves avoiding traps and wrecks that have devastated our lives in the past.

What's even more amazing as this transformation takes place is how we begin to be the father or mother that God created us to be. We become the sons and daughters we were meant to be. We now are allowing our loving Heavenly Father to mold us into the man or woman of God that He intended us to be! We actually become "blessings" to those we love. No more trashing our lives to appease our flesh and trying to be who the world wants us to be. What a relief, don't you think? Or, I suppose, we can go a few more rounds in life doing things "our way". Not to pry, but, how's that been working for you so far? I can honestly tell you, to borrow the cliché; I have never loved, lived, or laughed with such genuine intensity as I do now that Christ is behind the wheel in my life.

I love the saying that BIBLE Stands for Basic Instructions Before Leaving Earth. The late Miles Munroe made an awesome analogy that I could easily relate to as I have survived 13 vehicular total-outs in the dark desert nights of Nevada. All of them were high-speed (well over 90 mph) rollovers, except four that were end over end, and one where Stevie and I launched my 1970 Nova 67 feet in the air at over 110 mph, just outside of Tonopah. Almost all of them involved alcohol and a cow. Mostly, we would start drinking at the bar in Warm Springs, and then our flesh would start screaming "let's go to town and find some chicks". Middle of the night – 50 miles through cow and horse infested desert highway to the nearest town (all open range back then), and we were pretty much drunk…or whatever. And we did it over and over – literally, miracle after miracle. That's clearly deemed as "stuck on stupid", yet only God could save me so many times. But of course, I was an "invincible genius" – God bless you, A.V.Munoz for coining that phrase!

So Miles tells it something like this;

You go to the local car dealer and you buy a brand-new car. It runs good and everything is going great as you head out onto the freeway at full speed. Then, without warning, it begins to chug-a-lug, and the engine goes into spit and sputter mode, invoking memories of "Chitty Chitty Bang Bang" (of Mary Poppins fame) reruns in your mind. The engine finally just dies as you drift to a stop along the side of the road. You try turning the ignition key…nothing. "Oh, I can fix it myself" you proudly proclaim. You thump on the dashboard, fiddle with the radio, and then get out and kicked the tires, but nothing helps. Other cars are just a flash going by at 75 mph, but you try hollering to them anyway as they speed by you without even slowing down; "What's wrong with my car? Hey, what's wrong with my car?" you yell into the wind and noise of the other cars as they streak past you. That doesn't work, apparently. Oh yeah, no cell phone service either, so no "AAA", or calling the dealer for help.

Finally it occurs to you? What about the Owner's Manual in the glove compartment? It is all about your car! If anything goes wrong with your car it will be covered in the troubleshooting section of the Owner's Manual, right? Why? Because the Owner's Manual was written about your car by the Manufacturer; the One who created your car. The Manufacturer knows more about your car than anybody else. The Manufacturer knows every nut and bolt, accessory, piston rhythm, and hick up in your car because He created it. And what's more, no matter what happens, whether an internal malfunction, driver error, or even an accident, He can fix it! Asking other cars how to fix themselves, or you and your car, seems very foolish, now doesn't it? Often, according to the Owner's Manual that was written by the Creator of the automobile you're driving, the solution is usually a simple matter of hitting a breaker switch, a reset button or changing a blown fuse.

Sometimes the cure is often just taking a smoother, less dangerous road, with less bumps and potholes to rattle your car apart.

The more you read the Owner's Manual the better the vehicle's guidance system works, and you begin to avoid most road hazards as you start your journey over, once again, so keep reading it daily, by all means! Or, of course, you can choose to just throw it back into the glove compartment and forget about it until the next wreck or breakdown occurs, and redo this whole process over and over again, needlessly.

But the Manufacturer has provided the information we need, in the Owner's Manual, to fix the problems and we are off and running once again. Not only that but we now know much better how to properly drive or operate the car in the manner in which it was intended, and we can see the road hazards and warning signs much clearer now that the windshield wipers and washer are clearing the "bugs" of the world off of our windshield. We continue down the road much more cautiously and with so much less drama! And as an added surprise we find that people we love and care about feel much more comfortable riding with us! Thank You, Manufacturer!

I know you get this, but I'll point it out anyway; the car is your life, the Owner's Manual is the Bible, and that Manufacturer is God our Creator and our Heavenly Father, and you can fill in the rest.

Also worth mentioning, I have found through my experience that sometimes the car has to go into "the shop" for repairs and a tune-up. This could be a multitude of different things from Christian retreats, counseling, or group therapy, to the hospital, homeless shelters, rehab facilities, and incarceration. All these things have the ability to expedite our repairs and get us back on the right road, if we use them wisely, and never let them make us bitter. In these situations it's always good to ask the Manufacturer, "What needs fixed so badly that I am here? "and "how do I help You fix it?" When I was in the shop, I simply cried out "Fix me. Lord... Please". I think anything less might possibly delay our getting back out onto the road.

Well, let's go cruising... And while we're at it, don't pass up an opportunity to tell other drivers about the Owner's Manual, and how well it worked for us.

*"And do not be conformed to this world, but be transformed by the renewing of your mind, that you may prove what is the good and acceptable and perfect will of God"*, Romans 12:2.

*"For though we walk in the flesh, we do not war according to the flesh. For the weapons of our warfare are not carnal but mighty in God for the pulling down of strongholds, casting down arguments and every high thing that exalts itself against the knowledge of God, bringing every thought into captivity to the obedience of Christ..."2 Corinthians 10:3-5.*

## CHAPTER 21

## The Lure of Mohave Gold

*"If I have made gold my hope, or said to fine gold, 'you are my confidence'... This also would be an iniquity deserving of judgment, for I would have denied God who is above".* Job 31:24, 28

My cousin Jeff and I barely finished a staking job for Unk and got out of the high country of northern Elko County just before the first real heavy snow falls arrived. Mostly because it was Chukar and Sagehen season and the hunting was beyond phenomenal. My cousin Jeff taught me to eat vinegar on my fried eggs every morning at breakfast... I just thought I'd throw that in here somewhere, because I miss him.

When we got back to Reno we were pretty much set for the winter, financially. Lori said some Irish guy named Con had called several times looking for me. I called him back and within a few days he came to Reno to offer me a business proposition. He said we would be partners on a small gold recovery system that he wanted to build, and until it started making money, he would pay all my bills and expenses. He had a small trommel, a Gardner Denver jig, and a few other pieces of equipment to get us started and said that good gold properties were "dime a dozen" in the Mohave Desert. We just had to find a place to set up the test mill in the Randsburg area.

At any time now I was expecting him to pull the telltale 'vial of gold nuggets' out of his pocket to wave in front of me like a carrot in front of a donkey. That's usually the traditional BS play most "promoters" use when trying to "set the hook" in potential "investors/partners" (suckers, more likely), and this wasn't my first rodeo. I waited and waited, then finally I got impatient and just out and out ask him to his face, "Isn't this the part where you pull out a vial of gold and wave it like a hypnotist's watch in front of my face?" The smile left his face and he leaned back in his chair and studied me for a minute. Then he said, "Everyone I ever saw who pulled a vial of gold out of their pocket turned out to be full of BS". Well, we got that in common, I thought. "I'm not here to BS you, I'm here to see if you will partner up with me and make a lot of money".

Between the sincerity in his voice and that damn twinkle in his Irish eyes, I agreed to give it a go for a couple of months and see how it went. Con was smiling again, but Lori wasn't. And the truth is, she was right to be angry with me. The bills were paid up through winter and there was no excuse for running off on another "get rich quick" adventure searching for gold. I was an adrenaline junkie who was terrified of being bored all winter. How selfish is that?

I can't remember a time in my life when I wasn't looking or dreaming of treasure, in whatever form. And those that I have found have always wound up in a box somewhere or a safety deposit box or more likely, sold to finance my treasure hunting equipment and my next adventure. Sad to say, even at the time of this writing, if the opportunity presented itself for another adventure with even the slightest likelihood of successful treasure hunting as an endpoint, I would probably find some twisted way to make lame excuses, justify (i.e. Isaiah 45:3) leaving my life on hold, abandoning my responsibilities, and taking out on another probable wild goose chase… God forgive me. It's the lure of treasure; the hunting and possibility of actually discovering it that calls to me. Once found, it holds little or no more interest to me, be it gold, jewels, Spanish conquistador treasure, lost or hidden robbery caches, sunken shipwrecks, Knights Templar Silver, or buried valuables of any type or circumstance. As Jones said it, "The best days are those spent out in the middle of nowhere, treasure hunting… Nothing better than that." Yes, I confess, these same words whisper in my own heart as well. Especially in later years when my son, William, got old enough to do most of the digging! I will always cherish the days I spent with him in the mountains of central Nevada, digging for treasures as well as all the times I spent with my entire family prospecting and treasure hunting in the ghost towns and high desert mountains of Nevada.

Even when we dug up several old strong boxes, cast-iron kettles, and old rotting wooden chests, only to open them and stare into an empty void where treasure had once been, what makes it all worth it is that they were there to share it with me. Talk about "the thrill of victory and the agony of defeat" as they say, let me tell you; actually finding a buried strong box makes it impossible to breathe because your heart is pounding so hard in your throat. Then you pry open the lid only to stare into an empty box…there are no words to describe the heart pounding thrill that we endured.

The times that I left my family behind and took off to seek my fortune, most of which were not glorious at all, have caused me much regret for making the many poor decisions that left my loved ones hanging in limbo while waiting for me to come home again and usually with me showing up empty-handed, worn ragged and broke. Whether I was successful or not, I cannot buy back the time I lost with them or the damage I did to our relationships. The victories of the finds that I did make, whether large or small, were hollow and empty if my family wasn't there to rejoice with me. Believe me, being alone, even with treasure, and not having your loved ones present to share the experience with has proven itself to be heartbreaking. Yes, sometimes we sacrifice everything for nothing.

It's what addiction is all about. So many times I found myself out in the middle of nowhere and due to a sudden and unforeseen change in circumstances, found myself facing the reality that I may not make it back to my family "this time". Yet God would have mercy on me and allow me to survive, only to run right back out into a similar situation the first chance I got.

We really need to take time each day to thank God that His Son, Jesus, meets us right where we are, even in our addictions, and we really need to thank Him that He doesn't leave us there. And then, on top of that, the Lord turns the twisted wreckage of our lives into a reflection of the Love of Christ, to show others the way out! We are literally, individual treasure maps, if you will, to show others the way to the greatest treasure of all…HIM! Jesus! You and I are God's treasure maps in progress! Now if that's not worthy of praise and worship, what is?

When you think about it, within the story of each of our lives we hold a map that can and will lead others. The sobering truth is that our maps can lead others to only one of two destinations; Heaven or hell. To change our maps, we change our course and thankfully, it's never too late to change our courses. And someone is always watching us as we go, whether we realize it or not; a child, a friend or relative, a coworker, neighbor or cellmate.

I believe that Heaven is obviously the most magnificent homecoming party imaginable. All who knew us, friends, family and loved ones will be there to meet us, including all who gained direction from our "maps". And what a joyous celebration it will be! (Luke 15)

On the other hand, the only thing more devastating than finding yourself in hell for all eternity is the horror that will consume you when you realize that a son or daughter, or a loved one or friend is also there because they followed you. You lead the way.

So, is your map clearly readable? Is it accurate? Where does your map lead? Will it guide those who are watching toward their Heavenly destination or will it cause them to stumble and fall?

We have been warned by the Lord Jesus Himself, *"But whoever causes one of these little ones who believe in Me to stumble, it would be better for him if a millstone were hung around his neck, and he were thrown into the sea".* Mark 9:42.

I can't help but wonder about leaders, songwriters, music icons, Hollywood movie stars, filmmakers, teachers, and others who promote an ungodly agenda. These professed "role models" can easily destroy the faith of their audiences. And according to the Son of God, they will be held highly accountable.

***

I moved into my room at the "Whatever" Motel on Ridgecrest Boulevard, and it wasn't much. A box with a bed and toilet was about it, but the air conditioner worked, and it's about all that I required anyway. It was always hot, it seemed, in the Mohave Desert

The first thing we did was put the proverbial cart ahead of the horse, and went out looking at gold properties. True to his word, Con showed me several good prospects and it seemed everybody had one. Why weren't they mining and getting rich then? Simple. No water. It takes a lot of water to run even a small gravity placer recovery system if you're going to seriously mine. Otherwise you can just "play around" or promote like everyone else. The Yellow Aster Mine had almost all of the water wells in the area tied up.

One well that they didn't have under their thumb literally sold water by the gallon at a price that put profitable placer mining out of reach. Every place else on earth seem to live by the "golden rule of mining", which is "he who has the gold, makes the rules". Not so in the Mohave. We quickly learned that here, "he who has the water makes the rules". And one evening, in a barely alive, semi-ghost town called Red Mountain, in the Silver Dollar Saloon (nope! I kid you not!), we met the man who makes the rules.

His name was Bond…Fred Bond.

Fred was fairly small in stature but gigantic in heart, and he loved a good joke or a good story. And Con could tell both. It did not take me long, by just watching and listening, to ascertain the fact that, not only was Fred very wise, but he was also a man of integrity. I also perceived that he had a "line", so to speak, that you don't cross. I liked him from the get-go.

A few miles east of Red Mountain, down in the valley by the China Lake Testing Range, Fred had a mill site, including a mill building, shop and his living quarters…and Fred also had a lovely, producing water well.

As the evening turned late Fred sat there listening to my partner go on and on. He looked straight ahead, sipping his whiskey, with just a hint of a smile at the corners of his mouth. Once in a while he would shift his gaze over to me for a moment, and then back straight ahead without changing his expression at all. I was sure that he had heard all of this before, probably 1000 times over. He was obviously more than content to sell his water by the truck load and had no need of anyone's offer of a "big deal".

Eventually, Fred gathered up his money from the table and put it in his pocket, leaving a few bucks for a tip. He purposefully enjoyed sipping down the last of his whiskey and set the glass down on the table. I could almost feel the desperation in the Irishman's eyes. What else was there that he could say to convince Fred to let us on to his mill site and use his water? We definitely didn't have the money to pay our way into Fred's mill, even if Fred would let us. And it seemed obvious that he wasn't considering it as an option, for any price. Then, he did an odd thing; he leaned forward toward me, put his elbows on the table, looked right in my face and asked, "Well John, what do you think of all this?"

I looked him right back in his eyes and said, "I think Con's plan to set up a 100 ton per day test mill is a good one, and I've come here to help him build it and give it a go. All I can guarantee to you, Fred, is that I will do my very best to make it pay. If it does, good… If it don't, I'll go back home to my family with my tail between my legs. But I promise you this; that if it doesn't work, it won't be because I didn't give it my very best shot".

Without moving his gaze from my face he slowly leaned back in his chair. After a long moment he pushed back his chair and stood up to leave. He looked over at Con and said, "I would like to invite you to my place for dessert tomorrow evening. If you can find your way to the mill, I will look for you about sundown".

"Absolutely! We'll be there" said Con, grinning from ear to ear. "Thank you, Fred. We'll see you then", he finished. Fred turned to go, then in an apparent afterthought, he turned back to Con and said, "And bring a bottle of Black Velvet with you... Don't forget". Con laughed and agreed to the terms.

Fred was born back in Bluford, Illinois in 1921 and came to Red Mountain in 1967, and he was a Marine Corps veteran. He knew what honor was. You have no idea how rare that is in the gold mining business these days. Throughout our time together he always reiterated to me the vital importance of teaching my kids the 10 Commandments and getting them the best education possible. He was a plumber by trade and had owned his own company in Illinois. As we looked around the mill the next evening, he verified that by saying, "Not too bad for a plumber in the Mohave Desert, don't you think, boys?" And he was right. The centerpiece in his mill was a long, hand built concentrating table, made by a master craftsman in Johannesburg by the name of Bud Gamble. I had experience with Wilfley (not so good) and Diester (excellent) concentrating tables, but this was by far the most precision and well-balanced gold concentrating/separation table I had ever seen, or for that matter, have ever seen to this day. In the days to come I would watch for hours as gold nuggets, as well as fine flour gold, would separate its self from the black sands and amazingly seemed to stand up and walk itself across the riffles and drop themselves into a gold pan or Mason jar.

Bud told me it was all about the balance and fine tuning the exact movement of the table itself to match the signature of the ore you were running. I never forgot that and used it to my advantage, many years later, while successfully fine-tuning Diester Triple-decks and main con tables, to match complex ores, in Utah and Nevada.

As twilight settled in we sat down at Fred's kitchen table where we were served "Fred's finest", as he put it, cherry cheesecake. Sober this time, Con and Fred discussed the plan to build a 10 ton an hour placer mill here at Fred's place. Con explained that we had already spoken with several claim holders who, although they did not have water to put their own placer claims into production, would gladly pay us to run a minimum 100 ton bulk ore test through our little mill, so they could "establish their value". More like prove to their investors that their projects were worthwhile, not to mention, worth the continual funding necessary until they could get water and a mill of their own.

We agreed on an equal share partnership of a three way split. As business concluded Fred cleared off the table, brought three short glasses, and set the quart of Black Velvet whiskey in the middle of the table. "And here's the final condition of our agreement, gentlemen", he stated matter-of-factly as he poured our glasses full. "You will pay me, for the use of my water, one bottle of Black Velvet every day. No whiskey, no water. If you forget a day, the next day's payment is doubled. Agreed?"

"Agreed!" we both said in harmony. We were finally in business, and I was already dreading it. I hated whiskey…always will.

## CHAPTER 22

## The High Cost of Gold Fever

*"How much better to get wisdom than gold! And to get understanding is to be chosen rather than silver"* Proverbs 16:16

A lot of the equipment Con had was in the Reno area so I got to go home several times that month and see my wife and son. My always being away from them was causing extreme stress on our relationship. To make things worse, one night I was coming home through a snowstorm near Bridgeport, California and hit a deer with my pickup. The corner of my steel mine rail bumper caught the deer squarely in the side of the head, killing it instantly without damaging the rest of the meat or my truck (not that I am trying to justify anything here, either). To avoid being seen by approaching traffic, I quickly stuffed that deer behind the bench seat in my Chevy and resumed my journey. Just north of Bridgeport I got pulled over for going too fast on the ice. As the officer tore my citation out of his book and handed it to me through my open window, he just froze for a second, staring at the hooves of the deer sticking up above the back of the seat, behind my head. He then asked, "Someone reported a pickup hitting a deer south of town… Was that you?"

"Yes, sir", I answered, and before he could say more I told him, "I just couldn't see wasting it when I have a family to feed".

"You gonna slow down on the ice, now?" He asked.

"I sure am, sir", was my immediate response. Then, to my amazement he walked back to his car and drove away!

At 1:30 AM I arrived home in Reno, and it was only 5° above zero. I drug that deer into the kitchen, spread an old tarp on the floor, and without even kissing my wife hello, proceeded to gut the thing on the kitchen floor. What a moron I was. How my marriage survived this, let alone the first 20 years, is living proof that there is a God Who does miracles in people's hearts. She should have thrown me out, and God knows I would have deserved it. I think God also knew that I would never have made it this far through life without her. Even so, she kept trying to convince me to stay home and be a father and a husband, but I had already convinced myself that "I was doing all of this for my family", and wasn't having any of it.

The one person we cannot lie to his God. The one person we lie to the most is ourselves. Besides, in the Mohave I was fast becoming a "big shot" mining man. With the plant almost up and running, word was traveling fast that there was a mill that miners and claim owners could bulk ship a hundred tons to and have it ran in two day's for the cost of $1000, and we already had ore trucks rolling in, stockpiling material.

After fine-tuning our small mill we started running our first customers material and had it finished up in a day and a half. We cleaned out the primary sluice box between the trommel and the jig, cleaned out the jig itself, and drained and cleaned the fines out of the Knelson bowl. These concentrates were then run over Bud Gambles main concentrating table inside of the mill, which separated most all of the gold from the "mids" or final concentrate. Then, by weighing the gold and assaying the left over mids, and assaying a "head ore" (the material before it is processed), the value of the ore per ton can be established, as well as the recovery rate of the gravity milling process as applied to the customers particular ore that is being evaluated.

And our small mill system worked flawlessly. Our recovery rate was always in the high 80 to 95% area with simple placer (free) gold.

After the conclusion of our milling services, the results, the concentrates and the gold were given to our customers, the machinery was thoroughly cleaned out as not to contaminate the next batch of material, and we did it all over again; and we made pretty good money. It was a lot of work in extreme heat but my partners were both very hard workers as was I. After "clean-up" at the end of each day, weary and tired, we would make our way to Fred's kitchen table and the ever waiting bottle of Black Velvet. I can't remember how many nights I drove Con and I to Ridgecrest and upon arriving couldn't remember any of the one hour drive it took to get there. "Even after I limited myself to" just one", I would often "come to" as I was running off of the road and hitting road markers. As I was so exhausted from the day's work anyway, even adding one small drink to our drive home became deadly.

Then Dr. Johnson and the people from Riverside approached us to run two, 100 ton ore shipments through our mill, while they were still having difficulty getting their mill and mining project into operation. The people responsible for building and putting their 100 ton per hour plant into production had encountered many setbacks and "unforeseen" issues, resulting in the timetable for completion of the project being pushed farther and farther into the future. They were now almost a year behind schedule. They had also reiterated several times, to the group of investors, that the best recovery rate they could hope for would be in the 55 to 65% range, for various (whatever) reasons. All told, this didn't set too well with the group who had already invested an awful lot of money with nothing to show for it up to this point.

So they were ecstatic when we ran their material from Goler Canyon and, at the end of both runs, handed them several ounces of gold at a 89% recovery rate. Even though Banjo and Jesse Junior were present for the entire procedure, they falsely accused Con of "salting" (secretly adding gold into the concentrates) to produce such a positive, let alone prosperous, result. For "blaspheming" our integrity, I felt it necessary that we needed to "rebuke" them (kick their asses) and make them recant all statements made by them that were questionable to our honor. Fred would not allow it, and Con just laughed in their faces and told them "it is what it is". I couldn't begin to understand what Con thought was so funny, until two days later, when he announced that we were "taking over" the Goler Mine Operation on behalf of Doc Johnson and his fellow investors. He told them to give us 30 days to get the plant into operation and we would see who was telling the truth.

Even though we would still haul our concentrates to Fred's mill to do final processing, I was still sad to leave his place, as I was now very fond of him. However, I was elated not to be partaking of our nightly Black Velvet road trip to town anymore, even though when referring to his beloved Black Velvet, he would consistently say "I don't know how they make it so good and sell it so cheap". And besides all that, it presented the opportunity to get out of the motel and bar in Ridgecrest, as I convinced Con and Doc Johnson that a watchman was needed to stay on the mine site. I went to Reno and got my camp trailer, found some high ground to park it on along the canyon wall, and finally got myself back out into the mountains where I belong.

So we worked sun up to sunset building the plant and laying 2 ½ miles of 4 inch aluminum pipe from the well head down at Banjo's place on the highway, all the way up Goler Canyon, to the cement water reservoir above the plant. It was so hot that if you touched the pipe with your bare hands it would raise an instant blister. At one point, a 20 foot section of pipe fell off of the truck and broke my right hand, between my wrist and thumb. Because I had no insurance, the hospital in Ridgecrest would not treat me, even though I offered to pay cash. When Doc Johnson heard about it he drove all the way up from Riverside to make sure the bone was aligned properly and to splint it correctly, God bless him, as he proved himself to be a man of high integrity.

In the evenings, when the workday was done and the canyon filled with cool evening shadows, I would sample and pan my way up and down the sides of the canyon as well as the small ravines that drained into it. At one point I began picking up very tiny pieces of gold, that were very sharp and course, for lack of a better analogy. They were not rounded and smoothed down as was typical of the common gold particles normally found in the canyon floor. These particular pieces had not been worn down and smoothed due to "travel" or their movement caused by erosion and water over many years, wearing down their natural roughness. That meant that the gold had not traveled very far from its original source, or vein deposit. I continued panning my way up past the mill that we were building until eventually, the course nuggets I was following just stopped. They disappeared, and I could no longer find them in with the typical worn and rounded gold particles commonly found in the canyon floor material. So I went back to the last placed I had seen them, and started working my way up along a ravine near a Y in the canyon. The regularity of finding the course gold in my pan increased as I worked my way higher up the ravine. Then about 150 feet above the canyon floor, they vanished.

I examined several huge rock outcrops and cliffs to the left of the ravine, and satisfied that the gold had not originated from that direction, moved on to the brush and cactus covered area on the right hand side of the ravine, directly across from where I had last successfully panned the gold. There was much more "overburden" (dirt covering the outcrops) on this side and the going was much slower, as I had to dig test holes deeper into the hillside as I went. I persistently continued to dig and sample for several evenings without revealing to anyone what I was doing. Eventually I dug down into a greenish-brown decomposing rock ledge that held the source of the gold. The gold from the ledge was "jewelry quality" as it had not "traveled" or been moved at all, thus still retaining its original rough or "sharp" form with no signs of smoothing or wearing down whatsoever. It was really beautiful gold! Specimen quality!

How much of it there was, I had no idea. The plan had always been to try and reach bedrock in the bottom of the canyon floor, where thousands of years of gold had been accumulating, as the canyon flooded and redeposited more gold every year. And every year the canyon flashed flooded, which literally erased every excavation attempt to reach the gold at the bedrock level. So every year, you started over.

We'll see how well that goes, I thought, as I covered up all of my test holes and brushed out my tracks to eliminate any evidence of my being on the hillside at all. (P.S. this is how lost mines and lost treasures are born, by the way!)

(P.P.S. I just realized that I may actually be part of the lost treasure hunting addiction problem that is sweeping the land in epic proportions – how sad – too bad – my bad)

So far, I had been thrown just enough bones to keep me going and to barely cover our bills. They promised to get caught up with what they owed me as soon as the plant was running. If I hadn't have known for a fact that the gold was actually here, I would have "folded my hand" and gone home a few months ago. Besides, taking over the Goler project from the previous contractors had gone into "physical mode" on two different occasions so far, and when you have to literally fight for something, you just don't throw it down and walk away from it, right? And just a note of advice; when there is visible "free gold" present in your operation, you always sleep with your pistols. "Gold fever" is not a joke or a fairytale as Hollywood would like you to believe. It's a very real disease, like alcoholism or drug abuse, that affects even the "good guys", much less the unscrupulous men and women that make up the majority of the "get rich quick" gold seekers of this age.

When they see it with their eyes, they don't forget it. They go home or wherever and think about it. They remember its luster and how heavy its substance felt in their hands. There are however, a few, but rare, actual men of honor out there that will refuse to allow the human lust of gold to overpower their morals, values, and their integrity... but, in my half a century of experience, as I've said, they are very rare. As most people continue to think about the gold they have seen and held, it's not long it seems, before they begin to think really stupid thoughts. Almost every profitable placer or free (visible) gold mine that I have ever seen go into production, failed. Not because of running out of ore, flash floods, cave-ins, price drop, government "intervention", or anything of the normal situations responsible for a mine closure commonly found in the rest of the mining industry. What almost always closes a mining project where visible gold is present, is predominantly, gold fever that has perpetuated into greed, with lawsuits, litigation, and cease and desist orders soon following. The lawyers get rich, often making more in legal fees than the mine property would ever produce, and the property itself is tied up in litigation until no one even cares anymore. Years and years later, when it does come free of the court system, there is usually millions of dollars in fees, fines, restitution, and back taxes that must be satisfied before any consideration of reopening the mine can be spoken of. Now nobody can afford to mine it because there is too much owed against it.

Assayers are said to be the number one "mine killers" in the land because, for us prospectors, they reveal what we believe to be rich mineable ore that is nothing short of "the motherlode" quality, into the "leaverite" (leave her right where you found it because it's just a worthless rock), or the "fool's gold" (pyrite) that it truly is. If that be the case, then Gold Fever has to be the number one killer of existing Free Gold (where visible gold is present) mines, and is without question, more commonly understood when mentally interpreted as greed to about the $97^{th}$ power. Sadly, most of the true "high-grade" gold projects I have ever seen or been a part of, folded up because the so-called "partners" and their accountants spent more time counting everybody else's money instead of their own, and instead of being grateful for their share, spent way too much time trying to figure out how to get a bigger piece of everybody else's share. The saddest of all is the fact that all of these mines where I have witnessed this ugly phenomenon take place had the ability to produce enough gold to make them all wealthy, had they not succumbed to greed.

That's why gold fever, to me, is a cancerous disease. When the people at the top start fighting over the gold, the working miners and their families like mine suffers through needless layoffs, and unemployment as the result.

As always, when we succumb to the wants of our flesh, we inevitably sacrifice everything for nothing again, and the ripple effect usually hurts many others around us, as well. After a while the words "I'm sorry" become hollow and numbing, and forgiveness becomes more difficult as our hearts get a little harder each time, until bitterness takes up permanent residence within us.

*"Guard your heart above all else, for it determines the course of your life"* Proverbs 4:23 (NLT).

Bitterness... If we don't take our hurts to God in prayer daily, to receive our healing, it will spread poison throughout our lives if left unchecked. Are you bitter? Tell God why. Tell Him what they did and let Him deal with it so that you can be free. Tell Him what you did so you can be forgiven and healed. Don't keep it locked up inside you to wreak havoc in your life and spread to the lives around you. Release it to God in prayer...a lot of prayer, if need be, but get yourself free of it, because bitterness has the ability to consume you.

I love the way the Apostle Paul said it to a bunch of folks in a busted Roman copper mining town called Philippi. He said, *"Brethren, I do not count myself to have apprehended but one thing (I do), forgetting those things which are behind and reaching forward to those things which are ahead, I press toward the goal for the prize of the upward call of God in Christ Jesus"* Philippians 3:13-14.

I'll be happy to paraphrase that verse for you; "That was then, this is now. Let it go and keep moving forward in your walk with God, because, I guarantee, your best days are still out in front of you and not behind you".

It also helps when we learn from our past experiences, rather than repeat them, so, yeah, we'll see how the partners of Goler Canyon do when we fire this placer operation up and start making gold. Until then we will just keep the hidden gold ledge that I found, hidden right where it is.

***

We ran the plant for several hours each day to fine tune it, using random material from the excavation pit we had started ramping down into the floor of the canyon. Eventually we worked most of the "bugs" out of the system and got this huge monstrosity running fairly smooth. After we got our pit down past 20 feet or so the gold values showed a steady increase. Not so much in the course gold but definitely in the fine gold, and as a result, we slowed the feed down and reduced the volume of water as not to lose the "fines". Con was constantly panning the "tails" (waste material coming out of the mill) to make sure we were not losing the gold, and thus, telling me whether to increase or decrease the feed and water flows until we eventually found the "balance" or tons per hour that we could run through the mill safely and efficiently with a minimum loss of fine gold. This is critical, as the ore or material you are processing in this fashion is what determines your flow rate, or speed and tonnage you can efficiently operate at... Not simply how much and how fast you can shove dirt into the machine.

Case in point, we were now efficiently (very minimum loss of gold) running this 100 ton per hour mill at 24 to 28 tons per hour, with a recovery rate of about 80%. To substantially increase our recovery rate beyond 80% we would have to slow the feed down to less than 18 tons per hour. So the 20% loss of fine gold was acceptable considering the accumulated increase in recoverable gold we achieved by running the eight or ten more tons per hour, at around 28 tons per hour, due to the increase of gold being fed into the mill.

On the other end of the equation, if we increased our feed to over 30 tons per hour, the milling process would not have allowed enough time to extract most of the fine gold, as it is now moving at a much faster rate and combined with the increase in water needed to keep a steady flow, we would be washing a substantial amount of our fine gold right on through the mill and back out into the canyon floor in our "tailings" (waste or reject flow). We would simply be going too fast to catch the gold and it would literally run in one end of our processing plant and out the other... Hence, the age-old mining term "in one end and out the other".

Finding the "balance" is everything. It can only be obtained through constant and consistent feed, and by constantly panning the "tails" and making your adjustments accordingly. The fastest way to go broke is to allow a "bean counter" (accountant, etc.), investor, or anyone else with a calculator to call the shots and tell you "but if we are making X amount of gold at 28 tons per hour, according to my calculations, we can make XX (double, much more, etc.) the amount of gold at 56 tons per hour, by cranking up the machine and doubling the feed input." It doesn't work that way. What you double is your expenses in excavation, milling and manpower with little or no increase in gold recovery because your milling machine was already running at the maximum allowable speed with a minimum loss of gold. Now, at the over- increase of speed, you are just washing and sizing gravel and throwing the fine gold right back out the discharge end of the plant. You will eventually lose your...behind. This scenario in the placer mining business is so incredibly common, it is staggering. In recent years I have actually told one gravity mill owner, after inspecting his operation that his full retirement was in his tailings ponds. And, yup! Same root cause... Gold Fever.

Not so in our case, though. Con and I were allowed to have full authority of the operation, and we made gold. That's not to say that arguments didn't erupt with some of the investors who wanted to increase the feed (tons per hour), but Con always reiterated why we could not feasibly do it, and he was good at standing his ground.

Things seemed to be going good, so due to an epic lack of patience on my part, I waited until the next weekend when no one else was around and proceeded to take the dozer up the ravine to where the ledge of gold ore was hidden. I had it in mind to do a little scratching around with the bulldozer to see if I could get a better idea of how big of a deposit we had. As shallow as it was under the overburden, and as close as it was to the top of the hill or bench level, I felt confident that I could reclaim anything I tore up as long as I didn't get too carried away.

I pushed the overburden and topsoil up the hill at an angle because of the steepness, and stockpiled it above the discovery. Then I began taking slow, thin cuts with the dozer blade until I was down a few feet and the greenish-brown rock began to expose itself. The ledge seemed to run all the way across the hillside, about 40 yards from ravine to ravine. Instead of just running level or horizontally, it was at about a 35 degree angle, with the "dip and strike" running from the Northeast to the Southwest.

Then, as I removed the topsoil from below the gold bearing ledge, I hit two long outcrops of Hematite bearing rock that were both running parallel to the greenish-brown ledge. This was not good. First, we were already having a problem with hematite plugging up riffles in our mill as well as the riffles on the concentrating table that was causing us to run much slower in order to give the gold more of a chance to stay in the riffles and not wash away, and many times we had to rerun our concentrates several times just to make sure. And second, these two veins or outcrops of hematite were between the gold bearing ore and the bottom of the hill where I had to get it in order to be loaded out and moved closer to the feed hopper of the mill. To contaminate the rich gold ore by trying to push it straight down the hill over the hematite "dykes" would surely damage our ability to recover the gold effectively.

Ah, but wait! What if I fed the high grade ore by pushing it along its own 35° course until it got to the ravine, then pushed it down the ravine to the bottom of the hill, thus evading the other two ledges of hematite altogether? Brilliant, don't you think?

The Terex Dozer was not what you would call a powerhouse, but I managed to "strip and grub" all the brush, cactus, and topsoil off by pushing it uphill to a place in the ravine above where the rich vein intersected it. That way it would be much easier for me to put the topsoil and brush back into the ravine when I was done.

By the end of the day I had moved maybe 65 tons of high-grade to the bottom of the hill. I dared not take more for fear of not being able to reclaim, or more precisely, re-hide the rich outcrop of gold ore. It was a lot of work but I had it looking pretty good (not great) by evening, and I even worked until way after dark shoveling and transplanting bushes and raking out all of my bulldozer tracks. I was relying heavily on the fact that most people involved in this operation were "city Slickers" and probably wouldn't even look in this direction as they were so busy focusing on the placer plant, and the gold it was producing.

The next morning, after looking it all over in the morning light and making a few more "adjustments", I was satisfied. I put the dozer back where I got it from and used the loader to move the new stockpile to the mill. I piled it up behind an already existing 100 ton or more stockpile of material that was scheduled to be run the first thing on Monday morning. I still had not decided whether to run it separate, or blend it with the regular material we normally run in order to conceal its distinctive color, and just see what happens.

\*\*\*

Because Monday started off in such a flurry, I didn't even get a chance to tell Con about the discovery I had made or even show him the stockpile. We were up and running shortly after dawn and Con had people following him around like puppy dogs nipping at his heels. A week earlier, Con had wisely approached several local sand, gravel, and aggregate companies about selling them our discharge piles of washed sand and various sizes of clean rock. We were limited on room in the canyon, and would soon be out of places to stockpile our rejects (waste) without it ending up being in the way of our mining the canyon floor. It was a very smart idea on Cons part, but the local sand and gravel companies just laughed at us, even though our price was about $.10 on the dollar of what it was costing them to produce their own washed and sized aggregate. So Con ran an ad in the local papers offering free washed and sized sand and gravel to anyone who wanted it. I spent a huge amount of my day loading trucks of all shapes and sizes, and the local companies were now screaming bloody murder over an almost total collapse in their business sales. Now, a week later, here they all were begging Con to allow them to buy our rock and sand! Con, of course, was merciful and allowed them, and canceled the newspaper ads. Now that was just good business. Con did manage to look over at me and give me that famous, mischievous Irish wink with the accompanying grin as he walked past with the local boys hot on his heels, jabbering to him as they went. I laughed and went to work.

I started feeding both piles of the material into the grizzly at a 50/50 ratio of blending until my 65 tons of high grade was gone. We ran for about 6 ½ hours, depleting almost all of the remaining stockpiled material except maybe eight or nine tons.

Once the material was dumped into the grizzly by the front end loader, it was carried up a long conveyor belt and dropped into two series of large shaker screens that washed, sized, and separated the rock and gravel into separate piles. Everything ¼ inch and smaller was then divided evenly and fed into two parallel sluice boxes that were 12 feet long and 4 feet wide, each. The ripples were almost an inch tall and Afro turf carpet was used the full length of both sluice boxes to capture most of the course gold. From there it went over a series of Gardner Denver and Pan-American jigs (concentrators) to make the main concentrate, then on to a series of industrial Knelson centrifugal concentrators to capture the last of the very fine "flour" gold before discharging into the tailings pond. It was a very good gravity recovery system for the type of material we were mining. The sluices, jigs, and Knelson Bowls were cleaned out at the end of each daily run and the concentrates were then taken over to Fred's mill and ran across the main concentrating table to separate the gold from the black sands.

As the shutdown process began each day, the normal was for everyone to climb up onto the upper deck and gather around the huge sluice boxes to see how much course gold they could spot in the riffles as the water stopped flowing over them for the day. And this day was no exception, at least not until the water stopped and the riffles revealed their content. Eyeballs bugged out of their sockets and mouths dropped wide open as everyone stood silently in utter amazement and stared into those sluice boxes. The 1 inch riffles in the first 7 to 8 feet of those 12 foot long boxes were filled to the top with gold! More gold than I or anyone else there for that matter, had ever seen! No really big nuggets or "clunkers", but mostly granular, about 1/16 of an inch or smaller "pickers" with some of them almost up to 1/8 inch in diameter! The sun made the gold glisten and it was a truly beautiful sight to behold. Hysterical laughter broke out and exclamations of "we're rich" and a lot of patting each other on the back and shaking each other's hands. The sluices were cleaned and the contents placed in 5 gallon buckets, as was the concentrates from the jigs and Knelson bowls, during which time the excited talk and speculations got bigger and more boisterous. Then, loading all of the concentrates into his pickup, Con proceeded down the canyon to Fred's mill with a parade of investors following close behind.

  Then finally, once again, the canyon was silent, except for the slight breeze whispering through the sagebrush and greasewood, as it found its way from the top of the mountain, down through the cliff walls and arroyos, to the floor of the Mojave Desert, below. The silence sounded so sweet to me at the end of a hard, hot, loud day. I couldn't wait to tell my partner where all that gold had come from. I had been trying to convince him to sample the ravines and arroyos in the walls of the canyon to try and find where the gold in the canyon floor was coming from. Sadly he and everybody else could only focus on getting down to bedrock, as is typical of a placer operation. My point was simply that the gold in the canyon floor had to come from somewhere. Now I was beginning to rehearse my "I told you so" speech!

  And it was a really super good speech, too. Too bad I never got to use it.

***

  The next morning I got up at dawn and started servicing all of the equipment in preparation for another run. I greased, oiled, and fueled everything and by about 8:30 AM the plant was ready to go. I took the dozer to the bottom of our excavation pit and started pushing up material to replace yesterday's stockpile. By 10:30, no one had showed up yet, and I figured they were probably celebrating until the bars closed at 2 AM, so I got the loader and stockpiled everything I had taken out of the pit, by the feed hopper and grizzly. Still, nobody showed up. About suppertime I could clearly hear the sound of a vehicle echoing off the rock walls of the canyon below me. Two vehicles actually, that bore the insignia of the Kern County Sheriff's department. They pulled up to the Mill and proceeded to post signage around the entry way, and in the canyon above and below the mill site.

They were "cease and desist operations" orders. The deputy told me they were issued by a Kern County judge in response to multiple litigation suits being filed in the Bakersfield courthouse, concerning this mining operation.

Great, huh? And that pretty much killed any chance of me collecting the thousands of dollars in back pay they owed me. The gold and the means to recover it was right here in front of them, and instead of rejoicing and getting rich together, their greed had separated them and caused them to fight over it. I felt sick to my stomach. The deputy gave me 24 hours to get my camp trailer and personal belongings, tools, welder, etc. off of the property.

When they left, I just sat there gazing up at that hidden ledge of gold on the hillside and drank a cold beer. I never even got one tiny little flake of gold out of this whole deal and I had busted my hump to build this thing and get it into production. The irony is that they had no idea where all that gold they were fighting over had come from. Every outfit that ever tried to mine the bedrock of Goler Canyon went broke because of the depth they had to go and the floods that wiped out their efforts every year. So be it...

I was packed up and out of there by 8:30 AM the next morning and back across the Nevada border by noon. Don't know what it is, but there's something about crossing back into Nevada that just comforts and settles my soul.

## CHAPTER 23

## It's in the Blood

Not long after arriving back in Reno, Phil Davis contacted me with 100 more claims that had to be completely staked and filed before spring. That meant staking in the mountains of northern Nevada in the middle of winter, and that is dangerous business. Unpredictable weather conditions that high up can go from sunny and clear to blizzard mode in a matter of minutes.

The urgency stemmed from the fact that Phil was not the only one looking to stake this particular piece of real estate. His old friend at Cordex Exploration happened to mention that his company was sending out a claim staking contractor, the following spring, to tie up the ground adjoining Rossi mine, to the north. That was Unk's plan as well, so he made the decision to move up the timetable in order to beat them to locating the property, as well as hopefully avoiding a "claim war" in northern Elko County.

The claim war might have been a better idea. We preplanned every monument line in advance and filled out the certificates of location, except for the days date, and had them bagged and packaged with the exact amount of posts needed per line. We went in at 2:30 to 3 AM in the morning, under cover of darkness, as we had to drive directly through the Rossi mine to get to the property. All other access roads to the North were closed already due to snow. My "77" GMC had a fresh .427 Interceptor motor recently installed and was running 14.5 inch wide Kelly Springfield mud and snow tires. I had custom tire chains for all four wheels and I could shut off my tail and running lights on a separate switch, turn on my Army issue "glow lights", and maintain very low visibility in the dark.

As this was my primary staking vehicle, it also ran the exhaust from that .427 engine up through a really cool looking set of stacks, as not to set the dry grass on fire during the hot summer months. All the bumpers and roll bars were built out of steel mine rail. Besides mowing through brush and trees, if you hit a deer, you could keep it if it didn't go under my wheels, anyway. Yeah, it's so true... I loved that truck. My friend Ray Fisher built that .427 Interceptor motor for me, and when he got done I could smoke all four tires, and on many occasions, ate Chevy Iroc Camaros for lunch! Couldn't hardly pass a gas station, though. It had a Holly 780 double pumper carburetor, so mashing the gas pedal to the floor was like flushing a toilet that was full of gas and setting on top of my motor.

My brother and I knocked all those monument lines in, in just five days. Once the monument lines are in place the claims can be filed at the courthouse and with the Bureau of Land Management, which makes them legally yours for one year. You have 60 days to "perfect" them, meaning put in all the rest of the corner and (at that time) side center posts, and you had 90 days in which you had to file the claim from the time you put up the monument post containing the Certificate of Location. So once the monuments are in, you technically take possession of the properties mineral rights. The first one to get there monument up on any given piece of open ground, wins. That's how little guys like Phil could compete with major multimillion dollar mining corporations like Cordex, Newmont, etc. and actually win.

As I may or may not have previously stated, that was until they passed the law giving the $100 per claim that you would normally spend on the yearly assessment work on the claims themselves, to the BLM instead. They knew that small miners would never be able to afford paying their working money to the government and still be able to afford to work their claims as well. Big mining companies in cooperation with the government's greed wiped out tens of thousands of small miners and small companies like Phil's and our families, thus eliminating the competition issue and forming big company monopolies in the mining industry.

So after Bill and I got the monuments in, much to Unk's dismay, we took off for a week to go deer hunting, as was our custom, with our Dad and my wife, Lori. After all, (my religious argument to Phil) was it not God who invented Bar-B-Q (Leviticus 1:1-17)? And besides… If the Good Lord didn't want us to eat animals, He never would have made them out of meat.

Dad had always hunted the Diamond Mountains in Eureka County, behind grandpas silver mine at Black Point. He had always hunted with his Savage 250-3000 lever action and was a living legacy of the term, "one shot, one deer", that Johnny Pinola had drilled into us as young boys. Lori used Dad's rifle one time and fell in love with it, so I bought a new Savage 22-250 and custom seated the barrel and action into a set of 1909, .300 Savage handcrafted wood stocks, shortened the butt stock to an exact fit for her, and fine-tuned the trigger and the smoothness of the action. That seemed to put her and my father on equal terms, when it came to hunting, and I honestly never saw either one of them miss, regardless of a running target or the distance involved!

They were extremely competitive and the only way I could maintain any kind of edge was by using Lori's father's .300 Weatherby Magnum with a 12 power scope that I had inherited upon Bob's demise. Yes, I blew up a lot of meat, but talk about a long range, "reach out and touch someone" gun, this was it!

***

The Ultimate Marksman

I have always admired young David's marksmanship when he drilled ol' Goliath right between the eyes with that rock. With that first rock, at that (1 Samuel 17). I know in my heart that beyond a shadow of a doubt, when he did it, that God pumped out His chest and with a huge grin, probably put a little strut in His step while saying, "That's my boy! Did you see that shot?"

Well, maybe, maybe not, but that's what I envision because that's how I used to act when I would take my kids out shooting or hunting and they made a really tough shot. Both were then, and are now, excellent marksman.

Noteworthy is the often overlooked fact that, even though David nailed Goliath with that first round, he was packing a "full clip" of ammo, just in case. Hmmm. In case it took a second shot, or third…or fourth, I have to assume. The point being that David was prepared for a shootout (1 Samuel 17:40). He was ready for an extended battle if need be. It's good to be prepared, I think.

God's people have always had enemies and had to fight them, and always will, until the Lord Himself comes and deals with them personally (Revelation 19 – 20). And that's coming sooner than you think. These are the "End Times"…the "Last Days". And that is why, in one of His Old Testament appearances, Jesus professed Himself to be "the Commander of the Army of the Lord" to Joshua (Joshua 5:13-15).

Even more astonishing is the Lord's marksmanship. Most (about 90%) of the ozone layer resides in the layer that starts between 6 and 10 miles above the surface of the earth, and extends up to about 30 miles (also called the stratosphere). How's that for a long shot? Beyond that distance is space, and of course God can do anything He wants (Luke 1:37, 18:27, etc.) but, space does not have the ability to produce hailstones. So what about a shot, somewhere between 6 and up to 30 miles, with pinpoint accuracy? What about a whole bunch of them?

Five Canaanite kings joined forces to attack and destroy the town of Gibeon. So Joshua, all the people of war, and all the mighty men of valor with him, came down from Gilgal, marched all night and proceeded to give those Canaanites a good old-fashioned ass-whoopin'.

*"And it happened, as they fled before Israel and were on the descent of Beth Horon, that the Lord cast down large hailstones from Heaven on them as far as Azekah, and they died. And there were more who died from the hailstones than the children of Israel killed with the sword"* Joshua 10:11.

Using a storm of hailstones and the equivalent of a laser guidance system, God exhibited His own pinpoint accuracy as He directed each individual hailstone to selectively hit only the enemy targets, amidst the ongoing, running battle!

In the fast approaching End Time Tribulation period, Revelation 16:21 declares that one day God will unleash His Holy Wrath on the rebellious people of the earth who refuse to repent of their evil deeds. In so doing He will release a barrage of hailstones, probably doing about Mach 8, and weighing a "talent" (75 to 120 pounds, depending on who's teachings you adhere to), again with pinpoint accuracy, on His enemies. Those hailstones won't stop until they travel from the top of one's head to his heels, I'm sure.

Comforting to me is the fact that our Heavenly Marksman will be the One delivering and executing this final judgment. "He knows who to attack and who to spare," points out Skip Heitzig (The Daily God Book). I agree with him that we are not called to be spiritual pacifists as our enemy is always in attack mode.

Charles Spurgeon once said, "There is something comforting in the thought that the devil is an adversary. I'd sooner have him for an adversary than for a friend".

*"Now thanks be to God who always leads us in triumph in Christ, and through us defuses the fragrance of His knowledge in every place. For we are to God the fragrance of Christ among those who are being saved and among those who are perishing. For to one we are the aroma of death leading to death, and to the other the aroma of life leading to life."* 2 Corinthians 2:14-16.

\*\*\*

The really huge bucks that I preferred to hunt didn't get that way by being careless or stupid. They were very wise and very skittish. I would watch them through my spotting scope for hours, sometimes. They walked above or below, common deer trails. If the wind changed direction they would immediately go to ground or go into hiding. And they usually hung out with a smaller three or four point buck that seemed to "run interference" for them. There are so many times I have seen someone shoot a nice four point buck only to have one of these huge "cactus heads" stand up and run off in the other direction at the sound of the shot. And in Nevada, four point means four points or horn tips on each side, i.e. four on the left and four points on the right also, not four points all together. It was hard letting a nice big four point buck walk away from you in hopes of outsmarting and getting a shot at a trophy buck that may or may not be lurking in the shadows. Sometimes the younger buck would irregularly look back behind him or higher up the hill above him into the buck brush or trees where nothing seemed to be apparent. More often than not I was disappointed for my patients, but then there are those times when, after hours of waiting and scoping it out, that big huge old buck finally stands up or steps out of the mahogany's and you try desperately to control your pounding heart that just climbed up into your throat as your thumb flips the safety off and your forefinger gently curls around the trigger.

Yes, there are many different types of treasure hunting and many different types of treasures.

It was on such a hunt that I became the hunted. Dad and Bill had both shot their deer just at sunrise in the canyon behind Blackpoint. Lori and I had spent almost all of the morning gaining altitude and carefully moving along the ancient game trails about three quarters of the way to the top of the Diamond Mountains, and working our way north. We were sneaking our way above the upper tree line towards a large stand of Quake & Aspen, as that was where we had earlier seen several deer bed down for the day through my spotting scope, including a nice buck.

The going had been slow due to several areas of very little cover that required us to slowly crawl along using sagebrush and sheep grass for cover. A shifting breeze had also made progress incredibly difficult, but by midafternoon we were nestled in behind a nice rock out crop about 100 yards from the tree line that the deer had bedded down in front of. After a half hour of scoping out the thick sage and buck brush about 50 feet from the stand of quakes, we finally spotted just the tips of the buck's horns protruding up above a patch of high sagebrush. The shadows were becoming long now, and we knew as the day cooled that the deer would be up and feeding again so we decided to wait a little longer in hopes of spotting a second buck.

Sure enough within an hour they began to stand, stretch and graze. Although they had bedded down in the same area together, it soon became apparent that the four does were not with the four point buck, as they soon separated and began moving away from him working their way farther down the hill. As the buck gradually grazed his way closer and closer to the trees, he at no time looked around or focused on anything except his dinner. We decided to take him while we still had plenty of daylight left to dress him out and get him off of the mountain before it got too dark. Lori solidly rested her rifle on a large rock as I watched her target through my 12 power scope, as the buck stepped within 20 feet of the tree line. A split second before Lori shot him, that buck raised his head, twisted around over his right shoulder and stared straight up the hill above him. Oh, s_ _t, I thought as I tried to chamber a round, but Lori's perfect shot as usual, rang out across the mountain dropping that four point where he stood. In a fraction of a second, a monster sized buck jumped up from behind some buck brush, about 35 yards above Lori's now dead four point, and in three quick jumps, bound into the trees and out of sight! I knew better, and should have been ready…Aaargh!

I quickly tried to move straight uphill to gain enough elevation to cover the ridge on the far side of the stand of trees, but all I saw was a fleeting glimpse of that huge rack of horns disappearing over the skyline. I would be back at dawn to take up his trail, but for now Lori and I had our work cut out for us. We dressed out her deer, and with Lori packing our rifles and me dragging her awesome four point, we worked our way down the mountain making it back to the truck about an hour after sunset.

It was almost 10 AM the next morning by the time I worked my way back up to the ridge line behind Blackpoint, where I had last seen my buck. I was packing much more gear this time, including a bedroll and extra food, so when I finally topped out on the skyline at 8800 feet elevation, I again received the divine revelation that had flooded my mind on so many similar occasions... I gotta quit smoking.

    Because they were so large, the buck's tracks were easy to pick up. They dropped over the ridge and into Green Canyon and because he was at a full run, followed an old deer trail that ran horizontal to the mountaintop ridge line, about 200 yards below the skyline. The cold breeze was in my favor, coming out of the north, so after searching the upper canyon with my binoculars; I headed out after him at a pretty good pace. Although I was at least a quarter-mile above the tree line, the top of Green Canyon offered excellent concealment for my prey with large clumps of buckbrush and plenty of dense sagebrush all the way across to the next ridge, about a mile to the north. Even so, I was fairly confident that a wise old buck like this one would not stop until he had at least two canyons between him and the place where his younger companion had met his demise. At least I hoped so.

    Years earlier I had shot a nice buck in Green Canyon and paid a hard price. There is no access up Green Canyon from the bottom and the mahogany's and pine trees are so thick that when I got to the tree-line in the bottom of the canyon, I barely was able to get through with my deer. It was a long battle, to say the least, and one I would not soon forget. Now I avoided shooting game in Green Canyon at all costs.

    About half way across the top of the canyon the tracks left the trail and began angling upward through the natural brush making it much slower tracking. Several times I found where he had stopped to check his back trail from the concealment of rocks and high brush. His tracks now indicated he was moving along at a slower, steadier gate.

    After crossing over the next ridge into Water Canyon I followed his tracks about 50 yards until they disappeared. I backtracked until I found where he had purposely jumped into sagebrush to hide his tracks, as he changed direction and went straight uphill for over 15 yards! How amazing! How could it be that he would know to hide his own tracks? This was a very cagey and wise old mountain deer!

    After going up the mountain for 15 yards or so, he reversed direction and backtracked to the previous ridge line we had just crossed and he had stopped just before the crest of the ridge to watch his back trail, without making himself visible! How could I not respect and admire such amazing abilities? By the looks of it, he had spent a lot of time here just watching, probably until dark, as to be sure he was not pursued. Feeling confident that he was not, I'm sure he had bedded down close by, and a short time later I confirmed my guess when I followed his tracks to the spot he had chosen to spend the night, again, in a large cluster of buckbrush.

    Everything above was pretty much windblown and barren on up to the top of the Diamond Mountain ridge line at 8888 feet elevation. It was an incredible vantage point for him, and now, me as well. It seemed like I could see forever across the vast mountain ranges of Nevada to the West. And below me I could almost see the old charcoal oven hidden in the steep winding canyon below. But what I could see was my truck that Lori and Dad had painstakingly crawled up through the pines and mahogany trees and left for me right at the tree line, after they had dropped me off at Black point an hour before dawn this morning. It took a really good truck to make that climb and other than right at that old Coke oven, which was about half way up, and the narrow spot in a ravine where my truck was now parked, there was no place to turn around if you got in trouble. Dad was raised in these mountains, as were my brother and I, and we had a good handle on what we could and couldn't get away with. To get hurt or seriously injured in some of these canyons would allow the coyotes and cougars to scatter your bones before anyone could ever find you. One other time hunting up high like this about 4 miles south of where I was now, Dad and I found a few old crumbly bones and a gun belt that still held a Ruger six shooter in its holster.

The skies toward the West were turning gray and foretold of an approaching squall. This high up, that meant snow. It was going to be a really cold night on this mountain for me unless I could close the distance between me and that wily ol' cactus head before dark, and that didn't seem too likely. His tracks had showed me that he was no longer in a hurry and was in fact grazing as he went, but he had a huge head start on me and I had to move very cautiously now, as not to spook him again.

By late afternoon snow flurries were beginning to limit visibility and the wind ahead of the storm front had picked up to about 10 or 15 mph. The wind was now blowing out of the west and still very advantageous to me as my buck was still moving somewhere to the north of my current position. I was making much better time as I scrambled through the gully that led straight down through a forest of quakes, then on to my truck, on the other side of them.

But the game was almost over as snow began to quickly cover the ground, and the big bucks tracks, with large wet snowflakes. The front of the storm had passed and the wind completely calmed as I crested the hill I was on. Though I could move much more silently in the fresh snow, the tracks were all but covered over, and I would now stick out like the proverbial "sore thumb" against the bright white background of the snow-covered mountain side. It was probably less than two hours until sundown. In the heavy silence that accompanied the snowfall, I took off my pack and my gear, sat down using it as my backrest, and lit a smoke – something I never do when I'm hunting, because the smell will send the deer running. But it was over… "Another time for you, my friend" I softly spoke to that unseen granddaddy of a buck that had managed to elude me.

Then I heard brush cracking and dry limbs breaking in the stand of quakes below me and now to my left. Moments later a young three point buck and two doe's broke cover and ran out of the trees, crossed the gully and ran south towards the ridge of Green Canyon that I had just came from. About halfway to the ridge they all stopped and looked back at the trees, but I had no idea what had startled them. Maybe the echo of my voice, soft as it was, but I doubted it at this distance, and surely not the smell of my cigarette as the barely noticeable breeze was blowing my smoke uphill, not down.

Well, whatever the reason, a three point made really good eating and I wasn't looking forward to sleeping on this cold old mountain tonight, anyway. As slowly and quietly as I could, I slid a .300 Magnum round into the chamber of my Weatherby. It would be a downhill shot at about 175 yards. I rested my elbow on my knee in a sitting position and made a full wrap around my right forearm with the sling and pulled the rifle snugly into my shoulder. I had to be very steady, as anything other than a head or high neck shot, at this distance, would allow the .300 Magnum round to ruin most of the meat due to the velocity of the bullets impact and the extreme amount of air that would follow the bullet into the deer's body.

As I drew a bead on the young bucks head he, and the other two does, suddenly turned their heads all the way around and were staring almost right at me! What the…then I heard it. The sound of a deer moving through the barren windswept ground above me! I looked up the hill to see that wily old buck I had been tracking moving at full speed, back toward the south and the safety of the ridge that would drop him, again, right back into Green Canyon. That old Fox had double-backed on me again, and was probably just sitting up there above me laughing all this time as he watched me pass by below him! The fresh snow had hidden his tracks and I would never have known, had he not caught a whiff of my ciggy and spooked, as its smoke was carried up the slope to him on that ever so slight breeze.

Before I could swing my rifle around he disappeared over the crest of the hill we were on and down into the gully. All good by me, I thought, as there is only open country between the gully and the ridge to Green Canyon, and I would be ready. I laid my rifle across my pack and bedroll and steadied it preparing for a 250 yard shot, and I would only get one off before he made it over the ridge. I was calm and my mind, my again, became incredibly clear as he came into view at a full out run.

He seemed very small in my scope as he neared the ridge line and I relaxed my body, let out half a breath, and gently squeezed the trigger. BOOM! That .300 mag kicked like a dog-gone mule as it sent a tingle of pain into my shoulder. The bullet caught my buck in full stride, driving his head down into the brush ahead of him, and he went (for lack of a better term) ass-over-tea-kettle into the ground at full speed. The sound of the shot echoed down the canyon, then all was again silent, except for the sound of the fleeing three point and his two does. Then, that sound also faded out as they ran into the tree line below us and disappeared.

I gathered up all my gear and made my way back toward the ridge to almost the same place we had crossed over it hours earlier.

From the earliest hunts that my father took us on when we were yet small boys, he always emphasized the importance of always "returning the blood to the earth", as he would say it. I never really understood what he was talking about or why we did this until many years later, when reading Deuteronomy 12:23-25, and found that the Lord had commanded that, *"Only be sure that you do not eat the blood, for the blood is the life; you may not eat the life with the meat. You shall not eat it; you shall pour it on the earth like water. You shall not eat it, that it may go well with you and your children after you, when you do what is right in the sight of the Lord"*.

I can't even imagine how much all those vampire movies must anger God. Throughout the Bible from Abel's blood crying out from the ground to curse his brother Cain (Genesis 4:10-12), to Christ's return wearing a robe dipped in blood (Revelation 19:13), God adamantly stresses the fact that blood is sacred. And not just man's blood, but as Scripture makes clear, the blood of all living creatures is sacred as well. The Creator of all the universe has also made it clear that he will not be passive in this matter, either. As part of God's covenant with Creation, found in Genesis chapters 8 and 9, He made Himself very clear; *"So God blessed Noah and his sons, and said to them;' be fruitful and multiply, and fill the earth. And the fear of you and the dread of you shall be on every beast of the earth, on every bird of the air, on all that moves on the earth, and on all the fish of the sea. They are given into your hand. Every moving thing that lives shall be food for you. I have given you all things, even as the green herbs. But you shall not eat flesh with its life, that is, its blood. Surely for your lifeblood I will demand a reckoning; from the hand of every beast I will require it, and from the hand of man. From the hand of every man's brother I will require the life of man'." (*Genesis 9:1-5).

And of course, to God and to us there is no blood more sacred than the blood of Jesus. It is the most important gift our Heavenly Father has bestowed upon us. That's because the blood of our Lord has incomprehensible power. When the shed blood of Jesus is applied to your life it;

**Provides forgiveness of your sins**, *"and without the shedding of blood there is no forgiveness"* of sins (Hebrews 9:22 NIV).

**Gives you life**, *"Then Jesus said to them,' Most assuredly, I say to you, unless you eat the flesh of the Son of Man and drink his blood, you have no life in you'."* (John 6:53), *"And He took bread, gave thanks and broke it, and gave it to them, saying,' this is My body which is given for you; do this in remembrance of Me'. Likewise He also took the cup after supper, saying,' this cup is the new covenant in My blood, which is shed for you.'" (Luke 22:19, 20).* That's Communion. Finally, these words spoken by Jesus make perfect sense, knowing that the "life is in the blood", as stated in the verses above.

**Brings you close to God** (Ephesians 2:13).

**Cleanses your conscience** (Hebrews 9:14).

**Gives you boldness to approach God** (Hebrews 10:19).
**Sanctifies you** (Hebrews 13:12).
**Cleanses you** (1 John 1:7).
**Heals you** (1 Peter 2:24).
**Enables you to overcome the devil and his works** (Revelation 12:11).

This is why the church has instructed us for hundreds of years to, "plead the blood" over our lives, our circumstances, and our loved ones. And make no mistake; your words are incredibly powerful in declaring, speaking and praying the "Blood of Jesus" into your life. Blood is so important to God that it is mentioned over 700 times in the Bible. The perfect example is found in Exodus 12 when God sent Moses along with 10 plagues to free the children of Israel from 400 years of bondage and slavery to Pharaoh, and bring them out of the land of Egypt. The 10$^{th}$ plague sent on the Israelites final night in Egypt would bring the death of all the firstborn sons in Egypt, Egyptian and Israelite, man and beast (Chapters 11 & 12, specifically 12:12). On that night God's children were to kill a lamb and smear its blood on the sides and tops of their doorframes so that when the death Angel saw the blood, he would "Passover" their houses and not kill their firstborn.

*"The blood on your door posts will serve as a sign, marking the houses where you are staying. When I see the blood, I will pass over you. This plague of death will not touch you when I strike the land of Egypt."* Exodus 12:13.

The fact that they were Israelites meant nothing, as only the blood of the lamb would save them. And as it is today, that was the precursor to the coming of God's only Son, Jesus, THE LAMB OF GOD, (John 1:29, 1:36 see also Genesis 22:8, Revelation 5:6, 7:17, 14:10, 15:3, 19:9, 21:23, and 22:3) who shed His blood and died on the cross for you and me, to pay the full price for our sins and to deliver us from eternal death to eternal life. We're under His blood… That's why we plead the blood of Jesus over our lives and loved ones.

Your natural blood supplies life-giving oxygen and nutrients to every single cell in your body. If that blood flow were cut off from any part of your body, that part would quickly begin to die. (I'm writing this part mostly to show off to my daughter, Brandy, that I was actually paying attention!)

Sooo… From our spiritual perspective, any part of life that is cut off from the life-giving blood of Jesus is either dead or dying.

Your blood also carries away toxins, impurities, and waste from your cells. (And this part is so my wife, Lori, knows that I was also paying attention to her as well! Hallelujah!)

From our spiritual perspective, you would have your life completely filled with the filth and toxins of this world, without the cleansing power of Jesus's blood… Praise God!

The point is, the blood of Jesus Christ, shed for us – you and me – removes the dirt and filth of sin from our daily lives!

Also, our Wonderful Creator has equipped us with an immune system and white blood cells that kick butt and fight off sickness. When viruses or bacteria, for instance, try to get in, your white cells attack and immediately start destroying the invaders. So when your natural body is healthy and your immune system isn't already busy fighting off self-inflicted toxins like tobacco, alcohol, or drugs per se, you are protected from disease. Being spiritually healthy means that there is nothing that punk devil can bring against you that the all-powerful blood of Jesus cannot overcome! Yes! There truly is life in The Blood!

You apply the blood of Jesus when you say statements like, "The blood of Jesus Christ was shed on the cross for me". I believe that you can apply the blood of Jesus to anything God has given you authority over or influence upon, such as healing, protection of you and your children, their circumstances, etc. And I believe that what the blood of Jesus is applied to becomes redeemed by Christ. Although the blood of Jesus will never ever lose its power, it will only make a difference when you apply it in faith. There truly is power in the blood of Jesus!

All of us have sinned and fallen short of the glory of God (Romans 3:23). And our sins are what separate us from our righteous Holy God because no sin can stand in His presence. And even though God rightfully demands a "reckoning" for our sins, which would result in our death, He gave us this amazing gift of Jesus' shed blood, that His blood alone would be sufficient to pay the full penalty/price for our sins, reconcile us back to God, and give us eternal life (Romans 6:23). We are washed clean by the shed blood of Jesus (1 John 1:7 – 2:2).

Yes, that Blood of His Only Son is sacred. And it was poured out, back into the earth, to get you back home to your Heavenly Father. That's the Gospel truth. That's the true power of The Blood… To transform you from certain death to eternal life. There is no way to earn your salvation; it is a free gift to you (Ephesians 2:1-10). I pray that you will simply accept His gift, as He paid the ultimate price to be able to offer it freely to you.

## CHAPTER 24

## When the Hunter Becomes the Prey

So as Dad taught me, with its head downhill, I "bled out" the buck, and field dressed it. My bullet had just barely gone over the top of his shoulder blades and hit him at the base of his neck. He was probably dead before he hit the ground. I made a sling to drag it with, and then down the hill we went. How big, you ask? Six horns on one side and nine on the other. And even though the mountainside was very steep, I could hardly drag it down the hill and liked to broke my back every time his horns hung up in the brush.

Only the very peaks of the mountains above me were being touched by the last few rays of the day's sunshine. The snow squall had passed by and the sky was rapidly clearing, promising a very cold night. As I got closer to the large stand of Quake and Aspen trees below me, I crossed over the tracks of the buck and two does that I had watched exit the cover of the trees, earlier. I wondered what had scared them out of such a good hiding place. Pondering this question became very unsettling as I was about to enter into the thick trees. I had no choice. It would be a really long way around them and would require me to drag this huge deer carcass, which outweighed me by probably 100 pounds, uphill in order to skirt around the grove of trees. I had to follow the gully which led straight through the center of the trees, and eventually, to my truck parked about 70 yards beyond.

Warning bells were going off in my head and the hair on the back of my neck was standing up as the last of the sunshine disappeared from the high mountain peaks, and I dragged my deer into the dense trees. I know it sounds crazy, but I knew I was being watched. I could feel it.

Every few seconds I would stop and listen. It was even harder dragging my buck up over the fallen dead trees that were scattered throughout this mini forest. The walls were fairly steep on both sides of the gully and me occupying the lowest ground made me feel incredibly vulnerable. Then, as if on cue, I stopped to listen for a moment and in the silence that was only broken by my heavy breathing; I heard a distinct, yet soft, growl...above me and somewhere to my right. The next sound was the unmistakable sound of metal as I jacked a big fat long .300 Magnum round into the chamber of my rifle.

"Go ahead and growl at me again", I spoke calmly and clearly. I didn't have to speak loud in these silent trees to be heard. In fact, the soft growl I had heard wasn't very loud at all, but it could be heard as clear as crystal. I was losing daylight fast and I knew I didn't have the luxury of staying here with my back to the wall of the ditch. I had to move or darkness would make me easy prey. Every nerve in my body was tingling and my heart was pounding. No matter how hard I stared into the darkening shadows of the woods, I couldn't see what was stalking me, but I was sure I knew.

How to drag my deer down through the gully, over rocks, brush and dead trees while I moved backwards to cover the North Slope and the ditch behind me, seemed almost impossible, but I was not about to leave my monster buck after all I went through to get him. Besides, that ol' buck deserved better than to end up as food for a predator that he had spent his whole life outfoxing (this statement is what is called and "ironic oxymoron", as in "the pot calling the kettle black." I looked it up on Google. Well, alrighty then...).

I stumbled and dragged that buck another 20 feet or so down the hill before I heard the second, much more serious growl. I was being warned to leave the carcass and move off. Typical modus operandi from one predator to another. This growl was clearer and closer and I still couldn't see anything. I had backed down the ditch to a large dead tree lying across the narrow gully. I would need both hands to pull my deer up and over the deadfall. Man, I really needed to get a clear shot at this thing. In this close of quarters, as I had learned the hard way, to fire a warning shot could trigger a panicked reaction and cause an immediate attack. I wouldn't have time to cycle a second round before he got me. Warning shots on wolves, coyotes, and cougars had only worked in the past when they had enough distance between them and the carcass to rationally choose to retreat, and not be mesmerized by the smell of blood.

I climbed over the log, scanned the hill and gully, and then leaned my rifle against the fallen tree. I reached over the dead tree, grabbed those massive horns, and pulled with all of my strength. As I lifted the deer up on top of the tree I caught a glimpse of movement up the left side of the slope, then another movement in the brush right next to the gully where I had just come from.

Holy cow that thing was close! Try as I might, I couldn't find anything to shoot in my rifle scope as the range was too close for my scope to focus. It was all just a blur. Then came the telltale snarl that was clearly meant to give me my last warning. As in the past, my mind went incredibly clear and my pounding heart, calmed to a steady rhythm. I pulled out my long knife and cut one of the straps of belly meat off of the deer carcass and left it on top of the dead tree I had just climbed over. I shouldered my rifle, grabbed onto the buck by his horns and dragged him as hard and fast as I could. I made it to the bottom tree line before I was stopped by a smaller fallen tree. When I looked back this time the meat I had left behind on the log was gone. I could see my truck about 75 yards below, but even once I got out of the trees, the high sagebrush would easily conceal the attack of my stalker. About 10 feet below the tree line was a large outcrop of rocks on the south side of the ditch. I took out my long knife once more, and cut off the other slab of belly meat, putting it on top of the rock. The rock formation was such that, this time my deadly adversary would have to expose himself, and when he does, I'm gonna blow his head off...hopefully.

I drug my deer down the gully another 15 yards and dropped it, sat down on top of it, and got ready to take my one and only shot.

And he came. He moved with such grace and intensity. As he glided up the rock out crop to the meat I had left on the top, I remember thinking, "my God, this is the biggest mountain lion I have ever seen". Instead of snatching the meat off of the rock and trying to disappear, he just laid down on top of that rock with the meat between his gigantic front paws. I hadn't expected anything like that and it caused me to hesitate. As I stared at him over the barrel of my Weatherby he just stared right back, almost like he was saying, "go ahead". And he was obviously very ancient. By far the oldest cat I had ever seen, as well. Most of his face and his entire muzzle was gray-white in color and bore many old scars, as well as a long scar I had noticed on his right front shoulder when he was ascending the rocks. He had been through many battles.

The slight westerly breeze carried the smell of me and my buck's carcass right to him, and he looked hungry. He opened his mouth and gave me a kind of quiet snarl and I could see that one of his fangs had had the tip broken off. He looked at me for another moment then looked down at the meat and began eating it! No one would ever believe this! And you probably don't either, but it's how it happened. He looked at me while he ate, and I was stuck! I didn't know whether to pull the trigger or try to move away, and this old cougar didn't seem to give a damn one way or the other.

What kind of stupidity possessed me to do it, I have no idea, but I shifted my rifle to my right hand (I'm left-handed), and again moving very slowly, drew my long knife that I had made out of an old Nicholson file. I slowly took one step back over the deer carcass and, without taking my eyes off of that cat, knelt down behind it and gently set my rifle on top of the dead deer. I raised up the front leg with my right hand and slipped my razor-sharp blade under the armpit, and in a few slices cut the front arm and shoulder blade free of the carcass. The cougar had stopped eating and was just staring at me the whole time I did this. I laid the front severed shoulder on the ground in front of the buck's body, and picked up my rifle ever so slowly. His head came up and his ears went back.

"I don't want to kill you if I don't have to", I softly said. "I gotta go, so it's up to you now, ol' Timer. Just let me go...please."

With my rifle back in my left hand and my finger on the trigger, I reached over with my right hand and grabbed onto those big beautiful horns. I began backing down the gully dragging the deer with me. He just sat there and watched, as if he were contemplating his next move. Then he seemed to relax and his ears slowly came forward again. I could feel the relief flood through my body as I got a little farther and a little farther away from him. My entire body was aching, not just from the physical exertion of dragging this monster buck, but I think, more so from the extreme tension that had contracted every muscle in my body throughout this entire ordeal. As I finally got to my truck, I could still see him laying on top of that rock. He had not taken his old sharp eyes off of me the entire time, nor had I taken my eyes off of him.

At the rear of my truck I pulled the latch and lowered my tailgate. I put the safety on and leaned my rifle against the spare tire that was mounted just inside the bed of my truck. I took my eyes off of the mountain lion for just a moment as I climbed up into the back of my truck, and that was the last time I saw him. As I began to hoist the deer up into the bed of my truck, I looked up and he was gone. I can't begin to describe the relief and exhaustion I felt when I finally climbed into the cab of my pickup and shut the door, and let out a deep breath that I felt I had been holding inside me for hours. What a day!

I have often thought back on this day and wondered if God smiled. I hope so. Over many years of hunting on the Diamond Mountains of Eureka County, I have often looked upon cougar tracks I have encountered and thought back on that old majestic mountain lion with fondness; God bless him, too.

***

We are "fishers of men" according to Jesus (Matthew 4:19), so I suppose that adds credence to the old saying, "we catch 'em, and God cleans 'em" (I know... Probably unscriptural... Sorry).

I love to fish, but I have always been a hunter, so I guess that's why seeing Jesus calling several fishermen to be "fishers of men" just makes sense to me, especially in light of Holy Scripture clearly declaring that *"the Son of Man has come to seek and to save that which was lost"* (Luke 19:10). "Seek", to me, seems synonymous to "hunt". I have heard many argue that, "only those who God calls" can be saved, and I have heard a lot about "don't throw your pearls before swine" (Matthew 7:6) in reference to witnessing or sharing the Gospel with those who are deemed "not worthy" or who have already rejected Jesus, yet the Bible also clearly tells us that *"... God our Savior, who desires **all men** to be saved and to come to the knowledge of the truth."* (1 Timothy 2:4) and, *"that supplications, prayers, intercessions, and giving of thanks be made for **all men**,"* (1 Timothy 2:1). I don't have all the answers but I think it would really suck if I got to Heaven and found out that someone I knew or met didn't make it to Heaven and was roasting in hell because I didn't feel like they were worthy of me to attempt in sharing the Gospel with them.

Although I have been cussed, cursed, spit on, and I have even had my long ponytail cut off (Yup! By a female Jehovah's Witness! I never did figure that one out), whatever it takes to assure that, on my judgment day, I will not stand before my Lord and Master as He shows me so-and-so, who burns in hell because I decided not to at least attempt to share God's greatest gift with them. They can get all "pissy", I don't care. And what they do with it after I give it to them, is on them. And I must also humbly admit that, sometimes, every now and then, after attempting to present the Gospel message to some very hateful and volatile people, I am reminded that I am not the "Jackass Whisperer"; but I took my shot. I am also very aware that I am not Jesus' sharpest tool in the shed, but I keep myself close to the door, ready and willing, so He can use me whenever, wherever, to do whatever He wills.

It's the same choice all of us have to make while we are still on this side of the grass. The devil is not hunting you, he already has you, so don't be passive. If you do nothing you, and they, lose. Like Edmund Burke stated; "The only way for evil to triumph is for good men to do nothing". Like it or not, you need to pick a side, and to choose nothing is a choice in itself to remain on the same road of darkness that leads to the destruction of your soul. *"... And if it seems evil to you to serve the Lord, choose for yourselves this day whom you will serve... But as for me and my house, we will serve the Lord."* Joshua 24:15. *"I call Heaven and earth as witnesses today against you, that I have set before you life and death, blessing and cursing; therefore choose life, that both you and your descendants may live;"* Deuteronomy 30:19. If you have chosen to believe in Jesus as your Lord and Savior, then you have already missed out on Satan's perfect will for your life... Hallelujah! If not...

But they aren't going to hell because I didn't take my shot or plant a seed when God put the opportunity before me. After all, we are all in the "seed planting" business, "sowers" if you will (Matthew 13), and it's up to God as to what the "seed" (Word) accomplishes (Isaiah 55:11) and there is no partiality with God (Romans 2:11, James 2:1). Judging others spiritual condition, calling, or faith is forbidden for Scripture says, *"Who are you to judge another's servant? To his own Master he stands or falls..."* (Romans 14:4) and, it is God our Savior *"who desires all men to be saved and to come to the knowledge of truth"* (1 Timothy 2:4).

The most notable verse I have seen taken out of context and used as an excuse not to minister the Good News of Jesus Christ to "undesirables" is taken from John 6:44, where Jesus says, *"no one can come to Me unless the Father who sent Me draws him"*. It's important to notice in verse 45, the very next verse, that it goes on to say, *"...therefore, everyone who has **heard** and learned from the Father comes to Me"*. Note the word, "heard". Sooo... If we don't tell them, how will they hear about salvation or that God loves them?

Read John 1:1-5 and verse 14. Who is the Word of God? Get it? God reveals Who He is with His Word. The Word of God draws them! *"...Surely I will pour out my spirit on you; I will make my words known to you"*. Proverbs 1:23. With this in mind, let's look at Romans 10 starting at verse 8, *"But what does it say? The **word** is near you, in your mouth and in your heart (that is the word of faith we preach); that if you confess with your mouth the Lord Jesus and believe in your heart that God raised Him from the dead, you will be saved"*.

I believe that little word "if" in the above verse defines your calling of God. The Word calls you. "If" you confess and believe, you will be saved, according to God's Word, here. "If" you do not, and you refuse to accept the calling, or "drawing" of the Word, by your own choice, you will perish (see Romans 1:14-32).

Verse 10 goes on to explain, *"For with the heart one believes unto righteousness, and with the mouth confession is made unto salvation."* Interestingly, its God's Word that calls you, and your words that pronounce your salvation. Words mean everything to God (see "Our Words" in Appendix H). Verse 13 seals it clearly when it boldly says, *"For whoever calls on the name of the Lord shall be saved"*. You and I are "whoever"; and sin is sin to God, so it's "whoever" that is doing "whatever" that God has qualified to attain salvation – that's all of us! Go ahead... Stick your name in there where it says "whoever"; and do it in John 3:16-17 too!

Romans 1:16 confirms that the Gospel of Jesus Christ is the power of God unto salvation for **all** who believe. The rottenest person you can think of is "whoever", whether we feel they are worthy or not. Might keep in mind that Romans 3:23 clearly points out that you and I were once "unworthy" as well. Hmmm... Hence, the term "saving faith". Ephesians 2:8 declares *"For by grace you have been saved through faith, and that not of yourselves; it is the gift of God, not of works, lest anyone should boast."* Works cannot save. Period. And it doesn't matter how many good deeds you do, what "temple" you got married in, what dead person you got baptized for, or how many "infidels" you kill, your works count as absolutely nothing as far as your salvation is concerned.

But James 2:17 says, *"Thus also faith by itself, if it does not have works, is dead."* That's not what James, the brother of Jesus, is even talking about in James 2:14-26. What he is clearly saying is that true faith produces results, or works. He defines the contrast between two kinds of faith; living and dead. Living faith is the "real deal" that saves and is dynamic in its nature. Dead faith cannot save because, in itself, it is lifeless or stagnant, so to speak. Living faith isn't just intellectual knowledge, and it's not some emotional sensation that brings a temporary "warm and fuzzy" feeling of well-being. Living faith is the kind of faith that leads to willful obedience as a lifestyle, which produces a renewing of the mind and a change of character, rather than just some one time isolated event in a person's life. True faith works these works of faith in a person's life; it brings change.

And yes, it's our job to preach the Word to them, otherwise, how will many of them ever hear it, if not from us? You may be the only opportunity they will ever have to hear about the Good News. That's the bottom line. As versus 14-17 in Romans 10 goes on to explain how the "Word of Faith" (verse 8) is imparted to nonbelievers; *"How then now shall they call on Him in whom they have not believed? And how shall they believe in Him whom they have not heard? And how shall they hear without a preacher? And how shall they preach unless they are sent?*

*As it is written; how beautiful are the feet of those who preach the Gospel of Peace, who bring glad tidings of good things!*

*But they have not all obeyed the Gospel. For Isaiah says,' Lord, who has believed our report?' So then faith comes by hearing, and hearing by the Word of God."*

As the Holy Spirit leads me, I will always "take my shot" regardless of possible ridicule, rejection, or any other repercussions it may produce, in hopes that some may be saved.

As a hunter, I tend to look at it this way; Are you saved? If your answer is yes, then I'm not hunting for you.

Also, I really don't see a lot of "unsaved" people in church either. But just walk out the door and we have an unlimited hunting ground.

Good hunting.

\*\*\*

What it is to be hunted by a lion, and survive, is an incredibly rare experience. But I wonder what would it be to be stalked and hunted down by the Lion of Judah, the ultimate hunter of all, from whom there is no escape? Such was the case of this religious fanatic named Saul. Born in the year 5 A.D. in Tarsus (Turkey), he was raised and trained to be a Pharisee (one of a group of Jews who thought that they kept all of God's rules) like his father before him. Saul of Tarsus hated Christians. When exactly he began his bloody mission of savagery against the church of Christ is unknown with any degree of precision. The fear of him was very significant, and Christians everywhere trembled at the mention of the name of this "wolf" who stalked "the fold of the Lamb", and was considered by those he persecuted as a terrorist of the highest order.

In life, many types of people cross our paths. Some as friends, relatives, coworkers, neighbors and strangers that just seem to be beyond the reach of our prayers even though we have prayed for them for a long time, even years, and still don't see any results.

And if we are honest, there are those who occasionally cross our paths that it seems obvious that they were sent by the devil to torment us until Jesus comes. We would prefer to format our prayers for them more along the lines of "just go ahead and take him, Lord," or call on God to judge between us and them. Over the years, you would be surprised at how many times I have had well-meaning Christians who are fed up with hurt, pain, and seemingly unanswered prayers, asked me if they should "turn so-and-so over to Satan." Do they seem that far beyond hope?

Saul of Tarsus would have been one of those people. This guy never knew how to do anything in moderation. He first appears in the Book of Acts at the stoning murder of Stephen, a beloved disciple of Jesus. Not only did he watch over everybody's cloths (equivalent to coats, tunics and sweaters, I think) while they were stoning him to death, but he also consented and gave his approval (Acts 7:58; 9:1). After that, Saul relentlessly went door to door in Jerusalem finding people who believe that Jesus is the Messiah, and imprisoned them (Acts 8:3), and all the while, believing he was sincerely doing God's will (23:1, 26:9). Pursuing the Saints even unto foreign cities (26:11), he beat, imprisoned, and had them put to death (22:19). In his own testimony he told of how he persecuted the followers of the Way (Acts 22:4-5) and himself stated that, *"I persecuted the church of God beyond measure and tried to destroy it"* (Galatians 1:13).

Then, the Lamb became a Lion, and the hunter became the hunted.

*"Then Saul, still breathing threats and murder against the disciples of the Lord..."* (Acts 9:1-2) took off on another terrorizing "field trip" to Damascus to further his bloody rampaging mission of destruction on those of the Christian Way, some 140 miles to the north of Jerusalem. As Saul drew near the city, a light brighter than the noon day sun suddenly engulfed him, and he had an encounter with the true living Christ that brought his agenda and his life to a screeching halt and left the not so mighty Saul of Tarsus blind and helpless in the middle of the road. Saul, the mighty Christian Hunter had suddenly become the prey of Jesus! And yeah, I'm sorry to testify that some people just won't listen until they are knocked down.

King David even prayed, *"I use to wander off until You disciplined me; but now I closely follow Your word (Psalm 119:67).* And as we discussed earlier, God loves us, so He corrects us (see Hebrews 12:5-7, Proverbs 3:11-12, and Job 5:17-18).

The early church thought Saul was beyond reach and the mere mention of his name terrified them. Can you think of someone that you would consider a lost cause? Don't give up praying. The story of Saul's conversion to the beloved Apostle Paul on the Damascus Road proves beyond any doubt that no one is beyond God's reach. No one. Not even you. Not even whoever you're thinking about right now.

As the Lord taught us, don't give up praying! See Matthew 7:7-12, Luke 18:1-8, and Luke 11:5-8, then you will understand what I'm talking about. What's it about?

Persistence.

# REDEMPTION OF A HARDROCK MINER

## CHAPTER 25

## A Voice in the Cold

> *"Then He said,' Go out, and stand on the mountain before the Lord.' And behold, the Lord passed by, and a great and strong wind tore into the mountains and broke the rocks in pieces before the Lord, but the Lord was not in the wind; and after the wind an earthquake, but the Lord was not in the earthquake; and after the earthquake a fire, but the Lord was not in the fire; and after the fire **a still small voice.**"*    1 Kings 19:11-12

Uncle Phil was in a panic and throwing a pissy fit by the time we got back to Battle Mountain, because the decent fall weather was now gone and the forecast called for days of sleet and snow. He felt we had wasted the last of the good weather, but if he had been on that hunt with me, I'm sure he would have been singing a different tune. I tried to tell him about it but that only upset him because he loved us like his own kids, so we geared up as soon as possible and headed up north to finish the claims. The ground held water like a sponge, so we had to go in while it was frozen, work all day leaving the truck parked on solid ground as not to get it stuck in the mud, and we would have to come out long after nightfall, when the ground re-froze again.

That far up in the wilderness, miles and miles from the nearest paved road, it was risky business. We started putting in claim corner and side center lines at the farthest northern point and worked our way toward Rossi mine, to the south, so every day we had to go less and less deeper into the back country.

By the first week in November we were almost done, and hoping to finish up in just one or two more days. We had several snowstorms that had passed through the area, but the air had warmed up somewhat and we were having several days of rain and especially sleet. It was kind of odd for this time of year in the high country when we normally should have had steady snow and very cold temperatures, but we weren't complaining, even though we were usually very cold and soaking wet by the end of the day.

One night when we got back to town my brother's girlfriend from Reno was there to greet us, and she had brought their two dogs, Rocky and Heidi, with her. Rocky was a well-mannered Pitbull and Heidi was a playful Boxer, both shorthaired dogs who didn't do so well in the cold.

The story that they had conspired together was that Renée, Bill's girlfriend, had thought to surprise him and he, of course, knew nothing of her and the dogs coming, and was totally surprised as I was to see them. Even better, the next morning at 3 AM we all loaded up in the cab of my 77 GMC truck, dogs and all, and "hi Ho, hi Ho, it's off to work we go!"

When we got in to our work area we found a fairly solid, rocky area to park the truck on. Renée was "schooled" on what not to do, while she definitely stayed in the truck while Bill and I ran in our claim lines for the day. No honking the horn. No driving or moving the truck at all (I had to leave the keys so she wouldn't freeze to death, right?). Only start the truck to get warm and only when absolutely necessary. Don't leave it run all day or you will run it out of gas. Don't eat all the food. And don't mess with any of the switches, lights, or stereo, as not to run the batteries down, because "No dear, AAA don't work out here".

There was about 2 inches of snow on the ground at dawn, when Bill and I loaded up our bundles of claim posts and took off to work for the day. By 11 AM the light snow flurries had turned to a very wet sleet as the day began to warm, causing most of the snow on the ground to melt, thus turning the landscape into mud. We were soaking wet by 3 PM when the sleet turned back to big fat snowflakes that soon had the countryside changed back to bright white. It made seeing my brother, who was running his parallel claim line 750 feet south of me, fairly easy to see when the snowfall died down from time to time.

An hour and a half later we met up at the end of his line and began the long trek over the rolling hills and ravines back to the truck. We knew the sun had set as darkness was beginning to settle in, even though we couldn't actually see that the sun had gone down because of the snowfall and dark gray sky. As the day faded out, the winds calmed and a thick silence accompanied the snow falling all around us, broken only by the sounds of our breathing and our boots steadily trudging through the fresh snow. It was then, as we were still three quarters of a mile away, that we heard the faint sound of music breaking the stillness.

With a few muttered cuss words we took off running, even as dog tired and wet as we were. It seemed to take forever to cover the ground between us and the truck, and hearing the "Steve Miller Band" getting louder and louder as we got closer, put a heavy sick feeling in the pit of my stomach. My legs and lungs felt like they were exploding when I finally jerked open the driver's door and turned the stereo control knob to the off position, and turned the inside light off as well. I looked over at my brother and turned the ignition switch to the start position. Click, click, click... The engine would not turn over. Billy Bob was doing the ass chewing so I focused on cleaning the battery terminals on both batteries and checking and tightening all the other electrical connections, including the starter.

GRRR... Click, click, click. "It's gonna be a long night," I said, "We'll have to ride it out till morning." With no moon or stars, i.e. total darkness in a snowstorm, it would be practically impossible to walk the five or six miles back to Rossi mine.

And a long, cold night it was. The snow never let up and the cloud cover never broke up either, holding the colder air above the clouds. It still must have been in the high 20s or low 30s because by 3:30 AM things were trying to freeze. We cut my thick woven seat covers off of the seat to try and cover up with. Bill and I were shivering because we were still soaking wet, so we kept Renée, who was nice and dry, between us, and Bill and I each put one of those shorthaired shivering dogs on top of us, and that seemed to help. About 6 AM I opened the door and stuck a tape measure into the fresh snow fall and it measured 15 inches.

Phil and Lori were both very adamant about their evening reports I had to give every night when we got in, so by now, they knew something was wrong. About all we had left for food were eight bananas and a bottle of Comtrex cold medicine, after we split up the last of our Kipper Snacks and Pork & Beans out of our work gear. Renée argued that the dogs should have a share of the food – I argued that probably in the next 24 hours I was gonna eat at least one of them. She was horrified, and those poor dogs went hungry.

Phil would be coming for us soon. The snow let up some, but kept falling off and on throughout the day, adding at least four more inches. Nothing living moved in this much snowfall, no rabbits, no Sagehen... Nothing. Late in the afternoon we all thought we heard a distant motor to the south that we knew had to be Phil, and later we learned that it was, in fact, the Unk. Without knowing our exact location he had made it to within a couple of miles of us before getting his Bronco stuck. By the time he dug and jacked it out it was after dark and all he could do was follow his own tracks back out to safety.

About 4 AM the storm temporarily broke, the clouds parted, and the sky lit up with big, beautiful, bright stars like only Nevada can display them. And like nowhere else, the temperature plummeted to at least 15 or 20 below zero within less than an hour. Everything froze, including our wet clothes. When the sun finally came up it found us all huddled together under the seat covers and shivering uncontrollably. By 10 AM the sun had warmed things up to just about 10° below freezing, and we knew we probably wouldn't survive another subzero night like last night. I took out one of my two spare tires, deflated it, and cleared a large area of snow down to ground level, in preparation to burn my tire in an attempt to dry our cloths and get warm. A nice two or three hour plume of black smoke while the sky was clear was going to be a nice bonus as well. It would be seen for miles.

And it was! The midafternoon sky was beginning to darken with clouds again when a small Cessna airplane flew over us. On its second pass it was so close that we could see Unk's grinning face in the window, before it bee-lined off back in the direction of Battle Mountain. Now that he knew exactly where to find us, Unk would have us out by supper time, or so we thought. At least it was enough hope to spare the dogs from being eaten for one more night.

An hour and a half after the plane left, the snow returned with a vengeance, and by nightfall we had another 3 inches of fresh snow on top of the frozen, crusted 19 inches we already had. Hopes of Phil reaching us faded as the ferocity of the blizzard increased, as it raged on until way after midnight. Then, as quickly as it came, it just stopped, as if God simply threw a switch that immediately killed the howling wind and pelting snow, and then there was just this eerie calm, peacefulness.

The cloud cover held its place in the night sky but we knew if it cleared before dawn, we would probably be found frozen to death by the time Phil got to us. I could no longer just sit there and shiver as I waited to see if we made it through another night. I made Renée give me her dry socks which she did without a fight, but she went to wailing something fierce and held her ground when I tried to explain why I had to eat one of the dogs in order to get enough energy and protein that I desperately needed in order to walk out to Rossi mine for help. Better to die in the snow than sit here and listen to her ball her head off any more, was my reasoning, so as the skies showed the first gray hint of predawn, I took off.

The first thing that became obvious was that it would be impossible to keep any kind of steady pace in this deep snow. To make matters worse, underneath the top 5 inches of snow was a layer of frozen or "crusted" snow that I kept breaking through with my every step, then sinking about 18 or 20 more inches into the layer of snow beneath the crust. Every step was a battle, and I only had about 6 miles to go. I had to stop and rest about every quarter mile or so, and exhaustion was trying hard to overwhelm me. If it had just been about me, I probably would have quit and just laid down in the snow. "Where are You, God?" I wondered. Where is my God of the mountains that I knew so well as a boy? "Help me, God. Here I am in Your mountains, where are You?"

By midday the skies cleared once again and the cold air it produced burned in my lungs with every gasping breath. My legs would either tremble or cramp, for which I could only stop, eat some snow, or chew on sticks I broke off the sagebrush that was often under my feet when I couldn't make out exactly where the road was beneath the snow. I remember regaining my thought patterns that I had no idea I had lost, then looking at the long trail of tracks behind me and being aware that I had no memory of making them. I was drifting in and out of reality and becoming delirious. I went down in the snow many times. My wet long johns had frozen to the skin on my thighs and right calf.

I was just lying there in the snow, part way up the hill, when that joyful feeling of euphoria that I had battled for so long began to swim around in my head and swallow me. "Get up!" said a crystal clear voice in my head. So real that it startled me back to consciousness and I jumped up and looked around to see who had spoken. I was still all alone on the hillside. I began trudging up the hill once again. Soon, I was getting over the top of the rise, and sat down in the snow for a rest. I must have closed my eyes, for how long I don't know, but again I heard a voice say, "Open your eyes and look." I opened my eyes, and there before me was the dump and open pit of the Rossi mine just a couple of hundred yards ahead of me. New life ran through my veins as I stood up and "set my jaw" to make it to the mine.

Although the mine was shut down for the winter, there were still maintenance personnel and mechanics in the shop building when I threw open the door. You should have seen the look on their faces – true "shock and awe". I must have looked a site. They grabbed me and dragged me over to an old chair and sat me down in front of a "salamander" diesel and used oil burning stove. You can imagine how wonderful the heat from that stove felt to me. I told them my sad tale as I rotated and thawed my legs, feet and calves out. They had already eaten their lunch's hours before yet managed to come up with the most wonderful gourmet meal, consisting of Pork and Beans, potato chips, crackers, and two fabulous Baby Ruth candy bars.

I tried to tell them we needed a snowplow, grader or dozer to get back into my brother and Renée, but they weren't having any of it. They had this jacked up, souped up, chained up 1976 International Travel All that they had built for just an occasion as this, and, "By God, we'll get your brother out of there for ya", they all agreed with all heads bobbing up and down.

Although my tracks were clearly visible for guidance, I insisted on going with them, rather than stay in the nice warm shop. Mostly because, after trekking 6 miles through this crap, I had my reserves about their rescue truck. They had no idea how much snow had drifted up between Rossi and my pickup.

So all three of the Rossi boys and I loaded up in their International "monster rescue truck", and off we went. The snow was often plowing right up over the hood as we bashed our way from snowdrift to snowdrift, sometimes having to back up and get a long run at many of them, in order to break our way through. Within a couple of miles the snow compacted into the grill and radiator causing engine overheating as no air could pass through the thick four core radiator that was behind the now plugged up transmission coolant radiator. The snow stopped us on several occasions, but we would shovel it out and get the truck rocking back and forth and eventually get it unstuck again. Then finally, about 3 miles into the rescue attempt, the trucks chained tires broke through the frozen crust of the earth beneath the snow, and sunk to its axles in the mud below.

I told them that I was too weak to walk back to Rossi, and God bless them, they told me to stay put with the heater running until they got back with help. Then they single filed out in the tracks the International had just made, and began their long trek back to Rossi. I watched them go for about 15 minutes until they disappeared over the skyline, then I shut off the engine, opened the hood, and disconnected the battery with the tools they had conveniently left in the back of the Travelall. I tied the battery into an old sweatshirt I found in the back seat, and tied the arms and bottom together with mechanics wire. I threw the tied arms of the sweatshirt over my head and one arm, and started my way back to Billy and Renée. As I had already broken a trail through the deep snow, going was much easier and I got back to my pickup just before sundown.

To my surprise and delight, Bill had already shoveled out four long trenches in front of each wheel and had all four of my tire chains laid out in them! As I opened the hood and began removing one of my batteries and disconnecting the other so the dead battery couldn't draw power from the fresh Travelall battery, Renée came around beside me and said, "I was sure we were gonna die, John, but your brother never gave up on you. He knew you would make it. He knew you would come back for us". Knowing how many times I had gone down in the snow ready to give up and quit, I felt so ashamed and weak. My brother believed in me more than I believe in myself. If it hadn't have been for those "voices", real or hallucinated, whether I wanted to or not, I probably would have given up, laid down in the snow, and let my brother die. That "fact" would haunt me for years, until many years later when thinking back on it, the Lord revealed the "truth" as to where that (His) voice came from. Now those memories give me cause to praise His Holy Name! Abba Father! You saved me, again! When I am weak, you are strong! Hallelujah!

When I hit the ignition switch with that International battery bolted in place, that big ol' 427 Interceptor roared to life! Snow and soot belched out of those twin stacks and the night air was filled with our laughter! While Bill and Renée sat under the heater I chained up all four of those massive 14 ½ inch wide by 36 inch tall Kelly Springfield bias mud and snow tires and reconnected my second battery as to charge it up as well.

Snowflakes were beginning to whirl about us as we kicked on the lights and locked in the front hubs. This was gonna be one hell of a ride. "Keep the dogs off of me and give me room", I said as we turned around and headed for the Rossi Mine. And it was "all or nothing", full throttle, from then on. Those chains were slinging "rooster tails" all the way out. When we got to that buried International, we stopped nose to nose, and I took the borrowed battery out of my truck, as my second battery allowed it to stay running, while I put my original battery back in its place, and then properly bolted the battery I had taken, back into the International, where I got it from.

A half mile before we got to Rossi we met up with the boys from the shop. They had chained up a motor grader and were working their way back into save us! They were more than happy to head back to the mine and let their rescue truck set where it was until better weather conditions presented a more opportune time to "fetch it back", God bless them. I offered to pay them for their trouble, but being true Nevadans, they were hurt by this suggestion.

Two miles south of Rossi, low and behold, we found the Unk stuck in a ditch. He had slid off of the road. God bless you, Unk! Thanks for not giving up! He told us that the sheriff's department wanted to wait until morning so he came himself. What an awesome friend. *"Greater love has no one than this, than to lay down one's life for his friends" (John 15:13).*

And this wasn't even close to the first time Uncle Phil had come to my rescue. Back in 1975, when I was in high school, he rolled into my yard in Red Bluff, California at 3 AM, in that hot rod Ford pickup of his with the .472 Cadillac engine in it, slow down just enough for me to run and jump through his passenger window, and had me back in Reno, Nevada for breakfast by morning. What a ride that was!

In the winter of 1976, my cousin Mickey and I along with his wife Margie and their one and a half year old daughter, Patricia (Trish), were living up behind the Duval mine outside of Battle Mountain, Nevada, at the old Copper Queen mine. Besides some claims I had staked with my Dad and brother, and some high grading here and there, it was my first mining venture/partnership. We had taken out a lease on the old shutdown Copper Queen mine and took to following a vein of turquoise down a decline on one of the upper benches of the old open pit wall.

We were pretty much broke until we could get enough turquoise out to sell, so we just settled in to our little trailer house for the winter when the snows came, and kept on mining. We probably could have gotten out of the canyon before it got too bad, but we were hiding my new Chevy truck from the finance company until we got a "payday" and I could get caught up on the payments. Phil was running loader at the Duval pit and would come by every week or two to check on us and bring us some much welcomed canned goods, bread and stuff. We listened to the old time "Mystery Theater" program on the a.m. radio every night, but the funniest entertainment was giving Trish a plate full of spaghetti...you kind of had to be there and see it to understand...funny, funny, funny.

Anyway, a few weeks before Christmas, we found ourselves snowbound when the winds drifted over the road down the canyon and sealed us in. We killed a deer and lived off of it for a while, and then we could only manage an occasional jackrabbit now and then. We tried everything to make those old scrawny Jacks edible. We even tried soaking them overnight in salt water, but a jackrabbit can't be made into a "cottontail" no matter what you do. It's a nasty business, eating jackrabbits is. Even today, after 40 years, the memory disgusts me still. After the rabbits were gone, Mickey brought home some kind of bird, cleaned and completely skinned that he swore was a blue grouse. It was a lie, as the meat (if you could call it that) was so stringy we had to boil it and it tasted just wrong, but it's what's for dinner, so we ate it too.

Then two days before Christmas, here comes the Unk walking up the canyon through the snow with a burlap potato sack full of food! How awesome is that! The snow had stopped his truck about a mile down the canyon so he packed in the rest of the way on foot! We cooked up the real food that he brought us, then he gave us the money to go back home to our families in Ely for Christmas! Once we walked out to his pickup with him, he took us to his house, and loaned us his little Datsun car to get there in! I will always honor you in my prayers, Unk. Thank you.

So, back to finding the Unk in the ditch below Rossi mine, we pulled him out and went to town looking for four big, thick steaks. And I don't believe anyone was happier than the dogs – I think they knew…

## CHAPTER 26

## Let's Make a Deal

Tra-la-la-boom-de-yay! With our bills once again paid up in advance until springtime, Lori and I took off for a couple of weeks to Nassau, Bahamas to "get warm". Because my heart was set on finding Spanish doubloons, and Lori was the all-time limbo champion, which paid the winner in quarts of rum, we spent most of our days snorkeling and floating around in the warm, clear Caribbean ocean, nursing my hangover. Even though I found no booty from the Spanish fleet, we did good on conch shells and sand dollars. Dive boats that we hired took us to the outer reefs to dive on shipwrecks. Back in those days, Paradise Island was actually still a paradise, with the exception of only one casino on the south end. You could spend the day on deserted white beaches, and swimming with sea rays and dolphins was still pretty common. The fish as well as the vegetation and coral were the most beautifully vivid and colorful I have ever experienced, and the waters are crystal clear and warm.

And a word of warning to nonbelievers and backslidden Christians; NEVER let Satan talk you into being a seafood "Explorer" when your head and belly are full up with rum. The locals in the Bahamas and Jamaica, as well, eat things that probably ought not to be so; at least for a couple of mainlanders from Nevada, anyway. In the end, it will not only hurt, and rip out your insides, but it will also leave a carpet stain that shows up on your hotel bill.

The most sobering event in which I partook was when I decided to photograph a large group of jellyfish. When I came up out of the water with a very large one stuck between my shoulder blades, my wife and many witnesses said I was literally running on top of the water, still wearing my swim fins! I ran to my room and boiled that jellyfish off of me in the shower, and of course, had Lori sterilize my back with...you guessed it...rum. And, uh yeah, it burned the heck out of me.

It all ended when I accidentally rubbed my shoulder blade on the coral reef and filled the water with blood. We were yanked out of the water and taken to shore for the last couple remaining days of our vacation.

About nine months after getting home, our daughter, Brandy Ann was born. She was not only the light of my life (Yup! Daddy's girl to the max!) but would also prove to be my greatest inspiration, my confidant, and my counselor as the years passed. And I must say, although incredibly effective,

I have never warmed up to the idea of being "scolded" by my little girl, regardless of age (both of ours), how much I needed it or how devastatingly accurate my scolding's have been... So keep up the good work, 2C! Love you...Thanks!

***

"So here's the deal", Billy Bob said to me over the phone. He was working underground at the Ward Mountain Declines, which are two identical parallel tunnels/drifts being driven down at about a 12° angle underneath Ward Mountain to intercept a huge silver ore deposit, thousands of feet beneath the surface. It was boasting of being the world's longest underground conveyor system, when completed, and was located just a few miles south of Ely.

Unfortunately for Alta Gold Mining Company, that owned the mine, they had drilled into an underground lake that was pouring thousands of gallons of water into the mine through two drill holes at about the 2000 foot level. One Tamerak "Jumbo" drilling machine was underwater and the water level was rising. As the rock in the "ribs" (sidewalls) and "back" (roof) became saturated, they began to "peel" (caving off in big slabs), and obviously time was of the essence if the mine was to survive at all.

The mine superintendent, a man named Drip (kid you not) and the owners had a meeting with state and federal mine inspectors to discuss their best options, and oddly enough, my name was mentioned. Probably do to my surviving multiple other really crappy mines (Gooseberry, Savage, Pole Canyon, Common Wealth, etc.) where I had worked with the mine inspectors in applying various ground stabilization methods (spiling, steel sets, shotcrete, pony sets, crows nests, etc.), in order to maintain some degree of ground control, where extreme "bad ground" had pushed engineering methods and miner ingenuity to the limits, in order to re-create a semi-safe mining environment where almost impossible ore extraction had actually not only become possible again, but profitable. The truth be known, one of the mine inspectors that was present at the meeting, and I, had become friends over a series of years where I worked in some incredibly unstable mines, and custom timbering and ground control were becoming my specialties. In fact, a few years later, in Eureka, Nevada, I would design and install a one-of-a-kind timbering system called "floating timbers" that would use all of the weight in the center of the building to hold up the outer sandstone walls of the Eureka Opera House while we excavated below the walls and installed concrete foundations, a basement and an elevator shaft, in another broken agreement where I was screwed out of $175,000, for my trouble.

The original Ward underground mine which was farther up the mountain, was the mine that I had made mine wedges for when I was 15, and who I later worked for right after I got out of high school, as did my cousin Mickey, back when they were called Silver King Mines.

Bill went on to tell me, "The lowest bid they have gotten up till now, is a little over 1 million bucks. And that's just to get them through the currently flooded area and install steel sets, rock bolts and chain-link. I know you can beat that price," he said.

Those tunnels were 16 feet high and 14 feet wide. That's a lot of steel, rock bolts and chain-link. Coincidentally (yeah, right...Hahaha), my brother's call came at a time when I was deeply meditating within my inner self on how much I hated living in the city. The "gang" situation in Reno was up and running and gaining momentum in the schools. Billy was now three years old, and it was time to think about his future in the institutes of higher learning, available to us in the Reno area, and... Oh yeah, I hated living in the city.

So it ended up, the "deal" we made with Drip and Alta Gold was that we would work on pumping out the flooded ground, and re-gaining ground control, working straight graveyard shifts until normal mining activities could resume and the declines could be driven past the flooded area. "Gaso" pumps would be installed and run 24 hours a day until the water table of the underground lakes dropped and the ground was stabilized in order to continue driving the declines to intercept the ore zone. And the price? A cool million? Probably should have. A half a million? You would think so, but no (again, i.e. Pee-Wee Herman). How about "six bits and carbide"? – That's my Dad's term for days' pay, and it equals $.75 a day and free carbide for the old style carbide lamps we used to use before battery powered lights came along, FYI.

As bad as it sounds now, that was pretty much the deal with the agreement that my brother and I would maintain our employment with them for the life of the mine. At the time, the life of the Ward Declines Project was about 12 years – at least that's what they suckered their investors...and us...into believing. What it meant for me was, realistically, about 7 to 10 years of stability for my growing family, and my best excuse to get out of the city and away from all the drama Lori's friends and family were creating in my life and marriage; and besides, I missed my folks. Of course, later on, in Ely I would find out what drama really looked like when it's personified!

So it came to pass, that I loaded up Billy, now three years old, and took him with me to stay at Dad and Mom's house in Ely. Lori, pregnant with Brandy (we didn't know it was Brandy, yet), stayed behind in Reno because it was commonly believed at that time that doctors in Ely still did stuff like waving dead cats and chickens over your head, and such. So we agreed that Brandy, like her brother, would be born in Reno and I would be there when the time came.

The first thing I learned, being back in Ely, was that Ronnie and Stevie and just about everybody else I knew had also become "Dad's" about the same time I did, so driving around Ely became insanely treacherous. I'm talking about

"Diaper Wars"! Poopy, gloopy, droopy, stinky rotten diapers flying through the air at extremely high rates of speed. They were most commonly thrown from a moving vehicle, usually on Main Street while doing 35 mph, and connecting with an oncoming vehicle also doing 25 to 35 mph in the opposite direction, making the impact of the spinach baby food butt bomb at about 50 to 70 miles per hour…all over your windshield, or into your open side window (God forbid!).

The worst one I got was when I took my 66 GTO out on the highway to Cummins Lake, to get out of the war zone, and Ronnie got me dead center in the windshield while we were both doing over 70 miles per hour! What earthly food substance they could have possibly fed their kid to create this horrible concoction, I have no idea, but it was beyond rotten meat level. There really are no words to describe what he did to my car, and my "gag reflex" being very low anyway, I threw up inside my own hot rod before I could get stopped. I could clearly hear Ronnie's screaming hysterical laughter over our roaring engines as we passed each other, and it still haunts me to this day. Knowing Ronnie as I do, he probably had been saving that "blown ass-gasket" just for me, since the child's birth. And therein lies the issue; me and Stevie and everybody else always came out on the short end of the stick because our "poop bomb" attacks were fairly random, whereas, Ronnie's attacks were methodological, strategically planned and executed… Poop Terrorism taken to its most disgusting degree that, to this very day, commands my utmost respect and envy.

***

"I found the perfect house for us!" I excitedly exclaimed to my 8 ½ month along, pregnant, no-nonsense cuz I'm not in the mood, precious princess, and most loving wife. The response was silence… Dead air in the receiver… Then a low, intense growl; Grrrrrrr… Timing being everything, it was quickly becoming obvious that good timing was a skill I did not possess, nor had the ability to master.

The old (built in 1907!) rock house on Campton Street had been for sale for over a year. I had always loved that mini-castle looking house. The two old Basque's that built it surely never even owned a level or a plumb-bob, as was evident in the "wavy" pyramid shaped walls and ceiling, but the 8 x 8 timbering and 3 foot thick solid rock basement walls, that were founded on bedrock, made it the most solid and strongest house in Ely.

"Small? Sort of… The easier to clean, my dear… Cozy, would be a better description… And it's bulletproof!" I probably should've left that part out. However comforting to me, it was very unsettling for Lori, as I was constantly in the process of convincing her (and her mother) that I have successfully abandoned my "old ways and former associates" and was now a "responsible" (whatever that means) husband and father. Yeah… I should have thought my presentation (sales pitch) through a little better before I called her.

"The house and the brand-new steel shop building… What? Did I say shop building? Well, yeah, it comes with a… More of a "garage" than a shop building, actually... How big? Not very big... Well, I think it's only like 40' x 60' but it's fully insulated and on an 8 inch thick solid, one piece concrete pad that you could (and I have) drive a D8 dozer on to... Huge! No, now honey, I wouldn't say it's huge... But, hey, listen! There is a two-seater outhouse out back behind it with a built on chicken coop! How cool is that? And the best part is, it's on over an acre of land, and is built in its own little canyon (more of a gully or ditch) all by itself! No neighbors! Hallelujah! Just what WE been lookin' for, right Babe? If you want, I can sign the papers on it tomorrow! You're gonna love it!"

"GRRRRRRRR....... "(Louder, much more deeply intense).

"Oh..... You want to see it, huh...Hmmmm... Okay. But I just hope they don't sell it out from under us in the meantime... Can you come tomorrow? Your Mom's not coming, is she?" Yeah, 8 ½ months pregnant, 336 miles away, over 10 summits, and with winter once again bearing down on us... I shamefully admit that my selfishness knew no bounds... And yet, she loves me still. Amazing. If you can't see the miracle in that, you're blind. She has always been the essence of God's mercy and grace, and because of her, I am truly blessed to this very day. Thank You, Lord. And thank you, Lori, again, for not "kicking me to the curb" as I so justly deserved.

Two days later...

"And this can be the babies room", I said, as she systematically went through the house, room by room, for the third time. Her crinkled brow and silent demeanor told me it's best to shut up while she professionally evaluates every possible option and scenario for each room, and the house itself, as she mentally calculated the house's overall ability to meet her needs for a growing family (see Proverbs 31:10-28). This, of course, was galaxies beyond my ability to reason. I simply wanted to go into 30 years of mortgage debt because it was a cool looking house, and I wanted that shop. Cool and calculating, she was. Finally, she looked at me with that deep furrowed brow look, at what might be mistakenly (or not) taken as a scowl, and gave a slight nod of agreement.

"Better get your butt back to Reno, John, because it's about time," she said. A week and a half later my beautiful blue-eyed baby girl was handed to me in the delivery room of Washoe Med. The first thing she did was reach in and steal my heart, and then wrap me tightly forever around her finger, as it remains to this day (see Proverbs 31:29-31).

When I got back to the mine I found that the pumps that were barely keeping up with the flooding were now actually beginning to gain a little ground and the water level was beginning to slowly drop. Very slowly, at that.

One night, after we managed to hook a chain on to the Tamarack Jumbo and pull it out of the water with the mucker, we could tell by the water movement, about where the water was gushing out of the highest of the two drill holes. Even though I came away freezing and soaking wet, I climbed in the bucket of that Wagner ST8 8 yard mucker, had my brother raised the bucket and drive into the water as far as he dared, as not to kill the diesel motor. I was close enough to the face that I managed to jam a 6 foot drill steel with a rag wrapped around the end of it, up into the flooding drill hole, and drove wedges into the hole, all around the steel to hold it in place. With half of the incoming water volume shut down the big pumps would be able to pump out the mine at a much faster rate. We would be able to continue placing steel sets and rock bolting chain-link into the flooded area within a few days (weeks ahead of schedule), and thus reestablishing ground control as the water level decreased.

As Bill was backing the mucker up the decline and out of the water, "there came such a rumble deep down in the ground" (Big Bad John, by Jimmy Dean, 1961- check it out on YouTube!). The air blast almost knocked me out of the bucket and into the water and the ground shook so violently that I thought the whole mountain was coming down on us. The mine quickly filled with dust, so thick that I could barely make out my brother's light only a few feet away, in the operator's seat of the Wagner ST8.

As our self-rescuers are only effective in the event of a mine fire, they were useless to us in this dust, so we grabbed rags from under the seat of the mucker and did our best to tie them around our faces, as we choked for air. We felt our way through the thick dust and we made our way over rocks and boulders until we found the air manifold at the end of the 4 inch Victaulic pipe used to pump compressed air to the drill machines. Bill grabbed the handle of the end ball valve and yanked it open. To our relief, high-pressure air screamed out of the open valve and into the mine, meaning that the 4 inch steel Victaulic air supply line had not been severed in the cave in. We not only had air but it was clearing and settling the dust around us, slowly regaining our visibility.

Unfortunately, the first thing we noticed was the bent piece of 6 inch steel Victaulic pipe we had climbed over to get to the air manifold. It was the broken water line from the water intake to the Gaso pumps. The mine was quickly filling with water.

Great. In this business of hard rock mining, you try to keep all the different possible scenarios of how easily and commonly death can take you, locked up back in the dark recesses of your mind. Yet they always seem to escape and run free in your thoughts and dreams when you lose your focus and allow your mind to wander. You think of being "slabbed", in a cave-in, trapped alone in the dark, starving, suffocating, choking and burning to death in a mine fire, methane gas, drilling into a "miss" (a live, unexploded drill hole full of dynamite), etc., etc., etc.. But drowning? Naw…to slow. At least most other ways are usually quick and for the most part, painless. I remember at one point, agreeing that, if that's the way it plays out, we would shut off our lights so we didn't have to watch our own brother drowned.

That was sobering enough to get us moving on finding a way out.

I found my 1 gallon "lucky" (lucky because it survived the cave-in at Gooseberry, also… Now that I think about it, maybe it's not so lucky…) Stanley thermos on the back of the mucker and shared a cup of coffee with Bill, as we looked things over and discussed our options.

If we took the mucker back down to the edge of the water and raised the bucket as high as it would go, we could probably shimmy it forward and back enough times between the ribs (sidewalls of the mine) to get it turned around. Then we could use it to dig our way through the caved area. But the only place we have room to put the rock we dig out with the mucker would be in the water, which would cause the water level to rise with every bucket load of material, and the water was already coming up fast, as it was. We had nothing to "bar down" the loose rock that hung over us in the freshly exposed hole/area where the rock had collapsed in from, so at great risk, we climbed the pile of caved rock to almost the top, where the air pipe came out of the pile. As we did, we could hear the sucking sound of the Gaso pump echoing through the end of the buried 6 inch water line, somewhere within the pile of rubble. We looked at each other with wide eyes as the idea seemed to hit both of us at the same time. We scrambled back down off the muck pile and found the 6 inch piece of Victaulic pipe that had been knocked off of the pump line when the cave-in occurred. It was bent about halfway down its 20 foot length. Our hearts sank at the realization that we could not reconnect the pipe. Besides, the other end of the pipe line was buried somewhere under the rubble pile and the unburied end was still hanging about 12 feet up the rib, close to the back (ceiling) where it had broken out of its Victaulic coupler.

Discouraged, we sat down and poured our last cup of coffee and passed it back and forth between us in silence. That's when the miracle happened.

As I looked down at the rising water line, my light fell on the very end of a piece of 6 inch thick Victaulic pipe that was barely sticking up out of the water, against the rib! I know it wasn't there before, and even if it was, it must have been left there by the day shift when they were "hanging services" (installing air and water pipes) before the mine flooded. That, in itself would be a miracle because they are never allowed to leave tools, unused pipe or anything else in the work areas at the end of shift, as not to be in the way of the miners coming in to work on the next shift. Space, underground, is very limited. Both of us waded out, grabbed a hold of the pipe and pulled it up the decline onto dry ground. It was a full, new 20 foot long stick of 6 inch pipe! We just grinned and stared at each other in amazement! How could this be?

With no time left to ponder the question, we set about the task of rescuing ourselves. With a pick and shovel we climbed back up to the top of the pile and commenced digging out the end of the pipe, praying that it hadn't been damaged. About 4 feet into the pile we found it, not only in tact but with its Victaulic coupler still in place! Bill said he saw another Victaulic fitting on the mucker, and when he looked under my thermos it was still there. While Bill fired up the mucker, raised the bucket and began the process of turning it around in the narrow drift, I pulled out my spud wrench (steel crescent adjustable wrench with a long pointed handle) and began loosening the bolts on the Victaulic fittings. Once Bill was turned around he positioned the bucket directly underneath the hanging end of the 6 inch pipe that still remained in place near the top of the drift. We then dragged the 20 foot piece of steel pipe up the muck pile and placed the end of it right beside the pipe we had just unburied beneath the pile. God knows that pipe is very heavy, and as I look back I humbly thank Him for the strength he gave us that night. We set the other end of the pipe on the bucket of the underground loader, then I climbed in the bucket and Bill got in behind the controls.

Bill slowly raised me and the pipe up to the open hanging end of pipe near the back. It was a very difficult struggle, by myself, but by the grace of God, I managed to align the two pipes, end to end, work the rubber gasket into place over both of them, and finally get the Victaulic clamps into the precut grooves and tighten the nuts down all the way onto the bolts to secure the clamp tightly in place. Bill lowered me back down and as we both climbed back up the pile of cave-in rubble to reconnect the other end, a huge "slab" weighing about 2 tons, peeled off of the back and hit just inches away from us. So close...

"Come on, let's get it done and get out of here", Bill said to me in a calm, steady voice. "I got stuff (not exactly his words) to do today," he finished as we climbed over the 2 tons of rock that had barely missed us, and climbed the rest of the way up to the pipe.

Somehow the new piece of pipe came out about an inch too long, but we both pulled on it with all of our might and shoved it enough to get it to butt up against the other one. With a slight adjustment using a mine ax, for proper alignment, we were then able to get the rubber gasket and Victaulic coupling into place. As the pipes joined together and the pump began sucking water instead of air, the pipe began jumping and bucking violently. We could barely hold it in place long enough to get the nuts started and tightened onto the bolts, and as we did, it shook loose more rocks that fell all around us (Tommyknockers, more likely). It was a battle, to say the least, but we finished tightening the bolts as the weight of the water coming up the pipe stopped it from bouncing and knocking more rocks down on us (damn Tommyknockers).

We sat down and took a break back at the water's edge, and watched to make sure the water line was once again receding. We were shivering, but after we had a smoke, Bill climbed on the mucker and went to digging out along the rib opposite of where the other rib had collapsed. He ran the mucker up the right side of the decline and stacked the muck on the left side, as far back into the water as he could go. The mine soon darkened with diesel exhaust and it burned our eyes. Then suddenly, all the smoke and dust began moving in an upward direction to the top of the pile above where Bill was digging. Another huge slab peeled off the back and crashed onto the front end of the mucker, but other than scaring the crap out of us, didn't break anything.

After he took a couple more bucket loads out, Bill and I climbed up the pile to find a 2' x 3' opening. It must have been close to the predawn because, as we looked through the hole and up the decline toward the portal, we could see the bright red glow of the laser that was mounted just inside the first few sets of timber. It's beam shined all the way down 2000 feet to the face, and is used to keep the two downward parallel tunnels perfectly straight. Every morning, just before the predawn light crept across the eastern sky, the laser would emit an "aura" around itself that was nothing short of spectacular, and it usually lasted only for a few moments. As we looked up the long sloping tunnel toward the surface, that's what we saw.

As we gathered up our lunch boxes and gear I looked on the mucker for my lucky thermos, but to no avail. As I turned to leave I found it, right where Bill had turned the mucker around, smashed flatter than a pancake. Bill had killed my lucky thermos with the mucker. I'm not superstitious, but oddly, after he smashed that thermos I never got trapped in another cave-in…just sayin'.

Although the sun was still not quite up over the Schell Creek Mountains yet, the sky was very light when we walked out of the mine. Daylight felt especially good in my eyes today. Bert Cooper, the night mechanic, as well as my former truant officer, probation officer, baseball coach, and an all-around good man, was heading towards us in full underground gear. "What kept you boys?" He said, "You're late and I was just coming down the hole to look for ya." He was agitated about like a father looking out for a couple of overdue kids.

"Sorry, Bert" I said. "Yeah, me too, Bert. It won't happen again, pard", Bill added. Burt's crinkled brow relaxed and a hint of a smile crossed his face, "well, okay, I guess. I don't know about you two… Never know what you're up to next," he mumbled as I put my arm around his shoulder and we walked towards the "dry" (showers and changing room).

"Everything all right?" Bert asked, as we went by the shop.

"Tommyknockers gave us some trouble, but it's all good now." I said. Bill and I took a quick smile at each other and Bert looked back and forth at the two of us with an obvious look of skepticism, then reiterated, "Yeah…right…like I said… I don't know about you two… never can tell what you boys are up to".

Within a few days the caved area was mucked out and steel sets, chain-link and rock bolts were installed to stabilize the cross fault that had given way. The water level had dropped dramatically with the one drill hole plugged, and steel sets were being installed right up to the face. With the velocity of water flow in the remaining drill holes substantially decreasing daily, it would be a matter of a week or so until normal mining could be once again get underway and daily advancement of the twin declines would resume. I was so looking forward to getting back to simply mining again; round in, round out.

That bubble was quickly burst, when a few days later, Lori and I signed the final papers on the rock house before Bill and I headed to work. When we got to the mine there were notes pinned to our "diggers" (underground work clothes) that said Dip...oops...Drip wanted us to come to the administration office and see him. Yup... You guessed it. Over many years, I've often pondered why it is so difficult for most mining outfits to simply keep their word to their employees.

"Downsizing", Drip said. "Cutbacks due to unforeseen expenses", he dribbled. "Appreciated our good work, but..." He blabbered on in his well-rehearsed speech that he undoubtedly had perfected on countless employees before he ever put it on Bill and me. And creamy smooth, bull pucky it was, too. So much for our deal with Alta Gold. I now have taken on two full home mortgages and lost my job, all in the same day. Foremost in my mind was cracking this guy's skull and finding my wife a job, maybe two, to help out. Otherwise we don't have a chance of making it through the winter. Bill, knowing my temper, put his hand on my shoulder, leaned close to my face, and in a soft clear voice spoke just one word that everyone in the room clearly heard; "Jail". I let out a long breath that I didn't even know I was holding in, and Drippy just stared at me and went white as a ghost, realizing he was just a split second away from a beating.

To this day I'm not sure how I contained my rage, but I turned around and walked out of his office without uttering a word. As if sent by Satan himself, the greatest test came a few moments later when we stepped into the dry (changing room) to be greeted by two brand-new hands, in shiny new hardhats, boots, and gear belts.

"Hi", the taller of the two proclaimed as he stepped toward us with an outstretched hand. "I'm Danny Drip and this is my cousin, Butch. We just started working here, today", the dipstick proudly declared. Grabbing his outstretched hand, I squeezed as hard as I could until I could feel the bones in his hand grind together. I jerked his wide, terror filled eyes right into mine and screamed as loud as I could..."BAAAAAAAAAAAAAAAA!" When I let go of his hand he stumbled backwards until he fell over the wooden bench seat behind him and hit the floor on his butt. As his cousin rushed to help him get back up, Bill glared at them and said, "Get the hell out of here", and, POOF! Like magic, they were gone.

***

The ride back to town wasn't long enough. How was I gonna tell Lori about this. Our plans of all of us finally living together as a family had just gone out the window, as Alta Gold owned the only currently operating mines in the area. Now I would have to find work at another mine out of the area and leave my wife and kids in a strange town. At least my folks would be there for them, as they loved my wife as their own daughter and were very elated to have their grandkids so close.

I was kicking myself for at least not gaining the satisfaction of nailing that lying dimwit to the wall, but Bill's word "Jail" had rightfully hit a nerve in me. Not only had I swore to Lori that I would, to the best of my ability, not do anything that my kids would be ashamed of me for, but I had also not been to jail in Nevada in several years.

For some reason my thoughts drifted back to Tonopah when my cousin Mickey and I were (I feel, unfairly) arrested for 12 gauging a dozen Chukar that happened to be walking up the old mine dump that Bobby's Buckeye Bar (yeah, a cat house) was built upon. In our defense, I explained to the judge (over the jail phone on a Sunday afternoon, mind you) that we had come back to Hot Creek Valley from Reno, and searched for the elusive birds in question for the entire weekend, without so much as a feather to show for our hard effort and the vast expenses we had incurred, and vaguely alluded to the possibility that we may or may not have temporarily taken leave of our senses (more like, lost our minds).

Before leaving Warm Springs we had done a proper job of adequately drowning our misfortune in beer (Mickey's sober wife, Margie was driving) and were now headed back, empty-handed, to Reno. As we barely entered just a teensy-weensy little bit within the Tonopah city limits, a "whole herd" of the seemingly mythical game birds ran across the road in front of us!

As we skidded to a stop they took flight only to land a short distance away, but still within 12gauge range, on the old mine dump ... Upon which the house of ill -repute also resides. Overwhelmed with joy and believing the Good Lord responsible for this immense blessing, we set about "harvesting" our "bounty", until our shotguns were empty.

"Did we not hear the girls inside the building screaming?" asked the judge. "No, your honor, as my ears were ringing too loudly from the blasts of our guns", says I.

"Were we aware that we were blocking traffic on a federal highway?"

"Not really, your honor. I just figured they had stopped to cheer us on or watch... And besides, your grace, there was no place to pull off of the road, as you well know, that there are guardrails on both sides of the highway, so technically, your honor, sir, it's not totally our fault," I explained.

The judge was sympathetic in as much as he acknowledged how the dry season had made finding chukar almost impossible, as not many hatchlings had survived. He even went as far as to confide in us that he too, had spent many days out in search of the tasty game birds himself, but with similar results.

That's probably what prompted him to do what he did when he said, "Please hand the phone back to the jailer if you would Mr. Gergen, but before you go I would like to clarify that you and your cousin are both very remorseful for your idiotic crimes and confess that you acted out of pure ignorance because you two "mighty hunters" were slightly inebriated and somewhat confused as to your exact location, correct?"

"Yes sir, your honor sir, that is correct," we agreed. I think he must have been a new judge in Tonopah and obviously had no knowledge of my many "priors" here. I handed the phone to the jailer who nodded his head and said "Uh-huh, uh-huh," several times into the receiver, then hung up the phone. While he was talking to the judge, Mickey and I slipped our wallets to Margie.

"The fine is $25 apiece, in cash, no checks, and we will be confiscating the birds as evidence," he flatly said with a totally expressionless face.

Margie dug through our wallets and counted the money out on the desk as the jailer took the cuffs off and handed us back our empty shotguns. That was 1973, and I was 16 years old. The price of "redemption" went up dramatically from there, as the years passed. But back then, the price to be paid for our heinous crimes in order to regain our freedom were $25 apiece and 12 plump, juicy chukar birds.

It was also one of the last times I got in trouble with the law and could get out of it by myself. As I look back, I realized that if I were to actually write about all the other times I crossed it up with the legal system, the end of each chapter would carry the bold words, "**BUT GOD...**" as the solution to each particular incident as they unfolded in my life. When I could no longer pay the price to get myself set free, or in other words redeem myself, I look back and see God's intervention on my behalf. I, at the same time, naturally gave all the credit to my "good luck" and my "exemplary wit", not to mention my folks continually bailing me out and getting me really good lawyers.

Redemption. Interesting concept. Google defines it as;
1) The action of saving or being saved from sin, error, or evil.
2) The action of regaining or gaining possession of something in exchange for payment, or clearing a debt.

Sounds like "ransom" to me. And that "something"? To me that" something" is "freedom" in the truest-sense. Try this one… I understand it a little better, I think; Bible.org rightly says that Redemption means to free someone from bondage. It often involves the paying of a ransom, a price that makes redemption possible. Originally, the payment of a price to secure the release of a prisoner of war, also used it to describe the release of a slave, and sometimes a word that came to be used in terms of the release of a person under the sentence of death. Redemption always means the payment of a price to secure release.

I personally believe the Apostle Peter to have been a sort of, "loose cannon", like me in many ways. I can relate well to him, in any event, and love the way he explains redemption in his First Epistle, chapter 1, verses 17-21;

*"And if you call on the Father, who without partiality judges according to each one's work, conduct yourselves throughout the time of your stay here in fear; knowing that you were not redeemed with corruptible things, like silver and gold, from your aimless conduct received by tradition from your fathers, but with the precious blood of Christ, as of a lamb without blemish and without spot. He indeed was foreordained before the foundation of the world, but was manifest in these last times for you who through Him believe in God, who raised Him from the dead and gave Him glory, so that your faith and hope are in God,"*

What Peter is clearly telling us is that Christ has redeemed us (set us free) from an empty way of life, leading to our slavery to our sins and thus, to certain death, as it has been handed down to us by our ancestors. And this redeeming love of Christ was present even before sin entered the equation (vs. 18-19).

Wow. Have you ever given serious thought about the fact that Jesus Christ loves you knowing everything there is to know about you, even in your darkest sins? That deeply humbles me, knowing all I have done, and He loves me still… enough to do what He did that day on the cross to ransom me and pay the full price in His own blood… For me…ME!... And for you too!

Our worth is never again to be measured in bank accounts, abilities, IQ, gold, silver or any other type of monetary or worldly value, but only by the price that our Heavenly Father has paid for us on our behalf, which is the Blood of His Only Son, Jesus Christ, that horrific day over 2000 years ago on that Roman cross! Our worth is measured by what God paid for us… Period. You and I are now God's possession (1 Peter 2:9) and no one can snatch us out of his hand (or my son! Hold him tight, Lord!), (John 10:28-29).

Back in 1973 the price of freedom for Mickey and I was a mere $25 apiece and a dozen game birds. That's the cheapest I ever got off. As time progressed in my life, my sins and disobedience raised that price higher and higher until eventually, not me or anybody else could pay the penalty for what I had done…BUT GOD, loving me while I was still in my sins (Romans 5:6-11, check this one out!), sent His Son to pay the ultimate ransom price for me…for us! FOR YOU!

Do you long to escape your past? Do you wonder if you will ever be free of the pain, shame and guilt that are in your heart?

I use to think about my past and doubt that God could ever love me, and that was a lie from hell that kept me bound for many years. Get this: no matter what you have done or how you have failed, God loves you unconditionally and wants you to be free of your past and embrace the wonderful life He has in store for you. You and I need to trust Him to heal our hearts and the hearts of those we have hurt, and allow Him to change the course of our lives!

CHAPTER 27

## Deals & Covenants, Rainbows & Circumcision

With our Reno house still up for sale we were juggling not just one, but two mortgages when Alta broke their deal with Bill and me. Lori took it much better than I did, especially considering a new baby, two mortgages, a car payment, and winter in full swing. With her college degree as a legal secretary she was very limited on possible jobs in the field of law (actually, none at the time) in small-town Ely, but was gladly welcomed into employment at Eastern Nevada Realty as the owner/proprietor, George Swallow's executive secretary. It was a position my own mother had filled for many years when I was a young boy, until her retirement. I still remember the smells of the hair salon that used to be in the back of the office building and visiting with our dear friend, Dicie Johnson there, on my way home from school.

Even so, we were still coming up short on the bills, but looking back in my life, that's just typically how most mining deals go. I seriously have enough worthless mining stock certificates in my portfolio to wallpaper my bathroom, and that is about the full extent of their worth. Ya, ya, I made a lot of deals over the years that I always managed to hold up my end on, and usually ended up being the only one who did. Of course, at the time the deals were made, those stock certificates were the guarantee to my family's prosperous and carefree future, including the highest education possible for my children. I know...sucker.

To this day it still baffles and frustrates my brother and I how people and companies can raise millions of dollars to throw into a phony mining deal or scam, when we have a legitimate high grade silver/copper mine with over 20,000 tons of ore (currently, about $8 million) sitting in a stockpile, and can't raise a dime to build a small mill and put the mine back into production.

Yet over the years we have been contracted to stake claims, drill worthless properties and even build several of the highest quality free gold gravity mills for people who have no ore or any intention of mining anything. Where integrity used to mean everything in the mining industry, it is now taken as a sign of weakness.

I am convinced that the only One left to honors their "deals" is God Himself. Ooops! Did I say "deal"? My bad. I often have pastors get upset when I tell them that I made a deal with God. They barked back at me "God doesn't make deals!" Well... Whatever. Okay, for arguments sake we will use the term, "covenant". That's Mo Betta? And when God makes a covenant you don't have to take no "down the road" stock options, either. As a matter of fact, when God makes a deal (oops!) or covenant, He quite often seals it with a sign or pledge to guarantee its authenticity, or to "seal the deal" such as a covenant he made with Noah, including every living creature (Genesis 9:8-17) and all of creation, after the flood (Genesis chapters 6 – 9).

*"Thus I establish My covenant with you: never again shall all flesh be cut off by the waters of the flood; never again shall there be a flood to destroy the earth."*

*And God said: "this is the sign of the covenant which I make between Me and you, and every living creature that is with you, for perpetual generations; I set My rainbow in the cloud, and it shall be for the sign of the covenant between Me and the earth."* Genesis 9:11-13.

How awesome! Noah got a big beautiful rainbow! I didn't. And neither did it Abraham.

Mine came on Halloween, 1996; my darkest hour. All my money, power and attorneys had failed and could not save me from what was to come. I had no escape plan, no "plan B". We'll talk about this part a little later on, I think. I had just finished reading a paperback book that uncle Phil had sent in to me called 70×7 and Beyond, in which this, I think, intellectually challenged person calling himself Monty Montana, was saved and transformed, by God no less, from a life of drugs, crime and prison, and into a life of freedom, deliverance and righteousness. As I read his testimony about how he called out to Jesus in his despair, I could totally relate, and when he finally gave his life to Jesus I thought, maybe it's about time for me, too. So I said, "Lord, I don't know for sure how this works, so You gotta help me". I sat down on my bunk, contemplating several different ways I might force someone to kill me, as suicide seemed to distasteful, not to mention shameful for my family to bear as the end to my legacy, such as it was. As I sat down I accidentally (right) sat on my Gideon's Bible. I picked it up, and just for the heck of it, opened it somewhere close to the center. Psalm 51 stared back at me. King David's famous covenant with God is outlined in 2 Samuel 7:10-13, but I know in my own heart that Psalm 51 is the "deal" that David made with God that counted the most.

God was answering my prayer I had just made to Him for help. He was showing me how it works. It was David's prayer of repentance after he had sinned with Bathsheba, and paid a high price for the repercussions of those sins.

I read and reread Psalm 51 over and over until tears ran down my face, especially the "deal" part of it in versus 10-13. Did you catch that part? It's so worth repeating here that I'm gonna;

*Create in me a clean heart, O God, and renew a steadfast spirit within me,*

*Do not cast me away from Your presence, and do not take Your Holy Spirit from me.*

*Restore to me the joy of Your salvation, and uphold me by Your generous Spirit.*

*Then I will teach transgressors Your ways, and sinners shall be converted to You.*

(See also Psalm 19:11-14, Ezekiel 36:26-27, Isaiah 55:7, Isaiah 57:14-19, Jeremiah 29:11-14, and Job 22:21-30)

"I'll do it, Lord!" I cried, "I'll serve You if You save me and get me out of this." As I sat there boobin' like a baby, I dropped my Bible to the floor. When I picked it up my eyes fell on to Isaiah 41:10 *"Fear not, for I am with you; be not dismayed, for I am your God. I will strengthen you, yes, I will help you, I will uphold you with My righteous right hand."*

Don't you ever let someone tell you that God does not speak to you in and through His Holy Word! Only a fool would say such a thing, and you are no fool.

God has kept his promise to me all these years and I do my best to keep my end of the deal. Our God keeps His word, and He is a covenant keeping God!

Later that evening Armando Munoz was sent by the Lord to explain salvation through the shed blood of Jesus Christ to me. That Halloween night in 1996, Jesus Christ became my Lord and Savior, and forever changed the course of my life... But I didn't get a rainbow. And as I said earlier, neither did Father Abraham.

The account of Abraham's covenant is laid out in Genesis chapters 12 through 17. It begins in 12:1-2 where the Lord said to Abram;

*I will make you a great nation; I will bless you and make your name great; and you shall be a blessing. I will bless those who bless you, and I will curse him who curses you; and in you all the families of the earth shall be blessed.*

The covenant continues to in chapters 15 and 17. This covenant is really worth your time to study as it belongs to you as well, if you are Christ's, as Galatians 3:26-29 clearly explains. In particular, look at verse 29 which states;

*"And if you are Christ's, then you are Abraham's seed, and heirs according to the promise."*

Hallelujah! Those blessings are ours!

Now with all that, you would think Abraham would get something cool like the rainbow that Noah got as a sign to "seal the deal", rieeeght?

Nope. Read Genesis 17:1-11. Wow. At 99 years old, God tells Abraham; *"and you shall be circumcised in the flesh of your foreskins, and it shall be a sign of the covenant between Me and you."* (Verse 11). At 99 years old, mind you... Ouch!

Noah got a rainbow and Abraham got circumcision. God forgive me, I am ashamed to admit this, that I sometimes get angry at God when all around me, believers and nonbelievers alike, who mostly use the name of Jesus as a cuss word, are getting rainbows when I am doing everything I know to do to abide in Him and walk in His light (failing daily, mind you) and getting circumcision, so to speak. Man, I think I need to grow up and get over it. My Lord and Master has never left me or forsaking me, and has always kept His word. Life is not all rainbows, and I understand that.

I have friends who tell me "what doesn't kill you makes you stronger," but sometimes what doesn't kill you cripples you. It is in those times that I become the most vulnerable to doubt an offense. Especially when it involves a long waiting period, often many years, of clinging to my faith in hopes of getting my prayers answered concerning healing or deliverance of those I love the most."...*and having done all, to stand,"* (Ephesians 6:13) is often very difficult for me over these long periods of waiting.

Jesus said, *"Blessed is he who is not offended because of me,"* (Luke 7:23) yet in my insecurity, I echoed the cries of the prophet Jeremiah, *"Righteous are You, O Lord, when I plead with You; yet let me talk with You about Your judgments. Why does the way of the wicked prosper? Why are those happy who deal so treacherously? You have planted them, yes, they have taken root; they grow, yes, they bear fruit. You are near in their mouth but far from there mind"* (12:1-2).

Pastor Brian Houston said, "No mature Christian who is seasoned in the Word has any reasonable excuse to live their life offended." And like I keep saying, a casual Christian is ignorant of spiritual warfare, and will always be offended. Being routinely offended over the years had made me habitually resentful and negative, and nobody wants to be around somebody that just constantly drags them down with negativity. After paying attention to what was consistently coming out of my mouth, I now make a conscious decision daily, to do my best to be an encourager. And, wow! People started liking to talk to me! It's kinda nice not having everybody "drift away" from you when you're talking to them. And I love to laugh with people... It's much more fun than whining and bitching.

I thank God for His patience with me, and for His grace and forgiveness he abundantly bestows on me. I am so grateful that He knows and hears my heart and loves me enough to allow me to come to Him with my often incredibly foolish questions. I don't often get the answers I want to, but it calms my soul just to come to Him in prayer and ask my questions. Try it. It works. Its okay, you're not going to tick Him off. You're his kid!

Perhaps a greater awareness of our own vulnerability to be offended, as well as knowing the enemy's tactics will help us to be on guard against offense. In Matthew 13:18-23 (KJV) Jesus explains the parable of the Sower, and states in verse 20 and 21 what brings offense to us. He said, *"But he that received the seed into stony places, the same is he that heareth the word, and anon with joy recieveth it; Yet hath he not root in himself, but dureth for a while: for when tribulation or persecution ariseth because of the word, by and by he is offended."*

This parable describes five weapons the devil uses to choke out the Word;

1. Affliction
2. Persecution
3. Cares of this world
4. Deceitfulness of riches
5. Lust of the other things

That pretty much covers it. So it's not God's fault, as the father of lies would have us to believe, it is, in fact the lies of the enemy that caused me to be offended at God. That combined with my own selfishness. I wonder if the Apostle Paul struggled in this area when he said, *"... I myself always strive to have a conscience without offense toward God and men"* (Acts 24:16).

I am aware that most times "offense" is used in the Bible it's about me not offending God and others, but I am now also aware that I don't need to be letting the enemy, and my flesh, to cause me to be offended by every little thing. It's an attack that is designed to separate me from my Heavenly Father as well as others around me.

The really marvelous news is; BUT GOD..." *Who has begun a good work in me* (and you, and your kids) *will complete it until the day of Jesus Christ"!* (Philippians 1:6, author's translation). And to help us along, He gave us this awesome prayer in Philippians 1:9-11 to personalize and pray as much as we need, and it really helps! I pray it something like this;

**"And this I pray, that my love may abound still more and more in knowledge and all discernment, that I may approve the things that are excellent, that I may be sincere and without offense till the day of Christ, being filled with the fruit of righteousness which are by Jesus Christ, to the glory and praise of God. And Lord, please give me a spirit of calmness, peace, and self-control. In Jesus's name, Amen."**

It really does help, and it gives me peace and comfort to pray this prayer for others, especially for those I love, putting their name in it. Praying God's own Word will never fail...it's His Word!

Deals, contracts, mining leases and agreements; I can't even tell you how many of these have been "broken off in me" (gone bad, in mining terms) since those days at the Ward mine way back in 1984. What I can tell you is that God has never broken His deal with me, ever.

I am much better now at not getting mad at God or blaming Him for the work of the enemy, as some churches do. Sickness, disease, pain, sorrow, and poverty are not from God to teach you something. That's ludicrous. Those things are all part of the curse (see Deuteronomy 28) and are not from God to teach you something. Maybe the reason why so many people in the churches today look like they just got baptized in lemon juice is because they believe that stuff.

Remember how Jesus taught us to pray in Matthew 6:5-15? Remember verse 10?

*"Your kingdom come, Your will be done, on earth as it is in Heaven."*

Is all that pain, suffering, sickness, disease, poverty and evil in general, in Heaven? No. Then how or why would He give you what He doesn't have. We have an enemy and we have free will to make good and bad choices. Again, I reiterate the truth that, as a Christian, you are a child of the Most High God. If He put any of that stuff on you, it would be "child abuse". Would you put that kind of stuff on your kids? If God never answered your prayers, that would be child neglect. The answer may well be "no" or "wait", as well as "yes", and the "wait" may seem like an eternity, but the important thing is that He hears you and answers.

When it comes to troubles and suffering I believe no one ever explained it better than Joseph, after his brothers sold him into slavery, told his father he was dead, and he spent his life as a slave in Egypt, not to mention serving over eight years of it in prison after being falsely accused (I really relate to the story) as told in Genesis 37 – 50. His suffering I'm sure was beyond our comprehension, yet after it was all over and done, he tells his brothers *"But as for you, you meant evil against me;* **BUT GOD** *meant it for good..."* Genesis 50:20, emphasis mine. Even so, I sometimes still struggle with Romans 8:28, *"and we know that all things work together for good to those who love God, to those who are called according to his purpose"*, but that doesn't make it any the less true.

I don't even pretend to know everything and I surely don't have all the answers. I struggle like everybody else. I know it's not always easy but I guess I'll just keep on trusting Him, even when I can't see anything. How about you? Who else you gonna trust if not your Father in Heaven, Creator of the Heavens, the earth and the sea, and all that is in them?

Sometimes the best thing you can do is not think, not worry, not wonder, not imagine, and not obsess. Just breathe and have faith that God will work everything out for the best, knowing that your best days are still out in front of you and not behind you.

The Lord will see us through.

And remember... Only a faith that is tested is a faith that can be trusted.

# JOHN GERGEN

## CHAPTER 28

# Good Ol' Ely

Ah, Ely... Land of disenchantment. I remember growing up there as a boy. Hooky-Bobbin' was the popular winter pastime, usually done at night and in extremely sub-zero temperatures that were so cold your hair would freeze and the snow was too cold to compact into a snowball. Hooky Bobbin, by the way, is where you hide behind a fence or parked car near a stop sign until a passing vehicle stops for the sign. North Street and Ogden Avenue were my favorite. When they stopped you would come out of hiding behind the car or Sanford's fence and sneak up to it, hopefully unseen, and hunkered down and grab onto the back bumper. When the car took off you would "ski" on your feet over the snow and ice packed streets and roads to wherever the car took you. Manhole covers and dry patches of road were deadly, especially at high speeds with other cars behind you. We were very blessed to have Louie for our Boy Scout Master who allowed us to hone our Hooky Bobbin skills every Wednesday night as he took us home after our scout meetings.

Hitting cars with snowballs was also very popular as the cars couldn't hardly stop on the ice before you got away... And sometimes you didn't get away, and you usually got your ass kicked and your face very vigorously "washed" with icy snow.

One time my friend Ricky and I got caught but my brother made good his getaway on his bike. As our victim prepared to give us our usual beating he said, "Which one of you did it?" to which we both pointed at my totally innocent brother, who was over a half a block away, and in perfect harmony, yelled "He did it!" That guy chased my brother all the way down Crawford Street and right on into my Aunt Neva's house, where my Uncle Sam and my cousins Bob, Mickey, and Little Sam scared that guy so bad he peed himself! Ricky and I still laugh about it to this day... Bill, not so much. And if our folks knew we were listening to beatnik music back then, in the 60s, they would've whacked are behind's.

Summers were all about climbing Squaw Peak, lizard hunting, fishing, and rock fights that eventually got replaced with BB guns. Hot days were spent at the "rafting pond" in the old railroad yard (a big stagnant mud hole full of old railroad ties) or often as not, at a place below the old Jack Rice hog pens called "Boggy Acres" (a major black slimy gooey mud hole) down on Murray Creek near the railroad tracks.

The mud there was warm, black, thick and deep and when we covered ourselves completely from head to toe with it, and let it dry on us, it was like a second skin. So much that we could walk home up Orson Avenue, down North Street to Parker Avenue, and nobody could tell who we were! No one recognized us! Unlike brothers Clifford and Wendy who walked around the neighborhood with towels (capes) bobby-pinned around their necks as superheroes, but everybody knew who they really were. What I'm talking about is the ultimate disguise! We looked like tar babies, or walking piles of.......mud.

The two people who actually did recognize us were, first of all, my Aunt Neva who was often a co-conspirator in the shenanigans of my life. As we went by her house she would always laugh and wave, full well knowing that we were choosing to receive the same penalty as we had always received the last 20 or so times we came home like this, and would most often pull up to our house just about the time we got home, to enjoy the show. I guess that's why she was always such a positive inspiration to me, as no matter what, she would always cheer me on.

And secondly, my Mom always recognized us as well; however "inspiration" isn't exactly what I would say that we received, out on the back porch when we got home. Allowing even a fragment of that mud into her house was totally inconceivable and as she looked at us completely covered in it, the mere thought of it disgusted her.

But she also knew that underneath all that filth and grime was her two boys whom she loved with all of her heart. So the process of cleaning (kind of like the sanctification process) would begin. We would stand in one spot and slowly turn in circles while Mom sprayed us up and down with incredibly icy cold water, at full force, from the garden hose. At this stage of our "cleansing" we would holler and yell, and we could usually take a little solace as we listened to our next-door neighbor, and partner in mischief, Ricky, screaming and hollering as he to, was receiving his "cleansing" reward, just like us.

We had two duck's and an insanely demented chicken living in the backyard as well, and the more noise we made the more they squawked and quacked. Our dog, Dan, a purebred Silvertipped German Shepherd, was barking and carrying on throughout the entire process, from where he had been locked up in the house, as he would never allow anyone, not even Mom or Dad, to lay a hand to us kids. If we knew we had a spanking coming we would frantically run through the house screaming, "Here Dan! Here Dan!"

All of this noise, yelling and hollering, unfortunately to our extreme embarrassment, almost always brought the other neighbors out of their back doors to see what the cause of all the commotion was. Sad to say, I believe it eventually evolved into a common source of entertainment for them, in particularly for the members of the Stewart and Snow families living across the alley, as they both had young girls as spectators that we had to go to school with. That was really a drag, especially when considering that the next stage of the cleansing process required to allow us back into the house, required us to strip down to our "skivvies" (underwear), and God help you if you forgot to put any on that morning.

Once more we would then be hosed to perfection according to my mother's critical and loving eye. We could actually restrain ourselves from yelling at this point, in order to save ourselves further shame by attracting attention from anybody else that wasn't already watching and laughing.

At long last we were clean enough to pass Mom's inspection and receive a swat or two on our behinds for our outlandish behavior, if she chose to do so, which she mostly did not unless we got mouthy. We could now reenter our home and finalize our cleansing with a nice warm bath, and Dan would be loosened to run in and inspect us to assure we had no life-threatening injuries.

Sometimes Dan's inspection would require him to get into the bathtub with us, causing the entire bathroom to be drenched in bathwater, however, Mom always seemed to be preoccupied somewhere else, and this messy offense somehow was always overlooked regardless of the mess it created. Even Dad never scolded Dan for protecting us... Not even against a whipping from him despite however much we had it coming. I think Dad always knew that Dan would always be there for us, when he couldn't be.

I think we all know the moral of this story that reflects how it is with our Heavenly Father as well. Our filth and our sins have separated us from our Father and it makes it impossible for us to stand before Him. We are so grimy that we can't even get clean by ourselves. All the soap and water in the world won't do it, and trying to go back into the world to solve a problem that the world, itself created, is foolishness as well as futile... It's utterly hopeless. BUT GOD *"so loved the world that He gave His only begotten Son, that whoever believes in Him should not perish but have everlasting life"* (John 3:16). God sent Jesus and with His very own blood, He cleansed us from our grimy, filthy sins. We are now free to enter back into our Father's house! Yes!

*"The blood of Jesus Christ, His Son, cleanses us from all sin"* (1 John 1:7).

He didn't come to condemn you, He came to save you! (John 1:17-18). Do you believe this? That's the ultimate question that holds the key to your eternal destiny. Everyone will live forever; the question is, where? *"In my father's house"* Jesus has prepared a place for me (John 14:2). How about you? We could actually be neighbors! It's a free gift available to us right now, right where we are (Ephesians 2:4-10, Romans 5:6-11). When you're all set in knowing that you're gonna be around forever and your locked into your eternal destiny, you relax.

As Christians, I know many of us have heard that Jesus has cleansed us from our sins so much that these words seem dull and fail to have the proper impact on us that they should. We were cut off by our sins, from God, and the chance of ever getting back into our true Heavenly Home, forever! That's what the Bible means when it describes us as "lost"...we were that lost, as in wandering around lost! BUT GOD transformed our lives and our eternal destination the moment we received Christ as our Lord and Savior! NOT LOST, anymore! We're going to a destination, HOME, and that means that we are just passing through this place!

I think maybe that's what Peter was getting at when he said in 2 Peter 1:9, *"For he who lacks these things is shortsighted, even to blindness, and has forgotten that he was cleansed from his old sins"*. Never, ever, allow yourself to forget that day when you chose Jesus to be your Savior and never forget how that choice affected your eternal destination. That's your Spiritual Birthday! And for sure never let the devil or anyone lie to you and tell you different. You are His. If you haven't made that choice, now would be a really good time to do so. He is coming. If you receive Him now by faith, He will surely be your Savior. If you wait until you see Him, and *"every eye shall see Him"* (Revelation 1:7), it will be too late, as He will no longer be your Savior... He will be your Judge. We must accept Him by faith (Romans 3:21-26, Romans 10:6-13).

It's the "real deal".

\*\*\*

As I grew older and even long after I was married, stock cars and demolition derby's were still one of Stevie's, Ronnie's and my favorite past times and Ely flourished in these areas, way before Atari or Nintendo were ever invented. I think wrecking cars was a gift I had, both on and off the track.

To adjust to living in Ely, Lori put herself back through school, and soon L.A. Gergen Appraisal Service (both commercial and residential real estate) was incorporated and successfully implemented in the White Pine County area. Problems soon arose when clients would try to dictate to Lori what they wanted the value of their real estate to come in at, but Lori would never compromise her integrity. "It is what it is", she would tell them and many would take their business to certain other local appraisers that would accommodate their wishes. I will always be proud of my wife for standing her ground and not selling out her honor for money, in an industry where "selling out" was not only very common but profitable as well, even though it cost her a great many clients.

It was particularly hard for her while working at the real estate office on Altman Street as she would always dress appropriately in a nice dress or suit for work, which was apparently somewhat uncommon in Ely. My local friends used to half-jokingly say that throwing out the makeup, putting on a

T-shirt and a feed bag were the norm, right after the wedding ceremony. I wouldn't know. This led many of the local women of the community to say some of the most hateful and cruel lies about her you could ever imagine, from accusing her of being a hooker to being an ex-stripper. I will always regret moving her to Ely because of this evil gossiping and persecution she endured for so many years, for having "class" in a classless community.

After my "layoff" with Alta, a friend of mine in San Diego hooked me up with a series of short term not-so-gainful employment opportunities to get us through until spring. Two of which were bodyguard positions for "clients" who probably should have been doing life sentences. One nearly cost me my life on two separate occasions, and the other resulted in my barely making it back across the Mexican border and almost spending the majority of my life in a Mexican prison, where my "employer" should have been, had justice actually been served. In the meantime, my friend was bodyguard to a rich doctor during a very vicious and bitter divorce proceeding. The day the court proceedings were over the doctor told my friend that he had won and that he no longer needed his services, as he had a restraining order against his ex-spouse. That night, after firing my friend, his ex drove a car through the front window of the good doctor's house and killed him in his living room. Thus, like Mr. Wizard used to say in my favorite childhood cartoon series by the same name, (Drizzle-Drazzle-Drozzle-Drone, time for this one to come home," and Poof! I was out of there and back to Nevada.

A few years later, my friend rented out his house to a young woman, who later allowed her new boyfriend to move in. Then, within a very short time, all of his gang buddies moved themselves right on into her house as well. They started tearing the place up and she couldn't get them to leave, so she called my friend and told him of the situation, and said she was real sorry but she had to get out of his house, so goodbye. My friend then proceeded to go down to San Diego and "cleanout" his house... with a Mini 14 semi-automatic rifle, and although he wounded several of them, he somehow managed not to kill anyone. Years later he confided in me that killing them would have left bodies but just shooting them up some allowed them to get themselves and each other off of his property... food for thought, I figured.

Knowing the neighbors surely had called the police, he hid the rifle and his ski mask, and when the SWAT team showed up, he acted as surprised as they were, saying he had just arrived on the scene. Yup. They arrested him.

*In a dream I had*, two nights later, I entered the police taped crime scene through a second-story bathroom window. In the living room I removed the huge flat stone embedded in the living room floor, just in front of the fireplace (like you need a fireplace in San Diego, right?) that revealed a hidden compartment, and I left the house the same way I got in only the Mini

14 left with me. I figure I owed him that. He was a good friend to me. I was back in Nevada by just about breakfast time.

My friend was eventually exonerated of all charges, for lack of evidence, as the shell casings had no fingerprints on them and couldn't be matched with a weapon that would tie him to the incident. *What a crazy dream!*

Many years later, my friend would prove to be not only a dear friend and cherished brother in Christ, but also a valuable partner in my outreach ministry, McGill Christian Youth Group. Go figure!

It's an amazing phenomenon, who God chooses to use, in His work of ministering the Gospel to the lost! I suppose this rubs a lot of folks the wrong way who have been raised in the churches and have walked in their religion their whole lives, but that's all good by me. He used a couple of renegades like us, and you don't even know the half of it.

You wonder if He could use you? You bet... in a heartbeat.

Who's gonna listen to you? People just like you! That's the answer God laid on my heart when I asked Him the same question, many years later, and it goes for all of us!

You see, the mission "is to set prisoners free from the kingdom of darkness, and to establish the kingdom of God in their hearts," as A. V. Munoz rightfully explains it in his book, Radical Faith-Transforming the World, One Person at a Time from the Inside Out (page 184, a must read!).

And who is better suited to this task than those who know the kingdom of darkness intimately, yet have been freed themselves and now serve the God of light? (John 1:1-14).

He goes on to say, "This is the mystery, a perfect God living in an imperfect man reconciling the world to Himself" (page 26). As mentioned above, this may come as an offense to many "religious people", but as A.V.Munoz also perfectly stated, "God doesn't need anyone's approval to bless me" (page XVI), let alone use me. "You might call me a fanatic, a Jesus Freak, or whatever you like. However, you cannot condemn me to hell, and the only one who can, Him will I serve." (Page 2)

Amen and Amen! Those words joyously echo through my heart and into my very soul!

To hell with the "dark side". Come on over to the winning side; come on over to the kingdom of light! We are soldiers in the Army of the Lord!

CHAPTER 29

## A Clean Start

*"For nothing is secret that will not be revealed, nor anything hidden that will not be known and come to light."* Luke 8:17

Over the next 30 years or so, Ely became our "home base" for a vast variety of various types of adventures from treasure hunts in Florida and the Caribbean, to hunting lost conquistador gold and silver in the high deserts of Nevada and Utah, and many intense claim staking and mining adventures throughout the Western US. We even found a Spanish cannon on a treasure dive in Jamaica one year, but they wouldn't let us bring it home! I think it would have looked really cool mounted on my front deck and sticking out over Campton Street. But alas, no. In fact, the authorities made us watch as they hung some poor fellow for smuggling (third offense, if I remember correctly), to detour us from any notion of bringing "anything" out of the country illegally. It worked perfectly... We got the point. And after all of this and not being able to bring my cannon home I decided right then and there that if I ever do find a Spanish gold doubloon it's going up the secret hiding place before I ever come out of the water, however, it has been rumored that local customs officers and the Department of antiquities have store employees on payroll to watch for tourists buying screens, spaghetti strainers, and Ex-Lax. You don't mess around with the law in Third World countries. You think that because you are an American that you have rights, but I'm here to tell you, you have none. You cross the governing authorities and you can disappear pretty fast. If you happen to have rich relatives, your chances of survival are greatly enhanced, but otherwise, don't do anything stupid. There's my "travel tip" for the day.

We also brought several innovative and somewhat prosperous businesses and corporations into play, while based in Ely. As mentioned, LA Gergen Appraisal Service, Desert Enterprises Mining Company, Desert Enterprises Custom Painting (airbrush, murals, flames, stripes, glass etching, etc.), Renew You Laser and Dexter Mining Company, as well as several 501c(3) non-profits (after the Lord "ironed out my britches", so to speak) including McGill Christian Youth Group, Open Door Homeless Shelter, Open Door Project, and Second Chance Ink.

My extracurricular employment activities were always kept very low keyed and no one in town really had a clue as to my other less lucrative career choices (body guarding, armed escort service, bounty hunting, etc.), with possibly the exception of one particular local judge who became somewhat enlightened when, for my own personal reasons, I went after a "skip" from her court. As I see no measure in which to glorify the Lord in most of these matters, they are omitted, as not to give credence to the work of my enemy, the devil, in my life. Enough said.

The proverbial "cat" was almost "let out of the bag" when I rolled into town in an ambulance with a gunshot wound through my chest in 1990. We passed it off as a hunting accident, but over the next couple of years, questions began to arise that were becoming very annoying and unsettling such as, "Do you know" so and so questions, and "Have you ever heard about" this happening, or that incident? You know what I mean; people nosing around where they have no business.

In 1992 we closed up our home and moved to Gardnerville, Nevada "for a while", figuring the "out of sight, out of mind" policy would be best until the inquisitive parties involved found something or someone else to speculate about. Not that I was guilty of anything illegal in, and of itself, but the convicting analogy of "guilty by association" was a very real factor when applied to some of my business associates as of late.

So looking for a "clean start" we (I) went strictly legit. Lori got hired right away at a huge law firm in Lake Tahoe for her legal secretarial skills. I went to work for Art Wilson Corporation in Carson City, who owned and operated the gypsum mine and gold mill in the Moundhouse area, as well as the New Yorker mine in Virginia City, and the open pit mining operation just above Silver city.

Art Wilson himself was a man I will always hold in the highest regard as he proved himself to be a man of integrity, time and time again, as did his foreman, Al, who I envied for his ability to stay cool, calm, and collected in the most adverse situations.

One time in the mine at Silver city, Art offered me $500 if I would quit smoking, because he was genuinely concerned for my health! I, on the other hand, was not, and like a fool, offered him $500 if he would stop asking me to quit. Years later, $500 wouldn't even cover the Chantix prescription I used when I finally did get delivered from nicotine... and I probably quit 37 times before that, in the process. I loved smoking, I was an expert at it and yes, it really did make me look cool. Thank You, God, for getting me off of the hardest addiction I ever had to break, because I proved over and over that I couldn't do it by myself. It took a lot of faith, prayer, and Chantix. What a battle.

One day, after leaving the pit just north of Devils Gate, I crested the last hill just to the south of the Occidental Grade "Y" in the road. With a belly dump loaded with heavy ore I began my decent down the long grade to Moundhouse. As usual, I reached over and flipped on my Jacobs brake as the steep grade was causing the Kenworth to pick up speed at a very rapid pace. The moment the Jake kicked on my engine exploded with a horrendous "boom", throwing a piston rod out the left side of the engine block. The truck lurched and bounced violently as parts from the engine went underneath the dual wheels, and then another loud bang as something in the clutch or transmission broke, and I was suddenly freewheeling down the 2 lane Highway in a runaway truck! It was midmorning and right in the middle of tourist season in Virginia City. Heavy traffic in the uphill Lane was only spaced a few car lengths apart and I had maybe 60 yards between me and the cars ahead of me, and I was quickly picking up speed. The traffic lane I was heading downhill in was built right up against the steep mountain side that it had been cut out of. There was no chance at all of getting off the road, except on the left side which was about a very steep 2 to 1 sloped drop off down the side of the mountain.

    Driving many of the roads over the Sierras I had seen a few trucks that had gone over the driver side edge of the road, including one that had ended up in a river with a loaded 40 ton end dump of gravel piling up on top of the truck cab. I never saw anyone survive jumping out as they went over the left edge, as the trailer(s) behind them always crashed on top of them or ran them over. Staying in the cab with tons of rock, not to mention the trailer itself, landing on top of you when you hit the bottom was no chance at all.

    What I knew for a fact was that I couldn't turn this 40+ tons of rock and steel loose into oncoming traffic. To seriously complicate things, I was losing my air supply fast. Truck brakes don't work without air and if/when the emergency brakes kicked on, as fast as I was now going, the rig would be impossible to control. Not an option in this heavy traffic. All this went through my head in seconds. Then, as before, my head went incredibly clear.

    I looked down the road and saw that a slow moving motorhome coming up the hill had created a space between it and the station wagon ahead of him of about 7 or so car lengths. It wasn't much but it was something... a chance, maybe. I un-buckled my seat belt and opened the driver's door. As soon as that station wagon goes by I will crank the steering wheel hard to the left, and maybe if I can hit the ground running as I go over the edge... maybe I can outrun that belly dump full of gold ore.

    It was the only option I had coming to me. I didn't have enough air to stop the truck on this grade and locking up the emergency brake system would surely throw this old truck out of control, and going this fast, in heavy traffic, would imminently cause extreme havoc in an area of this mountain road that didn't even have any guardrails. For a split second I thought of Lori and my two little ones and nearly choked up.

    With my left foot holding the driver's door part way open, I focused on the station wagon that was now almost up to me. The driver in the car ahead of him gawked up at me with his eyes bugging out and his mouth wide open as he went past me, disbelief shock and awe clearly etched on his face. He could tell what I was about to do, I think. After all, not that many people drive a speeding Kenworth that's billowing out smoke, down the road while hanging halfway out the door with one foot on the step. I probably would have laughed had I not been a second or two from being dead...somehow that killed the humorous side of things.

Then, as I took one last look up the road to gauge the space between the motorhome and the station wagon that was now just coming by me, my eye caught sight of a mailbox on the right-hand side of the road! And there with it someone had carved a wide spot out of the mountainside just big enough to accommodate a pullout spot for a U.S. Postal Service vehicle.

What happened next was so much more than a miracle that I'm not sure I can explain it properly. The station wagon whizzed by me on my left and the open space between it and the motorhome opened up at the exact same time that I came upon the small turnout area where the mailbox was. Every aspect of what happened is still crystal-clear in my mind, but just as it was then, I could see myself doing the same things that I did but it was as if I was a spectator. I guess I'm trying to say it was as if I was watching myself do it, but it wasn't me doing it. Yeah, if you had any doubts about my sanity, (or insanity, as the case may be) up till now, this should probably clarify it for you.

Anyway, with the space momentarily open, I sat back down in the driver's seat; I swerved hard into the left lane then immediately cranked the steering wheel back to the right. As the nose of the truck entered into the pullout area I grabbed the trailer brake lever on the steering column and jammed it all the way down, then reached over and pulled out the red emergency brake knob. Starting with the trailer brakes first, every brake on that rig locked up. I pulled the steering wheel back to the left as my right front tire hit the dirt hillside, and yeah, I took that mailbox out like it was the thing to do. The side of the trailer slammed into the soft dirt embankment as the truck skidded parallel to the highway, half on the pavement and half in the ditch. As I slid toward the rock and dirt wall at the end of the turnout, I braced myself for the impact. A wall of dirt and dust flew up over the cab and windshield making it impossible to see anything as the front of the truck smashed into the mountain at the end of the turnout... Only it didn't! The truck didn't smash into the rock! It just stopped!

I sat there, still clenched tightly to the steering wheel, in my "brace for impact and prepare to die" position, but it didn't happen. As the dust settled I could see the mountainside right in front of me as I stared out the windshield. All traffic was stopped and staring at me, and to my delight, I was alive! Visibly shaking I got out of the truck and walked to the front of it to see the front bumper was only 2 inches from the rock wall! How could this be? I looked back and saw that the tail of my belly dump was only a mere six or seven feet from the cutouts embankment wall on the other end, yet fully within the tiny cutout! It's as if the truck had slid sideways into the slot that was barely big enough to fit the entire length of the 18 wheeler into, at all! With only six or seven feet to spare, I couldn't possibly begin to comprehend what had happened here.

It was impossible, yet here it was.

The next thing to add to this mind spinning dilemma is Art Wilson himself, slapping me on my back and yelling, "That's the best piece of driving I ever saw!" I never knew it but he had been following right behind me the whole time in his El Camino.

Still stunned I said, "Wasn't me, Art. It wasn't me... Just dumb luck I guess."

Then a lady in the car beside us chimed in and said, "no, that was a miracle of God, son," smiled at me, and drove away.

Now, as I look back, I see Psalm 91 becoming a reality. To this day, I believe I was spared that day because of the prayers of my daughter, my mother and my wife. God was calling to me, and sadly, I refused.

That night when I got home there was another package from Phil Davis sitting in my stack of mail. As usual, knowing that it was just another "God book," I threw it, unopened, into a box with all of the others. When Lori got home I told her what had happened, and for some reason, I even told her what the lady in the car had said about a "miracle of God" thing, and asked what she thought about it. Without hesitating, and with no doubt whatsoever, she said "absolutely a miracle".

Hmmmm...

Later that night I went back and picked that last package from Phil out of the box and opened it. It was a book,( of course) by Hal Lindsey called "The Late Great Planet Earth." I sat down on the couch, but instead of starting at the beginning of the book, I instead opened it randomly to a page somewhere near the middle and began reading a quote from the book of Revelation as Lindsay portrayed his rendition of the End Times and God's judgment on mankind;

*"...he himself shall also drink of the wine of the wrath of God which is poured out full strength into the cup of His indignation. He shall be tormented with fire and brimstone in the presence of the holy angels and in the presence of the Lamb."* Revelation 14:10.

Wow. Fire and brimstone... Seems like that's all I've heard my whole life.

Unbeknownst to me, as he has always done throughout time (see Genesis 3, and Luke 4:1-13), Satan took the Holy Word of God and twisted it around and used it to support his lies, as "he is a liar and the father of it," and just as Jesus foretold how and why in John 8:42-47, I fell for it. I was deceived into believing that God hated me, and unfortunately this wasn't the first time. As I threw Lindsay's book back into the box with all the others, my mind had already gone back to my boyhood in Ely, to when and where this deadly lie was first planted in me.

After our beloved Boy Scout Master, Louie, retired his position to his new predecessor, things changed rapidly. Within a few scout meetings most of the original members of our troop quit and were replaced by active members from the LDS church. My friend Dick and I held on and tried to make the best of it, but soon it was obvious that we didn't fit in. Meetings became sermons based on the Book of Mormon and their church doctrine, and camping trips became nothing more than weekend lectures often directly focused on Dick and me as examples of what not to do. About the only two actual Bible scriptures I remember were used in conjunction with Mormon teachings and consisted of Ephesians 5:3-7, and Colossians 3:6 to illustrate why Dick and I could never be "married in the temple" and thus, why we would never go to Heaven. In short, the wrath of God was reserved for "people like me and Dick."

Although it was another lie from the pit of hell, I didn't know it, and it severely affected my view of God, and yes, "I took offense" is a gross understatement. In the years following it became very easy for the Master of Lies to build on the foundation that I would never be "good enough" for a holy God, and His wrath would always be upon me. Henceforth, everything bad that ever happened to me was God beating me down. That's how demonic influences work, and over the years I got comfortable hating Him, and that made it easy for the devil to reinforce his lies to me on the few occasions that I did honestly try and seek the Lord.

Listen my friend, above all you must read and study the Bible, especially the New Testament, and I recommend the New King James Version. If you do not know the truth within its pages, then you, just like me, will be a slow moving easy target for the father of lies. In his first Epistle the Apostle Peter warned us, *"Be sober, be vigilant; because your adversary the devil walks about like a roaring lion, seeking whom he may devour."* (1 Peter 5:8).

And as he's doing this and killing, stealing and destroying the lives of his victims (John 10:10), this treacherous, murderous enemy of ours is all the while pretending and convincing us that he is our friend.

But if you know the truth in your heart, then no one, not even that lying punk from hell, can tell you different. That's why Jesus explained in John chapter 8, right before he describes the above mentioned versus that depict the lies that the devil uses to deceive us, that,"...*if you abide in My word, you are My disciples indeed. And you shall know the truth and the truth shall make you free"*. (John 8:31-32) Satan lies to us because he knows our sins separate us from God, and he must at all costs keep us from turning back to God who "abundantly pardons" us and forgive us our sins when we confess to Him and repent, and thus, become reconciled to our Father in Heaven.

I guess what they didn't tell me when I was a boy was that Jesus paid the price for ALL of my sins, and freed me from the penalty of sin and death. Jesus tells us in versus 34 and 36 of the same chapter, *"Most assuredly I say to you, whoever commits sin is a slave to sin... Therefore, if the Son makes you free, you shall be free indeed."*

Now when the devil tries to lie to me, I enjoy slapping him in the face with my sword, the true Word of God. Maybe it's time for you to pick up your sword as well, found in Ephesians 6:17 and start smacking that liar upside the head the next time he tries to plant his trash into your thoughts. In His Word you will be assured of his immeasurable love for you and that God has a good plan for your life and your future. It's time to get into the Word... You've been lied to long enough.

\*\*\*

The next day at work was Friday and everybody employed by Art Wilson Company had to complete their tasks by sundown. My truck boss, Al, God bless him, knew I was shook up from the previous day's accident and felt the best remedy was to "get me right back in the saddle" before I had much time to think about it.

Just before noon I pulled up on the dumpsite at the Mill and kicked open the gates on my belly dump as I slowly moved forward. My gates had barely fully opened when the truck came to an abrupt stop and my drivers (wheels) started to spin. I was stuck. I got out and looked and found I was hung up on a very large rock that was jammed against the open air gates of the belly dump. Standard procedure was to let the 988 loader operator lift up the back of my trailer until I was safely free from the rock. I looked around but could not see the loader anywhere. I waited...but not long enough. In my impatience, I locked in my differentials, stuck the transmission in the lowest gear and jerked and twisted myself off of that rock; and tore up my gates in the process.

The head mechanic at the truck shop was a real "bear", and I avoided him at all costs, as he had the ability to make or break you as far as service time and scheduling were concerned. And there he was, standing there watching me as I pulled into the shop area, with that stone cold poker face of his. I had rehearsed my story (lie) all the way back to the shop, and I was ready. There were already eight or nine trucks in the service line waiting their turn to get into the shop for repairs, and there were three trucks inside of the shop itself. My heart sank as I realized I could be off work a long time until my rig got fixed. The head mechanic and his assistant with the scheduling clipboard were already walking towards me, across the parking lot, as I set my brake and shut down. I hope he buys my BS story or I'm sunk. I had heard a lot of horror stories about this guy from all the other drivers.

I opened my door and stepped down to the ground as he rudely walked right past me to inspect the damage. I fell right in behind him and just as I was opening my mouth to spew my "sad sad story" that I had concocted, he stopped short and spun around. Man, is he mad, I thought. Shoving his face in front of mine he stared into my soul with his cold steel eyes and blurted out two words – "What happened?"

"I really screwed up, Mike. I got hung up on a rock and pulled myself off instead of waiting for the loader," I said in a calm voice, "I'm sorry". Where the heck that came from I have no idea. My lie would have been much better and it wouldn't have come with the shame I was feeling right now. "What's wrong with me", I thought to myself.

The mechanic took a step back and looked at me, his face totally expressionless. Then he nodded his head toward the line of busted trucks awaiting their turn in the shop and said, "See all these trucks? They are sitting here not because we are so busy in the shop but because every one of these "Cab lizards" (drivers) tried to give me a line of crap about how it's not their fault that their trucks are busted." I didn't know what to say so I just kept my big mouth shut as he stood there looking me over and sizing me up.

Looking back at the line of trucks he said, "And they are going to stay right where they are until I'm damn good and ready to work on them." Then he stepped around me to the guy with the clipboard and said to him, "Get Gergen's truck in next, and make damn sure it's ready to go on Monday morning." He glanced back at me, with what I think was a hint of laughter in his eyes, and maybe a hint of respect as well, and then walked off toward the shop.

I never, ever forgot that, and lying never came easy for me after that day. Maybe, for the first time I began to understand what personal integrity stood for. All I really knew for sure was how good I felt by telling the truth, and how good it felt to tell Lori about it.

## CHAPTER 30

## ...What Is Truth...?
John 18:38

That Sunday my daughter Brandy talked her Mom into going to church with her and her friends, and I went to my "church" of the NFL. Dan Marino and the Dolphins knocked Joe Montana and the Kansas City Chiefs (you read that right) out of the playoffs. When Dan saw a blitz coming he started licking his chops. He mastered the flea flicker and the fake spike and made good on his statement that "there is no defense against a perfectly thrown pass." We miss you, Dan... Sniffle, sniffle, sniff, sniff... (Sad face).

Even so, I couldn't stop thinking about the events of the last few days, what was the truth? Something inside me was hungry for it, even though I had no idea what the truth was. Over the next couple years I began searching. At first I just dabbled at it and later I had times where my search was frantic, with the answers I sought becoming completely elusive. That's because I searched in all the wrong places, and that just kept magnifying my hunger. The bright side is, that through intensive and very thorough searching over many years, I found out where the truth wasn't; Very notably, not unlike a lot of my treasure hunting adventures. After months, and sometimes years of digging through research data, maps, and tons of personal testimonies and journals, no matter how good or "right" it seemed, it just wasn't there.

The God of the Bible would be the last place I searched, because I was sure He hated me and there was this whole thing about being accountable for my "sins". So I figured Buddhism or Hinduism would produce answers to what I was experiencing in the events of my life, so I started there. But as with my study of Islam and the Quran, getting into the history of their founders and the often crumbling foundations that these belief systems are founded on, I wound up even more frustrated and confused than I was to start with.

Then came my years of "new age" searching for "enlightenment". Scientology, Dianetics, Celestine prophecy, and many others had me, at one time, out in my backyard on a full moon with quartz crystals, a crystal ball and incantations that were to guarantee my ascension to being my own god, who is within me, and, oh yeah, believing I could hear the thoughts of people riding on an airplane that was passing over my head at the time... And they say the 60s and 70s were "far out". Funny how most stuff like this now becomes laughable when you look at it with a clear head. Not so funny was how I almost drove Lori over the edge during this part of my search, and amazingly...Yes!... I'm still married to her... Miracle of miracles!

Right... So who exactly does orchestrate these miracles that have been happening in my life lately? Hmmm...

Raised as a boy with the Pinola family I witnessed, learned, and sometimes partook in various rituals, of the Shoshones and the Native American culture. Especially if I got sick. And I must be honest, the cures that they used, such as "root", sweat lodges, etc. for the most part, really did work good on me and made me well. There were vast differences, but also there were uncanny similarities between some of their beliefs and those of my grandmother, who believed in the God of the Bible, the Creator of the Heavens, the earth, the sea, and all that is in them.

All those other religions had much less accountability than the Christians had, so I suppose that's why they were so appealing to me, however digging into the facts and, in many cases, simply applying common sense as to right and wrong, revealed the true nature of their messages. Listen folks, when researching anything you always start at the source. When you study the source or person that these beliefs are founded on, you can actually "weed through them" pretty fast. There's a lot of "fanatics" out there, as you will see, and most had an alternative motive (i.e. avoid legal persecution, justify wrong doing, lunatic, exaltation of polygamy, psychopath, personal gain, etc. etc.) for creating their belief system and convincing others to follow them (strength in numbers). Some, but very few, where men simply seeking to understand a higher power.

Over the years, one very unsettling common factor I found was several young boys between 14 and 16 years of age, that received the demonic message of "everybody else has it wrong, but I'm going to give you the right way", from untested (see Appendix C, Test All Things) angelic "beings", particularly in the last few hundred years. This always seemed to lead to a "new" twisted doctrine or "interpretation" of the Bible, that denies the divinity of Jesus Christ (Gnostics, etc.) and the Holy Trinity, and demonically leads the lost away from the only true means of salvation (2 John 1:7-11). And we are warned of this when Paul explains, *"Now the Spirit expressly says that in the latter times some will depart from the faith, giving heed to deceiving spirits and doctrines of demons..."* (1 Timothy 4:1).

*"And no wonder! For Satan himself transforms himself into an angel of light."* (2 Corinthians 11:14).

Therefore, *"But even if we, or an angel from Heaven, preach any other gospel to you than what we have preached to you, let him be accursed."* (Galatians 1:8)

Twisted Scripture is the trademark of all cults (2 Peter 3:16). Cults are a perversion of God's Word, the Holy Bible (see Appendix A, False

Prophets and Religions – Cults). Any teaching about Jesus Christ that is contrary to the teachings of the Holy Bible should and must be rejected. Don't be letting anyone tell you that "God, Himself has revealed (or given me a new revelation of) something new to me". Don't buy into it. God has revealed Himself and given you what you need already, in the Bible.

The bottom line is, it's either Jesus Christ or anti-Christ, as clearly explained by the beloved Apostle John when he gave us the means to discern between the two in 1 John 4:1-6. Here is the test... *"Beloved, do not believe every spirit, but test the spirits, whether they are of God; because many false prophets have gone out into the world. By this you know the Spirit of God; every spirit that confesses that Jesus Christ has come in the flesh is of God, and every spirit that does not confess that Jesus Christ has come in the flesh is not of God. And this is the spirit of the anti-Christ, which you have heard was coming, and is now already in the world.*

*You are of God, little children, and have overcome them, because He who is in you is greater than he who is in the world. They are of the world. Therefore they speak as of the world, and the world hears them. We are of God. He who knows God hears us; he who is not of God does not hear us.* **By this we know the spirit of truth and the spirit of error.**"

In a "nutshell", they either exalt the biblical Christ (Messiah) and his work or they deny it. Christ or anti-Christ.

As far as Satanism, Wicca, and the occult in general, in my search as well as in my life, I always recognized raw, dark evil when I came across to it, and I never intentionally crossed that line (see Appendix B, False Prophets and Religions - Occult). I crossed it unintentionally, when I was much younger, through Ouija boards, séances, and other so-called "kids games", and it opened doors to the realm of darkness that eventually had to be dealt with, renounced, and shut over 20 years later. And, oh yes, there were consequences. That's why I highly recommend Neil T Anderson's books, Victory Over Darkness, and especially, The Bondage Breaker in dealing with the occult intrusions in your life.

The occult is rebellion against God, defiance of God's Word, and always satanic, although it is often presented in various "innocent" packages. Some examples are communicating with the dead, fascination with the dead and death (i.e. vampires, zombies, etc.), divination, sorcery/drug use, witchcraft, soothsayers, mediums, astrology, horoscopes, familiar spirits, New Age religion, worship of stars, moon, sun, "mother Earth", etc., evolution, magic charms, psychics (only God can read your mind, 1Kings 8:39), fortunetellers, magic, black magic, rebellion, satanic worship and rituals, and that's only to name a few (scriptural references are in the Appendix B, False Prophets and Religions – Occult).

Even false dreams, are to be compared to the Word of God (Jeremiah 23:25-32).

The Epistle of Jude, written by the younger half-brother of Jesus, and brother of James, is often referred to by many as our "Call to Arms", and rightly so. In verse three he admonishes us to "contend" earnestly for the faith; *"Beloved, while I was very diligent to write to you concerning our common salvation, I found it necessary to write to you exhorting you to contend earnestly for the faith which was once for all delivered to the saints."* He then goes on to explain why in the rest of his Epistle. The word "contend" that he used here is from the Greek word "agonizomai" meaning fight, fighting, fought, laboring earnestly, strive.

I know, right? Christians aren't supposed to fight...are they? According to Ecclesiastes 3 there is a time for everything (see also Psalm 18, 144). I had a brother in Christ tell me just the other day, how no Christian needs an assault weapon. I thought about it then asked him, "Can you hunt with a bow?"

"Of course", he replied.

"Can you hunt with a spear or a sling?" I asked.

"Yes", he answered, a little more wary now.

"Can you hunt with the sword?" I asked.

"No, that's not what a sword is designed for." He answered matter of factly.

"What's it for?" Says I.

"Killing men; it's a weapon of war." Says he.

"Ahhh... Probably the first assault weapon then, wouldn't you agree?"

"No, a rock would be the first," he stated.

"No, you can hunt with a rock", I countered.

"Oh, yeah," he confessed, "now that I think about it, I think you're right about the sword being the first assault weapon."

"In any event I think we can agree that assault weapons have really evolved from Jesus's time up till now, don't you think?" I offered.

"On that we can agree," he allowed, "but they are all still assault weapons," he added.

"Yes, I agree," says I, "so what do you suppose Jesus was thinking when He instructed his disciples **that did not already have a sword** or "assault weapon" of that time period, to sell their garments and buy one, as He did in Luke 22:36?"

"Uuuhhh... I'll get back to you on that," was his final word on the subject.

Listen up... I am not advocating anything as I really have no idea what my Master had in mind when He told His disciples to buy swords.

*"Then He said to them,' But now, he who has a money bag, let him take it, and likewise a knapsack; and he who has no sword, let him sell his garment and buy one."* (Luke 22:36)

Note the "he who has no sword", part. Apparently some of them already had swords? And Jesus not only knew about it but was okay with it? Just a very short time later in the garden, when Judas betrayed Jesus with a kiss and it became apparent what was about to happen, Scripture speaks of the disciples in Luke 22:49 when it says, "**they** said to Him, Lord, shall **we** strike with the sword?" confirming that the disciples were armed, and Peter wasn't the only one who was "packing". Furthermore, when Simon Peter pulled his blade and cut off Malchus' ear, not only did Jesus NOT freak out, or condemn Peter for his action and tell him to throw his sword away and never pick it up again, He actually "*said to Peter,' put your sword into the sheath"* (John 18:10-11) knowingly allowing Peter to keep his sword, for whatever reason. Interesting, in light of scriptures like Psalm 149:5-9. After all, who else is there to fight against evil? That's all I'm saying, so please don't read anything more into this than that, as it's a mystery to me. I just wanted to point out, that the Disciples went "healed", as John Wayne would put it.

Obviously during this particular time period, exactly as it was prophesied, Jesus came as The Lamb of God that takes away the sins of the world, and He Himself, of course, would not have wielded a sword... yet in times past, as the Commander of the Army of the Lord, He appeared "with His sword drawn in His hand (Joshua 5:13-15), as well as in the very near future times He will again lead the armies of Heaven as the Word of God, King of Kings and Lord of Lords at which time "out of His mouth goes a sharp sword, that with it He should strike the nations" ( Revelation 19:11-16), proving that Jesus is no stranger, then, now or in times to come, to wielding His sword ( or whip, for that matter- John 2:15).

Kinda adds a whole new twist to the age old question, "What time is it?" don't you think?

Just wondering though, when was the last time you heard these verses preached from the pulpit of your church...or any church? We sure seem to have the whole "turn the other cheek" part down pat, but... *"To everything there is a season, a time for every purpose under Heaven; a time to..."* Ecclesiastes 3:1, 2.

***

Monday morning, that bear of a mechanic was found to be true to his word. My truck was in the ready line, as good as new. Actually it wasn't my truck, as my truck had blown up a few days ago. This truck was the pride and joy of my boss's son. It was on loan to me until another regular truck became available for me. And it was the nicest, prettiest, fanciest candy apple red Peterbilt I had ever seen. It had all the "bells and whistles" you could imagine! Just after 7 AM I took on a load of gold ore at the mine just above Silver City, and headed down the mountain to the mill at Moundhouse. When

I got to the dump area by the jaw crusher, I found that several trucks had dumped ahead of me but their long piles of ore from their belly dumps had not yet been cleared by the loader, so there was no room for me to dump.

As I watched, the 988 loader came roaring up on to the dump pad, obviously late, and in high gear. The operator hadn't taken time to scrape or defrost his windows and could barely see out of a couple "holes" made by the defroster vents. He pulled up to my driver's door and told me to back up, as he "guided me" until the back of my trailer was against the road berm behind me, in order to give him room to clear the previous dump piles. He seemed a little wound up, so that was fine by me. I got out my thermos, and was just beginning to pour myself a lovely, hot cup of coffee, when the loader came flying at me in a half circle turn, in reverse, and smashed into the front end of the Peterbilt!

His left rear tire came up over my bumper and my right tire, crushing my fiberglass hood and smashing in the windshield and passenger side of the truck with the rear bumper of the loader. How he didn't flip over on his side is beyond me. It happened so fast that I was still holding my thermos in my right hand and my cup in my left when the loader "bounced" off the Pete and came to a stop.

As I sat there in total shock, still holding my thermos and cup, the loader operator (either hung over or still drunk) opened his door, stepped out of the cab on the upper deck, and started screaming profanities at me and calling me dirty names! I came out of shock and out of that truck so fast it would make your head swim.

"You're a dead man!" I screamed as I rounded the front of the truck and leapt onto the ladder of that loader. He believed, jumped back into the cab and locked the door. Then Al and another driver had me by my legs and pulled me off of the loader. And good thing, as something had snapped in me. They had seen the entire episode as it happened and with no doubt in my heart, stopped me from mindlessly killing that fool.

Looking back on the incident now, I realize that the split-second timing of those boys getting to me, let alone just being there in the first place, could have only been orchestrated by God, Himself. I alone know what was really in my heart, and it wasn't nothin' nice. So in working the last three days, I had three wrecks, and three miracles. Not knowing the Lord's handywork at the time, it was God who I inevitably blamed for all of it. You have no idea how it shames me to tell of this, and it still shames me to this day. Yes, even now I have many such regrets, as I look back over the years of my life and recognize the obvious times God was saving me and helping me yet, all the while I was cussing and blaming him for everything. I was a fool.

And among some of the greatest of my regrets is, even though Art Wilson was getting me my inoculation shots for the mine managers position I was to fill, near Lingbao, China, my dream job, I quit the best outfit I ever worked for.

## CHAPTER 31

## Back to the Mohave

### The Lure of Gold and Another Partnership

Lori called me one afternoon from the legal firm where she worked, to ask on behalf of one of the partnering lawyers, if I knew where one of their clients could invest in a "serious" gold venture. Goler canyon in the Mohave Desert came immediately to mind. Two days later I met with them and told them the story of my previous experiences many years earlier, leaving out the location, of course.

The job I was holding with a local excavation company was increasingly becoming more dissatisfying (boring) and I had just had my butt handed to me by my loving wife, who had recently received a call from Pah Wah Loo elementary school revealing that my daughter Brandy and her older brother Billy had exceeded the maximum amount of "excused" absences they were allowed. Our Friday afternoon fishing trips to the river were unveiled when some wannabe do-gooder, called the cops because an obviously stolen Mercedes (my work car) was bouncing down a rocky trail by the old Carson River dam, apparently to the do-gooder, to be stripped. Even more unpleasant was the fact that the fish were biting like never before when the cops showed up.

They ID'ed me and called in my plates, and the car came back registered to Lori (because I hate going to the DMV) so they called her... And they called the school to see if Billy and Brandy had the day off for parent-teacher conference, like I told them. The school reported that they were out of school for their grandmother's funeral and their records further showed that it was the third grandmother's funeral in eight months (oops. How brilliant could I be?).

To top things off, Calador, my half Red Wolf and half Malamute had just eaten the neighbor's cat, "Fluffy", and left the tail, paws, and pieces of the fur and a few other miscellaneous parts all over my front yard.

So... I shot the "client" the price it would cost him to retain me (and my dog) to go down to the Mohave Desert, check the status of the mining property, and the availability, if any, of the water that would be required to build and operate a gravity gold mill (in other words, "get the hell out of Dodge"). My retainer fee was agreed upon, handed to me, and Va-Voom!

Calador and I were out of there, at least until everybody simmered down, anyway.

The first couple of nights we just spent camped out on the desert as we were both elated to be out of the city, where obviously neither of us belonged. In the Desert Mountains of the Mohave we could "breathe" again. It was a good environment for me and that dog of mine, other than the heat, maybe.

The canyon and mine site were completely deserted, with only a few pieces of scrap iron and busted machinery parts lying about to give any hint of the huge mining and milling operation we had built here, over 16 years ago. The yearly wall to wall flash floods had seen to that and everything else that the waters hadn't been able to ravage was now overgrown with brush and cactus. That included the area where the hidden ledge of gold was, farther up the ravine, however I could tell that someone had tried to mine it after I had left. There were old dozer cuts and old holes, probably dug out with a loader, where someone had removed 15 or 20 tons of material, but far down the hillside below the ledge, which had remained untouched all these years. They had dug out of those hematite dikes trying to find where the gold had come from not knowing that they were close enough to the gold to spit and hit it.

I just sat there with Calador and smiled as the afternoon shadows filled the canyon.

A trip to the courthouse and the BLM office in Bakersfield revealed that Dr. Johnson had, in fact, retained his full ownership of the property. Yet after all the years of legal smoke had cleared, all apparent attempts to reproduce the rich ore that they had all witnessed the last day we ran, 16 years ago, had failed and further attempts to mine the canyon floor had been abandoned.

The water well down by the highway where Banjo and his family used to live, had "sanded" (filled in with sand) years ago. That was most unfortunate, as drilling a new water well in the Mohave Desert was very cost prohibitive, to say the least.

Even Fred's mill, below Red Mountain, had been abandoned and fallen victim to time and looters. Although Fred had moved into Red Mountain and retired, so to speak, he was a blessing to see again, as I didn't have a lot of true friends, like Fred had always been to me. We enjoyed "breaking bread" together and caught each other up to speed on what life had unveiled over the years, since we had last seen each other. When I showed him pictures of my wife and children he grabbed hold of my forearms, looked into my eyes, and told me, "There is nothing here in the Mohave that is more precious than what you already have, son. Not even all the gold in the world. Don't you ever forget that." If I would've taken his words to heart I probably wouldn't have had to lose everything, including nearly losing my life, to realize the truth he was desperately trying to impress upon me. Over many decades Fred had witnessed firsthand how the lure of gold had robbed countless men of everything they held precious, family, integrity, honor, dignity, and often even their lives. It was a hard business that hardened men's hearts.

Fred also told me about an "abandoned" mill site with "a sanded" water well on the property, just northwest of Randsburg, about halfway between the town and Goler Canyon. Upon investigation, it looked well suited for my milling purposes. Fred also told me I could use his old mill site, such as it was, if it would help me. Such good friends are extremely rare these days. I will miss him dearly until I see him again on the other side, where we will then laugh together again, of that I'm sure.

I took an extra day to go back to the courthouse and the BLM to check on the mill site Fred had told me about, and found that the owner had only filed his last yearly "intent to hold" with the county courthouse, and not with the BLM. This technically made the two claims that the mill site sat upon, invalid... and ripe for a hostile takeover. It would also provide a fantastic opportunity for me to install an "insurance policy" on my own behalf, considering I didn't know my partner at all, and after all, this was the gold business. So far he was paying my retainer and I didn't require a gun to do my job, so he had that going for him. The fact is, I had never even met my actual partner, the investor/money man in person. All my dealings up to this point had been through his "representative" (promotor), and I had never been able to find it in my heart (due to plain old common sense, I think) to trust a promoter. Though I had even met a few that I liked, and maybe even respected to some degree, I still never trusted them.

So, I relocated the two claims the mill and all of its equipment were sitting on, in my name.

I filed the claims, then headed back to Nevada to put together my report and research the previous mill owner to see just how hard I could push, so to speak. By the look of things so far, I was confident that I could give him a 30 day notice to move everything, knowing that he couldn't afford to move anything in 30 days, and end up taking ownership of the entire shebang for nothing. I would double check on his financial situation just to be sure, and make sure there were no hidden "undesirable" connections (mob, etc.) to jump up and bite me in the gluteus maximus. Where gold is concerned, one always has to be sure before he makes such a move. Overlooking such a serious detail could easily prove deadly, especially when you're doing business in the Mohave Desert, because you're already located where they are gonna dig your shallow grave. I try not to make it any easier than it needs to be for those types of people, and avoid dealings with them much more than I used to, as I was now a family man. Life was a lot different when I only had to look out for just me. Maybe Marriage and family came with a bit of a byproduct, a kin to wisdom, or maybe a little more caution, but in any event I found myself becoming much less reckless over the years. Of course, learning from my errors and making a point not to repeat them weighed in heavy in this regard, as well, such as being shot and stabbed, for example.

It seems that not paying for the same mistake twice had been a huge key to my survival over the years, considering you don't usually survive the first traumatic episode, let alone survive a repeat performance because you were stupid enough to do it, or fall for it, a second time, as the case may be. Sometimes a little paranoia can save your butt. I guess in a strange way, I always held a sense of respect for the enemies I faced, win or lose, but I always felt that the deepest pits of hell were reserved for my skulking enemies, often disguised as friends, whose vicious attacks I never saw coming. It's kind of like being "Sunday punched" by the only friend you trust, except it's on a life or death basis. You can't imagine the raging torment and agony within me when, in the near future, God would require me to forgive them all.

CHAPTER 32

## Animals, Unicorns and Dragons

*"And the unicorns shall come down with them...and their land shall be soaked with blood..."*
Isaiah 34:7 (KJV)

*"Praise the Lord from the earth, ye dragons..."* Psalms 148:7 (KJV)
*"I am a brother to dragons..."* Job 39:29 (KJV)

Paying attention to my wolf/dog Calador, saved me on a multitude of different occasions, concerning the amount of trust that I put in other people, and I should have paid more attention to him than I did. You could smooth talk me into believing what you wanted me to believe, but not Cal. Your words meant nothing to him. If he didn't like you, it's because he could see what's really inside of you, and all the times I trusted that hybrid dog of mine, I never got burned. I know it sounds kind of weird but I tried to have Cal with me whenever I met a possible new business associate and insisted that he come with me to as many business meetings as possible, as well. Eccentric? Yes, but I didn't get BS'ed when Cal was around. Years later, when the time came that I had to put him in the ground, a large piece of me got buried with him that day, and I won't get it back until I see him in Heaven.

Is he in Heaven, you ask? That's what I had to know, because it wouldn't be Heaven without him and my other True Blue canine companions that were essential to my ability to survive many of the most painful elements of my life, here on good old planet Earth.

Well, I found out through a lot of research, and I'll share some of the high points with you. First of all, I found that the only two true sources that I could trust, when it comes to the subject of Heaven, are God's word, because it's proven itself as the only reliable book written by the One who created the Heavens, the earth, the sea and all that is in them. The other source is the testimonies of those who have been there and returned, and this source is, at best, "ify". And here's a warning; you had better be solidly rooted and grounded in the true Word of God, the Holy Bible, before you start a study in this area because the devil will always be waiting with his elaborate lies to get you sidetracked down some pretty dark paths. And let me tell you, there's a lot of "trash" out there as far as "near death experiences" are concerned, however, after sifting through almost a hundred of them after my Dad died, I managed to find a few that passed the "acid test" by adhering and agreeing totally with the Holy Bible.

Then, just to be safe, I omit the ones given by adults, even though I believe many of them, and focused on testimonies of very young children who couldn't possibly have made up such a story, or been coached into such detail as these kids describe when they speak of what they saw and heard while in the presence of our Lord (*we are confident, yes, well pleased rather to be absent from the body and to be present with the Lord,* 2 Corinthians 5; 8).

Among my favorites, topping the list is the account of a three-year-old boy named Colton Burpo, as portrayed in "Heaven is for Real" (book and movie), where at one point he tells his Mom of meeting his unborn sister, miscarried by his mother, details of his great grandfather who had died 30 years before Colton was born, and my personal favorite, he told of seeing their deceased family dog now walking around with Jesus!

But what does the Bible say about all this? Well, let's talk about that.

Starting in Genesis (pun intended) 1; 21–22, we see that when God created them he also blessed them. Most theologians agree that when man received a "soul" was when "God formed man from the dust of the ground (earth), and breathed into his nostrils the breath of life (soul); and man became a living being", as stated clearly in Genesis 2: 7. Every argument against animals going to Heaven that I ever heard was based on the assumption that animals have no soul, but here's a "clincher" for you. Job 12:7–10 declares that animals not only know God's ways but also "that the hand of the Lord has done this, in whose hand is the soul (the word "nephesh" in Hebrew) of every living thing and the breath of all mankind (KJV). Animals have souls... No if's and's or buts! And, by the way, Genesis 2:11–12 tells of a land called "Havilah", where there is gold, which I have spent a lot of my life looking for. And the gold of that land is good. This has nothing to do with our study on animals... I just thought it worth mentioning, so I threw it in here... Sidetracked...happens a lot lately..... My bad.

Anyway, Genesis 2:19 shows us that animals were also formed from the ground, like man, and included in the Covenant that God made with man AND animals after the flood. Got also declared that He would require a "reckoning" from animals, as well as man, for the blood of man that they spill (Genesis 9:1–17, and see also Hebrews 4:13). If God demands a "reckoning" from animals, what would it matter, if they just die, anyway??? Note that in the above-mentioned versus, God makes and includes animals in his covenants, including the Law of the Sabbaths (Exodus 23:10–12), and the "New Covenant" as foretold by the prophet in Jeremiah 31:27–34! James simply confirms this in referring to our redemption in James 1:18, and

Psalm 50:10–11 reiterates that God Himself declares that ALL beasts belong to the Lord!

Animals are accountable to God (Hebrews 4:13), animals cry out to God, have a relationship with God, and God provides for them (Job 38:39–41, Psalm 147:9, Joel 1:20, Joel 2:22, Luke 12:24, Psalm 104; 21), as Psalm 104:27–30 beautifully illuminates this for us; *"these all wait for You, that You may give them their food in due season. What You give them they gather in; You open Your hand, they are filled with good. You hide your face, they are troubled; You take away their breath, they die and return to the dust. You send forth Your Spirit, they are created; and You renew the face of the earth."*

Critters are also not forgotten by God (Luke 12:6), not now, and not ever!

1 Kings 17:4 6 gives a nice example of how animals, in this case Ravens, serve and obey God by supplying food for Elijah, and in the book of Jonah the people of Nineveh knew to make the beasts, as well as humans, to neither eat nor drink, be covered in sackcloth and cry out to God in repentance that they would be spared from the prophecy preached to them by Jonah, and it worked! (Versus 5–10).

And what about that whole Balaam and the donkey thing? (And Jesus! See "Old Testament appearances of Jesus" in Appendix O ). I think I'll just put that one on your plate, leave it there, and let you deal with it. In any case, you can't tell me the Lord doesn't have a sense of humor, because you will never convince me that He did all this to Balaam with a straight face (Numbers 22:22–33).

The wild beasts were with Jesus in the wilderness (Mark 1:13). The Bible really nails it down for us (pardon the pun) in the next two passages;

Psalm number 36:6; *"Your righteousness is like the great mountains; Your judgments are a great deep; O Lord, You preserve man and beast."*

The operative word here is "preserve". According to Strong's Concordance, the word is a direct translation of the Hebrew word "yasha", that is translated as "save" 149 times in the Bible, "Savior" 15 times, "salvation" 3 times, and "deliverer" 13 times, as well as "preserved" not "preserve" as in this case, 5 times. So the literal translation of the last line of Psalm 36:6 truly reads, "O Lord, you save man and beast". How awesome is that?

Oh, but wait! You get a second verse free! Luke 3:6 in the New Testament affirms our findings in saying, *"and all flesh shall see the salvation of God"*. And yes, the operative word here, is "flesh", and according to Strong's Concordance, is derived from the Greek word, "sarx", predominantly meaning "flesh (the soft substance of the living body, which covers the bones and is permeated with blood) of both man and beasts", and denotes its detailed definition in this Scripture as, "a living creature (because possessed of a body of flesh) whether man or beast".

Although all "flesh" isn't the same, as clearly stated in 1 Corinthians 15:39, this verse unquestionably declares and confirms that animals are "flesh", under the Greek definition of the word, "sarx", that is used in Luke 3:6. Thus, all "flesh" (man and beast/animal) shall see the salvation of the Lord!

And "salvation" means what? I love Theopedia's definition the best; "Salvation refers to the act of God's grace in delivering His people (and animals, as we have proven!) from bondage to sin and condemnation, transferring them into the Kingdom of His beloved Son (Colossians 1:13), and giving them eternal life (Romans 6:23), all on the basis of what Christ accomplished in His atoning sacrifice. The Bible says *"We are saved by grace through faith; and that not of ourselves, it is a gift of God* (Ephesians 2:8)".

There can be absolutely no doubt. This is why Romans 8:19–23 explains that animals, as a part of all creation, eagerly await our redemption.

Interestingly, Hebrews 9:23–24 depicts things on earth as a "copy" of things in Heaven. Hmmmmm... And what about Heaven and the New Creation during Jesus's reign, which is coming very soon?

Job 5:22–23 tells us that we shall be at peace with the beasts of the field and we shall not be afraid of the beasts of the earth.

Isaiah 43:20 says that the beasts will honor God.

Isaiah 65:25 explains that the wolf and the lamb shall feed together, and the lion shall eat straw like an ox.

Speaking of wolves, I'm not sure how all this works, but just to be safe, I pray those rabbits in Heaven had wings and were moving when my wolves, Calador and Kiesha, got there... At least until the Lord got them calmed down to eating "whatever".

By far, my favorite "peek" into all of this that the Lord has given us, is found in Isaiah 11:6–9, *"The wolf also shall dwell with the lamb, the leopard shall lie down with the young goat, the calf and the young lion and the fatling together; and a little child shall lead them. The cow and the bear shall graze; their young ones shall lie down together; and the lion shall eat straw like the ox. The nursing child shall play by the cobra hole, and the weaned child shall put his hand in the viper's den. They shall not hurt nor destroy in all My holy mountain, for the earth shall be full of the knowledge of the Lord as the waters cover the sea"*.

Check out that last verse. Sooo... Animals will know what we know of the Lord? Is that what it says? I don't know... It's hard to wrap my head around!

Not even done yet, either! Here's a question for doubters; if there are no animals in Heaven, then where did Jesus get his white horse that He is gonna come riding on in Revelation 19:11? And, a chariot and horses of fire picked up Elijah and gave him a ride to Heaven, in 2 Kings 2:11.

Yeah? You like that, huh? Well don't stop reading! Go on down to Revelation 19:14 and be amazed because that's where the Bible says you get a white horse, too!

"And the armies in Heaven, clothed in fine linen, white and clean (that's you!), followed Him on white horses". Yippee-Ki-Yay! Incredible! I can hardly wait! I hope my cowboy hat makes it to Heaven! Yes, truly, our best days are still out in front of us, surely not behind us!

Have you ever experienced the unconditional love and devotion of a dog or other pet? Did not God create this love? Love is of God (1 John 4:7), and God is love (1 John 4:8), so how could anyone consider God creating such profound love, as part of his own nature, and then throwing it away? In lieu of knowing who God is and what scriptures have revealed, to accept that assumption would take a special kind of ignorance.

Think about this; Besides Jesus Himself, a dog is the only creature on Earth that loves you more than he loves himself.

I also believe that people who train dogs will be accountable for their "students" actions that they have taught them...some to honor and some to dishonor. It blows my mind to see all of the amazing things dogs can be trained to do, when I simply "Google" Dog Training....guard dogs, protector dogs, bomb and cancer sniffing dogs, companion dogs in Hospice, and on and on. Wow! As far as being held accountable by the Lord, my brother and I have speculated on the possible ramifications due us for training our dogs to be lunatics. And the crazier the stuff they did, the more we rewarded them, for instance; Calador would grab and hump first one then the other of the pairs of the various types of "religion" sale people that frequented my door; I would cook him a steak after they fled. I've never been able to bring myself to full repentance without laughing over the matter, so I suppose that I rightfully have that "reckoning" coming.

Animals go to Heaven. The Bible proves it. My dogs are in Heaven waiting for me. Your dog is in Heaven too!

If you have taken all this in, up to this point, I might as well go a little over the edge, rieeeght?

Back in the "old days" before translators got concerned about "political correctness" or possible embarrassing and "uncomfortable" scriptures, there was the original King James Version of the Bible. Yup, it had a lot of " thee's, thy's, and thou's" in it and "th" added to the end of about every other word, it seems, like "shalt" and "shalt not", making it a little difficult to understand in these "modern" times we live in today. Kinda like me trying to understand Ebonics. But... The King James Version also had "dragons" in it! True story! 16 references to them in the plural form and 18 times it uses the singular form, "Dragon"!

I don't even allude to knowing what all is going on here, but keep in mind, the word "dinosaur" didn't even exist until the 1800s, yet Job, believed to be the oldest book in the Bible, makes not only detailed reference to them in chapters 40 and 41, but also to "sea monsters" as does Isaiah and the Psalms in telling of Leviathan the serpent of the sea! (Job 41:1, Psalm 74:14, Psalm 104:26, Isaiah 27:1)

Please treat yourself to an awesome study of dragons in the old original King James Version of our Bible, and every time you read one of the 34 Bible references to them, take time to sit and ponder what you just might really see when you get to Heaven! Whatever they are, they are definitely animals, and animals go to Heaven. I sincerely hope dragons are there, not to mention the Unicorns! Yeah, baby! That's what I'm talkin' about!

They can whitewash it, explain it away, sugarcoat it, and laugh at it, but no one can deny it... Unicorns are mentioned three times in the King James Version Bible, Deuteronomy 33:17, Psalm 22:21, and Isaiah 34:7, and six scriptures reference the singular form of "Unicorn", Numbers 23:22, Numbers 24:8, Job 39:9, Job 39:10, Psalm 29:6, and Psalm 92:10.

I bet you haven't heard anybody preaching this from the pulpit lately, except maybe Dr. Kent Hovind or Dr. Carl Baugh and they have some incredible material out there on these subjects... very enlightening, I assure you.

When we think about our loved ones in Heaven, with our Lord, it comforts us. When I think about what else may well be there, it fascinates me! I think we may seriously be guilty of grossly underestimating Heaven. I think we are all gonna be in for a big, wonderful shocker!

## CHAPTER 33

## Calador and the Wildcat

**1995.** Back in Nevada I presented my findings and recommendations to the promoter and soon got a phone call from the actual investor, allowing me to speak directly to him. We discussed several possible scenarios then settled on a 50/50 deal and I began putting together a new cost analysis. A feasibility study would follow after I had the opportunity to make a deal with Doc Johnson and do some serious bulk grid sampling of the potential areas to be placer mined within the canyon.

My new partner also agreed to pay all of my expenses, including moving my family to Ridgecrest, as well as a modest salary that would eventually be deducted from my part of the proceeds, when we went into production. It all sounded good until one evening I got a distraught call from my partner in California wondering why my overhead costs and projected expenditures were so "alarmingly" high on my initial cost analysis. As we started going over the numbers for the first phase, two things became blatantly clear; the first was that the promoter had no idea that my partner and I were directly communicating with each other, and second, he had obviously "padded" (added extra money on to) my cost analysis before submitting it to my new partner. This was commonly done by some of the more unscrupulous promoters to allow them to "skim" extra money for themselves off of the top of the original costs and expenses. In this particular case, it was done with such an astonishing lack of talent on the promoter's part, I was led to surmise that when it came to thinking in general, he had incredibly bad luck.

Even though he was my partner's buddy, I insisted that adjustments had to be made, considering the nature of the free gold business, and I stood my ground knowing that if he can't be trusted with our money, then we darn for sure won't be able to trust him with our gold. My partner assured me that the promoter would not have any more to do with our mining venture, and I made a mental note that he did not say the promoter was fired. Hmmm...

The whole incident left me feeling uneasy. I told my brother about it when he came to visit that weekend, and also told him that living in the city (Gardnerville), as it were, was having an adverse effect on my young son.

When he and I went to pick up my son at his "friends" house, and altercation ensued involving my brother and I and five of Billy's "friends".

The sheriff's department was very understanding and sympathetic to our "response", agreeing that we were "justified", after seeing what a piece of chain had done to my upper back and left shoulder. So no charges were incurred upon my brother and I, but because one of the young "friends" that took a beating was barely 18 years old the investigating officers were eager to suggest that we expedite our moving plans, as well as informed us that the "friends" had a bunch more "friends" who would surely be arriving soon. The funny thing was that Billy wasn't even at the house... He left right before we got there.

Billy went to live with my brother in Kingston, Nevada and Lori, Brandy and I moved to Ridgecrest, California. Lori and I found a great house, virtually on the very outskirts of town, on the southwest end and it was surrounded by open desert on two sides. Odd enough to be noteworthy, on the left side of the property were an old 63 Chevy pickup and an old Volkswagen minivan that had both been sinking into the desert floor for quite some time. In and around the bushes surrounding them we noticed the remaining fur and miscellaneous domesticated housecat parts (legs, tales, etc.) left over from "somethings" dinner. With the ground being too sandy to read tracks I guessed that maybe a hawk or coyote was keeping the local cat population in check.

As Christmas drew near, Brandy's enthusiasm hit the boiling over stage because of her anticipation of a white Christmas (snow) that surely would be a wonderful and welcome change from the sand and heat of the desert that now surrounded us. Lori and I tried redundantly to explain that it just doesn't snow at all in the Mohave Desert, but she firmly stood on her faith that she had always had a white Christmas and, although her geographical location may have changed, this year would be no exception. "I told God we needed snow for Christmas so it will snow," she said and defiantly held her ground. Whatever...about time she learns the truth about Santa Clause, tooth fairy and the Easter Bunny, too, I thought to myself. Then Christmas arrived...and with it came four or five inches of wet, sloppy, slippery snow! Brandy went ballistic! Every time she smacked me with another snowball she would holler, "Miracle!", and, "Here Dad! Have another miracle!"...splat! Her and her mother had this smug look on their faces for days...and in my heart I knew that somehow, my little girl had brought this "real" miracle to pass.

When we tried to make our way to the store that afternoon we had to abandon our attempt and go back to the safety of our house, as other drivers were smashing each other to smithereens! You would have to see it to believe it. Every intersection we came upon had bashed up cars in them! As we watched in dismay, other cars would come sliding on up and into the intersections with all four wheels locked up tight and totally out of control, and crash into the pile. We ducked down a couple of alleys and made our way back home to await the melting of the "miracle". But no denying it: it truly was a Christmas miracle.

I was excited to get the "gold claimer" portable trommel to begin bulk sampling and testing the property. I built a nice little trommel and cleanup vibrating sluices to use with my new gold wheel for my final tests on the concentrates that I brought in from the field. The gold claimer had a water recycle system so I could run all day on two 55 gallon drums of water.

I told my partner that I was going to notify the former owner of the mill site that he had 30 days to get anything he wanted off of the property, however, my partner said he would handle that for us. There was a lot of equipment at the Mill, including two huge proto-type 200 ton per hour wheel mounted trommels. I had hired a small crew to help clean up the site, and start putting things in order. I hired mechanics to make repairs on the machinery, fabricate a working feeding system, and put brakes on the Terex loader (the same one I had used years earlier) that Doc Johnson had graciously supplied for us.

When my partner came to see the mine and mill site for the first time, he said he had come to see what he had bought for his $18,000. When I pressed him to explain, he confessed that he had "made a deal" with the previous mill owner and paid him the 18 grand, and that's all he would tell me. The hair was going up on the back of my neck and I couldn't figure out why. I was beginning to "smell a rat", so to speak. A month or so later my old partner Cornelius showed up at the Mill "just to look around". Before he left, he mentioned my new partner by name, twice, and referred to him on a first name basis.

I kept Lori, my only true partner, up to speed on all of this, and we agreed that something was going on but we had no idea exactly what that was, and I soon started losing sleep over it. My partner was consistently coming up short on his financial obligations, and for over three months Lori and I not only had to borrow money from her Mom for food and our bills, but also to make up for shortages in the payroll.

Then the mechanic who stayed out at the mill site had his dog, a German Shepherd about the size and color of Cal, shot in the middle of the night. He up and quit, moved back to Carson City, and I started packing my guns and leaving Cal at home. I had no idea what was going on, but I knew it was escalating.

We were still a few weeks away from going into production on a small scale of about 150 to 200 tons per day, but even at this rate we should just barely gross a little over 1 million bucks a month. I kept thinking to myself that I just had to hang in here a little while longer and going into production would make everything okay. I'm pretty sure that I don't have an inner child that's trying to get out, but I do have an inner idiot that surfaces from time to time and this line of reasoning is the best example I have produced, thus far. I was getting the hair up on the back of my neck almost all the time now, and warning bells are playing songs in my head, and because I can't pin the exact problem down I kept pushing forward instead of pulling out. I just couldn't let this opportunity go, being this close to making it pay, and I suppose I would have always hated myself if I had pulled out and left.

I finally sent Lori and Brandy back to our home in Ely, and I should have gone with them. I changed out my pickup trucks, my 77 GMC 4 x 4 for my 75, two wheel drive because the 75 Chevy had a fresh 454 engine, a top end of over 150 mph (I have a copy of a 154 mile-per-hour in a 55 mile per hour zone speeding ticket I got), and most importantly, it had steel plating in the doors and cab plus an excellent hidden compartment in the dashboard that held my Colt CAR 15, .223 caliber semi-automatic rifle, along with several 30 round magazines. A steel framed canopy over the bed of the truck made a cool place for Calador to ride out of the sun...yeah, I really should have sent him home with Lori and Brandy but I trusted him and I knew I could count on him in a "situation".

As always I had put all my faith and trust in myself, my dog and my guns. My arrogance knew no limits. At one point, Cal and I had both taken up sleeping outside of the house under some trees in our yard, as it was cooler and much more comfortable than trying to sleep within the confines of the house. Somehow my sleeping bag, army cot and mattress under the stars always felt more like "home" to me than any house I ever lived in. One such evening, just at sunset, we were laying there listening to the sounds of the desert, when we heard the sound of a "scuffle" at the west side of the property, followed by the sound of a muffled catfight that ended very abruptly, then silence. In the dwindling evening light we could see a small cloud of dust rise over by the old 63 Chevy pickup, then all was silent again. Calador was standing in his no BS stance with the hair on his back sticking straight up, his teeth bared, and his eyes fixed in the direction from which the dust cloud had appeared. I pulled on my boots and stuck my Beretta in the back of my pants, and we slowly and cautiously moved into the west side of the acre, toward the old abandoned vehicles. As we approached the old truck and VW van we heard and saw nothing. We stopped to listen several times, then I began moving between the 63 Chevy pickup on my left and the Volkswagen van on my right. There was only about 3 feet between the two causing Cal and I to go single file, with me in the lead.

With absolutely no warning, Cal slammed me against the VW van as he lurched past me with all his strength. It happened so fast that I never had a chance to reach for my pistol as my Companion lunged past me, just as the

Desert Wildcat dove out from under the Chevy pickup right in front of me. The cat's intent was to dive underneath the VW van and it almost made it, as its head and front shoulders were already underneath the van when Cal grabbed onto its back, just in front of its hips. Cal planted his feet, and gave a mighty jerk, pulling that cat out from under that rusty old van and right into his face. And that old wildcat came out fighting!

The fight that ensued right at my feet was nothing short of terrifying. Cal had fought and killed many dogs, including two huge pit bulls, but he had never faced anything like this wildcat. It was almost as big as he was, smaller than a cougar, yet much bigger than a bobcat or lynx. Fur and blood flew everywhere as I frantically grabbed for my pistol and tried to get lined up on an impossible shot that never came.

Just as suddenly as it began, the cat broke free of Cal's 185 pounds and of the grip Cal now had on the back of its neck, shot around the front corner of the van, and disappeared into the open desert beyond. I never saw any animal live, let alone escape once that half wolf got ahold of them by the neck or throat. Calador started to take off in pursuit but with a single word I told him to stay, and he obeyed. Cal was hurt bad and bleeding, making me feel horrible for not at least getting a shot off or being able to help him. Razor-sharp claws had gouged long cuts on his face that had just barely missed his eye, but had put a nasty split in his right ear. His front right shoulder and ribs were flayed open as well. Looking at the blood trail that cat had left behind, it apparently had not fared any better. That blood trail was definitely trackable and I wanted to track that wildcat down and finish this, yet a part of me figured that having survived a fight with Cal, maybe he earned the right to live, if he in fact survived at all considering the blood he was losing.

Cal hated vets and the feeling was mutual, with the exception of the vet up in Elko, Nevada, which was way too far away to help us now. He allowed me to put a few stitches in his shoulder and ribs, but wouldn't let me touch his face or ear. When I called the vet in Elko the next morning, he told me to try and superglue Cal's ear together until it healed, and by the grace of God, which I knew nothing about at that time, it actually worked!

Also that morning we re-investigated the scene from the previous night's battle, and found a partially eaten house cat beneath the old 63 Chevy pickup, solving the mystery of the "cat parts" found in and about the property.

My Dad came down from Ely to help look after Calador for a few weeks while I left him at home. It was really great to see Dad, even though he constantly badgered me to "let it go" and head back to Nevada with him. But I wasn't having any of it... Not when we were this close. I was a fool.

# JOHN GERGEN

## CHAPTER 34

# Summary of Freedom and Hippies-1972

My nerves were frazzled and I became suspicious of everybody and everything. Sleep became a time of mental torment as I would lay awake running hundreds of possible scenarios through my head hoping to find one that would make sense of what was going on, but without actually knowing the facts, all I could do was guess, and make up worst-case scenarios in my head. Hopefully our "plan of operation" we had submitted for approval to the BLM should be finalized within this week and we will begin extracting and shipping material the short distance to the mill. I couldn't remember what it was like to have a "carefree" day, when it was actually fun to go to work.

I did manage to find a "portal" through which I could drift into dreamland for a short time. I would simply make a little trip down memory lane to the summer of 1972, when at 15 years old; I spent the entire summer hitchhiking the back roads of Northern California and the Sierra Mountains. My friends Chris and his brother Scott and I concocted the plan, lied to my folks and told them Chris's Dad was taking us to their grandparents' ranch up in the Sierras near North San Juan, California. Chris's Dad even backed up our story, and at daybreak in the first week of June, with $16 in my pocket, we started walking and "thumbing" our way out of Ely. That was the trick; getting out of Ely without someone recognizing me and telling my parents, but just as we were approaching the train tunnel on the west side of Ely, we hooked our first ride in the back of a pickup, all the way to Reno! Well, Sparks actually.

That's where my cousins lived in a house right on Fourth Street. Mickey and his wife Margie, and Mick's sister Pat and her husband Ron took us in, fed us and swore an allegiance of secrecy to our cause, whatever it was, because I can't remember what I had told them. After a few days Mickey and his pal Cody gave us a ride up to Verdi in Cody's 56 Chevy, and let me tell you, that two door hardtop was incredibly fast. Pat made us a nice lunch and Ron schooled us on what to be careful of hitchhiking around California. Especially informative and inspiring was the schooling he gave me on the pitfalls of "free love" that was so popular during these times. A lasting impression was made on me when he graphically explained venereal disease, free clinics, and the means and proper application of a product called A-200. The impression he made on me served to stop me from making and carrying out some really stupid decisions that were set before me throughout the summer...thus, I remained a virgin. Thanks Ron, for caring enough for me to "school" me and save me (postponed, more like) from my own treacherous, screaming hormones. Of course, even the pretty girls with very hairy armpits were a deterrent as well.

After leaving Nevada, rides came fairly easily, the reason being that probably 90% of them were with "hippies". When they picked you up and you climbed in their car or van, they always seem to ask the same question, "What's your story, man?" It got really fun making up BS stories, i.e. looking for our lost sister, brother, mother, house burned down, ran from the orphanage, etc., and they always said, "that's groovy", "that's deep", or "right on", and almost always followed up with "groovy baby, wanna hit?"

We made it to Della and Herman's house, Chris's grandparents, above North San Juan, just after dark as we had to walk the last 2 miles up the dirt road through the forest to the ranch. We moved into the bunkhouse and it was an awesome, groovy, summer. Many times we hitchhiked the back roads from North San Juan to Grass Valley, Nevada city, Marysville, Chico and Red Bluff, where Chris and Scott's family were originally from, so they knew lots of people who helped us out, fed us, and let us sleep in the orchards.

A lot of the time the hippies would take us to their "pads" or more often their "communes", get us stoned and we would sit around a campfire singing "Kumbaya", "Puff the Magic Dragon", "Me and Bobby McGee", as well as many other Janis Joplin, Bob Dylan, and Carol King songs. They shared "everything" with us, and we learned a lot from them that summer. We learned how to tie-die stuff, make flowers out of napkins, how to "get our minds blown", take "trips", and the vast qualities and benefits of "staying mellow".

The thing is, even though we were very young, they treated us with respect and took us into their midst and accepted us as one of their own. They often talked about Jesus and quoted Bible verses, but by then I had had enough "religion" shoved down my throat, and I was not willing to accept that Jesus could really love the "rotten sinner" that my LDS upbringing had convinced me that I was. I respectfully declined their attempts to enlighten me as to the truth of the Bible.

It usually didn't take long before their preachy religious persistence became annoying and we would hit the road again to continue on our adventure, in a purely "Coddiwopple" fashion (to travel purposefully toward an as-yet-unknown destination). It always seemed good to be on the move again, as if we had a goal or destination, even though we really didn't. We were just bumming around the countryside. We partied a lot in Red Bluff as the "Keggers" and parties seemed to never end. Then we would work our way back south to Grass Valley and North San Juan. We would hitchhike through the Sierra Nevada Mountains every day to get down to the forks of the Yuba River and swim all day long, or go deep into the forest to Arlo's Place.

Arlo was the oldest hippie I ever met. He had long gray hair, a long gray beard and hardly ever wore a shirt over his wiry frame. He made his living in "horticulture", but he had only two plants. One was a towering 14 feet tall and the other was almost a full 16 feet tall, and their "trunks" looked to have "bark" on them. Over many years of cultivation, Arlo had spliced or implanted other plants from around the world into his plants and the "buds" were commonly over 15 inches long and potent enough to drop a rhinoceros. Arlo himself had obviously built up an immunity to the effects of his plants over the years, but for us, it only took being in close contact with them for about 30 minutes before our heads were swimming and our legs became wobbly.

And Arlo had a still. It wasn't that big as far as moonshine stills go, but the high quality and blinding potency of his product (shine) was respectfully held in the highest regard throughout the Sierras, including certain upscale nightclubs in Chico, Marysville, Oroville and Sacramento. He used custom-built milk jugs for the travel containers for his elixir, that were at least three times thicker than any milk jug I had ever seen. They fit snugly into the custom-built square slots in the huge trunk compartments of either his 1969 Plymouth fury or his 1969 Chrysler New Yorker. Both of these cars were extremely customized for Arlo, for the specific purpose of running shine through the twisting mountain roads of the Sierra Nevada Mountains. Both had high performance 440C.I.D.engines, custom exhaust systems to keep them almost silent, and huge air shocks on the rear ends as to keep them riding even under the heavy loads of shine they carried, and double shocked front ends with cross stabilizer bars for extremely high speed cornering. All this and they looked just like my Mom's New Yorker, as plain and common as could be... They were truly what were referred to as "sleepers".

I was fortunate enough to make a "night run" with Arlo as he round-tripped Chico all in one night and had us back to his place before dawn. As we were empty on the way home, he showed me what that New Yorker would do, and I will never forget that ride. After I received a driver's license of my own six months later, I ran my Mom's New Yorker practically into the ground within a few short years... Sorry Mom. And thank you, Arlo, for putting up with such a "Rattle mouth" kid.

All things considered, even though I spent the entire summer with the total freedom to make all my own decisions for myself, I think I did pretty good...for the most part. I remained a virgin when several opportunities to the contrary presented themselves (thank you Cousin Ron for that). I tried a lot of "psychedelics" for the first time, which actually taught me not to do them again in the future, and at least I was in an environment where I was looked after when I did, as not to be hurt or taken advantage of. I wish I could thank all of my hippie friends that took such good care of me, right here, by name, but one of the unfortunate side effects of my "experimenting" is that I can't even remember one of your names because I think the brain cells that I killed that summer are the very ones that held your names in my memory...sorry, but with all my heart, thank you for being such good friends. I believe most of them are probably holding political offices by now. I also realized at my young age that my system (metabolism) could not handle cannabis like my friends, or anybody else for that matter, could. This is obviously a blessing from God and I'll bet He had a good reason for it. It just "nuked" me. Even just a little bit of it was all it took to immobilize me, and I hated that feeling. I learned moderation and to be very careful with that stuff in my forthcoming teen years, and early 20s, after which I just didn't have any use for it at all anymore.

I don't regret it, but climbing into that car full of dope and moonshine to run through the twisting back roads of the Sierras with a half-lit old hippie probably wasn't my wisest choice. The ramifications could have been devastating if we had been apprehended, as well as fatal had we hit a deer or missed a turn, and for this I can only attribute my well-being to God, who looks after young fools like me, and old ones like Arlo, too, I believe, even amidst my denying Him at the time. He is truly a long-suffering and forgiving God.

As summer came to a close we hitched our way back into Nevada, but only made it as far as Fallon, where we sat by the road on the east side of town for 2 ½ days. No one would help us at all and several times a day local "cowboys" would drive by and throw stuff (beer cans, mostly) at us and call us "blankety-blank" hippies.

And then, with no food or resources for over two days, I called my parents with the concocted story that Chris's Dad's car broke down and we were stranded in Fallon. Within an hour, my really awesome Aunt Alice, who lived here, picked us up and took us to her place. She fed us and let us clean up before my Mom came the next day to get us. All the while she listened to our sad, sad story with a half-smile and a raised eyebrow, not falling for any of it, but kind and gracious enough to not out and out tell us we were full of crap.

Aunt Alice was a news reporter and she could smell BS a mile away. I wish now that we had either shut up or told her the truth, rather than compromising our rapport with her with our made-up tales. She was considerate enough as not to embarrass us further, by calling us on the errors in our story, as she felt, I'm sure, that that privilege was reserved for my Mom and Dad when we got home; which it was. You're still awesome to this day, Aunt Alice, and I love ya!

I survived that summer, by the grace and mercy of our Heavenly Father who refused to let me throw Him out of my life, and I grew up some because of it as well. Thank You, Father, for not letting me train wreck my life back then... At least until I was a little older, anyway.

I believe that there is only so much abuse that the Lord will take until He lets you have it "your way".

## CHAPTER 35

## Here We Go

### Deliverance Begins — What a Nightmare

February, 1996 — I was just loading up the last 5 gallon bucket of samples into the back of my pickup when the rifle shot echoed off of the cliff walls and on up the canyon to where I was working. I snuggled a little closer to my CAR 15 that was leaning on my spare tire by the tailgate. The shot sounded quite a bit farther down toward the mouth of the canyon, but echoes can fool you. Definitely a rifle shot though. I closed the tailgate then scanned the cliff tops and ridges with my binoculars. I was working in this part of the canyon to confirm bulk samples I had previously taken to determine where we would begin excavating, hopefully, in a week or so, when our permits came through. 20 minutes passed with no further shots or sounds at all other than a slight February breeze whispering through the narrow desert canyon.

As I prepared to head for town and travel in the direction the gunshot had originated from, I opted to put my CAR 15 in its driver door gun rack rather than back into its hidden dashboard compartment as I always did. My Beretta 9 mm was on the seat beside me. I put my maps and sample locations into my map case on the floor board and began my slow descent down the canyon. At the mouth of the canyon I stopped when I topped out on the canyon rim. From this vantage point I could scan the trail ahead on down to Garlock Road, and even look over the mill site across the valley floor through my binoculars, as well. All seemed quiet...almost to quiet. I would've thought to hear a vehicle motor or off-road machine from whoever fired that shot, as the canyon walls were an exemplary natural amplifying system. I had heard nothing, and Calador was at ease. My paranoia may have been getting the best of me, but just to be safe I kept my guns handy.

We drove down the hillside and hung a left on Garlock Road, without incident. In a horrific display of stupidity I left my CAR 15 rifle in the driver's door gun rack instead of putting it back into the hidden dashboard compartment. A few miles later, Cal and I made a left on Highway 395 and headed north towards Ridgecrest.

Still several miles from town we passed a sheriff's car parked on the side of the road. As we went past him, he pulled out behind us. I always took it easy with Cal in the back so we were doing a few miles under the speed limit as we turned right onto China Lake Boulevard with several miles of desert remaining between us and town. As we made the turn the sheriff's vehicle turned on his lights and we pulled over.

My friend Cliff was also coming into town from the mill and pulled over in front of my truck and tried to hang out until he could find out what was going on, however the deputy told him to leave. Unknown to me at the time, Cliff went to town and called Lori – thanks, my friend.

I slipped my pistol into my map case.

The deputy approached my driver's door and asked for my license and registration, which I gave him. I asked him why he had pulled me over and he said "they" were looking for so-&-so, a wanted man driving a pickup similar to mine, and had heard that he was traveling on this stretch of road. Then, looking again at my driver's license, which proved I wasn't the person they were looking for, he put my driver's license into his shirt pocket, handed me back my registration, and asked "Do you have any guns in your vehicle?" So much for probable cause.

Loud warning bells exploded in my head, Cal gave out a low growl, and the deputy dropped his hand to his gun. At that very moment it became crystal clear that he knew exactly who I was and this was no random stop. I slowly placed both my hands on top of the steering wheel and replied "Yes, I do".

One look at this guy was all it took to know he was on a definite mission with a definite purpose, and just looking for an excuse to pull his pistol on me. Without taking his eyes off of me or his hand off of his pistol, he slowly opened my driver's door with his free hand and told me to "Step out of the vehicle, and clasp my fingers together behind my head." I complied, talking softly to Calador as I did, as not to get him shot in the process. Cal's hair was up on his back but he obediently remained silent, never taking his eyes away from the deputy.

I was then walked back to the hood of the police car, pushed over it, and then handcuffed behind my back.

"Why are you doing this?" I asked, but he just shoved me into the back seat of his car and shut the door, as a California Highway Patrol car pulled up behind us. The exhilaration I felt, and actually thinking "thank God" for this highway patrolman, that I was sure to save me, was short-lived. As the two officers met beside the deputy's car, the young highway patrolman looked in at me and asked, "Is this the guy?" The deputy smiled and said "Yep".

The deputy had pulled my CAR 15 out of my truck and was showing it to the highway patrolman and they both laughed. Then they went around to the passenger side of my truck, and pulled out my map case, removing my Beretta 9 mm. They stayed there for several minutes in an intense conversation as they took turns handling my guns and looking back and forth from each other to me. Apparently, when they had corroborated their story the deputy held up my map case in one hand and a small bottle or film canister in the other and said "Look what we found".

"Bullshit!" I screamed, "Why are you doing this to me?" Thank God that I had leashed Cal in the back of my truck, because when I yelled he went off, scaring the hell out of those two cops.

The CHP pulled his Glock and pointed it at Cal but the deputy reached up and pulled the gun down as there were cars coming down the highway. I was in a panic, yelling and kicking the inside of the squad car trying desperately to save my dog. The cops came around the passenger side of the deputy's squad car, open the back door and drug me out by my hair and right arm, jerking me up on my feet. The cars went by and the CHP "officer" pulled out his Glock 9 mm again and shoved it in my face. One look in his eyes and I knew he was going to kill me and he was going to enjoy it. As he held me up against the deputy's car he told the sheriff's deputy, "Go over by the dog so they can hear him barking in the background and call it in that we gotta put it down." As the deputy called in on the radio about my dog the CHP "officer" looked me in the eyes and said, "And you went crazy and we had to put you down next."

With his gun to my head and me still handcuffed behind my back, he grabbed me by my arm and led me to the side of the road between my pickup and the sheriff's car, where I know he was taking me to shoot me.

Here it is... The, BUT GOD moment that I didn't recognize until later.

As the CHP raised his pistol to my head while saying, "I'm gonna pop a cap in you", suddenly an Animal Control Truck pulled up, and a female Animal Control Officer jumped out, came around the front of the truck and loudly exclaimed, "Don't do it!"

I believe the two officers were caught "flat-footed" (by surprise... Pardon the pun) by the "deer caught in the headlights" look on their faces. They looked at the Animal Control Lady and a back and forth at each other with "what now" looks on their faces. Before they could recover their wits, the lady walked over to me and said, "Can you get your dog into the side compartment of my truck?"

I said, "Yes ma'am!"

"Okay, but no tricks" said the CHP and to emphasize the point he put his pistol back up to the side of my head again and said, "or I'm gonna "pop a cap" in you... You hear me?" I said I understood as the deputy uncuffed me.

I climbed up into the bed of my truck and gave Cal a quick hug and said, "Its okay, Cal, let's go for a ride." I unhooked the "D" ring that attached his leash to the "I" bolt in the back of the truck, led him out and over to the side compartment of the Animal Control Vehicle, and said "load up!" Without hesitation Calador jumped into the open compartment, and I shut the door.

The CHP grabbed me and slammed me against the truck and re-handcuffed me.

"Is that necessary?" The lady asked him. She looked back and forth at the two officers and when she looked back at me her eyes and pale facial expression told me that she obviously had a good idea what was going on...and also that she was shaken up over it.

"Thanks for your help," the deputy told her, "We got it from here."

"Yeah," she said. "I'll follow you on into town, if you're ready to go." What intense courage she had to have to do this! The ugly glares she received from the two cops in response were blatantly intimidating, but thank God, she held her ground and after a long moment, they shoved me back into the back seat of the deputy's squad car. True to her word, she followed the car I was in until we reached the Jail in Ridgecrest. The CHP flipped a "U" turn and disappeared.

I never saw or heard from her again after that, but pray God to honor and bless her for saving me and Cal that day. I have no doubt we would both have died on that secluded stretch of desert highway had the Lord not put her there at the exact right moment.

On the way to town I asked the deputy, "I'm in serious trouble here aren't I? Why?"

He said, "No, not too bad." I knew better and I was scared. These people are above the law and have no remorse whatsoever about breaking it. What a setup. I was never even read my rights, I mused. I guess they don't give you your Miranda rights before they execute you.

The fact that they were actually doing this and getting away with it caused such a deep feeling of helplessness in me that I had to turn it immediately over into hatred or I wouldn't be able to bear it. At this point in my life I had developed hate as the primary survival mode I would go into in order to handle the extremely painful things that had the ability to debilitate me mentally, emotionally, and also physically.

Insane? Possibly. Demonic? Probably. But I came to understand over the years that many things beyond my control had the ability to mentally and emotionally cripple, if not outright kill me. But converting the debilitating and sometimes deadly, incapacitating things that I couldn't control or process, such as pain (emotional, mental and physical), depression, injustice, helplessness, hopelessness, insecurity and low self-esteem, etc., into hate and inner rage, robbed them of their ability to kill me. The bottom line is, I could live on hate. And as time progressed, hate began its work of consuming me. To be free of this, to me, is the ultimate freedom. Nowadays, I can say with all my heart that the true reality of "Who the Son sets free is free indeed" (John 8:36) radiates all throughout my soul and my entire being, even though I will be haunted with regret until I get home to be with my Lord.

***

Although I had been to jail on several other occasions, this time we did things different. I was put in a "holding cell" for several hours before I was booked. During that time I was taken out and held with my back against the wall while the arresting deputy held my head against the wall with one hand and shined an intensely bright flashlight into one of my eyes with the other hand. After what seemed like forever he removed the flashlight and, after looking back and forth from one of my eyes to the other, beckoned to a detective (tie and sport coat) walking by and asked, "Does this eye look dilated to you?" After looking back and forth that my eyes the passerby said, "Yeah, I guess, but you better work on the other eye."

Then the deputies said the words out loud as he wrote them in his report, "Eyes of the suspect were dilated, and confirmed by detective so-and-so upon his observation."

He then un-cuffed me and handed me a solo-cup, not a urine test specimen bottle that I could close and seal, and told me to pee in it. I crushed it in my hand and dropped it on the floor. He slammed me face first into the wall, handcuffed me behind my back again and through me back into the holding cell, which had no toilet, and told me to let him know when I got to "go to the bathroom" (not his exact words).

Several hours later he came by my cell and said, "It's been a long day and I'm tired of messing with you. Are you ready, or do we do this the hard way?" I conceded. He had me turn around and back up to the bars and he unlocked the cuffs. When I turned around he handed me another solo-cup, which I filled. Passing it back through the cell bars, he took it into the bathroom and several minutes later, came out with an official sealed urine specimen bottle with my name on it. The test results would come back later showing positive for a trace of methamphetamine. This would guarantee that I would never get my legally owned and registered guns back.

You know, after all these years (over 20) I would've thought I could have handled writing about all this a little better, but I don't have the words to describe the deep emotional grief I still feel while recollecting these injustices and evil things that they did to me. It's much harder than I thought it would be.

After that I was booked and taken back to an empty cellblock and locked up entirely by myself. About two hours later a jailer came by and slid a cordless phone into my cell, and whispered, "Now is your chance to tell somebody where you are," before he disappeared around the corner. God bless that jailer. I called Lori, and she took care of everything else; Calador, my truck and my bail, and my daughter who had come back to finish this school semester out.

    Worse than going through the ordeal of her father going to jail was her seeing my rage as I swore vengeance on those responsible, and went to an all-time low of blaming God and His hate for me. I shamefully told Brandy that God created us simply for his personal entertainment. It broke her heart.

## CHAPTER 36

## The "Criminal" Justice System

I got a certified letter from the BLM requesting more information on the extraction data, ground disturbance and reclamation methods (yearly flash flood wasn't acceptable – kidding), so the permits were held up until I submitted the information they wanted. It was a simple enough fix, but in lieu of current circumstances, I hid the letter until I could see my way clear of this new legal entanglement and exact revenge on whoever was responsible for it.

The only thing I knew without a doubt was the fact that whoever set this little ditty up for me was gonna wish to God they had killed me. My vengeance would be a unique, one-of-a-kind, work of art that would allow them to know the source without a chance of proving it, and it would eventually be fatal, after I made them suffer for a while. No amount of gold would compensate them for what I had in mind. I was never a big bodybuilder or martial arts expert, but I learned at a very early age that within the "law of equalizers" I can always find a way to get a blade or bullet inside one's rib cage… figuratively speaking, of course. The evilest part of me was begging to be unleashed yet my mind was calm and very composed. It would be done "right". They want to play dirty? I'll show them how dark I can really be.

Lori came back down and got me hooked up with my first "dump-truck" lawyer who recommended a private investigator, who we also hired. After a few weeks the P. I. Told me he was convinced that my ex-partner was probably innocent and my current partner was behind all of this and that evidence would (as always) be forthcoming. I had to have proof and told him so. I was also beginning to suspect that he might just possibly be saying things that I already suspected, just to keep himself in a paycheck. As time passed, he would feed me tidbits of "secret information" he had attained, such as the police were actually looking for my new mechanics son on the day they arrested me. Hmmm… We looked nothing alike, and neither did our vehicles bear even a remote likeness. He suggested I tell my new mechanic about how the law was looking for his son. When I did, they packed up and left, as now I am sure, was what that "Private Dick" was hoping for. Thus, I also lost my watchmen at the Mill.

The investigators tidbits of information would continue to alter how I operated my business, in slow progression and reducing key personnel.

At my arraignment I was totally shocked to find myself charged with ex-felon in possession of a firearm. I had never been an ex-felon in my life!

Everything I ever got in trouble with the law for was just misdemeanors or the charges had been dismissed. I asked him to explain to me how they could just make these charges up. He said it was based on a case 22 years earlier, when I was in my senior year of high school in Red Bluff, California, because I spent five days in jail on a burglary charge. He explained that my lawyer at the time, Mr. Pugh, had a motorcycle accident before filing the final paperwork. I explained to him, and later produced all the paperwork to prove it, that because my truck was involved and I refused to "snitch" on others, I did the five days in jail and probation. I also gave him the court stamped order where all charges had been dismissed, including a letter stating there would be no criminal record of any of it!

He explained that under California three strikes laws that I was looking at a minimum of eight years in prison for the two strikes, if convicted. My case was kicked up to the courts in Bakersfield for trial and my lawyer said we could submit the "evidence" (my paperwork) at that time and get the ex-felon thing dropped, and I would probably just have probation.

What about my Miranda rights I never got? What about subpoenaing the dogcatcher lady? What about the two witnesses in the jail who saw that deputy hold me against the wall and dilate my eye with a flashlight? What about probable cause and pulling me over? My lawyer said that would all be taken care of at my hearing in the Kern County courts in Bakersfield.

Lori was coming down from Nevada and going to each court appearance with me, as she not only had extensive training and background in law but also had many resources from her previous employers to which she had access to legal advice and second opinions. At my first hearing in Bakersfield the "head judge" presided over my case. It was at this hearing that we were to present our evidence and list of witnesses. The judge said that not being read my rights was "irrelevant to the case". He said that we could not subpoena a sheriff's deputy/jailer to testify against another deputy, and that other "criminal suspects" who may have seen what they did to me in the jail could not be considered "reliable witnesses" to testify against a sheriff's deputy. When we submitted our request to subpoena the Animal Control Officer who witnessed my "arrest", he simply said "Sure", with a devious smile, then said "Let me know how that works for you". He also ruled that "In the line of duty a Kern County Sheriff often has to exercise his best judgment, which is acceptable to the court", concerning probable cause, or the lack thereof, as we tried to submit photos of the person and vehicle they were looking for, compared to mine. Then he said he would "consider" all our documentation that proved I was not and ex-felon and that, other than traffic tickets and one misdemeanor from 1978, I had a clean record for over 20 years.

The White Pine County Sheriff in Ely also gave me a letter to verify that I was not a felon. We submitted documentation from Alcohol Tobacco and Firearms that also cleared me to purchase explosives for several mines I had been involved with over the years. All of my guns that they took from me were sold to me and legally registered to me after I had undergone and successfully passed multiple background checks, and we submitted that paperwork as well.

The next day my PI told me that in talking to my attorney, he had discovered that the judge had privately intimidated him and my attorney had told him that I was going to have to do some "serious time", several years in prison, at the least. The PI convinced me that my lawyer was "rolling over on me", and just by chance, had the name of a really good "crackerjack" lawyer friend that I needed to hire. I did as he instructed, as I was still reeling from that judge not allowing me to enter any of our evidence or witnesses.

In trying to subpoena the lady dogcatcher, according to my PI, she simply disappeared; quit her job, cleaned out her house, and left with no forwarding address.

Then Lori got pulled over twice in her custom Camaro and harassed by the same highway patrol officer that had put the gun to my head. The third time, Brandy and I were in with her. As both times before, it was after dark and in a residential area, definitely out of CHP's jurisdiction. He came up to Lori's driver's window, leaned in toward her and said, "Hi baby. Remember me?" He looked over at me and said, "Awe! What a nice surprise!" As he continued his overbearing line of demoralizing and accusing line of crap, he soon noticed Lori was writing in shorthand and everything he was saying she was putting down on a yellow legal pad. "What the____ is that?" He snarled. "Just getting it all down for court", she said, calmly and matter-of-factly.

"I'm outta here", he said, turned and went back to his cop car, turned off the flashing lights and sped away. Brandy started to cry and Lori and I did our best to comfort her, while I realized in my rage that, no matter what, I had to protect my family. This was now very personal. No cop on this earth has the right to terrorize innocent women and children, even though they may otherwise be above the law. Not my law. How much would a man take before he acted to protect his loved ones? There was no one to help us. No one wanted to "get involved", so they just turned their heads.

Two midsized sedans took turns showing up parked about a half a block north of our house, and through my spotting scope I could clearly see the driver hunkered down in the seat for hours on end. This was turning into my worst nightmare. I sometimes would have Brandy or Lori set in my car or outside on the porch, wearing my jacket and hat while I slipped out the back and had Cliff pick me up a block away, just so I could go out to the job sites and take care of business, without giving them the opportunity to catch me out on the desert highway away from witnesses, again.

And then, just after dark one evening, I fired up my truck and casually drove to the other side of town with the "stakeout" car following me. I went to Walmart while Lori, Brandy and Cal left for Ely under the cover of darkness, and undetected. Lori took with her a large manila envelope with a topography map containing an "X marks the spot" and several pieces of ancient Indian pottery shards, some arrowheads and flint chips. I told her to mail it to the Bureau of Land Management office in Ridgecrest if anything else happened to me. It was my insurance policy that if I couldn't mine that gold deposit this time, then nobody would – ever. Matching pot shards, flint chips, arrowheads and a grinding stone would be found on the level ridge top directly above the hidden gold ledge to seal it as a Native American archaeological site for all time. Looking at Google Earth, it remains untouched to this day...Que-sera-sera. So be it.

Then the PI told me that he had discovered that the reason the head judge of Kern County was personally overseeing my case was because he was a close friend or relative of my partner's wife.

With this new information combined with the judge not allowing us to submit our evidence, we petitioned for a change of venue (new judge in a different jurisdiction). Not only did we get denied, but the intimidation and harassment against me increased. One time after a court appearance, my wife and I were talking with my lawyer in the main hall of the court room when the CHP officer came down the stairs, pointed his fingers imitating a gun at me first, then at Lori, and said, "Boom! Boom! I'll be seeing you." My lawyer saw the whole thing, and said and did absolutely nothing.

The best piece of evidence to prove my innocence emerged when my lawyer got a cassette copy of the conversations between the deputy and the CHP officer, through the dispatcher, that talked about me and how they would "bust me", hours before I was pulled over. One voice said, "Get it in his lunch box or wallet, if you can," and, "It's not a bindle", my lawyer excitedly told me, as we entered the courtroom to submit our new evidence.

Upon making the request to submit the cassette tape, the judge told my attorney and the prosecuting attorney to approach the bench (so the court reporter could not hear, I'm sure). The conversation started to become "heated" and the judge called for a 10 minute recess and both attorneys were to join him in his chambers. After the recess my attorney emerged back into the courtroom, visibly shaken and without the cassette tape. When I asked him what was going on, he turned to me and as calmly as he could, said, "The judge will not allow us to submit any evidence that could compromise or question the integrity of the Kern County Sheriff's Department." He finished with, "He took the tape. You should probably find a new lawyer to represent you."

He later told me outside the courtroom that he had been "severely threatened", and, "there is nothing more I can do for you." As horrifying as that was to hear, it couldn't compare to what he said next. He said, "The judge also said that the next time your wife shows up in court with her notepad she will be drug tested, just like you were, and jailed until the court sees fit to hear her case."

Lori and my Dad had been coming down from Ely to be at all of my court appearances, and because they would not give my lawyer a copy of the minutes from the court reporter, Lori had been documenting everything that was said.

How could such blatant evil and injustice come from a justice system that was supposed to protect the innocent? It was maddening...a sick, bizarre nightmare that left no avenue of escape, and no thread of hope for a fair trial. At my next court appearance the judge, true to his threat, smiled at me and set a urine specimen cup on top of his bench.

Lori, my lawyer and I systematically and chronologically listed all this "evidence of injustice" in a complaint we filed with the Judicial Committee, in hopes of getting a change of venue. Here's how that went; according to my lawyer, the judge in question is notified of the complaint within 10 days but the said judge has 90 days in which to respond to the complaint. That means that my life became a living hell for those 90 days, with the judges intended end result being my imprisonment, thus making it impossible for me to continue with the Judicial Committees complaint proceedings.

Spotlights would randomly shine through my windows and into my house all hours of the night. Lori could no longer safely come to my court dates, or cross into California for that matter. The judge, from this point on, would schedule court appearances for me, week after week. I would have to drive almost daily from Ridgecrest, 113 miles and about two hours one way, just to sit in his courtroom, all day long, and never have my case called. I would drive back to Ridgecrest that evening, and then do it all over and over again, throughout the entire summer months. My lawyer told me that I absolutely must be there when court began session and not move from my seat until court is adjourned at the end of the day. Otherwise, the moment the judge does not see me in the court room he will immediately call up my case and, in my absence, issue a bench warrant for failure to appear, thus invoking my supposed "third strike" which comes with a mandatory 25 to life sentence in California. My "punishment was disproportionate to my crime" (Capt. Barbosa, Pirates of the Caribbean, Curse of the Black Pearl, a Disney production). My lawyer told me not to even go out to the bathroom.

At one point my lawyer asked to change one court date so I could go to my son Billy's graduation ceremony from the Marine Corps' "Devil Pups" program in Camp Pendleton. "Absolutely not" was the judge's response. I sent Cliff and another friend to video Billy's graduation for me and pick him up and take him to a certain beach where, after sitting in court all day long until 5 PM, I was able to meet with my son before sending him back to Nevada. There are so many scriptures in the Bible that condemn evil judges and those who take bribes, especially in Proverbs, but I feel the need to restrain myself from listing them all here. Evil is evil and that is what I was contending with. With Billy back safe in Ely, I went out to see my old friend, Fred Bond, in Red Mountain, and enjoy a peaceful dinner with him.

In passing conversation I mentioned some of the things my private investigator had told me. With a puzzled look on his face Fred asked me what his name was. When I told him his eyes widened and he exclaimed, "I know that guy! He's Con's buddy!"

Everything started to fall into place. So if the PI was "railroading" me, what about the attorney he insisted that I hire? I suppose that it didn't matter much this late in the game, as I had no money left to pay him anymore, and like Proverbs 11:4 explains, money isn't going to help me out of this anyway. And yeah, the realization that I was never gonna see that half $1 million a month was now crystal-clear. The bittersweet satisfaction I took knowing that no one else would see it either, did little to console me as my life had imploded around me. Just from the implications of some of my "adventures" that I've covered in the previous pages of this book, let alone the ones that I will carry to my grave with me, we can surmise that there are instances in my life that should have resulted in my incarceration, however, this particular situation wasn't one of them. Had I known what was coming, I would've walked away from the Goldmine and given it to them, but there is no way I could have foreseen this. They had planned it well and the trap had been sprung. I am certain now that I will probably never know all of the details, or the degree of involvement certain people played, and I have finally reached a point in my life and in my relationship with the Lord that I can truly say, I don't care anymore. It is now between those involved and God (Deuteronomy 32:35, Psalm 21:1-13, John 20:23, Romans 12:17-21, 2 Corinthians 2:10-11).

*"It is a fearful thing to fall into the hands of the living God."* (Hebrews 10:31)

Only with God's help have I finally been able to forgive them.

The last conversation I had with my attorney ended with him telling me that the least amount of prison time the judge would sentence me to was eight years, and the most would be 25 to life if I went to court, and he said I would have to plead guilty to get that eight year sentence. If I went to trial it would surely get me 25 to life, he said. I knew I would never survive either sentence, being locked up in prison for that long. He also told me, "By the way, not that it matters but all the evidence, your guns, the dope; everything has disappeared out of the evidence room in Ridgecrest." Wow.

Probably doing exactly what the PI and my so-called partners obviously were hoping for, and to the obvious delight of the corrupt judge, CHP, and Sheriff's deputy, I left for Nevada under the cover of darkness, the night before my next court appearance. I "jumped bail" and again became the hunted instead of the hunter. Now they could shoot me on site, and I would do likewise. It kind of evened things out, to my way of looking at it.

I fueled and took on supplies in Tonopah just after sunrise and headed to the only place I had ever known true peace – Keystone Mine in Hot Creek Valley.

# JOHN GERGEN

CHAPTER 37

## Back to My God of the Mountains

*"Hear what the Lord says: Arise, plead your case before the mountains, and let the hills hear your voice."* Micah 6:1

*"Therefore let the Lord be judge, and judge between you and me, and see and plead my case, and deliver me out of your hand."* 1 Samuel 24:15

It was quiet and peaceful, like I remembered; only the torment in my soul robbed me of any tranquility the mountains of my youth had to offer me. I watched and listened for approaching vehicles as the days and nights passed with devastating slowness.

*"Oh, that I had in the wilderness a lodging place for travelers; that I might leave my people, and go from them! For they are all adulterers, and assembly of treacherous men."* Jeremiah 9:2-3... Amen.

I would sneak down to Warm Springs for a bath and even though the old place was abandoned, the payphone still worked and I could check in with Dad and Lori every now and then. Dad brought me a fresh supply of food and essentials and I would meet him at Rattlesnake Springs, across the valley.

I could see anyone coming up the road from miles away. If they came after me here, then let them come. This was my country and I would make them pay dearly if they did. You are not going to find me in these mountains unless I want to be found, and if I didn't want you to leave, you never would, and no one would ever find you, either.

The warm August nights put the skies ablaze with stars, comets and a full moon. As the warm breeze whispered its way through the pines and junipers, maybe I sensed His presence. Maybe my boyhood memories of Him reminded me of how we use to walk together and I would talk to Him for days on end, in my youth.

*"And I will bring you into the wilderness of the peoples, and there I will plead My case with you face to face."* Ezekiel 20:35

At first I yelled and screamed at Him in my rage and my words radiated from a stone cold heart, but He just silently waited. "Why are You doing this to me?" I blamed, and "I hate You for destroying my life and my family – kill me now – be done with it." My voice would echo from the canyons and mountainsides. Sometimes I would swing my fists at the air as I yelled hateful threats. Days of rage, bitterness and anger eventually passed into days of brokenness and weeping.

"What have I done, God? I can't fix this. I can't live without my wife and kids. My God of the mountains, I beg you…help me."

*"I will lift up my eyes to the hills – from whence comes my help? My help comes from the Lord, who made Heaven and earth."* Psalm 121:1.

"I don't want to die and I don't want to live without them."

*"Those who survive will escape and be on the mountains like doves of the valleys, all of them mourning, each for his iniquity."* Ezekiel 7:16. See also Micah 4:1, 1:3, 1 Kings 19:11-13 (Elijah), and as Jesus did – Luke 5:16, 6:12, 9:28, Mark 6:46, Matthew 14:23.

Then, with a totally broken heart I cried, "I'll do whatever it takes, God, just please… Only You can save me. Tell me what to do."

*"Who treads the high places of the earth – the Lord God of hosts is His name."* Amos 4:13.

That evening, with my soul empty, I could cry no more, and God gave me rest.

*"The mountains will bring peace to the people, and the little hills, by righteousness. He will bring justice to the poor of the people; He will save the children of the needy, and will break in pieces the oppressor."* Psalm 72:3-4.

I slept the whole night through for the first time in many months.

*"I cried to the Lord with my voice, and He heard me from His holy hill. Selah. I lay down and slept; I awoke, and the Lord sustained me."* Psalm 3: 4-5.

I weighed my options and rejected the option of suicide that had been plaguing me for weeks. That left getting out of the country. It gave me something to focus on – a plan, or at least a goal. Unknown to me at the time, God had heard my cry and had a plan of His own, forthcoming – that's what Divine Providence is all about – "divinely ordained events and outcomes" (Wikipedia).

I spent the next night across the valley, near Highway 6, up the canyon at Rattlesnake spring. Dad came with fuel and supplies and I told him of my decision and I believe he was more grieved over it than I was. I explained that, sooner or later, they would back me into a corner and I would fight, and blood would spill. More than likely it would be innocent blood, probably just some poor smuck of a cop trying to do his job, so to my reckoning, this was the best plan I could come up with to avoid it, not to mention avoiding my own personal demise or even worse, prison.

I had always been fairly meticulous in my attempt to not get on the wrong side of the law, and now, here I was, a wanted outlaw and not even of my own choosing. This sucked.

Not knowing if we would ever see each other again, saying goodbye was literally *excruciating (*from the word "crucifixion", synonymous with agonizing, unbearable, torturous, tormenting, etc.). My father was my best friend and the emotional pain of possibly being permanently separated from him somehow finds its proper placement and definition where Jesus was Himself separated from His Father as well. Although unworthy in comparison, I'm sure, yet still it is worthy of noting as to its ability to deeply compound my suffering, from my perspective, at least.

We loaded up our rigs and Dad left a few minutes ahead of me. We came out of the canyon right across the highway from the Hot Creek Ranch Road. Dad turned right on Highway 6 and headed north east toward Ely. A few minutes later I pulled up to the highway as well, with the intent to cross over it and take the dirt road toward Hot Creek, and eventually back to the safety and seclusion of Keystone. Then, Providence happened; Supernatural design within a series of natural events.

Good and proper driver that I am, I stopped at reaching the pavement and looked both ways before crossing over onto Hot Creek Road. A white pickup was fast approaching from the direction of Tonopah so I waited just a few seconds for it to pass by. When it did I saw it was a Nye County Sheriff's vehicle and the driver was seriously "rubbernecking" me out of his back window as he went on up the road. I waited a few more seconds to see his brake lights come on as he disappeared around the corner. If I crossed over the highway now he would see my dust plume and could easily follow me wherever I went, and leading him to Keystone would result in very bad consequences… for both of us.

I made a left and headed southwest on the highway knowing that, if he followed me, he probably could not keep up with my 427 Interceptor engine for very long and I could ditch him in the mountains behind Warm Springs after the sun went down shortly.

I blew past the Blue Jay Maintenance Station at over 135 miles per hour, but as I leveled out on the valley floor I had a real clear view of the road behind me, and he wasn't there! Later I would learn that my father had broken down just around the corner from where I had last seen the Nye County deputy hit his brakes, and the Sheriff's deputy had in fact stopped to help my Dad! Thank You, awesome Lord, for looking out for my Dad!

I have gone weeks and sometimes months without seeing Sheriff's or Nevada highway patrol vehicles out this far into the "Badlands", unless of course, there was an accident (fairly frequent, especially at night, as this was still open range back then).

And whoever said Nevada State Highway 50 was the "loneliest road in America" obviously never got around Nevada very much. Highway 6 would educate you as to what "lonely" really was, if you ever broke down between Ely in Tonopah.

In any case, I slowed down to about 60 and watched my back trail as I approached Base Camp. It was now getting late enough in the day to warrant turning on one's headlights, although not fully dark. Soon it would be dark enough to hide my dust plume and I could turn off at Base Camp and take the dirt road along the foothills of the Hot Creek Mountains and back to Keystone.

Not. Providence, again.

A half mile or so before I got to the Tybo turn off at Base Camp I passed a Nevada highway patrol vehicle heading in the direction that I had just come from, and after we passed, he pulled over to the side of the road and stopped. No way could I turn onto the road to Keystone without him seeing me as we were right in the middle of a long flat stretch on the valley floor. I cruised right on past the turnoff and thought about two other roads coming out before Warm Springs that also led north into the Hot Creek Range but both would allow the NHP to see me exit the paved road in the late evening light, should he turn around and come after me... which he did. As he flipped around he turned on his "blue and red's" and the chase was on. I hammered the throttle to my Holly 780 double pumper carburetor (very similar to flushing a toilet) and when my 427 roared to life that ol' Big Block put the back of my head against the head rest. Somehow I had to buy a little time and distance between us so he wouldn't be able to see me when I left the main highway under cover of darkness, but man he was close. Maybe only three or 4 miles back and he was coming on steady. In retrospect, I can see it was clearly God who flushed me out of the safety of my mountains. Definitely not what I had in mind when I begged Him for help. The chances of seeing a cop on this road at night were slim and none, BUT GOD...

My truck was just starting to "stretch its legs" when I blew past Warm Springs at over 140 miles per hour, barely (by the grace of God) missing one of Joe Fallini's head of prime beef standing in the left lane of the road. That got the old adrenaline rush up to full power! There was a road past the microwave station that circled the mountain behind Warm Springs, that was coming up but the NHP would top the summit a mile later to look out over the next flat stretch, the Stone Cabin Valley, and know immediately that I had bailed off the road, and backtrack on me. I would have to make it across the valley, past Colvin's ranch, around the first turn as I entered the Monitor Mountain Range, and then I could safely jump off on the Stone Cabin Road that led past Clifford's ranch. Just before Clifford's I would cut right, and connect up to the adjoining road that would bring me right back out at Tommy Colvin's ranch again. From there I would backtrack on the NHP and get my butt back to Keystone.

I had to move it though, because I soon heard him call into Tonopah on my scanner, and another Sheriff's deputy was now headed my way from Tonopah. That can't be good. The good news is that he did not identify me personally as the "suspect". So I wonder why (God) he flipped around and came after me?

I dodged a couple more cows in the road while going by Colvin's ranch and oddly found myself hoping that cop who was chasing me didn't catch one of them in his windshield. For me it was a matter of taking it in the grill, and at this insane speed I couldn't be sure my steel homemade mine rail bumper and grill guard would save me as it had in the past, at much lower speeds. Usually, if I hit a deer, I got to keep it, but a cow in excess of 140 miles per hour would be fatal. That NHP cruiser would take the legs out from under ol' Bossy and put her in the front seat with the driver, and that would be a hard thing to survive. Growing up in Warm Springs, I had seen it happen many times, horses being the worst, and both were all over the road at night. I had four off-road KC Daylighter Hilites at 130 Watts and 279,000 cd candlepower each, and two airplane landing lights at over 300,000 cd candlepower that were given to me after I had hit my last cow, by none other than "The Unk" (Phil Davis) himself, God bless him, as they were now saving my life, minute by minute! The upside was that it lit up the road in front of me like a hot summer day, the downside was #1, when you shut them off you were temporarily almost completely blind until your eyes readjusted, and #2, my 135 amp alternator could only run all six lights together for about 10 minutes at a time before sucking all the power out of my huge twin batteries. Then I would have to shut down at least half of them to recharge, and sometimes all of them for a quick recharge if I let them run too long.

At any rate I would momentarily be going around the upcoming right hand bend in the road that would render me invisible to that cop who was in "hot pursuit" (Sheriff Roscoe P Coletrain, Dukes of Hazard). While temporarily out of his sight I cut my lights down, made a right turn onto Stone Cabin Valley Road, and as not to raise a lot of dust, slowly cruised over the crest of a small rise and dropped out of sight from the highway. That cop would have to make it over two summits, past Sand Springs, and into the next valley before he could see far enough ahead to know I was no longer out in front of him. By that time he should probably run into that deputy coming out of Tonopah, but regardless, I would be long gone by that time.

Stone Cabin Road was a well maintained dirt road and I cruised it at 70 miles per hour, cooling my engine temperature and restoring full power to my batteries. After several miles I came to the road junction just south of Clifford's ranch and made a right turn, ran a couple of miles southeast and came to the main Stone Cabin Road that ran from Colvin's ranch all the way north up the valley, behind Hot Creek Canyon, and eventually ended at Highway 50 between Austin and Eureka.

I turned right and headed south back towards highway 6. I went about a half a mile and pulled off the road about 50 yards at the bottom of a few low-lying foothills where I could watch the road ahead of me, just to make sure I didn't get any more surprises. If someone came down the same road behind me they would pass me by without seeing my truck as it was tucked in against the slope of a hill that would be behind and to the right of them when they came down the road that dropped over the same little ridge, 50 yards away. I shut my engine down so I could listen, and lit a smoke. The silent desert night was sweet music to my ears.

***
## Shoshone Intervention

By the time I finished my cigarette I was ready to get moving, but as I started to climb back into the cab of my truck I could hear the faint hum of an engine. It was coming closer from the direction I had just come from. As the sound became louder and closer in the night air I fired up my truck and waited. My eyes had become used to the night so I flipped the toggle switch that shut down my brake and taillights as an older pickup truck ambled over the ridge and down the road.

Then it stopped! I couldn't believe it! I quickly shut off my motor, as the inside cab light came on and a person got out on the passenger side and proceeded to take a leak. As he was finishing up, he spotted the dark outline of my black truck against the lighter hillside behind me. I thought of turning on my off-road lights and blinding them, but decided to see what happened. As long as they didn't go in to gun mode I wouldn't push it. I didn't want them to take me for a rustler either, and open up on me. The man turned and said something to whoever was in the cab of their pickup and to my surprise, they shut their lights and engine off. I had seen Johnny Pinola do the same thing while hunting, several times while growing up and working with him at Blackpoint Mine. He did it to hear and to quickly adjust his eyes to the night – that's how I knew these people here were Indians, probably Shoshone. I heard the driver's door open.

"Tsanku yeike" (good evening) I said into the night air.

After a moment of silence, "E aise hakate" (who are you?), and "an-na-ne-ah" (what is your name?), came the reply.

I thought I heard a faint metallic "click". My left forefinger slowly and quietly took the safety off of the Ruger Mini 14 rifle I was holding just behind my open driver's door, then came to gently rest on the trigger.

"John Gergen", I said.

Their eyes would be used to the dark by now, as mine were. There were three of them, and by her size and stature in what little moonlight there was, one was a woman. If she was young they would try to impress her, if she was older they would be in no hurry to start anything crazy.

It kind of surprises me when she spoke next, "We know Billy Bob – you Billy Bob's little brother?" she asked in English. Her voice was not young at all, and I had played out just about all of the Shoshone I could remember.

"Yes", I said, knowing my brother had ridden with most of the valleys ranching outfits, especially during roundup season.

"You from Warm Springs – long time ago – what are you doing here?"

"Hiding from a speeding ticket", I said, trying to put a little humor in my voice.

They spoke in low tones to each other for a minute or two then one of the men spoke up and said, "You need to leave here. You always in trouble."

"Okay," is all I said, but the relief I felt may have been heard in my voice.

Then, out of the blue, the woman asked me, "You hungry?"

Kind of stunned I answered, "No, but thank you."

The other male voice concluded, "We like Billy Bob." With that they climbed in their truck, started it up, turned on the lights, and headed down the road.

I was watching them go down the road when several miles beyond them I saw two sets of headlights come off of highway 6 and onto the Stone Cabin Road, headed right towards me.

If those people had not picked that exact spot to stop and relieve themselves, seen me, and held me up as they did, I would have left earlier and driven right into those two cops! That's Providence!

Man, I can't get a break, I thought as I fired up my engine and headed north with my tail and brake lights turned off and a nice dust cloud left by my new Indian friends, hiding the glow of my Army issue nightlights. Once again, Providence had put me on a different path. I thought it was all just bad luck. I had no idea if the people from the ranch would tell the cops that they had seen me, or not.

There was a slight westerly breeze that I was trusting in to make my dust trail disappear long before the cops, who were several miles behind me, I hoped, could see it in their headlights.

I passed by the Kiln Canyon Road that came in the back side of Tybo, as it was more like two parallel cow trails rather than an actual road, and I would have to go to slow across the valley to reach the canyon without being seen. Besides, I was much more familiar with the road up Little Fish Lake Valley and could make good time. On a rise just before entering the Hot Creek Mountains I stopped where I could see for several miles back down the valley I had just passed through. I was probably directly east of Keystone on the west side of the mountains that separated me from the safety of my hideout.

The only option left to get there would be the approaching road that went down through Hot Creek Canyon and that would entail going through several ranch yards and home sites in the middle of the night, not to mention God knows how many closed gates that I would have to stop and open. I was heading deeper into the mountains and whatever I did, it had to be done before sunrise. If the ranchers told them my name there would surely be a plane or two in the air come daylight, and I would not be able to hide my dust plume from them, and you cannot out run a two-way radio in daylight.

When I got to the sharp right hand turn off that led east down Hot Creek Canyon, I slowed down enough to make the turn and leave a clear set of telltale tracks for them to follow. A few hundred feet down the road I turned around and pulled my truck off to the side of the road into the sagebrush, got out, and with a piece of brush, wiped out my tracks where I turned around and pulled out into the brush. Then I locked in the hubs and bounced through the brush until I was well back around the corner to the north and back onto the road to Little Fish Lake Valley. Again, I hurriedly wiped out my tracks where I came back onto the road and then wedged several large chunks of brush into my back bumper to drag the ground behind my tires, eliminating the clear track I made when I stopped in the road. This cost me a great deal of time but hopefully they would take the bait and head down Hot Creek Canyon.

If they didn't, because I had let them draw much closer, more aggressive measures would have to be taken.

CHAPTER 38

## Running the Backroads

"Outlaw running from the law but he's got nowhere to run to. Big law he broke it and ran, faster than the lightning bolt."
From, 'Wild as the Western Wind' by REO Speedwagon-1974

When we were younger and living in Keystone, Reveille, Blackpoint, and many other mines and mountainous jobsites, all of us, my brother, Festus, Steve, Ronnie, Mongo and others were locked in a continuous, seemingly never-ending game of "ditch". If you knew one of the others was ahead of you, you chased him. If you looked back behind you and saw one of your pals coming up behind you, you did whatever you had to do to ditch them. This took place for years, at high speeds over highways and dirt roads throughout the entire state of Nevada. The trick was to go fast enough to gain that needed distance between you and the one following you to allow enough time to pull off one of many hiding techniques or various shenanigans.

    Yeah, we had some wrecks, especially when alcohol was involved. The most commonly utilized trick was finding a place in the trees, a gully, or on some cow trail of a side road and pulling off the main road good enough, without being seen, and hiding until the one chasing you went by. Then you would pull back out of hiding and chase him down, or attempt to do so, at least. Touching his back bumper with your front bumper was the ultimate form of "counting coup". On dirt roads you ate a lot of dust in order to get close to your prey.

    In the Hot Creek, and Reveille mountains we often used vehicles that we "found", "abandoned" along Highway 6, after they sat by the road, "unclaimed" for a time. These particular vehicles always seemed to sustain an extreme amount of damage in playing ditch, as that's all they were used for and eventually wound up buried in a ditch or garbage dump when we broke camp and moved on to the next job (because we didn't have titles to them).

    So it occurred to me that ditching my pursuers this night, in the thick pine and juniper forest that I was now passing through would be a simple thing. However, it would put them to the north of my position with the probability of backup units already coming out of Tonopah to the south, and they could "squeeze" me between them as optional roads and trails that didn't dead end were somewhat limited, and thus, very predictable. No, its best if I stay out in front of them. The road we were on would eventually come out on Highway 50 to the north and I'm sure they knew that. I would ditch them long before that, and hopefully be hidden someplace far out of the area by sunrise.

Sometimes I could hear bits and pieces of conversations on my police scanner but radio reception in these mountains was sketchy, at the least. As I sped past Little Fish Lake I caught just enough of their conversation to know that they had split up and one of them was going down hot Creek Canyon. The other was coming after me.

Soon the road up the valley I was on forked and I went to the left along the monitor foothills, then headed up a ridge line of the Toiyabe National Forest. As I gained altitude it allowed me a few opportunities to look back down my back trail and see the headlights of my pursuer in the foothills below. Man, this guy is very persistent, I thought to myself.

Sometime before midnight I would be making a total change of direction in open country, and I had to get rid of him here in the mountains before then, preferably in an area or canyon where his radio wouldn't work. The road soon left the ridge line, traversed around the face of the mountain side and then dropped into a canyon with a couple of hair-pin turns in the bottom of it. Just past the first right hand turn I stopped, jumped into the back of my truck, and grabbed one of two gunny sacks containing "nail traps".

The nail traps consisted of 6 or 7 foot long strips of rolled up roofing tar paper that held 2 inch roofing nails that had been poked through the tar paper about every 3 inches apart, for the entire length and width of the material. I unrolled it across the road on the right hand turn as not to give the driver a chance to see it in his headlights while navigating the turn.

Then I continued on up the canyon road until I reached Dobbin Summit. There I parked just over the crest of the hill as not to "skyline" the shape of my truck, and again shut off my motor to listen and watch my back trail. Just to make sure, I laid out the second nail trap just over the crest of the Summit on the downhill side, again to assure he would not be able to see it when and if he topped over the pass. Not many people carry more than one or two spare tires, with the exception of claims staking outfits, and I doubt this guy had the three or four that he would need to continue his pursuit of me. By the time I was finished I still had not heard the sound of his engine echoing up the canyon behind me. Probably still changing tires or he has settled in for the night to await his rescue.

I fired up my truck again and began my decent down the mountain road. Part way down, the road forked again and I stayed to the left on the main road that led to Monitor Valley. At the crossroads just a few miles east of Diana's Punch Bowl, I left the main road that went to Potts Hot Spring and Highway 50 to the north beyond that, and took a left turn on an older road that led me to the Southwest where I eventually tied into the well-groomed main dirt road #82, that ran the full length of Monitor Valley from the old town of Belmont in the South, to Highway 50 in the north end of the valley. It was a super good road, and although it was still dirt, I could open up that 427 pretty good.

Not a light flickered in the windows of the houses and buildings as I did my best to tiptoe down Main Street, in Belmont, as I made my way through. Belmont was literally a ghost town that still had a few people living in it; my kind of town, I guess. On each end of town stood silent sentries looming up into the dark sky; towering old smokestacks that are all that is left of the long gone huge silver mills of 100 years ago, that ran 24 hours a day processing the millions of tons of silver ore that the mines here produced in its heyday.

Some miles south of Belmont I turned west onto E. Manhattan Rd. and another climb back up into the mountain range. After topping over the pass I had a slow, easy descent down into the town of Manhattan where my recently married brother Bill was running a mining and milling operation.

To my amazement, in front of the first mobile home on the left side of the street, as I came into town, sat my brothers' truck! It was a company bunkhouse/office so I didn't dare wake him not knowing who else was in the trailer, and I had to keep moving anyway. I scribbled a quick note on a piece of scratch paper and quietly opened the door of his truck and put the note on his steering wheel. As I did so I saw his "brick phone" in the charging cradle on the dashboard. I didn't dare call Lori or Dad in the middle of the night, about 2 AM actually, and tell them "Hi, I'm in Manhattan and I'm running for my life. Just thought I'd call and say hi." They didn't deserve that.

So I called my would-be partner and woke him up instead. "Hello," he says. "This is John," says I. Long pause..."You need to come back and turn yourself in", he tells me. Yup. That sealed it for me, full well knowing I would spend the rest of my life in prison, or more likely, pushing up daisies from the wrong side of the grass, and he tells me to come back. Wow. But I suppose it had to sound better to him than having me running around loose and not knowing where I'm gonna show up next.

"Be seeing you around", I told him and hung up the phone. Sweet dreams, "partner.

The road turned to asphalt as I rolled through town and in a few minutes and 7 miles later I hung a right turn and headed north on Highway 376. The ride past Round Mountain Mine and through Carver station was quiet and uneventful, as usual this time of night, but shift change at the mine in an hour or so would change all of that. I was dog tired as I cruised up Big Smoky Valley and on past Smokey Joe's.

A trace of light was beginning to show over the mountains to the east when I found an old dirt road that took me due west and into a canyon just a few miles south of Kingston. There was a small creek and the trees were tall enough to get my truck tucked underneath them as not to be spotted from the air or a passing vehicle, as long as they didn't get too close. I was too tired to cook so I made a dry camp and ate a couple of cans of whatever. Then I climbed into my sleeping bag and immediately fell asleep under the last fading stars, and far enough away from the brook that I could easily hear a car if it came up the canyon.

"I woke up in the morning, and I raise my weary head,
I got an old coat for a pillow, and the earth was last night's bed.
I don't know where I'm going, only God knows where I've been..."
La la la la... (Blaze of Glory—Bon Jovi—1990)

I rested throughout most of the day and that Friday evening went to visit my brother and sister-in-law, Lori (yes, I am aware that we both married Loris... There are now two Lori Gergens! How cool is that?).

Bill re-armed me with his CAR 15 and another Colt .45 automatic and suggested that I contact our old friend Mike (Mongo) in Fallon to get moving on my new passport, Social Security card, and drivers license, which I did. My Lori sent the thousand dollars for the new identification papers over to me, and as it was unnerving to wait and see if or when the local town cop was going to pull up in the driveway at any moment, I left after nightfall.

Lori had arranged a place for me to hide out with friends in the Virginia foothills, near Reno, while I waited for my new IDs to be produced, so after I dropped the money off with Mongo on my way through Fallon, that's where I went.

***

## Rental Car Providence

And good friends they were, at that. They fed me, hid me and gave me a safe place to stay. When my new IDs were nearing completion, and just before my long trip to Belize was about to commence, our friends rented a car for me to go home and see my family in Ely one last time before I left. I parked my truck at Mongo's house in Fallon for safekeeping. Mongo gave me a ride to get the rental car, and I took a nice easy drive to Ely. I hid the rental car at Festus's house, then just after dark, I laid down in the back of his Ford pickup and he drove me right up my driveway. While he went around to the front door to knock, I snuck around the back unseen...except by Calador and Keisha who promptly knocked me down, mauled me and mug washed (slurped my entire face) me. I barely managed to get through the back door before Lori came to turn on the back porch light looking to see what the commotion was all about.

My nerves were shot and I spent half my time at home peeking out windows and looking at cars and motel rooms below my house, to see if my house was under surveillance. I was making everybody's life miserable, that was plain to see. Because I had used up all of our money trying to fight this thing, we couldn't afford another lawyer and Lori was doing everything she could, doing real estate appraisals and working full time for the realty company to pay bills and feed the kids.

My family needed me badly and I was getting ready to skip the country – how terrible is that? None of us could see any other option, though. Maybe, after a while, I could afford another lawyer, and maybe this, or maybe that. One thing was blatantly clear out of all this; the justice system only served those who could afford it. No money, no justice. "Liberty and justice for all? Hahaha! Liberty and justice for those who could buy it, was a better analogy. My hate and bitterness ran to the core of my being. Sadly, my young son watched and listened, and learned from me.

With hollow promises of "everything will work out in time", I said goodbye to everyone who loved me and left. On my way back to the Reno area I drove for hours through the cloudless night sky. Several times I stopped just to get out, look up at the stars, and cry. "Please help me", were my only words. My heart hurt so bad from being shattered that it was suffocating me and I hoped I would die. To me, there was no life without my loved ones.

I fought a raging mental battle back and forth between making my escape good and sneaking back into California and settling things up with as many of those bastards as I could. After all, for nothing at all they had just taken my entire life from me. The least that I could do was return the favor. And killing me at this point would literally be a favor, and other than that, what else could they do? Besides, that whole going out "in a blaze of glory" thing really was calling to me. At least it would be quick, not like rotting away in some prison cell or some third world South American crap hole of a country, knowing that everyday your family was suffering because of you. And, to quote the cliché "we have the technology". They would never see or hear me coming. Whatever I was and whatever I did was a creation of their greed and injustice, and it was on them. They made me, now they would have to deal with it, and me.

I knew that I was getting on a fast track to hell, and that was okay by me, as there apparently wasn't any justice in Heaven. Anyways, Heaven or hell or whatever, I would settle things there as well, when I got there... I just have to figure out how to take my guns with me, that's all.

As hate began to take over my emotions once more, it began to suppress the deadly stifling pain in my heart, and I could breathe again.

***

When I left Fallon I decided to take the 2 lane road, highway 50, to Carson City and avoid the whole Reno thing. Driving through Mound House, just before Carson City, I was reminded how good life seemed when I worked here just a year earlier. I wish to God I had never quit that job with Art Wilson. They always treated me good. How rare is that nowadays?

Coming into Carson City on Highway 50, for whatever reason (spaced out, or more likely, divine providence), I drove past Arrowhead Drive which I normally took to skirt around the main part of town in order to head north. Oops. I didn't think much about it, figuring that I would just go on into town and make a right turn on the main drag, N. Carson St., which turned into Highway 395, and would take me all the way to the Virginia foothills anyway.

As I went past the 7-11 a Nevada highway patrol car pulled out of the parking lot and into my lane about a half a block behind me, which shouldn't be any big thing. He stayed behind me as we went past Mills Park and Roop Street. He was getting much closer so I changed lanes as we approached Stewart Street, just one block before my upcoming turn onto Carson Street. He changed lanes and got in behind me as the Stewart Street traffic light went red, so I pulled into the left turning lane, which he did also. When my light went green I proceeded to make a left onto Stewart Street going south, and as we made the turn the patrol car turned on his lights to pull me over.

Racked with fear, I made him follow me a block down the road where I turned right onto a nice, dark, road called Washington Street. It was secluded and I could see no one around, so I pulled over. The rental car obviously wasn't in my name so there is no way he could know who I was, so I played it cool, roll down my window, and put both my hands on the steering wheel as he approached. I politely gave him my driver's license and the car registration when asked for it, and then he asked, "Do you know why I pulled you over?"

"No sir", I replied.

"Come out of the car and I will show you", he told me. I got out and we, oddly enough, walked to the front of the car where he shined his flashlight on my front license plate, and said, "I figured as much".

There on the front plate was a yearly registration sticker that should have been on the back plate.

"Rental cars", he said, shook his head and we both laughed. Of all the rental cars on the road today, the chances of the rental car company putting the registration sticker on the front plate instead of the back, then me getting that particular car, then getting a cop behind me to notice it, had to be a gazillion to one. Yeah, right. Definitely providence because nobody on this planet could consistently have this bad of luck.

As I got back into the car and shut the door the officer handed me the registration and said, "I'm just giving you a warning and you can go...just give me a minute to run your license and you'll be on your way." My heart was pounding up in my throat as he walked back to his car.

"No choice. I gotta do this," I told myself as I pulled the Colt .45 out from under my seat and cocked the hammer back, full well knowing I already had a round in the chamber. I quickly looked all around to make sure there were no witnesses in the vicinity. I reached over with my right hand and grabbed the door handle, as I prepared to open the door and swing out with the pistol in my left hand. I started to turn my body to the left as I pulled on the door handle when a crystal clear voice in my head said "DON'T DO IT."

It resonated throughout my mind and body so clearly that I froze in place. What the hell was that? Who was that? I was shaking profusely as I obediently took my hand off of the door handle and reached down with my left hand and set the Colt .45 auto on the floorboard between my legs. Without a thought in my head I slowly turned and stuck both of my hands out the window. When I did I watched the patrol officer in my side mirror sit upright as he watched me do it. He slowly opened his car door and walked up to me with his hand on his holstered weapon.

"Step out of the car, please," he said, as he opened my door with his free hand.

I knew the routine. I stood up, turned, and leaned over the car with my hands behind my back. As I did so, he proceeded to handcuff me as the dispatcher came on his portable radio and described my "wants and warrants". When he shined his flashlight into my car, he went white as a ghost upon seeing my cocked pistol lying on the floorboard. Still a little numb in the head, I began getting small shaking tremors, and from past experiences, I half expected a beating would soon follow, but it didn't.

He keyed his mic and reported that he had me in custody and requested backup. He patted me down and found my ivory handled 3 inch folding knife tucked in its custom sheath behind my back. The sheath was designed so when you pulled on the knife handle to remove it, the knife would automatically open on its way out. He patted down my legs and the outside of my boots. When he turned me around I told him, "You missed one inside my right boot. "There in its boot holster, was my Cobray 410/45 Long Colt double-barreled derringer. He pulled it out, looked at it, looked at me and just shook his head. He pulled my pack of Camels out of my shirt pocket, took one out and put it in my mouth, and as he lit it for me, he said, "You're white as a ghost. What's going on here?"

"You too," I said. "It's a long story and I bet just about everybody you arrest tells you that they are innocent, right?"

He walked me to the passenger side of his patrol car, opened the back door and helped me set down on the seat sideways without putting my feet and legs inside the car, so I could smoke my cigarette without getting ashes or too much smoke inside the car.

"You behave if I leave you here for a minute?" He asked. "Yes. You have my word." I told him. He nodded and gave me another long look of confusion and bewilderment, then went back to my car and pulled out all my guns, unloaded them, and place them on the roof of the car.

Backup must have been on coffee break because it took a pretty long time for them to show up, but when they did, it was typical "police cadet" style. A K-9 unit showed up and then two officers with SWAT insignias on their uniforms. They began examining my guns and looking through all of my stuff. The police dog thought he smelled something, and regardless of the fact that it was a brand-new car and I was its first rental customer, they cut and shredded that car apart; seats, trunk liner, dashboard, everything.

Finding absolutely nothing, a very heavyset female sheriff's deputy walked back to the patrol car I was sitting handcuffed in, jerked me up and out of the backseat, dragged me to the front of the car (so everyone could see the show, obviously) and threw me down on the pavement, face first, in front of the headlights.

Then, as she called me filthy names, she shoved her boot down on the side of my face smashing my head into the asphalt. She then pulled out her handgun, cocked it, shoved it in front of my face and yelled, "Where is it, scumbag."

"That's enough – get your foot off of him." the arresting highway patrolman told her as she moved back, and he reached down to help me up. I don't know what happened in that car but I was really starting to regret my surrender. Something about the NHP officer's demeanor helped me to stay calm, in light of the circumstances, and this overweight female version of "Barney Fife" that had attacked me. They always seem so tough when you're handcuffed behind your back and they got a gun in your face.

The highway patrolman took me back to my seat in his patrol car, sat me down, and gave me another cigarette! I truly marveled at the respect and kindness he showed me, as he lit the cigarette and said, "You better have another one while you can. You won't have any more for a while after tonight."

"Thank you," I told him.

***

Three hots and a cot...again. Yippy Yie O Kie Yay! The word "Kie" means "cows". I bet you didn't know that. But, I am sure that you, like me, couldn't care less. You know what the word "Yie" means? Me neither. I'm pretty sure it don't mean squat. But if you combine them together it defines what I did when one of the attorneys that Lori previously worked for, showed up as my legal counsel. Yup, it's true. I "Kai Yie'ed", whined, sniveled and swore if he didn't find a way to get me out of jail that I was gonna die for sure. He (rightfully) told me that he understood that this wasn't the "Taj Mahal" (ivory-white marble palace in India, acclaimed to be one of the wonders of the world), but I needed to "man-up" and calm down. The Taj Mahal was literally a mausoleum built in 1632 by the Mughal Emperor to house the tomb (carcass) of his favorite (dead) wife. Be that as it may, I saw no point in a futile attempt at explaining or correlating the "dead wife" thing to my current circumstances, as the lawyer was adamant about standing his ground on this issue. Frankly, me not having a cigarette for almost 3 days has seriously compounded my already "train wrecked" emotional state and reduce me to what is best described as a "raging, blithering, hateful, wise ass."

In truth, he explained that my standard procedure court appearance was nothing more than a legal prerequisite formality before my extradition proceedings could take place. Nonetheless, he said it was a good opportunity to get on an official court record of the fact that, as of yet, I still had no mention of a felony conviction on any current police records in spite of the fact that California was claiming "ex-felon in possession of a firearm" as my current crime, and despite the fact that I was being extradited for jumping bail.

In light of this, it enabled him to explain to the judge that all of my guns taken from me, both here and in California, were sold and legally registered to me, following background checks (my brother Bill's CAR 15 was a gift from me which I purchased in my name, the Colt.45 auto was purchased by me but I traded it to Bill for a basket case 1964 Harley Davidson chopper, and the 410/45 Long colt Derringer, which was a bit of an awkward subject, as it was holstered in my boot, nevertheless was likewise legally registered to me, as well.

The judge ruled that, as I had no felonies on my record, and the guns were legally mine, my guns could be released to my brother Bill. The judge sincerely told me that, unfortunately, there was nothing he could do to help me with my California case, and he hoped that I had a really good lawyer there, and wished me the best of luck. He said I would remain in custody for a maximum of 30 days from my arrest date, and if Kern County failed to proceed with extradition within that time period, I would be released with no further California warrants having the ability to be invoked upon me, concerning this matter.

The pressing matter more at hand was my survival back in my cellblock at the county jail. Nicotine withdrawals and fear had me yelling and ranting at whoever would take my phone call. I had been so close to getting out of the country and away from all of this insanity. How could this be happening when I was so close? There must be a way out of this jail and somebody had to find it. I thought about escape and may have found a way, but "something" held me back from the attempt.

As God was just getting started with this whole providence and deliverance thing, I got a cellmate who was over 6 foot tall and an accomplished 3rd degree black belt. When he spoke, which he rarely did, I had a tendency to listen to him. His presence in my cell is probably the single most factor why half of the inmates in my block didn't come into my cell and beat the heck out of me. Lord knows I had it coming with all my raging, especially yelling at them to shut up so I could hear when I was on the phone. Alan Tawney's demeanor was very calm and always in control, sometimes bordering on menacing, and he had a definite calming effect on me. Definitely not one to be trifled with; kinda reminded me of Cobra, in that regard. He never raised his voice or threatened me, but when he would say "calm down" or "lower your voice" I would always comply.

The inmate in the next cell had all my issues figured out and introduced me to what I needed to solve all my problems; Scientology. I have always loved to read and a few years earlier, with a much more "open mind", I had begun reading Ron L Hubbard's book, Dianetics. Now, reading the copy the inmate next-door had given me, just seemed too grate on my nerves. Let's see... We are going to fix everything that's wrong with me by "auditing" (erasing) one of three parts of my mind, the "reactive" part, which contains all the painful and crappy parts of my past, and which is the responsible cause of why I'm so screwed up now. By deactivating this one third of my mind (sounds like a lobotomy to me) I will calm down, regain my ethics, my awareness, my happiness, and my sanity. Don't they make a pill for this now? Sitting in this jail cell reading this horse crap with a clear head made me realize just how ridiculous "Scientology" really was.

At one point I asked Alan, "What do you think of this stuff?" A man of few words, his response was, "its trash." Then, kind of surprisingly, he reached under his pillow, pulled out a Gideon's Bible and as he handed it to me, said "What you are reading is designed by Satan to keep you out of this." Well there you have it then. Wow. That's deep, I thought, as he started out the cell door to go to the commons area. I looked at the Bible and muttered, "God has abandoned me." To my astonishment, Alan whirled around and knelt down right in front of where I was sitting, looked me in the face and said, "God did not abandon you." He looked into my eyes to make sure I got what he was saying, then stood up and walked out of our cell. I never forgot that, Alan. Thank you. It stuck with me, and I began a refocusing process that ushered in a new direction in my life.

Carson City jail is what I would consider an "old school" type of jail, with the exception that you couldn't smoke. You got plenty of hot coffee in the morning and the food was pretty darn good for a jail. Other than one "hostile" female jailer, most of them were decent folks, and if you treated them with respect, then that's what you got back from them.

On several occasions as the weeks passed the arresting NHP officer that brought me in would come by just to visit. After a few visits it became obvious that he was not only sincerely interested in my well-being, but that he, as I was, was struggling to understand exactly what had transpired that night he pulled me over. It was obvious to him that I had gone fully into gun mode before holding both my hands out the window to surrender myself. It was haunting him, and me as well, yet I was afraid to tell anyone, even Lori, what had really happened as I felt I would be forfeiting any claim I had left on my sanity. I mean, really? Was I losing my mind? What actually did happen? It all seems so very surreal to me. More bizarre was this cop who was genuinely concerned about the plight that I was locked into.

Finally, after several weeks of incarceration, I broke down and told him about the voice in my head that told me, "don't do it", and stopped me from shooting my way free of him. He just sat there quietly looking at me, then starting to tear up, he told me, "Listen John, I don't know what's going to happen to you, but I do know that God is moving in a powerful way in your life."

I'm thinking, "Yeah, I think you're right. I finally pissed Him off enough that now He's sending me to rot and die, all alone, in a prison cell."

Unlike me, he knew a miracle when he saw one, and this one probably saved his life, and mine as well.

Horrifically heartbreaking, on the final day possible, the 30th day of my jail term and only a few hours before my release, I was extradited. I was cuffed and chained to a "D" ring on the floor of a single engine Cessna airplane, by a nice middle-aged lady deputy whose favorite saying, that she repeated many times over, was "Kern County – come on vacation, go home on probation." Isn't that witty? I found it to be repulsive and quite dismal, but it apparently amused her, as it continually came up in conversation all the way to Bakersfield.

Belize wasn't that bad of a plan, considering the options available to me now. I would've taken my snorkel gear.

Bye-bye, Belize.


Another wind will dry me, and the sun will make me warm,
 ... But to me my life will always be, the calm before the storm (From the song "Lightning" by REO Speedwagon-1976)
 Amen.

## CHAPTER 39

## Lerdo

Lerdo Pretrial Facility (jail) is unlike any jail I have ever seen. Google it and read the first five articles that come up at any given time and you will see news reports of a consistent pattern in inmate deaths, riots, beatings, and brawls. And that doesn't even come close to what really is happening on the inside that never gets reported. The facility I was in was run by the gangs, not the guards. I never saw so much blood in my life as I saw spilled on the walls and floors of my cellblock in the 7 ½ months I was there. At the time of this writing they are mopping up after a "brawl" involving 75 inmates, with many being transported to the emergency hospital in Bakersfield. The term "brawl" may be a slight understatement, ya think?

Gang beatings, blanket parties, shankings, cuttings and clubbings were almost a daily occurrence. Shives were used to bleed you, Shanks were used to stab and kill you. One-on-one fights were very rare, as the preferred method was a large group of men ganging up on one lone victim. The guards never came in until the "beating" was over, then all cells would be locked down for a short period of time.

Transfer requests to get moved to a different block were rarely ever approved without the permission of the "shot callers" (head member of each ethnic group) of the cellblock. The only way many men got transferred to a different cellblock was right after they got released from the intensive care unit after the severe beating they had just received.

Upper echelon gang members were often allowed special treatment, food, usually brought to them by trustees after mealtimes, daily and evening escorted (by guards) trips to the yard for smoking, etc. Certain cells were not included in "shakedowns" where guards would take virtually everything out of the cells and throw every item, down to the last toothbrush and scrap of paper, out the cell door, over the tier railing and onto the floor below in the "commons" area, piling everybody's stuff together in big piles. Then we would have 30 minutes to clean it all up and put it all back. This was a frequent event that was designed more to humiliate and demoralize you (in that, it was very effective) than the pretend search for weapons and contraband that they said it was used for.

During my booking, humiliation and degrading were the primary goals of the scrawny little jailer who, backed up by two huge gorilla looking jailers, took extreme pleasure in running his mouth with a constant flow of insults, taunts, disrespect and filthy verbal abuse that would have gotten his neck snapped anywhere outside these walls, where he wasn't protected. I would have laughed had I not known it would have surely gotten me a beating. "You're here to be punished, not rehabilitated," he and most of the guards kept reiterating throughout my time in Lerdo, and, as my arresting deputy in Ridgecrest told me as well, "My job is to infringe on as many of your rights as possible while you are here," they would say.

I knew I was in for a fun time when the lady deputy that brought me from Carson City, looked over that mouthy jailers shoulder and onto his computer screen while he was booking me and said, "You can't put him in there". The jailer responded, "That's where I was told to put him". The female deputy shook her head, said "Jesus" and walked out of the room. I soon found out the hard way that it was a predominantly "gang occupied" cellblock that I wasn't expected to survive in. Whether orchestrated by the corrupt judge that I filed a complaint on with the judicial committee, the crooked cops, or whoever, life got interesting from that point on.

The two bunkbeds in my cell were simply made of solid sheets of steel that you covered with a very thin mattress, and you were only allowed one blanket. Should you get caught with two blankets or mattresses, you would wish that you hadn't. So you slept cold every night as they intentionally kept the thermostat turned down and the temperature set at a constant "chilly" as not to allow you to be comfortable or restful during your stay with them.

Around 4 AM you were "awakened" for "count" and you are required to be dressed and standing in line out front of the cellblocks, in military fashion. If you went back to bed afterwards, you forfeited breakfast which immediately followed count.

Before leaving Carson City, Alan had recommended a new fancy (expensive) lawyer before I left, that would supposedly "fight for me". Lori had to sell my retirement property on top of Atlas Hill in Eureka, Nevada to pay for him. It was a terrible loss considering the new lawyer was a true "dump truck" like the others, and eventually traded losing my case, with the prosecutor's office, in order to win another man's case who was paying him much more for his "services". My new dump truck did, however, explain to me that Lerdo was literally a "pre-trial" facility with a much darker intent and meaning. All of the "quirks" and discomforts explained above are intentionally designed to push inmates to accept plea-bargains to hasten the endpoint of their miserable incarceration time at this facility. This plea settlement sometimes ended in a period of probation, but usually meant "catching the chain" (being moved) to a much more preferable mainline prison facility where serving time was substantially easier and significantly more comfortable with coffee and tobacco readily available at the commissaries (prison stores).

Several years later I was sitting with my father watching the news when a "special report" claimed that over 30% of LA and Kern County convicted felons were wrongfully incarcerated in prisons throughout California after being threatened with three strikes (mandatory 25 to life) in order to force them to take a lesser prison sentence of 1 to 18 years. Furthermore, the report went on to state that of the majority of these 30%, most were innocent of their crimes that got them incarcerated, but because of past criminal activity (often just suspicion) and a lack of attorney fees, they were forced to accept a plea bargain set up with the District Attorney's Office by their "court appointed" legal counsel. This was justified by eliminating long trials and Justice Department costs at the poor taxpayer's expense, overpopulation in the jails, and the practice of forcing suspects to plea bargain "kept the criminal court system flowing smoothly". Not smoothly if you're the one losing everything (life, family, job, integrity, etc. etc. etc.) and having to do prison time because you can't afford to go to court with a real lawyer, and it's the only deal your court appointed "dump truck" is willing to put on the table. I believe "railroaded" is the proper term for this. No upcoming changes to the system were mentioned and I'll bet the court system isn't considering any, either.

I watched young gang members who had "financial backing" walk free of "thrill kills" (drive-by shootings that they admittedly bragged about), on a "technicality", while others got 18 years for stealing a chainsaw and another old guy who got his 25 to life, third strike, sentence for stealing a carton of cigarettes. Both tried to fight their cases with "court appointed" lawyers. Yeah.

My cell was on the ground floor, in the farthest corner away from the entrance and the guard station, and it was tucked under the stairway to the upper tier cellblocks. Because of its location, it was the favorite "go to" place for fights, beatings and settling disagreements among my fellow prisoners. I later found out from one of my guards that my placement in this particular cell was no accident, either. And neither was the fact that in the 7 ½ months I spent surviving this place I had 11 different cellmates and nine of them were heroin addicts, coming in fresh off the street.

In my best hypothesis, I believe that 85% of newly arrested inmates coming into our cellblock, fresh off the streets, were definitely high on something, and this fact accounted for many of the bloody beatings that I witnessed. If I had been incarcerated here instead of Carson City jail for the first 30 days of my arrest, acting here the way I did in Carson City, I would surely be dead now. That's Providence and thank You, Lord, for that. I surely would not have survived had not the 30 days I spent in Carson City jail with Alan, who himself had been here on a couple of other occasions, helped to somewhat prepare me (nothing can actually prepare you) for this beforehand. The shot-callers and other inmates here wouldn't have put up with me for 15 minutes, and I am convinced that those responsible for putting me in this particular cellblock were not only well aware of this, but were counting on it.

Notwithstanding, heroin addicts are by far the worst cellmates, at least for the first few days. The torturous physical pain, convulsions, vomiting, and muscle spasms they endure while agonizing through their withdrawals makes them extremely dangerous, and explosively volatile. If they were lucky they would get a few shots of methadone, or some other drug that I can't seem to remember the name of, that would help with the pain, and weaning them off the extreme heroin cravings they endure, thus helping them make it through the hardest first three days or so. If you were unlucky enough to get locked up in my cell with me, you would get nothing to help you. Not only am I grateful for God's providence, but most assuredly for his divine protection as well.

They would bring these guys in fresh off the street, throw them in my cell, and as horrible and frightening as it was I really don't think I can find words to justly depict what it was like being locked up for days in a 5 x 10' cell with them. The first couple were terrifyingly gut-wrenching, and even though survival seemed a minute by minute thing on many occasions, I soon could not help but feel empathy for these poor souls. I would put a mattress on the floor for them, as they lived and sometimes slept on the floor next to the toilet and spent almost every hour of the first two days writhing in agony on the floor. To make matters worse, if they couldn't make it to the lineup for morning and evening count, often as not the guards would come into the cell and knock them around for not following the mandatory count rules. I would do my best to get them up and help them to the line. Once there, they could only lean on me until count began, then they would have to stand without assistance. Sometimes they didn't make it.

My court appearances took up right where they had left off before I bailed, only this time I was chained and shackled with up to 10 other men. Lori and Dad came down to many of them and that same old judge would put his urine specimen cup up on his bench when he saw her, to keep her from taking notes.

I would sit or stand in holding cells in Lerdo from about 3 AM that were so packed like sardines with other handcuffed and shackled inmates, that there was only room to stand, shoulder to shoulder, most of the time. And yet wearing ankle chains and our wrists handcuffed to a chain around our waists, not only would stupidity rear its ugly head but would take center stage as a surprising number of rival gang members would be thrown into the same holding cell and go to head-butting, biting and trying to literally grab each other at the only points their hands could reach. About 6 AM we were put on a bus to the old jail facility beneath the court house where we waited in the old cells, for however many hours until it was your turn to go up to the court room. And then back to the holding cells until long after dark when they took you back to Lerdo, where you were strip-searched for contraband and given a mustard sandwich for diner.

This went on and on, I can't even remember how many times, for 6 ½ months. Finally I told Dad and Lori and other family members to stop coming down from Nevada, as this judge was not going to stop his games.

One day at mail call I got a package from "the Unk". It was, of course, a "religious" book. This one was a "testimony" written in novel form, called 70×7 and Beyond. As I had no pressing engagements at the time, I read it. It was about this guy calling himself Monty Montana whose life of drugs and crime destroyed his family and bounced him in and out of numerous jails and prisons. Then to my astonishment, God saved him, and he turned from the trash in his life, after several failed attempts, and got his life and family back. He often talked of freedom and victory in Jesus and the last page was a call for repentance and a prayer of salvation that I said without really understanding the implications, but it caused me to ponder what the whole Jesus thing was about. (See, Appendix N, Victory in Jesus) Regardless, a sense of peace and calmness came over me, and for the first time that I can remember in I don't know how long, I got a decent night's sleep.

The next day I got locked down with another heroin addict from Fresno. He was an older man in his late 60s, who was surprisingly well spoken, and polite. He struggled like all the rest but did his best to keep it to himself, and I found myself wishing I could do more to help him. Another older white guy, I think out of the sense of obligation to our shared ethnic background, would come by our door, softly knock or whisper and asked if we needed anything. Like what? I kept thinking, a TV would be nice, or a jackhammer maybe. On the second day my new "celly" was throwing up nothing but blood and his stomach lining and I was just doing my best to stay out of his way and be quiet for the few short periods he would doze off between "episodes". When the old man came by that day, I answered his usual inquiry with "get me something to read", as I had counted not only all the cinderblocks in the walls of my cell, but was now trying to count the holes in the individual cinderblocks. There was only one newspaper a day allowed into the cellblock and it always fell apart from use before the white guys ever got a turn at it.

Yet after dinner, which a guard had brought to my cell, that old man came back and said, "This is all I could get", then proceeded to figure out how to shove a Gideon's Bible under my door. Finally, he tore the cover off, opened it at about the center, and thus managed to smash it enough to get it under my door.

Providence.

God now had a captive audience (pun intended). Fine. I got a few questions, anyway, I was thinking as I started reading. At one point my cellmate woke up and asked, "What are you reading?" I told him.

"What are you looking for," he asked without moving from his position on the floor next to the toilet.

"I'm trying to figure out this whole God-Jesus thing", I told him.

His breathing had been coming in short, shallow breaths since about the middle of the day, and I was getting a little more than concerned that this old-timer may well die here. He hadn't moved from his spot or eaten in going on three days, except for when I helped him to the line for count. He was thin and very frail, and at the last two counts I had to hold him up, figuring that I could take a beating better than he could. But God wasn't having any of it, and during the counts that I held him up we had a brand-new guard who allowed me to do it without saying a word.

About two hours later in the night his voice broke the stillness of our cell as he told me, "Find a chapter called Matthew and start reading there."

The next morning he ate a little, but it came right back up. He would ask me to read out loud sometimes and I would until he dropped off to sleep again. The calming effect it had on him was very apparent. His color was better and soon he started to hold food down. Shortly before his release due to a technicality (evidence missing from the evidence room-imagine that) he confided in me that, in years past, he had killed several men for money, and for my trying to help him, he would consider it an honor, at no charge to me, to rid me of the two key persons that were responsible for putting me in here. Though he was of small stature and long in tooth, to look into his dark eyes was to know it was truth he was speaking, and he meant what he said. The thought of such an easy fix delighted me.

As I marveled at the good fortune that had just seemingly dropped into my lap, George Embry, my friend who shoved that Bible under my door, just "happened" to come by our cell and our conversation was temporarily postponed. George's celly (cellmate) had "caught the chain" (been taken to prison) the night before and had left his Gideon's Bible behind, as you were not allowed to take them with you. George wanted to give it to me to replace the torn up one he had slid under my door several days earlier. George also explained that sometimes he just liked to pick up the Bible and randomly open it to whatever page happened to appear, and read whatever it said. He went on to tell me that after breakfast, he picked up his ex-cellies Bible, opened it and commenced reading Psalm 31, and when he did, it reminded him of me, so that's why he felt he was to give me this Bible. That's a little odd, but, okay, whatever, I thought. He was excited to have me read it, so I did. The second time I read Psalm 31 I became aware that my situation was by no means unique and others before me had cried out to God under similar circumstances. I guess it just seemed really "personal" to me, somehow.

My pondering soon turned into a ruthless soul-searching, wrestling match in my head, as I so wanted those two evil snakes spawned from the pit of hell to get what they deserved (according to my reckoning, anyway). That whole "... I trust in You, O Lord;... You are my God. My times are in Your hand; deliver me from the hand of my enemies, and from those who persecute me", part, wouldn't let go of me. I wanted to pray that prayer with all of my heart to God, but somehow, having my celly kill these two clowns gave me the impression that my prayer may not have the effect or impact that I was hoping it would have.

As absolutely stupid as I felt, I very respectfully declined my cellies offer, and with a convicting sense of "I'm a frigin' moron" on my part, I bid him farewell as he "rolled up" a few hours later.

Trusting in Someone I have blamed for every bad thing that ever happened in my life seemed pretty idiotic to me, yet I felt drawn to do just that. Maybe if life was a bed of roses it would make a little more sense, but this was my life we were talking about. And when life turns dark and ugly, "trust God" can become a cheap cliché very easily, or a "crutch" for the weak who haven't the ability or "intestinal fortitude" to fight back. Yet here I was. No ability and no hope, unless God is real and somehow inclined to help the likes of me.

"Are you real? Will you help me?" I whispered into my empty cell. I decided, okay George, here we go, and picked up that Bible, closed my eyes and stuck my thumb into the pages and opened it. When I open my eyes I read these words;

**"Fear not, for I am with you;**
**Be not dismayed, for I am your God.**
**I will strengthen you,**
**Yes, I will help you,**
**I will uphold you with My righteous right hand".** Isaiah 41:10.

## CHAPTER 40

## The Deal that Saved My Soul

*"To crush under one's feet All the prisoners of the earth,
To turn aside the justice due a man Before the face of the Most High,
Or subvert a man in his cause—The Lord does not approve."*
Lamentations 3:34-36

Every once in a great while we would be given the option to go outside on the "yard" for 30 minutes to an hour. I was elated to get out of the musty cellblock and into some fresh air. The term "yard" was a gross misuse of the word, and "outside" was almost in antonym (opposite) of the physical design of the place we were led into. In reality we were actually "inside" a huge concrete hole, and not a very spacious place by any means. The concrete floor had just enough room for a handball court, and a small basketball half court, with concrete walls over two stories high all the way around and topped off with chain-link fencing covering the entire open top. If you looked straight up you could see the sky, and as dismal as that sounds, I was very happy to be able to do that, if nothing else. And it had real air, not "manufactured" air, even though it was kind of stinky as there must have been a dairy farm close by. But it was all good to me, and I was grateful.

A little awkward however, was the not really overlooked detail that I was almost always the only white guy out there. Why, I don't know, and most of the Hispanic guys just gave me a curious look, like "what are you doing here?" I knew nothing of gangs or racial dividing that predominate these California jails and prisons, but I knew it was a very dangerous thing. In any event, I was content to just try and find a place against the wall, where I was out of the way and could sit down, enjoy the air and sky, and maybe read a little bit. I got a few aggressive looks now and then, so when it was time to go back in I would always be the last in line.

Truthfully, I was totally ignorant of the dos and don'ts of this volatile environment and that's why some of the guards would sometimes walk by me and snicker, "Still alive, I see" or "Wow! You're still alive?"

I knew nothing of the "rules". Walk too fast – aggressive. Walk too slow – mocking. Eye contact – challenging. Eye contact, especially while turning your head to look at them – disrespectful. Eye contact with another gangs "shot-caller" gets you a beating for certain. Staring only at the floor offers total submission and invites really bad trouble. And on and on and on…

I was basically a hick from the sticks who had no business at all playing in someone else's totally unfamiliar backyard. Looking back it is clear as crystal to see that God knew I badly needed help in this area as well, and He had my back. So he "arranged" for a man to look out after me, and more importantly, to "school me".

So it happened, I was out on the yard one afternoon following dinner (usually about 4 PM), sitting against the wall, when oddly, a guard came out onto the yard and approached a fellow named Munoz and handed him the most beautiful black and gold Bible I had ever seen. Then the guard abruptly turned and left this guy standing by himself with that Bible. What possessed me I got no clue, but fool heartedly, reckless and extremely idiotically I just stood up and walked over to him while staring at that Bible, and said, "That's the most beautiful Bible I have ever seen."

He looked at me and said nothing, but half of the men on the yard stopped what they were doing and glared at me. Just as quickly, recess was over. Even a hick from Nevada like me could spend one day in my cellblock and know that Munoz was at the top of the food chain, and harebrained me was on the bottom.

The same guard, who had allowed me to hold up my sick cellmate at count a few days earlier, appeared out of nowhere, took me by my arm and escorted me to my cell and locked me down. I was alone, as I had not received my last cellies replacement yet. A few minutes later the whole cellblock was locked down and I was hoping to God that it wasn't because of me, or I'm a dead man when they let us out again.

The last time I talked to her, my Mom told me that her favorite books in the Bible were the Psalms, as she said they always comforted her. Comfort would be nice about now. She told me to find them, simply open my Bible to the very center of the pages, and she of course, was right. She, more than most, was tickled pink to find out that I was reading Scripture. I imagine it put a lot of light at the end of her long blackened tunnel, as far as her prodigal son was concerned.

So sitting in my despair on the edge of my bunk, I picked up my Bible and opened it randomly to Psalm 51, again. As I began to read it, the words seem to come alive, and with pinpoint accuracy, they echoed the cry of my own soul. It reverberated throughout my entire being as I reread it over and over, astounded that someone in the Bible had not only experienced my desperation and anguish, but had also cried out for deliverance as my heart was now doing... Hopelessness, crying out for a shred of hope, with no one else to call upon but God, Himself, and desperately wanting to believe He is listening.

*"Have mercy upon me, O God, according to your lovingkindness; according to the multitude of Your tender mercies, blot out my transgressions.*

*Wash me thoroughly from my iniquity, and cleanse me from my sin.*

*For I acknowledge my transgressions, and my sin is always before me.*

*Against You, You only, have I sinned, and done this evil in your sight – that You may be found just when You speak, and blameless when You judge.*

*Behold, I was brought forth in iniquity, and in sin my mother conceived me.*

*Behold, You desire truth in the inward parts, and in the hidden part You will make me to know wisdom.*

*Purge me with hyssop, and I shall be clean; wash me, and I shall be whiter than snow.*

*Make me hear joy and gladness, that the bones You have broken may rejoice.*

*Hide Your face from my sins, and blot out all my iniquities."* Psalm 51:1-9.

Anointed by God and written by the giant killer, David, after he had victoriously become the king over all God's people, this Psalm was his intense plea to set things right again with the Lord, after he committed adultery with a married woman named Bathsheba and then had her husband, Uriah, killed so he could keep her (2 Samuel 11). It seemed to me that these verses were David's "reset button", or plea for a pardon, as to restoring his relationship with God, and it apparently worked, although God allowed him to live out the consequences of his sins. The point being that God did indeed hear, and granted His mercy and forgiveness to David.

When I got to verses 10 through 13, it was just as if God was saying to me "Here's the deal".

*"Create in me a clean heart, O God, and renew a steadfast spirit within me.*

*Do not cast me away from Your presence, and do not take Your Holy Spirit from me.*

*Restore to me the joy of Your salvation, and uphold me by Your generous Spirit.*

*Then I will teach transgressors Your ways, and sinners shall be converted to You."*

Create... Renew... Restore... Uphold! Yes! I wanted to make the same "deal" so badly, and as I continued on I realized that verses 16 and 17 qualified me, just as they had qualified David;

*For You do not desire sacrifice, or else I would give it; You do not delight in burnt offering.*

*The sacrifices of God are a broken spirit, a broken and contrite heart – these, O God, You will not despise."*

I was finally broken, and it's how it had to be. For me, there was no other way. I pray to God that it doesn't have to be this way with you, too, but if that's where you are right now, or where you have been in the past, know that you are in very good company. Joseph, Moses, David, Peter, Paul, etc., etc., etc., are your previously broken mentors that our Father used to change the world.

Welcome.

Yes, YOU are welcome here! It don't matter what you did to get broken, what matters is that out of God's love, God's own Son paid our sin debt and restored our right standing (righteousness) with our Heavenly Father! See John 3:16-18, Romans 5:17-19, and Romans 10:3-13, and please don't neglect to study the Scriptures.

As I keep trying to tell you, it's a free gift that you can't earn or achieve (Ephesians 2:4-10). God simply declares that you are innocent, as far as He is concerned, because you believe in Jesus, knowing that He paid your debt in full, with His own blood, at the cross.

You are righteous if Jesus is your Lord, and nothing you've done can change that, because nothing can undo what Jesus did, for us.

And for me, here's the miracle of this whole thing... It was Armando Munoz who explained all of this to me, and here's how it happened;

By 4 AM the severe dread of what was going to happen to me had subsided considerably, though still very real. I had earnestly prayed Psalm 51 and had asked God to make the same "deal" with me that he had made with David. However, it is very difficult for me to exhibit patience, when in fact I have none, so in waiting for the cell doors to unlock I surmised that I had taken some pretty bad beatings before (of course, being drunk seem to make them somewhat less severe), and even if they killed me, so what? Better than 25 to life, as this would be the rest/end of my life, regardless.

At some point I drifted off to sleep. In my dream there was a set of closed gigantic double doors, maybe 50 feet tall, a foot or so thick and each was over 10 feet wide. They made me feel very tiny as I stood before them, staring up at them in my dark and dimly lit surroundings. I could sense His presence on the other side of those enormous doors, and as I stood trembling, in a faint whisper I asked, "Can I come in... Please?"

A crack of light appeared where the two huge doors joined together and the warmest, loving voice I've ever known gently said, "Yes... Of course you can."

I stepped up to the doors and bracing myself against one of them, I began to push. To my astonishment, they moved quite easily and as they parted, light completely flooded the dark place I had previously stood. As the doors separated and I moved between them to enter into His presence, His powerful, yet loving voice penetrated my entire being, body, soul and spirit, with the words, "I have heard your prayer... It's a deal".

Many times since then, in giving my testimony, I have been rebuked by "religious" folks that declared to me that "God doesn't make deals", but in truth, it is what it is. He made one with David and he made one with me.

To my dismay, at that point, I was startled awake by the metallic clash of the electronic cell door locks being deactivated to lead us out of our cells for count and breakfast. But this time, no guards came into the block and there was only the sound of one set of footsteps coming down the stairs, instead of the usual entire second tier of inmates.

Then I sat up to see Armando Munoz standing in my doorway, looking at me with a definite look of inner turmoil and agitation in his eyes. As I carefully stood to my feet he said, "What's up with you?" As there seemed no point, I said nothing.

His eyes were penetrating, and then he glanced down at the Bible, lying where I had left it, on my bed. When he looked back up at me he asked, "What are you reading?" It's been over 10 seconds now and I'm still alive. Wow. Caught by surprise at the question, I simply answered, "Psalm 51."

After a very long moment he gave a slight nod, and then said, "I feel led by the Lord to come here; to help you, maybe. We'll talk after breakfast." And with that he turned and was gone.

As soon as he appeared back out in the commons area, the place came alive with the usual hustle and bustle of guards and inmates lining up for morning count and breakfast. All I knew was that I was still alive, and I was in awe. What had just happened? Was I still dreaming?

During breakfast no one even looked at me or talk to me, not even George or the other white guy in our cellblock. I was okay with that as I really didn't feel chatty anyway. After breakfast was done, as usual, everybody in the entire cellblock went back to bed, except me and Armando. We sat down together at a table where he explained the origin and circumstances in which Psalm 51 was created, as well as the purpose for which it was intended, as I have attempted to explain to you in the previous pages. When he asked if I had made Jesus my Lord and Savior, I told him about the "70×7 and Beyond" book I had just read, and confessed that I didn't understand all of it. We retrieved our Bibles from our cells, with which he, step-by-step and Scripture by Scripture, explained the Gospel message to me very clearly, and thus, that evening on October 31, Halloween night (also Nevada day!) 1996, I received Jesus Christ as my Lord and Savior, as ministered to me by Armando Munoz, and I became "born again". Hallelujah! Glory to God! That's my spiritual birthday! When was yours? If you don't know then perhaps today would be a fine day to be your new birthday.

Therein lies the greatest miracle of all time, for all of us! Our ticket to eternity in Heaven, and the best part is, it's free!

Meeting with my brother in Christ, Armando, in the stillness of the early morning, after breakfast, became our daily routine. We played chess every day and studied God's Word. One time in the wee hours of dawn's earliest light, I actually won a game of chess while playing against Armando. I like to think that I won by superior strategy, and God bless my brother in Christ if, in fact, he let me win, and never let me believe otherwise in that I had attained my hard sought victory on my own accord. In any event, over the next week at least, I could not restrain myself from letting anyone who would listen know that I, in fact, had won one of the hundreds of chess games we had played. Major personal victory, here. If I could remember the play-by-play action as it went down, I would have written it here, but the Lord, in keeping me humble I'm sure, has spared us all by letting it slip from my memory. Yeah, and it was the only one I ever won.

The first fruits of the seed that Armando planted in me became evident when, in December, I was able to minister the gospel message to my son Billy and later my brother Bill as they visited me, resulting in both of them receiving their salvation through our Savior and Lord, Jesus Christ. How awesome is that! Knowing positively that the ones you love the most will be in Heaven with you is priceless. The alternative to those who reject Jesus and his sacrifice is beyond horrifying. Everyone will spend eternity somewhere – Heaven or hell – but it's a personal decision we will all make, determined by what we did with God's only Son, while we were here on planet Earth… whether we rejected Him or accepted Him. That's the bottom line with nothing else added.

In the days and weeks that followed my salvation, Armando and his friend Bobby schooled me in the crucial art of survival in the pandemonium of a gang atmosphere as related to a jail and prison environment. And what's more, because of their "influence" on the others in our cellblock, I was shown great mercy by many others for several mistakes that I unknowingly made in my education process, and they would explain to me what I had inadvertently done, as well as how to avoid repeating my offense. The truth is, I believe almost all of them just kind of looked out for me, God bless them, as God's Divine Providence continued to rule in my life.

Through the winter months I often found myself outside on the handball court all alone, as nobody else wanted "yard" when it was raining or cold. I would go out by myself with a handball (racquetball) and stay warm by vigorously practicing, well, mostly chasing, that little blue rubber ball all over the place for about an hour. I wasn't great but I could finally at least "hold my own" and sometimes, was allowed to play "Kulo". I was almost always matched with a partner who was exceedingly good in order to give the other team a chance of winning. I guess I was like, the handicap, if you will. And the Hispanics were the ultimate Masters of this game and played it with fervent intensity and fierceness as, the losers would be required to stand bent over against the wall, with their hands on their ankles, and allow each of the winners to take a turn at throwing the rubber ball, with all of their might, at the "exposed parts" of the losers, from the "out of bounds" line at the back of the court.

In the meantime, Armando loaned me two books to study by Neil T Anderson, Freedom in Christ Ministries, entitled Victory Over the Darkness, and The Bondage Breaker. Aside from the Bible itself, these two scripturally based books on "deliverance" were vital to not only understanding how I, as well as others in my life, had "opened doors" to my enemy the devil, and allowed him and his dark forces into various areas of my life where they eventually controlled them. It explained so much and gave me, in the power of the Holy Spirit, the knowledge to throw out the dark forces that were firmly embedded in my life, and close the doors, so to speak, thus not allowing them back in. They detailed what I had done to allow them into my life through, alcohol, drugs, Ouija boards, seemingly innocent new age and occult practices, séances, false doctrines, etc. etc. etc. (again, please see "test all things" in Appendix C). And finally, it revealed how, through the wrongful admonition of my Mormon counselor, I had eventually been led by my enemy to believe that God hated me, I would never be good enough for Him, I could never go to Heaven because I could never be married in the Mormon Temple, and of course, everything bad that ever happened to me was God's fault.

I can't begin to describe the true freedom in Christ that I experienced when I was able to confess, repent, renounce and cast out each and every one of these abominations to God that I had participated in and rid myself of the deceitful chains they had placed on my soul.

Who the Son sets free is truly free indeed! I am truly free through Jesus Christ! (See John 8:34-36).

Needless to say, I highly recommend these two books. Jesus is the absolute Almighty Chain-Breaker!

As to God being responsible for every bad thing that ever came into my life, even to this day I have devout Christians who love and worship God with all of their hearts tell me that all of the demonic attacks, bad things, and junk (evil) that happens to me on a day-to-day basis is God's will because He allows it, imposing that I should just "roll with the punches", and accept these atrocities of the evil against me as part of God's purpose for my life. If everything bad that happens to us is God's will because He allows it, then what about when we search the Scriptures to find out what they clearly say is God's will for a particular situation, we pray about it and we don't receive it? I don't think God would contradict Himself, and isn't that what this would indicate? We really need to look at that for a minute, in order to avoid creating a bad balance in our belief system.

The truth of the matter is always in Scripture so that's where we will start. And we will start at the beginning with the good news for Heaven and the bad news for Earth;

*"Therefore rejoice, O Heavens, and you who dwell in them! Woe to the inhabitants of the earth and the sea! For the devil has come down to you, having great wrath, because he knows that he has a short time." Revelation 12:12.* Earth is now the main battlefield, as the devils time on the earth is now. The earth has now become his kingdom and we are right in the middle of it.

Jesus referred to the devil as "the ruler of this world", and John 12:31, John 14:30 and John 16:11, and 2 Corinthians 4:4 describes him as *the god of this age.* In Ephesians 2:2 he is referred to as, *the prince of the power of the air.*

Satan's authority and kingdom are defined when he tempted Jesus in the wilderness as outlined in Matthew 4:8-9, and Luke 4:5-7 which tells us, *"Then the devil, taking Him up on a high mountain, showed Him all the kingdoms of the world in a moment of time. And the devil said to Him,' all this authority I will give to You, and their glory; for this has been delivered to me, and I give it to whomever I wish."* Notice he didn't have to ask permission to do as he wanted with his kingdoms.

Jesus clearly made reference to Satan's kingdoms in His teachings, such as in Luke 11:18, and Matthew 12:26. I believe it was common knowledge to everyone in Jesus's time where sickness disease and the "bad things" that happened to the people, originated from. The Gospels are full of references to this, such as Luke 13:16 where *"Satan has bound – think of it – for 18 years,"* a Hebrew woman that Jesus *"laid His hands on her, and immediately she was straight, and glorified God."*

Revelation 2:13 tells us that Satan has a throne.

So the earth we are standing on, our world, is the current and temporary kingdom of the devil, according to the Bible. That sounds very depressing to me.

*"We know that we are of God, and the whole world lies under the sway of the wicked one."* 1 John 5:19.

Because the works of the world are evil, the world hated Jesus (John 7:7) and that's why the world hates us who choose to follow Christ, as the Lord told us in John 15:18-20, and John: 14.

I don't think it's possible to be in the world without being subjected and exposed to the influences (junk) of the world, but these things are not from God (1 John 2:15-16). Acts 10:38 clearly and profoundly states *"how God anointed Jesus of Nazareth with the Holy Spirit and with power, who went about doing good and healing all who were oppressed by the devil, for God was with him."* So, who did all the oppressing with sickness, disease, demonic possession, and all the other junk and bad things in the four Gospels? Who did the healing? And who was with Him? Are you seriously going to try and tell me that God "allowed" all this evil on all these people just so he could put on a good show? You gotta be sick in the head to believe that. Of course, like I used to do, I'm sure our enemy is just tickled every time we blame the bad things in our lives on the sovereignty of God, as many folks do as a means to justify why healing didn't manifest itself in a particular scenario, so to justify things, they make statements like, "Well you know, God is sovereign".

BUT GOD...IS GOOD- ALL THE TIME!

I don't believe God will violate his own spiritual laws, and so he sent Jesus to set things straight.

Jesus made clear reference to this when the 70 disciples he sent out," *returned with joy, saying,' Lord, even the demons are subject to us in Your name.'*

*And He said to them,' I saw Satan fall like lightning from Heaven. Behold, I give you the authority to trample on serpents and scorpions, and all the power of the enemy..."* Luke 10:17-19.

Jesus verified this in Acts 26:18 when he told Paul, *"... I now send you, to open their eyes, in order to turn them from the darkness to light, and from the*

***dominion*** *of Satan to God, that they may receive forgiveness of sins and an inheritance among those who are sanctified by faith in Me."* (NAS)

And remember the importance of "the blood" thing we talked about?

*"He (Jesus) has delivered us from the dominion of darkness and conveyed us into the kingdom of the Son of His love, in whom we have redemption through His blood, the forgiveness of sins." Colossians 1:13-14,* NAS.

*"Inasmuch then as the children have partaken of flesh and blood, He Himself (Jesus) likewise shared in the same, that through death He might destroy him who had the power of death, that is, the devil, and release those who through fear of death were all their lifetime subject to bondage." Hebrews 2:14-15.*

*"Having disarmed principalities and powers, He made a public spectacle of them, triumphing over them in it. Colossians 2:15.*

And, I really love this one;

*"For this purpose the Son of God was manifested, that He might destroy the works of the devil." 1 John 3:9.*

And here's God's plan for us;

*"And the God of peace will crush Satan under your feet shortly."* Romans 16:20 Glory to God!

For now, Satan runs things here, but not for much longer. Even so, I believe we do a great injustice to the Lord when we accredit God for the devil's work. I believe the right to test us came to the devil as a package deal when he received his kingdom. People commonly and rightfully point out the fact that the devil had to ask permission of God before he could test Job (Job 2) and Peter (Luke 22:31) but I think the fact that is greatly overlooked is that the devil had the right to ask in the first place; we miss that part, and the fact that Job (Job 1:10) and Peter (Luke 10:19) were both specifically under the divine protection of Almighty God and Jesus at the time. That's why the devil had to ask for permission.

By the way, none of this has anything to do with God's correction; that's a whole different issue, and we are never to return evil for evil (Romans 12:17, 1 Thessalonians 5:15, 1 Peter 3:9).

I guess the point I'm trying to make is that when you are in a kingdom, you are subject to that kingdoms King or Ruler. If you find yourself in England you are subject to the Queen while you are in her country because she is the ruling authority there. The same goes for any other country on the planet... And the same goes for the planet itself.

In my opinion, the fact that God allows the devil's kingdom to temporarily exist is not an excuse to say it's God's will for every evil thing that happens to us because He "allowed it". I think that's a copout as far as the believer's duty to understand and engage in spiritual warfare, and I repeat, a casual Christian is ignorant of spiritual warfare and what it entails.

Through prayerfully studying the Scriptures I have become convinced that, as to our time on this planet, this is a time of choosing; good or evil, right or wrong, light or darkness, Heaven or hell, God or whatever else you may choose to put above Him or in His place, including nothing. The temporary existence of the kingdom of darkness and all the temptations, trash and evil that comes with it are what gives you the options to choose from and are crafted and designed by the devil to sway (1 John 5:19) your decision away from God, as it has already throughout most of the world. Think about this... If the kingdom of darkness and all that goes with it wasn't here you wouldn't have a choice, and that would be terribly wrong (see Deuteronomy 28, and Deuteronomy 30:19-20). We would simply be like programmed robots.

The current problem being, that living in the very midst of all the "junk" of this world, it's just a matter of time until it spills over, or for a better analogy, slops over on to all of us. It's nice to know, however, that in choosing the Lord and His kingdom we will one day continue our existence in a place where none of this junk (evil) is allowed to reside or exist at all. And if none of this were true, then why would we have so many warnings and instructions in the Bible to deal with it, let alone, why would we need the full armor of God as outlined in Ephesians 6:10-18, if we are to just roll over and submit every time evil touches us, in any form, as we would have to do had we succumbed to the belief that "God allowed it, so it must be His will." Well, maybe it's not His will. I don't know what you're going through right now, but what does the Bible say about your situation? We all have challenges to our faith and we all have tribulations and if we are not careful they can easily be misinterpreted and side-track us into doubt and unbelief, so it's vital to know what the Bible actually says about our specific situations. Once unbelief and doubt begin to spread, the momentum gains quickly and becomes very hard to stop. Your enemy the devil knows this, as it is his primary goal for your life.

Why would the Bible refer to us and admonish us to endure *"as a good soldier of Jesus Christ"* (2 Timothy 2:3), when a soldiers purpose and function is in the realm of warfare and no soldier, who is truly a soldier, ever just rolled over and submitted themselves to the enemy in battle... Let me tell you folks, as long as your feet are on this planet you're on enemy territory, and like it or not, you're in a continuous battle. The battle is for your soul, and it begins in your mind.

Maybe we should stop letting the devil kick our butts so much, at least not without a fight. Search the Scriptures concerning your situations and pray those Scriptures that you find.

I am just an old Soldier of the Cross who has fought many battles of spiritual warfare, and have my scars to remind me. I don't believe in a "roll over and play dead" theology.

That's why the Bible is so adamant about warning us and training us to walk in our victory in Jesus while we are here. For example, 1 Peter 5:8-9 instructs us to *"be sober, be vigilant; because your adversary the devil walks about like a roaring lion, seeking whom he may devour. Resist him, steadfast in the faith,"*... But if he does go ahead and eat ya, its okay, cuz it's my will because I allowed it," said God NEVER! Really? What about something as horrible as child rape for instance? If that's God's will then I need a new God. That's evil, folks... That's not from God! And we are to hate evil (Psalms 97:10, Proverbs 8:13, Amos 5:15, etc.).

*"Because he has set his love upon Me, therefore I will deliver him;*
*I will set him on high, because he has known My name.*
*He shall call upon Me, and I will answer him; I will be with him in trouble;*
*I will deliver him and honor him.*
*With long life I will satisfy him, and show him My salvation."* Psalm 91:14-16.

I'm real sure that we all need to be praying Psalm 91 in its entirety, over our lives and the lives of our loved ones.

## CHAPTER 41

## Oh, Hell No!

Each of my court appearances painted a bleaker and more hopeless scenario than the one before. To make matters much worse, that December I lost my greatest friend and mentor, as Armando caught the chain to Wasco main reception prison then on to Mule Creek State Prison. As grievous as this all was it didn't compare to the bitter painfulness I underwent as the Lord began dealing with my unforgiveness, which had probably allowed the devil his greatest foothold of all in my life, as Ephesians 4:26-27, and 2 Corinthians 2:10-11 warned us. What a long and miserable battle. Especially when considering the long hours of strategic planning I had invested in each unique design and sequence of events that would be implemented in taking my revenge, should I ever get out of here. Looking back through my perfect 20/20 hindsight vision, I see clearly that my Heavenly Father wasn't about to let me out of there with all of this hate and vengeance in my heart... After all, we had a deal. Therefore, the battle raged on in my soul; my flesh demanding vengeance, and my new "Helper" the Holy Spirit demanding forgiveness.

To those who were to be the recipients of my raging vengeance, you have truly been blessed by God, and I pray you make the most of it, as the Lord persistently fought with me exceedingly hard and unrelenting, on your behalf. And I might add that He tackled this battle within me, relentlessly, one person at a time, and one incident at a time. Otherwise it would have been too gigantic of an obstacle for me to overcome, and even so, I cried out to Him constantly and admitted that I could not forgive them on my own, and swore to my own hurt. Without His help it was an impossible task for me. Relishing the thoughts and plans of my revenge is what had kept me going through this entire nightmare, and now, one piece at a time, God was taking it from me. The Lord would continually drop scriptures on me, as I tried to read my Bible, that were ceaselessly telling me why I had to forgive, but I would incessantly search the Psalms and Old Testament stories to find His own Scriptures that would justify my cause.

By the way, trying to use God's own words in order to win your point of view while arguing with Him is an exercise in futility, just so you know. I really believed that I had some pretty good ideas and couldn't understand why the Creator of the Universe wouldn't even consider my well-planned schemes, let alone take my advice seriously. At first, I looked at it as a waste of really good talent and resources on His part. He looked at it as purging His beloved child from a life threatening disease that had all but consumed what was left of me.

So He began the process of extracting it. Interesting to note that the more I fought against His forgiveness "program", the more court postponements I had to endure, and the more time I spent locked up. Hmmm. The reason being, for this to work in me, the Lord needed a "captive audience", and my undivided attention, which He had. Back then I pleaded with Him to set me free and now, looking back, I thank God that he didn't cut me loose at that time.

Unforgiveness had poisoned my soul.

As it always comforted me to say the Lord's Prayer that I had been taught at a very young age, I often took solace in visiting the familiarity of Jesus's Sermon on the Mount (Matthew 5 – 7). One evening I was once again there in chapter 6 as the Lord was saying;

*"In this manner, therefore, pray:*
*Our Father who art in Heaven,*
*Hallowed be your name.*
*Thy kingdom come,*
*Thy will be done,*
*On earth as it is in Heaven.*
*Give us this day,*
*Our daily bread,*
*And forgive us our trespasses,*
*As...*
As...
**As...**
**AS...**
*As we forgive those who have trespassed against us,...* (Emphasis mine).
And that's where God started this whole ball rolling.
"As". Matthew six verse 12.

You probably have a different opinion, but to me, this little two letter word became the hardest word in the entire Bible. When I tried to find scriptures to "whitewash it, sugarcoat it, or contradict it", I only kept coming up with stuff that confirmed and validated it. Two verses later in verse 14, it's like the Lord was saying to me, "It's not that hard to understand – no mystery here, son. Let me break it down for you";

*"For if you forgive men their trespasses, your Heavenly Father will also forgive you.* ***But*** *if you do not forgive men their trespasses, neither will your Father forgive your trespasses"* Matthew 6:14.

Yeah... Right. I am truly remorseful for my sins and they are not. That's not fair. But God wouldn't let it go, and when I started flipping through a few pages in order to change the subject, I hit on Matthew 18:15 that seems to justify my perspective in saying if my brother (which he ain't) sins against me, then I can go tell him about his "fault", just between me and him alone (my paraphrase of verse 15).

Now that sounded much better, and don't worry, we won't have any need of "witnesses" as verse 16 goes on about. I should've called it good and closed the book, for the time being, but I kept reading right on into the whole 70×7 thing in verses 21-22. Apparently Peter, like me, had issues with this whole "let them off the hook" thing (Peter – fisherman – off the hook – ha ha ha!). Then Jesus goes into this story (parable) of this unforgiving servant who (coincidently? Not!) got himself turned over to "the torturers" for not forgiving others, in Matthew 18:23-34! I can relate…sort of.

Then, on top of all that, as if to drive home His point, which He did, He goes off on me in the next verse (verse 35) with, *"so My Heavenly Father also will do to you if each of you, from his heart, does not forgive his brother is trespasses."*

I took it as a threat, so I said, "Okay Lord, I forgive them." Now maybe we can move on. Oh, but no. *"From his heart"*, jumps off of the page at me.

I can't. Besides, he's not my brother! (Good point, don't you think? Well, it didn't work either).

This went on and on for months, every day and every night. Sometimes Scriptures would conjure up faces and memories of my "enemies" and the things they had done. Sometimes they would bring back to my memory ugly things that I had done and needed to bring before God in true confession and repentance, after which I would notice a definite sense of relief and peace.

*"If we confess our sins, He is faithful and just to forgive us our sins and to cleanse us from all unrighteousness"* 1 John 1:9.

That little shred of relief and peace I experienced got my attention, and I soon became quick to repent and renounce those things I had done, as the Holy Spirit brought them to mind. Looking back, I thank God for being so gentle with me, and not making me face my sins all at once, for surely the deep anguish of the things I had done would have surely ended me. At the end of the day, there are those times when I am to ashamed to pray and all I can say is I'm sorry, and all I can do is close my eyes and allow the night to pass, putting all of my hope in the dawning of the new sunrise, knowing that His mercy is new every morning;

*"My soul still remembers and sinks within me.*
*. This I recall to my mind, therefore I have hope.*
*Through the Lord's mercies we are not consumed, because His compassions fail not.*
*They are new every morning; great is Your faithfulness.*
*'The Lord is my portion,' says my soul, therefore I hope in Him!"* Lamentations 3:20-24.

Once He brought me to the "turn the other cheek" thing in order to kill my whole "eye for an eye" attitude (Matthew 5:38-40). I countered with Psalm

144:1, *"Blessed be the Lord my Rock, Who trains my hands for war, and my fingers for battle –"*. Yeah, maybe a little hardheaded, I was.

Then, while reading in the Gospel of Mark 11:20-24, Jesus is explaining how faith based prayers can accomplish amazing things (miracles!), and without any breakage in this script, verses 25 and 26 again declares His command to forgive others or God will not forgive me. Was this alluding to, or directly connecting my unforgiveness to hindering my faith from working in my prayers? Because, right now I'm in the fight of my life, facing 25 to life with a $20,000 dump truck of a lawyer and a miracle is what I'm praying for! Alrighty then... We'll give it a whirl, just to be safe.

I could easily think my way back into my very distant past, where friends and morons alike had instances where they out and out "done me wrong". As I drug up these old irritating memories and thought individually back on the ones who had vexed me, I realized that their offenses against me, however large or small at the time, were over and done, and what's more, comparing them to some of the things that I had already confessed to God, I found it not that difficult to forgive them.

So then one of the trustees finds a Believers Voice of Victory magazine put out by Kenneth Copeland Ministries out in the yard and decides, "for whatever reason" (Providence), to bring it to me. Amazingly, the main articles are about trusting God to handle the wrongs done to us in our lives, and one thing jumped out of that magazine to me;

Because God forgave me, I **choose** to forgive.

"Okay, Lord. I truly forgive so-and-so for doing this-and-that to me. Really. Don't hold their dumb asses accountable on my part. Just let it go, Lord. After all they're your kids, and You can deal with it anyway you want, or not at all, but I'm done with it. Amen."

Every time I did it, sincerely, I would get a sense of relief, and always a sense of peace within myself. Several times the devil would try to throw them back up in my face but I would stand my ground; "Nope. I have forgiven that person, with God's help," I would say, and move on to something else in my thoughts (2 Corinthians 10:3-5 is a "must read" in this regard).

It began to dawn on me that, after forgiving several offenses in my past and experiencing the sense of freedom that came with each occurrence, this forgiveness thing was working wonders for me. I was also aware that the people that I was forgiving not only more than likely couldn't care less, but hadn't even given what they had done to me a second thought, since they did it however many years ago that it may have been. And, yes, it seemed very unfair that they had hurt me and gotten away with it "scot-free", but forgiving them was becoming very liberating for me, as long as I stayed on guard as not to allow malice (the desire to see someone suffer) a foothold in my heart. Now I realize it's me I'm helping, not them, when I forgive. There really is something to this forgiveness business... But there is also a line you don't cross with me, and that line has been crossed. Premeditated as it may be, not everybody is gonna get off my hook, and I just figure that me and God will have to deal with it when the time comes, to my way of thinking anyway. In the remaining blackness of my heart I was convinced that certain people would be much easier to forgive after I'm done with them and I have successfully orchestrated their "face to face" appointment with God.

Of course, God's thinking not being anything close to mine, was making sure that time just didn't come.

As time wore on the Lord showed me through 2 Corinthians 2:10-11 and Ephesians 4:26-27 that I may genuinely have some serious issues due to the access I had allowed the devil into my life through my inability to forgive; serious spiritual issues.

*"Now whom you forgive anything, I also forgive. For if indeed I have forgiven anything, I have forgiven that one for your sakes in the presence of Christ, least Satan should take advantage of us; for we are not ignorant of his devices."* 2 Corinthians 2:10-11.

*"Be angry, and do not sin; do not let the sun go down on your wrath, nor give place to the devil."* Ephesians 4:26-27.

I knew I needed understanding to all of this so that's what I prayed for. By way of my unwillingness to forgive, was it possible that I had allowed my hate and inner rage, over many years, to metamorphosis into an addiction that fueled my desperate need for revenge? Is that why I considered vengeance as an art form to be held in such high regard as I had placed it in my life? Am I a demented nutball? Or more likely, had I been so deeply hurt that I couldn't face my pain and shame without the soothing thoughts of possibly getting revenge? Had I allowed the evil one that much access into my heart?

Don't know, but breakfast sucked and without Armando there for morning chess and fellowship, I went back to my bunk and tried to sleep. That's when I got celly #11, a fellow named George who, when he saw my Bible, informed me that he was a self-proclaimed "evolutionist". Oh, isn't that great. Just gets better by the moment.

By his pale clammy skin tone, his jittery, argumentative demeanor and his profuse sweating in a cold cellblock, he was starting his withdrawals from heroin. Maybe this one will just kill me and get it over with, I sarcastically and only half-jokingly mused. I was weary of all this.

To my relief, they didn't lock me down with my new celly and our door stayed open throughout the day. I would check in on him every couple of hours to see if he needed anything, but mostly I tried to give him his privacy as this was obviously "not his first rodeo".

I spent most of my day reading and rereading Armando's, as well as my own favorite psalm, #37. It was like applying a healing, soothing balm to my aching heart, as the reality of being without my wife and children was ripping me to the core.

*"Trust in the Lord, and do good; dwell in the land, and feed on his faithfulness.*

*Delight yourself also in the Lord, and He shall give you the desires of your heart.*

*Commit your way to the Lord, trust also in Him, and He shall bring it to pass.*

*He shall bring forth your righteousness as the light, and your justice as the noon day.*

*Rest in the Lord, and wait patiently for him; do not fret because of him who prospers in his way, because of the man who brings wicked schemes to pass.*

*Cease from anger, and forsake wrath; do not fret – it only causes harm.*

*For evildoers shall be cut off; but those who wait on the Lord, they shall inherit the earth.*

*For yet a little while and the wicked shall be no more; indeed, you will look carefully for his place, but it shall be no more.*

*But the meek shall inherit the earth, and shall delight themselves in the abundance of peace.*

*The wicked plots against the just, and gnashes at him with his teeth.*

*The Lord laughs at him, for He sees that his day is coming."* Psalm 37:3-13.

FYI, when I looked up the word "meek" the definition is "strength under control".

I like that. I could live without inheriting the earth, but I would love to know more about that "abundance of peace", part. What would that be like? I recall the bumper sticker I had read that professed, "No Jesus – No Peace, Know Jesus – Know Peace". As I pondered it I realized that although my existence on planet Earth was quickly imploding all around me and the circumstances were, for the most part, way beyond my control, I had this deep inner sense of calmness, or I guess, "peace" that kind of "anchored" me down and kept me from going ballistic when things went wrong or overwhelmed me. That definitely wasn't there before Jesus became my Lord and Master. So was peace achievable for me? Amidst all of this that I was going through? Doubtful. Being a hermit in the mountains with nobody hunting me, maybe. *"The mountains will bring peace to the people, and the little hills, by righteousness,"* Psalm 72:3… Now that, I could wrap my head around. I just had to get out of here first, and for that I started praying Psalm 35 back to Him to remind Him that he is not only my Vindicator and Champion but also, in fact, my only hope.

Besides, verses 12 and 13 of Psalm 37 said that *"the Lord laughs at him, for He sees that his day is coming."* Well, I'm glad that Somebody thinks all of this is funny, but just to be safe, I'll keep reminding God of my need, and His promises to help me, as clearly told in Psalm 37:39-40;

*"But the salvation of the righteous is from the Lord; He is their strength in time of trouble.*

*And the Lord shall help them and deliver them; He shall deliver them from the wicked, and save them, because they trust in Him."*

As crazy as it sounds, all of this did give me a small, yet consistent sense of peace, and convinced me that it was definitely worthy of further study. Looking back, I see now that I could never have been purged from my need for vengeance without His peace to replace my hate, eventually. If any of this sounds like you, please see my scriptural study notes on "Keys to Peace" in Appendix G.

*"Mark the blameless man, and observe the upright; for the future of that man is peace"* Psalm 37:37. Well, I'm not exactly blameless or upright, so maybe I need a little more work... And I knew this doggone forgiveness thing was holding me back from receiving a lot of what I was asking God for. I'm really screwed up here. Even if I could attain peace, without my loved ones, what's the point?

The court system was becoming bored in dealing with me and I needed some help really soon.

Though vengeance didn't seem to be such a bad thing in the Old Testament where it was orchestrated quite often, I suppose that deep down, I knew in my heart that my revenge would be the direct result of my unforgiveness. Trying to find a way to have one without the other was stupid, and trying to deal with one without including the other was just as ridiculous, and no matter what, if God doesn't help me I will never be able to deal with either my need for revenge or my unforgiveness.

"Please, God, I can't do it alone. I can't forgive them unless you change me."

One night, a week or so after George became my new cellmate, even he could see the obvious struggle I was going through with all of this. As I was sitting on my bunk despairingly holding my head in my hands, he asked what was eating at me so bad. Somewhat irritated, I told him, as best that I could. He then simply shrugs his shoulders and says, "Oh. Well, vengeance is mine, says the Lord, I will repay." Aaargh!

"Yeah, well, God's pretty busy these days, so I figured I'd help him out and handle this one for Him," I threw back at him.

"Let me know how that works out for ya," George responds.

"I thought you were an atheist?" I asked.

"Didn't say that. I said I was an evolutionist. There's a difference." He responded.

"And what's the difference?" I prodded him.

This went on night after night after lockdown, and all we did was frustrate each other to the max, but I got the subject changed away from the most blatant Scripture in the whole Bible that I must avoid;

Hebrews 10:30 – *"Vengeance is mine, I will repay"* says the Lord. And again, *"the Lord will judge His people."*

But thinking about it, what could I do in extracting my revenge that could possibly surpass what the "Living God" could do? The question is, can I get God to do it? Can I trust God to do it? There it is. The bottom line is, can I trust God to handle it? That's... That's... A lot. I have never really trusted anyone without getting burned, sooner or later. I have what the Bible refers to as a bad case of "malice" (hate, vengefulness, animosity. The desire to inflict injury, harm, or suffering on another, either because of a hostile impulse or out of deep-seated meanness. The intention or desire to do evil. Revenge. The desire to see another person suffer.). Yeah, I guess that nails it... If I got a case of anything, it's malice.

It finally sunk in to my thick head that there was no weaseling out of this, as far as the Lord was concerned.

"Can I trust You in this? Can I trust You with my life? You're asking me to give up the only thing that has kept me going, up to this point. And be that as it may, I'm not sure I can. In fact there's no way. You said the Holy Spirit is come to live inside of me and this is gonna have to be an inside job, Lord. So start shoving it out of me Holy Spirit, because I can't get it out of me by myself. And if You do get it out of me, what's left? A vacant hole? A spiritual lobotomy?"

I panicked away on into the night, and then a verse came into my head from Philippians 4:6-7, *"Be anxious for nothing, but in everything by prayer and supplication, with Thanksgiving, let your request be made known to God; and the **peace of God**, which surpasses all understanding, will guard your hearts and minds through Christ Jesus."*

Sooo... God will "replace" my malice and unforgiveness with peace. Have I got that right? And these verses are the instructions to attain this peace? "I wish it was that simple, Lord." I muttered out loud. George, who I thought was asleep, replied, "Try Romans 12, something."

Sure thing, Pal. I bet you got this all figured out, I was thinking as I turned to Romans 12. My celly the prophet. I don't think he knows whether Christ was hung on a tree or killed with an ax. Glad I didn't say any of this out loud or I would be eating crow; that said, I apologize, George, for thinking it.

Romans 12:17-21 – *"Repay no one evil for evil. Have regard for good things in the sight of all men. If at all possible, as much as depends on you, live peaceably with all men. Beloved, do not avenge yourselves, but rather give place to wrath; for it is written, "Vengeance is Mine, I will repay," says the Lord. Therefore "if your enemy is hungry, feed him; if he is thirsty, give him a drink; for in so doing you will heap coals of fire on his head." Do not be overcome by evil, but overcome evil with good."*

That, *"but rather give place"* in verse 19 literally means "leave room for" the wrath of God.

"So if I don't "avenge" myself, You will handle it, right Lord? Okay, okay. At least I'm not having to worry about that "feed em' if they're hungry" part, although I like the part that says that if I do, it will heap coals of fire on their heads. Technically speaking, Lord, if I send them all free gift certificates at McDonald's, anonymously of course, will that suffice the requirement to cook their brains a little? Maybe burn off some hair, anyway, right? Even better, Carl's Jr. gift certificates, as I got food poisoning two out of two times there. Sorry... Just kidding... But would it work – just asking. Paul and those guys sent hankies to people to heal them, sooo... Same principle, I'm thinking, right?"

*"For the wrath of man does not produce the righteousness of God"* James 1:20. Ouch.

"I suppose, if You promise to handle it, I'll try my best to let them go, but You gotta help because I'm really good at hating them."

Oh yeah... In flipping that coin, for future reference, if you ever receive a free fast food gift certificate in the mail, anonymously, just to be safe, **don't use it!**

I began by trying to forgive those who haven't done me too serious of damage at first, with some limited success. As weeks wore on and I got closer to my next court date, I was down to anguishing over the cops, the judge, that private investigator, and my would-be ex-partners. I would, one at a time, "forgive" them about 20 times a day and know beyond any doubt in my heart, that I had failed, as I still hated their guts. Progress had come to a standstill. I was frustrating myself with every attempt and just couldn't let it go. Then I got a letter from my daughter in which she told me that she, her Mom, and my mother were all praying for me. That morning after breakfast, I sat alone in the commons area rereading the letter and picturing my mother, my wife, and my little girl all praying before God on my behalf, when the question interrupted my thoughts, "Do my enemies have loved ones praying for them? A wife or child? A mother maybe?"

I kind of felt my calloused heart begin to soften, just a little. "God bless them, if they are praying for those bastards", I whispered. "That's gotta be tough." Thinking of the possible broken hearts of their loved ones somewhat humbled me. "Okay, Lord. If that may be the case, I'll make you a deal. I will be avenged if You just bring them to their knees before You, whatever it takes, and make them admit/confess what they did to me, and repent, in the same manner that You have brought me to my knees before You and done the same to me."

As if hard scales fell from my heart, relief flooded my soul and I began to weep. I was all in... throwing in the towel, in a manner of speaking.

I then began moving from person to person on my "revenge" list, and picturing them kneeling before God and confessing what they had done to me, in my mind, as I prayed to forgive them, one at a time, day after day, some much more difficult than others, and being real with God when I couldn't.

Next came the spiritual "kick in the guts" I felt, when right in the middle of our little Bible study group, we hit on Luke 6:27-28 – *"But I say to you who hear: love your enemies, do good to those who hate you, bless those who curse you, and pray for those who spitefully use you. To him who strikes you on the one cheek, offer the other also. And from him who takes away your cloak, do not withhold your tunic either."* Said Jesus.

Oh, come on! Oh, hell no! Pray for them to bless them? Love them? Turn the other cheek for what? So they can have another go at me? I got a better idea – they need to pray that I don't ever see them again. Now that I think about it, I need to pray that I don't ever see them again or all this will be for nothing. So that's what I did. I told God nothing He didn't already know. I could only forgive them through His grace and mercy as I definitely don't have enough of it in me to get the job done, and it's only gonna work if He makes sure I never lay eyes on them ever again (except maybe in Heaven, and I'm pretty confident at this point, that ain't happening), because I am just flat out and out too weak to handle such an encounter. I prayed that my conditions would be good enough for Him, because it's all I got left to give; "We just hit the bottom of the barrel. Listen, Lord; Remember, You're the one who said,' **If it is possible**, as much as depends on you, live peaceably with all men' (Romans 12:18). Well, please Lord, this is the "if it is possible" part, and it ain't, and You know it. Please help me in this, Father."

In his mercy, God honored my prayer.

Shortly thereafter, the miracles of Divine Providence began to unfold. I have heard some preachers say you can't live from miracle to miracle, but I say you can, and I'm living proof.

But before I tell you about that, I need to tell you about this; if you wait to forgive until you feel like it or you get an apology, that time will never come. The enemy of your soul will see to that. That's how he got his "foothold" in your life in the first place, and he can't be letting you close the door on him. Do it anyway. Forgive and be free of that lying, hateful punk. It's what freedom in Christ is all about. As long as you can't forgive, you can't throw him out, and he will always be there trying to run your life… whispering to you in your hurt and despair.

Even to this day, the only way I know I have honestly forgiven them, is when I think about them, I have peace with God about them. I don't think about revenge or malice. I don't think about them at all. I'm much too busy seeking peace, knowing that from God only can it come. Nothing on this earth can give me what I now seek, and that's all good.

My flesh could never and will never forgive them. But telling God truthfully how I must have His help, or I won't be able to do it on my own, is what has made it possible for my spirit and soul to forgive them, and bring my flesh into submission to the Holy Spirit.

And that's how I know is because I have peace with God about them. They are in His hands now, and not mine. They are not mine to deal with anymore. I'm done with them. That was then, this is now.

It's not about peace **with** them. It's about peace with God **about** them.

And who was the hardest of all my enemies to forgive, you might wonder?

Myself.

And even so, the regrets always remain, and are always with me.

## CHAPTER 42

## The Miraculous Begins

*"For I know the thoughts that I think toward you, says the Lord, thoughts of peace and not of evil, to give you a future and a hope.
Then you will call upon Me and go and pray to Me, and I will listen to you.
And you will seek Me and find Me, when you search for Me with all your heart.
I will be found by you, says the Lord, and I will bring you back from your captivity;"*
Jeremiah 29:11-14

Three days before my court date to file my plea, my illustrious dump-truck of a lawyer, to my absolute shock, came to see me. He came to tell me of the "deal of a lifetime" that he was authorized by the District Attorney's Office to offer me. They would drop the third strike if I pled guilty to ex-felon in possession of a firearm and took an eight year sentence. Knowing full well that I wouldn't be able to take eight years of this crap, I told him I would think about it but we would probably be going to a jury trial. He became insistent that if I choose to go to trial, it would be best to go before the judge only, and forgo the jury trial. Yeah, $20,000 we paid this clown, in advance, and he was selling me out. No way was this guy going to fight for me, and he made it clear that my $20,000 didn't cover going to trial.

He did mention that the corrupt private investigator that had helped to set me up and encouraged me to jump bail had been in an auto accident and was paralyzed. He also told me that the corrupt deputy sheriff that had set me up was also under investigation.

True or not, as he had already proven himself untrustworthy, I refused and rebuked myself from celebrating their possible but not likely calamities, as I had fought so hard to forgive them and move past it. That was between them and God.

I called Lori and my folks to let them in on the bad news. "Yeah, I bet it's because of stuff like that, that the Lord Jesus specifically pronounced all those 'woe unto you lawyers 'in the Gospel of Luke (11:45-54) Johnny, so apparently the Lord didn't like em' any more than we do," Dad said. And we all wonder where I get my really cool sarcastic sense of humor!

Our troubles were compounded when I called Lori, as Billy was having a great deal of trouble and my Calador had withdrawn into a severe and possibly lethal state of reclusiveness. Cal had lost over 45 pounds over the past several months. He would not come into the house unless he was forced, as he seemed to just lie in the same spot in the yard every day, looking down Campton Street for me. Brandy could make him eat a little every day but as of late, he wasn't even doing that now. Keisha, our female wolf, would take food to him as well, but he refused it.

How much more could my heartbreak. I was shattered with all this and so was Lori. For several minutes the phone was quiet while we silently wept together. How could I have put this on my loved ones? And yes, this was on me. We had to always do things my way – always what I wanted. I had to take full ownership of the repercussions of my decisions. I knew fully now, what it was to be broken, and knowing that there was absolutely nothing I could do to help them, or me.

Lori had my daughter bring Calador into the house, and said, "You have got to talk to him and get him to eat something." He lied down and they put some half cooked meat in front of him and set the phone close to him on speaker. The love talk between a man and his wolf is very personal (and somewhat embarrassing) so forgoing that part, I said as best I could in a fun-loving voice, "You eat that, Cal. You don't get no treats till you eat that." He started eating as I just kept talking to him. Afterwards I would call every couple of days, running the monthly phone bill into the hundreds because of the jails and prisons insane greed that sets the telephone prices per minute, (what a scam!) And once he started to eat, we would leave the speakerphone on while we talked. Even so he would still only eat very small portions, but it was something. The thought of Cal, or anybody else I love, dying while I was incarcerated, began to re-stir my anger and I had to fervently fight back the option to go to rage mode. I had to get out of here, and now, only God could pull that off.

When I hung up the phone I went back to my cell, got a piece of paper, and wrote down a list of everything I was grieving over in what remained of my shattered heart.

"Well God. Here we go. You said you would supply all my needs in Philippians 4:19 and this is what I gotta have. You said if I trust in You, You would give me the desires of my heart. I have committed my life to You and I am trusting You, with all I got left, and I pray it's enough to get You to bring it to pass (: 3-6). So bring forth my justice as You promised!

Here goes…"

"Dear Lord, as your servant Hannah cried out for a son and promised to give him back to serve You all the days of his life (1 Samuel 1:9-11), I give You back my only son, as he is in trouble now, and I can't help him. I put Billy in Your loving hands, Father. He needs you now, so shield him with Your blood and build a hedge of protection around him, and deliver him, as only You can do. And I pray that he may serve to glorify Your Holy Name, all the days of his life." As Hannah did, *"Now I am giving him to the Lord, and he will belong to the Lord his whole life"* 1 Samuel 1:28.

There is a part of your heart that never hardens... It always breaks... That part of your heart is reserved for your son (or daughter). As you read this, I ask you to please just take a second and say a small prayer for my son, Billy, regardless of what you believe, for his deliverance, protection, and God's love to shine brightly in him, on him, and through him to others, in Jesus's name, Amen.

With all of my heart, thank you.

Next, I prayed for God to spare and preserve my Calador and to comfort his grieving heart until we would be reunited, based on Psalm 36:6. Amazingly noteworthy is the Hebrew word "yasha" translated here in this Psalm as "preserve", which is also translated as "save"! I didn't even know that at the time! Thank You, Holy Spirit!

Recognizing the unmistakable animosity I was harboring against my two-faced moneygrubbing, sell-me-down-the-river lawyer, I stayed on my knees before the Lord for what seemed like forever, until I was confident that I had let him go and repented of my bitterness towards him. "He's in Your hands, Lord. You deal with him."

As, not so long ago, I was comforted in relishing the vision of my enemies flesh melting in the fires of hell, again, as before, the epiphany now struck me that my own, as well as everybody else's, salvation could only come via true and sincere confession and repentance. However, this time without vengeance as my motive, I started with my lawyer and going through the entire list of my adversaries from the dark side, I prayed individually for their salvation and deliverance from evil influences, again. How or when, was left in the Lord's hands, but I was now 100% free.

Up until now, my bunkie was content to lie in his bunk and listen as I prayed for my family members and even my dog, but lost it when he heard me pray for my adversaries and of my corrupt lawyer to be saved. "Awe, come on! You gotta be kidding me!" He blurted out.

"I know you can't get it, George, but now they no longer own a piece of me. I'm free of them."

"What do you mean?" He asked. I went on to explain, as best I could, how as long as I held anger, malice or unforgiveness towards anybody in my heart, that they owned a piece of me. They controlled that part of me, and nobody had the right to own me except the One who bought me with His own blood. And besides, I told him, God requires it of me, and Proverbs 16:7 says, *"When a man's ways please the Lord, He makes even his enemies to be at peace with him"*.

As he sat back on his bunk and thought about what I had said, I began whispering a prayer for God to "water the seed" inside of my cellmate, George. Then I continued on down my prayer list, praying for God to take out the hearts of stone in my former enemies and especially that ungodly judge, and put a new spirit in them and give them a "heart of flesh" just as He had recently done in me. This He promised through His prophet Ezekiel, in chapter 36:26-27, saying;

*"I will give you a new heart and put a new spirit within you; I will take the heart of stone out of your flesh and give you a heart of flesh. I will put My Spirit within you and cause you to walk in My statutes, and you will keep My judgments and do them."*

Lastly, I prayed for God to strengthen me and make me able to endure all of this, and to give me a quick release from either my incarceration or my life, and I left that choice in His hands as well, thinking, I'm just about done with all this, either way. Enough is enough.

*"He who loves his life will lose it, and he who hates his life in this world will keep it for eternal life"* John 12:25.

I am hating my life beyond words right about now and welcome the move right on into "the eternal life", if the Lord is willing. Either way, get it done, Lord. I'm "all in".

***

## Billy's Letter

Two days later I experienced one of the greatest uplifting realities an inmate is allowed to enjoy; they called my name at mail call, for which I received a letter from my 15-year-old son. And here's the kicker; it was postdated and mailed only two days earlier (when I was praying for him in earnest) from a little town in South Eastern Nevada, with nothing more for an address than "to John Gergen Bakersfield jail"! No street address, ZIP Code, or even the state was written on the envelope! Considering the US Postal Service, a blind man can see that the guard who gave me my letter had just handed me a miracle! And of all things, my son had written me a letter to tell me he believed in me and to encourage me in the faith to "stay strong in the Lord"!

I had my face against the wall as I lay on my bunk and cried. No words had brought me such hope and encouragement up to this point in my life, more so for the fact that he too was struggling with his own issues in the boys' facility in Caliente.

That afternoon, like most of the time we spent together, George and I passed the time arguing about creation versus evolution, and as usual, as soon as I started to gain ground in the altercation (squabble, more like it), George would blurt out some idiotic "scientific" babble that made no sense at all, then walk out the cell door before I could respond.

In my frustration I cried out to the Lord, "God, why must I tolerate this fool?" Immediately a gentle voice inside me clearly said "So you will learn".

I jumped to my feet with tears welling up in my eyes, looking around the empty room.

"It happened. I really heard You," I whispered.

I sat back down on my bunk, closed my eyes and listened, hoping for more.

"Here I am, Lord," I prayed, but that was it. After a while I went out in the commons area to the phone, and called Lori to tell her (which had to have freaked her out a little, I'll bet), and to tell her of the miracle letter I had received from our son. She patiently listened until I finished, then with a sense of urgency in her voice, she told me I needed to call my Dad before they shut off the phones tonight because he had something to tell me.

I hung up and called Dad, ticking off another inmate waiting to use the phone. The other inmate was getting himself pretty worked up by the time Dad picked up the phone and I was just getting ready to drop the receiver so I could have both hands free to deal with him. Out of nowhere, Bobby who was now calling the shots in our cellblock, stepped between us, put his hand on the other guy's chest and immediately stopped his advance. Bobby turned and looked at me and I said, "I'm really sorry Bobby and I apologize, but I go out shackled in the morning and this call is really important." There would be no phone use available in the morning before they chained me and took me to court. Bobby, speaking very softly as always, said something to the other inmate who turned and walked away. Thank God and thank Bobby! An incident would have immediately got the phone and television shut off and not only would I not be able to talk to Dad before court tomorrow, but I would have a beating coming for getting the TV turned off! Thank You, Jesus, for sending Bobby!

Dad was excited, and I had a very difficult time processing what he was telling me to do, even though I could hear and understand him clearly.

"Okay Dad, say it one more time," I told him. Again he said what I thought he said, "Take the plea bargain for eight years, Johnny. You have to. Jack Grimm said he hired a lawyer for $10,000 to show up at your sentencing and take care of things," he repeated. "That's all I can tell you on this phone, but you have got to trust me, and Jack has faith in you!"

Jail phones are monitored and recorded. What he was telling me was to commit judicial suicide tomorrow in court. Yet, I had always trusted my Dad and had no reason not to now. This was nuts!

"Okay Dad, I'll do it." I told him, just before the phone shut off and the buzzer went off for nightly count.

Wow, what a day!

So Jack had hired some guy for 10 grand to simply show up at my sentencing and "take care of things". Sentencing usually takes about five minutes. For 10 grand this guy better come with a magic wand or explosives strapped to his chest. And knowing Jack, it could go either way and not surprisingly, as he always seemed to have an "ace in the hole" as long as I have known him.

***

Jack F. Grimm was a Treasure Hunter Extraordinaire, on a gigantic scale. Inspired by his Grandfathers tales of buried treasure, at age 11, Jack bought some dynamite from the local hardware store and used it to blow up a creek bed, near his home, which turned up a few arrowheads, some lead bullets, and an old frying pan. Jack said in later years, "That was it. That was all it took to hook my imagination."

A few years later he served as a demolition expert in the Marines in World War II, and afterwards found out his Navy buddy from the war, Bunker, was the son of the billionaire oil tycoon H. L. Hunt. Spurring each other on through many years and many adventures together, Jack became an oil wildcatter as well, striking oil on his very first oil well that he drilled.

He and his wife Jackie spent their honeymoon panning for gold in the high Sierra's! Now that's dedication to treasure hunting! Their searches in Nevada for silver and gold put many small mines into production in the late 70s including the Keystone Mine, which eventually was handed down to my father, then to my brother Bill and I. When Jack or Bunker came to Nevada to check on their projects, they would gather up our entire crews and their families for a night of feasting, celebration, and Jubilee just to show how much they appreciated their dedication. They were truly the last of the mining "tycoons".

I remember hunting deer in the mountains of Nevada every year with Jack, and the treasure hunting stories he would tell, and of his adventures, and many expeditions in search of Sasquatch (Bigfoot) in the Pacific Northwest, the Abominable Snowman in Nepal, the Loch Ness Monster in Scotland, the Titanic in the North Atlantic, and of course my personal favorite, Noah's Ark on Mount Ararat in Turkey.

On his third expedition he and his fellow searchers, high up on the mountain side of Ararat, managed to dig a hand carved timber out of the ice. Jack returned to the US and enlisted the help of my father to design a machine that would free the Ark from the ice it was encased in, using steam.

Unfortunately, when word of the expedition's discovery and probable location of the Ark itself reached the Turkish and Russian governments, a ban of all further expeditions to the site was implemented, and was reinforced when ballistic missiles were pointed at the location to emphasize the seriousness of the issue. So the Ark was again lost over many years until the ban to explore Mount Ararat was raised.

I remember the chunk of wood that Jack always carried in his briefcase, and I remember him letting me and my brother hold it in our hands. Jack best described his own life as "a continuous search for the unknown."

I have tried my best to follow in his footsteps, but again, it's been more like Indiana Jones on an incredibly pathetic budget. And like Jack, I will always cherish my adventures, even the scary ones, and especially the adventures I shared with my wife and eternal partner, Lori.

In any event, through their exploits and sometimes their shenanigans, Jack and Bunker made a lot of work for a lot of people, often during a time in the economy when you couldn't buy a job, and me and my family will always be grateful, and God bless them for all they have done for us.

## CHAPTER 43

## Going Out Shackled

*"Then they cried out to the Lord in their trouble,
And He saved them out of their distresses.
He brought them out of darkness and the shadow of death,
And broke their chains in pieces."*
Psalm 107:13-14

At 3:40 AM I was roused out of bed, taken into the foyer, and chained. A chain was wrapped around my waist like a belt and my wrists were handcuffed to the front of it, then shackles with a very short chain in between my feet, were clamped around my ankles.

Before transport to the old jail cells in the basement of the courthouse, I would be chained together with nine other inmates, but for now, we were all shoved into a very small room with a couple of dozen other inmates who were also chained and shackled. There was standing room only and that's what we did…for hours. All part of the plan, my lawyer reassured me, to make us suffer enough to take whatever plea-bargain they threw at us, just so a person could move on to the "comforts" of prison life. And again, I would always marvel at the complete stupidity and madness that would break out when two opposite gang members, both chained and shackled, would again go at each other by head-butting and biting on one another until the guards came in and beat the daylights out of them. And if, in fact, you got some of their blood spattered on you, when you got back to your cell block late that night and lined up for evening count, if the guards saw the blood on your clothes, you would likely get worked over for fighting. They didn't want to hear an explanation; they just wanted an excuse to do what they do.

On this particular day, I'm just standing there with my head in the "zone" when I get slapped out of it by one of the two inmates next to me mentioning my dump-truck lawyer's name. "He's really good, man. It costs us a lot of money but he made a deal with that blankety-blank she-devil prosecutor to get me probation in exchange for her getting to give some white guy eight years. But it all depends on how this blankety-blank white guy pleads today, so I don't know how it's going to go yet." the one inmate told the other.

"Did you hear that, Lord?" I said under my breath. "Are you getting this, God? Are you gonna let this happen to me?" As I started to get angrier and angrier, this undeniably ridiculous Bible first pops into my head that I never understood regardless of how many times I read it, "... *And the Lord said, I am Jesus whom thou persecutest: it is hard for thee to kick against the pricks."* Acts 9:5 KJV.

I'm thinking, well now, isn't that funny.

Yes it is, and yes they are. Please forgive me, but at that time, I had no understanding of what this verse really meant. Instead, I went to my "go-to" verse, Isaiah 41:10, and just kept repeating it over and over in my head.

Hours later, when I finally got to court, I asked my "babbling backstabber attorney" for a pen and a piece of paper. He gave me one of his business cards on which I wrote, "it's hard to kick against the pricks" on the back, and slid it over to him, as it seemed appropriate that the message concerned him as well as it did me, at least from my perspective. Over 20 years later, I still have that card, by the way.

He read it and leaned over to me and whispered, "What the hell is this supposed to mean?"

As I nodded over toward the inmate I had overheard in holding, I answered, "I know you sold me out to get that other guy off on probation, you piece of blank (poo), but its okay. I want you to know that I forgive you even though you're an ------- (synonymous with anus).

The look on his face was almost worth the 20 grand he had ripped me off for. As he stared back at me in red faced, shock and awe, I smiled and winked at him. He never looked me in the eyes after that.

Then the judge read my charges and told me to stand and asked me "How do you plea, Mr. Gergen?" It was very apparent that everybody, the judge, and that battle-ax of a prosecuting attorney from the DAs office, as well as my very own dump-truck were simply going through the motions and were expecting a "not guilty" plea, to put in motion a jury trial, against three strikes and a 25 to life sentence.

"Guilty, your honor." I said.

You could've heard a pin drop. If it didn't hold the possibility of being the biggest mistake of my life, it would have been comical. With eyes wide and mouths gaping wide they all three looked back and forth from one to another. Finally the judge smiled and stammered, "You may be seated," and looking like a cat that just swallowed a bird, set a date for me to reappear before him in 30 days so he could have the pleasure of passing sentence upon me.

After a very long and weary day of being chained and shackled, the chains were finally removed and I was put back into my cell block. I called Lori and Dad to tell them what I had overheard and what had transpired in court. Then I went to my cell to wait for last count so I could finally go to bed and just let this day be done. When I got "home", I found another Believers Voice of Victory magazine, published by Kenneth Copeland ministries, lying on my bunk. I asked George about it but he knew nothing of its origin other than the fact that it was there when he got back from lunch. I read it before count and found it very bold and encouraging. One article that caught my attention was about praying actual Scriptures that pertain to your circumstances in order to know that what you are praying is, in fact, the will of God. That made sense to me.

I started praying Psalm 91 over me and my son Billy, and putting Billy's name into it to make it a personal prayer for his protection.

A few days later a very atrocious fight broke out and we were locked down for several days. I stayed in my Bible most of the time, searching for God's promises that I could pray for to help me and my family. In its own way, it was kind of like treasure hunting through the Scriptures and I would often get excited to find very specific promises that directly applied to my circumstances.

I was sleeping better than I had since before my arrest in Carson City, and two nights before the lockdown ended, I had an exceptionally vivid dream where angels opened the doors of the prison to release me and take me high into the mountains of the Sierra Nevada's. Most noteworthy was that, in my dream, I had just barely arrived at the prison when it happened, and yet I was reunited with my wife on her next birthday, being July 21. I thought that was a pretty cool dream! Then I had the same dream the next night, even much more real than the previous one, and the Lord Jesus was walking me out through the prison gates this time!

Dreams have always been a sore spot for me as I have had the same reoccurring nightmare of falling down a mine shaft, ever since I was a boy, right down to the exact details of my Aunt Neva trying to save me, to my rib cage breaking as I bounce off of mine timbers on my way down. My brother has always had the same exact dream in every detail. The difference is, as we grew older, Bill's dream occurrences grew farther and farther apart and became almost non-existent, but mine grew closer and closer together and would often awaken me, yelling as I fell, every few weeks or so by this time, as I endured my 40$^{th}$ birthday. What's even more astounding is the fact that, since Halloween night 1996 when I was led in a prayer of salvation by my friend Armando, I have not, even to this very day, had a single reoccurrence of my nightmare! Ever! Hallelujah! Praise be to the Holy Spirit who booted that demonic spirit of fear out of my subconscious when He moved in!

Having said that, and knowing that dreams are a very touchy subject with me, I was beside myself when, after lockdown ended I found myself blabbering to others that I felt God was telling me that I wasn't going to do even one year in prison. It made enough people nervous enough to request that I be locked down again, as they thought I was in the process of "nutting up", or losing my mind because of the heavy sentence that I was about to receive. Even my friend George Embry agreed with George, my bunkie, that I needed to shut up for my own protection. When they finally let me back out, a few days before court, most everybody avoided me like I had the plague, even a lot of the guys in my Bible study.

And truthfully, I was starting to wonder if I was losing control of my senses. It just seemed so real, that dream did.

\*\*\*

*"... And when they had gone aside, they talked among themselves, saying, "This man is doing nothing deserving of death or chains."*
Acts 26:31

"So be it", I'm thinking, as I read the account of the Apostle Paul when he went to court before King Agrippa and Festus. It was the last thing I had time to read before being chained and shackled and herded off to court for sentencing. This time there were several other fellows from my cell block chained up together with me.

And, oh! Lucky me! When we got to the court room I was the first one on the agenda.

The shrew from of the DAs office was here, as well as my dump-truck, and they were happily chatting away as we waited for his Eminence, the judge to grace us with his presence.

Then a very dignified elderly gentleman with white hair and a polished demeanor entered the courtroom. Aristocratic would well describe him as he gracefully walked down the center isle of the courtroom, through the small wooden swinging door/gate that separated the spectators from the participants (combatants?), and walked right up and stopped in front of me.

The dump-truck and Jezebel from the DAs office had stopped midsentence in there conversation to watch him walk into the room, with a look of respect, mixed with "what's he doing here" all over their faces. This courtly gentleman, in his well-tailored three-piece suit, with actual gold cufflinks I might add, held out his hand to me and in the perfect courtroom voice, said, "John Gergen? It's a pleasure to meet you. I have heard good things of you from your friend, Mr. Grimm." His smile was genuine, his grip very firm as he shook my hand, and the twinkle in his deep blue eyes was unmistakable, as he seemed to look into my soul as his eyes looked into mine.

As dump-truck came closer to us, the Real attorney turned slightly as to allow Dumpy to hear as well when, with a very polite smile, he stated, "I am so-and-so, attorney-at-law and your legal counsel, and I will be representing you during these sentencing proceedings." Dump-truck introduced himself and shook the real attorney's hand as he began to babble something about the plea bargain that the DAs office had so mercifully offered me, when, at over 30 minutes late, the bailiff loudly proclaimed, "All rise for his honor, judge So-And-So."

Except for my new attorney, who stood there with a slight but very professional smile on his face, the rest of us just stood there in bewilderment as a judge I had never seen before in my life, stepped up behind the bench and seated himself!

"Please accept my apology for the delay in today's proceedings as judge so-and-so (the possibly demon possessed one) was unable to be here this morning," he stated, short sweet and to the point, as he shuffled through and organized the paperwork on top of his podium.

Wow! This fellow was also a man of considerable years, late 60s or early 70s I dared to venture, also with white hair, and an aura of professionalism and dignity that gave one the impression that he wasn't one to be trifled with. I was later told he had retired from law to become a Methodist minister! As he called up the first case on the court docket, mine, I distinctly remember certain verses from Psalm 37, popping into my head.

*"The wicked watches the righteous,*
*And seeks to slay him.*
*The Lord will not leave him in his hand,*
*Nor condemn him when he is judged."* Psalm 37:32-33

The judge then sat there for several minutes reading through my case file until the diabolical prosecuting attorney stood up in exasperation and curtly said, "Your Honor, we have a full day ahead of us and we are almost an hour behind..." Where she was cut off by one finger raised by the judge to "shhhhuush" her. Was that a foot stomp I saw? Her eyes widened and her mouth dropped open as if she had been slapped! His honor took his eyes off of my paperwork only momentarily to glance over at her and respond, "I am well aware of the time and the agenda... You may be seated."

I have never fought so hard to restrain a "Yeee Haww" in my life.

*"The wicked plots against the just,*
*And gnash is at him with his* (or her) *teeth.*
*The Lord laughs at him,*
*For he sees that his day is coming."* Psalm 37:12-13.

*"Commit your way to the Lord,*
*Trust also in Him,*
*And He shall bring it to pass.*
*He shall bring forth your righteousness as the light,*
*And your justice as the noon day."* Psalm 37:5-6.

Almost another 20 minutes passed, to the disdain of the debauched prosecuting attorney, before the judge, putting down my paperwork, said, "Mr. Gergen, I don't see where you did anything wrong... I mean that, of course, you have done something wrong, as you are apparently **only a felon in California**, but I would like your counsel and the representative from the District Attorney's Office to approach the bench, please." Which they did.

> *For the Lord loves justice,*
> *And does not forsake His saints;*
> *They are preserved forever."* Psalm 37:28.

Most of the conversation seemed to be the Fair and Just Judge talking to the unscrupulous prosecutor who, during her useless attempts at a rebuttal, did in fact, stomp her foot a couple of times. I wish I could have heard what was being said. How all this was going to turn out, I had no idea, but I really wished Lori and my Dad could have been here to see this, but of course, it had become far too dangerous for them to attend my court appearances anymore, thanks to the subtle threats of the former inequitable judge. I have no idea if it applied to my case at all, but my former dump-truck once suggested that unless the possibility existed for the presiding judge or prosecutor to accept a "gratuity" (bribe), it would be impossible to win my case without a change of venue (see also, Isaiah 10:1-4, Exodus 23:8, Deuteronomy 16:18-19, Deuteronomy 27:25, Proverbs 17:23, Isaiah 5:23, and Micah 7:3). I don't know if that's the case here, but I do know that with God, nothing is impossible! God can change everything, including the judge, if need be, Amen?

I knew that I was standing smack-dab in the middle of a gigantic miracle, and so did several of the other inmates from my cellblock, as they had become somewhat of a low, murmuring cheering section.

When the attorneys finally returned to their places, Dumpy looked... Dumbfounded... No, flabbergasted... No, wait... Stupefied... Yes, that's it... Stupefied, and befuddled (I could go on and on). My new Real Counselor had simply, slightly enlarged his smile and kept his continence completely professional in poise and expression.

Her Royal highness from the DAs office was looking as if she had been spanked and was dangerously bordering on a pissy-fit (tantrum).

My Real Lawyer leaned over to me and whispered, "There seemed to be some concern about retribution for wrongful incarceration that I had not anticipated." Before he could explain, the judge smacked his gavel three times and told me to rise. "What the hell was my lawyer talking about", I wondered, as I stood focused on the judge as he rendered my sentence upon me.

Although I was ruled and ex-felon only in California, and my guns were legally purchased and registered to me, the court has accepted my plea of guilty to the charge of ex-felon in possession of a firearm, for which I am to receive a 16 month prison sentence, which shall be reduced to half time (eight months) with the time I have already served in jail to be deducted from the prison sentence (time served), and three years parole.

By the blank look on my face, it obviously had not sunk in, so my Real Attorney whispered to me, "You should be out in a month or so".

The judge wrapped his gavel on his bench and said "next case". My "inmate cheering section" went off cheering, Dumpy continued on with his dumbstruck look of shock, the Queen of Halloween glared over at me with a look of death, and the Faithful Judge beat his gavel to regain order in the court.

My Real Lawyer turned to me, put his hand on my shoulder, and with a warm smile, said, "It's been a pleasure to meet you." With tears running down my cheeks all I could say was, "God bless you," to which he grinned and said, "Yes indeed. And God bless you as well."

I never saw him again after that, as the bailiff, a lovely young woman, took my arm to lead me out of the court room's back door. As I went past the judge's bench I pulled my arm free of the deputy and stopped, looking up into the face of that judge, and with all the sincerity in my heart, said, "Thank you". Sternly, he turned his head and looked down on me, as an ever so slight smile raised one corner of his mouth and gave me a small nod. He then turned his face toward the court and called the next case, as I was led through the door and down the long hallway that would eventually take me to the old jail cells, in the basement, where I would wait for the rest of the day to catch the bus ride back to Lerdo, for the last time.

At one point in the hall, the young bailiff turned to me and said, "I can't believe you can be a felon only in California and nowhere else". "Yeah," I said, "Me either. This state definitely has their own way of doing things."

Dumpy later came by the jail to explain to me that my plea bargain came with a promise that I would receive a full pardon after seven years, if I so choose to apply for one.

I applied after seven years and their response was that the law had changed and it was now 10 years before I could apply. At 10 years, I requested my pardon they had promised and received no response at all, as with many, many other requests over the past 20 years. Hence, it's safe and easy to assume that the California Justice Department is functioning just as it always has, with little or no improvement, God have mercy on them.

> *"But the salvation of the righteous is from the Lord;*
> *He is their strength in time of trouble.*
> *And the Lord shall help them and deliver them;*
> *He shall deliver them from the wicked,*
> *And save them,*
> *Because they trust in Him."*
> Psalm 37:39-40!

## CHAPTER 44

## Catching the Chain

Well, not to anyone's surprise ever, the California penal system manipulated the numbers, and to their way of reckoning, they came up with me doing 4 ½ months in prison, instead of about one. How typical.

That night after court I got back to my cell block in time for dinner. I barely had time to call Lori and my folks to tell them how God and Jack Grimm had saved my bacon because I was constantly being hounded to tell and retell the story to other inmates. I had caught the early bus back to the jail, and later, when the other inmates got back from their court appearances they confirmed the miraculous events of that day in the Kern County Courthouse. Apparently my fellow inmates had concluded that I may not have been as crazy as they first perceived me to be, a few days before. Maybe God really did tell me something… Maybe God would really not only listen to their prayers but maybe help them like He had obviously helped me.

Myself and others from our little Bible study group of five did our best to explain through the Scriptures how much God really loved them and didn't want them in jail any more than they wanted to be here. We explained the ramifications of sin and our own choices and how the Lord intended for our lives to be different and promised to help us change, just as he had helped me and others. Some were let down when I couldn't give them a scriptural "get out of jail free" verse or two, and some fell away when I told of how God had personally required me to forgive those who had hurt me the worst, but even so, several inmates received Jesus as their Lord and Savior that very night and in the days and weeks to come. Some joined in hoping that the guards would see and give a good report of them, and some came with open hearts searching for hope in a forgiving God.

Regardless, many seeds were planted and the Gospel, the Good News, was preached to many with broken hearts and yearning souls. When I finally caught the chain about a month later, our little Bible study now had over 25 steady members.

Of all the greatest blessings that the Lord had bestowed upon me that day I went to court, none could compare to leading my cellmate, George, in receiving Jesus Christ as his personal Lord and Savior, after we had been locked down for the night. I prayed with George every day for weeks until I left, and pray for him, Armando, and George Embry still to this day, May God bless them.

Then one late night, about 1:30 in the morning, just as my friend Armando and so many others before me, I "rolled up" and "caught the chain" to Wasco State Prison – reception center for intake, classification, and diagnosis.

Before I left Lerdo jail, I was humbled to call Jack Grimm on his private line and try in vain to find the words of gratitude to properly thank him. He just laughed and told me to get my butt back to Nevada, where I belonged (Roger that). I told him that I was good for the 10 grand and he said, "I know you are, Johnny, you have never let me down and I'm proud to have been able to help you, son."

It was a good thing that I made that call when I could because Wasco had no inmate phones, so no calls, for the two months that I was there.

I was really worried about Calador, even though Lori's letters reassured me that she and Brandy were diligently making sure he ate a little something every day.

Wasco was massive, with 634 acres of concrete, chain-link and razor wire, some referred to it as "a city within a city." I didn't get it, but the place was huge, and compared with the last 7 ½ months I had just spent in that hellhole of a jail, Wasco was like a country club. Because I was "short" (soon to be released – short sentence), I was removed from the high risk profile I had, and placed in a minimum risk cellblock. That meant dormitory living instead of a cell (I actually preferred cell living), a small outdoor patio that I could access all day long (including real sunshine, air and everything!), A large yard with real grass and a "walking track", a cart full of books that came around twice a week, and best of all, commissary (a store)! A piece of Heaven was my way of looking at it.

There was no church, no religious books, and no Bibles, (they never let us bring our Bibles from jail – they would throw them away if you tried) but I could sit outside in the fresh air, read a Louis L'Amour cowboy book, smoke roll-your-own's and drink Folgers instant coffee all day long. With nothing else to do, I could finish a paperback Western in one day. A country club, all right… A country club that tolerated no drama at all from its occupants.

After spending over nine hours on the floor of a cell (overcrowding to the max) in reception, I and about 25 others were led into the main corridor of the facility, where we were made to stand naked in a line, at attention. At this time we had the "rules" explained (screamed into our faces) to us, as well as a clear and vivid understanding of what happens to those who violate Wasco's rules, including visual effects. Lining the walls of the corridor were "man – cages" that were similar but slightly smaller than an empty telephone booth. They had no glass like a phone booth but were constructed entirely of steel bars, with a drain in the floor. As I said, they were empty, meaning there was no seat or anything else in them and they were built narrow enough to where the occupants didn't have enough room to fold up their legs and body to allow them access to sit down on the floor. And every one of them was occupied by cons who had been stripped down, and by the look of many, had been "encased" in these cages for so long that they could no longer stand on their feet, so they just "slumped" against the bars as best they could.

Disrespecting the guards, in anyway, and fighting were the foremost activities you could partake in to guarantee your spot in one of the "man–cages", and I must say, this method of "correction" was very efficient in keeping the peace. I only saw two fights the entire time I was here, and never saw any guard disrespected. The penalties seemed understandably harsh as, it seemed that at least half of the guards were female and verbal abuse was rightfully dealt with quickly. As the sergeant concluded our "orientation" (threatening us), he yelled, "Do you understand the rules?" We all said, "Yes sir".

"Good. Then if you do not follow the rules you understand and accept your penalty?" He questioned.

A lone voice from a group of men at the far and of the corridor responded, "We're all 'violators', Sarge. If we could follow rules we wouldn't be here." He took a really hard hit in the stomach from a nightstick.

The flip side of this coin was that every day the showers, having no walls or curtains, would not be opened up for use until all of the female guards that chose to participate, lined up for "the show", with cat-calls, whoops and hollers included. Very humiliating and degrading, to say the least, as their remarks were always of the very cruel nature.

One day I paid another inmate "two fingers" of tobacco and one envelope to cut my now long and shaggy hair. This was done right next to the guard station where the scissors were issued to an inmate and never left the watchful eyes of one of the guards on duty. While sitting in a chair next to the wall, getting my haircut, I noticed a short message written on one of the bricks of the wall beside me. Written in light pencil lead as not to be noticed by passersby, it simply read, "If you need a Bible write to Kenneth Copeland Ministries, Fort Worth, Texas, 76192.

I remembered them from that "Believers Voice of Victory" magazine someone had placed on my bunk, in Lerdo. Nine days later I received my New King James Version Bible in the mail! It was specifically designed for Prison Outreach, with a message from Kenneth, and Stephen Morin's testimony (1951 – 1985, death row – Texas state Department of Corrections), and a vast study notes section that covered a multitude of subjects, verse by verse. Although having been "rebuilt", I still have and use this Bible today, as I have for the past 20 years. Thank you, "for remembering me in my chains," Kenneth Copeland Ministries! You, God, and Mike Barber were there when nobody else was. Well done.

Whenever the guards offered the opportunity to work, I took it. Especially outdoor work, such as shoveling, weed pulling, etc. as it felt so good to use my hands and muscles again, although I had gotten very "soft" and blistered easily.

My bunk was on the second tier, next to a 4" x 3' long vertical window that overlooked the big yard. To my delight, one day an outreach ministry set up their stage out on the yard and I watched as, every hour, Mike Barber Prison Ministries put on a modern musical presentation that defined the Gospel Message and our need for a Savior, as he led hundreds to give their lives to Jesus Christ! To this day, the biggest revival I have ever personally witnessed is going on behind prison walls, where broken men are being healed and restored by the love of a gracious and merciful God!

I pray this isn't the path you must take in order for God to reach your heart, but if it is, know that He will be there for you, with forgiveness, mercy, and open, loving arms.

Two months after entering Wasco, I "caught the chain" again to my mainline prison facility, in Coalinga. I understand, by the way, that this facility has been turned into a marijuana farm in 2016, after it was closed in 2011. Ironic is the fact that many of my fellow inmates at Coalinga were there for growing and selling pot. Different, I guess, when the government receives revenue from it, rieeeght?

It was probably California's smallest of prisons (about 500 inmates), especially compared to Pleasant Valley State prison (2308 inmates) just down the road. It was, however, big enough to have a formidable baseball team. Me being 6'1" tall and left-handed made first base one of my favorite places to be on the planet. I loved playing baseball. Try-outs for the team were just starting when I arrived at the prison, and until the 30 day lock down for new inmates had been completed (again, classification, psych evaluation, job assignment, and bed assignment upon availability) I was confined to cellblock "B" and couldn't even go outside to the small yard, let alone to the baseball field.

Even though an inmate was housed in "B" block, once he had completed classification, his new ID card would have a barcode on it instead of a red colored bar along the bottom of the card. This, when held up to the guard station, would allow him to go through the electronically locked door and into the outer yards, if the guards felt like opening the door for him at the time.

To be on that baseball team meant that I could travel around to other prisons and get out into the world a little bit. Sooo... I disassembled a plastic shaving razor and used the blade to carefully cut, shape and remove the white and black barcode from my deodorant stick and (perfectly, I must say) reinstall it on my ID card over the top of the red bar. When I held it up to the guard station above the electronic steel door, it opened and out I went!

It was tough, day after day, competing against guys half my age for that position, but "I can do all things through Christ who strengthens me", (Philippians 4:13) so by His Grace, I secured the position of the first baseman on a team called "the Paybacks".

May 6, 1997 was our first game against a team from neighboring Pleasant Valley prison and, as God's divine providence would have it, I got called into my counselor's office for final processing and classification an hour before the game began. I quickly changed into my long-sleeved "prison blues", buttoned my top button and shirt cuffs and hustled down the hallway of the prison offices. I had to pull the fake barcode off of my ID card as I went, as I would have to turn it in to get my new one with the real barcode on it.

My counselor was really great. He was an elderly Christian man who allowed me to plead with him to get an "outside" job (cleaning the yard before dawn) rather than washing pots and pans in the kitchen, as they had me scheduled for. Thank You, Jesus! It meant so much to me to be able to start my day outside on the yard, all alone, with my cup of coffee, my smoke, and my God as the dawning of a new day began. Yes, it's so true; sometimes it's the little things in life that matter the most.

By the time my final classification was over I was moving as fast as I could without catching a rubber bullet from the guard tower. I got to my bunk and peeled off my good clothes and changed into my regular stuff, T-shirt, jeans, and Bob Barker tennis shoes, then headed for the door. Two of my cellmates were telling me to get moving or I would be too late and they would give my position on the baseball team to someone else, if I wasn't there in six minutes, when the game started.

As I hurriedly came to a stop in front of the big steel door and the guard station above it, I held up my shiny new ID card. I heard the electric locks disengage as I put my ID card in my teeth while I tried to tuck in my shirttail. As the door began to open, and overwhelming feeling of grief and intense dread washed over me like a tidal wave. My legs started shaking and turned to rubber, my stomach began churning, and my peripheral vision disappeared as tunnel vision reduced my ability to see to only what was directly in front of my face. In seconds I didn't know if I was going to vomit or pass out, so I doubled over, turned around, and with sweat dripping off of my face I weakly made my way back to my bunk, where I flopped down, face first on the bed.

The guard was furious at me for the disrespect I had blatantly shown him by troubling him to open the door (push the button) and then not going through it, but instead turning around and walking away. The guard, in retaliation, locked down the cellblock, and turned off the TV and showers.

I had no clue what was wrong with me but I knew I was about to get a pretty bad beating from the raging inmates in "B" block. I remember seeing a tall slender black man standing in front of my bunk with two of the other white guys, trying to yell over the approaching inmates that were coming to pay me back for getting us lockdown, "He's sick – it's not his fault – something's wrong with him."

Suddenly, with earsplitting volume, every alarm in the prison went off, but I was divinely blessed to be on my bunk. As it is drilled into all inmates during orientation, every single man in the prison immediately hit the floor on their stomachs, wherever they were at. Seconds after the alarms go off, if you are in any type of upright position you would be shot, at best, with a rubber bullet, or clubbed down by guards or the "goon squad" (riot squad) as they came running through to deal with whatever situation had warranted the sounding of the alarms. This was particularly nasty if you happen to be in the shower or toilet facilities at the time, and wound up face down on the floor.

Just as suddenly, when the alarms went off, my head instantly cleared, the wretched pain in my belly stopped, my temperature dropped back to normal, and all the queasiness left my body!

As we were already locked down prior to the beginning of the May 6, 1997 prison riot at the Claremont Facility in Coalinga California, we were the only cellblock that was spared from the violence and chaos that day. To tell it truthfully, we didn't have a clue what was going on, other than there was a riot going on "somewhere". We heard yelling, screaming and shots, mostly sounding as if they were coming from out on the yard, and sometimes coming from just on the other side of the wall in the next cellblock. These were gang oriented prisons, for the most part. A Christian guard that befriended me later told me that the riot had "gone off" on the baseball field, when members of a rival gang on the Pleasant Valley baseball team, clashed with opposite gang members on our baseball team. In the frantic mayhem, everybody went to swinging on whoever, and the fighting spread quickly to all of the cellblocks, as Whites, Blacks and Hispanics segregated into groups to "protect their own". As soon as each group began to grow, it posed a threat to the other groups, and in a very few short minutes, the devil had men trying to kill each other that were, just moments before, playing volleyball, cards, handball and socializing together. They went at each other with several baseball bats, shives, shanks and fists.

It spread so fast that the regular guards locked themselves down and waited for the "goon squad" from Pleasant Valley prison to arrive and "restore order". It was a bloodbath... One that God's divine providence had spared me and all my cellmates in "B" block from being involved in, and many, if not most of the guys in B block realized it. Mostly in part to Preacher Mike. That's the name of that tall black guy, now laying on the floor beside my bunk, that had tried to stand with a white guy named Jeffers, and this old skinny guy named Ron (who, by his own admission, looked as if he had spent the best part of his life on the "Jenny crank diet plan") to defend me just before the alarms went off. The four of us had about 4 ½ hours to get acquainted, as we laid there not moving, until the guards finally said they could get up and go to their assigned bunks.

As the cafeteria workers were still locked down as we were, that evening they brought us sack lunches (mustard sandwiches and an apple) for dinner, and allowed us to use the tables in the commons area (without TV), as B block had no involvement in the riot. As I sat down at a table with my newfound friends to enjoy the cuisine, a man at the table next to ours looked over and said, "You're lucky that alarm went off when it did". Preacher Mike responded, "Really. Let's talk about that. I think you are the lucky ones. In fact, we are all blessed because of what this guy did; otherwise we wouldn't have been locked up, safe and sound, when things went off." He went on to ask how many men actually saw what had happened to me and several raised their hands or acknowledge that they had. One guy said, "I thought he was having a heart attack, or stroke or something," and several others agreed with him. Preacher Mike said, "Yes, I saw it too, and I'm here to tell you that what we saw was God's hand of protection on this guy, and on all of us because of him. If you can't admit that what you saw was a miracle then you're lyin' to yourself."

Man, this guy was good! Within about 10 minutes of witnessing he had a lot of men saying "Amen! Amen!" and after dinner, such as it was, he was praying with many of them to repent and receive Jesus as their Savior. There were several who prayed to recommit their lives to God and renounced their sins and backslidden ways!

We had a mini-revival happening in B block! Then, Preacher Mike goes to singing, "Amazing Grace" and a couple of really good songs that he himself had written, and gets over half of these guys singing and humming background and clapping their hands! I never saw anything like it!

> "This train is runnin', do-do do-doot.
> Yeah, from coast-to-coast, do-do do-doot.
> The conductors name, do-do do-doot.
> Is the Holy Ghost, do-do do-doot. (Larry "Preacher" Mike 1997)

I leaned over to Jeffers sitting next to me and said, "Wow! This is awesome!"

"I don't know about all that," he responded, "I just never was any good at staying out of other people's beatings," he said with a sarcastic smile. I knew I liked him right off – reminds me of someone I used to know…or be.

Old Ron, with a big grin and a cackle, reached over and patted Jeffers on the back with a sarcastically resounding "Hallelujah! Amen, brutha! Me too!"

I knew I was in good company.

Preacher Mike was really good at writing worship music. Better than most, as I think everybody in prison eventually tries their hand at songwriting, poetry, art, or different types of "sculpture", namely carving bars of soap or making super cool picture frames and stuff out of gum wrappers, etc. and a lot of what I've seen these men create is some of the best that I have ever seen. I have seen some of the most beautiful art work and sang worship songs that opened my heart. So many behind these walls are so amazingly gifted… Even though I tried I'm relatively sure I'm not included in that circle, however.

I opted for the more common "ballad" type of songwriting, as to vent my own personal pity party and forever immortalize my sad, sad, tale. As Mike's songs were fun to sing and spiritually inspiring, my song, my one and only song, was not.

But so that I may say with all honesty that I am a published songwriter (looks good on a resume), it is thus, forthcoming and published right here in this book.

## AN OUTLAWS PRAYER

I pray each day for forgiveness
For the outlaw I've become.
And curse each night for the loneliness
Of livin' on the run.

And the devil be damned
Cause I'm comin' home
Let 'em take me if they can.
And with my blood, I'll pay the price,
With the six-gun in my hand.

Chorus:
God who made the Heavens,
God will make it right,
It was God who gave your love to me,
To hold all through the night.

As the day turns into darkness,
Another long night settles in.
My soul cries out for deliverance.
From the torment locked within.

Instinct tells me I should run,
But desire rules my heart.
Baby I just can't take the pain,
Of them keeping us apart.

The Lord knows that I love Him,
And He knows I love you too,
And to hold you in my arms once more,
There's nothin' I won't do.

## JOHN GERGEN

**Chorus:**
**God who made the Heavens,**
**God will make it right,**
**It was God who gave your love to me,**
**To hold all through the night.**

**Well my love I held you,**
**Long into the night.**
**And with a broken heart I left you,**
**As darkness turned to light.**

**The laws of God I live by,**
**But I broke the laws of man.**
**Soon the law caught up with me,**
**With its cold and vengeful hand.**

**Chorus:**

**Now prison walls surround me,**
**As I long to be with you.**
**Memories haunt my days and nights,**
**But the Lord will see me through.**

**I'm sorry for the things I did,**
**I'm sorry for the pain,**
**But time will pass by the grace of God,**
**And our souls will join again.**

**Baby I know your waitin',**
**I know that you'll be true,**
**Cause soulmates are forever,**
**And my heart belongs to you.**

**Chorus:**

**I'm comin' home----**
**Baby, I'm comin' home---**

**A song, written by John Gergen, June, 1997**

Kinda lengthy, I know, but I had the time (chuckle, chuckle).

And it's okay if you don't like it, as it should be a comfort that it's the only and final attempt I have made to contribute to the music industry... Still though... A published songwriter, none the less!

AND, a published Artist, as well!

Baahahahahaha!

**There you have it!**

## CHAPTER 45

## Free Indeed

*"You believe that there is one God. You do well. Even the demons believe – and tremble!"*
James 2:19.

Music has always calmed the beast inside of mankind (1 Samuel 16:14-23, Psalms 1 – 150). Above all, in calming and comforting the troubled and anxious souls of men (and women), are songs written from the heart, by those who have been where we have been, and experienced the similar emotional ups and downs of life, as are the Psalms (songs) found in the center of the Bible. These types of songs help us to cope with life as well as celebrate it. They allow us to semi-sanely get in our cars, merge with the cluster, and navigate the highways, byways, and bumper-to-bumper streets and roads of this land during rush hour, to some extent, anyway.

Knowing this, I can't wait to hear the music in Heaven! There, in Heaven, I will finally be able to "lift my voice on high" singing praise to my King at the top of my lungs. Here on earth that's not an option. If I did, churches would no doubt take up a collection to pay me not to sing, because I sing like a crow. God will fix that when I get to Heaven, of that I have no doubt... No way is He going to put up with my current singing ability. I believe that's the reason that, God in his mercy, blessed me with a singing wife whose beautiful voice fills the air of our home every day and keeps me calm (for the most part) and grounded (kinda... Sorta... Maybe... To some extent, anyway). Truthfully, her singing sooths my soul, and I am so blessed by it.

I have also learned a little secret over the years, that to change the song she is currently whistling or singing, I need only to sing a few lines or whistle a few bars, and Wa-Lah!

*Note: definithing.com defines "Wa-Lah" as "Viola" for idiots. "Viola" is French for "look here" and they go on to explain that people who are clueless sometimes say or spell it "Wa-Lah" because the French do not pronounce the "V". My thoughts are, then why the heck did you put a "V" in it, in the first place, if you're not going to use it? Duh!

I remember one time in the early 80s at the Depression Delicatessen on Fourth Street in Reno, Lori and her bluegrass band were performing up on the stage. She always made it a point to sing my favorite song, "Fire on the Mountain" (Marshall Tucker band, etc.) with the most awesome mandolin and banjo accompaniment you could ever imagine. That night, standing at the bar next to me was this old bowlegged cowboy who leaned over to me as he stared at my beautiful wife up on that stage, and respectfully said, very matter-of-factly, "I'd drink her bathwater". I thought about it for a second and said, "Me too, pard". Probably the greatest compliment ever that a man could receive in regard to his wife, to my way of thinking. And, "She is absolutely hotter than a blow dryer on disco night", I heard another man say.

And dance? Man o' man could she dance! But like my singing, I just tried not to embarrass her too much, even though it seemed at times, the more I drank the better I got (or, depending on whose perspective you viewed it from, the bigger fool I made myself). Another prime example of why I don't need to drink anymore.

Meanwhile, back at the ranch, or prison, as the case may be, I was delighted to find that church services were held twice a week in a conference room in the main building. Although there was rarely a speaker or pastor from the outside to conduct the services, the inmates who presided over the gathering were some of the best Holy Spirit filled church leaders I have ever had the privilege to be ministered to… by…from… Whatever. They had a sincerity that cannot be understood by someone who hasn't been broken by the Lord, in order to receive divine deliverance and healing and be "fixed" (please see the Potter and the Clay, Jeremiah 18:1-11). And there was no "sugarcoating, whitewashing, or watering down" the Gospel Message and the need for repentance that they delivered, as they were living the reality of it. It was "the real deal" according to their personal experiences with their Creator. To put it in simpler terms, it was the difference between knowing the Word of God, and personally knowing the God of the Word. I actually miss those Holy Ghost filled meetings, as crazy as it sounds. They were real to me, full of encouragement in the faith and edification through the Word, without the presence of "religion" or judgment, if you can understand what I'm trying to say.

Similar to Wasco, this prison was dorm type living for me. One of the byproducts of a prison riot is that it opens up a lot of vacancies in a very short amount of time. So much that me and all my new friends from B block received our new bunk assignments within the next two days. The inmate next to my bunk was a young kid from Vietnam and the bunk across the walkway from me was an Apache Indian, I believe from a town called White River, Arizona on the Fort Apache reservation, if I recall correctly. Both were decent young men and soon became curious as to what the Bible says, as I was constantly reading it all the time. On the other side of the concrete petition that my bunk was up against was a man named Mike W who was very strong in the Word and would often help me to answer my two young Bunkie's questions, which came more and more frequently as time passed. I enjoyed helping them find their answers and I was getting pretty good at presenting and explaining the Gospel Message and really looked forward to telling others about the miracles God had recently orchestrated in my life. The latter, combined with showing them in the

Scriptures that God wasn't mad at them, seemed to give the most hope to those who previously had none.

I would tell them that God doesn't want them in here anymore than they want to be here, but there are consequences for sin, and left unchecked, this is a very popular way, to my way of reasoning, for God to put us in "timeout" so He can have our full attention. And don't worry, I would tell them; if this timeout session didn't do the trick then there's always the next one, however, I have noticed that they always get a little longer each time, and time isn't what we have a lot of to be wasting. Life is short.

We all definitely need to make better decisions and that's what the Lord and His Word are here to help us with. In essence, we have all based our decisions on what the world says is right and acceptable instead of what the Lord says is right and wrong, in His Word. By making the Bible the foundation of all our decisions, we don't have to do this entire prison thing ever again. I emphasized that God didn't give us a book of rules because He didn't want us to have any fun, He gave us the Rules because we have an enemy pretty much running things on earth and that punk devil has come to "steal, kill and destroy" our lives (John 10:10). The rules are meant to keep us from wrecks, and Jesus came to give us an abundant life, here and in eternity as well, by paying the full price for our sins, with His own blood, instead of our own as we justly deserved.

Sometime after midnight, on the first of June, I was awakened by what I thought at first was the low growl of an animal. As I lied there and became more aware of my surroundings, I recognized the deep growling sound was coming from Sonny, my young Indian neighbor across the way from me. In the dim light it seemed like he might just be having a nightmare, until snarled words began to form and the low growling noise he was emitting turned less and less human in nature.

This can't be good.

Hoping the guards didn't see me, I dressed and crept over to Sonny's bunk. He was lying on his back with his eyes open but his eyeballs were rolled back in his head. His mouth was slightly open and the sounds and some words, "hate you", "rotten flesh" and "own you", came out of him but his lips didn't move.

This can't be real. I can't handle this. It shook me to the core.

I turned to sneak back to my bunk, then for whatever ridiculous reason, I turned back to him, put my hand on his shoulder and shook him; "Wake up, Sonny". Then it happened.

His eyes rolled back to their proper place, his mouth closed and he woke up… No head spinning, no levitation, no freaking out…

"What's up?" He said.

"You okay?" I asked him.

"Yeah", he answered, "and you?" He whispered.

"I'm good," I said, and sat down on the floor against the concrete petition beside his bunk so the guards wouldn't see me. We just sat there in the dim light as I rolled a smoke, and cupped my lighter so the flash wouldn't be detected when I lit it up. I took a long draw with the ciggy cupped in my hands as to hide the glow, then handed it to Sonny. He likewise took a couple of puffs then, when he handed it back, I asked, "What the hell was that I just saw?"

"Did it speak?" He asked.

"Yeah" I responded in a whisper.

"What did it say?" Sonny asked me.

"Nothin' good" I told him.

"I think it wants to kill me. Did it say it was gonna kill me?" He asked.

"No," I told him as I realized that this was surely the creepiest conversation I had ever had in my life.

"Is it a demon?" Sonny asked, but I think he already knew the answer.

"Well, it ain't from God, for sure, and it ain't you, so… Yeah."

Even in the dim light I could see excessive moisture forming in his upturned eyes.

"We'll figure this out, Sonny. I'll help you get through this, okay?"

The night guard would be doing his walk-through at any time. "I better go. Are you okay for a bit?" I asked.

"Yeah, sure. I'll be fine. Talk to you in the morning."

I started to move when he reached out and grabbed my elbow. I stopped and looked back at him.

"Thanks." Sonny told me.

"No sweat," I smiled at him then went back to bed and prayed hard for him. I prayed equally as hard for God to tell me what to do and show me how to help him. The book, "Bondage Breaker" (Neil T Anderson) had given me a lot of insight into these matters but it's different when you're facing the real thing for the first time, and not just reading about it. There had to be a "right way" to help Sonny, I just had to find it.

At 4:15 that morning I heated my coffee in the microwave and scurried through the open door and out onto the yard for my morning ritual of time with God before I started cleaning the place up. Surprisingly the night guard didn't mess with the door by starting to close it early to make me move a little faster, as was our custom. In fact as I squatted by the west wall and lit my smoke I noticed that he hadn't closed the door at all. As I watched he came walking through it and made his way over to where I was.

"What is Sonny having trouble again?" He pointedly asked.

"Some," I responded, still a little surprised.

"I can put him in solitary" he stated.

"I can't help him if he's in solitary," I answered.

"Maybe you can, and maybe not. I saw what happened to you just before the riot, so maybe you can, with the Lord helping you the way He does," and he ended with "we'll see," then he turned and started to walk away.

"If you fire up another cigarette in my block again, you'll be the one in solitary," he said over his shoulder as he walked away.

Dang.

"I think he's a good man, Lord," I mused with a smile, as he shut the cellblock door behind himself, "so go ahead and bless him on my behalf, for not busting me."

I knew James 4:7 says *"Submit therefore to God, resist the devil and he will flee from you."*

Considering all that I had experienced in the last year or so, I also knew that trying to resist the devil without first submitting to God always results in a vicious dog fight. And like me, if Sonny doesn't come to know who he really is in Christ, he would have no ground to stand on in his battle with the powers of darkness. So, first things first, I reasoned.

Then we better be figuring out, with prayers for God to reveal it to us, is what spiritual doors he has opened to allow this creature of darkness to gain such access into his life, just as I had done. And also as with me, we would have to go through the process of confessing, repenting, seeking forgiveness and renouncing each one of these things in order to "close the doors and clean the house," so to speak.

After breakfast Sonny and I sat down and I started off by repeating something I had read that Neil Anderson had said; "Demons are like cockroaches. They scurry around in the dark, but when the light of God's truth shines, they run for cover" (see John 1:1-9, John 8:12, John 3:18-21). I went on with, I promise you Sonny, that Jesus has this covered and He is gonna set you free. He came to "destroy the works of the devil," and I showed him 1 John 3:8. I told him that "we are going to do a lot of praying together and submit to God every part of our lives so he can show us the parts we need to address and the people we need to forgive. Are you okay with that?"

He thought about it, and then said, "Yes. I'm ready. I should have done this a long time ago, but I don't know how to pray."

And that's where we began.

We prayed for God to open up the Scriptures to him and reveal who he really is in Christ, his real identity, as we studied the New Testament together.

Then we prayed for God to reveal where and what events had allowed the demon access to his life. As we went over certain Scriptures that uncovered specific areas of sin and idolatry of things forbidden (in this case, 1 Timothy 4:1) by God, we encountered "resistance". His eyes would become cloudy, he would start sweating and fidgeting, then find an excuse to get up and go somewhere, i.e., bathroom, wash hands, have a smoke, etc. We had undoubtedly found at least two incidents in his life that the dark ones (possibly two) had gained entry.

When I started reading Ephesians chapter 1 and praying the prayer in verses 17-23 over him, he up and bolted out into the yard.

Mike W was just getting off work when Sonny took off right past him, and came over to ask about him. I told him what was happening and he said he would help, as he had substantial experience in the area of deliverance, thank God! I was starting to get a little frazzled, myself. After that, Mike W, Preacher Mike, Sonny and I would study/counsel together, but Mike W and Preacher Mike both insisted that I lead in the formatting and laying out the necessary Scriptures and prayers. Both "Mike's" agreed that it was for my "edification" as they felt that God was clearly leading and schooling me in the Ministry of deliverance, or I never would have been allowed by the Lord this far into this situation. They said it was rare to be called into this. I was thinking this is going beyond being "nuts", let alone beyond my ability to handle, even though they were guiding me.

They instructed me to show Sonny that, *"whoever is born of God does not sin; but he who has been born of God keeps himself, and the wicked one does not touch him"*, as John 1:12, 1 John 5:4-5, and 1 John 5:18, clearly state. Upon revealing this to him I said, "That's you Sonny! You can tell that old devil 'I am a child of God. The evil one cannot touch me!"

Poof! He couldn't say it! He up and bolted again. I felt that I was making a mess of this.

"Duh! The cart is ahead of the horse," I explained to my colleagues in Christ.

When Sonny came back after dinner, I shifted gears and went back to the basic Good News of Salvation through Jesus Christ, and had Mike W pray with me and we bound the demons to silence so they would stop talking to Sonny.

Just before bedtime, Sonny prayed out loud and confessed his need for a Savior because of his sins, and gave his life to his Lord and Savior Jesus Christ! Hallelujah!

Before we turned in I asked him again to declare out loud that, "I am a child of God and the wicked one cannot touch me!", and he did! And with a big victorious smile, he kept saying it over and over.

Mike W, Preacher Mike and I anointed Sonny with oil, laid our hands on him in a prayer of agreement, and in the Mighty Name of Jesus, I commanded the demons to come out of Sonny, and my friend was immediately set free! I had never even imagined anything like it. With the Holy Spirit now indwelling in Sonny's heart, it was a done deal. An "inside job" if you will!

I spent part of everyday was Sonny, reaffirming his loving relationship with God through the Scriptures, and praying through difficult areas in his past, as one by one, doors were closed, repentance, forgiveness, and renouncement's were accomplished and our Heavenly Father's love, grace and mercy flooded into my friend's life, bringing the true freedom that only deliverance can attain.

*"Then Jesus said to those Jews who believed in him, "If you abide in My word, you are My disciples indeed. And you shall know the truth, and the truth shall make you free."... Jesus answered them, "most assuredly, I say to you,*

*whoever commits sin is a slave of sin. And a slave does not abide in the house forever, but a son abides forever. Therefore if the Son makes you free, you shall be free indeed."* John 8:31-32, 34-36. Yes, free indeed!

***

On his birthday, June 8, 1997, I was blessed to minister to my very own brother Bill, over a prison phone, as he received his Salvation, gifted to him by his Lord and Savior Jesus Christ. What an honor and privilege for me! Thank You, my awesome Lord!

I know he's a little rough around the edges, Lord, but I know he will "polish up" real good!

Funny how that works!

***

On June 29, 1997, by the mercy and providence of my Master, I have rolled up and was released from prison. No more Menudo. No more "mystery" meat.

And yet, even to this day, I occasionally mix up a cup of instant coffee, in the quiet times, to spend a little time with God and remind myself of the pre-dawn mornings on the yard and where my Lord saved me from.

## CHAPTER 46

### No Greater Feeling

*"Thus says the Lord: In an acceptable time I have heard You,*
*And in the day of salvation I have helped You;*
*I will preserve You and give You*
*As a covenant to the people,*
*To restore the earth,*
*To cause them to inherit the desolate heritages;*
*That You may say to the prisoners,*
*'Go forth'*
*To those who are in darkness,*
*'Show your selves'"*
Isaiah 49:8-9

Lori had sent in my street clothes for my release but they apparently got lost in the mail. I found a pair of sweat shorts and a T-shirt in "personal lost and found" that was good enough to get me through the doors. It definitely wasn't what Lori, Dad and Brandy were expecting or looking for, as they would look right past me through the window at the other end of the sally port while I underwent final processing. My hair was over my shoulders and down my back and my beard, which I had never had before, was long enough to touch my chest. There were no glass mirrors in prison and the old stainless steel plates above the sinks in my block were so old and scratched up that you couldn't see anywhere close enough to properly shave, so with no one to impress, I had just let it go. Or at least, that's the story that I was sticking to. And then there was the fact that I was 50 pounds heavier... No comment.

The shock was real when they finally opened the last door and my family realized it was me stepping out to greet them! I thought it was funny, and they were aghast.

For me, it was the absolute greatest feeling in the world, bar none. To be in the company of those who love us is something that should never be taken for granted. I thought of many things I needed to say when this day finally arrived; "I am so sorry for putting you all through this", "Please forgive me for my selfishness that caused all this pain that I have put you through," etc., etc. I even rehearsed many of them, but when I saw them, and when I hugged them, particularly my daughter, I choked up and came out with, "Well, that was fun."

I was definitely a "changed man" and the ride back to Bakersfield was somewhat awkward for all of us. We had to go to the parole office in Bakersfield to pick up my "interstate compact" that I and my counselor had put in for over two months ago. It is what would allow me to cross the state line and go back home to Nevada.

We arrived at P&P (parole and probation department) at 11:20 a.m. and were taken to the office of the parole officer who was handling my case. Before I could even get a few words out the officer rudely cut me off and said, "You're not going anywhere. There is no interstate compact for you, convict. What you're going to do for the next three years is move into the homeless shelter downtown and do dishes to earn your keep. I'm here to see to it, and make you wish you were back in the joint, where you belong." He insulted my father when he tried to speak, and had Brandy on the verge of tears, all the while making it obvious with his contemptuous smile that he was enjoying himself.

"So you can go say goodbye to your little friends here, and then have your butt back here after lunch to get your bed number and your job assignment. For the next three years, I own you, pal, you got that?"

Yeah, well... That definitely isn't from God... That's an attack of the evil one.

We were totally devastated, and with nowhere to go we pulled into a motel and got a room. I had no idea if this was the work of that ungodly judge, someone else, or the devil himself, but trying to survive in the very heart of the impious judicial system that had done its best to destroy me, was unimaginable. Daniel in the lion's den came to mind, but the difference between one night and three years was very significant, from my standpoint.

We needed to cry out to God and I hoped that my family could handle the new me.

"Listen, I know this is a terrible thing that's come against us, but I need all of you to just please help me pray. I know I sound a little crazy but just bear with me. Let's all of us just kneel down by the edge of the bed and agree in prayer that we need our Heavenly Father to intercede in this thing, on our behalf."

They took it fairly well... Sort of. It felt clumsy and very inelegant as we knelt and joined hands to pray together for the first time in our lives. But once I started, the words came easily (bless You and thank You, Holy Spirit!) and our prayer for deliverance from this present evil affliction just seemed to flow with Scripture and ended asking God to forgive and put a new heart into my new parole officer. I asked them to agree in the name of Jesus, and we all felt quite a bit less terrorized by the situation, when we had finished.

Dad said Jack Grimm had asked to be notified when they had me back home, so Dad called Jack and we stepped outside so I could have a cigarette. I told Lori and Brandy that I was sure God wouldn't let us down, but if God wanted me in that homeless shelter, then it's all good (Romans 8:28). I knew He hadn't brought me this far without a purpose and a plan.

When we got back to P&P at 1 o'clock the secretary lead us back to the same office, but this time there was a different person at the desk. As we entered the room Dad sneezed, and without looking up from my paperwork, the guy said, "God bless you". In perfect unison, we all raised our eyebrows and looked at one another. It was funny and I know God giggled. He looked up at us, then said to me, "I have no idea what has held up your interstate compact. It should have been done a month ago. I'll have to reapply for it, but the bad news is that it will take about 30 days." As he spoke, the secretary came in and handed him a piece of paper. He read it then said, "This fax from Grimm Oil Company says you have at least 30 days work for them, sampling and evaluating a mine in Mariposa, is that right?"

You could've knocked us all over with a feather. Except maybe my Dad; he was just standing there, grinning. He told us the other parole officer had been called away to Fresno, very suddenly, and that he would now see to my case, himself.

THAT'S THE POWER OF PRAYER, and JESUS IS LORD! No one can ever tell us different... Not ever.

We had to check in with the parole department in Merced and they said they would call us when my interstate compact went through. From there it was up into the Sierra Nevada Mountains to Mariposa. Lori, Dad and Brandy left me at the Miners Inn to look for a place to rent for a month while they went to Mongo's place in Fallon, to get my truck for me. It was there that a wonderful lady named Kathy C introduced me to my 1st cup of real "Americana" coffee.

I was setting at a table in the restaurant drinking coffee and looking through newspapers for some place to rent. I know a lot of this stuff sounds pretty weird, but sometimes things get somewhat bizarre when you totally submit to God and let Him call the shots in your life. That said, every now and then I would look up from the papers and noticed this stately looking lady with her arms folded, practically staring at me from behind the counter.

She probably thinks I'm a bum, by the look of me, and she's contemplating throwing me out, as she is undoubtedly a person of high influence in this establishment. I tried to ignore her gaze. Then she walked over to this odd looking machine on the back counter, poured 2 cups of something, and carried them over to my table. She set one of the cups of Heavenly smelling coffee down in front of me and asked if she might join me. When she sat down directly across from me, with a warm smile and a distinctive twinkle in her eyes, she introduced herself as the manager of the Miners Inn. Out of embarrassment for my former place of residence, I simply responded with my name.

"Try this", she said, nodding to the cup of coffee she had set before me, "I have a feeling that you'll like it."

Coo –Coo –Ka –Choo, I'm thinking.

What was going on, I had no clue, but the term "strange" didn't begin to cover it. As I picked up the cup the aroma of its contents was captivating. Just as I took a gentle sip of this Heavenly brew, she said, in more of a statement of fact, than a question, "God sent you here, didn't He?" I all but spit coffee all over the table.

She never even flinched; she just broadened her smile little. "I thought so," she said, as I inadvertently gave validation to her claim.

So God evidently takes great amusement in blowing my mind... Okay... Now that we've established that...

Divine Providence is so far beyond amazing, it is... Astonishingly miraculous! (Biggest words I could think of).

Looking back, I guess that my spirit witnessed with her spirit, or something of that nature, because I felt I could relax around her, like I could one of my old friends. She made some suggestions in helping me find a short-term apartment, and also told me that most apartment complexes probably would not consider renting one out for just a month or two.

She was right. All of them that I called wanted at least a six month lease agreement with first and last months' rent up front and a large security or cleaning deposit, and I couldn't afford to stay in the motel more than two more nights.

The next day when Lori, Brandy and Dad showed back up with my truck, we went looking at everything from camp trailers and garages to small houses and apartments but most were taken by the time we got there, or wanted more than I could pay.

The next morning Lori, Dad and my daughter headed back to Nevada. I checked out of the motel, loaded what little stuff I had in my pickup, and went over to the restaurant to have coffee. Everything seemed better over a cup of Americana.

I confided in Kathy that after praying for the Lord to guide me, I had found several nice apartments in good neighborhoods, one even right next door to the church that I felt sure the Lord was providing for me but none of them panned out. I also confessed that my funds were limited and that I had recently been released from prison so if the parole and probation people found out I was living in my truck, I would "violate" and go back to prison. I was bewildered, to say the least. She reached across the table, and taking my hands, prayed for God to show me where He had already arranged for me to live, and we agreed in His Name.

After a few moments of silence she said she remembered one more place a few miles down in the canyon, towards Yosemite, about halfway to the Merced River, but she also stated that "it ain't nothin' nice".

An hour later I made a left turn off of Highway 140 onto a side road, and then made a right turn by an old sign that said "Bear Creek Cabins". As I crossed the old one lane wooden bridge that brought me into a dirt parking lot, I slammed on my brakes as two young (around four years old) stark naked kids ran screaming in front of my truck. More accurate, the first naked kid was screaming as he ran as fast as he could from the second naked kid that was chasing him with a long stick, about 10 feet behind him. In a flash they disappeared around the corner of the building to my right, and as the small dust clouds settled that their little feet had raised up in passing, it was like, "Yeah, this is it. This definitely looks more like the Lord's doing."

I found an old "office" sign in a window to my left and a heavyset young mother with a baby on her hip gave me directions to the "recently vacated" (as in, police raid, style) small apartment that her husband was working on at this very moment. Parking my truck under a huge pine tree, I climbed up the old broken, sagging concrete steps, across the 20 foot piece of sidewalk, and knocked on the open door jam. What was left of the front door was lying strewn about the place in pieces, as it had surely been broken down with a police RAM.

The landlord, a man in his mid-30s, 6 feet tall with very long hair, shirtless and weighing all of 85 or 90 pounds, came to the door and standing in the middle of a huge blood stain on the carpet, asked me, "Well, you still interested?"

"Does it come with the front door?" I countered.

"Yeah, it does, but it won't be ready till tonight. You got cash?" He inquired.

"Yup. My name is John," and I held out my hand. He took it and as we shook hands he said with a smile, "I'm so-and-so, and I don't care what your name is as long as you got cash money."

It was just starting to get dark when I returned to my new "penthouse suite". From what I could tell, the only piece of sidewalk in the vicinity was in front of my door which explains why I had to step over a couple of partially disassembled bicycles to get to my humble abode. The apparent "head mechanic" was a long-haired, shirtless skinny kid of about 12 or 13 years, who took only a brief moment to look up from his work, eyeball me up and down once, then returned to his project. And it appeared that when the sun goes down on these apartment complexes, the party starts. Loud music and revelry were abundant, both inside and outside of several units. How nice.

The new (very old, used) door stood open on its shiny new hinges as I walked into the room and stopped a few feet behind a man on his knees with his back to me. He kneed the carpet that he was laying tightly against the wall and nailed it down. He sat upright and with his back still to me, he chuckled, and in a voice that sounded just like Dracula or the count on Sesame Street, said, "Ah, so you're a Christian."

"Ah, for the love of God," I thought to myself. "Can't I just go to sleep somewhere? I'm tired and all this eerie macabre stuff You keep popping on me may be hilarious to You, Lord, but it's starting to get a little spooky for me. What now?" As the thought culminated it flew out of my mind, not at the men before me, but precisely aimed at God, whose smile I now realize, I had learned to "see" and recognize. Along with this newfound epiphany I was having, came the comprehension that I, of all people, held the ability to make God smile! Knowing this bit of wisdom led down some very zany trails in the years that followed, and to this very moment, I still wake up some days hitting the floor with my feet, and declaring "No matter what, Lord, today I'm gonna find a way to make you laugh." Everyone should try it, just to see how wacky a day can really get.

Joe was his name and he was a veteran Soldier of the Cross. He was a Czechoslovakian who had spent most of his career in the service of Her Majesty, Queen Elizabeth, as one of her personal bodyguards. After the Queens 1983 visit to the RMS Queen Mary, permanently anchored in Long Beach, California, as they boarded the airplane for their return trip home to England, Joe heard the Lord distinctly tell him that he could not return with the Queen, that he loved and served, back to their home in the United Kingdom. He was crushed, but obeyed and after saying his farewell, he turned away from the airplane and just started walking… until he reached Mariposa where, until the Lord directs him further, is currently his home. Although he owns the local antique bookstore, he works at various construction and handyman jobs, as the Lord sees fit. He does not ever wear a watch as he refuses to be bound by time. He became my counselor and one of my greatest mentors, leading me into the great depths of the Scriptures and the comprehension of the spiritual laws that govern not only our physical world, but also transcend into the spiritual realm as well.

Humbling was the realization that if I spent every day of my earthly life prayerfully studying the spiritual laws of God, found in the Bible, I would barely be able to scratch the surface of all we will come to know when we are finally at home with our Heavenly Father. What I do know for sure, is that we are going to be profusely astounded and lavishly amazed.

My next trip to town for mail, supplies and Americana found Kathy very frazzled. She had been at the Inn since the wee hours of the morning, cleaning up after what she called a "disturbance". The evening cook and a dishwasher had quit as a result, and she mentioned something about a flying fire extinguisher. To me, it was starting to sound like a bar fight that started in the kitchen, but I was very wrong.

She led me to the back office and showed me the security camera footage from the night before, just after closing time. The cook was singing "Lord I Lift Your Name on High", a popular Christian song, as he moved about the kitchen doing his end of shift work. The dishwasher loudly began singing, "highway to hell" in order to tease the cook, who in turn increased his volume by several decibels, to which the dishwasher responded to, in-kind. Both men were obviously taking it all in good humor as the cook stopped in the middle of the floor, raised his hands to Heaven and instituted another verse of his favorite worship song in his loudest voice. The next part we played and replayed at least a dozen times, mostly in slow motion.

As the cook stood there presenting his best opera voice, a fire extinguisher that hung on the wall about 15 feet away, "tore itself" off of the wall, bracket and all. It flew across the room and hit the cook in the stomach with such force that it drove him backwards through the double swinging doors that lead into the restaurant, past the counter and finally crashing backwards to a stop into a table set.

I asked to examine the fire extinguisher, which I found completely intact, and unused. I struggled to believe what I was seeing.

Claiming it to be a ghost, and the Inn to be haunted, both men quit. Kathy and I both knew it was no Casper. We knew beyond any doubt that it was a demon.

She showed me other security camera videos from the past several months that showed several other "incidents" including three where the thing seemed to manifest itself on or up through the small dance floor in the bar area, long after closing. These last three were the only ones where you could detect, or "see" its presence, which was akin to a dark vapor maybe like a tall patch of dark, transparent smoke.

It made my skin crawl, and I felt like running out the door, just looking at the security videos. Kathy let me into the bar, now closed for the morning, before she went back to work. I went in and sat down alone at a table, to just see if I could "feel" anything. All I felt after about 10 minutes was the same "ebby-jeebbies" I had before I entered the bar room. This was way too creepy for me, and I started feeling like that really stupid person in all the horror flicks that goes snooping around in dark places with a dim flashlight, asking to be eaten/bitten/attacked/murdered or whatever.

Before I left I walked out on the dance floor and stood there in the silence for about a minute. As best as I can describe it, I felt a deep sense of dread…probably from realizing I was moronic enough to stand here in the first place…yet, the feeling seemed to have substance to it, kind of "chilling", as it were, so when the edginess began to overwhelm me I left and went back to my happy little apartment. This was all way too much for me to deal with. I just want to go home to my family and get on with my life. Yes, I was afraid. Ironically, one thing for certain that occurred to me was how useless my guns would be in comforting me now. Regardless of how good I once was with them, they had been my source of (false) security my whole life, but their ineffectiveness in the battles that really matter in a person's life, had now become blatantly clear.

*"For the weapons of our warfare are not carnal but mighty in God for pulling down strongholds"* 2 Corinthians 10:4.

## CHAPTER 47

## Guns for a Sword

*"Finally, my brethren, be strong in the Lord and the power of His might. Put on the whole armor of God, that you may be able to stand against the wiles of the devil. For we do not wrestle against flesh and blood, but against principalities, against powers, against the rulers of the darkness of this age, against spiritual hosts of wickedness in the Heavenly places.*
*Therefore take up the whole armor of God, that you may be able to withstand in the evil day, and having done all, to stand.*
*Stand therefore, having girded your waist with truth, having put on the breastplate of righteousness, and having shod your feet with the preparation of the gospel of peace; above all, taking the shield of faith with which you will be able to quench all the fiery darts of the wicked one.*
*And take the helmet of salvation, and the sword of the Spirit, which is the Word of God;"*
Ephesians 6:10-17.

In the weeks to come, I tried to submerge myself in my studies, yet every subject I delved into always gently carried me back to the same spiritual laws and the use of our spiritual weapons (see, Weapons of Mass Instruction – Appendix P). Joyce Meyers currently has written a book called "Battlefield of the Mind" that I have found instrumental in gaining deliverance on a personal level, as with my friend Sonny, but this thing at the Inn wasn't "in" anybody, it was running around loose. As totally inapt as I felt myself to be concerning this phenomenon and finding the whole concept extremely perplexing, I still couldn't put it down.

In my frustration, one afternoon, I said, "Gee Lord, maybe if I go in waving a dead cat and a chicken's foot or two, I could run it off like that. What do You say?" As if slugged in the heart, I immediately felt a deep conviction and apologized, the Lord then putting it on my heart that this was serious. Again, I felt fear.

Afterward, for three days and nights the Lord taught me, armed me for battle, and instilled within me the skill to wield my sword of the Spirit. At times the Word would fill me with such confidence in His power that I would get up, put on my long coat and declare, "I'm ready! Let's go, Lord, and get it over with," and another time, "Let's do the deed, Lord! I'm really ready." Somehow putting on my long coat always made me feel cocky, as I usually adorned it to conceal my Mossberg 12gauge pump sawed-off shotgun, even though that was no longer the case…but it still felt good to put it on.

But, case in point; you're not ready until God says you are ready. I would sometimes head for the door, only to turn back around for something, and find myself sitting in my chair at my small kitchen table, several hours later, staring into my Bible.

On July 19, 1997, in full preparation of the Lord, I stepped out of the door of my apartment and drove to town, brandishing my Sword (the Word of God), a small bottle of oil, and the Anointing of the Holy Spirit that gave me the power and the authority to use them, in the Name of my Master, Jesus Christ.

The young boy I had met working on his bike the night that I moved in, was sitting out in front of my unit where we had spent many evenings talking about "things" pertaining to our Heavenly Father. He looked up at me and said, "What's going on? You look like you're gonna go kill somebody."

Taken aback by his comment I smiled back at him and told him, "It's all good, son. I just got a little business for the Lord to tend to." This kid was coming up the hard way and it surprised me when he got up and gave me a quick hug.

"See ya later, okay?" He asked.

"Yup!" I confirmed and climbed into my big black truck and built a fire in that 427 engine. I was tingling, and the anointing I felt inside of me left absolutely no room for fear. I had it in me, and I had it on me. It surged throughout my being and seemed to emanate from me. God was using me; ME! Hallelujah!

I felt as if I was God's "man of power for the hour," and best of all, my full confidence that what I was experiencing was in Him, not me. I'm just the "delivery boy," so to speak! There was no doubt of victory. I knew that with the Creator of the Universe upholding me, there was nothing that could defeat me. I stated earlier that getting out of prison was the best feeling in the world, which it surely was, but this… This was Divine. I was "cloud walking" and God was with me. How can it get better than that?

As I drove the dark winding road up through the mountains I sang songs to the Lord and was filled with such joy that I laughed, whooped and hollered, giving praise and all glory to God!

Once I arrived, Kathy met me and we prayerfully "cleansed" and anointed each room, starting in the back at the offices and working our way all the way through the building and ending up in the bar. The bartender was trying to wake up the only patron, a very intoxicated customer at the bar, and when we walked into the room the intoxicated individual sat bolt upright as if he had been slapped awake. With eyes wide and profusely blinking he looked at me, looked around the room, then scrambled for the door leading to the parking lot! When the bartender looked at her in amazement, Kathy just nodded toward the front door and the bar keeper disappeared as well, through the last and only doorway we had not anointed with oil…yet.

We went directly to the center of the dance floor.

"In the Name of Jesus we 'plead the blood 'over this place and claimed it all for Christ. "We bind you, spirit of darkness, to absolute silence and command you to leave this place, NOW, as Jesus is Lord of all! In His Holy Name, you shall bow before the Son of God, and then be gone from here forever!"

As I spoke I poured drops of oil on the dance floor as Kathy prayed Scripture. Something fell on the floor at the back end of the bar, by the door to the restaurant, but we had anointed that door earlier, when we came through it, after cleansing the restaurant itself. The only door that was left undone was the front door leading outside. I pointed to it and yelled, "Get out, in Jesus's Name!" After which a silent stillness settled into the room.

I felt no weight or sense of dread any longer as I stood in the center of the dance floor. I moved over to a table and sat down as a great weariness came over me. Man, I was so tired. Kathy sat down to, and after a few minutes of silence, she said with a smile "It's gone; and not a peep out of it." I knew it was gone as well. I anointed the front door on my way out and headed home.

It was late when I got to bed that night. I slept so soundly that the next thing I remember was Joe and the kid knocking on my door. When I opened it I could tell it was late afternoon. "You okay, John?" Joe asked, in that Dracula voice I had come to enjoy.

"Yeah. What's up?" I asked.

"The kid told me he hadn't seen you since two days ago, when he saw you headed off for town in the middle of the night, and he was worried."

Two days ago?

I got to a phone and called Lori, knowing that she would be concerned. She told me that my Interstate Compact had gone through so she and Brandy were coming to spend a couple days with me exploring Yosemite National Park, where we found the most wonderful Little Rock church. Lori also found out that my boyhood Pal, Ricky, was in Mariposa jail and we managed to get some books into him before we left.

We shared a wonderful dinner with Joe, his fiancé Chris and her boys, and they prayed in earnest over each of us, and then we were off to our home in Nevada, and on to the next series of Divine Providence and miracles in our lives.

***

**"If I find in myself a desire which no experience in this world can satisfy, the most probable explanation is that I was made for another world"** – C.S. Lewis, Mere Christianity.

Crossing over the Nevada state line was such a wonderful feeling that I couldn't contain my happiness. I whooped, and yeehawed, praised my Lord and Savior, and swore, that by the grace of God, I would never cross that state line into California again, as my lawyer had warned me that, "There is usually no escape from this high level of corruption in the justice system," he told me, "so count yourself lucky."

Count myself blessed, I mentally corrected him in my thoughts, as I passed the "Welcome to Nevada" sign, which was to me, surely a sign from Heaven.

My truck had been "rode hard and put away wet" before I had been arrested almost a year ago in Carson City, and the drivetrain was giving me cause to "pray without ceasing" for it, all the way home. As we pulled into our driveway in Ely, the rear driveline literally fell out on the ground! Bless the Holy Angels that held it together for me until we made it home. Not even caring, I parked and set the emergency brake, bailed out and ran into the backyard for my long overdue reunion with Calador and Keisha. It was all love, fur and slobber as they trounced all over me, rolling me all around in the mud from the days earlier rainstorm, and I had it coming for causing our needless separation.

Later that very evening Brandy asked Lori and I to clearly explain salvation to her to make sure she had understood it correctly, and in so doing, we ministered Salvation to our beautiful daughter – thank You, Jesus!

The next morning we got a visit from P&P about Billy Bob running a mining operation in Manhattan, Nevada, as he had vouched for my employment for validation of one of the conditions of my Interstate Compact. This guy was verbally abusing, and the way he arrogantly stared up and down my wife's body with his filthy innuendos made me consider hitting him in the throat, especially as he did all this right in front of my little girl. He told me I would be taking a job out of town with my brother, and he would "check in with Lori if he needed anything." He said he would kill my dogs if they even looked at him, said that I could no longer run my own corporation, could not work for Nathan Ministries (Phil Davis's outreach ministry) or preach at all for that matter. Sometimes, the evil and corruption never seem to have an end, but if someone "snaps", then they are considered the bad guy, as their side of the story never sees the light of day. There is good and evil in every person, regardless of position or job title, and it's horrible when the evil attains a position above the law, as I have witnessed. Everyone has within them that "fight or flight" line that, when crossed, causes some people to "fight" rather than flight, especially when it involves protecting family and loved ones from evil.

So once again, we went to our knees and cast it on the Lord in prayer, this time including Uncle Phil's ministry, and they put it on several prayer chains as well. In less than a month this guy was called back to Elko, without further incident, thank God! My new parole officer was a fair and decent man, for the most part.

In the meantime I had my truck almost back together but I needed a U joint and a muffler. Lori and I went to Ely motor supply and were told that the U joint was $12 and the muffler was $90. I only had $30, so we decided to go to C.B. Auto Parts. Upon parking out in front of the store, Lori and I prayed and asked the Lord to help us by stretching our money for enough to get what we needed. At the counter I purchased a U joint for $9.25 but they didn't have the muffler I needed. As we got ready to leave, a man who had overheard our conversation said that he had that exact muffler in the back of his truck, and lo and behold, he actually did.

"How much?" I asked.

"How much you got?" He countered.

The muffler cost us $20.25!!! God really does care about the small stuff, Glory to God!

\*\*\*

Very comforting were the Christian books, magazines, and devotionals I received in the mail from Kenneth Copeland Ministries, as they took the time to track me after my release, and encourage me in the faith, at a time I felt very much alone.

On the other hand, I'm not sure what spooked off most of my friends more, the fact that I got out of the 25 to life prison sentence, or the Jesus thing, but most of them didn't know how to handle the "new me," so they just stayed away. I know beyond doubt that they still loved me as a brother, and I them, and if necessary we would, as always, be willing to help each other or even die for one another if need be (John 15:13). Yet, it often made them uncomfortable to be around me, and it would hurt when they would "duck me" in the grocery store or other places. I was still the same friend as I had always been, I just couldn't go back down the same old path I had always been on, and I couldn't stop bringing up the Lord in our conversations (1 Peter 4:1-4)... Except for Gary B... He didn't give a hoot. He was my dear friend before all of this happened and because of his genuine concern for me, he showed up at my door a couple of days after I got home. He came up all the way from Henderson Nevada just to check on me and make sure I was okay, and he will never know how much that meant to me at a time when I felt so abandoned.

*"... But there is a friend who sticks closer than a brother."* Proverbs 18:24.

Although we didn't hang out much anymore, the Boys from the Brush always remained loyal to one another as did Ricky, too. The truth is, when you commit yourself to the Lord, you're going to lose a lot of friends that *"think it's strange that you do not run with them"* (1 Peter 4:4). However, the Lord will send you new ones that will pray with you and have the ability to strengthen and encourage you in the faith. Sometimes you will have the awesome blessing and opportunity to share your faith with your closest friends, without them running off, but I have found that to be very, very rare.

In this regard, the bottom line is, that time is short and the Lord is coming soon to get those who are His (1 Corinthians 15:51-52, 1 Thessalonians 4:13 through 5:11, etc.) out of the way of His wrath, that is also coming (see, Rapture, Appendix J).

*"For God did not appoint us to wrath, but to obtain salvation through our Lord Jesus Christ, who died for us, that whether we wake or sleep, we should live together with Him."* 1 Thessalonians 5:9-10.

*"...and to wait for His Son from Heaven, who He raised from the dead, even Jesus who delivers us from the wrath to come."* 1 Thessalonians 1:10.

*"But take heed to yourselves, least your hearts be weighed down with carousing, drunkenness, and cares of this life, and that Day come on you unexpectedly. For it will come as a snare on all those who dwell on the face of the whole earth. Watch therefore, and pray always that you may be counted worthy to escape all these things that will come to pass, and to stand before the Son of Man."* Luke 21:34-36.

*"Because you have kept My command to persevere, I also will keep you from the hour of trial which shall come upon the whole world, to test those who dwell on the earth."* Revelation 3:10.

The Rapture is the event where all who have put their trust in Jesus Christ will be suddenly caught up from the earth and taken into Heaven by the Lord, Himself. The word Rapture is a translation from the Greek word "harpazo", and it occurs 14 times in the New Testament. It has four predominant meanings; 1) carry off by force, 2) to claim for one's self eagerly, 3) to snatch away speedily, and, 4) to rescue from the danger of destruction.

It is a soon coming imminent event that will be spectacular!

The Rapture will be the all-time mega-reunion of the universe. All of your loved ones who have gone before you will be present. Their souls that descend from Heaven with Jesus will then be reunited with their resurrected bodies that rise first when the Rapture begins.

Then we who are still alive will rise to meet the resurrected believers in the air!

And finally, at long last, we will all experience the unspeakable joy of our reunion with our Lord, face to face! *"Beloved, now we are children of God; and it has not yet been revealed what we shall be, but we know that when He is revealed, we shall be like Him, for we shall see Him as He is."* 1 John 3:2. Hallelujah!

Come Lord Jesus!

Sooo… It occurs to me that you may be reading this and the Rapture has already happened, and multitudes of people (with the Holy Spirit, 2

Thessalonians 2:6-7), worldwide have simply vanished, so here's the short course that we will call "tribulation 101". A very charismatic world leader has risen with the ability not only to say what everybody wants to hear, but also backs it up with (lying, –2 Thessalonians 2: 8-10) signs and wonders, and has managed to put in place a seven year peace treaty with Israel (Daniel 9:27). This will trigger the "End Times" as detailed in Daniel, Revelation, Matthew 24, Mark 13, Luke 21, etc.

The first 3 ½ years will seem peaceful as global laws are enacted to allow everyone to take the "mark of the beast" (Revelation 13:15-8), which might possibly be a computer chip placed in the right hand, as well as the new world religion and its leader to be implemented (Revelation 13:11-18), namely the Beast.

This new world leader is the antichrist (2 Thessalonians 2:8-12, 2 Thessalonians 2:3-4, Daniel 7:19-27, 11:21-45, Matthew 24:15, 24:24, 1 John 4:1-3, Revelation 13:1-10, 17:8, 6:2, and 20:1-3), and if you take the "mark", you're not going to see Heaven at all (Revelation 14:11, Revelation 13:8), and you will suffer God's wrath (Revelation 16:2, Revelation 19:20, Philippians 3:18-19).

In the last 3 ½ years (of the now broken) seven year peace treaty, if you don't take the mark you will be hunted and killed (probably beheaded if you're caught, Revelation 13:15, Revelation 20:4), BUT, you will have eternity with God and us and Heaven (Revelation 14:12-13, Revelation 15:2, Daniel 12:12). During the last three and half years of the tribulation period (Daniel 7:25), until the Lord finally comes and sets things straight (Revelation 19:11 through 22:21) you will be hunted.

Thus, *"Here is the patience of the saints; here are those who keep the commandments of God and the faith of Jesus."* As Revelation 14:12 instructs you, you have need of patience and endurance if in fact, you now find yourself in this seven year time period immediately following the Rapture.

Even so, by God's grace and mercy, it's still not too late! You must accept Jesus Christ as your Lord and Savior, and if the Rapture has happened already, you must hold to your faith no matter what, at any cost, and endure to the end. **It's still not too late!**

And interestingly, here's a little food for thought; with at least nine warnings about being drunk (that I know of, Matthew 24:49, Luke 12:45, Luke 21:34-36, 1 Thessalonians 5:6-10, Ephesians 5:14-18, 1 Peter 1:13, 1 Corinthians 6:9-11, Romans 13:11-14, Titus 2:12-13) when the time of the Rapture occurs, if you're drunk, do you go? Hmmm.... Or are you left behind? This study is by no means conclusive.

And that's my Tribulation 101 short course, such as it is.

So, if you truly value your friends, you have to take your shot at bringing them to know the Lord, or, without Christ, they will surely be "left behind." This is what will likely cause the separation between you and them, but you have to try… If not you, then who? Time is short. The urgency is real. You have to take the chance, for their sake. How do you know you are His? **John 14:1-6, and Romans 10:8-13.**

At one point, the loss of friendships led me to argue with the Lord about sending me back to my hometown, in the first place. I reminded Him of His own words, *"A prophet is not without honor except in his own country, among his own relatives, and in his own house"* Mark 6:4.

"I'm no prophet... I got that. But they all know me here, Lord. Who is gonna to listen to the likes of me?" Good argument, don't you think?

In my soul I heard, "𝔓𝔢𝔬𝔭𝔩𝔢 𝔧𝔲𝔰𝔱 𝔩𝔦𝔨𝔢 𝔶𝔬𝔲."

"Fine. I'll be a hermit then," I'm thinking.

"𝔗𝔥𝔞𝔱'𝔰 𝔴𝔥𝔞𝔱 𝔍𝔬𝔫𝔞𝔥 𝔱𝔥𝔬𝔲𝔤𝔥𝔱."

"But Lord, I'm so ashamed because I've been in prison."

"𝔖𝔬 𝔴𝔞𝔰 𝔍𝔬𝔰𝔢𝔭𝔥, 𝔞𝔫𝔡 𝔦𝔱 𝔴𝔬𝔯𝔨𝔢𝔡 𝔬𝔲𝔱 𝔭𝔯𝔢𝔱𝔱𝔶 𝔤𝔬𝔬𝔡 𝔣𝔬𝔯 𝔥𝔦𝔪."

"Good. I'll go to Egypt and run things, then."

"𝔍 𝔫𝔢𝔢𝔡 𝔶𝔬𝔲 𝔥𝔢𝔯𝔢."

This is how my thought process worked, anyway, because when I consistently study the Bible, Scriptures and Bible stories seem to constantly pop into my head when I ponder life's daily questions.

*"But the Helper, the Holy Spirit, whom the Father will send in My name, He will teach you all things, and bring to your remembrance all things that I said to you."* John 14:26.

Was God actually speaking with me in my mind? Beats me, but His Word definitely was, and John 1:1-5, 14 defines the Word as God, and becoming flesh and dwelling among us in the form of Jesus Christ.

Regardless, if you're not studying God's Word daily, you can clearly see how you are missing out. It works the same for everybody. It's the predominant spiritual law of reaping and sowing. You get out of it what you put into it.

*"But this I say: he who sows sparingly will also reap sparingly, and he who sows bountifully will also reap bountifully."* 2 Corinthians 9:6.

*"Do not be deceived, God is not mocked; for whatever a man sows, that he will also reap. For he who sows to the flesh will of the flesh reap corruption, but he who sows to the Spirit will of the Spirit reap everlasting life."* Galatians 6:7-8.

And please... I'm not saying that I got all this talking with God thing figured out because I don't. Especially at times when it seems God is talking crystal clear to every other believer on the planet and not to me. Like when God tells Super Sister Christian to quit her job, sell her house, moved to Jamaica and start the most successful reggae worship band on the planet, while I'm praying as hard as I can trying to get the Lord to reveal to me why my truck won't start, 10 minutes before I have to be to work.

I do know He guides me with His Word and with His Peace, again as Philippians 4:6-7 explains, and His Divine Guidance in my life, through

Providence, is unquestionable. Proven over and over, time and again is the fact that as long as I adhere to his Word and obey what He tells me in it, I suffer much fewer wrecks in my life. I can come to no other conclusion than to trust Him completely.

Albert Einstein explained it so wonderfully to the Saturday Evening Post, in 1929, proclaiming "As a child I received instruction in the Bible and in the Talmud. I am a Jew, but I am enthralled by the luminous figure of the Nazarene... No one can read the Gospels without feeling the actual presence of Jesus. His personality pulsates in every word. No myth is filled with such life."

Amen to that.

## CHAPTER 48

## Stumbling into My Calling

*"The harvest truly is great, but the laborers are few; therefore pray the Lord of the harvest to send out laborers into His harvest."*
Luke 10:2.

I don't always get a miracle when I pray for one, and I pray for miracles every day. When I do get one, it's always phenomenal and it always glorifies my Lord, as well as drops me to my knees in humility and worship, whether they directly affect me or someone I'm lifting before the Lord in prayer. If you don't believe in miracles, then don't bother praying for them. I believe, and I pray for miracles. I grow so weary of super Christians telling me that "You can't live from miracle to miracle" when that's exactly what I've done for over 20 years. Sometimes they are few and far between, yet when they happen it's usually in a way that is totally unexpected and reflects the unmatched majesty and power of our loving Father in Heaven.

In October 1997, I removed the valve cover on my Chevy big block to find a stuck valve, busted valve spring, and a bent pushrod. Very disheartened and in despair I sat down in my shop and said to God, "Lord, You know I don't have any money for this, and You know I can't do Your work or mine tomorrow without a vehicle. I can't do this by myself. I need Your help."

I went down to the house to have a cup of coffee and see if I could think my way out of this problem. As I was scratching Calador's ears on the back porch I heard the phone ring inside the house. It was Phil Davis in Battle Mountain. He said that he didn't know what was going on, BUT (GOD) about 15 minutes ago, while he was in the shower, "The Lord laid it on his heart" that he was to give Lori and I two vehicles! He told me to get a ride up to his place and he would have the titles ready when I got there! I told him what had happened 15 minutes earlier, up in my shop, and we both went off shouting and praising the Lord!

God really cares about us. Not just the big things, but the small stuff as well. And as His Providence proves, He's real good at getting us to move in the direction we need to be going. In November, with winter once again setting in, I took a layoff, but with my new parole officer I was allowed to come back to Ely to look for something closer to home. Unfortunately, this time of year meant reductions in crews and everybody seemed to be laying off until better weather returned. In Ely, being about 6500 feet elevation that could be a long wait.

That morning I was getting ready to take my resume up to Alta Gold's office and see if they had anything available at one of several mines that they had going. I had managed to get myself in a hurry, for no reason, other than I felt so ashamed of being in prison that I almost talked myself out of going, so now I was in a "hurry up and get it over with" frenzy. I am particularly grieved about the part of a job interview where they asked "And what exactly were you in prison for?", because if you can't give a one, maybe two word answer, which I can't, you're screwed. I say "ex-felon in possession of a firearm." Then they ask, "What was your first crime that made you an ex-felon?" Yeah. "Well, I was never an ex-felon, actually, but what happened is...blah, blah, blah..." Then they come back at you with, "Well, yeah. Right. We'll be in touch. Thank you for your application. Goodbye."

I might as well say my previous employer got on my nerve (I only have one left) so I bludgeoned him to death with a long sharp rock, chopped him in little pieces, ran him through my wife's brand-new Hamilton Beach blender, then through the garbage disposal and down the ol' waterslide of darkness (sewer system), where he now sleeps at the bottom of the great Brown pond, with the other fishes, well not exactly fishes... But I'm better now... I have meds. Thank you for asking. What time do you want me to start...boss?

So, with woeful anticipation I grabbed a copy of my resume and headed out the front door, but before I reached the bottom step, I "remembered" that I was to call Gracyne. I flipped around and by the time I reached the top step, I realized that I don't know anybody named Gracyne, thus proving beyond any doubt, that I have successfully blown what few brain cells I had left. Dumbfounded, I went back in the house, poured another cup of coffee, and sat down at the kitchen table. Where that thought had come from I had no idea, but it was so clear that it seemed like one of my normal thoughts, like it was part of me. I'm not very good at describing this, obviously, so please bear with me. And yes, just like you are probably now thinking, I too rationalized that I was more than likely losing my mental faculties.

I needed some help figuring this out. I thought of calling Dad and Mom, but this kind of drama would probably freak them out a little bit more than I usually do, so I called Lori at her work.

As soon as I began speaking I felt blindingly stupid telling her that I essentially "hear voices in my head".

"Voices?" She says.

"Well, more like thoughts," I explained.

"Really?" She quips.

"Yeah. It's not funny. I'm having problems, for real, in my head, I think."

"What do the voices say?" She asks, more seriously, probably trying to humor me and get me off the phone so she can get back to work. I didn't want to say, but I was kinda committed at this point.

"Call Gracyne," I responded. There. I said it.

"Maybe it's God. You better call Gracyne then."

Now I really feel like an idiot as I tell her, "I don't know anybody named Gracyne."

I'm such a moron, I'm thinking. I never should've called her. After all, she is the one and only person on the planet that I'm trying to impress, and I call her up with this little tidbit of insanity while she's trying to work and pay the bills.

"There used to be a lady that worked here by that name. I'll ask Lois," she said. Lois is like, Lori's other Mom, a true and committed Christian woman who cheerfully serves the Lord in whatever capacity in which she is called, and is known in many elite circles as "the Great Knower of All Things", and she also keeps the books for the real estate firm Lori works for.

Well, okay, I thought. At least Lori didn't hang up on me, so I got that going for me. And actually offering to help is an added bonus as well. Much better than another one of those tedious psych evaluations, by my way of reckoning, which is where I would have guessed this whole thing was headed. Of course, I may not be "out of the woods" yet, as she may have me on hold while she calls on the other line to make my extended appointment in the Rubber Room Hotel.

As I weigh my options and consider whether or not I should hang up the phone and flee for my life, as I'm pretty sure insanity is a parole violation, I hear my wife's soothing voice come back on the line, "are you still there?" Was she reading me? Did she expect me to flee?

"Yes," I countered.

"Lois said her name is Gracyne Parker and here's her phone number in McGill..." then, "Okay? I gotta go... Love ya," click. I didn't even get a chance to say goodbye, or "Can you call her for me?"

I know...it's a guy thing, but cold calling a woman who doesn't know me from Jack the Ripper, who I never met in my whole life, and telling her, "Hi there! As insane as this may sound, I think, maybe, God told me to call you, for what, I have no idea, and no, I'm not a psycho insane murderer person, so please don't call the cops on me, as I just got out of prison and I kinda like it this way, on this side of the wall, and all."

Maybe I'd be better off telling this Gracyne person that Lois told me to call her. I'm sure it would be Lois's first offense and she would only get probation, maybe a month or two in County at tops. Naw... Lori loves the heck out of Lois and I'd never hear the end of it. Besides, that eatin' is a hard habit to break, and I get tired of my own cooking really fast, not to mention that every now and then, Lois treats me to my favorite homemade banana cream pie and it's the best I ever had.

Fine. I'll call Gracyne myself. I hope Lois can get one of those pies to me in jail if things don't go good with this poor lady I'm about to traumatize.

"Hello, I'm trying to reach Gracyne," so far so good.

"This is her, what can I do for you?" Wow! A Texas accent just like Jack Grimm – very comforting... Here goes...

"My name is John Gergen, and this may sound a little strange, but I think God wants me to call you…"

"Hahaha hahaha!" She busts out laughing at me, and then with the sweetest sounding Texas drawl I ever heard, she explained, "Well John, that's real good. Me and the kids in our youth group have been praying for God to send us someone to help out."

Caught totally flat-footed, I said, "That would be me."

She Giggled and said, "We happen to be having our meetings in the back room of the McGill Methodist Church every Wednesday night at seven, so that's tonight if you would like to come by."

And that's how it all started, with a still small voice (1 Kings 19:11-12) that I thought was my own thought. Gracyne, my soon to be best pal, is the original founder of what would soon become the McGill Christian Youth Group, a nondenominational 501©3 Christian outreach.

I spent way longer than any man should ever admit to, trying on slacks and shirts in front of a mirror, not to mention trying to remember how to tie a tie. I rejected the tie first; "Sorry, Lord." Then the jacket; "I'm trying hard to look good and make You proud of me at church, tonight," I mumbled. It was when Brandy came home from school, took one look at all my "fancy clothes" lying around the house and me gawking into the mirror, and she asked, "Whose funeral is it," that I gave up.

"You knew what You were getting when You saved me, Lord."

I pulled on my comfortable Levi's, one of my "Jesus" T-shirts, my boots and my black leather riding jacket and told Brandy that "I'm going to church tonight." She looked me over with what I think was an approving half smile and told me what I desperately needed to hear; she said, "Right on, Dad. Don't ever try to be someone you're not, especially in front of God." That's my girl!

I was getting very nervous by the time it came for me to leave, but at least I was very comfortable in what I was wearing. "Wait till they get a load of me," was the cliché that I spun as I fired up the Bronco that the Unk had given me, and headed for McGill.

It was way cold and just after dark when I got to the church. I found the door unlocked and let myself in, only to find myself all alone. The sanctuary as well as the main meeting room was empty, but I heard the faint sounds of voices coming from beyond the kitchen. I felt entirely out of place here, and was having serious enough regret about my attire that I thought of leaving and coming back next Wednesday when I would be more appropriately dressed for a "church" event, instead of being dressed like a biker.

Oh, wait – I was a biker.

Brandy's words popped back into my mind, and God bless her, I held up my head, straightened my shoulders, and did my best John Wayne strut (that I sucked at) right on through the kitchen, to a small door in the back. The voices that I had heard were coming from behind the door I was now opening, but went silent as I stepped into the room and down a few stairs to the floor level of a very small room, closing the door behind me.

There were about 9 or 10 kids huddled around the propane wall heater or sitting at the long table with Gracyne, who was reading out of the Book of Luke before I interrupted them, and now they were all staring at me. Then one kid said, "John, what are you doing here," and another said, "Yeah, my old man said you was dead," and then, "I heard you got a life prison sentence in California." I had ridden my Harley with almost all of these kid's parents! It was almost like old home week! The questions poured on to me, "What happened?" and, "Heard you got shot up pretty bad – what's up with that?" And again, "Why are you here?"

The last one was the one I answered; "Well, that's why I'm here. To tell what happened to me, and it's totally amazing!" I went on to tell them the short version of how God saved me from a 25 to life prison sentence, emphasizing the "deal" that I made with God and how He kept His part through the series of miracles that brought me back to Ely... "And to this very room we are in right now, tonight. God sent me back with a message to give to you. Above all, He wants me to make sure that you know how much He loves you (John 3:16), and no matter what anybody says, He's not mad at you! (Isaiah 54:9-10)"

I told them it would take some time for me to show them what I was talking about, but if they would let me, I would come back every week if it was okay with Gracyne and all of them.

The words God spoke to me in my previous argument with Him echoed through my mind, "People just like you!" That's who will listen to me! Glory to God! And here's God's sense of humor; the last time these young people saw me, I was wearing the same outfit I am wearing right now, save the black T-shirt that has a biker kneeling and praying beside his Harley on it and says, "bless em' all and let God sort em' out." How cool is that? He must have got a real laugh out of watching me try on all those clothes, not to mention watching me try and tie that tie!

Here, with Gracyne and these kids, I felt at home, as if I had finally found my "niche" in the "Body of Christ". Their faith was small but growing stronger every week, and it was real, as was their search for a better way of life and the possibility of something different than street life.

So we searched together throughout the Scriptures, for a better life, a way out of our old ways, and especially for God and His Jesus. And with Gracyne at the helm, we found answers and so much more than we had ever even hoped. We discovered the love of a Heavenly Father that loved us just the way we were, and who empowered us to become His sons and daughters.

Over many years we had to deal with some very hard issues that the other churches in our town either scorned us for, or more commonly, played like they didn't exist so they could easily ignore them. Drugs, alcohol, abusive parents, sex, rape, abortion, cuttings, demons, and suicide are just some of the hard-fought spiritual battles these young kids faced. They fought like true Warriors of the Cross and gained their victories in Jesus's Name and to the glory of God, and mere words cannot describe the devastation we endured when a battle of these types and magnitudes was lost. Never have I, or will I ever, be more proud to have stood beside anyone involved in spiritual warfare, as I am to have fought beside these brave, yet often scared, young kids. They fought through their own life's battles, and then turned to help their friends and others fight for their victories from the never-ending onslaught of attacks' spawned against them in the realm of darkness.

Worthy of our adoration was God's extremely quick response to their prayers of faith for healing, especially in our local hospital. God's miracles and provision were commonplace, as hundreds witnessed, and years of my journals testify. And, yes, we had our share of problems, rebellion, and circumstances that come with this type of ministry, but by the grace of God, we worked through them and moved forward (Philippians 3:12-14).

And one time, on a very cold winter night at youth group, a young boy named Keegan decided we needed a boat to take south to Lake Mead so we could get out of the snow and go get warm. At the end of the evening we all joined hands in a circle, as usual, to pray in agreement (Appendix L&P) for each other and our loved ones, and at the close of prayer Keegan threw in, "And Lord, we need a boat". Whatever, we thought, but we all agreed with him anyway, then closed with the Lord's Prayer. The very next afternoon, an 18 foot, open bow, Bayliner Ski boat rolled up my driveway!!!

I will always be proud of these, my young friends, and I will always hold them dear in my heart, and honor them in my prayers before our Heavenly Father. God bless them, in Jesus' Name. And for sure, Lord, blessings and honor on my dear friend Gracyne.

## CHAPTER 49

## Angels, Demons, and Jailhouse Religion

*"I, the Lord, called You in righteousness, and will hold Your hand;*
*I will keep You and give You as a covenant to the people, as a light to*
*the Gentiles,*
*To open blind eyes, to bring out prisoners from the prison,*
*Those who sit in darkness from the prison house.*
Isaiah 42:6-7.
As is Isaiah 49:8-9, this Scripture is part of our Covenant, and I pray these scriptures for my brother in Christ, Armando.

To not have a job for very long was a parole violation, and the prospects of finding any kind of work at the beginning of winter, was daunting. Everybody I talked to were in the process of laying their workers off for the long, cold months of winter here in the high country. On the last day in November, Lori, Billy, Brandy and I joined hands at the breakfast table to give thanks for His provision and asked the Lord to "make a job opening for me." Dropping the kids off at school Brandy told me she thought I would have a job soon, and not to worry. Without thinking about it, I told her that tomorrow would be the day. At 4:30 PM the next day, Alta Gold called and said that even though they had just told me that they had no job openings available, less than an hour earlier, and that they "weren't sure exactly how it happened", but they now had a job for me 90 miles north of town at Kinsley mine. It wasn't an equipment operators position like I had applied for, but I could start immediately as an "oiler".

Hallelujah! Oiler is a much better occupation than inmate any day! Abba, Father! Thank You, Lord!

Within a week I found myself, every morning as the sunrise broke onto the top of Kinsley Mountain, on my knees asking God for the strength to get me through the physical requirements of my job, in the day ahead. I also asked the Lord to keep me warm as the winter winds blowing at nearly 7500 feet elevation were usually bitter cold and often sent the outside temperatures way below zero. I always felt reassured when I finished my time at sunrise with Him on top of these mountains, and my favorite scripture, Isaiah 41:10 would usually come to mind, as if the Lord were saying to me, "I will be with you."

On the day before Christmas I pulled my service truck into its usual position to service all of the 50 ton ore trucks as they came down the steep and twisting haulage road from the upper pit. I was parked on a widened out area on a hairpin corner where I could have the haul trucks pull off the main hall road, one at a time, to be fueled and serviced. The front of my truck was pulled into the bank and the rear of my truck, which held a work platform and all of the fuel and lubricant hoses, was facing the hairpin turn. As I stood on the work platform of the truck, with my back to the haulage road, the first fully loaded ore truck pulled off of the haul road and into the open area where I was waiting to fuel him.

As he tried to apply his brakes he lost control and went into a slide on ice that had been covered with 3 or 4 inches of fresh snow the night before. As the gigantic truck slid sideways towards me from behind, I never had an inkling as to what was happening as the service trucks air compressor was running loudly at high rpm to power the grease and pump systems on the truck, and I never saw it coming. Not more than one second before the 12 foot tall rear tires smashed into the back of my service truck, completely crushing the rear bumper platform I was standing on, "something" hit me and grabbed me in the middle of my back, and literally flung me 35 feet through the air like a ragdoll, where I landed "spread eagle" and face first in the snow. It happened so incredibly fast that there wasn't even time for the "pucker factor" to engage, and I know you know what I mean.

The impact of the haul trucks rear wheel crashing sideways into the rear of the service truck was tremendous, and completely totaled the back of the service truck. I would have been crushed into mush had not a Guardian Angel thrown me clear of the wreckage, of that, there was absolutely no doubt whatsoever!

I began yelling "Thank You, Jesus", praising God, and laughing and whooping! Charlie, the driver of the haul truck, came running around the back of his truck yelling, "I saw! I saw! I saw you fly through the air in my mirror! I saw it all!"

The Lord said, "I will be with you," and He was!

Soon, Rick the mine safety coordinator, the mine manager and the foreman all showed up to "investigate" the accident. Charlie and I both went to proclaiming the blatant miracle that had just happened, but they weren't having any of it. While Rick was coming up with all of these reasons why the accident should have been avoided, I kept telling him to "Look way over there in the snow where I landed! No human can jump that far! How many sets of tracks do you see? One! Just one! And it's my tracks coming FROM where I landed! There are no tracks going TO where I landed are there? I "flew" through the air! MIRACLE! Hello? Are you hearing what I'm saying, Rick?"

All the while Charlie is chiming in with, "That's right! I saw! I saw it all! He flew through the air! It's an angel that did it just like John's tellin' ya!"

Rick got frustrated, told Charlie to get back in his truck, and snatched the clipboard with the accident report form that I was in the process of filling out in complete detail, out of my hands, saying, "You ain't puttin' any of that Angel stuff in the report."

That night after work, Charlie knew what he had witnessed was the "real thing" and he gladly received his salvation through Jesus Christ, Who had shown Himself to be real to him through this miracle.

Charlie really did see! We'll have us a couple of laughs about it when we get to Heaven, for sure.

\*\*\*

"Jailhouse religion" is a phenomenon that has always intrigued me. Quite commonly, the ramifications from our sins eventually catch up with us, and often we find ourselves in jail. I look on this period or "season of life," as God's own version of "timeout". The calamity of worldly noise and distractions are removed, or more appropriately, you are removed from them, in order to address specific sin issues and areas of our lives that need altered and immediate change. Often, jail time becomes obvious instances of God's knocking on the door of our hearts (please see the Correction section in Appendix F). This, in many instances, evokes repentance and the humbling of one's self before Almighty God in search of redemption, and more often, deliverance from the consequences of our sinful actions.

Future time travel as a form of discipline was a commonly accepted practice when I was growing up as a kid. Up until recently, when we inadvertently "grew too many pansies in the garden", so to speak, my Mom, like most Moms of my generation, upon having had enough of our misbehavior, would offer us; 1) the option of behaving rightly in the here and now, or 2) forgoing this entire moment in time by "knocking you into the middle of next week," hence, time travel.

Once, when I was very young, I am told that, while trying to lean over the edge of Grandma Gergen's garage roof to catch a sparrow in its nest, I fell headfirst from the roof and knocked myself unconscious. That's the story my cousins swore to, who supposedly "eye-witnessed" the event, so God knows what really happened. In any case, I don't remember any of it, except waking up on our couch and upon seeing my mother, asking her, "Is this the middle of next week?"

I never could understand why we couldn't travel back in time, either, but it was always a one-way ticket into the future, for me anyways.

Regardless, America by far leads the rest of the world in the amount of men and women that are in "timeout," not only in prisons but in jails as well, and I can't help but wonder if part of the reason we have so many people of these latest generations in timeout (incarcerated) isn't largely due to the fact that we forgot to mention the possibility of "future time travel" to them when they were younger. I'm just saying that the rising numbers of incarceration rates greatly coincide with the last few generations of almost total decline and lack of disciplinary parents. But God...please see, Job 5:17, Proverbs 3:11-12, Hebrews 12:5-11, 2 Corinthians 7:9-11, 1 Corinthians 11:31-32, Job 36:8-12, and as mentioned a little earlier, the Correction Bible study in Appendix F.

God is merciful and compassionate, eventually allowing the iron doors of our incarceration to be opened to once again grant us our freedom to make our own decisions. And amazingly to me, is the first decision some folks make as soon as they are set free; namely, "Thanks God. Praise the Lord! I'll call You if I need You again." And that's okay, I guess, because you shouldn't worry too much if your Heavenly Father didn't knock loud or hard enough this time...and the next...and the next...and even harder after that.

*"What do you want? Shall I come to you with a rod, or in love and a spirit of gentleness?"* (1 Corinthians 4:21).

Sooo... How do you want it? The easy way or the hard way? As I said before, some of us just insist on having it the hard way. It didn't need to be that way, but it was our choice. We knew right from wrong and we chose poorly.

The White Pine County Sheriff graciously granted me permission to counsel and do jail ministry, on a one-on-one basis, with young inmates back in 1997, and over many years I have gotten very good at discerning "jailhouse religion", (probably second only to jailers themselves) as is the case with many repeat offenders going on their second, third, fourth or more times through the system.

*"As a dog returns to its vomit, so a fool repeats his folly."* Proverbs 26:11.

Then there are those who truly recognize the error of their ways, repent, and commit themselves to living up right before the Lord, but within a short time after their release, they fall prey to the traps, temptations and wiles of the enemy. It is these latter inmates that I do my best to focus my jail ministry on. I find it vital to their survival to prepare them, as best I can, for the intense temptations and battles that the devil will try to force upon them, particularly within the first few weeks of their release from jail or prison.

I'm not necessarily there to tell them that they need Jesus. If they didn't already know that, they wouldn't have requested my counsel in the first place. I'm going to do my very best to prepare them for all the drugs, booze, sex, lure of wealth, and other things the devil is going to shove in their faces, immediately upon their release. The evil one has to break their faith and get them dragged right back down into the pit, before they can tell anybody else how God got them out of it. That's always his demonic plan, every time, and if he has a plan, you better have one too. Go ahead and leave Jesus at the jail or prison when you go and let me know how that works out for you. If you're incarcerated right now while you're reading this, you really need to know what you got coming when you get out, because next time you may not get out at all. In case you haven't noticed from a lot of the people that you're doing time with, or your own experience, the length of time one must serve is very progressive in years for repeat offenders, and we only have so much time before life is over.

When you get out, any friend, relative, stranger or especially, romantic relationship that greets you with the same stuff that got you locked up in the first place, is being used by the devil to "kill, steal, and destroy" you, your life, and your testimony (John 10:10). If you don't have that one fact firmly etched in your mind when you get out, you're doomed to return. Don't sugarcoat it, whitewash it, or water it down, either. Your weakest area is where Satan will attack you. He will never face you in your strong points or head on. He will stab you in the back if you let him, "It's okay... No one will know... Everybody's doing it... Just this once... I won't get caught... I won't get addicted like everybody else..." He will whisper to you, as he plunges his knife deeper between your shoulder blades, all the while convincing you that he is your best friend.

*"Now a word was secretly brought to me, and my ear received a whisper of it. In disquieting thoughts from the visions of the night, when deep sleep falls on men, fear came upon me, and trembling, which made all my bones shake.*

*Then a spirit passed before my face; the hair on my body stood up. It stood still, but I could not discern its appearance.* Job 4: 12-16 describes the voice of evil, and is why we must train ourselves to take every thought captive to the obedience of Christ in order to survive spiritual warfare as we are instructed in 2 Corinthians 10:3-5.

Listen what the Apostle Peter said, *"For when they speak great swelling words of emptiness, they allure through the lusts of the flesh, through lewdness, the ones who have actually escaped from those who live in error. While they promise them liberty, they themselves are slaves of corruption; for by whom a person is overcome, by him also he is brought into bondage. For if, after they have escaped the pollutions of the world through the knowledge of the Lord and Savior Jesus Christ, they are again entangled in them and overcome, the latter end is worse for them than the beginning. For it would have been better for them not to have known the way of righteousness, than having known it, to turn from the holy commandment delivered to them but it has happened to them according to the true proverb: a dog returns to his own vomit, and, a sow, having washed, to her wallowing in the mire."* 2 Peter 2:18-22.

Please read all of 1 and 2 Peter and Ephesians as to prepare yourself for battle, and make a plan, for your success. Think about where you will go and who you will see. The alternative is simply step out the front door, get your brains beat out by your punkass enemy the devil, and try this all over again next time. It is vitally important that you eventually succeed as there is a limit, as Proverbs 29:1 when invoked, will bring and "endpoint";

*"He who is often rebuked, and hardens his neck, will suddenly be destroyed, and that without remedy."*

How far do you really want to push this? How much farther before your "endpoint" is invoked?

*"Seek the Lord while He may be found, call upon Him while He is near. Let the wicked forsake his way, and the unrighteous man his thoughts; let him return to the Lord, and He will have mercy on him; and to our God, for He will abundantly pardon."* Isaiah 55:6-7.

Sorry to be so graphic but if I sugarcoat it to you, it could cost you your life... Besides, it's just not my style.

Like it or not, we all enter the battle at Salvation. Satan hates God so he attacks what God loves the most... You.

And just because someone doesn't believe in Jesus it doesn't change the truth/fact that He did and does exist, it simply means that they refuse to accept any amount of the insurmountable, undeniable, historical evidence that He did and does exist. Jesus is recorded history, even more so by those who do not follow him and are non-Christians, than by Christians themselves. He is a historical fact, and His existence is undeniable. However, people will always choose to ignore this obvious truth and "bury their heads in the sand", rather than acknowledge that they are, in fact, accountable for their sins, when it is Jesus Himself who is the One who paid the price for their sin debt, so they could be forgiven!

That's why truth sounds like hate to those who hate truth. It's like, "I already have my mind made up, so don't confuse me with the truth." I think the bottom line for most of them is the whole "repentance" and "submission" part of the equation, because it requires them to acknowledge and turn away from their sins, and frankly, they don't want to. If sin wasn't fun, and addicting, it wouldn't tempt us, the devil wouldn't have any bait, and no one would be doing it. For instance, the so-called "free love" movement of the 1960s led to the extreme perpetuation of the age old sin of premarital sex (lust, adultery), to a current point of sacrificing millions of baby girls and boys (abortion) to demons, under the false guise of the "Jesus movement". It wasn't "free" if it costs millions of humans their lives.

Psalm 106:37 cries out, *"they even sacrificed their sons and their daughters to demons"*.

The sacrifice is now called abortion, and the demons name, as always, is Lust. But to speak against their sacrifices or their demons is now considered hate rather than the truth that it is.

The awesome alternative is when we get born of God, turn from our sins, and the wicked one cannot touch us (1 John 5:18).

Will we still have battles? You betcha, but our victory is guaranteed in Christ! (Appendix N, Victory in Jesus Christ). Read the last four chapters of the

Bible (Revelation 19, 20, 21, and 22)....WE WIN! Hallelujah! And all glory to God!

***

Kinsley mine shut down in late winter, and I was back on "forced vacation". Lori goes in to work one day to find Lois a little shaken up, saying that the phones in the back offices were making terrible noises and the adding machine "went crazy". We went down to the office after closing, prayerfully and spiritually cleansing and anointing each room, which eliminated the problem.

A couple of days later a fellow named Ron, from Boston, called me from his room at the Hotel Nevada, wanting to discuss his experimentation with a new theory on gold exploration. I met with him and he seemed like a very nice man, yet I felt very "edgy" around him. We discussed the possibility of my helping him with his project. When I got up to leave and was walking to the door, in a low voice I had not heard before, he said "Maybe your Jesus will help us find the gold". I had not spoken at all about my faith, God, Jesus or anything of that nature, and that "tingle" ran down my spine, again.

Ron moved into an apartment behind the Sheriff's department and I made it a point to spend most of our time together talking about the Bible, as we waited for the snow to melt and dryer weather, which would allow us to go out prospecting. He told me of serious stress issues he was having as well as "flashbacks" from his tour in Vietnam. Because I felt somewhat out of my league, I called the VA (Veterans Administration) and his sister back in Boston as well. Both stressed their deep concern for Ron but neither felt that they had any options for helping him, and although the counselor at the VA couldn't reveal any personal information, he did indicate that he was delighted that Ron was getting "spiritual" help, as those were "variables" that the man could not "deal with".

Spring comes around, and on a beautiful May morning, Lori picks up the phone and its Ron (or maybe not), and in his deep weird voice he says he has three messages from God that he was to deliver to me. I knew it had to be good by the way she raised one eyebrow and got that "yeah...right" look on her face while she handed the phone across the kitchen table to me.

"It's for you, dear," she said, then silently mouthed the word "demon" as she nodded her head slowly up and down. I almost told her to take a message.

"Yeah, well, that's nice, Ron... Wouldn't want to miss that... I'll be right over".

I was still on my knees praying at the kitchen table when Lori got done putting her makeup on (not that I am insinuating that it takes an exceedingly long time...that's not what I'm saying at all). She anointed my head with oil, prayed with me, and knowing that Ron was not "saved" I went to his house to "test" (1 John 4:1, see Test All Things in Appendix C) this spirit from which the "messages" were to be delivered.

Upon arriving, I found Ron to be very nervous and twitching, confused, upset, and babbling about his fear of repercussions of these messages upon our friendship. Because revelation from God always causes inner peace, I could discern immediately that he was under demonic influence, not to mention that I was "tingling" from my head to my feet with the power of the Holy Spirit! Again, I can't begin to explain the inner calmness that overwhelmed me, knowing and anticipating the battle I was about to partake in, and knowing that I could not be defeated. Scriptures were flowing through my mind, Jesus was with me, and the battle was the Lord's!

I opened my Bible to Ephesians chapter 1 (my authority through the blood of Christ), told Ron that I needed a minute to prepare for the "messages", and began reading out loud. Ron's voice became louder and more frantic, and when I casually set my small bottle of anointing oil on the table, he grabbed it and threw it over on the couch! Then he went over and sat on it!

When I read 1 Corinthians 12:3, *"therefore I make known to you that no one speaking by the Spirit of God calls Jesus accursed, and no one can say that Jesus is Lord except by the Holy Spirit,"* and then I pronounced loudly "Jesus is Lord", Ron went off yelling his asinine messages at me.

I said, "That's kinda like what this says", which it wasn't, but he slowed down long enough for me to read Jesus's parable about "binding the strongman" in Matthew 12:29. As he began his next message, I slowly walked through his front door, with him following right behind me as I went outside, opened the hood of my truck, and pulled out the oil dipstick. With a blob of black 30 weight motor oil on my thumb, I turned around as he was "commanding me to allow others to follow Mormonism, and stop denouncing it, as there are many paths to God". In a loud voice, right in front of the neighbors, I said, "By the power of Christ's shed blood, I bind you to silence in the Name of Jesus", and stuck my oily thumb on his forehead, and he shut up right in midsentence!

His legs started wobbling so I helped him back inside to his couch, where I read several scriptures that the Lord gave me concerning false doctrines and the doctrine of demons (John 14:6, Galatians 1:6-9, 2 John 1:7-11, 1 Timothy 4:1, 1 Timothy 1:3, etc.), then after rebuking the lie with the truth of the Word, and in the power of Jesus' shed blood, I commanded the lying spirit to come out, and in the Mighty Name of Jesus, cast it out.

With tears streaming down his face, Ron slumped over and relaxed. The Truth had set him free (John 8:32). I asked him if he was ready to accept Jesus into his life as his Lord, master and Savior, and he did, to the glory of God! His victory was claimed in Jesus.

When I got back home, I found that Lori had been praying without ceasing for me the whole time! God bless her, and all glory to God! Thank you, Lord!

\*\*\*

I really can't recall how many of these battles the Lord has called me to. With God's empowerment, I have won many, yet the ones that I can't forget are the ones that I lost...and I live with the catastrophic anguish that they have left in their wake. I will not speak of these. They haunt me, as some were very close to me.

Darlene, however, was an easy "win", at least as far as deliverance ministering goes. I list her here simply to emphasize one of the most common ways used to allow demonic activity into our lives, and as an absolute rebuttal to those who think Christians can't fall prey to dark spirits.

She was 67 years old when, through divine Providence, we met. She was a gentlewoman of short stature, blue eyes, gray hair, a genuinely loving smile, and the sweetest disposition, and she was sleeping in her car across the street from my house when I found her. She was from back east, where she was raised a Christian, practiced her faith, and lived with her childhood sweetheart and husband for almost 50 years, until he was called home to Heaven. Unable to contend with the passing and bereavement of her "soulmate", she fled her home and everything that reminded her of her agonizing loss. She just drove off, and kept driving. Along the way she became "obsessed" with her desire to once again know the comforting presence of her departed husband, and so she squandered her life savings going from city to city as she searched out psychics and mediums who proclaimed their ability to "seek the dead" and reconnect her to her true love. In the spiritual realm, second only to devil worship, this would probably be considered the fastest way there is to inadvertently open wide the doors to the realm of darkness and allow demonic activity, and very possibly, demonic possession into one's life. When you open "the door", it's never a question of whether or not he, the devil, is coming in; he's coming. And he never leaves politely; you have to throw him out.

Well, to make a short story long, she realized what she had done by the "voices" now living in her head, but didn't know how to free herself of their presence. With my friend Leslie's help, we got her off the streets and into a small apartment where we could study the Bible truths concerning her predicament, confess each offence, renounce her involvement in them while asking her loving Heavenly Fathers forgiveness, then rebuked the demonic spirits with the truth of God's Word, and commanding them to leave, in Jesus's name. It was the simplest deliverance I was ever allowed to participate in.

The predominant Scriptures we covered were;
Leviticus 19:31 – psychics, mediums and familiar spirits defile you.
Leviticus 20:6, 23, 27 – causes you to "prostitute" your self – idolatry.
Isaiah 8:19-22 – mediums, wizards and "those who seek the dead on behalf of the living", bring trouble, darkness, gloom, and anguish, and will be

driven into darkness. We are too, instead, "Seek God", comparing everything to "this Word".

Ezekiel 13:22-23 – God Himself has promised to deliver you! Also note that in here and in the verses above, 3-21, that it is God's people, His righteous ones that are being preyed upon. No one is exempt. The Apostle Paul emphasizes this fact, when talking to the Spirit filled Christian believers (and us) in the church in Corinth telling them that he, "does not **want** them to have fellowship with demons", and clearly says we can't have both, the things of the Lord and of demons (1 Corinthians 10:19-22).

Notice, he did not say, "**can't have**" fellowship with demons. But, believe what you want; I have seen what I have seen. Quench the Holy Spirit enough times and see what you get (1 Thessalonians 5:19).

And while we are noting notes, noteworthy is the eyewitness account of Paul's deliverance of a slave girl who was "possessed" with a "spirit" of divination and thus, fortune-telling is equated to demonic possession, and Paul casts out the "spirit" accordingly, in the name of Jesus (Acts 16:16-18).

To my delight, for many years after this, Darlene and I would sit and discuss the Scriptures for hours, over a hot cup of Postum (that really shows our age, doesn't it) that she would always make for the occasion. I so look forward to her hug that I will receive when I, too, get home to Heaven...and maybe a cup of Postum...you never know. Seeing my beloved bacon in Heaven might be a little "iffy" though.

## CHAPTER 50

## Integrity

*"Let me be weighed on honest scales, that God may know my integrity."*
Job 31:6.

*"As for me, You uphold me in my integrity, and set me before Your face forever."*
Psalm 41:12.

*"The righteous man walks in his integrity; his children are blessed after him."*
Proverbs 20:7.

I believe that being able to restore a man's integrity and dignity, once it has been lost, is a precious blessing that God bestows on very few. I also believe that having the ability to do so, and not doing it, is a horrible waste of a divine gift and the loss of a God given opportunity. A sin? I don't know, maybe. A crime against the soul of another, definitely.

My Dad, like many others I know, faced their imminent demise with only one achievable goal, before leaving this earth and going back home to Heaven... to die with their dignity intact. I pray that I may do so as well, should I not outlive the coming of the Rapture.

I helped to put together a "deal" for Phil concerning his 1000+ mining claims on the north end of the Carlin Trend, and a world class mining company, that was beyond our ability to hope for. What I didn't know was that another "company" had been whispering "sweet promises" in Phil's ear that I knew nothing about. When the highly respectable company representatives came from Japan to Phil's place in Battle Mountain to begin finalizing our deal, Phil, like a mad man, went off on them about "their" atrocities committed during World War II, and insulting them deeply, to my shock and dismay, which of course, ran them off.

The other "company" had promised Phil the moon, so to speak, as long as he didn't sign the deal with the Japanese firm to take over his claims. Worse, they promised to file the annual assessment work and pay all of the filing fees as well, which was something Phil could no longer afford to do himself. If the claims were not filed and the fees paid by September 1, Phil would lose all of his claims. The people Phil were listening to were a disreputable group I had advised him not to get tangled up with a year earlier, and that's why he felt he should keep it from me, his property manager, until after he made the deal with them. I was deeply grieved that he kept it secret from me, and yes, had I known I would have thrown a first class pissy-fit. But my hurt was nothing in comparison to his when the realization of what he had done finally set in.

Phil called on the afternoon of August 31, and told me he couldn't pay the filing fees on his claims and the con artists that had recently promised to pay them were nowhere to be found. He asked if I would come up to northern Elko County and re-stake his claims (that night) and told me he couldn't pay me unless he made a deal with someone before the 90 day filing period was up. That's 1076 claims for free, with absolutely no payroll to hire a crew with, at least $15-$20,000 in expenses, and no money to rebuild, repair and replace my trucks, bikes, off-road equipment, supplies and personal gear that I would run into the ground, and winter was coming early this year.

Sure. What are friends for?

Dad and I left that night for Battle Mountain.

On September 1, we moved on to the "Phil" claims to find other stakers already there, making it very obvious that Phil had been set up. Feeling very "naked" without my guns, I unloaded my Honda 300, and geared up with claim posts and equipment. I rode first to the west end of the other stakers' progressing monument line and planted a double set of monuments in front of them, stopping their progress, as they yelled threats at me. Then to the east end and planted another set of double claim monuments at the beginning of their claim line. For them to stake over the top of my newly established claims would be "claim jumping" and could/would evoke very serious consequences, and according to the 1872 mining laws still in effect, they could legally be shot, if caught in the act. They, of course, had no idea I was unarmed, but surely nobody would be fool enough to do what I had just done to them, unless they were willing to back it up "in spades", and I was counting on them not being willing to incite a shooting incident out here in the middle of nowhere.

I also had Dad take our truck up on top of a high ridge behind them where it would seem as if they would be caught in a crossfire from higher ground. It was a very bad gamble and an ugly show of aggressiveness that invited gunplay, but it paid off, as they loaded their gear and left.

As near as I could guess, we had lost over 100 claims in the first day, which told me that, judging by the size of their crew, they must have been staking several days before Phil's filing fees were even due, and postdating the location notices to September 1. Dad talked me out of setting "nail traps" in the bottom of Soldier Creek where the road crossed, in order to give them a long days walk to Rossi mine and time to think about how they had double-crossed my dear friend, Phil. Dad was mad enough to let me do it, maybe, had I not mentioned the second part of my plan was to set their truck on fire so they could watch the plume of smoke rise into the air for miles as they hiked out of the high country. I repented for my malice, even though I felt I had barely averted a perfect opportunity to backslide. You think you have "killed your old man" (former nature), then the devil pushes a button you forgot you had, and presto! Resurrection time for that ol' worldly piece of…you that you thought was dead and buried.

Trying to convince my Dad of all this didn't exactly fly, as he pointed out (rebuked me) the blatant fact that me still packing nail traps in our gear in the first place, made it a premeditated event.

So, anyway, we staked everything you could see from the only access road in the area first, then did the southern end just above the Rossi mine.

We moved camp up to Willow Creek Reservoir so that hopefully, Dad could get in a little fishing while I staked the hard ground on the north end of the claim block. Day by day I was running myself into the ground at a very accelerated rate, as it was almost just too much to do for one person. I rode my four wheelers and climbed mountains from sun up to sunset, regardless of the weather, and after a while every part of me hurt. Dad did all my paperwork and set up my monument lines with the location notices in numbered film bottles, so all I had to do was grab them, load the claim posts on my bike, and go. One evening I came dragging back to camp with a gash on the left side of my left calf that I had received from slipping down a sharp rock face. It was too jagged of a cut for Dad to stitch up properly but he did the best he could. The next morning I returned to camp at about 10 AM with the same leg, including the gash, full of cactus thorns. Some days are just like that.

I was hurting now to where I could hardly sleep and Dad insisted on taking the other bike and helping me run some of the claim lines in. I shouldn't have let him, but I couldn't have stopped him. Shortly after the third week, Dad got his bike tangled up in some sagebrush and broke his leg, God bless him. But God…used his downtime! Dad spent most of his time in the trailer, after he got his leg in a cast, reading my Christian books and my Bible and his spiritual growth was obvious to everybody! We prayed together every day and God blessed us.

Soon we woke up to a half inch of snow on the ground and subzero temperatures. I knew I couldn't do this without God's supernatural strength and help, and I clung to his promise from Isaiah 41:10.

I would *"Plead my case before the mountains, and let the hills hear my voice,"* every day, as the Lord instructed in Micah 6:1, and He heard my anguished cry. The power of the Holy Spirit caused me to sleep and regain my strength, and He gave Angels charge over me. My greatest strength came when the Lord showed me Amos 4:13 saying, *"Who walks the high places* (mountains!) *of the earth? The Lord God of Hosts is His Name."* From that moment on, I knew He was there with me in these desolate mountains, even though blizzard conditions were becoming common.

At one point I stuck my bike on its side in very high sagebrush and broke my big toe. The cold amplified the pain, but as it had become my custom, I always stopped on top of the highest mountain that we called "the Little Hilton" on the way back to camp each evening, to pray and give thanks to the Lord. It was easier on some days than others, believe me. As I neared the top of the mountain, a "hole" suddenly appeared in the sky of solid clouds. In the center of the "hole", the sun burst brightly through revealing the most beautiful deep blue sky that I had ever seen. A beam of light streamed right through the snow storm and engulfed me on top of that mountain top, with its brilliant light! I looked around in every direction and as far as the eye could see, the only place it shined was on me and a space of maybe 30 feet around me! The snow swirled all around me and glittered like diamonds, kind of like in a snow globe...or like around one of those Disney princesses in the movies (I know, not the best analogy... Whatever).

I instinctively dropped to my knees in the snow, giving praise and worship to my Lord God, Creator of the Heavens and the Earth and the Sea, and all that is in them, because He loves me so much to do such a wonderful thing for just me! And I love Him back.

I felt as if He told me that, even though storms will come and go, no matter what I'm going through, He is with me. He knows! No matter how hard the situation becomes, He will never leave me or forsake me. No matter what trials I, and you, face, we will never face them alone.

HE LOVES ME! HE LOVES YOU!

From then on, until we finished the job and went home, signs and wonders commonly accompanied my days. Most amazing was that antelope, lynx, coyotes, rabbits, badgers, ravens and other animals were no longer afraid of me. I sat down and shared a can of peaches with a badger! I believe that perhaps, their spirit was witnessing with my spirit. To me, this is what it means to walk with the Lord, and pray without ceasing.

And again, thanks be to God, because we managed to save 946 of Phil's original claims.

***

Working for a road construction company near Kinsley mine, I hurt my lower back very badly when a load of huge electrical cable accidentally slid out of the loader bucket and on to a flatbed semi-truck I was loading for transport. Looking back through my journals I now realize that was when the healing miracles actually began to consistently manifest.

About the same time my dear friend Barbara Laskey, Pastor of the Open Door Church in Ely, was taken ill and together we began researching and praying various healing scriptures together. Naturally, our prayers and studies rolled right on over into my weekly youth group lessons, and everyone has somebody that needs God's healing touch.

As a corporate unit of the Body of Christ, praying prayers of faith in agreement (James 5:15, Matthew 18:19-20), these young people, whose angels always see the face of our Heavenly Father (Matthew 18:10), reigned in massive undeniable miracles of healing.

And then almost in equal proportion, the attacks of the enemy also increased upon us and others. In the winter months of November 1999 through March 2000 we spent so much time at the hospital, ER, and Care Center that they allowed us to come and go all hours of the day and night, as was needed. Certain nurses would recommend our young prayer group to their patients, as the results that the Lord was supplying to our prayers, became overwhelmingly obvious.

During this amazing time of miracles my own healing needs for my back pain went un-met, but the pain actually increased, making it difficult to stay on my feet for more than an hour or so at a time. Then my orthopedic surgeon who was handling my case, told me my options were limited because of the bone damage to my vertebrae's and that first we would try a series of steroid injections directly into my back (that hurt), then probably surgery with only a small chance of success, as fusion may not be possible due to the damage, and more than likely, I would be in a wheelchair within a few short years.

Yeah, I know what you're thinking, and I agree... Dumb ass lying devil, shut up in the Name of Jesus, *"Who Himself bore our sins in His own body on the tree, that we, having died to sins, might live for righteousness –* **by whose stripes you were healed."** *(*1 Peter 2:24).

That same doctor said that irregardless of even a successful surgery, I would never be able to drive truck or run heavy equipment ever again.

Hahahaha! Somebody, either God or my doctor got it wrong and doesn't know what they are talking about...Hmmmm... I choose God's Word as the Truth in this matter! God said, *"I can do all things through Christ, who strengthens me"* (Philippians 4:13), because, *"He who is in you is greater than he who is in the world" (*1 John 4:4). Please see Healing Scriptures in Appendix Q.

Thus began one of the most difficult battles of faith I have ever engaged in.

## CHAPTER 51

## Mayhem to Miracles, and a Peek at Heaven

*"And the prayer of faith will save the sick, and the Lord will raise him up".*
James 5:15.

November 29, 1999 – Tammy, a 14 or 15-year-old member of our youth group, came over to our house tonight to ask if I would go with her to the hospital and pray with her, her sister and brother-in-law for the healing of their 18-month-old baby boy, named Daniel. Little Daniel was in intensive care because he had "severe pneumonia" and things had taken a turn for the worst. X-rays showed that his tiny lungs were full of liquid.

Just as I was about to enter his room, a certain agitated doctor looked at my Bible and pulled me over to one side in the hallway, and harshly whispered to me, "This is what religion has done. Jehovah Witnesses they are and they refused to bring their baby to the hospital until now and now it's too late. I'll try to start an IV, but..." He then just shook his head in apparent disgust and walked off. I had no idea what he was talking about.

The poor little baby couldn't breathe hardly at all, and could barely cry and had turned pale white and going to blue in color. The room was swarming with doctors and their staff. As they were assembling an oxygen tent around him, I managed to work my way over to the back side of the crib and gathered Tammy and both of Daniel's parents together for a prayer of faith. As we prayed, I anointed baby Daniel with oil (James 5:14, Mark 6:13) and called on the Lord to use it as a shield of the Blood of Jesus for protection, then I reached in under the oxygen tent and grabbed hold of his tiny little foot to lay hands on him (Mark 16:17-18), at which time I felt the sudden urge to release the hand of Daniel's mother that I was holding and instead grab onto young Tammy's hand. Tammy and I prayed healing Scriptures and thanked God for the baby's recovery, and his parents prayed and agreed with us. Afterwards I found a place over against the wall and prayed Scripture over that little guy.

No longer able to stand on my feet for the intense pain in my lower back, I left the hospital and went home for about 30 minutes to rest. When I got back to the hospital I knew something had happened. When I entered Daniel's room I was greeted with hugs and overwhelming joy by Daniel's father! Then a nurse, with tears on her face, walked into the room, grabbed me and hugged me and walked back out without saying anything.

They told me that only moments after I left, Daniel stopped crying and began breathing easier! His color had returned before the IV had been fully set up or started! As I approached the crib, Daniel saw me and started smiling and making happy baby noises at me and got very excited. He was also coughing out all the junk in his little lungs and they were clearing rapidly, Praise and Glory to God!

I told him, "You have been talking to your Daddy in Heaven, haven't you Daniel, and your Daddy in Heaven loves you, doesn't He?"

At this, he actually rolled over and stood up in the crib, grabbed my finger I had stuck through the little oxygen tent door, and jumped up and down, rocking back and forth and laughing!

I blessed him in the Name of Jesus.

With most of the commotion over with, someone had brought a couple of chairs back into the room, and Daniel's mother was sitting in one of them, sobbing. I sat down beside her and cried too.

After hugging them all and emphasizing the importance of praising the Lord for this miracle of healing, I went home, praising, honoring, and glorifying Yahweh Rapha (the Lord who heals you – Exodus 15:26). And incredibly, as I went, the pain in my back stopped for the rest of the night, allowing me a much-needed full night's sleep.

Even 20 years after the fact, I sometimes run into a person who was there that night, and it's like, "Do you remember...?" And then we praise and glorify God all over again for it!

I will never forget, Lord.

***

And that's pretty much how all of December went as well. "Divine Healing Technicians" as Kenneth Hagin referred to them. Our young prayer group grew to a half dozen kids who just simply believed the Gospels and expected the results that the Word of God promised. We prayed over sicknesses and diseases, drug overdoses, and car wreck victims. We prayed for nonbelievers as well as believers. We even went to the Care Center when Lori asked us to come to the Hospice care room, where her dear friend and employer of 21 years, George, had been sent "until he passed" by the doctors at the hospital. Five days later George was back at the office working again!

On New Year's Eve my friend Barbara was care flighted into Reno. Barbara's daughter and I left Ely at 8 PM and Barbara had just come out of surgery at 1 AM when we got there, and was doing well. I arrived back home in Ely at 8 PM that night in time to go up to the hospital with Tammy and Paul to pray for Tammy's stepdad who was in ICU with internal bleeding. The doctors could not determine the source of his bleeding. As we held hands and prayed for our spirits to unite to do God's will for this healing, the "surge" (for lack of a better word) of the Holy Spirit up my arms and then through my body was very intense. The next morning, a CAT scan that was done on Tammy's stepdad found no trace whatsoever of the internal bleeding, and they released him shortly thereafter!

\*\*\*

A few days later I again drove the 325 miles over nine summits to get back to my friend and mentor in Reno. Barbara, even though very ill, was in a cheerful demeanor. I immediately went about anointing her with oil, laying hands on her and praying for several days for her health to be restored. Then one day she asked if I "would stop for a few minutes so we could just enjoy each other's company, without all the fuss, Sweetie?"

I was afraid, and she knew it. I didn't have a lot of "spiritual" friends, and Barbara and Gracyne were kind of my pals, so it hurt my heart when she smiled at me and told me, "Maybe it's just my time to go home, John. I'm okay with that." The problem was, I wasn't. The remainder of our time together was spent talking about her childhood, family and all the things God had done in her life. She accepted everybody as children of God, just like Jesus did. Her whole life was centered on the teachings of Christ, her goal was sharing Jesus with others, and her hope of glory was knowing that eventually she would be there with Him, where she is right now. The last thing she said to me was, "See ya later, Sweetie". And she will. What about you?

2 Corinthians 5:8 says, *"To be absent from the body is to be present with the Lord"*, and because Barbara as well as "uncle" Phil Davis, my mother and father, and so many others that have gone before me knew this in their hearts, they not only had no fear whatsoever of death (thanatophobia), but they anticipated going home to be with the Lord with joy.

*"Death has no sting"* the Bible says in 1 Corinthians 15:54-55, and *"is swallowed up in victory"*.

Jesus took care of that on the cross, *"that through death He might destroy him who had the power of death, that is, the devil, and release those who through fear of death were all their lifetime subject to bondage,"* Hebrews 2:14-15.

That's the true freedom we have to live our lives out, knowing that when it's over, we simply go home. The tragedy of all this death business is found in not realizing that we are **Citizens of Heaven** and all of this here on planet Earth, is not our home (Hebrews 11:13-16). Of course, it goes without saying that if you have chosen not to accept Jesus's sacrifice on the cross for the full payment of your sins, then you better be afraid, and rightly so, because your fear is justified.

And furthermore, there is a homecoming party for all of us who have been redeemed by choosing to make Jesus our Lord and Savior! Isaiah 51:11

tells us, *"So the ransomed of the Lord shall return, and come to Zion with singing, with everlasting joy on their heads. They shall obtain joy and gladness; sorrow and sighing shall flee away."*

Did you get the "everlasting joy" part? Everlasting, meaning... Lasting forever! Hallelujah!

Death is nothing but a curtain between us and our next life in eternity, *"Some to everlasting life, some to shame and everlasting contempt,"* Daniel 2:2, depending on what you do with Jesus, here and now, in this lifetime. As Jesus explained in Matthew 25:46, some *"will go away into everlasting punishment, but the righteous into everlasting life."*

It's up to you. It's your choice. Choose life.

God said, *"I have set before you life and death, blessing and cursing; therefore choose life, that both you and your descendants may live",* Deuteronomy 30:19.

God designed and created each of us to be an "overcomer" (Genesis 1:26-27, Romans 8) so, for God's sake, as well as your own, be one. How?

*"And they overcame by the blood of the Lamb and by the word of their testimony, and they did not love their lives to the death."* Revelation 12:11.

*"Who is the one who overcomes the world, but he who believes that Jesus is the Son of God?"* 1 John 5:5.

*"You are from God, little children, and have overcome them; because greater is He who is in you than he who is in the world."* 1 John 4:4.

As there are specific blessings for overcomers, please see also, John 16:33, Romans 8:31-39, 1 John 2:13, Revelation 2:7, 2:17, 2:26, 3:5, 3:12, 3:21, 12:11, and 1 John: 4-5.

In a nutshell, *"He who has an ear, let him hear what the Spirit says to the churches. He who overcomes shall not be hurt by the second death."* Revelation 2:11.

Jesus took it for you.

His death was your death.

His resurrection was your resurrection.

You and I have been raised up together with Christ! (Ephesians 2:1-7).

Because He endured the crucifixion to get me back home to Heaven, I have no issue living and serving Him with my life, as without Him doing what He did, I wouldn't have a life that didn't end in hell.

If God would give us all a quick peek behind that curtain and let us glimpse what's going on in Heaven, and then let us make the choice of where we wanted to be, we'd all be hanging out with Him, and Barbara, and all our loved ones who went home before us, right now, Amen?

But we have to accept Him by faith. Barbara knew this, as did so many of my friends and family, and that's how they got to Heaven. They are now standing in *"an innumerable company of angels."* (Hebrews 12:22). Try, for a moment, to picture all this in your mind. Jesus said in John 14, *"In my father's house are many mansions: If it were not so, I would have told you."* If I know my Mom, she is probably running upstairs and sliding down banisters about now. Dad, a devoted miner, is surely digging potholes in the streets of gold (Revelation 21:21).

And they have heard Jesus's very own words, "Well done, good and faithful servant." Today, this day, they walk with the Master. I love this subject!

Here's a little of what they are experiencing…imagine, please, yourself, or someone you love who has gone to Heaven, being led about the place with Jesus's arm around their shoulder as He shows them these things for the first time;

*"Now I saw a new Heaven and a new earth, for the first Heaven and the first earth had passed away. Also there was no more sea.*

*God Himself will be with them and be their God. And God will wipe away every tear from their eyes; there shall be no more death, nor sorrow, nor crying. There shall be no more pain, for the former things have passed away. Then He who sat on the throne said, "Behold, I make all things new".*

*And he carried me away in the Spirit to a great and high mountain,* (J. G.: I can't wait to see the mountains in Heaven!) *and showed me the great city, the Holy Jerusalem, descending out of Heaven from God, having the glory of God. Her light was like a most precious stone, like a jasper stone, clear as crystal. Also she had a great and high wall with 12 gates, and 12 angels at the gates, and names written on them, which are the names of the 12 tribes of the children of Israel; three gates on the east, three gates on the north, three gates on the south and three gates on the west.*

*Now the wall of the city had 12 foundations, and on them were the names of the 12 apostles of the Lamb.*

*And the construction of its wall was of jasper; and the city was pure gold, like clear glass. The foundations of the wall of the city were adorned with all kinds of precious stones; the first foundation was jasper, the second sapphire, the third chalcedony, the fourth emerald, the fifth sardonyx, the sixth sardius, the seventh chrysolite, the eighth beryl, the ninth topaz, the tenth chrysoprase, the eleventh jacinth, and the twelfth amethyst. The 12 gates were 12 pearls; each individual gate was of one pearl. And the streets of the city are pure gold, like transparent glass.*

*But I saw no temple in it, for the Lord God Almighty and the Lamb are its temple. The city has no need of the sun or the moon to shine in it, for the glory of God illuminated it. The Lamb was its light. And the nations of those who are saved shall walk in its light, and the kings of the earth bring their glory and honor into it. The gates shall not be shut at all by day (there shall be no night there).*

*And he showed me a pure river of water of life, clear as crystal, proceeding from the throne of God and of the Lamb. In the middle of its street, and on either side of the river, was the Tree of Life, which bore 12 fruits, each tree yielding its fruit each month. The leaves of the tree were for the healing of the nations. And there shall be no more curse, but the throne of God and of the Lamb shall be in it, and His servants shall serve Him. They shall see His face, and His name shall be on their foreheads. There shall be no night there; they need no lamp nor light of the sun, for the Lord God gives them light. And they shall reign for ever and ever."* (Excerpts from Revelation 21 and 22).

Relax, and let that vision just sink in for a minute.

Jesus offers peace and wholeness through salvation.

He offers forgiveness and healing with no condemnation.

He offers guidance and protection through the storms of life.

He offers unconditional love.

And He offers eternal life with Him in Heaven.

No strings attached. It's free to you... It wasn't free to Jesus... He paid for it, so you could have it for free.

He doesn't care who you are or what you've done in the past. He wants you right now, as you are. He promised.

*"All that the Father gives Me will come to Me, and the one who comes to Me I will by no means cast out"*. John 6:37.

And now is a very good time.

\*\*\*

Upon arriving back in Ely I was called back to the hospital to pray for the mother of a boy in my youth group. Jesse said his Mom was in the ER suffering from a heart attack. I anointed her and we said a prayer of faith over her, as she was being taken to the airport to Care Flight her to Salt Lake City. Jesse called a few hours later from the hospital in Salt Lake, whooping and hollering praise to God! He said that the doctors were "going in" after the blood clot that had caused his mother's heart attack. While they were just beginning the procedure, the blood clot vanished! It disappeared right before them! He went on to tell us that she would be coming home the next day, Glory to God!

While I was at the hospital I was asked to come into a room and pray for a boy named Alan who was in critical condition, and he was released to go home that same night! God was on the move!

Every single incident that happened created a massive platform from which to proclaim God's love, mercy and grace!

People were humbling themselves before Him and receiving Him as their Savior at every manifestation of healing!

## CHAPTER 52

## Dances, Road Trips and Doing Business for the Lord

*"For the Son of Man has come to seek and to save that which was lost."*
Luke 19:10.

It's astonishing to me, how many people, through misinformation, believe that in a 1963 Supreme Court case known as Abington School District versus Schempp, the Bible and prayer were banned from public schools. Man, the devil really twisted what actually happened and the people bit into the lie, hook, line and sinker.

At the time, Pennsylvania had a law requiring Bible reading at the beginning of each day. A guy named Schempp challenged the law and the court agreed that the state cannot require someone to read the Bible – the state shouldn't be in the business of requiring students to be devoted to a particular religious faith. Making it "mandatory" or forcing kids to read the Bible in school is unconstitutional.

However, the court did not declare all Bible reading in school unconstitutional.

The court went on to clarify that it was not ruling out Bible reading when it wrote; "...the state may not establish a 'religion of secularism 'in the sense of affirmatively opposing or showing hostility to religion, thus preferring those who believe in no religion over those who do believe." But what most teachers and administrators are doing today is acting exactly as the court warned them against. They are definitely establishing a religion of secularism.

The Supreme Court went on to say; "It might well be said that one's education is not complete without a study of comparative religion or history of religion and its relationship to the advancement of civilization. It certainly may be said that the Bible is worthy of study for its literary and historic qualities."

Folks, that's not just allowing it, that's encouraging it! They said it's worthy of study!

Betcha didn't know that.

With this, and mountains of legal data, and curriculum suggestions, I went to the school board in White Pine County, until I was blue in the face, and found I was having a battle of wits with a group of seemingly unarmed people. Regardless of the facts they said things like, "Oh, that can't be right", when it was the true facts I presented, and "it's illegal", when I proved over and over that it wasn't.

"No", they said.
"Why not?" I asked.
"Because it's in our bylaws", I was told.
"What bylaws? Where?" Lori asked.
"Next item on the agenda", they went on.
So, here's what God did…

With a "tip" from a friend, who to this day, still wishes to remain anonymous (still works for them), Lori targeted specific "glitches" in her research of the school board's "bylaws". She found that for us to use the gymnasium of the middle school (former high school to us old folks) for any event, they could not charge us the usual fee because we are a 501©(3) nonprofit organization. Not only that, but as long as the majority of the participants in our "event" were from their student body, they had to underwrite us on their insurance! Ha ha ha ha! And boy howdy, that made some people really mad, especially the principle of the middle school, for some reason.

With extremely super generous monetary donations from the Laskey family and Nathan Ministries, we managed to purchase the two big 110 pound "disco" speakers from the old Bank Club, a moderate light show, a 200 Watt Yamaha amplifier that I wired my daughters "boom box" stereo into, and a couple of smoke machines.

And with gigantic donations of time, prayer and commitment from our friends from the Methodist, Foursquare, Calvary, Baptist, Episcopal, and Lutheran churches, we put on youth dances every first Friday of the month, for all the local kids!

Month after month at the school, we gave away hundreds of Bibles, tracts, Christian music CDs and Christian movie videos and novelties. None of the pastors, reverends, or ministers from any of the churches or "Ministerial Association" would condone our dance outreach to the kids in the community with the exception of Angelo from the Methodist Church, and in fact the rest of them condemned it, but the actual "Body of Christ" was always there to help out. Especially at the New Year's Eve dances and carnivals we put on. The menstrual (oops!) Ministerial Association told us that the reason we had such a huge turnout was because the parents just wanted someplace safe to "dump off their kids" while they went out and partied…Ya think? That was kinda the whole point.

Many friends and officers from the Sheriff's Department donated their personal time to do "walk-throughs" so everybody behaved themselves, God bless them, and would often pray with us and our friends from all the other churches long before the doors opened to start the evening's festivities. We, by God's grace, managed to create an environment where it was comfortable to present the Gospel, witness, pray, counsel, and minister to about 80% of the teenagers in the White Pine County area, encourage them to make good life decisions based on godly principles, and they were quite receptive! How awesome is that?

The miracles, like this one, that God performs for us are amazingly mind-boggling, yet by far, the greatest work God does is in the hearts of men when by love, grace, and mercy, He redeems them from the curse of sin, death and hell and adopts them into His celestial family, heals their souls, and grants them eternal life with Him in Heaven. And it is a very humbling thing to be used by Almighty God to help accomplish His greatest work. Telling others of the free gift of Salvation should never be done without seeing the high price Jesus paid for our redemption, because we couldn't. Helpful to keeping it in its proper perspective is remembering that planet Earth is simply a spiritual battleground for human souls, but thanks to Jesus, everybody has the opportunity to win the war. He made victory possible for everybody.

Celebrate Easter, always, and every time we see the symbol of a cross we should be reminded how valuable we are to Him who paid such a remarkably high price to bring us back home to Him.

Thank You, Jesus.

Remember the cross...and tell others...time is short.

***

Seeins how (is that a word?)... Seeing how – seeing as how – seeing as... As practically all of the kids who signed up for, or showed interest in joining our Youth Group on Wednesday evenings had no means of transportation available to them, it was a tremendous blessing when the Lord provided us with our first 12 passenger van. It was very well worn as it came from the Bald Mountain Mine public auction when it had over 100,000 miles on it, but it had been well maintained, as was the second one we bought when the first one filled up. The vans quickly became the "lifeblood" of our outreach ministry because we could now safely pick up and bring home the kids we transported weekly to the church in McGill, 13 miles from Ely.

Whereas we were the only ones in the area to offer this service, and the highly criticized fact that we had no criteria that the kids had to meet to join us, the results were that we had the largest Youth Ministry in White Pine County. Every week we picked up kids from all the low income housing complexes throughout Ely as well as kids from the "ritzy" part of town, and virtually all neighborhoods in between, and eventually we soon were nicknamed "low income housing on wheels" by many. Oddly enough, our critics who came up with these witty names and hurtful little comments were almost always from the professed Christians in the established local churches, mostly because we were considered "unchurched" (rabble).

The kids worked hard doing yard and house work, and repairs through realty companies, as well as fundraisers and the like, and we were completely self-supportive with God supplying all of our needs through Christ Jesus. Even when we outgrew the two vans, God moved in men's hearts, and Barrick Gold Mining Company gave us a 21 passenger bus! We also rounded up anyone who wanted to go to church on Sundays, but sadly, many of the "Street kids" had already tried going to church at one time or another, and felt overwhelmingly rejected, unwanted and uncomfortable, and stated they "didn't fit in" or "belong".

He said that He would make us "fishers of men". Did you ever go fishing without any bait? What did you catch? Nothing. Well, thanks to God, the fishing was great, and "road trips" were the primary bait. And thank God for the yearly Creation Festivals held in Washington State! If you haven't been, make it a point to go! We fit right in and for the first time most of these kids actually knew they "fit in" and belonged to the Body of Christ! For three days we praised and worshiped our Savior with thousands of other kids just like them, with every background, every lifestyle and every color of hairdo you can imagine. They prayed with us and we prayed with them. Most every Christian band we knew was there.

Because almost all of these kids had never seen the ocean, we left Ely two days early and went to Lincoln City, Oregon and spent a whole day playing at the beach. Three days later, at the Creation Festival, in the 90° heat, we began the pungent task of finding and removing all of the hidden starfish, snails, sand crabs, and miscellaneous sea creatures the kids had hidden in the vans to take home and show their friends and family. It was bad… Really bad.

On the way home we always stopped off at Shoshone Falls, near Twin Falls, Idaho to go cliff jumping at our favorite swimming hole (Hippie Head). We camped at state parks for 12 to 16 bucks a night which included a barbecue pit and showers. Our meals were preplanned and precooked (mostly, except for breakfast) for all our road trips, which were many. We went to Salt Lake City on one of our trips to see Carman in concert, and it was fabulous! My sister in Christ and pal Leslie, cooked up enough chicken so that each person could have two pieces each. However, late that night after the concert, when we set up our food table in the parking lot, so many hungry people came by to ask if we had any extra that we wound up feeding over 100 people, and still had enough chicken left over that, when we got home, each of our kids could take some home to share with their families! What a crazy miracle God did that night! Everybody saw it and we will never forget!

And thank you and God bless you, my dearest friend, Tim Lujan for always riding shotgun over many roads and many years, with more kids than sanity could survive. Tim has been there always to encourage me and help me grow in my faith... And he has been there to help me pick up the pieces of my shattered faith when I lost battles, sometimes maybe even making the difference between whether or not I got back up again. Thanks bro.

The same goes for my pal, Mark Drain, who on the second morning of our first road trip ever, woke up with me and 16 kids in "pet cemetery"! We had left Ely that morning, went through Winnemucca Nevada and on up to Burns Oregon on our way to the coast, but when we got to Burns way after midnight, all the camping grounds were full up, so we kept going into the night until I saw a small dirt road leading into the forest. Exhausted, we pulled off the road and just threw our sleeping bags out on the ground around the two vans Mark and I were driving. As dawn peeked its lovely head through the trees, we woke up in and on every kind of dead animal skeleton you can imagine! Apparently the highway department had at one time not too long ago, used this side road to drag all of the road kill out of the traffic lanes. Deer, mostly, with dogs, coyotes, badgers, and various others I had trouble identifying after being run over several times. Then we walked maybe 150 feet around the bend in the road, hearing the sound of water, to find a plush grassy meadow by a beautiful stream! I think the Lord had the perfect place for us picked out to rest, but I was so tired, I gave up just a few feet before we got there.

And yes, we all see the moral to this story, rieeeght?

Don't give up. I know you're tired. Just a little ways further. You're almost there, and then you can rest.

We even toured down inside Boulder Dam, before 9-11 of course, and Zion national Park was one of our favorite camping destinations. We always tried to format our trips around the Lord, His Creation, Christian events and the Body of Christ as to provide experiences that honored God and revealed His love through others. In particularly, we enjoyed going south to camp in warmer temperatures as the frost level came so early to Ely's 6500 foot elevation, and we were always welcomed with open arms at the Word of Life Christian Center, on Buffalo Drive in Las Vegas. We smelled like campfire and Lake Mead yet these people, strangers at that, hugged and loved on us like no other church I have ever been to. They prayed with us and the several times we invited our nonbelieving young friends from our neighborhoods, they often received the gift of salvation and the baptism of the Holy Spirit through our brothers and sisters in Christ that worshiped here, God bless them, especially my friend Calvin. Hi Calvin! Hope you read this! We even saw the famous preacher, Jesse Duplantis there one time!

***

Oh, yeah. Then there was this, like, ninja warrior type guy who I need to mention who gave his life to Christ and entered into discipleship with me. Paul Williams and I would often spend time just hanging out at the city park below my house, as that's where most of the "Street kids" would be in the warmer summer months. We would sometimes set up a volleyball net and invite others to join us for a few games while we took the opportunities the Lord set before us to give witness and testimony of what God had been doing in our lives. Many received our invitation to join our Wednesday evening Youth Group meetings as well as allowing us to pray with them about what they were going through at the time. Those were awesome summer days, well spent. And at 6'1" tall I was pretty good at volleyball too… Paul…well…anyway. He wasn't too bad at handball, though.

Getting a metal detector turned out to be a very good investment for witnessing at the parks, as well. Turns out, they are a "kid magnet", calling out to the "inner treasure hunter" instinct in all of them. As (at least at the time of this writing) every United States coin gives witness and testimony to the value of trusting God (the "in God we trust" imprinted on all United States coins), I could tell them, "Look! I found a message from God saying to trust Him! Who do you trust?" and the like. Great icebreaker and a fun and profitable hobby, not only for me but for hunting true treasures (souls) for the Kingdom of Heaven.

Good bait; good fishing. We catch 'em, God cleans 'em. Gotta love it!

\*\*\*

That summer, as always, Lori was doing one of hundreds of routine home inspections, when she opened a door to an outside hot water heater compartment and was smashed on the head by soaking wet drywall and insulation. The hot water heater had been spewing water from a leaking pipe that soaked the interior of the compartment for a long period of winter in the unoccupied mobile home. Because the water drained through the floor and went underneath the foundation, it went undetected. The weight of the overhead drywall ceiling and wall crushed several vertebrae and discs in Lori's neck and would eventually require several surgeries and fusions. The constant sharp pain was and is unrelenting in her neck and head.

Throughout our many years of marriage we were always able to look out for each other. When one of us was down, the other always was there to take up the extra load, so to speak, and handle things. This time we were both hurt and down at the same time, yet we did our very best to help each other and encourage each other in the faith, and Jesus handled the rest. That's what soulmates do. Even though pain engulfed most of our days, sometimes incapacitating us, somehow we seemed to always manage a laugh or two. I never would have made it through these dark days without her, and God knew this… That's why He sent her to me, I am very sure.

Ecclesiastes 4:9-12;

*"Two are better than one, because they have a good reward for their labor.*

*For if they fall, one will lift up his companion.*

*But woe to him who is alone when he falls, for he has no one to help him up.*

*Again, if two lie down together, they will keep warm;*
*But how can one be warm alone?*
*Though one may be overpowered by another, two can withstand him.*
*And a threefold cord is not easily broken."*

That threefold cord? That's me, Lori, and Jesus!

And, *"assuredly, I say to you, whatever you bind on earth will be bound in Heaven..."* Jesus promised. Noteworthy is the fact that Jesus thought this statement is important enough to repeat Himself twice and Matthew 18:18 and 16:19. Therefore, Lori and I have joined together and become one flesh and are bound together, in the name of Jesus. So be it.

## CHAPTER 53

## The Open Door

*"To the present hour we both hunger and thirst, and we are poorly clothed, and beaten, and homeless. And we labor, working with our own hands. Being reviled, we bless; being persecuted, we endure; being defamed, we entreat. We have been made as the filth of the world, the offscouring of all things until now."* 1 Corinthians 4:11-13.

It was late fall and snow was coming early to the high country of Nevada. With the help of some of the boys from our youth group, I had recently just finished replacing the drywall in the entire basement and re-carpeting the beautiful five-bedroom home of my dearly departed friend, Barbara. I had been working on the house for the past seven months or so, fixing, cleaning and repairing as best I could, with the ever present pain in my lower back. Now, as I finished walking through and inspecting every room for the umpteenth time, I ended up in the living room and sat down on the couch.

"Lord, the magnitude of this blessing is just too big for me to deal with on my own. I hear all these other preachers and Christians always telling me, 'God told me this, and God told me that' and Your Bible says You're no respecter of persons, so when You tell me what I'm supposed to do with this house, I'll do it. I've done the best I could to fix it up so, until then, I guess I'll just lock it up until I hear directly from You and You alone."

Barbara's family had gifted the house to our ministry and I was having a hard time wrapping my mind around such a huge blessing. I didn't know that God obviously had a purpose for doing such a thing. It was all done. Every bedroom was furnished with beds, nightstands and dressers, the kitchen was completely stocked with housewares, a dining set, and microwave, and the living room was also modestly furnished including an extra television set Lori and I had.

I locked the front door and went home.

\*\*\*

Because of our extremely cold winter temperatures often with a chill factor over 30° below zero at night, Ely was a terrible place to be dropped off if you were a homeless person. There were absolutely no facilities available to help them. No place to sleep, no food, not even a bus to get you out of town even if you could find someone to help with a bus ticket. And Ely is in the middle of nowhere, far from the interstate highways. Yet because it is on the shortest two lane highway route from the northwestern states to the southwestern states, drifters were often picked up heading north from Vegas or heading south from interstates 80 and 84, to be dumped off in Ely. Coming out of Las Vegas, they very often would arrive in Ely to find themselves in bitter subzero temperatures without so much as a jacket or sweater. Many had destinations they were trying to get to, and most were just drifters. The small casinos in town were open 24/7 but had no tolerance for "bums", so either I or my friend Karen at Support Incorporated (of which I was a board member for many years) would get calls all hours of the night from the Sheriff's department or the local churches to help them, and between all of our friends, we usually handled it.

Support Incorporated Family Crisis Center was a nonprofit crisis intervention service dealing with everything from domestic violence and abuse to substance abuse and feeding the poor. And the people who ran it had a heart to help people in need, so between all of us and our friends from various churches, we always seemed to be able to pool our resources and help the homeless people of our community, as the needs arose.

One cold night, just before Christmas, Karen called me trying to raise funds for food and hotel rooms for a family of seven that had hit an elk, totaling their car, several miles south of Ely. They were all at the ER getting treated for non-life-threatening injuries and were soon to be released with nowhere to go and very little money. Complicating our efforts was the fact that all of the fairly inexpensive motel rooms (if there is such a thing) were completely sold out for the holidays and everybody we knew, including myself, was close to flat broke anyway.

"Well, Karen," as divine epiphany smacks me upside the head, "listen; I got Barbara's old house back in pretty good shape. It has 30% propane for the furnace and stove, and the water and power are still turned on. We got lots of beds, so all we have to come up with is bedding and food. Lori even stocked the kitchen with pots, pans and dishes."

Awesome God and awesome friends!

Bedding and sleeping bags poured in and with the generosity of many friends, the fridge and cupboards were stocked to overflowing within an hour! How magnificent is the Body of Christ when God is on the move! Such an honor to be a part of His plans.

At 1 AM we moved the entire family into the house, and the Open Door Project was born that night, by the grace of God. Even though they couldn't speak hardly any English, their constant heartfelt blessing of "El Senor Este Con Ustedes" was perfectly understood (the Lord be with you).

From that night on, for almost a decade, the Open Door Homeless Shelter never once sat empty or turned anyone away. And for the life of me, I can't even begin to understand or explain how, week by week, month by month, and year by year, the bills all got paid and hundreds of people were fed, clothed and housed, except by the obvious and amazing hand of God. El Shaddia,

Yahweh Jira, our God who is more than enough and the God who supplies all our needs, as He promised in His Word (Philippians 4:19).

And we learned a lot about the homeless, and they learned a lot about Jesus.

We learned there are different types and reasons for homelessness. Some are the result of simply "falling on hard times", such as unemployment, house fires, etc., and these people often just need a "hand up", so to speak to get back up and on their feet. These are the easiest to help. Through the Open Door Project many folks found work in the area and eventually were able to support themselves and re-enter society. Some even found love and got married here.

Others are "professionally homeless". They have made a lifestyle out of wandering and never settle too long in one place before their "feet get itchy" and they feel compelled to move on. They are always moving, and life, though extremely difficult, is somewhat of an adventure. Many of these have proven to be highly skilled and excellent workers, yet seek no form of permanence. They are often driven by great pain or loss in their past that has led them to forsake jobs, careers, businesses, homes, family, and all aspects of stability. Loss or death of a loved one, divorce, imprisonment, Post-Traumatic Stress Disorder (commonly found in our veterans) failure, committed crimes, warrants, injustice, guilt, depression and anxiety are just a few of the root causes that enabled them to drop everything and just walk away from their previous lives. They have experienced some sort of trauma that they are unable to mentally process or deal with. In theory, as long as they keep moving, the painful experiences remain behind them, and thus don't have to be faced or dealt with.

Even so, these types adhere to a self-set "code of ethics" that helps them maintain a level of integrity and dignity, as best they can. Many not only know the Lord, but have come to rely on Him completely.

Not so much with the more self-abusive type. They, like the last mentioned group, have something that has driven them to the streets, highways and byways of this nation, but these have given themselves over to alcoholism and drug abuse as a means of daily escapism, and no longer have the ability or oftentimes even the will to get themselves free. PTSD is one of the leading causes, and this type is by far the most heartbreaking.

These folks usually have a "circuit" that they travel. They are not really interested in picking up work or odd jobs, except out of absolute necessity. They have nothing left of life except their addiction(s) and they are completely given over to it/them. They commonly travel to shelters in the southern states during winter and migrate to the northern states in the heat of summer. From town to town, city by city they know which shelters will harbor them and feed them and for how long, as well as which churches, organizations and some businesses they can "hit up" for the usual "contributions". They can almost always plan the amount of days they will stay in each location based on the time it will take to exhaust all the resources available to them, before they move on to the next one, in their yearly "rounds".

So, excluding the bondage to their addictions, who is really more free…us or them. Hmmm…

If you're like most people, we are in bondage to our possessions such as mortgages, bills, payments, careers, taxes, insurance, etc., and to all the things we feel are necessary for life, whereas they are not. Our possessions often own us, and we are slaves, or at best, maintenance people to our belongings, whereas these folks are truly free to come and go where they wish, as they please.

What would it be to own nothing and be debt-free? What would you do? What if I could take even one of my paychecks and do with it whatever I wanted, except buy material possessions? Truthfully, I can't even think of anything I would want to buy anyway. Interesting… Probably best for me if I change the subject.

\*\*\*

Glenn was a Vietnam vet. He arrived back in the states from the war in 1973, with a fierce addiction to heroin, and has been homeless ever since. That same year his mother died. At the time I met him he had spent well over 30 years wandering without a home. Along the way, and over many years, rescue missions and the Veterans Administration helped him break free of his heroin addiction, but it left deep "scars".

He is a very kind man, yet his thoughts are often "scattered" and foreboding, causing confusion, paranoia, and mental discomfort. Inside, he is trying so very hard to again be that brave young boy who went off to Vietnam to make his mama proud, before the atrocities of war and heroin stole his innocence. Glenn was a true drifter, one of the few who did not follow a "circuit" or any type of pattern in his wanderings.

Untreated mental illness is a very common trait shared in homelessness, as is alcoholism. A "friend" is often mentally created by many to sustain a form of companionship in order to offset their horrific loneliness. Open communications and conversations with these "friends" or mental companions become progressive among them, and are accepted as the "norm" in circles of the homeless. No big thing, until these entities begin to speak or talk back to those who have opened this door by inventing them and creating a place in their lives for their existence. Friendly "conversations" soon turn ugly and condemning. Subliminal "guidance", suggestions and directions lead so many into the service of the evil one or at least into an ongoing "mental war" between the kingdoms of darkness and light, right and wrong, good and evil.

Needless to say, when folks come into our homeless shelter, or anywhere for that matter, who proclaim to hear voices, I become very wary. Even more so, when the voices they are listening to proclaim to be, or are "divinely" delivering "messages from God", I tend to keep them in the "corner of my eye" and not turn my back on them. This lesson was hard earned, not once, but twice and both times almost cost me my life.

This is as it was when James came into the shelter, "sent to me" with three (yes! Not one or two, but three!) "messages from God". I have a wonderful, close, personal, open relationship with my Heavenly Father and I am confident that if He needs to say something to me, He has no need to send a messenger boy, as I am always available to hear from Him.

The truth you need to know about this is found in Mark 15 where, at the crucifixion of His beloved Son for all of mankind's sin that had separated us from Him, God demonstrated our re-conciliation to Himself in a very visible and tangible way. At the precise moment of Jesus's death and the completion of payment in full of our sin debt, an amazing miracle happened.

*"Then the veil of the temple was torn in two from top to bottom"*, Mark 15:38. Significant to notice is that it was torn not from bottom to the top, it was torn from God's end first, not ours. That veil or curtain is what separated common mankind from the presence of God in the temple. It marked the entrance to the holiest part of the temple where only God resided, and because no sin can stand in His presence, no man could enter with the exception of the high priest, once a year, on the Day of Atonement. The curtain was 60 feet high and separated the Holy Place from the Holy of Holies. The high priest would have to carry out, with exact precision, the instructions for the sprinkling of blood for the people's atonement for their sins, found in Leviticus 16. Any deviation from the instructions and he would die. He went in with a cord attached to his leg just in case they had to drag his dead body back out. It was serious business. Then came Jesus, who took all of our sins to the cross and paid the full price, once and for all, making us "clean" in God's eyes! The curtain or veil was the barrier put in place to keep us and our sins out of His presence. But thanks to Jesus, we can now *"come boldly to the throne of grace, that we may obtain mercy and find grace to help in time of need"* (Hebrews 4:16), *"For there is one God and one Mediator between God and men, the Man Christ Jesus."*

And even when we don't know what or how to pray, the Holy Spirit will make intercession for us! (Romans 8:26-27).

That doesn't really seem to leave a lot of room for a messenger boy, does it? It's really that simple, thanks to what Jesus has done. Any system that endeavors to complicate or add a bunch of ritualistic dogma to what the Lord has already provided for us, through His supreme sacrifice, is an insult to Him, as is any system or theology that puts a person between you and God.

What Jesus did was open wide the way for all of us to have a personal relationship directly with God! You have that opportunity before you, right now! There are no barriers, curtains, walls, sin or hierarchy between us and God, and you don't need anybody's approval or permission to enter into the presence of the Creator of the Universe, your Heavenly Father! It's as easy as just saying, "Hello Father", and go from there.

Anyway, back at the Open Door Homeless Shelter, James was dogging my heels for days, always clutching a Bible and a notebook, asking if I was ready to hear the three messages God had told him to give me, and it was getting very annoying. He was very meek and timid in character, yet adamant and aggressive about delivering his messages, especially after I had told him, "No, I don't want to hear them," over a dozen times.

There were several other men at the house that also needed my time, as well as maintenance and repairs that I was trying to deal with around the property. I was distracted. When Lori had come by the house with groceries and gas for the lawnmower, I courteously and properly introduced her to James, who openly stared at her before she left. After her leaving, James actually went silent and stopped pursuing the issue for an hour or so. Then, with new fervor, he started back in on me.

Finally, out in the backyard, I told him, "Let's hear it, if you agree not to bring it up ever again."

He agreed, stood upright with his heels together and his head held very high, and told me the first message, about how I was to show no partiality to the people in the shelter and help them in any way I can, as long as it takes, with all of my resources, especially with my money.

As he spoke I listened carefully and realized that my spirit was not discerning anything demonic in him or dark in the words he used (other than moronic), as he went on to the second message. I believe this was all just stuff he had come up with all by himself, with obviously no "spiritual guidance", good or bad, involved. I was somewhat relieved; until he dropped the second message. This one came with an apparent nervousness, visible discomfort and fidgeting, as he told me that Christian leaders, such as myself, are to always be prepared to be a living example for others of martyrdom. In no circumstance am I to lift a hand to another human being, not even in defense of my own life. "As a matter of fact," he goes on, "even if someone breaks into your home to rape and murder your family, and your wife, you are only allowed to stand in front of her and offer up your own body and life first."

What a test. To those who may have witnessed the event I may have seemed like an epic fail, as far as the test went, but I didn't knock him out, so I personally think I passed. Only God knows.

However, I did grab him by the shirt and shoved my face in is, in order to make myself perfectly clear, and calmly said, "Choose your next words very carefully, James, because they will determine whether you spend the rest of the day here, or in jail. We're done here. No more messages… Ever. Don't bring it up again. Do you understand?" With bulging eyes he nodded agreement, and I let him go. He turned without a word and scurried back into the house, and I immediately felt bad about the terrible way I had mishandled the situation. Not very "Christian" at all and I felt ashamed of myself. But, on a good note, it's worthy of praise to God for the work He has done in me up to this point, (though obviously not yet complete) as a few years ago I would have been apologizing to James when he came out of his coma, after seemingly threatening my family.

I found out later that James had gone to several other local pastors with the similar messages – they apparently handled it better than I did, but, if you think that because I am a Christian that makes me a victim, you better rethink it. God gave me a family because he knew he could trust me to look out for them as best as I can.

In all of this, I had missed a few telltale signs of deeper issues with Glenn. This came to manifestation with a panicked phone call from one of the other men in the shelter, right after supper time.

When I arrived back at the "recently vacated" homeless shelter, the hair on the back of my neck went up as I went through the front door and on through the living room. As I approached the kitchen, I heard Glenn yell, "Leonard says, Satan has asked for you, James, so he can sift you as wheat, and I am the sifter!" I walked into the kitchen and quickly took in the situation, noting the absence of blood on anyone or anything. Glenn was standing in the middle of the room and James was cowering down in the corner created where the refrigerator meets the wall, still clutching his Bible and notebook.

"Don't tell me, let me guess..." I said to James, "You tried to tell your three messages to him, didn't you?" Without waiting for a response, I turned to Glenn and asked, "Who is Leonard?"

"Ask him yourself," Glenn responded as he turned his head to look toward the empty corner of the room by the back door, "he's standing right there."

I looked at the empty space Glenn was looking at and said, "Who are you, Leonard?"

Nothing.

Then Glenn said, "He said for you to butt out. This is none of your affair."

Great... A battle of the "no-see-em's". Unfortunately, or more precisely, fortunately, James was "unarmed", as he really didn't have a "spook" giving him his "messages".

"Please, sit down, Glen," I asked.

"I'm not going to tell you again..." Glenn began to say before I cut him off with, "Leonard, in the mighty name of Jesus Christ, I bind you to silence! Speak no more to Glenn, in Jesus's name."

Then, with the same authoritative voice, I said, "Glenn... Sit down, now," and he did.

As he pulled out a chair from the table and sat, he looked up at me and said in a small, scared voice, "Help me".

"It's all gonna be okay, my friend," I told him in as soothing of voice as I could come up with, under the circumstances. "Glenn, today it's gonna be over and you are finally gonna be free from him, I promise." I told him, as I pulled a bottle of cooking oil out of the cupboard.

I washed my hands over the sink with the oil, and started praising the Lord.

"Jesus is so awesome, Glenn. Thank You, Lord, for setting Glenn free! Say it with me Glenn – thank You, Jesus, for setting me free."

He chimed right in as I laid my oily hands on his head.

"I plead a blood covering of protection over you, Glen, and by the power of Jesus's shed blood, and in His Almighty Name, I command this spirit of darkness to forever leave you in peace. In the name of Jesus Christ, Son of God, come out of him, now, Leonard!"

Glenn closed his eyes and slowly raised his hands to his head and put them on mine, and began to weep.

I looked over at James, still in the corner, trembling in shock, and said, "Go James. Get out of here for a little while," and "poof" he was out of there.

"He's gone." Glenn said. "He's really gone. And my head doesn't hurt anymore."

I am sad to say that James never came back and I never got another opportunity to minister to him. My mishandling James the way I did will always cause regret in my soul. I pray that one day I see him again and have the chance to try and make things right with him. I'm so very sorry, James… Please forgive me.

As for Glenn, with the help of my awesome pal, Leslie, and the Veterans Administration, we managed to get him into his very own one-bedroom apartment, complete with furnishings, a phone, and food assistance. It was his first and only home of his own since going off to war, over 30 years ago, as he was now 49 years old. The first call he made on his very own phone was to me, asking if I would come bless his new place. When I got there he explained that it was so much room that he felt I should rent out most of it as all the room he needed was where he had "set up camp" in the large walk-in closet. Trying not to tear up, I told him no, that it was all his and he deserved it as the blessing of God to His own boy, that it was. It took a while but he finally started using the rest of the apartment.

Every year I would take him to the ice fishing derby at Cave Lake so he could have a chance to win "big money" by catching the lucky fish, with the winning tag attached to it.

He made it almost 2 years. Then one day my phone rang and Glenn asked if I would come by and see him. I somehow knew before I got there, and it broke my heart in 1000 pieces. He had to go. He just had to go. He had stayed as long as he could, but the open roads call to him was too great. He was thankful for all we had done, and especially for bringing him to meet and know his

Savior, but the life of a wanderer was too ingrained in his being to stay put in one place, and it was his time to go.

I wanted to "fix" his life, but I couldn't. Only Jesus could. True freedom for my friend, Glen, could only be found on the highways and byways of this beautiful country. The comforts and confines of his apartment could no longer hold him, and so he left. God bless you, wherever you are, my brother. Amen.

***

"Hey, did you see this?" Exclaimed my dear friend, Tim, as he shoved a local newspaper in front of me. On the front page was a large picture of the old **condemned** Ely grade school building, which I had attended from first grade to the eighth. The headline and following blurb read something about the city of Ely turning the old closed Ely grade school (did I mention condemned?) into a mass homeless shelter with the millions in grant money they were trying to get, as part of President Bush's "Faith-based Initiative" grant policy.

Right. Whatever, I thought.

At the time, we were getting about 80% of our homeless people brought to us from the Sheriff's Department and the Nevada Highway Patrol as they were found by them on the streets and highways in the area. The officers of the Sheriff's Department did an awesome job of looking out for us by checking for potential problems such as violent backgrounds, etc. and were always there when we needed them (a special thank you to officers Penny, Luke, Scott, Lester, Jim, and Bernie! God bless you for your compassion and your kindness). About 11% were referred by the local churches, and the rest were sent to us by the folks in the community.

Several months passed until I received a call from a grant research group in Washington DC asking for this exact information as well as inquiring as to the primary sources of our financial support, which was "none" except the Lord, at that particular time.

"Not even from the local governments (city of Ely, etc.) that bring you most of your homeless people?" They asked.

"Nope", I responded.

Several more months passed, when the City Council held a meeting in which they shut down our homeless shelter. A few months later I got another call from the people in Washington DC telling me that they had re-applied, stating that there no longer existed a homeless shelter in the area, so I told them what happened with the City Council.

To this day there still no longer exists a homeless shelter in the area. How sad is that. It's all "coincidence" I am told. Like I said before; right... Whatever.

What do you think?

I do know what the Lord thinks. Jesus made it very clear in Matthew 25 versus 31 through 46. Important to note in versus 41 and 45 is the Lord's defining response, "He **will** answer them…"and, "He **will** also say…" It does not say "maybe" or "He might". **HE WILL**. I think it's safe to say the Lord has already judged this issue.

*Then He will also say to those on the left hand,' depart from Me, you cursed, into the everlasting fire prepared for the devil and his angels: for I was hungry and you gave Me no food; I was thirsty and you gave Me no drink; I was a stranger and you did not take Me in, naked and you did not clothe Me, sick and in prison and you did not visit Me.'*

*Then they will also answer Him, saying,' Lord, when did we see You hungry or thirsty or a stranger or naked or sick or in prison, and did not minister to You?' Then He will answer them, saying,' assuredly, I say to you, inasmuch as you did not do it to one of the least of these, you did not do it to Me.'*

*And these will go away into everlasting punishment, but the righteous into eternal life."* Matthew 25:41-46.

The most chilling is the word "will" in the last sentence.

May God have mercy and forgive them.

## CHAPTER 54

## Breakfast With An Angel

The prophecy;
*But He was wounded for our transgressions,
He was bruised for our iniquities;
The chastisement of our peace was upon Him,
And by His stripes we **are** healed.*
Isaiah 53:5.

The prophecy fulfilled;
*...who Himself bore our sins in His own body on the tree, that we, having died to sins, might live for righteousness – by whose stripes you **were** healed.*
1 Peter 2:24.

As the elevator at Washoe Medical Center came slowly to a stop on the floor designated as the Intensive Care Unit, I stood waiting for the doors to open, with my Bible tucked under my arm and feeling like God's Man of Power for the Hour. Recent months had produced an exceptional amount of "fruit" for the Kingdom of God by means of a consecutive series of healings, salvations, deliverances, and other miracles. In response, the attacks from the enemy were seemingly proportionate to the workings of God we were experiencing. We withstood them, at least for the most part, by prayer and worship, speaking The Word over our situations, and encouraging and edifying one another in the faith.

It's vital to know your enemy when you are a soldier in the armed forces, and so much more so when you are a Soldier of the Cross operating in the service of the Lord.

Dumbfounding is the knowledge of how many people really believe that the devil is sitting around in hell waiting for them to get there. Not hardly, and believing such nonsense will be their undoing. Satan will eventually end up there, but until then, he is cruising the earth, raising havoc and destruction in the lives of God's people.

The Bible calls him "the god of this world" (2 Corinthians 4:4). His career is set on killing, stealing and destroying (John 10:10). And he is a "people watcher". Devil means "slanderer, false accuser" as exampled in Revelation

12:10, *"For the accuser of our brethren, who accused them before our God day and night, has been cast down."* That's what he does, with what he sees, in us. He accuses us before God.

*"And the Lord said to Satan,' From where do you come?' Satan answered the Lord and said,' from going to and fro on all the earth, and from walking back and forth on it".* (Job 2:2, and also Job 1:7).

That's where he is…right now.

As he did with Job (Job 1 and 2) Satan had to ask permission to test Peter, (Luke 22:31) that he may "sift you as wheat", as interestingly, Peter and Job both had God's supernatural protection around them (see Luke 10:19 and Job 1:10). However, I doubt seriously that the herd of pigs in Matthew 8:30-31 had His protection around them when the legion of demons had to ask permission of Jesus before they could enter into them. Hmmm… I have no idea what one has to do with the other, but anyway…

If God allows us to be tested by the enemy and go through the fire, so that our "impurities" can come to the surface during the refinement process, know that His eye never leaves us and His hand is on the thermostat.

Peter, after surviving being "sifted" by the enemy, offered up this warning, *"Be sober, vigilant; because your adversary the devil walks about like a roaring lion, seeking whom he may devour. Resist him, steadfast in the faith…"* (1 Peter 5:8 and 9). Advice well received but often difficult for me to apply, it seems.

I believe that death secretes an odor. It's the smell of death. I believe I have smelled death on several occasions. Perhaps it's just an odor present as people succumb to death by certain causes or diseases, but I have smelled death, and it's not likely a smell I will forget. It's a very pungent odor and I have never been exposed to anything else that comes even close to being similar to it.

I find it to be a tremendous blessing that this smell will never exist in Heaven.

Death is the last enemy to be destroyed (1 Corinthians 15:26).

And the smell of death slapped me hard in the face when the elevator doors opened and I stepped out onto the ICU floor of the hospital. It was an unexpected and very unwelcome surprise.

Approaching the nurse's station, a dark-haired, middle-aged woman behind the desk looked at me, then at my Bible, and with what may have been a smirk, pulled a clipboard full of charts and data from its place on the shelf beside her.

"Andrea's mother said you would be coming by, to…" she said, stopping in midsentence, without looking up from the clipboard as she began flipping through its pages. Then her eyes moved from the clipboard to my Bible, and as her eyes slowly began to raise up to my face in some sort of assessment of me, she tilted her head slightly to one side and finished her sentence, "…to pray."

Was she taunting me?

Again, I had to ponder the possibility of certain people being sent into my life, by the antichrist, to torment me until Jesus comes. I even wonder sometimes about certain machines and vehicles I have operated that have managed to defy every effort to get them to run or just function properly... Yeah, anyway...

Moving from behind the counter, she came alongside me, and page by page, went into the details of Andrea's condition; no brain activity, when her kidneys and liver had shut down and how long it had been, her lungs, heart, and other organs that had failed, and all the machines that were now hooked up to her while in her comatose state of "existence".

"This way," she said as she abruptly turned and walked down the corridor to the very end room. As I entered the room behind her I was overwhelmed by all the machines, I.V. units, and monitor screens covering the wall behind the young patient. Hoses and electrical lines ran everywhere, and when I looked down on the young 19-year-old girl lying in the bed before me, I could not prevent the tears from running down my face.

She was small. Needles with hoses attached to them protruded from all of her arms, and legs, and the jaundice from her liver failure and breakdown of red blood cells had turned her entire skin tone a deep yellowish color, and her body was puffed up and swollen beyond what I could ever imagine. Her little knuckles were mere dimples in her huge, round, swollen fingers. So many tubes had been installed down her throat that they had taped her lips around them. Tubes were even running up into her little nostrils. She was so distorted from all of this that I could not tell what she could have possibly looked like before she had contracted this rare form of pneumonia, while spending time in Europe, last summer.

"Any life that is in her is supplied by these machines", the nurse said as she waved her hand in front of all the apparatus, machines and monitors that filled the room. Then, without another word she turned and left the room, leaving me standing there, beaten, with tears running down my face.

Andrea's parents were former Ely residents, now living in Reno, and had asked me to look in on their daughter, Andrea, the next time I came to Reno for my doctor appointments pertaining to my back.

My so called "prayer of faith" was incredibly feeble and lacked conviction. The beeps, bleeps and humming of the machines made them seem as if they were laughing at me. Loud moans and groans of painful anguish arose from the room next door, and instead of going in to the neighbors room to try and minister and comfort them, I gathered myself up, and with my eyes on the floor ahead of me, walked to the elevator and the nearest exit, like a whipped dog with his tail between his legs. I cannot accurately express the shame and failure I felt at that moment. Again, I just don't have the words. I felt as if darkness had engulfed me. Like underground darkness, only much more intense, and the pressure it created felt alive, somehow, as if it was wrapped around my soul and was squeezing the life (or light, perhaps) out of it.

When I stepped out the front door of the hospital into the night, I was gasping for air, on the verge of throwing up, and I was trembling.

What, the hell (literally), had just happened to me? I was shaken to the core of my being.

The only ones I told of this were Lori and my Dad.

\*\*\*

The phone was ringing but when I tried to get out of my recliner, the pain in my lower back and down my right leg forbid me from doing so. It finally quit ringing when Lori came upstairs and picked it up. The look on her face told me it was serious.

"Yes... Just a moment and I'll put him on", she said as she handed me the phone. It was Andrea's mother, and she was trying desperately not to cry as she asked, "Would you come to Reno and give my little girl her last rites, please?"

"Yes, of course," was my immediate response, even though I had no idea what "last rites" were. It just so happened (yeah, right. More like God on the move...again. Providence) that her last day before shutting down all of the life-support systems was the same day as my scheduled back surgery at the same hospital. That was pretty tricky, Lord, considering I was 325 miles away at the time, and couldn't stand or sit upright for more than a few minutes at a time, before the pain drove me back to a horizontal position lying flat on my back. After hanging up the phone I laid in my recliner trying to sort all of this out.

Finally, in frustration, I said, "How Lord? What do I do? Lord, forgive me but sometimes Your Words just seem like words. Sometimes the light of Your being seems so dim and distant. How can I help her when I'm like this? Father, I cannot lie here and say with my lips that my back doesn't hurt – in the name of Jesus, because it would be a lie. I need You, Lord."

Immediately, the pain was taken from me! As I lay there (mostly afraid to move) thanking and praising God for making Himself so very real to me, I saw so very clearly the vision of Peter stepping out of the boat and onto the water (Matthew 14:23-33). He stared into Jesus's loving eyes as he took his first steps, totally focused on his Master. The sea roared around him and the waves crashed. The wind slapped water against his face and pulled desperately at his clothes, trying frantically to take Peter's focus off of Jesus, if only for a second, and eventually it succeeded. Peter began to sink. In so doing he cried out to his Lord, and **immediately**, regardless of Peter's inability to stay focused, Jesus reached out and saved him!

"Forgive me for my lack of focus, Lord," I humbly prayed. "Help me to see You more clearly in the storms of life. And always hold my hand tightly in

Yours when I stumble or sink. Thank You, Lord, for the re-establishment of my faith and trust in You. Give me a fresh anointing to do Your work."

Lori and Dad had set up a bed for me in the backseat of my Chevy extended cab pickup, and so, down the road to Reno we went. Lori and Dad took turns driving, for six hours, while I laid in the back seat with my Bible searching for whatever this whole "last rites" thing was. I'm still to this day not quite sure what rights you think you have, just before you die, but in any event, I couldn't find it in the Word.

What I did find was that our God, known as Yahweh Rapha (Exodus 15:26) is "the Lord who heals you," not only in the healing of our souls by pardoning our iniquities, but in our bodies also by preserving us from diseases as well as curing them. Although God said He would heal (Isaiah 6:9-10) and Jesus repeated Him (Matthew 13:13-15), I found that teaching the traditions of men rather than the actual Word of God had empowered religion to rob us of our healing, and many other promises of God found in His Word and embedded in His Covenant with us, that is written in the blood of His Son (Colossians 2:6-9, Mark 7:6-9, 13, etc.).

Jesus provided our healing at the cross as prophesied by Isaiah;
*Surely He has borne our griefs*
*And carried our sorrows:*
*Yet we esteemed Him stricken,*
*Smitten by God, and afflicted.*
*But He was wounded for our transgressions,*
*He was bruised for our iniquities;*
*The chastisement for our peace was upon Him,*
*And by His stripes we **are** healed.* Isaiah 53:4-5.

Malachi 4:2 also prophesied of the Sun of Righteousness rising with healing in His wings, in reference to Jesus. And Peter reiterated it in the New Testament after the crucifixion and resurrection of Christ, when he said;
*Who Himself bore our sins in His own body on the tree, that we, having died to sins, might live for righteousness – by whose stripes you **were** healed"* (1 Peter 2:24).

If that doesn't get a "Hallelujah" out of you, it should!

In the Gospels we find all the many different ways and circumstances that Jesus healed the sick, delivered the possessed (Matthew chapters 8 and 9, for example) and even raised the dead back to life (Luke 7:11-17, Luke 8:40-56, John 11:1-44). He even spit in the dirt and made mud and stuck it on a blind guy's eyes and restored his sight! (John 9:6). I believe that the Lord and the Holy Spirit, throughout the Gospels and the Book of Acts, constantly used very different methods to heal and deliver in order to emphasis that there is NO FORMULA or magic ritual to accomplish these Devine manifestations---its about faith in Jesus!

Because Jesus was God in flesh form (John 1:1-5, 14, Colossians 1:13-18) it's easy for me to believe and accept these "divine" accounts of healing as truth, but then He makes the profound statement; *"Most assuredly, I say to you, he who believes in Me, the works that I do he will do also; and greater works than these he will do, because I go to the Father"* (John 14:12).

I believe in Him...but greater works than what Jesus did? It hurts my head just trying to wrap my mind around these words...trying to get some kind of handle on all this is tough for me...because we're talking about... Me... John Gergen. Yet the Lord said it, so it's true. He reaffirmed it in the Great Commission found in the Gospel of Mark, chapter 16, verses 14 through 18, ending with, *"...and they will lay hands on the sick, and they will recover"* (verse 18). He notably gave His disciples this power along with instructions on how and when to use it (see Matthew 10:1-15, Luke 10:1-20) which apparently also included anointing the sick with oil (Mark 6:7-13). It worked for them just as Jesus said it would, and that's why we should do the same thing. What really helped me come to the reality of all this was prayerfully studying the healing accounts done by the disciples, who were but mere men like you and me, in the Book of Acts.

The last thing Jesus said to His Apostles just before He ascended up into Heaven before their very eyes was, *"But you shall receive power when the Holy Spirit has come upon you: and you shall be witnesses of Me..."* (Acts 1:8), and He wasn't kidding when He said it.

The Holy Spirit is the power of the Lord, as Isaiah 61:1, Luke 4:14 and 18, Matthew 12:18, Luke 5:7 make clear to us, as does Acts 10:38 which states perfectly, *"how God anointed Jesus of Nazareth with the Holy Spirit and with power, who went about doing good and healing all who were oppressed by the devil."* So this verse clearly establishes that sickness and disease are an oppression of the devil (and NOT from God, for any reason, i.e. to teach you something, God's will for you because he allowed it, etc.) and are to be combated in the same manner that Jesus and his disciples did. All things of this nature are done through the power of the Holy Spirit. The power of the Holy Spirit is what heals us. The Word of God activates the power of the Holy Spirit according to Ephesians 6:17 and 18, and it's Him, not you, doing the work. Never forget this.

The Book of Acts (the history of the Acts of the Apostles), is jam-packed full of signs, wonders, and healing miracles, all designed and orchestrated by the Holy Spirit as a witness to the Lord, and examples of instruction for us. The last 2000+ years of our history bear uncountable documented accounts of miracles and divine healings, as do these last days we are living in right now.

I believe, without doubt, that there are as many signs, wonders and healing miracles going on every day around us that the media of these last days blatantly refuses to report. Yet, as always, charlatans, the deceptionists, and fallen ministers of the Gospel will always be exploited with front-page headlines as the assault on Christianity progresses, as prophesied by the Lord in Matthew 24, Luke 21, Mark 13, Revelation, Joel, etc., etc., etc.).

Sooo... Who, do you suppose, controls the media? For "God's sake" (literally), don't be foolish enough to believe anything you hear on the news media these days. I am convinced it is all designed to desensitize us and set us up for the rise of the anti-Christ, his false prophet, and their predecessors and minions (Revelation chapter 13 – note verses 13 and 14). If you don't study the Scriptures that foretell of the coming of these false ones, and the events they bring about, you will not recognize them, and you will be deceived. If you are still here because you rejected Jesus Christ as your Lord and Savior, and you take "the mark", it's over (Revelation 13:15-18, 14:9 and 11, 15:2, 16:2, 19:20 and 20:4). You can see the severity of how intensely serious it is that you know what is about to come, as your eternal destiny hangs in the balance.

Jesus said, *"Unless you see signs and wonders you will not believe"* in John 4:48, and Peter quoted the prophet Joel confirming God's signs and wonders in the last days, during his sermon in Acts 2:17-21;

*"I will show wonders in Heaven above and signs in the earth beneath: blood and fire and vapor of smoke. The sun shall be turned into darkness, and the moon into blood, before the coming of the great and awesome day of the Lord.*

***And it shall come to pass that whoever calls on the name of the Lord shall be saved.***"

Satan heard them say it and knows this as well, and boy, because of our hardened hearts, does he have a show he's about ready to put on for you! An extravaganza of deception!

And, yes, the days are soon approaching when the worldwide news media will actually be broadcasting all about signs and wonders. Will you know it when you see it? Seek the truth and the truth will make it impossible for that father of lies to deceive you. You must be sanctified by the Word of Truth.

*"Your Word is truth"*, the Lord said in John 17:17. If you know the truth, you cannot be lied to. There is no other way.

*"False Christ's and false prophets will arise and perform great signs and wonders, to deceive, if possible, even the elect,"* Jesus warned us in Matthew 24:24. The "if possible" part is determined by you.

Get this part right... What you choose to believe will by no means change what is coming. It will determine whether or not your soul survives it.

You should probably also know that atheism is a temporary condition as, *every knee will bow, and every tongue confess that Jesus Christ is Lord, to the glory of God the Father* (Philippians 2:5-11, and see also Romans 14:11).

As to the current fakes and the ones that are coming, please see also; Matthew 24:3-28, Mark 13:22, 2 Timothy 4:3-4, Acts 20:28-30, 2 Peter 3:14-18,

1 John 4:1-6, Matthew 7:15-20, 2 Peter 1:12-21, Titus 1:6-16, 2 Peter 2, and Matthew 23:1-29.

There's something in the wind. Something's coming. To me it seems that when things are quiet, you can almost hear it being whispered on the cool evening breeze. Can you perceive it? In the quiet, listen to your heart; what's it telling you?

As to the "real deal", let's get back to the Acts of the Apostles, as I studied them that day, long ago, while lying in the backseat of my Chevy pickup on my way to Reno (man, I really get sidetracked, don't I?).

As the road wound its way down the twisting east slope of Austin Summit, and passed several old played out gold and silver mines, I read Peter's words in Acts 3 to a man lame from his birth, *"Silver and gold I do not have, but what I do have I give to you; In the name of Jesus Christ of Nazareth, rise up and walk."* (Acts 3:6). And he did! Peter took him by the hand, helped him up, and they all went into the temple with the healed man *"...walking, leaping, and praising God"* (verse 7), and I'm betting that was a gross understatement! I'll bet John and Peter had their "mojo" going on just like that ex-lame guy! I would! Bustin' multiple moves, I'm guessing they were. The whole crowd goes wild, seeing this lame guy up and running around and they go off praising God, too! And Peter, being Peter, goes to preaching it (Acts 3:11-26) and tells everybody how and why this miracle came to be;

*"And His Name,* **through faith in His Name**, *has made this man strong, whom you see and know. Yes,* **the faith which comes through Him** *has given him this perfect soundness in the presence of you all* (verse 16, emphasis mine).

And of course, the religious fanatics who were running things at the time, weren't having any of it, and had them arrested and locked up, while they, all the big-shot religious leaders, tried to figure out how best to shut them up (Acts 4).

Yup...and it hasn't changed much in over 2000 years, from what I've experienced. So painfully sad when the Creator of the Universe, out of love, grace, compassion and mercy, miraculously heals someone of a terminal disease in front of everybody, and He gets denied. "Well, maybe they weren't that sick... Maybe the doctors were wrong... Maybe they had a good reaction to the medicine... Maybe, maybe, maybe. Maybe if the sun didn't come up tomorrow we wouldn't need a cure for skin cancer... Maybe if we had a cure for greed then we would be able to get on with a cure for cancer, itself... Maybe if a frog never jumped he wouldn't bump his butt on the ground. Maybe they are fools; *"The fool says in his heart,' there is no God'"* (Psalm 14:1, 53:1).

I love how the Apostle Paul said, *"For what if some did not believe? Will their unbelief make the faithfulness of God without effect? Certainly not!"* (Romans 3:3-4).

Just as with Jesus' parables (a worldly story with Heavenly meanings), some hearts the Word and works of God awakens, and others it hardens. Yet, there are always those who see it and do believe (Acts 4:4), and God is glorified, thus fulfilling God's spiritual law found in Isaiah 55:11, *"So shall My word be that goes forth from My mouth; it shall not return to Me void, but shall accomplish what I please, and it shall prosper in the thing to which I sent it."*

I wonder, rather than just sitting around all our lives being complacent about the matter, maybe such things are sent or happen to make us choose...to accept or reject His very existence...Hmmm...

I love Peter, and God knows we both share the trait of running our mouths, often before engaging our minds. Thank the blessed Holy Spirit for giving us the right words at the right time (Luke 12:12, Luke 21:15), as He did for Peter when the religious big-shots dragged him and John before them to explain themselves in Acts chapter 4. I really like how Peter, without fear or doubt, "nailed them to the cross" (so to speak – pun intended), about what they did to Jesus, in Acts 3, then as a reminder of this, he told them, *"Let it be known to you all, and all the people of Israel, that by the name of Jesus Christ of Nazareth, whom you crucified, whom God raised from the dead, by Him this man stands here before you whole"* (4:10), and nails it down with, *"nor is there salvation in any other, for there is no other name under Heaven given among men by which we must be saved" (4:12).*

What awesome confidence, after spending days with the resurrected Lord, including breakfast by the sea with Him (my favorite! What would that be like, let alone fishing with Jesus!), and all coming from the same scared man that had denied even knowing Jesus a few days earlier! Wow!

Then, after finally being released and told to be quiet about this entire "Jesus thing", I find this fantastic treasure of a prayer outlined in Acts 4:23-31, that I use in part, to this day;

(Verse 9*) Now, Lord, look on their threats, and grant Your servants that with all boldness they may speak Your Word, by stretching out Your hand to heal, and that signs and wonders may be done through the name of Your Holy Servant Jesus."* Major prayer!

And the Lord complied with their prayer request as documented throughout the Book of Acts, such as 2:13, 2:7, 5:12, etc., etc., etc., as well as the past 2000 years of history. Then, even though I had read Acts 9:36-42, hundreds of times in the past, it seemed to jump off the pages at me as I read it this day on my way to minister to a young girl living totally on life support machines.

The first thing that grabbed my attention was, who on this earth would name their daughter Dorcas? Granted, Dorcas translates to Tabitha, but, still... Dorcas? And she was a disciple, and she was dead. Even so, the other disciples in Joppa sent for Peter, anyway. That's magnificent faith in the unseen, while staring at the blatantly obvious dead girl, as she was seen by the non-believers that were present.

Note to self; if seriously ill, take account of who is around you and what they believe in, making adjustments as necessary.

Peter obviously took notice of this as well, and did exactly what his Master, Jesus, had done in Luke 8:48-55. The first thing he did upon his arrival was to throw out all the well-meaning doubters, *"...then kneeled down and prayed; and, turning to the body, he said 'Tabitha, arise!' She opened her eyes and, seeing Peter, she sat up."* Acts 9:40.

Perfect. He ousted the doubters and got down to business without overthinking or even evaluating the situation, like I am so guilty of. Just get it done. It suddenly became clear to me that it was overthinking and evaluating the so-called "facts" that had allowed doubt and defeat into my last encounter at the ICU in Reno on my last visit to minister to Andrea.

I know, above all else, that there is no formula, ritual or magical verse to recite to make God's healing manifest itself, as my studies have once again confirmed. It is faith that releases the power of the Holy Spirit, which has been activated by the spoken Word of God. Please see healing Scriptures in Appendix Q.

For me it always comes back to chapter 5 of the Epistle of James;

*"Is anyone among you suffering? Let him pray. Is anyone cheerful? Let him sing Psalms. Is anyone among you sick? Let him call for the elders of the church, and let them pray over him, anointing him with oil in the name of the Lord. And the prayer of faith will save the sick, and the Lord will raise him up. And if he has committed sins, he will be forgiven. Confess your trespasses to one another, that you may be healed. The effective, fervent prayer of a righteous man avails much."* James 5:13-16.

Faith filled words are what changes things, moves mountains, heals the sick and brings miracles to pass.

Feeling the confidence, peace and power of the Holy Spirit confirming that my full armor of God was properly adorned and fitted into place, as it had been so many years ago in Mariposa California, I knew I was ready.

\*\*\*

It was an hour after sunset and a dark moonless night had settled in. To save me as many painful steps as possible, Lori and Dad pulled right up to the front doors of Washoe Medical Center to let me out. It took a moment to force myself to stand fully erect when I got out of the pickup, as hot searing pain shot through my lower back and down my right leg, yet as I entered the building and headed over to the elevator, the pain began to subside dramatically.

"Thank You, Jesus," I muttered as the elevator doors closed and seemingly left my severe back pain behind in the lobby. I kid you not; I actually felt pretty dang good by the time the elevator doors reopened on the ICU floor. As before, the pungent smell of death immediately filled my nostrils and lungs as I took in my first breath, but as I let that first breath back out I smiled and said, "Not this time. Oh, death, where is your sting?"

Still wearing that same smile I walked past the nurse's station just as that same nurse as before was reaching for Andrea's status clipboard. I turned my smiling face to look directly at her, and before she had a chance to speak, I said, "Sshhhhhhh – I don't need to know. Thanks anyway," and still smiling, I just kept walking right on into Andrea's room, leaving the nurse standing there with her mouth hanging open.

After anointing the young girl with oil I knelt beside her bed, and laying my hands on her head, I offered to God my prayer of faith with all of my heart. I cast out the spirit of sickness and pneumonia from her and I told her that Jesus loved her and wanted her healed. I prayed until a tremendous sense of peace overtook me, then thanking and praising God for healing her, I gathered myself together and got back into the elevator. When the door opened again in the lobby, Lori and Dad were there to help me back to our vehicle, and both were quite surprised, as was I, when I told them I was okay and I didn't need assistance. It felt so great to walk back outside and over to our pickup without pain!

We checked into our hotel for a few hours' sleep before we returned to Washoe Med at 3:30 AM so they could "prep" me for surgery.

\*\*\*

The first chance I got I snuck out of pre-op and went up to Andrea's room to continue to pray over her. I was blown away to find all of her swelling gone, her skin color returned to normal, the restraints removed, and Andrea was responsive to commands!!!!!!! Yee Haw! Yippee Ki A! Yeah, Jesus!

That evening after surgery I awoke to my wife's beautiful eyes filled with tears, as she sat on the bed beside me. I had absolutely no feeling in my legs.

Before she could speak, I said, "Its okay honey, they did their best," as it seemed obvious to me that my lower back surgery had taken the worst case scenario. She looked at me kind of funny, then her eyes widened and she laughed!

"No, no, John, your surgery went pretty good. The feelings in your legs will return in an hour or so. They couldn't fuse your back because of the damage to your vertebrae's so they could only cut some of the bone away from your sciatic nerve, to relieve the pain down your leg," she said. Then the tears started to flow as she exclaimed, "God did a miracle!"

Lori had gone to check on Andrea and she was doing great! Better than great! She was coming out of her coma and they were disconnecting the life-support machines! She told me a dozen or so nurses and doctors were packed into her room to see what they couldn't believe with their ears. They told her "They couldn't explain it," and said, "We don't know what's happening but Andrea is emitting the sickness!"

Lori set them all straight, God bless her!

This is the most powerful healing I have ever witnessed. All glory to God! Jesus is Lord!

My doctor also told Lori that during surgery, I awoke and proclaimed that an angel was standing behind the doctor with his hand on Doc's shoulder, for which they all took a moment and sedated me back into La La Land, but I don't remember any of that. Regardless, Lord please bless that Holy Angel for looking after me! Thank You, Jesus!

After almost a year of physical therapy in Reno had passed, I answered my phone to hear the sweet voice of another angel. She said, "Hi. We've never really met before but you prayed for me...for my healing. My name is Andrea and I heard you were in town and wondered if you would like to come to my Mom's house so I could cook you breakfast."

I squeaked out a "Yes, I would love to," as best I could, hung up the phone, sat down and cried like a baby.

That beautiful morning, right here on planet Earth, I had breakfast with an angel.

## CHAPTER 55

## Healing on the Mountain

Several years later, I was tending the hot chocolate and coffee as I huddled around the campfire we had built at the base of Robinson Summit. That was my job, this cold January day, as my friend Tim and I had rounded up a dozen or so young kids (some from our Youth Group and several that we had simply invited along as we met them on the street) for a day of snowboarding. A recent lightning brush fire had burned all the sagebrush and most of the trees off of the north facing slope of the mountain and left it fairly hazard free and a perfect scenario for growing huge, windswept snowdrifts.

At 20° it was still an abnormally warm day for Northern Nevada, especially considering the top of Robinson is 8078 feet in elevation, the summit of the highway, where I now stoked the campfire on a blustery January day, was over 7500 feet high, and we had about a 15 mile per hour wind. Regardless, the kids were having a blast as Tim hauled them, over and over again, up the mountain on his snowmobile so they could slide and crash their way back down the white slopes of the mountain, usually in about 30 or 40 foot increments, as none of us knew how to snowboard. In fact, no one had even actually witnessed snowboarding firsthand other than on TV, let alone any of us ever having even one lesson. To us it seemed like what rich kids did, as ski passes, accommodations, equipment rental, and transportation to the closest ski resort calculated out to be well over a couple hundred dollars per kid, per day.

But…we had Robinson Summit and a bunch of used (slightly dinged up) snowboards that Lori and I had managed to pick up from several rental shops over the summer, as they restocked their inventory. We got a really good deal on them, (pennies on the dollar) for top brand boards, as apparently, most rich kids don't want to rent a scuffed up or damaged board for the kind of money they put out.

So Tim was laughing as he raced up and down the mountain, the kids were laughing and squealing as they hit the snow for the hundredth time and I was sulking by the campfire, wishing I could join them. The cold was horrific on me and magnified my lower back pain to the extent that moving just a few feet away from the fire pushed my pain level beyond my ability to bear for more than a few minutes.

"Woe is me," was my primary utterance as I whined and smiled and laughed outwardly with the kids at each new cr[...] that found its mark on my back.

Eventually, I mentally succumbed to "such is my lot in life,' deep sigh, sipped my coffee and reverted my thoughts back to the reoccurring dreams or visions of Peter stepping out of the boat, and on waters of the sea of Galilee (Matthew 14:22-33).

Galilee is the lowest fresh water lake in the world at levels between 6 feet and 705 feet below sea level, is 13 miles long, 8 miles wide, 141 feet deep, and has an average temperature of 86°, and Peter probably spent his whole life on it, up to the point where the Lord called him. He was a commercial fisherman, whose very name in Greek means "rock" and in Aramaic "stone" (see Matthew 16:13-20), and I'll bet nobody was more aware of the fact that if you step out of the boat while in the middle of the sea, during a storm, you're gonna sleep with the fishes, or more precisely, "sink like a rock."

As I sat alone by the fire looking up at the beautiful snow-covered mountains surrounding me, *"Now hear what the Lord says, plead your case unto the mountains and let the hills hear your voice"* (Micah 6:1) came to mind.

"Okay, Lord. I need to know, so please tell me… What was Peter thinking? What, literally in God's name, could have possibly been in his head at the exact moment he swung his leg over the side of that boat? What could he have been thinking of when he actually placed his foot on the surface of the water and then put all of his weight on it?" I asked.

How many times had Peter bailed over the side of the boat, every day for years, for a swim or launching his small ship out to fish, or landing it back onto the shore? Never in all those thousands of times had the surface of the water posed any resistance, but gave way every single time. But now…this time…

*"Lord, if it is You,"* Peter replied, *"tell me to come to You on the water."*

*"Come"*, He (Jesus) *said.*

*Then Peter got down out of the boat, walked on the water and came toward Jesus.* (Matthew 14:28-30).

As I sat there staring deep into the flames of the campfire, Devine epiphany seemed to smack me up-side the head, and I could envision Jesus before me, walking atop the surface of the water, as if through Peter's eyes.

It was all about his focus, and that was totally committed to Jesus. He could see Jesus before him walking on the water, making the impossible, possible, and Jesus' personal one word command to Peter, "come", is what made it possible for Peter to do the impossible with Jesus! That command made it possible for Peter to actually see himself stepping out of the boat and walking to his Master, in his mind's eye! If he saw himself doing it, he could do it, based on the Lord's say-so, but if he saw himself sinking he would sink, according to his worldly thinking. He locked his faith onto Jesus and stepped down out of the

The ultimate example of 2 Corinthians 5:7, *"We walk by faith, not by sight."*

And he did it, full well knowing he was going to walk on the water like Jesus was, because he could see himself doing it in his mind, and the Son of God had ordained it!

Sooo... If you are living a life strictly by what you can see, touch, feel, taste, and hear, you are living an extremely shallow existence;

*"... We do not look at the things which are seen, but at the things which are not seen. For things which are seen are temporary, but the things which are not seen are eternal"* (2 Corinthians 4:18).

If that be the case then, according to the Word of God, and Peter himself who walked on the water, *"who Himself* (Jesus) *bore our sins in His own body on the tree, that we, having died to sins, might live for righteousness –* **by whose stripes you were healed."** *(*1 Peter 2:24).

I was – am healed! It's all about faith. That's the bottom line. Is what the Lord said in His Word true or not? Absolutely. I am sure of it... I believe.

I stood up and walked over to several snowboards sticking straight up out of the snow and selected the longest, widest one there, just as Tim pulled up to the fire on the snowmobile. One look at his face, as he stared at me wide-eyed standing before him with a snowboard slung over my back, told me of his mixed emotions of disbelief and "Oh, my God, please tell me he's not gonna really do this," mindset. I walked over, climbed on behind him, grabbed a hold of him tight and said, "Take me up to the top."

He opened the throttle, the engine howled, and the snow machine launched forward and upward at full throttle in order to make it all the way up the mountain. As the machine began to stall out in the deep snow near the peak, Tim turned it sideways and came to a stop with the snowmobile pointing downhill, and said, "This is it – as high as we can go. Are you sure about this, John?"

"I'm good, bro. See you at the bottom."

Moments later, he was gone, and I sat down in the fresh snow and strapped my boots to the board. The view was spectacular, at almost 8000 feet elevation. The wind stung my face a little as I looked down the long mountain slope to the now tiny campfire by the highway. Tim and most of the kids were gathered around the fire staring up at me. They looked like ants at this distance, and probably had the same look of anticipation on their faces as NASCAR fans, full well knowing a horrific wreck is about to happen.

Running a bulldozer atop the high walls of Cortez mine, as well as several others, brought the same look from the loader operator and truck drivers, sometimes hundreds of feet below, when the wall would "peel". Everybody would stop and stare, to see if the dozer flip-flopped over the edge or not. I (God actually) disappointed the onlookers on more occasions than I care to recount.

Thank God that they don't cover those dozer seats with Naugahyde anymore. Oops, sidetracked. Sorry.

My eyes scanned the mountain side that lay between me and them, and it began to overwhelm me with its long distance and many obstacles, so I shut my eyes and held them tightly closed. Soon I could see (envision, imagine, hallucinate, whatever) myself floating down the mountain below me, turning and cutting around the rocks and half burned trees that were scattered along the slope. But when I opened my eyes and looked down the reality of the slope, I lost it. I think mostly because of the first, half-burnt twisted and blackened juniper tree closest to me that looked like Halloween personified and, I'm sure, by the look of it, had its roots grounded in hell itself. One ugly-assed, evil looking tree...very intimidating. I closed my eyes again, saw myself swooshing down the hill, and then opened them again. Then I closed them again...and again and again.

"Help me, Lord," I whispered.

Taking a deep breath and slowly exhaling, I relaxed and opened my eyes again, and smiled.

"I can do all things through Christ who strengthens me," (Galatians 4:13) I said in confidence, as I stood up on the board. With my eyes open, I could see it, in my mind, as I looked down the slope.

To keep my focus, I decided I would recite Psalm 91 (the one where God gives His angels charge over me so I don't hit a rock... Verses 11 and 12, my paraphrase).

That lasted for about the first four words of the psalm. With a slight hop I turned the nose of my board downhill, and within seconds, I was doing Mach 1. The only sound was the edges of the snowboard slicing through fresh virgin powder, at what seemed the speed of light. Though truly just a soft "swishing" sound, it seemed to roar in my ears and flood my heart and veins to the max with pure adrenaline, as I yelled at the top of my lungs, "Jesus! Jesus! Jesus!", the only word capable of coming out of my mouth! Just past that crappy tree, I leaned back a little and cut to the right just enough to miss an ambulance-sized rock that would have turned me to vapor at this insane speed. Oh my God!

I never anticipated such intense velocity, but should have, as Robinson Summit is very steep... I realize that now. Duh.

I bent a little more at my knees, and my speed increased even more, as I screamed "Jesus" over and over, all the way to the bottom of the mountain, where I slowed to a glide as the steep terrain gave way to the gentler slope of the foothill. I stood straight up on the board as I glided to a stop about 20 feet from the campfire. It was then that I became aware of the whooping and hollering of my friends, and it was then that I suddenly became aware of the total absence of any pain, whatsoever, in my back!

I was laughing hysterically with Tim and my young friends as a flood of tears rolled down my frozen face. Dropping to my knees in the deep snow I raised my hands and face skyward to praise my awesome Heavenly Father, and my friends joined me in awe of our Lord for the crazy miracle they had all just witnessed! Then they witnessed it three more times, just like the first time, as I got in three more rides before it finally became too dark to see.

In the many years to follow, I have had my "moments" but, all in all, by the grace of my Master and Lord, I am still healed, thank You, Jesus!

I have used this experience to counsel many young people over the years, on that very mountainside, and I pray above all else, that I honor You, Lord, every day of my life, for all You have done and all that You are. Amen.

## EPILOGUE...EULOGY...WHATEVER

*"It has seemed good to me to show the signs and wonders that the Most High God has done for me".* Daniel 4:1 E.S.V.
I agree, and it has been a long time coming.

My story is a paradox – something that can't be true...but is. My life has been orchestrated by Divine Providence. God, regardless of my many bad decisions, never gave up on me, and always found a way to use me. And, of course, I guess it's all about how God has pieced my life together, or pieced it back together, as it may be, after the many years that I did things my way while shaking my fist at Heaven. If God had not saved me when He did, there surely wouldn't have been enough left of me when I got to this point to matter, let alone be of any use to the Kingdom of God.

Apologetics? Theology? Religious doctrines, traditions and dogma? Don't bother with me. I have experienced His love, power, mercy, grace, compassion, and of course, His correction firsthand. I don't really care what anyone thinks or believes to the contrary.

I have experienced God.

As my friend Joseph taught me, a man with experience is never at the mercy of a man with an argument, and a man with an argument is only one experience away from renewing his mind. There is nothing anyone can say to change that or take it from me.

What church? I am an active member in the Body of Christ, as proclaimed in Romans 7:4, 1 Corinthians 10:16, 1 Corinthians 12:27, and Ephesians 4:12.

I like my current pastor's usage of the analogy of a car as the Body of Christ, and we are the various parts that keep it all working. He tells how almost everybody wants to be the turbocharger or maybe even the nitrous oxide system. I think I'm probably more like a dipstick, wingnut or maybe a lug nut. I'm good with that.

If the Word of God is in your mouth and heart, and you have confessed with your lips the Lord Jesus Christ and believe in your heart that God raised Him from the dead, you are saved (Romans 10:8-9), a member of my church, and you're stuck with me. If so, we now know the Lord not only through His Word, the Bible, but more so through our personal relationship with Him. If not, now is the time.

*"Seek the Lord, while He may be found. Call upon Him while He is near"* (Isaiah 55:6).

I have experienced Him working miracles, divine intervention, and specifically answering many of my prayers throughout my life. Because of the damage "religion" has done in my past, I am now very protective of my relationship with my Lord. As my dear friend Armando said it, "It is not a matter of 'do I believe in God'; the truth of the matter is that I have experienced God." No one, not even the devil, can undo what God has done in my life or how He has revealed Himself to me. He is real.

Truthfully, it has been a long, hard road and I have fought many battles. I have also known fear and doubt, which caused me to lose several battles. These losses were often catastrophic to my soul. My friend and pastor, Joseph, wisely stated that "God leaves His mark on us, and so does the devil. I believe in both God and the devil as I have experienced both, and I have scars from both."

Yeah, I guess that nails it pretty good.

And I also know enough about "religion" to stay away from it. Jesus did in an instant what religion could never do in a lifetime. If your Christianity wearies you or seems to be a burden, then you are practicing religion, not a relationship with the One who is cheering you on. Religion is man's attempt to shove God into a box, where He can be contained, understood and managed, usually through rituals, rules, and traditions. Religion never saved anybody. Truly, as the famous cliché rightly points out, "Jesus didn't come to give me a religion; He came to give me a personal relationship with Him."

No one can take that relationship from me, or you, and no one has the right to tell you "how it has to be", if you too are in a relationship with our Heavenly Father and He is guiding you with His Word.

*"For there is one God and one Mediator between God and men, the man Christ Jesus"* (1 Timothy 2:5).

That means no Bishop, no elder, no profit, no pope, no priest, no president, no counselor, no preacher or pastor, no man… ever again, coming between me and my Lord and Master. And definitely not the great Liar (John 8:42-47, Revelation 12:9) and the great Loser (who *"did not prevail"* Revelation 12:8), that loudmouth devil.

Unless they have walked where I have walked, they definitely don't have the ability to mentor me, judge me, or have any authority over me and my relationship with my Master (1 Corinthians 2:15-16). I was bought at a very high price, and I will not become a slave of man. I will remain with God in the state in which I was called (1 Corinthians 7:23-24). That last verse took a little while to sink in, as, in the beginning, I fantasized my ministry as pastoring a nice little country church somewhere, where nobody had any really serious issues and life would be like floating on a feather. Reality check – my ministry, where I serve my Lord at my best, is in "the pit". I was raised in the pit, I know the pit like the back of my hand, and I have flourished in the pit…for both God and the devil at different times in my life. And I now know my enemy, because I have done business with him. After all, was I a surprise to God, when He saved me, or did He know exactly what he was getting?

He knows you and me from the beginning to the end, and loves us still. Amazing! And on top of that, He uses us, yes us, to expand the Kingdom of God. That's beyond amazing! And you are no surprise to Him either, by the way, and yet His love for you is so deep it is beyond our understanding. It don't matter what you've done, He loves you still, I promise. Now do you see why I vigilantly guard my personal relationship with Him? Nobody loves us more.

And that's why, as the Apostle Paul himself so rightly put it, *"All things are lawful for me, but all things are not helpful. All things are lawful for me, but I will not be brought under the power of any"* (1 Corinthians 6:12).

Ditto.

And to all those other skeptics and critics within the church (God bless them!), we say again with Paul, *"But by the grace of God I am what I am, and His grace toward me was not in vain"* (1 Corinthians 15:10) and, *"Who are you to judge another's servant? To his own Master he stands or falls. Indeed, he will be made to stand, for God is able to make him stand"* (Romans 14:4).

Why do you suppose the Creator of the Universe bothered to save the likes of me? Aside from his great love for us, Scripture says He did it so that I may be an example to you and others that they may believe on Him, and be saved as well;

*"And I thank Christ Jesus our Lord who has enabled me, because He counted me faithful, putting me into the ministry, although I was formerly a blasphemer, a persecutor, and an insolent man; but I obtained mercy because I did it ignorantly in unbelief. And the grace of our Lord was exceedingly abundant, with faith and love which are in Christ Jesus. This is a faithful saying and worthy of all acceptance, that Christ Jesus came into the world to save sinners, of whom I am chief. However, for this reason I obtained mercy, that in me first Jesus Christ might show all long-suffering, as a pattern to those who are going to believe on Him for everlasting life. Now to the King eternal, immortal, invisible, to God who alone is wise, be honor and glory for ever and ever. Amen.* 1 Timothy 1:12-17. I pray it may be so.

My friend, hold your head up high! You are a living testament to the grace and power of a God who loves you!

To quote one of my favorite inspirational writers, David Roper, who not only has authored many books but also writes for "Our Daily Bread" devotional, and who has blessed me enormously when he wrote;

Ponder this gracious assurance; "That *our God may count you worthy of his calling, and that by His power he may fulfill every good purpose of yours and every act prompted by your faith"* (2 Thessalonians 1:11). He has instilled in you the desire to do better. He who prompted the desire is able to fulfill it. In the meantime, while you wait for His perfect work, don't worry about your failures. Offer up to God all that worries and annoys you and wait for Him in peace.

Phyllis McGinley writes, "The wonderful thing about Saints is that they were human. They lost their tempers, scolded God, were egotistical or testy or inpatient in their turns, made mistakes and regretted them. Still they went on doggedly blundering toward Heaven."

So blunder on. Don't dwell on present failings, or on the dead past. Every day has its mishaps and memories of something we should have done or not done. "Never look back" must be our motto.

Press on! Though in the process and incomplete we are freely loved, fully forgiven and on our way to glory. Sin may frustrate us for a day, but God's Favor goes on forever and on ahead lies perfection. Someday soon we shall see God face to face and we shall be like Him – "holy as the Holy One."

"Rivers know this," Winnie the Pooh assures us. "There is no hurry. We shall get there someday." (End quote – David Roper – In Quietness and Confidence, The Making of a Man of God –page 47)

Yes! That's me... Blundering on!

As the saying goes, I am now getting pretty long in tooth (I like that saying because I don't want to say old), and I am now just a well-worn soldier of the cross who has fought many spiritual battles, winning many victories to His Glory, and losing maybe a few too many battles, to my shame. As to the latter, I cannot un-know or un-remember the ugly evil things I have seen the enemy inflict upon the human race, nor the evil that mankind inflicts upon each other. In many instances, all I could do was try to pick up the pieces and clean up the mess as best I could, while experiencing the anguish of, for whatever reason, not being able to stop or at least intervene to avoid the horrific end results.

What's done is done. Setting things straight has always been a very difficult temptation for me to overcome. Sometimes still, even after all these years, the sound of my pistols and my sawed-off shotgun yet makes my ears ring, in my dreams, and causes me to bolt upright in bed with my heart pounding adrenaline through my veins, as the devil plays in my subconscious to remind me where I came from and what I have done...and my Heavenly Father always quickly intervenes and turns it so I can see what His wonderful grace, and mercy have forgiven me of, and what is completely cleansed and washed away by the shed blood of His Son, Jesus Christ. It goes without saying that there are so many more miracles and wonders I could add to all of this in the glory of His name, as well as many stories I will not write about that He, through His amazing grace, has forgiven me of. Through my repentance and God's love, I am forgiven.

You are too. And God's mercy endures forever! What incredible love! God loves you just as He loves Jesus (John 17:23)!!! This is why we praise and worship Him.

Laying down your worldly weapons is incredibly difficult when you have spent your whole life learning to master them with extreme proficiency, and trusted your life to them for so long. I am not, by any means, saying that it's something God is telling to everyone, but for me, it's how it had to be. The truth is, I don't want to kill anything, anymore... I've done enough...except maybe a few Chukar would be nice.

God's people have always been in the forefront of the war against evil, bearing arms to protect the innocent and uphold what is right; I think it's part of our job...part of why we are here. For some, it may be part of their calling, i.e., soldiers, police, militia, etc. and of course, hunting (as in, feed the family!). Remember Luke 22:36?

*"Let their throats voice hymns of adoration to God, with the two-edged sword in their hands"* says Psalm 149:6, *"... This honor have all the saints. Praise the Lord!"* Verse 9 goes on to say.

Although, I believe, Psalm 44:6-7 now speaks the loudest to my heart, as the years go by;

*"For I will not trust in my bow,*
*Nor shall my sword save me.*
*But You have saved us from our enemies,*
*And put to shame those who hated us."*

Only total trust in my Lord and Champion and His Holy Word make it even conceivable to me, let alone the reality it has become in my life. Now there's a miracle.

Yet I remain very optimistic, and encourage you to be the same, as not to be discouraged by what you see happening around us in these end times. Even though godliness and morality seem to be crumbling all around us, and the world seems more chaotic every day, know that God is still on the Throne. He has a plan of redemption that is on time and on course.

I know that, in these last days, there appears to be no real fear of God left in the world, or even inside some churches, and sin and its repercussions are indeed running rampant.

**Hold your ground!** (See Ephesians 6:10-13).

Shortly, sin will be judged and dealt with accordingly.

*"For the wages of sin is death but the gift of God is eternal life in Christ Jesus our Lord,"* Romans 6:23 promises.

"Given the slightest chance, sin will infiltrate your life and affect every aspect, including your faith, job and relationships. Nothing is off limits. If you're thinking, "I don't have any weakness with the potential to destroy my life," then Satan has already blinded you to a spiritual reality in your midst. You have a choice to face temptation as Joseph did (Genesis 39) – or as Sampson did (Judges 16)... Charles Stanley.

These are the end times or last days, I believe, that Paul warned us of, just before the Rapture (see Appendix J) and the rise of the anti-christ, the times known as "the falling away" or "great apostasy".

2 Thessalonians 2:1-4; *"Now, brethren, concerning the coming of our Lord Jesus Christ and our gathering together to Him, we ask you, not to be soon shaken in mind or troubled, either by spirit or by word or by letter, as if from us, as though the day of Christ had come. Let no one deceive you by any means; for*

*that Day will not come unless **the falling away** comes first, and the man of sin is revealed, the son of perdition, who opposes and exalts himself above all that is called God or that is worshiped, so that he sits as God in the temple of God, showing himself that he is God."*

And 1 Timothy 4:1-3 describes the Great Apostasy as; *"Now the Spirit expressly says that in the latter times some will depart from the faith, giving heed to deceiving spirits and doctrines of demons, speaking lies in hypocrisy, having their own conscience seared with a hot iron, forbidding to marry, and commanding to abstain from foods that God created to be received with thanksgiving by those who believe and know the truth."*

Again, I say, stand your ground and hold to your faith in our Lord Jesus Christ, as we watch for His imminent return. *"Even so, come, Lord Jesus!"* (Revelation 22:20).

No amount of unbelief, bad theology, misinterpretation of Scripture, or simply ignoring it can change the truth, that our Lord is coming back to get us very soon. Nor can it change what is coming upon the earth afterward, either.

Jesus said, *"See that you are not troubled; for all these things must come to pass..."* (Matthew 24:6), while speaking of these last days. I don't know about you, but it's hard sometimes for me not to be troubled, as many believers around me are near to "falling away", as evil rises and God often feels distant, prayers seem long in being answered, if at all, and Heaven seems silent...times of great testing.

But I will cling to my faith. Especially my faith in God's love for me. It is God's love that mends broken people. I will not "fall away". Psalm 44 is a good example, and like the song says, "I will praise him in this storm... I will lift my eyes to the hills. Where does my help come from? My help comes from the Lord, the Maker of Heaven and earth (Praise You in This Storm – by Casting Crowns, from Psalm 121).

Let's cut to the chase...about when prayers are within biblical boundaries and criteria, yet still don't get answered, we sometimes feel as if God is holding out on us. Brother Christian then tells us, "Well, you know, God is sovereign" (which we already know) and we nod, and choke it down with a smile.

More than ever, this is when we need to cry out to our Heavenly Father, "I don't understand and I don't know why this is what it is, but I will cling to You, no matter what, and You will get me through it. My eyes are on You, Lord, in all of this." Never give up, never fall away. Many will abandon their faith in these last days, as prophesied, but I won't be one of them. I will, *"hold fast the confession of our hope without wavering, for He who promised is faithful."* (Hebrews 10:23).

Even when Sister Christian tells me that I must have hidden sin (who doesn't), I don't have enough faith (my personal favorite), I didn't pray right (like there's a wrong way to pray!), and, oh yeah, I didn't do or obey the last thing God told me to do (I get that one a lot lately). It's the devil (a.k.a. lying punk) that tells you "you're not good enough", when Jesus saw you, just as you are, and died for you so you could live!

*"But God demonstrates His own love toward us, in that while we were still sinners, Christ died for us. Much more then, having now been justified by His blood, we shall be saved from wrath through Him"* Romans 5:8-9!!!!!!!

Cling to the truth. Cling to the Word! Cling to your victories! Nothing spiritually bonds us to God and establishes our intimacy with Him more than our victories over the battles we face in life.

Victory builds faith.

In a small town, several years ago, I attended a Sunday service at the invitation of a friend. The preacher presented John 14:13-14 as somewhat of a "magic formula" (which it is not) when applied with enough faith, to get you anything from God. He concluded with something that sounded to me like, "Due to a large influx of prayer requests the answer to your prayer may be delayed for up to several years. While the answer to your prayer is being processed, please enjoy the worship music, or in some cases, the suffering and drama, while you wait (my sarcastic paraphrase... My bad).

Our God is not Santa Claus or some Cosmic Cop waiting to punish you every time you mess up. We all stumble and we all sometimes fall, and He always picks us back up, dusts us off, and lovingly says, "Its okay. Let's try again."

Our living hope is what Peter was talking about when he wrote to the early Christians who were suffering for their faith. Peter had witnessed the incredibly brutal execution of the One he thought was about to deliver Israel from Roman rule. In unparalleled awe he must have marveled at how this Man could now not only be alive, but whole again! How He had indeed risen from the grave and again was alive! He was truly the Risen Lord!

Peter's message then, as it is to us now, as explained by Dr. Jeremiah (Is This The End, page 107) was this; "You have a living hope based on what Jesus Christ did when He walked out of the grave. Jesus defeated our greatest enemy – death – and thereby promises that no matter what happens in this life, you will defeat that enemy as well. If you are looking for hope while the nation descends into apathy around you, you need to look no further than the resurrected and living Christ."

He goes on to conclude, "The present world has only limited hope to offer – the hope of a life no better than our best efforts can make it, all of which eventually crumbles into the grave. If that is the best hope we have, we are of all men the most pitiable (1 Corinthians 15:19). How much better is it to have a "living hope" – the resources of Heaven itself – when we are facing a hopeless situation?"

To me, that's perfectly said, especially in the last days in which we are now living.

The Word of God (Bible – King James and New King James Versions are my preferences) is where I got my faith, as *"Faith comes by hearing, and hearing by the Word of God."* Romans 10:17.

Trials and suffering never built my faith; they tested it, and formed my character, as made clear in James 1:24 and Isaiah 48:10.

Only a faith that is tested is a faith that can be trusted.

What grew my faith strong and built my trust were my victories in Christ through answered prayers in times of need and despair.

1 Thessalonians 5:18 says, *"In everything give thanks; for this is the will of God in Christ Jesus concerning you"* (KJV). I noticed that Scripture tells us to give thanks **IN** all things, not **FOR** all things. Does that not make perfect sense? When tragedy, temptation, or suffering strikes, we are not to thank God for them. He isn't the author of these things, even though He has allowed them, He is the One who provides the way of escape from them or the spiritual strength to make it through. That's what we are to thank Him for.

Interestingly, the most terrible affliction I have ever experienced, even above the intense pain I have endured, was being chained and shackled... nothing worse than that. It stands to reason that the greatest euphoria I have enjoyed came when those chains and shackles were finally removed, and yet I thank God for both of them.

Never did Jesus give thanks for sickness or death. Jesus always gave thanks for the victory that God has given us over these things, and so should we. Over the years I have learned to ask not "why", but "Show me where You are in all of this, Lord." But never give thanks for Satan's activities in our lives as they are part of the curse (see Deuteronomy 28) and not from our Heavenly Father. In fact, as I mentioned earlier, Scripture affirms that sickness, etc. is an oppression of the devil that Jesus healed people of (Acts 10:38). Thanking God for such things, as ridiculous as it sounds knowing the source of them, is like telling your Heavenly Father thank you for allowing the enemy of my soul to kick my ass.

Psalm 97:10 says we are to hate evil, as does Romans 12:9, Proverbs 8:13 and Amos 5:15. It does not say we are to passively put up with it, and we are definitely not to try and manage it. After all, didn't Jesus Himself make it clear that there is no "gray" line when he told us in John 10:10, *"The thief does not come except to steal, and to kill, and to destroy. I have come that they may have life, and that they may have it more abundantly."*?

Paul emphasized this to the church at Ephesus when he told them, *"And have no fellowship with the unfruitful works of darkness, but rather expose them"* (Ephesians 5:11).

I know... Try letting that determine who you cast your vote for next Election Day, and see how that works.

Have we been desensitized? Many things that are now acceptable in many mainline churches today are clearly and abomination to God. That's why you need to know what's in the Bible.

So hang in there. Cling to your faith. Fight the good fight of faith by staying daily in the Word, so you, yourself, will know what is, and isn't good and pleasing to the Lord, and not have to fall into deception by some of these "new age" preachers, or gurus, that profess to be of God, but *"These people draw near to Me with their mouth, and honor Me with their lips, but their heart is far from Me. And in vain they worship Me, teaching as doctrines the commandments of men"* Matthew 15:8-9.

Jesus referred to these false prophets as wolves in sheep's clothing in Matthew 7:15.

For this reason I now pray for you, the reader, the same prayer that Paul prayed for the Colossians in chapter 1; I *"pray for you, to ask that you may be filled with the knowledge of His will and all wisdom and spiritual understanding; that you may walk worthy of the Lord, fully pleasing Him, being fruitful in every good work and increasing in the knowledge of God; strengthened with all might, according to His glorious power, for all patients and long-suffering with joy; giving thanks to the Father who has qualified us to be partakers of the inheritance of the saints in the light. He has delivered us from the power of darkness and conveyed us into the kingdom of the Son of His love, in whom we have redemption through His blood, the forgiveness of sins."* Amen.

Did you notice the "long-suffering with joy" part? That doesn't mean we take joy in suffering, it means that the joy of the Lord is what gets us through our long-suffering.

As Nehemiah 8:10 declares, the joy of the Lord is your strength. When God makes you strong, that's what he uses – not pain and anguish. Your strength to get through pain and anguish comes from our joy in the Lord and his promises! So rejoice! Find out what the Word says about your situation, cling to and pray out loud his promises concerning it, and rejoice and thank the Lord for getting you through it!

People these days love to throw around the saying, "What doesn't kill you makes you stronger", and in many circumstances, it's true. Yet I noticed in the story about how Jacob physically wrestled with the Lord (please see, Genesis 32:22-31) that Jacob did not "cling" (totally depend) on the Lord until after he had been crippled/broken. Jacob depended on his own abilities (conniving, etc.) to deal with his issues, in this case, his brother Esau, and, like me, had to lose those abilities he had all his life put his trust in, before he could fully trust in the Lord, and cling to Him. Jacob no longer had the options to fight or run from his brother who had sworn to kill him (Genesis 27:41), but now was so much stronger as he went to confront his brother in the power of the Lord.

As with Jacob, I learned to cling to God in my brokenness.

I pray that you are growing strong in the Lord and walking daily in His blessings, as many are. In these times our hearts seem to automatically send a stream of thanks, praise, and adoration Heavenward. But sometimes, what doesn't kill you breaks you or cripples you for life, and day by day, minute by minute, not only will the Lord our God walk with us through every painful moment, but He will also create a way to bring something good from it (Romans 8:28), even though sometimes it may be next to impossible for us to see through our anguish. Honestly, if He never did anything more than forgive our sins and guarantee eternal life in Heaven for us, with no more pain, sorrow, suffering or tears, wouldn't that still make us abundantly blessed, and Him worthy of our worship? Yet, always remember Isaiah 41:10 –

*"Fear not for I am with you,*
*Be not dismayed for I am your God.*
*I will strengthen you,*
*Yes, I will help you,*
*I will uphold you with My righteous right hand."*

We must trust Him in this and give Him thanks for getting us through these bad times, looking to the cross and resurrection, and full well knowing that our best days are definitely still out in front of us, and not behind us...all the while, clinging to our faith, however battered and shattered it sometimes may be.

This world is not our home. Heaven is our home. We are just passing through this place, on our journey back home, *"strangers and pilgrims on the earth...seeking our homeland"* (Hebrews 11:13-16), Glory to God!

Moreover, what's even more exciting is the truth that our Lord Jesus is about to come back and get us! Whoot! Whoot!

So blunder on, my dear friends.

As David prayed in one of his last Psalms, I too now will pray;
*Oh God, You have taught me from my youth;*
*And to this day I declare Your wondrous works.*
*Now also when I am old and gray-headed,*
*O God, do not forsake me,*
*Until I declare Your strength to this generation,*
*Your power to everyone who is to come.* (Psalm 71:17-18)
Amen.

Therein lies the point of all of this...and my mission.
And I bless you, now, dear reader, according to God's instruction;

**The Lord bless you and keep you;**
**The Lord make His face shine upon you,**
**And be gracious to you;**

*The Lord lift up His countenance upon you,*
*And give you peace.* (Numbers 6:24-26)

And, yes, of course,

*Amen. Even so, come Lord Jesus! The grace of our Lord Jesus Christ be with you all. Amen* (Revelation 22:20).

Considering the countless battles I have endured, win, lose or draw, know this; **I am not a survivor…I am a Warrior.**

And as to the unwritten part of my story, God knows, and I'm good with that.

The best is yet to come.

# WHAT A RIDE!

By John Gergen
    A servant of the Lord,
    An old Soldier of the Cross.

# APPENDIXES

Before using the following scriptures in these appendixes/study notes, please STOP now, and PRAY for God to reveal His truth that is contained in each verse, and not just my, or anybody else's opinion, for that matter, as I am only a man and I am not yet perfected, making me prone to mistakes.

The only opinion or view that truly matters is, of course, our Heavenly Fathers.

Thank you for taking this most important step, as I know you will be blessed by it.

John Gergen

## FALSE PROPHETS & RELIGIONS

*"But the prophet who presumes to speak a word in My name, which I have not commanded him to speak, or who speaks in the name of other gods, that prophet shall die. And if you say in your heart,' How shall we know the word which the Lord has not spoken?' – When a prophet speaks in the name of the Lord, if the thing does not happen or come to pass, that is the thing which the Lord has not spoken; the prophet has spoken it presumptuously; you shall not be afraid of him."* Deuteronomy 18:20-22
THE TEST!

# APPENDIX A

## CULT
Perversion of God's Word

### Old Testament

| | |
|---|---|
| Deuteronomy 13:1-9 | false prophets and gods |
| Jeremiah 2:8-19 | false idols – generational curse |
| Jeremiah 7 | false religions – "Queen of Heaven" |
| Jeremiah 8:8-12 | false doctrine |
| Jeremiah 13:1-17 | pride, apostasy= alcoholism |
| Jeremiah 14:14-16 | divination – false prophets |
| Jeremiah 23 | End time false prophets – false shepherds |
| Jeremiah 23:25-32 | false dreams – Compare it to the Word! |
| Jeremiah 23:33-40 | Saying "oracles of God" is forbidden |
| Jeremiah 29:8-7 | false dreams |
| Jeremiah 44:25-27 | "Queen of heaven" |
| Jeremiah 48:10 | deceitful servants cursed |
| Jeremiah 50:36 | soothsayers |
| Micah 2:6-11 | lying prophets |

### New Testament

| | |
|---|---|
| Matthew 12:6 | Jesus is greater than the temple |
| Matthew 15:3-9, Mark 7:6-13 | religious tradition |
| Matthew 16:6, 12, Mark 8:15 | beware of religious doctrine |
| Matthew 23, Luke 11:37-53 | woe scribes and Pharisees |
| Matthew 24:5, 10-12, 23-27 | end time warnings |
| Matthew 24:36-44, 2 Thessalonians 2:1-3 | false "end of the world" predictions |
| Luke 10:7 ? | House to house? |
| John 7:17 | must know doctrine |

| | |
|---|---|
| John 12:42-43 | praise of men, not God |
| Acts 13:6-11 | example |
| Romans 10:1-3 | "zeal" is real-but **not** according to knowledge |
| 1 Corinthians 15:29 | baptism for the dead – please refer to appendix D |
| 2 Corinthians 11:13-15 | demonic angel of light (see also 1Timothy 4:1-3, then Google "Moroni"!) |
| Galatians 1:6-9 | other "gospels" **accursed** |
| Galatians 4:21-31 | Muslim, Islam |
| Philippians 3:17-19 | materialism |
| Colossians 2:20-23 | religious tradition |
| Colossians 2:16-17 | festivals/holidays |
| 2 Thessalonians 2:1-12 | date setting/the end-antichrist |
| 1 Timothy 1:3-11 | no other doctrine-genealogies |
| 1 Timothy 4:1-3 | Doctrine of Demons |
| 1 Timothy 6:20-21 | false knowledge |
| 2 Timothy 3:1-9 | Last Days, form of godliness/denying the power-instruction |
| 2 Timothy 4:2-5 | instruction |
| Titus 3:9-10 | instruction |
| Hebrews 13:9 | strange doctrine |
| **James 1:26-27** | **True religion defined-based on compassion!** |
| 2 Peter 2 | false doctrines, prophets & teachers |
| 2 Peter 3:16 | twisted Scripture-the trademark of all cults |
| **2 John 1:7-11** | **false doctrines, deceivers, – Instruction** |
| Revelation 2:2 | tested false apostles |
| Revelation 2:9-10 | synagogue of Satan |
| Revelation 2:13-15 | Satan's throne-doctrine of Balaam |
| Revelation 2:6, 15 | Nicolations= religious dictatorship |
| Revelation 2:20-23 | Jezebel-false prophetess |
| Revelation 13, 14:9-20, Revelation 17, 18, 19:19-21, 20:10 | the ultimate false religion and its judgment |
| Revelation 22:18-19 | Warning! |

# APPENDIX B

## OCCULT
Rebellion Against God – Defiance of God's Word – **satanic**

Examples; Communicating with the dead, devination, sorcery, witchcraft, soothsayers, mediums, astrology, horoscopes, familiar spirits, New Age religion, worship of – stars, moon, sun, mother earth, etc., evolution, magic charms, psychics, fortunetellers, magic, black magic, rebellion, satanic worship and rituals.

### Old Testament

| | |
|---|---|
| Leviticus 19:26, 31 | eating blood, divination, soothsaying, mediums, familiar spirits |
| Leviticus 19:28 | no cutting's or tattoos for the dead |
| Leviticus 20:6, **23**, 27 | mediums, familiar spirits, sexual immorality defined |
| Deuteronomy 17:2-7 | false gods-sun, moon, stars |
| **Deuteronomy 18:10-14** | **occult defined** |
| 1 Samuel 15:23 | rebellion as witchcraft, stubbornness as idolatry |
| 2 Kings 21:6 | witchcraft, mediums, etc. – provokes God to anger |
| **1 Kings 8:39** | **Only God can read your mind!** |
| 2 Chronicles 33:6 | sorcery, occult practices – provokes God to anger |
| Ecclesiastes 7:14 | can't foresee future events |
| Isaiah 8:19-22 | mediums, wizards, seeking the dead-compare it to the Word |
| Isaiah 19:3-4 | Egypt's occult practices |
| Isaiah 47:19-15 | astrologers, horoscopes, results of drugs |
| Isaiah 57 | New Age, end time drug use, etc. |
| Jeremiah 2:27-35 | New Age, evolution |
| Jeremiah 3:9-15, 23 | new age |

| | |
|---|---|
| Jeremiah 10 | idols |
| Ezekiel 13:3-9 | false visions, devination |
| Ezekiel 13:17-23 | magic charms, psychics |
| **Ezekiel 28:1-19** | **Satan, the enemy of your soul** |
| **Isaiah 14:3-20** | **Satan, the enemy of your soul** |
| Daniel 1:20 | magic, astrology |
| Daniel 2:27-28 | not astrologers, magicians, soothsayers, idols – only God |
| Micah 5:12-15 | sorceries, soothsayers, idols |
| Nahum 3:4 | sorceries |
| Zechariah 10:2 | idols, diviners, false dreams |
| Malachi 3:5 | sorceries, adulterers, liars, cheats |

## New Testament

| | |
|---|---|
| Matthew 6:24, Luke 16:13 | can't serve God and money |
| 1 Timothy 6:10 | the love of money |
| Matthew 10:32-33, Luke 9:25-26, 12:8-9 | denying Jesus |
| Matthew 12:30 | either with Jesus or against Him |
| Acts 12:21-23 | **man is not God** |
| Acts 16:16-19 | fortune-telling= demonic possession |
| Acts 19:19 | magic |
| Romans 1:18-25 | New Age |
| 1 Corinthians 10:19-22 | the Lord or demons-can't have both |
| Colossians 2:8 | philosophy, new age |
| Colossians 2:18 | worship of angels – new age |
| Colossians 3:5-6 | covetousness= idolatry |
| 1 Timothy 6:20-21 | New Age-"knowledge" |
| James 3:14-18 | Heavenly versus demonic wisdom |
| 2 Peter 3:1-7 | scoffers in the last days |

Note: Sorcery = from the Greek word "pharmakeia" = which means "to administer **drugs**" – pharmacy (English)

Examples; see Revelation 9:20-21, Revelation 22:14-15, etc.

# APPENDIX C

## TEST ALL THINGS

*Test all things; hold fast to what is good.*
1 Thessalonians 5:21

### Old Testament

Deuteronomy 18:20-22 false prophets
Jeremiah 28:8-9, 15-16 false prophets
Isaiah 8:20 compare it to the word – false prophets
Isaiah 41:21-24 false Prophets and their followers
Jeremiah 23:25-32 False Dreams-compare it to the Word
Ezekiel 34 false shepherds-description

### New Testament

#### Religions

Matthew 7:15-20, 12:33 know them by their fruit – false prophet, etc.
Matthew 25:31-46 by their works-example; one John 3:17-19 helping the poor
Matthew 16:6, 12 beware of religious doctrine
John 8:47 must receive God's Word
John 7:17 must know doctrine
Acts 20:29-32 compare every religion to the Word!
1 Timothy 6:3-5 No Other Doctrines – Instruction
Romans 10:2-4 "zeal" is real-but not according to true knowledge
Ephesians 4:14-15 False Doctrine – Instruction
Colossians 2:20-23 self-imposed religion and tradition

John 3:18-21, 36, must believe in Christ
John 14:6, "
Acts 4:12, "
1 John 5:11-12 "

John 1:1-14, Jesus is God and flesh form
John 8:58 "
John 10:27-30, 33, 38 "

| | |
|---|---|
| John 17:10-11 | " |
| John 12:45 | " |
| John 14:7-11 | " |
| | |
| Matthew 24:26-28 | false Christ's (end time) |
| 1 John 2:3-11, 3:10 | test of knowing Jesus |
| Matthew 25:13 | no one knows when (date setting) |
| | |
| Luke 8:16-17, 12:1-3 | do nothing in secret |
| John 3:20-21 | " |
| Luke 9:5-56 | save, not destroy lives |
| Revelation 22:18-19 | don't add to or take away from the Word |

Spiritual
Ephesians 6:10-18

| | |
|---|---|
| 1 Corinthians 12:3 | **Jesus is Lord** see 2 Corinthians 11:13-15 angel of light |
| James 3:14-18 | heavenly versus demonic wisdom |
| 1 John 4:1-6 | **test of the spirits** – truth and error |

# APPENDIX D

## BAPTISM FOR THE DEAD (FORBIDDEN)

Why you cannot "baptize for the dead"

1 Corinthians 15:29    notice Paul used the word "they" twice to specifically separate himself from it
Deuteronomy 26:14    give nothing for the dead
Psalm 49:6-7    can't redeem others
Psalm 106:28    sacrifices for the dead provokes God to anger
Psalm 115:17    the dead don't praise
Isaiah 26:14    can't return
Isaiah 38:18    no hope in hell
Hebrews 9:27    die once, then the judgment – baptizing for the dead is basically saying God's judgment was wrong, and you're going to fix it.
Job 7:9-10    the dead can't return
Job 14:12    the dead can't return
Isaiah 26:14    the dead can't return
Isaiah 38:18    no hope in hell
Ezekiel 18:20    non-transferable

Luke 16:26    the dead can't return or cross over
Philippians 2:12    must work out our own salvation
2 Corinthians 5:8-11    to be absent from the body is to be present with the Lord
2 Corinthians 6:2    salvation is now, not later
1 Timothy 2:5    only one Mediator between God and man – you ain't it
Ephesians 4:5    there is only one baptism
Romans 14:12    personally/individually judged
Matthew 25:1-13    those who slept= died, note; when it's over it's over
Acts 11:13-18, & Ephesians 1:13    baptism occurs **after** salvation – baptism has no saving power

Romans 1:18-20 + Hebrews 6:4-6 = Romans 2:12-15

Colossians 2: 11-13 baptism (in the New Covenant) same as Circumcision (in the Old Covenant)
Romans 2:28-29,

Romans 4:10-11,
**Galatians 6:15** circumcision is an outward sign only and has no saving power as is baptism

In summary, to think that you can save a dead person by "baptizing them for the dead" is essentially saying that God's judgment was incorrect concerning that person, and you are now going to save that person by being baptized for them on their behalf – it's essentially a slap in the face to God and his ability to judge us rightly.

# APPENDIX E

## THE GOSPEL
## THE HOLY WORD OF GOD

**John 1:1-5, 14**
God and His Word are one
Jesus and His Word are one
Jesus is the Word of God! (Vs.14)
To see God, we look to Jesus,
To hear God, we look to His Word.
His Word, the Bible, is God speaking to you.

Matthew 13:18-43 – the parable of the Sower and the seed – seed= the Word, Sower= Jesus, ground= you
*It is sobering to note that in this parable told by Jesus, 75% of the "seed" (Word of God) that is planted has absolutely no effect because Satan comes immediately to take away the Word from their hearts, by applying his five primary weapons of affliction, persecution, cares of this world, deceitfulness of riches, and lust of other things. Only 25% of the "seed" is planted in "good ground" and survives the devil's attempt to steal it. What ground are you? Guard your seed.

| | |
|---|---|
| 2 Timothy 3:16 | The "Good News" |
| 2 Peter 1:19 | origin |
| Romans 1:16-17 | power |
| Romans 10:8-17 | **Salvation** |
| 1 Corinthians 9:14, 18 | live from-no charge |
| 2 Corinthians 4:1-6 | veiled to those who are perishing |
| Galatians 1:6-12 | any other is cursed |
| Ephesians 6:17 | is your sword |
| 1 Timothy 1:3-1 | no other doctrine |
| 2 Thessalonians 2:13-15 | called by – standby |
| 2 Timothy 1:10 | life and immortality |
| 2 Timothy 4:2-5 | Preach the Word! Some will turn away |
| Hebrews 4:12-13 | two edged sword |
| 1 Peter 1:22-25 | endures forever |
| 2 John 1:7-11 | antichrists |
| Acts 20:32 | build you up |
| Matthew 24:14 | determines when the end will come |

**Pray The Word!**

**Obviously, God's will is his Word.**
**Effective prayer that brings results must be based on God's Word.**
John 15:7
1 John 3:22
1 John 5:14-15
Isaiah 55:8-11
Isaiah 43:26-26
Isaiah 51:16
Psalm 119:49-50
Hebrews 1:3

# APPENDIX F

## CORRECTION

A Biblical Roadmap Through the Valley of Correction.
It's time for a change.

**Here's The Facts;**

| | |
|---|---|
| Romans 3:23 | **all** have sinned |
| Galatians 6:7-10 | the Law of Reaping and Sowing |
| John 8:44 | Satan is a liar |
| John 14:6 | Jesus is the truth |
| John 8:24, & | |
| Deuteronomy 30:19-20 | THE CHOICE |

**What Happened;**     (you chose the lie)

| | |
|---|---|
| 1 Peter 5:8 | it's Satan's will |
| John 10:10 | It's NOT God's will for you to be in this trouble |
| Jeremiah 2:17, 19 | you believed Satan's lies **and acted on them** |

Example;   "its okay, no one will know, you won't get caught, everybody's doing it," etc. etc.

**What To Do First;**
Stop blaming everyone else.

Acts 4:10-12, &
Romans 10:8-13         SALVATION! Say a prayer of salvation!
Dear Jesus, I call on You to be my Lord and Savior.
I'm sorry for what I have done and I ask You to forgive me of my sins.
Please fill me with Your Holy Spirit.
I give my life to You, in Jesus's name,
Amen.

| | |
|---|---|
| 1 John 1:5-10, 2:1-2 | Confessed to God and be forgiven |
| 2 Corinthians 2:10-11 | unforgiveness and guilt are **devices** (thoughts) of Satan |

Matthew 6:14                 Forgive all others (I know it can be tough, but it's mandatory)

## What Correction Is;

Hebrews 12:3-15, Job 5:17-18, and Proverbs 3:11-12;
It's the manifestation of God's **grace** and **love** towards those who are perishing.
It's your "**wake-up call**".
It's important to note that Genesis 50:20 tells us that Satan meant it for evil – but God uses it for good.

## Why Correction Comes;

John 3:16-21,
1 Corinthians 11:31-32     God loves you too much to let you be condemned!

## What Correction Produces;
1 Peter 4:19             Commitment
Acts 3:19-21             Salvation
1 Peter 5:5-11           Humility
Colossians 1:13-14       Deliverance
2 Corinthians 7:9-11      Repentance

## How Correction Works;

Isaiah 55:6-7
Hosea 5:15, 6:1-3
*Job 36:8-12*

## Why It Won't Work;

Proverbs 10:17
Proverbs 12:1

## Something Else You Need To Know;

Psalm 1,
1 Corinthians 15:33,
1 Peter 4:4-5            Choose friends very carefully! After all, your friends can't save you – only God can!

## What To Do Next;

John 8:31-36             Seek the Truth

2 Timothy 3:16
John 17:17
Psalm 119:9-16, 49-50,     Study the Bible daily
65-77, 92-94
Romans 5:6-11,             Turn from sin
Romans 8
2 Corinthians 10:3-5       Control your thoughts
Hebrews 10:19-25           Get involved in a Bible (un-altered) preaching Church
Ephesians 6:10-18          Dress for success!
Philippians 4:6-9,
Luke 21:34-36
1 Thessalonians 5:16-18    PRAY CONSTANTLY – keep your line of communication open at all times!

**What Not To Do;**

Proverbs 26:11
2 Peter 2:18-22

**Promises;**

Job 22:21-30
Isaiah 57:15-18
Isaiah 41:10
Isaiah 42:5-8
Isaiah 43:1-3
Psalm 40:1-3
Psalm 69:32-33
Psalm 145:14-21
Jeremiah 29:11-14
John 6:37

**Here's The Deal;**

Ezekiel 36:26-28
Psalm 51:1-17
Hebrews 8:10-12    New Covenant
Ezekiel 18:21-23

**And Finally……**

Deuteronomy 30:19

**As always, the choice is yours.**

# APPENDIX G

## KEYS TO PEACE

#1 Key = No Jesus, No Peace – Know Jesus, Know Peace

Deuteronomy 29:19 – No God-no peace
Judges 6:24 – the Lord is peace
Job 22:21 – peace in knowing God
Isaiah 9:6-7 – Jesus is the Prince of Peace
Micah 5:8 – Jesus is peace
Luke 1:79 – Jesus will guide us to peace
John 14:27 – Jesus gives peace-not fear
John 16:33 – peace in Jesus
Acts 10:36 – peace through Jesus
Ephesians 2:14-18 – Christ is our peace
Colossians 1:20 – peace came through The Blood of Christ

### Covenants of Peace
### Isaiah 54:10

Numbers 25:12-13 – priesthood-a zeal for God
Malachi 2:5-7 – messengers of the Lord
Job 5:23 – peace with all of creation (beasts, etc. included)

### The New (Blood) Covenant

Colossians 1:20 – peace came through the Blood of Christ, and free reconciliation to God through forgiveness of sins= Peace
Jeremiah 31:31
Ezekiel 16:60-63
Zechariah 9:11-12 – Promise-return double!
Hebrews 8:10-13
Hebrews 10:16-18
Hebrews 12:22-24 – Jesus is Mediator!
Hebrews 13:20-21
Isaiah 59:21

### Key Requirements

Psalm 119:165 – peace and loving God's law
Ephesians 6:15 – the Gospel of Peace is our foundation
Proverbs 3:1-2 – peace in keeping God's law
Romans 2:4-11 – peace comes through obedience
Proverbs 3:13-17 – peace and wisdom
Proverbs 16:7 – in pleasing the Lord/it makes your enemies be at peace with you
Isaiah 32:17-19 – works of righteousness-law of reaping and sowing
*Romans 14:17-19 – The Kingdom of God is righteousness, **peace** and joy in the Holy Spirit.
Galatians 5:22-25 – fruit of the spirit
Ephesians 4:1-6 – peace through unity
Hebrews 12:14 – peace is a requirement
2 Peter 3:14 – we must be found in peace in the day of the Lord!
*James 3:18 – peace is sown in peace (law of reaping and sowing)
**Psalms 72:3 – Mountains bring Peace!** See Micah 6:1 for further study
Isaiah 57:19 – peace for **backsliders**
1 Corinthians 7:15 – peace concerning divorce
*Romans 5:1 – faith= peace with God
*Romans 8:1-6 – Spiritually minded= peace
*Romans 12:18-21 – peace through forgiveness (that's a biggie)

Peace Comes Through Thanksgiving

Leviticus 7:13
**Philippians 4:6-9!**
Colossians 3:15

The Holy Spirit Always Guides Through Peace

John 14:27 – Law – Jesus gives peace-not fear
1 Corinthians 14:33 – Law – God is the Author of Peace-not confusion
Psalm 37:37 – peace through obedience
Colossians 3:14-17 – **Major Key** – instruction – guidance
Philippians 4:6-9 – **Major Key** – instruction – guidance

Psalm 34:14, 1 Peter 3:11-seek peace= Matthew 6:33= Romans 14:17-19 – Keys to the Kingdom of God

Prayers, Promises, Blessings

Psalm 29:11 – a blessing
Isaiah 26:3-4 – promise, as is Isaiah 26:12-13
Isaiah 27:5 – use God's strength for peace with God
Isaiah 55:12 – promise

Matthew 5:9 – Blessed are the peacemakers...
Romans 15:13 – prayer for peace
2 Corinthians 13:11 – benediction
2 Thessalonians 3:16 – benediction
1 Timothy 2:1-2 – prayer for peace
2 Timothy 2:22-26 – things to avoid
Isaiah 48:22 – no peace for the wicked
Romans 7:14, 8:13, and 1 Peter 2:11 – avoid "flesh" wars
2 Timothy 2:4 – avoid the affairs of this world, as is Colossians 3:1-10
2 Thessalonians 3:16 – prayer
Jeremiah 29:7 – pray for your town

## Numbers 6:23-27 – THE BLESSING

# APPENDIX H

## OUR WORDS

Matthew 12:33-37 – What you speak is what you bring to pass, for good or for evil, because words are governed by the spiritual law of sowing and reaping (Genesis 8:22, Galatians 6:7-9)
Matthew 4:1-11 – By His example, Jesus taught us how to defeat the devil by speaking out God's Word; this applies to any situation we face – Find out what God's word says about your situation and speak it out of your mouth.
Psalms 103:20 – Angels heed the spoken Word of God.
Joshua 1:8 – Success!
Romans 4:17, Hebrews 1:3 – The Word= Power
Matthew 12:36-37 – We are judged by our words-see also Matthew 15:11, 18.
James 3:2-10 – blessing and cursing.
Proverbs 18:20-21 – death and life.
Proverbs 21:23 – protection
Psalm 141:3 – Guard Your Mouth!
Hebrews 4:14-16 – Holdfast our confession.
**Mark 11:22-24 – Speak out words of faith!**
Romans 10:8-10 – Confessing God's Word is what brought about your salvation! Speak God's Word!
Romans 4:17 – it is words that change things; ours as well as God's.
James 3:2 – The power lies in consistency.
Hebrews 3 – Jesus himself is the high priest of our words.
Proverbs 13:2, 3 – A man shall eat good by the fruit of his mouth.
Proverbs 12:18 – the tongue of the wise is health.
Proverbs 4:24 – put away from you a disobedient mouth.
**Psalm 141:3 – Major Prayer – Set a guard, oh Lord, over my mouth; keep watch over the door of my lips.**

What you have in your life right now is a direct result of what's coming out of your mouth; if you don't like what you have, change what's coming out of your mouth. If you speak blessings from the Word of God you will have those blessings in your life – if you speak trash, you will have trash.
The topic of "our words" is worthy of much further study, as this study is by no means complete.

**The Power of the Name –**

Acts 3:16
Acts 4:10
Acts 4:29-30
Philippians 2:10
Luke 9:48
**Luke 10:17-20 – "even the demons are subject to us in Your name."**

## YOUR WORDS ARE YOUR POWER
Choose them wisely

# APPENDIX I

## BAPTISM

Matthew 28:19 – In the name of the Father, Son and Holy Spirit-The great commission
Mark 16:16 – Great Commission
John 3:5 – Born of water and the Spirit
John 3:22 – Jesus and the disciples baptized followers
Acts 2:38 – For remission of sins
Acts 10:48 – Peter commands to be baptized
Acts 22:16 – Why are you waiting? Arise and be baptized!
Romans 6:3-14 – Dead to sin-alive to God
1 Corinthians 1:10-17 –NOT into religion
1 Corinthians 12:12-14 – Commitment to take your place in the Body of Christ
Galatians 3:26-29 – All one in Christ
Ephesians 4:1-6 – One baptism-One body
Colossians 2:11-15 – baptism/circumcision-both our public and spiritual displays of commitment

# APPENDIX J

## RAPTURE

**1 Thessalonians 4:13-5:11 – The Rapture**
**1 Corinthians 15:50-56** – In the twinkling of an eye
Matthew 24:32-51
Mark 13:28-37
Luke 12:35-48
Luke 17:32-37
Luke 21:34-36 – Escape
Acts 1:9-11
**Revelation 3:8**
**Revelation 3:10**
**Revelation 4:1-2**
Jeremiah 30:7 – Saved "out of"
2 Peter 3:10
2 Peter 3:3-4 – scoffers
Zephaniah 2:1-3 – Escape
Psalm 37:39
Hosea 6:2 + 2 Peter 3:8
John 14:1-3
Philippians 3:20-21
2 Thessalonians 2:6-8 – **Holy Spirit removed**
2 Thessalonians 2:1-4 –?
Isaiah 26:19-21
Daniel 12:1-3 – Delivered from
Jonah 3:10 –?
**1 Thessalonians 1:10**

Sooo… What if you're drunk when the rapture comes?
Matthew 24:49
Luke 12:45
Luke 21:34-36
1 Thessalonians 5:6-10
Ephesians 5:14-18
1 Corinthians 6:9-11
Titus 2:12-13
1 Peter 1:13

# REDEMPTION OF A HARDROCK MINER

# APPENDIX K

I AM's

Who Am I?

Exodus 3:14, John 8:24, 28, 58 – I am NOT the "Great I Am"
1 Corinthians 15:10 – But by the grace of God, I am what I am
Matthew 5:13 – I am the salt of the earth
Matthew 5:14 – I am the light of the world
John 1:12 – **I am a child of God**
John 15:1, 5 – I am part of the true vine, a channel of Christ's life
John 15:15 – **I am Christ's friend**
John 15:16 – I am chosen and appointed by Christ to bear his fruit
Romans 6:18 – I am a slave of righteousness
Romans 6:22 – I am enslaved to God
Romans 8:14, 15, Galatians 3:26, 4:6 – I am a son of God, God is spiritually my Father
Romans 8:17 – I am joint heir with Christ sharing His inheritance with Him
1 Corinthians 3:16, 6:19 – I am a Temple, a dwelling place, of God, His Spirit and life dwell in me
1 Corinthians 6:17 – I am United with the Lord and I am Spirit with him
1 Corinthians 12:27, Ephesians 5:30 – I am a member of Christ's Body
2 Corinthians 5:17 – I am a new creation
2 Corinthians 5:18-19 – I am reconciled to God and am a minister of reconciliation
Galatians 3:26, 28 – I am a son of God and one in Christ
Galatians 4:6-7 – I am an heir of God since I am a son of God.
Ephesians 1:1, 1 Corinthians 1:2, Philippians 1:1, Colossians 1:2 – **I am a saint**
Ephesians 2:10 – I am God's workmanship-His handiwork-born anew in Christ to do His work
Ephesians 2:19 – I am a fellow citizen with the rest of God's family
Ephesians 3:1, 4:1 – I am a prisoner of Christ
Ephesians 4:24 – I am righteous and holy
Philippians 3:20, Ephesians 2:6 – **I am a citizen of Heaven, seated in Heaven right now**
Philippians 3:3 – I am hidden with Christ in God
Colossians 3:4 – I am an expression of the life of Christ because he is my life
Colossians 3:12 – I am chosen of God, holy and dearly loved
1 Thessalonians 1:4 – I am a son of light and not of darkness

Hebrews 3:1 – I am a holy partaker of the Heavenly calling
Hebrews 3:14 – I am a partaker of Christ, I share in His life
1 Peter 2:5 – I am one of God's living stones, built up in Christ as a spiritual house
1 Peter 2:9-10 – I am a member of a chosen race, a royal priesthood, a holy nation, a people for God's own possession!
1 Peter 2:11 – I am an alien and a stranger to this world in which I temporarily live!
1 Peter 5:8 – I am an enemy of the devil
1 John 3:12 – I am a child of God and I will resemble Christ when he returns
1 John 5:18 – I am born of God, and the evil one cannot touch me

**That's who you truly are!**

# APPENDIX L

## PRAYERS FOR MY KIDS

This the way you shall bless the children of Israel. Say to them:
**The Lord bless you and keep you;**
**The Lord make His face shine upon you,**
**And be gracious to you;**
**The Lord lift up His countenance upon you,**
**And give you peace.**
So they shall put My name on the children of Israel and I will bless them.
Numbers 6:23-27

***\*\*\*<u>Intercessory Prayer</u>\*\*\****
It's loving in the spirit (Colossians 1:8-9).
It's an application of spiritual force by the Holy Spirit (Romans 8:26) for someone else.
That force will overpower the evil spiritual forces that have that person bound – whether it be for salvation, healing or any other area of deliverance.
Intercession is not just getting God to do something.
It's combating principalities, powers, rulers of darkness and wicked spirits in behalf of others.
**It's because of prayer that the power of God will overpower the forces that have that person bound and prepare them to receive.**

### Old Testament

1 Samuel 1:27-28
1 Chronicles 4:9-10 – Jabez
2 Chronicles 30:9, 19
**Job 22:21-30** – delivered by purity of my hands
Psalm 5:11-12
Psalm 36:7-9
*****Psalm 51** – create in them a clean heart, O God
Psalm 72:4
Psalm 90:16
**\*\*\*Psalm 91\*\*\*– Major Prayer of Protection**
Psalm 20:1-5 – blessing
Psalm 102:28
Psalm 103:17-18
Psalm 112:1-3
Psalm 115:14 – blessing

Psalm 119:9-12*
Psalm 121:7-8 – going out and coming in
Psalm 127:3-5 – are a reward
Psalm 141:1-4 – guard my mouth
**\*Psalm 143:7-11 – Guidance**
Psalm 144:12
Proverbs 13:22
Proverbs 14:26-27 – refuge
Proverbs 20:7 – Blessed
**Isaiah 8:18 – four signs and wonders**
**\*Isaiah 29:23-24 – come to understanding**
**Isaiah 41:10**
**Isaiah 44:3 – Major promise of blessing**
**\*\*\*Isaiah 49:25 – God will save my kids!**
**Isaiah 54:13-15 –PEACE!**
**\*\*\*Isaiah 57:15-19 – By my prayers-Deliverance**
**Isaiah 55:11 – my guarantee!**
Isaiah 65:23-24 – kids in "New Creation"
Isaiah 66:22-23 –"           "
Jeremiah 3:12-15, 22-Matthew 9:37 – pray for God to send help
**Jeremiah 31:16-17 – By my works-they will come back!**

## New Testament

Matthew 9:37 – send His laborers
Matthew 18:18-20 – binding and loosening – agreement\*\*\*
Mark 2:5 – the effect of faith of others
Mark 3:27 – Binding the strongman on their behalf
Mark 9:17-29 – prayer and fasting
Luke 8:5 – remove those who doubt
Luke 18:1-7 – **Don't give up! Ephesians 6:10-18 stand!**
Acts 2:38-39 – promise
**Romans 5:8-10 – reconciled by the Blood**
**Romans 6:14 – sin has no dominion**
Romans 7:24-8:2 – free from sin and death
**Romans 8:31-34 – Promise – Jesus will help!**
Romans 8:37-39 – nothing can separate them from God
Romans 11:30-32 – Mercy
Romans 12:2 – **pray for the renewing of their minds**
1 Corinthians 10:13 – escape temptation
1 Corinthians 13:8 – love Never fails
1 Corinthians 15:57-58 – promise
**2 Corinthians 1:9-11** – intercessory prayer for deliverance
2 Corinthians 2:6-8 – forgive and comfort

2 Corinthians 4:16-18 – Don't lose heart
2 Corinthians 6:16-18 – promise
**2 Corinthians 10:3-5 – Warfare/Pulling Down Strongholds**
2 Corinthians 13:1 – Law of agreement
Galatians 1:3-5, Galatians 4:3-7 – Deliverance is God's will-It's why Jesus came!
Galatians 6:1, 9 – promise-in gentleness
**Ephesians 1:17-21 –MAJOR PRAYER**
**Ephesians 2:13 – Promise-Plead the Blood**
**Ephesians 3:14-19 –MAJOR PRAYER**
Ephesians 4:17-24 – Battle for the mind – Colossians 1:21
**Ephesians 6:10-18 – Spiritual warfare and the real enemy**
Philippians 1:6 – **God won't give up!**
**Philippians 1:9-11 –MAJOR PRAYER for discernment**
Philippians 1:19 – deliverance through intercessory prayer
***Philippians 4:6-7 – The Peace of God
**Colossians 1:9-14 –MAJOR PRAYER**
**2 Thessalonians 1:11-12 –PRAYER**
**2 Thessalonians 2:16-19 –PRAYER-comfort**
**2 Thessalonians 3:1-5 –PRAYER-Deliverance**
1 Timothy 2:1-6 – God's desire
*Hebrews 4:14-16 – Boldness, Mercy, Grace
*Hebrews 7:25 – Jesus will help
**Hebrews 9:14 – Plead the Blood!**
**Hebrews 10:16 – my New Covenant – promise!**
2 Peter 3:9 – God is patient
1 John 2:12-14 – promise
1 John 5:14-15 – Answered Prayer – Promise

**I have no greater joy than to hear that my children walk in truth.**
**3 John 1:2-4**

***

**Laws of Deliverance** (action/reaction)
Deuteronomy 28:32, 41 – The Curse
**Jesus Freed Us From The Curse!**
Galatians 3:13-14
Galatians 4:1-7
Romans 8:1-4

**Job 22:21-30**
Isaiah 55:11

**Isaiah 57:15-19**
Jeremiah 29:11-14
Matthew 18:18-20
Acts 4:9-12
Philippians 2:10 – **The Name**
Romans 11:30-32
Galatians 6:7-10 – Reaping and Sowing
Ephesians 6:10-18
Philippians 1:19
Philippians 4:6-7
Hebrews 4:14-16
**James 4:7**
1 John 5:16
2 Corinthians 4:6
Hebrews 7:25
Isaiah 55:6-7

## <u>Plead the Blood</u>
Matthew 26:28 – communion
Romans 5:6-11
Ephesians 2:13
Hebrews 12:24
Hebrews 9:14, 22
**Every single drop of Jesus's blood carries the redemption of God, for us and our loved ones!**

# APPENDIX M

## THE VOICE

**But this is what I commanded them, saying, "Obey My Voice, and I will be your God, and you shall be My people. And walk in all the ways that I have commanded you, that it may be well with you."**
Jeremiah 7:23

**But whoever listens to me will dwell safely, and will be secure, without fear of evil.**
**Proverbs 1:33**

**The Right Voice**

1 Kings 19:11-12 – "still small voice"
Isaiah 30:21 – Voice behind you
Deuteronomy 4:12-example
Isaiah 22:14-example
We have all heard the inner witness, or "Voice" inside of us at certain times, that tells us, "Somethings not right here," or, "Don't do it," and, "Don't go that way," or "Don't go there", etc., etc., etc., even though we can't see with our eyes that anything is wrong. The more time you spend in the Word of God the louder this voice becomes, and the easier it is to recognize. As we all have learned, disobeying this voice almost always comes with consequences and repercussions.

**The Wrong Voice**

Job 4:12-16 – the voice of evil
In order to achieve his goal of killing, stealing and destroying our lives, the evil one is constantly whispering to us in order to sway the choices and decisions we make to use us and to accomplish his evil agenda for us.
As with God's voice, the voice of the Holy Spirit as mentioned above, we have all heard the voice of our enemy as well; "It's okay... No one will know... Everybody's doing it... I won't get caught... Just this once... I won't be addicted... Etc., etc., etc." How did that work for you? ... Yeah, me too.

If you ignore God's Word, then soon enough, this will be the only voice you are able to hear.

**John 10:10** – What you get, depending on which voice you obey.

**The Voice, Through the Word**

John 1:1 – His Voice/Word
John 15:7 – Major Promise
John 14:26 – Bring to remembrance
**John 16:13-15 – Discernment**
1 Thessalonians 1:5 – power in the Holy Spirit and assurance
*!*John 14:21-23 – God/Jesus manifest themselves to us through the Word!

**The Voice, Through Peace**

*John 14:26-27 – **The Holy Spirit works through Inner Peace, not through fear!**
2 Timothy 1:7 – Fear versus Faith
*1 Corinthians 14:33 – Confusion versus Peace
James 3:13-18 – Discernment through Peace
**Philippians 4:6-7 – How it works! – Instruction – note; "Thanksgiving"**
**Colossians 3:14-17 – How it works! – Instruction**
2 Thessalonians 3:16 – Prayer – **"Now may the Lord of peace Himself give you peace always in every way."**

# APPENDIX N

## VICTORY IN JESUS

John 16:33
1 John 5:4-5
1 John 4:4
1 Corinthians 15:57
2 Corinthians 2:14
Mark 16:15-18
Luke 9:1-2
Luke 10:17-20
Philippians 4:13
Philippians 2:10
Ephesians 6:10-18
Deuteronomy 20:4
Isaiah 41:10
**Romans chapter 8**
1 Thessalonians 5:9-10
**Revelation chapters 20, 21, and 22!**

I am asking you, dear reader, to continue to add to this list yourself, as I know without doubt, this list is inexhaustible, especially as we are to add our own personal victories through our Lord, to it.

**Psalm 103!**

# APPENDIX O

## OLD TESTAMENT APPEARANCES OF JESUS

Genesis 12:7
**Genesis 14:18-24 – Melchizedek** (to Abraham)-see Hebrews 7
Genesis 16:7-13 – The God Who Sees (to Hagar)
Genesis 18 – "Is anything too hard for the Lord?"
Genesis 22 – Yahweh Jira = The-Lord-Will-Provide
Genesis 28:13-15 – Two Jacob (Jacobs Ladder) vision
Genesis 32:22-32 – Wrestling with Jacob
Genesis 35:1 – Jacob wrestled with God/Jesus, confirmed in Hosea 12:3-6
Genesis 35:9-15 – changed Jacob's name to Israel
Exodus 23:20-23
**Joshua 5:13-15 – The Commander of the Army of the Lord!**
Judges 13 – to Samson's mother
Judges 6:11-24 – two Gideon – **The Lord is Peace!**
Isaiah 6 – vision
Ezekiel 1 – vision
**Daniel 3:25 – in the Fiery Furnace**
**Daniel 7:9-10 – Vision of God**
**Daniel 7:13-14 – Vision of Jesus**
**Daniel 10 – Vision of Jesus** (?)
**Daniel 12:5-13 – Vision of Jesus (End Time Prophecy)**
Zechariah 3 – vision of the High Priest
Numbers 22:22 – Balaam, the donkey, & the Angel

## To Moses

Exodus 3 and 4 – The Burning Bush
Exodus 24:9-18 – On the mountain with God
Exodus 33:11 – To Moses
Exodus 33:18-23 – God's Glory – Jesus, because, no one can see God's face and live!

Enjoy referencing – Psalm 22, Psalm 45, Psalm 72, Psalm 110, Revelation 1:9-20, **Revelation 19:11-16** and Isaiah 53, etc.

# APPENDIX P

## **WEAPONS OF MASS INSTRUCTION**

Finally, my brethren, be strong in the Lord and the power of His might.
Put on the whole armor of God, that you may be able to stand against the wiles of the devil.
For we do not wrestle against flesh and blood, but against principalities, against powers, against the rulers of the darkness of this age, against spiritual hosts of wickedness in the heavenly places.
Therefore take up the whole armor of God, that you may be able to withstand in the evil day, and having done all, to stand.
Stand therefore, having girded your waist with truth, having put on the breastplate of righteousness, and having shod your feet with the preparation of the gospel of peace;
above all, taking the shield of faith with which you will be able to quench all the fiery darts of the wicked one.
And take the helmet of salvation, and the sword of the Spirit, which is the Word of God;
praying always with all prayer and supplication in the Spirit, being watchful to this end with all perseverance and supplication for all the saints —

Ephesians 6:10-18.

**Pray the Word**
Isaiah 43:25-26
Isaiah 55:11
Psalm 119:49-50
Isaiah 51:16
Hebrews 1:3

Therefore...
Matthew 9:37 – send laborers (help)
Matthew 17:19-21 – Prayer and fasting
Isaiah 58 – Prayer and fasting
Matthew 16:18-19 – The gates of Hades shall not prevail against us!
**Matthew 18:18 – Binding and loosening**

2 Corinthians 1:9-11 – Intercessory prayer – **use prayer lines** – see APPENDIX L

**Prayer of Agreement** – Very Powerful!
Ecclesiastes 4:9-12 – a threefold cord
Psalm 34:3-7 – together
**Matthew 18:19-20 – Agreement – Use Prayer Lines!**
**2 Corinthians 13:1 – Agreement – Use Prayer Lines!**

Matthew 9:18-26 – **Remove those who doubt – faith killers**
Luke 8:54 – Remove those who doubt
Acts 9:40 – remove those who doubt

Romans 8:26-27 – Holy Spirit

**Plead the Blood**
Matthew 26:28 – While taking Communion
Romans 5:6-11
Ephesians 2:13
Hebrews 12:24
Hebrews 9:14, 22

**Authority**
Mark 16:18-19
Mark 16:17
Luke 10:17-20
Luke 24:47
2 Corinthians 10:8
Ephesians 1 – 3
Romans 3:21-28

**Words**
Genesis 8:22 – Creation Covenant – Reaping and Sowing
Galatians 6:7-9 – The Law of Reaping and Sowing
Joshua 1:8
Psalms 103:20 – Angels heed the Word
Psalm 119 – God's Word – see Appendix E
Romans 4:17 – The Word= Power
Hebrews 1:3 – The Word= Power
Matthew 12:33-37 – Law of Judgment
James 3:10 – Blessing and Cursing
Proverbs 18:21
Proverbs 21:23
Hebrews 4:14-16 – Holdfast! – Our High Priest (Jesus) will help – Don't be shy!

Psalm 141:3 – Guard your mouth! Do not say words that are contrary to your prayers!

**Law of Love**
1 John 4:16 – God is Love
2 Timothy 1:7
**Jude 22 – Love the person-hate the sin.**
Romans 5:8
Romans 8:28 – God will make it work out for good.
Hebrews 6:10
1 Corinthians 16:13-14 – instruction
2 Corinthians 2:6-8 – instructions

**Power of the Name**
Luke 9:49, Luke 10:17, 20
Acts 3:16, Acts 4:10, Acts 4:29-30
**Philippians 2:10 – Every knee will bow – EVERY KNEE!**
**"Let us therefore come boldly to the Throne of Grace, that we may obtain mercy and find grace to help in time of need." Hebrews 4:16**

# APPENDIX Q

## HEALING

Is anyone among you sick? Let him call for the elders of the church, and let them pray over him anointing him with oil in the name of the Lord. And the prayer of faith will save the sick, and the Lord will raise him up. And if he has committed sins, he will be forgiven. Confess your trespasses to one another, and pray for one another, that you may be healed. The effective, fervent prayer of a righteous man of avails much.
**James 5:14-16**

**Healing is God's Will.**
Deuteronomy 7:15
**Exodus 15:26 – He is Yahweh Rapha-The God Who Heals You!**
Proverbs 4:20-23 – The Prescription
3 John 2
Luke 5:12-3 + Hebrews 13:8= His Will for You
Acts 10:38 – Sickness is an oppression of the devil requiring spiritual warfare, and His will is to heal you.
**Isaiah 53:4-10 – After Jesus paid such an extreme price for it, how could we ever say that healing is not his will?**

**Prayers** – please note that all healing Scriptures should and could be used in prayer form. The following Scriptures are just a few of my personal favorites as well as applicable instructions. God bless…
**John 11:4** – not unto death, but to the glory of God
**Acts 4:29 – Speak the Word-Jesus**
**1 Peter 2:24 – by His stripes we WERE healed**
**Isaiah 53:4-5 – by His stripes we ARE healed**
Psalm 41:1-3 – Promise
Psalm 103:1-5 – Promise
Psalm 107:17-22 – By His Word-Thanksgiving
Exodus 23:25 – Healing for His servants
Jeremiah 17:14
Ezekiel 37:9 – Raising the dead

Matthew 10:1, 7-8 – Our Authority

**Mark 16:18 – Our Authority-The Great Commission-we do it in obedience to Jesus.**
Matthew 17:19-21 – unbelief-prayer and fasting
Luke 6:17-19 – **Healed them ALL**
Matthew 13:15 – The prescription, as is
Proverbs 4:20-27 – Also the prescription.
Matthew 8&9 – How Jesus healed
Luke 4:39 – Jesus rebukes fever
Luke 8:54 – **Remove Those Who Doubt!**
**Acts 3:6, 16,**
**Acts 9:34, 40**
**Romans 8:11**
 Hebrews 12:12
**Psalm 30:2-3**
Psalm 139:14-16 – made whole and intact
Mark 6:6--Jesus could not heal because of unbelief.
**Mark 7:6-13 – Tradition of men will rob you of your healing!**
**Colossians 2:8-9 – Tradition of men will rob you of your healing**
2 Corinthians 12:7-10 – Paul's thorn – note: sickness is not mentioned! In verse 10 the word "infirmities" means "want of strength, weakness, indicates inability to produce results", not sickness. And according to 2 Timothy 4:6-7 and Philippians 4:12-13, Paul was **not** a sick man.

**Anointing with Oil**
James 5:14 – **In the Name of Jesus**
Mark 6:13 – The disciples

**Laying on of Hands**
Mark 16:18 – Done in obedience-The Great Commission
Mark 5:23 – Jesus
Luke 4:40 – Jesus
Mark 2:5 – "their" faith
2 Timothy 1:6

## HEALING SCRIPTURES

Exodus 15:26
Exodus 23:25
Deuteronomy 7:14, 28
Deuteronomy 30:19

Deuteronomy 32:39
Joshua 21:44
1 Kings 8:56
2 Kings 20:5
1 Chronicles 4:9
Job 5:18
Psalm 6:2
Psalm 6:9
Psalm 9:13
Psalm 22:21
Psalm 23
Psalm 30
Psalm 34:19
Psalm 41:3
Psalm 91
Psalm 103:1-5
Psalm 118:17
Psalm 147:3

Proverbs 3:8
Proverbs 4:20
Proverbs 16:24
Proverbs 17:22
Isaiah 19:22
Isaiah 40:31
Isaiah 41:10
Isaiah 53:5
Isaiah 54:17
Isaiah 55:10
Isaiah 57:18
Jeremiah 1:12
Jeremiah 3:22
Jeremiah 17:14
Jeremiah 30:17
Jeremiah 33:6
Hosea 6:1
Hosea 14:4 to
Joel 3:10
Jonah 2
Nahum 1:9
Haggai 2
Zechariah 1:3

Zechariah 13:9
Malachi 3:7
Malachi 4:2
Matthew 4:23
Matthew 7:7
Matthew 8:2-17
Matthew 9:20
Matthew 10:8
Matthew 12:15
Matthew 14:14
Matthew 14:35
Matthew 15:28
Matthew 17:18
Matthew 18:18
Matthew 19:2
Matthew 20:32
Matthew 21:14
Matthew 21: 21
Mark 1:41
Mark 3:10
Mark 5:23
Mark 5:34
Mark 6:13
Mark 6:55
Mark 7:31
Mark 7:32
Mark 10:51
Mark 11:22
Mark 16:14
Luke 4:18
Luke 4:40
Luke 5:13
Luke 6:10
Luke 6:19
Luke 7:7
Luke 7:14
Luke 8:44-56
Luke 9:2 to
Luke 9:11
Luke 9:42
Luke 13:10
Luke 14:1

Luke 17:11
Luke 18:40
John 3:16
John 4:46
John 5:6
John 6:2
John 8:32

John 9:6
John 10:10
John 11:25
John 14:12
John 15:16
Acts 3:6
Acts 4:27
Acts 5:16
Acts 8:7
Acts 9:34
Acts 10:38
Acts 14:8
Acts 28:8
Acts 19:11
Romans 4:16
Romans 8:12
Romans 8:11
Romans 8:26
1 Corinthians 12
2 Corinthians 10:3
Galatians 3:13
Galatians 6:7
Ephesians 6:10
Philippians 2:13
Philippians 4:6
1 Thessalonians 5:23
2 Timothy 1:7
Hebrews 4:16
Hebrews 10:23
Hebrews 10:35
Hebrews 11:11 to
Hebrews 13:6
James 4:7
James 5:14
1 Peter 2:24

1 John 3:21
1 John 4:4
1 John 5:14
3 John 1:2
Revelation 12:11
**Revelation 21:4-5! Hallelujah!**

## About the Author

Amazingly, although very worn John still manages, by the grace of God, to show up for work every day, hold down a full-time job and draws a paycheck, as he patiently (term used very loosely) awaits the return of his Master. Lori is with him, still compassionately (more like, pitifully) putting up with him (for the most part), knowing that probably nobody else would. They reside in Idaho to be near their beautiful daughter and her wonderful family, the youngest of which still believe their Grandpa is a Pirate (wonder where they got that idea?).

*"Live happily with the woman you love through all the meaningless days of life that God has given you under the sun. The wife God gives you is your reward for all your earthly toil."*
*Ecclesiastes 9:9 NLT*
Thank You, Lord.

Made in the USA
Middletown, DE
21 January 2025